HANDBOOK FOR WRITERS

HANDBOOK FOR WRITERS

GRAMMAR
PUNCTUATION
DICTION
RHETORIC
RESEARCH

CELIA MILLWARD
Boston University

HOLT, RINEHART AND WINSTON

New York   Chicago   San Francisco   Atlanta   Dallas
Montreal   Toronto

Editor Kenney Withers
Development Editor Lauren S. Bahr
Cover and Interior Designer Diane Daugherty
Production Manager Vic Calderon

Library of Congress Cataloging in Publication Data
Millward, Celia M
  Handbook for writers.

  Includes index.
  1. English language—Grammar—1950-   2. English
language—Rhetoric.   3. Report writing.   I. Title.
PE1112.M49   808′ .042   79-22306
ISBN 0-03-017796-0

0 1 2 3 4 5   032   9 8 7 6 5 4 3 2 1

ACKNOWLEDGMENTS

Excerpt from *Without Feathers* by Woody Allen. Copyright © 1972 by Woody Allen. Reprinted by permission of Woody Allen and Random House, Inc.

Reprints from the *Art Index*. Copyright © 1978 by the H. W. Wilson Company. Material reproduced by permission of the publisher.

Excerpt from *Patterns of Culture* by Ruth Benedict. Copyright 1934 and © renewed 1962 by Ruth Benedict Valentine. Used by permission of Houghton Mifflin Company.

Excerpt from "Brass Buttons, Fingertips, and the Fluid Mosaic" by William Bennett. Copyright © *Harvard Magazine*, 1977. Reprinted by permission.

Excerpt from *Mountaineering* by Alan Blackshaw, pp. 139–140. Copyright © Alan Blackshaw, 1965, 1968, 1970, 1973, 1975. Reprinted by permission of Penguin Books, Ltd.

Excerpt from *If Life is a Bowl of Cherries—What am I Doing in the Pits?* by Erma Bombeck. Copyright © 1978 by Erma Bombeck. Used with permission of McGraw-Hill Book Company.

Excerpt from *The Americans: The National Experience* by Daniel J. Boorstin. Copyright © 1965. Reprinted by permission of Random House, Inc.

Excerpt from *The I Hate to Cook Book* by Peg Bracken. Copyright © 1960 by Peg Bracken. Reprinted by permission of Harcourt Brace Jovanovich, Inc.

Excerpt from *Strong Family Strong Child: The Art of Working Together to Develop a Healthy Child* by Barry Bricklin and Patricia M. Bricklin. Copyright © 1970. Reprinted by permission of Delacorte Press.

Excerpts from *History of Greece* by J. B. Bury and R. Meiggs. Reprinted by permission of St. Martin's Press, Inc.

Excerpt from "Polluting Our Language," by Douglas Bush. Reprinted from *The American Scholar*, Volume 41, Number 2, Spring 1972. Copyright © 1972 by the United Chapters of Phi Beta Kappa. By permission of the publishers.

Excerpt from *The Edge of the Sea* by Rachel Carson. Copyright © 1955. Reprinted by permission of Houghton Mifflin Company.

Excerpt from *Gods, Graves, and Scholars*, second edition, by C. W. Ceram, translated by Edward B. Garside and Sophie Wilkins. Copyright © 1967. Reprinted by permission of Random House, Inc.

Excerpt from Review of *Mara* by Jerome Charyn. Copyright © 1978 by The New York Times Company. Reprinted by permission.

Excerpt from *Easy to Kill* by Agatha Christie. Copyright © 1945. Reprinted by permission of Dodd, Mead & Company.

Excerpt from "Indians in American History," *Collier's Encyclopedia*. Reprinted with permission from Collier's Encyclopedia. Copyright © 1957 Macmillan Educational Corporation.

Excerpt from *Six Men* by Alistair Cooke. Copyright © 1977. Reprinted by permission of Random House, Inc.

Excerpt from *Antiquing from A to Z* by Michael De Forrest. Copyright © 1972 by Michael De Forrest. Reprinted by permission of Simon & Schuster, a Division of Gulf & Western Corporation.

Excerpt from *Our Own Words* by Mary Helen Dohan. Copyright © 1976. Reprinted by permission of Random House, Inc.

Excerpt from "Global Satellite Communications, "*Scientific American*, February 1977, by Burton I. Edelson. Reprinted by permission of W. H. Freeman and Company Publishers.

Excerpt from *Arts and the Man* by Irwin Edman. Copyright 1928, 1939 by W. W. Norton & Company, Inc. Copyright renewed 1956, 1967 by Meta Markel. Used by permission of W. W. Norton & Company, Inc.

Excerpt from *The Natural History of Nonsense* by Bergen Evans. Copyright © 1960. Reprinted by permission of Random House, Inc.

Excerpt from the Introduction to *The Great Comic Book Heroes* by Jules Feiffer. Copyright © 1965 by The Dial Press. Reprinted by permission of The Dial Press.

Excerpt from "Midnight Egg and Other Revivers," *Bon Appétit*, May 1978, by M. F. K. Fisher. Copyright © 1978 Bon Appetit Publishing Corp. Reprinted by permission.

Excerpt from *The French Lieutenant's Woman* by John Fowles, by permission of Little, Brown and Co.

Excerpt from *The Structure of American English* by W. Nelson Francis. Copyright © 1958. Reprinted by permission of John Wiley & Sons, Inc.

Excerpt from *The Scotch* by John Kenneth Galbraith. Copyright © 1966. Reprinted by permission of Houghton Mifflin Company.

Excerpt from *The Life and Times of Chaucer* by John Gardner. Copyright © 1977. Reprinted by permission of Alfred A. Knopf, Inc.

Excerpts from *The Sunlight Dialogues* by John Gardner. Copyright © 1973. Reprinted by permission of Random House, Inc.

Excerpt from *Mohammedanism* by H. A. R. Gibb. Reprinted by permission of Oxford University Press.

Excerpt from "Sun Valley: The Compleat Resort," *Skiing*, December 1977, by Al Greenberg. Reprinted from *Skiing Magazine*. Copyright © 1977 Ziff-Davis Publishing Company. Reprinted by permission of Ziff-Davis Publishing Company.

Letters to the Editor, *The Greenville News*. Printed by permission of *The Greenville News*.

Excerpt from "Will There Always Be an England?" *The American Scholar*, by William Haley. Reprinted from *The American Scholar*, Volume 47, Number 3, Summer 1978. Copyright © 1978 by the United Chapters of Phi Beta Kappa. By permission of the publishers.

Excerpt from "Learning on the Tube Has Finally Arrived," March 4, 1979 "Week in Review," *The New York Times* by Fred M. Hechinger. Copyright © 1979 by the New York Times Company. Reprinted by permission.

Excerpt from "Meteorite Photography," *The Illustrated London News*, April 1978 by Keith Hindley.

Excerpt from "On Using Words," *Encounter*, July 1978 by Philip Howard.

Excerpt from *Improving Your Spelling*, Third Edition, by Falk S. Johnson. Copyright © 1979, 1965, 1959 by Falk S. Johnson. Reprinted by permission of Holt, Rinehart and Winston.

Excerpt from *Biological Science* by William T. Keeton, W. W. Norton & Company, Inc., New York, N. Y. Copyright © 1967 by W. W. Norton & Company, Inc.

Excerpt from *Cacti and Other Succulents* by Jack Kramer. Reprinted with permission of the publishers, Harry N. Abrams, Inc., 1979.

Excerpt from *The American Indian* by Oliver La Farge. Copyright © 1960 by Oliver La Farge and Western Publishing Company, Inc. Used by permission of the publisher.

Excerpt from *An Experiment in Criticism* by C. S. Lewis. Cambridge University Press, 1961.

Excerpt from *Time and the River Flowing: Grand Canyon* by Francois Leydet. Copyright © 1964 by Sierra Club Books. Reprinted by permission of Sierra Club Books.

Excerpt from "Rented Rooms," *The Atlantic Monthly*, August 1978, by Paul Malamud. Copyright © 1978 by the Atlantic Monthly Company, Boston, Mass. Reprinted with permission.

Excerpt from *American English* by Albert H. Marckwardt. Copyright © 1958 by Oxford University Press, Inc. Reprinted by permission.

Excerpt from *The Woman He Loved* by Ralph G. Martin. Copyright © 1974 by Ralph G. Martin. Reprinted by permission of Simon & Schuster, a Division of Gulf & Western Corporation.

Excerpt from *The Cloud Forest* by Peter Matthiessen. Copyright © 1961 by Peter Matthiessen. Reprinted by permission of Viking Penguin, Inc.

Excerpt from *Plagues and People* by William H. McNeill. Copyright © 1976 by William H. McNeill. Reprinted by permission of Doubleday & Company, Inc.

Excerpt from "D. H. Lawrence: Katherine Mansfield and 'Women in Love,' " *London Magazine*, May 1978, by Jeffrey Meyers. Reprinted by permission of *London Magazine*.

Excerpt from *Centennial* by James A. Michener. Copyright © 1975. Reprinted by permission of Random House, Inc.

Excerpt from "Affirmed's Kentucky Derby," *The New Yorker*, May 15, 1978, by Audax Minor. Reprinted by permission of *The New Yorker*.

Excerpt from *The Uses of the Past* by Herbert J. Muller. Copyright © 1952 by Oxford University Press, Inc. Reprinted by permission.

Excerpt from *I Can Teach You to Figure-Skate* by Tina Noyes with Freda Alexander. Reprinted by permission of Hawthorn Books from *Figure Skating* by Tina Noyes with Freda Alexander. Copyright © 1973 Associated Features Inc. All rights reserved.

Excerpt from *Culloden* by John Prebble. Copyright © 1963. Reprinted by permission of Martin Secker & Warburg Limited and Curtis Brown Ltd.

Excerpt from "Public Sector Bargaining and Strikes." Reprinted by permission from "Public Sector Bargaining and Strikes," Public Service Research Council, Vienna, Va., 1978.

Excerpt from *The Pirates of Colonial North Carolina* by Hugh F. Rankin. Used with permission of the Division of Archives and History, North Carolina Department of Cultural Resources.

Reprints from *Readers' Guide to Periodical Literature*. Copyright © 1978 by the H. W. Wilson Company. Material reproduced by permission of the publisher.

Excerpt from *Graffiti: Two Thousand Years of Wall Writing* by Robert George Reisner. Copyright © 1971 with the permission of Contemporary Books, Inc. Chicago.

Excerpt from "Gas Guzzlers Becoming Alcoholics in Brazil" by Larry Rohter. Copyright ©1978 *The Washington Post*. Reprinted by permission of *The Washington Post*.

Excerpt from "Richard the Bold," *The New Yorker*, June 19, 1978, by Richard Rovere. From an article in *The New Yorker*. Reprinted by permission. Copyright © 1978 The New Yorker Magazine, Inc.

Excerpt from *Senator Joe McCarthy* by Richard H. Rovere. Reprinted by permission of Harcourt Brace Jovanovich, Inc.

Excerpt from *The Egyptians* by John Ruffle. Copyright © 1977 by Phaidon Press Ltd., Oxford.

Excerpt from "They're Battling Again at Bennington," by Marjorie Ryerson. Marjorie Ryerson, *Vermont Life Magazine*.

Excerpt from *The Real Isadora: A Biography* by Victor Seroff. Copyright © 1971 by Victor Seroff. Reprinted by permission of The Dial Press.

Excerpt from *The Russians* by Hedrick Smith. Copyright © 1976 by Hedrick Smith. Reprinted by permission of Times Books, a division of Quadrangle/The New York Times Book Co., Inc.

Excerpt from *Inside the Third Reich* by Albert Speer. Copyright © 1970 by Macmillan Publishing Co., Inc.

Excerpt from *Names on the Land* by George R. Stewart. Copyright © renewed 1972 by George R. Stewart. Reprinted by permission of Houghton Mifflin Company.

Excerpt from "Those Baffling Black Holes." Reprinted by permission from *Time, The Weekly Newsmagazine*. Copyright Time Inc. 1978.

Excerpt from *Roofs and Siding: Home Repair and Improvement* published by Time-Life Books, Inc. Reprinted by permission of Time-Life Books, Inc.

Excerpt from *Of Mites and Men* by William Tucker. Copyright © 1978 by *Harper's Magazine*. All rights reserved. Reprinted from the August 1978 issue by special permission.

Excerpt from Helen Vendler's review of *Pudding Stone* by Steven Gould Axelrod. Copyright © 1979 by *The New York Review of Books*. Reprinted with permission of *The New York Review of Books*.

Excerpt from *Your Dog: His Health and Happiness* by Louis L. Vine. Copyright © 1971. Courtesy of Winchester Press, Inc.

Excerpt from *The Vogue Sewing Book*. Reprinted by permission of the publisher.

Excerpt from *The Wall Street Journal* feature "No Fiesta Ahead" 8/30/78, with permission.

Excerpt from *The Sense of the Past* by C. V. Wedgwood.

Excerpt from *Stress, Sanity and Survival* by Robert Woolfolk and Frank C. Richardson. Copyright © 1978. Reprinted by permission of Simon & Schuster, Inc., a Division of Gulf & Western Corporation.

contents

preface

Handbook for Writers is a handbook designed primarily for use in college composition courses. Students can use it as a text within the classroom and as a reference outside the classroom, both in connection with their composition courses and in writing papers for other courses. The purpose of the book is to help students improve their writing and to help their instructors assist them in achieving this improvement.

I have in general tried to take a commonsense approach to writing. In other words, I treat poor writing as a practical, not a moral, problem. Because acceptable written English is not the same as acceptable spoken English, I often make overt distinctions between the written and the spoken language, particularly in areas where spoken habits tend to lead to violation of written conventions. Although I have tried, insofar as possible, to take a positive approach to writing, a certain amount of negativism is unavoidable. Space prevents the inclusion of all the many things students do well and, after all, people consult handbooks to find out what they are doing wrong, not to learn what they are doing right.

The book is primarily descriptive. I describe good written English, and in so doing, prescription is often implicit. However, I do not hesitate to use such clearly prescriptive labels as "Incorrect," "Inappropriate," "Wrong," and even "Substandard" because I believe that most writers want to know what is acceptable and what is unacceptable. To me, it is crueler to imply that anything students may write is going to meet with universal approval than it is to tell them outright that some of their habits are generally frowned upon in the circles in which they wish to move. Good writers know that conventions exist and know what these conventions are. They violate the conventions as they see fit—but deliberately and not through ignorance.

The descriptions of appropriate usage are based on the dicta of recognized authorities; on my own experience as reader, writer, teacher, linguist, editor, and observer of the linguistic scene; and, occasionally, simply on my own preferences and prejudices. On the whole, the approach leans more toward the conservative than toward the "permissive"; my justification is that conservative usage is always acceptable and will always keep the struggling writer out of trouble. Nonetheless, I do accept certain usages that some may find objectionable. For example, I treat the split infinitive and the clause ending with a preposition as something less than cardinal sins. In instances where usage is mixed, complex, or poorly defined, I try to provide a rule, in the simplest form possible, that will never be wrong. In the sections on usage and punctuation, I have deliberately avoided extensive discussion of possible options. Such refinements are taken for granted by the experienced writer, but are all too often only confusing to the insecure writer.

With few exceptions, I use traditional grammatical and rhetorical terminology throughout the book. Although this terminology is sometimes unsatisfactory from a linguist's point of view, I feel that its use here is justified because (1) it is the terminology most likely to be familiar to the greatest number of students and teachers, (2) it is the terminology of dictionaries and other reference works, (3) it is the terminology of most of the foreign-language courses that students will have taken, and (4) it is the foundation of other, more "linguistic" vocabularies of grammar and rhetoric. I have attempted to keep the amount of technical terminology to the minimum necessary for concise explanations. On the other hand, if a term is needed to explain a principle that creates difficulty for student writers, I do not hesitate to employ it. Thus, for example, I introduce the term *mass noun* because the simple distinction between singular and plural nouns is inadequate to explain why we ask students to write *less furniture* but *fewer chairs*. All technical terms are defined and usually exemplified when they are first introduced.

The coverage of grammar and mechanics here is more comprehensive than in many handbooks. This completeness is intentional. There is, of course, no need to explain rules to the student who never makes grammatical or mechanical errors. But such students are rare indeed. For more typical students, some understanding of the nature of their errors and of the principles of the language underlying the accepted usage is essential if they are to develop habits of correct usage. My own classroom experience has taught me that the less complete coverage of most handbooks is inadequate to handle the questions that arise in the classroom and the errors that occur in actual student writing. On the other hand, I have by no means attempted to write a complete grammar of English. Rather, I concentrate the discussion on topics that are perennial troublemakers and ignore areas where native students rarely make errors (for example, the use of definite and indefinite articles).

Throughout the entire book, all principles and explanations are copiously illustrated by examples. The examples are drawn from a wide variety of subject areas and include an extensive range of stylistic levels. Most of the examples are from contemporary English, but I also include, without apology, some examples from earlier periods of written English.

Handbook for Writers is divided into five major parts: (I) Grammar and Grammatical Problems, (II) Punctuation and Mechanics, (III) Diction, (IV) Rhetoric, and (V) Research. Each part is self-contained insofar as possible. When it is necessary to use technical terms that have been discussed in other parts, a brief definition is usually provided on the spot and a cross-reference is given to the fuller explanation elsewhere.

Although there is a certain abstract logic to the order of the parts as they appear here, I do not assume that instructors will necessarily assign chapters sequentially or ask students to read the book from cover to cover. In my experience, there is no ideal organization for a handbook of composition. Many instructors, because they want to have their students begin writing immediately, will prefer to begin with "The Whole Paper." Others may prefer to begin with "Paragraphs" or "Words into Sentences." Still others may prefer to spend the first few classes on a review of grammar or punctuation. Probably many teachers will do as I usually do—use various sections of the book simultaneously, even returning to some sections several times during the term.

Part I, "Grammar and Grammatical Problems," is divided into two separate sections, the first providing a review of written English grammar and its terminology, and the second concentrating on major areas where students make grammatical errors. The grammar section begins with the major components of sentences and the basic sentence patterns and continues with more detailed descriptions of the parts of speech. The section concludes with discussions of phrases and clauses; the concept of nominals, adjectivals, and adverbials; and definitions of the various kinds of sentences. "Grammatical Problems" focuses on six major problem areas of grammar for student writers: verbs and verb phrases, subject-verb agreement, pronouns, modifiers, comparisons, and sentence form. Ample cross-references to the grammar section are provided as necessary. Problems are illustrated copiously with sample sentences.

Part II, "Punctuation and Mechanics," covers the use of marks of punctuation, capitalization, abbreviations, numbers, and spelling. Preceding the discussion of each mark of punctuation is a very brief summary of its uses; the entire section concludes with instructions for typing punctuation. The spelling section includes a brief analysis of spelling difficulties caused by the mismatch of spelling and pronunciation, the four standard spelling rules, and spelling of noun plurals and third-person singular present verbs. In addition, the section contains material on prefixes and suffixes designed to help the student both with spelling problems and with vocabulary building.

Part III, "Diction," treats appropriate diction in English, with special emphasis being given to the difference between spoken and written English. The section on the dictionary contains, not only a full explanation of dictionary entries, but also a brief comparison of the features of the most important college dictionaries.

Part IV, "Rhetoric," includes sections on sentences, paragraphs, the whole paper, logic, and special types of writing. "Words into Sentences" focuses on achieving clarity, emphasis, and variety in written sentences. "Paragraphs" stresses and exemplifies unity, completeness, and coherence in paragraph construction. Particular attention is paid to topic sentences, paragraph development, and transitions. "The Whole Paper" traces the process of writing a paper from choosing a topic to revision. "Making a Good Argument" discusses and illustrates the most common logical fallacies and provides advice on how to avoid them. "Special Types of Writing" treats the preparation of outlines, letters, résumés, paraphrases and summaries, and essay examinations.

Part V, "Research," has separate sections on preparing a research paper, the library, and documentation. The material on documentation and using the library has been made into separate sections that can easily be assigned or consulted apart from the section on writing the research paper, saving the student and the instructor the common annoyance of having to search through a single cumbersome section in order to find out how to read a library card or prepare a footnote for a book with two authors. The sample research paper itself is reproduced in full; its topic (sleep) is one of universal interest.

To avoid having the flow of the text interrupted by useful but bulky lists of various kinds, some materials have been put into appendices. These include "A Brief History of the English Language," "Glossary of Usage," "Frequently Confused Words," "Glossary of Grammatical Terms," "Complete Conjugation of an English Verb," and "Frequently Misspelled Words."

The entire book is coded by numbers and letters, and correction symbols are associated with major headings. A correction chart appears on the endpapers at the front of the book. The book is fully indexed. For students who need even more practice than that provided by exercises interspersed throughout the book, an accompanying workbook, cross-referenced to *Handbook for Writers*, is available. Diagnostic tests and a complete instructor's manual are available.

This book has benefited from the perceptive criticism and suggestions of many scholars and teachers, among them Robert Bain, University of North Carolina (Chapel Hill); Helen Brooks, Stanford University; Joanne Cockelreas, East Texas State University; Wallace Douglas, Northwestern University; Robert Gorrell, University of Nevada (Reno); Patricia Graves, Georgia State University; Jule S. Kaufman, University of Cincinnati; Joanne McCarthy, Tacoma Community College; Russell J. Meyer, University of Missouri (Columbia); Walter E. Meyers, North Carolina State University (Raleigh); James Raymond, University of Alabama; Robert Rudolph, University of Toledo; David Skwire, Cuyahoga Community College; and Joseph Trimmer, Ball State University. Very special thanks are due Richard Beal, who has been a continual source of wisdom and encouragement, and Linda Bowie, who has worked closely with me throughout the entire preparation of the book and who prepared most of the exercises.

Among those at Holt, Rinehart and Winston who have contributed to the production of this book are Vic Calderon, Diane Daugherty, Yvonne Freund, Cecil Golan, Susan Katz, and Maribeth Payne. I am particularly endebted to Lauren Bahr, Kenney Withers, Judy Rothman, and Norma Scheck.

Although my typist prefers to remain nameless, without her patience, accuracy, and willingness to work at any hour of the day or night, this book would never have been completed. Finally, I want to state publicly my affectionate gratitude to my husband Dick and my son Jim, who have for many months served as emergency clerical help, guinea pigs, and untiring cheerleaders. Both have always assumed that my work was as important as theirs.

CELIA MILLWARD

grammar and grammatical problems

A fundamental fact about English is that what is acceptable in speech is not always acceptable in writing. When we speak, our listeners understand that we are composing our sentences on the spur of the moment, and they are fairly tolerant of deviations from Standard English. There is, however, little acceptable variation in the grammar of written English. When writing violates grammatical rules, the violations distract the reader's attention from the content of the writing. Unfair as it may seem, readers often judge the value of what we have to say by the grammar we use in expressing it. Grammar is, then, one of the basic tools of writers, and writers, like all other craftsmen, should know how to use their tools.

Fortunately, most of the grammatical rules of written English are identical to the grammatical rules of spoken English. As native speakers of English, we know these rules intuitively and do not need to memorize them the way we memorize the grammatical rules of a foreign language. Normally, problems arise only in those instances where acceptable written English differs from acceptable spoken English.

The following pages present, first, a review of the types of written English sentence structures and of the parts of speech that make up phrases, clauses, and sentences. Following this review is a more detailed discussion of the specific areas of written English grammar that are most troublesome to writers: verbs and verb phrases, pronouns, subject-verb agreement, modifiers, comparisons, prepositions, and sentence form.

In a discussion of almost any subject, it is necessary to use a certain amount of technical terminology. When we talk about automobiles, we use the technical term *muffler* as a kind of shorthand for "a device to deaden the noise of escaping gases from an internal-combustion engine." The sports announcer who says, "They are going to try for a field goal" is using the technical term *field goal* to avoid having to say, "They are going to try to earn three points by place-kicking or drop-kicking the ball over the crossbar between their opponent's goal posts." Similarly, in a discussion of a sentence, it is, of course, possible to say, "The word used to define the action does not have the right form to match the form of the word used to indicate what is being talked about." But it is much more efficient to say, "The *verb* does not *agree* with the *subject*"; the words *verb, agree,* and *subject* are all technical terms with specific meanings that make discussion of grammar both easier and clearer. Thus, although it may seem tiresome to have to learn or relearn a certain amount of grammatical terminology, in the long run it will save you much time and frustration. In the following pages, each grammatical term is defined and usually exemplified at the time it first appears. Appendix D, "Glossary of Grammatical Terms," provides an alphabetical summary of the grammatical terms used in this handbook.

1 SENTENCE PATTERNS

The basic unit of the written language is the sentence. A **sentence** is a group of words that includes a subject (S) and a predicate (P) and that is not subordinated to (dependent upon) any other group of words; that is, a sentence can stand alone as a single utterance. The subject of a sentence is what or who is talked about, and the predicate is what is said about or asked about the subject. In many but not all sentences, the subject is the first word in the sentence.

    S   P
Elsa bought some green paint yesterday.

          S
Last week Peter was sick.

                        S
Because of budget cuts, the library will close.

     S
Did you feed the dog?

The predicate of a sentence must contain a verb phrase (VP). (Although the word *phrase* is commonly thought of as referring to two or more words, in grammatical and rhetorical usage, the term *verb phrase* is applied to single words as well.) A **verb phrase** is a word or words that express an action done by the subject or a state of existence of the subject. As the fourth sentence below illustrates, the parts of a verb phrase are sometimes separated by other elements of the sentence.

      VP
Elsa bought some green paint.

          VP
Last week Peter was sick.

                          VP
Because of budget cuts, the library will close.

VP   VP
Did you feed the dog?

All complete sentences contain a subject and a verb phrase. (Imperative sentences and some exclamations are an exception; these are discussed later). In many sentences, the predicate also requires elements other than just a verb phrase. Depending on the nature of these other elements, sentences are classified into five basic patterns.

1a SUBJECT + VERB PHRASE (S + VP)

A sentence may consist of only a subject and a verb phrase.

S   VP
<u>Money</u> <u>talks.</u>

S   VP
<u>The rains</u> <u>came.</u>

S   VP
<u>Swallows</u> <u>are nesting.</u>

1b SUBJECT + VERB PHRASE + SUBJECT COMPLEMENT (S + VP + SC)

When the verb phrase of a sentence contains a special kind of verb called a linking verb (see 4b), the verb phrase is followed by a subject complement (SC). A **subject complement** is a word or words that define or describe the subject.

S   VP   SC
<u>Time</u> <u>is</u> <u>money.</u>

S   VP   SC
<u>Time</u> <u>is</u> <u>valuable.</u>

S   VP   SC
<u>My sister</u> <u>became</u> <u>an archaeologist.</u>

S   VP   SC
<u>This milk</u> <u>has turned</u> <u>sour.</u>

Note that the subject complement refers to the same thing as the subject. The verb phrase in such sentences is like an equal sign: saying, "Time is money" is like saying, "Time = money." Or saying, "This milk has turned sour" is like saying, "This is sour milk."

1c SUBJECT + VERB PHRASE + DIRECT OBJECT (S + VP + DO)

In some sentences, the verb phrase is followed by a direct object (DO). The **direct object** of a verb is the person or thing that receives the action of the verb.

S   VP   DO
<u>Our business</u> <u>lost</u> <u>money.</u>

S   VP   DO
<u>Marilyn</u> <u>contradicted</u> <u>her mother.</u>

S   VP   DO
<u>The kindergartners</u> <u>are eating</u> <u>clay.</u>

The direct object can be thought of as answering the question *"What?"* or *"Whom?"* Thus, to the question *What did our business lose?* the answer is the direct object *money.* To the question *Whom did Marilyn contradict?* the answer is the direct object *her mother.*

1d SUBJECT + VERB PHRASE + INDIRECT OBJECT + DIRECT OBJECT (S + VP + IO + DO)

In some sentences, the verb phrase is followed by two objects, an indirect object (IO) and a direct object. The **indirect object** names the person or thing affected by the action of the verb or for whom or which the action of the verb was done.

```
       S   VP       IO          DO
     Paul sent his brother some money.
            S       VP    IO     DO
     The cowboy gave his horse a kiss.
        S     VP   IO     DO
     Ginger knit Andy a sweater.
```

1e SUBJECT + VERB PHRASE + DIRECT OBJECT + OBJECT COMPLEMENT (S + VP + DO + OC)

In some sentences, the verb phrase is followed by both a direct object and an object complement (OC). An **object complement** is a word or words that refer to the same thing as the direct object.

```
     S   VP       DO       OC
     I consider money an asset.
        S    VP    DO      OC
     Judy likes ice cream soft.
             S        VP      DO      OC
     The Andersons named their baby Tricia.
```

Note that, just as a subject complement refers to the same thing as the subject, so the object complement refers to the same thing as the direct object.

Every English sentence will be one of the above five types. In the examples given above, only one or two words have served as subjects, objects, and complements. In many sentences, the basic elements of subject, verb, subject complement, direct object, indirect object, and object complement are accompanied by modifiers (M). **Modifiers** are words that describe, define, or limit other words (see also 20).

```
         M    M     M    S       M       VP  M   M    DO
     The large Persian cat contentedly licked its white paws.
```

In this sentence, *the* and *Persian* modify the word *cat* by limiting it to a particular cat of a specific breed. *Large* describes the *cat*. The word *contentedly* modifies the verb phrase *licked* by describing how the cat licked. The word *its* modifies *paws* by limiting the paws to the cat's own paws, and *white* modifies *paws* by describing the paws.

EXERCISES: Sentence Patterns

Write *S* above the subject and *VP* above the verb phrase in the following sentences. Then, using the letters corresponding to the five sentence patterns listed below, identify each sentence by type in the margin. If the group of words is not a sentence, write *NS*.

A. Subject + Verb phrase
B. Subject + Verb phrase + Subject complement
C. Subject + Verb phrase + Direct object
D. Subject + Verb phrase + Indirect object + Direct object
E. Subject + Verb phrase + Direct object + Object complement

1. The dachshund barked ferociously at the burglar.
2. Elena gave Juan a cold stare.
3. The vivid colors in the rainbow following yesterday's storm.
4. From his cage, the gerbil greeted the restaurant's customers with a loud, squeaky voice.
5. After the tragedy the silence seemed deafening.
6. The boys at the garage judged Leroy's old Chevy the best for the drag race.
7. The cathedral chimes broke the eerie predawn stillness.
8. Before the race, the horse's owner gave the jockey an ultimatum.

2 PARTS OF SPEECH

We have thus far discussed the basic elements of sentences (subject, verb phrase, subject complement, direct object, indirect object, object complement, and modifiers). All of these elements are made up of words. But a moment's reflection will make it clear that not just any word can serve as a subject or as a verb phrase or as an indirect object. Words differ according to whether they name things or describe things or make assertions about things or connect things. Some words take certain kinds of endings that other words do not. Different words combine in different ways with other words. Different words typically appear in different positions in the sentence.

Native speakers of English will understand what you mean if you say, "Jimmy slept peacefully in his crib." But they will not know what you mean if you say, "<u>The</u> slept peacefully in his crib" or "<u>Peacefully</u> slept in his crib" or "<u>In</u> slept in his crib." Clearly, *Jimmy* can serve as the subject of a sentence, but *the, peacefully,* and *in* cannot. Because different kinds of words have different kinds of meaning and serve different functions in a sentence, it is useful to classify words into **parts of speech** according to their meanings and functions. We usually identify seven parts of speech: nouns, verbs, adjectives, adverbs, pronouns, prepositions, and conjunctions. An eighth part of speech, the isolate, is unique in that it is not grammatically related to other words in the sentence.

All these parts of speech are discussed in detail in the following pages. At this point a brief working definition and some examples of each of them will give us a vocabulary to use as we go along.

PART OF SPEECH	FUNCTION	EXAMPLES
Noun	Serves as subject, object, or complement in a sentence	table, law, Marilyn
Verb	Serves as the main element in a predicate	take, distribute, suppose
Adjective	Modifies nouns and pronouns	hairy, impossible, large
Adverb	Modifies verbs, adjectives, and other adverbs	quietly, already, very
Pronoun	Substitutes for a noun	him, anyone, itself
Preposition	Is used before a noun or pronoun to form a modifier of some other part of the sentence	toward, upon, to
Conjunction	Connects words, groups of words, and sentences	and, until, although
Isolate	Is not grammatically connected with other elements in the sentence	hello, ouch, yes

2a INFLECTIONS AND DERIVATIONAL SUFFIXES

Of the eight parts of speech, five (nouns, verbs, adjectives, adverbs, and pronouns) have characteristic endings that help to identify them. These endings are called **suffixes.** There are two kinds of suffixes, inflections and derivational suffixes. **Inflections** are endings that indicate such meanings as "more than one" (the plural inflection) or "action that took place in the past" (the past-tense inflection). For example, in the word *nations,* the -s is a plural inflection. In the word *showed,* the -ed is a past-tense inflection. Sometimes meanings are indicated by changes within a word; for example, *wrote* is the past tense of *write.* Such changes are also called inflections.

Derivational suffixes make new words by adding endings to existing words. They usually change the part of speech of the word to which they are attached. For example, the derivational suffix -*ment* makes a noun out of a verb: *establish/establishment.* The derivational suffix -*en* makes a verb out of an adjective: *sharp/sharpen.* Some derivational suffixes make a new word without changing the part of speech. For example, -*hood* makes one kind of noun out of another kind of noun: *mother/motherhood.*

In addition to suffixes, English words may also have prefixes. A **prefix** is an element that is attached to the beginning of a word but that is not an independent word itself. Examples of prefixes are *dis-*, *semi-*, *re-*, and *anti-*. Most prefixes change the meaning of the word to which they are added but do not change the part of speech: *happy* and *unhappy* are both adjectives; *assign* and *reassign* are both verbs. A few prefixes also change the part of speech of the word to which they are added. The prefix *en-*, for example, can be used to change a noun or adjective to a verb: *joy/enjoy; dear/endear*.

2b PHRASES AND CLAUSES

Two other terms needed in any discussion of the parts of speech are *phrases* and *clauses*. A **phrase** is a sequence of words arranged grammatically but not containing both a subject and a predicate (see 11).

> over my dead body
> a dilapidated green Volkswagen van
> would have liked to have seen

Note that the definition states that a phrase is arranged grammatically; this is important. *Over my dead body* is a phrase because the words are arranged grammatically. *Body over dead my* is not a phrase. It is just a string of words because the words are not arranged grammatically.

A **clause** is a sequence of words arranged grammatically and containing a subject and a predicate (see 12). Some clauses (**independent clauses**) can form complete sentences; some (**dependent clauses**) cannot.

INDEPENDENT CLAUSES	DEPENDENT CLAUSES
the traffic was light	although the traffic was light
you aren't home	if you aren't home
I hit my thumb	that I hit my thumb
this is what he wrote	which is what he wrote

A more complete discussion of kinds of phrases and clauses appears in 11 and 12.

3 NOUNS

The traditional definition of a **noun** is that it is the name of a person, place, thing, quality, or state. This definition by meaning is often accurate because most nouns do indeed name something or someone. Many nouns can also be defined by their form, that is, by their characteristic endings. And nouns can also be defined by their function or by the position they fill in sentences.

3a CHARACTERISTICS

Nouns are characterized by special endings, or inflections, for number and case, by derivational suffixes that make nouns out of other parts of speech, and by their function in a sentence as subjects, objects, and complements.

Inflections.   Noun inflections include those for number and case. The **number** of a noun indicates whether it is referring to a single thing (a singular noun) or more than one thing (a plural noun). Most English nouns have no inflectional ending in the singular and add *-s* or *-es* to form the plural. Some nouns have an irregular plural (see 46c for the spelling of irregular plural nouns).

SINGULAR	PLURAL
ribbon	ribbons
ditch	ditches
foot	feet (irregular plural)

The **case** of a noun shows its grammatical function in the sentence. English nouns have two cases, the **common** case and the **possessive** (sometimes called **genitive**) case. The possessive case is used to make the noun a modifier of another word; otherwise, the common case is used. (See 34a for the rules for forming possessive nouns.)

COMMON CASE	POSSESSIVE CASE
the burglar	the burglar's escape
a week	a week's vacation
sisters	my sisters' disappointment
men	men's clothing

Even when a noun is used as a modifier, it is often in the common case.

money market	*college* degree
coffee cup	*city* officials
weather forecast	*nail* clippers

Derivational Suffixes.   There are many derivational suffixes for making nouns out of other parts of speech (including other nouns).

-ance/-ence	elegance, prominence
-tion	condemnation, relaxation
-er	talker, destroyer
-ery	slavery, nunnery
-ism	realism, socialism
-ity	rapidity, elasticity
-ment	equipment, amazement
-ness	softness, thoroughness
-ship	friendship, dictatorship

Function and Position in Sentence.   Nouns have characteristic functions and positions in a sentence.

FUNCTION	EXAMPLES
Subject	Familiarity breeds contempt.
	One cup of water is enough.
Subject complement	Honesty is the best policy.
	John F. Kennedy was elected president.

Object complement	The Snapps named their daughter <u>Ginger</u>.
	Who appointed Irwin <u>boss</u>?
Direct object	We demand <u>justice</u>.
	Which <u>book</u> is the dog chewing up?
Indirect object	They wrote the <u>governor</u> a letter.
	Jeff baked his <u>mother</u> a cake.
Object of a preposition	Jill climbed over the <u>fence</u>.
	Our boat was damaged beyond <u>repair</u>.
Appositive	My brother <u>Bob</u> lives in Texas.
	He found the problem, a loose <u>nut</u>.
Direct address	<u>Brian</u>, your hamsters are loose again.
	Don't be so sure, my <u>friend</u>.
Nominative absolute	All <u>things</u> considered, I'd rather be home.
	A vote was taken, the <u>majority</u> abstaining.

Note: An **appositive** is a word, phrase, or clause that follows another word and that refers to the same thing or person (see 14). A **nominative absolute** (also called an **absolute phrase**) is a noun together with a particular form of a verb; the two together modify an entire clause or sentence (see 11c).

3b CLASSES

Nouns are traditionally divided into a number of different classes, depending on their formation, their meanings, and the kinds of modifiers that appear with them.

Simple and Compound Nouns. **Simple nouns** consist of a single word: *pan, miser, question, day*. **Compound nouns** consist of two—or sometimes more—parts of speech used as a single noun: *dustpan, tightwad, tossup, afternoon*. See also Appendix D, "Glossary of Grammatical Terms" and 46c.

Countable and Mass Nouns. **Countable nouns** have both a singular and a plural form. The singular form may be modified by either *a* or *the*. **Mass** (or **uncountable**) **nouns** are a special kind of singular noun that has no plural form and cannot be modified by the words *a* or *one*.

COUNTABLE NOUNS	MASS NOUNS
a chair, chairs	furniture
a pebble, pebbles	gravel
an enemy, enemies	hatred

Proper and Common Nouns. **Proper nouns** are those that name specific entities such as one particular person, place, building, holiday, or the like. Proper nouns may consist of more than one word, and all important words in a proper noun begin with a capital letter. All nouns that are not proper nouns are **common nouns.**

PROPER NOUNS	COMMON NOUNS
Helen Keller	a woman
White Plains	the city
Independence Hall	that building
Thanksgiving	a holiday

Concrete and Abstract Nouns. **Concrete nouns** designate tangible, physical objects that we can see, hear, touch, smell, or taste (*child, carrot, dime, rain*). Concrete nouns may be either countable or mass nouns. **Abstract nouns** designate ideas, concepts, or anything that we cannot experience directly with our senses (*childhood, nutrition, materialism, variation*). Most abstract nouns are also mass nouns. Many nouns may be used either as concrete or abstract nouns. In such instances, the concrete noun is usually a countable noun, and the abstract noun is a mass noun. See also Appendix D, "Glossary of Grammatical Terms" and 47b.

ABSTRACT AND MASS	<u>Beauty</u> is in the eye of the beholder. The concept of <u>honor</u> has changed over the centuries.
CONCRETE AND COUNTABLE	Though plain as a child, Caroline grew up to be a <u>beauty</u>. Dr. Miles has received numerous <u>honors</u>.

Collective Nouns. **Collective nouns** are used to designate an entire group of people or things (*audience, swarm, team, group*). Collective nouns are countable and may be made plural. See Appendix D, "Glossary of Grammatical Terms" and 18b.

SINGULAR COLLECTIVE	The <u>team</u> is best known for its post-game celebrations.
PLURAL COLLECTIVE	Four <u>teams</u> of workers are reseeding the oyster beds.

EXERCISES: Nouns

Underline every noun in the following sentences. Then write the letter from the list below over each noun to identify its function in the sentence.

A. Subject	F. Object of a Preposition
B. Subject Complement	G. Appositive
C. Object Complement	H. Direct Address
D. Direct Object	I. Nominative Absolute
E. Indirect Object	

1. Dixie tells her dreams—in vivid, tedious detail—to the entire family.
2. Our cat, Beethoven, has an inordinate hatred of the piano.
3. But the driver did not stop for the light, officer.
4. Alfred considers bathing a waste of time.
5. The lawyer raised his eyes from his briefcase and surveyed the woman.
6. Their son Gene became a surgeon and moved to Alaska with his wife.
7. The first orbit completed, the satellite beamed its signals to earth.
8. Jessica mailed her representative the petition.

4 VERBS

Verbs are traditionally defined as words that express an action, an occurrence, or a state of existence. This definition by meaning is not always satisfactory because other parts of speech, such as nouns, also express action or existence. But verbs can also be defined by their forms, that is, by characteristic endings, and by the function they serve in sentences.

4a CHARACTERISTICS

Verbs are characterized by inflections for tense, person, voice, and mood; by derivational suffixes that make verbs out of other parts of speech; and by their function in a sentence as the main element of the predicate.

Inflections. Verbs have five forms, an infinitive and four inflected forms. The **infinitive** is either the base form of the verb (*carry*) or the base form preceded by *to* (*to carry*). The four inflected forms are (1) third-person singular present tense, (2) past tense, (3) present participle (also called progressive participle), and (4) past participle.

TYPE OF INFLECTION	FORM OF INFLECTION	EXAMPLES
Third-person singular present tense	-s	she talks, he sings, it works
Past tense	-ed (or irregular)	she talked, he sang, it worked
Present participle	-ing	she is talking, he was singing, it has been working
Past participle	-ed (or irregular)	she has talked, he had sung, it has worked

The infinitive, the past tense, and the past participle of a verb are together called the **principal parts** of the verb.

PRINCIPAL PARTS	EXAMPLES
Infinitive	(to) talk, (to) grow, (to) work
Past tense	talked, grew, worked
Past participle	talked, grown, worked

Every form of a verb is either finite or nonfinite. **Finite verbs** are those that may stand alone as complete verb phrases or even as complete predicates. Infinitives, present participles, and past participles are **nonfinite verbs;** they cannot stand alone as complete verb phrases.

FINITE VERBS	NONFINITE VERBS
(The canary) sings.	(to) sing
(The canary) sang.	singing
	sung

In verb phrases containing more than one verb, only the first verb is finite, and the remaining verbs are nonfinite. Hence in the verb phrase *has been singing, has* is finite, but *been* (past participle) and *singing* (present participle) are nonfinite.

Derivational Suffixes. There are fewer derivational suffixes and prefixes for forming verbs out of other parts of speech than there are for forming nouns.

-ate	operate, designate, originate
-en	widen, ripen, sadden
-fy	quantify, liquefy, codify
-ize	civilize, recognize, legalize
em-/en-	empower, enable, endanger

Function and Position in Sentence. The primary function of a verb is to form the main element of the predicate; in simplest terms, the verb explains what is going on. Because the most common word order of English sentences is subject + predicate, the most common position of the verb phrase is after the subject. In certain kinds of sentences, however, at least part of the verb phrase precedes the subject.

AFTER SUBJECT	The ambulance <u>was racing</u> across the square.
BEFORE SUBJECT	<u>Have</u> you any ideas for a costume?
BEFORE AND AFTER SUBJECT	<u>Will</u> Elmer <u>be eaten</u> by the lion?

Tense, Mood, and Voice. Every verb phrase, whether it consists of a single verb or several verbs, conveys three categories of grammatical information—tense, mood, and voice.

    1. **Tense** is the time or duration of the action or state named by the verb or verb phrase. The following table summarizes the five tenses of English.

TENSE	FORMATION	MEANING	EXAMPLES
Present	-s for 3d person singular; no ending for other forms	Universally true; not limited to a particular time	she talk<u>s</u>, we talk
Past	-ed (or irregular)	Action completed at an earlier time	she talk<u>ed</u>; we talk<u>ed</u>
Progressive	A form of *be* plus the present participle of the verb	A continuing but limited action	she <u>is</u> talk<u>ing</u>; we <u>are</u> talk<u>ing</u>
Perfect	A form of *have* plus the past participle of the verb	Action begun earlier and still relevant at a later time	she <u>has</u> talk<u>ed</u>; we <u>have</u> talk<u>ed</u>
Future	*Will* or *shall* plus the infinitive	Future time; prediction	she <u>will</u> talk; we <u>will</u> talk

The progressive and perfect tenses may combine with each other and with the present, past, or future tenses to form numerous compound tenses.

PAST PERFECT	she had talked
FUTURE PROGRESSIVE	she will be talking
PAST PERFECT PROGRESSIVE	she had been talking

A complete list of all the possible tenses and their combinations is given in Appendix E, "Complete Conjugation of an English Verb."

2. The **mood** of a verb or verb phrase expresses the attitude of the speaker or writer toward the statement—as a fact or question, as a command, or as a possibility or something contrary to fact. English has three moods: the **indicative,** the **imperative,** and the **subjunctive.** See 17c for the uses of the different forms of the subjunctive.

MOOD	FORMATION	MEANING	EXAMPLES
Indicative	(as in the preceding chart of the five tenses)	Ordinary statement or question	she <u>is</u> quiet; <u>is</u> she quiet?
Imperative	Infinitive with no subject, but "you" understood	Request or command	<u>Be</u> quiet.
Subjunctive	Infinitive or plural past tense of verb	Unreal, hypothetical, or doubtful statement	that she <u>be</u> quiet; if she <u>were</u> quiet

3. The **voice** of a verb indicates the relation of the action of the verb to the subject of the clause or sentence. The **active voice** means that the subject is the doer of the action. The **passive voice** means that the subject is the receiver of the action. The passive voice consists of a form of the verb *to be* and the past participle of a verb.

ACTIVE VOICE	Surgeons sometimes <u>make</u> mistakes.
	The surgeon <u>has</u> not <u>taken</u> a sponge count.
	Whom <u>will</u> the surgeon <u>blame</u>?
	The irate patient <u>is filing</u> a malpractice suit.

PASSIVE VOICE	Mistakes <u>are</u> sometimes <u>made</u> [by surgeons].
	No sponge count <u>has been taken</u> [by the surgeon].
	Who <u>will be blamed</u> [by the surgeon]?
	A malpractice suit <u>is being filed</u> [by the irate patient].

EXERCISES: Tense, Mood, and Voice of Verbs

Part A: Underline all the verb phrases in the following sentences, and identify the tense, voice, and mood of each. If necessary, see Appendix E for a complete listing of tenses.

1. The bell had rung five minutes earlier when Don stumbled into the class.

2. Her mother does not know that she has been working at the club.

3. Karen will be furious when she learns that her roommate wrecked her car last night.

4. "See your lawyer first thing in the morning," Dmitri begged.
5. The wedding is being planned for the first week in October.
6. David insisted that Abraham attend the party.

Part B: Complete the following sentences by writing in the specified tense and voice of the italicized infinitive. If necessary, see Appendix E for a complete listing of tenses.

1. The neighbors _____ on their vacation tomorrow.
   (*to leave*—future progressive)
2. The committee _____ already, before we
   (*to decide*—future perfect)
   _____ a chance to present our argument.
   (*to have*—present perfect)

3. "She _____ here all evening," the landlady
        (*to be*—present perfect)
   _____ the police.
   (*to assure*—past)

4. You _____ everything that _____ to the rest of us.
        (*to know*—past)   (*to know*—past passive)
5. The theory _____ on a colony of ants.
        (*to test*—past progressive passive)

4b CLASSES

Verbs can be classified in a number of different ways according to their forms and their functions in a clause or sentence. The most basic division is that of main verbs vs. auxiliary verbs.

Main Verbs.   **Main verbs** (or **lexical verbs,** as they are sometimes called) are those that carry most of the meaning of the verb phrase in which they appear. Properly inflected, a main verb can stand alone as a complete verb phrase or even as a complete predicate.

> Insurance rates have <u>increased</u> by 52 percent.
>
> You will have to <u>redraw</u> all the maps.
>
> The lights <u>flickered</u>.

There are three major classifications of main verbs: (1) regular or irregular, (2) transitive, intransitive, or linking, and (3) finite or nonfinite.

1. Main verbs may be regular or irregular. For purposes of writing, a **regular verb** forms both its past tense and its past participle by adding *-ed.* An **irregular verb** forms its past tense or past participle in a different way, such as by changing the vowel, by adding *-t* instead of *-ed,* or by having no endings at all in the past tense or past participle. Out of thousands and thousands of verbs in English, fewer than two hundred are irregular, but the irregular ones are among the most frequently used verbs.

REGULAR VERBS	IRREGULAR VERBS
talk, talked, talked	speak, spoke, spoken
drop, dropped, dropped	run, ran, run
amaze, amazed, amazed	cut, cut, cut

The verb *to be* is the most irregular verb in English. Unlike any other verb, it has a separate form for the first-person and third-person singular present, and for the plural in both the present and past tenses.

PRESENT TENSE OF *TO BE*	PAST TENSE OF *TO BE*
I am	I was
you are	you were
he/she/it is	he/she/it was
we/you/they are	we/you/they were

2. Another classification of main verbs is made according to the kind of objects or complements that accompany them in a sentence.

Intransitive verbs are those with no direct object or subject complement.

> The old man <u>slept</u>.
> Time <u>passes slowly</u> here.
> Snow <u>is falling</u>.

Transitive verbs are those with at least a direct object. Some transitive verbs are also accompanied by an indirect object or an object complement.

> The old man <u>swept</u> the porch.
> Time <u>changes</u> all things.
> Snow <u>is covering</u> the shrubs.
> Mother <u>handed</u> me a spoon. (direct and indirect object)
> Schweitzer's work <u>made</u> him a hero. (direct object and object complement)

When the direct object of a transitive verb refers to the same thing or person as the subject, the verb is called **reflexive**. The direct object of a reflexive verb is always a pronoun ending in *-self*.

> The old man <u>hurt</u> himself.

Linking verbs are those that are followed by a subject complement.

> The old man <u>is</u> tactless.
> The old man <u>is</u> a coin-collector.
> The snow <u>feels</u> wet.
> Benedict Arnold <u>turned</u> traitor.

Some verbs are used only intransitively (*lie, rise, fall*), and some verbs are used only transitively (*have, need, want*). A few transitive verbs are used only reflexively (*pride, perjure, avail*). A very few verbs are used only as linking verbs (*seem*). Many verbs can be transitive or intransitive, reflexive or nonreflexive, linking or nonlinking.

TRANSITIVE	He turned the dial.
INTRANSITIVE	He turned slowly.
TRANSITIVE REFLEXIVE	He turned himself around.
LINKING	He turned green.

Auxiliary Verbs. Auxiliary verbs, also called **helping verbs,** are those that are used in forming verb phrases but that cannot form a complete verb phrase by themselves. The number of auxiliary verbs is limited, and they have no characteristic derivational suffixes. There are four major kinds of auxiliary verbs, each of which performs certain functions: (1) *be,* (2) *have,* (3) modal auxiliaries, and (4) *do.* (*Be, have,* and *do* can also be main verbs: I *am* your captain; Oscar *has* athlete's foot; Can you *do* a split?)

1. *Be* is used in forming the progressive tense and the passive voice.

| PROGRESSIVE TENSE | she <u>is</u> helping, she <u>was</u> helping, she has <u>been</u> helping |
| PASSIVE VOICE | she <u>is</u> helped [by her friends], she <u>was</u> helped, she has <u>been</u> helped |

2. *Have* is used in forming the perfect tenses.

she <u>has</u> helped
she <u>had</u> helped
she <u>has</u> been helped

3. The **modal auxiliaries** are *will, would, shall, should, can, could, may, might, dare, need (to), ought (to),* and *must.* Unlike other verbs, the modal auxiliaries have only one form and are followed only by the infinitive form of the verb. (*Dare* and *need* can also be main verbs: Bert *dared* Cecily to jump off the slide; Mrs. Ryan *needs* a hearing-aid.)

The modal auxiliaries *will* and *shall* are used in forming the future tenses. The other modal auxiliaries are used to express some degree of ability, necessity, obligation, uncertainty, or the like.

ABILITY	He <u>can</u> read.
NECESSITY	He <u>must</u> read.
OBLIGATION	He <u>ought to</u> read.
UNCERTAINTY	He <u>may</u> read.

4. *Do* is used when the grammar of the clause or sentence requires an auxiliary but no other auxiliary is appropriate. Thus, *do* is used primarily in asking questions and in negative sentences (those that deny an assertion).

He reads, <u>doesn't</u> he?
<u>Does</u> he read?
He <u>does</u> not read.

Do is also the so-called **emphatic auxiliary;** it is used to contradict a previous assumption or statement.

Despite what you say, he <u>does</u> read.

In addition to the four kinds of auxiliaries, there are a number of other verbs that sometimes precede the main verb and that act like auxiliaries. These **semiauxiliaries** are really idioms, that is, expressions whose meanings are not predictable from the meanings of their individual words.

He <u>kept on</u> reading.	She <u>is going to</u> read.
He <u>started to</u> read.	She <u>is to</u> read tomorrow.
He <u>has to</u> read.	She <u>is not about to</u> read.
He <u>used to</u> read.	She <u>is about to</u> read.
He <u>is supposed to</u> read.	She <u>happened to</u> read.

EXERCISES: Auxiliary Verbs

Underline all forms of the verbs *be, have,* and *do* in the following sentences. Indicate over each its function as either auxiliary verb (A) or main verb (M).

1. Have Alice and Don ever done such a thing?
2. Alfie is having some problems with his parents.
3. Kirsten had taken the pictures without removing the lens cap from the camera.
4. The man did promise to return the coat.
5. The child has never had a very stable home.
6. "I am being good," the four-year-old assured his mother.
7. Kittens should be inoculated for distemper.

5 ADJECTIVES

Adjectives are traditionally defined as words that modify nouns or pronouns by defining, describing, limiting, or qualifying those nouns or pronouns. Many adjectives also can be defined by their form, that is, by typical endings, or by the positions they take in sentences.

5a CHARACTERISTICS

Many adjectives are characterized by inflectional endings showing comparative and superlative degrees or by derivational suffixes that make adjectives out of other parts of speech. Adjectives are also identified by the positions they take as modifiers of nouns or noun substitutes.

Inflections. Some adjectives can be inflected for comparison. The three degrees of comparison are **positive, comparative,** and **superlative.** The positive degree of an adjective has no ending, the comparative ending is *-er*, and the superlative ending is *-est*.

POSITIVE	COMPARATIVE	SUPERLATIVE
fine	finer	finest
poor	poorer	poorest

A few adjectives have irregular inflections.

POSITIVE	COMPARATIVE	SUPERLATIVE
good	better	best
bad	worse	worst
a little	less	least
many/much	more	most
far	farther/further	farthest/furthest
old	older/elder	oldest/eldest

Many English adjectives do not form their comparative and superlative degrees by inflection but with the separate words *more* (or *less*) and *most* (or *least*). As a general rule, adjectives of one syllable are inflected, and adjectives of more than one syllable form comparative and superlative degrees with *more* (*less*) and *most* (*least*). However, two-syllable adjectives ending in *-y*, *-ly*, *-le*, *-er*, and *-ow* are usually inflected.

accurate/more accurate/most accurate
brutal/more brutal/most brutal
curious/less curious/least curious

-y	heavy/heavier/heaviest
-ly	early/earlier/earliest
-le	little/littler/littlest
-er	clever/cleverer/cleverest
-ow	shallow/shallower/shallowest

Derivational Suffixes.   There are many derivational suffixes that make adjectives out of other parts of speech or from Latin roots.

-able/-ible	comfortable, possible	-ic/-ical	comic, historical
-al/-ar	final, perpendicular	-ish	foolish, reddish
-ant/-ent	important, prominent	-ive	native, active
-ary	military, necessary	-less	hopeless, countless
-ed	bearded, wretched	-ly	kindly, earthly
-en	wooden, silken	-ous	generous, enormous
-ful	beautiful, careful	-y	messy, lumpy

Function and Position in Sentence.   In their function as modifiers of nouns and pronouns, adjectives appear near the words they modify. The following are four common positions:

(1) before nouns and the indefinite pronoun *one,*

The <u>tiny</u> nest was full of <u>delicate</u> eggs.
He'll take a pear if you have a <u>ripe</u> one.

(2) as subject complements following linking verbs,

Her explanation sounds <u>fishy</u>.
This fireplace is <u>elegant</u> but <u>impractical</u>.

(3) as object complements after direct objects,

I want that floor <u>spotless</u>.
You are driving us <u>mad</u>.

(4) after indefinite pronouns.

Anything <u>small</u> and <u>furry</u> delights Rupert.
None <u>better</u> could be found.

5b CLASSES

Adjectives can be divided into a number of classes, depending on their formation, their relationship with other parts of speech, and their function in the sentence.

Descriptive.   The great majority of adjectives are **descriptive adjectives,** which specify a quality or state of the noun or pronoun they modify. Descriptive adjectives are the only adjectives that have derivational suffixes.

WITHOUT SUFFIXES	large, rare, old, strong, sweet
WITH SUFFIXES	hasty, fatal, gracious, significant, merciless

A subclass of descriptive adjectives is **proper adjectives,** made by adding a derivational suffix to a proper noun.

Italian, Turkish, Romanesque, Shakespearean

Others.   Other classes of adjectives include the personal possessives used to modify nouns. When the demonstrative pronouns, interrogative pronouns, indefinite pronouns, relative pronouns, and cardinal and ordinal numbers are used to modify nouns, they are also classed as adjectives. Finally, the **definite article** and **indefinite article** are also kinds of adjectives. (See also Appendix D, "Glossary of Grammatical Terms.")

TYPE OF ADJECTIVE	FORMS	EXAMPLES OF USE
Possessive	my, your, his, her, its, our, their, one's	*my* hat; *its* completion
Demonstrative	this/these, that/those	*this* song; *those* stations
Interrogative	what, which, whose	*Which* path should we take?
Indefinite	another, each, both, many, any, some, no, etc.	*both* sides; *no* complaints
Numerical	two, five, third, eighth	*two* bricks, the *ninth* item
Relative	what(ever), which(ever), whose(ever)	He lost *what* little hair he had.
Definite Article	the	*the* noise; *the* beachcombers
Indefinite Article	a/an	*a* picture; *an* octopus

EXERCISES: Adjectives

Part A: Write sentences that include the specified form of the adjective given.

1. the comparative of *stubborn*
2. the superlative of *fragile*
3. the superlative of *bad*
4. the comparative of *much*
5. the superlative of *furry*
6. the comparative of *supple*

Part B: Underline *all* adjectives in the following sentences. Write above each one the letter from the list below that identifies the kind of adjective it is.

A. Descriptive
B. Proper
C. Possessive
D. Demonstrative
E. Interrogative
F. Indefinite
G. Numerical
H. Relative
I. Definite article
J. Indefinite article

1. That Irish dance is the most captivating part of their program.
2. Which mechanic worked on my car the last time?
3. Jon did not have enough money to pay for all of their tickets.
4. Those prices were the highest they had been in three years.
5. Millie loved to read German poetry aloud, but her awkward pronunciation greatly detracted from its lyrical cadences.
6. Kelly did not have any idea which tapes Randy had already bought.
7. Timid about making speeches of any kind, Dolores was especially upset when she had to deliver a welcome to the new supervisor.

6 ADVERBS

Adverbs are traditionally defined as words that modify verbs, adjectives, or other adverbs and that express such ideas as time, place, manner, cause, and degree. Many adverbs can also be defined by characteristic endings or by their position in the sentence.

6a CHARACTERISTICS

Many adverbs are characterized by inflectional endings showing comparative and superlative degrees and by derivational suffixes that make adverbs out of adjectives or other parts of speech. Adverbs are also identified by their position near the words they modify.

Inflections. Adverbs that are derived from adjectives or that have the same form as adjectives may take comparative inflections (*-er, -est*). *Soon*, although it has no corresponding adjective, also takes *-er* and *-est*. The rules for forming and using the comparative inflection with adverbs are the same as the rules for adjectives (5a). A few adverbs have irregular comparative inflections.

POSITIVE	COMPARATIVE	SUPERLATIVE
well	better	best
badly	worse	worst
far	farther/further	farthest/furthest

Derivational Suffixes. By far the most common derivational suffix of adverbs is -*ly*, which makes adverbs out of adjectives (*gently, normally, thoroughly*). The suffixes -*wise* and -*where* also form adverbs (*otherwise, elsewhere*). The derivational prefix *a*- makes adverbs out of both adjectives and nouns (*anew, aloud, aside*).

Function and Position in Sentence. Adjectives modify nouns and pronouns; adverbs modify almost everything else, including verbs, adjectives, other adverbs, and entire clauses or sentences. Adverbs express many different kinds of meaning, as the following examples illustrate.

MANNER	Mr. Potter speaks <u>eloquently</u>. (*Eloquently* modifies *speaks* and tells the manner in which Mr. Potter speaks.)
DEGREE	Mr. Potter's speech was <u>rather</u> long. (*Rather* modifies *long* and tells the extent to which Mr. Potter's speech was long.)
FREQUENCY	Mr. Potter <u>often</u> makes speeches. (*Often* modifies *makes speeches* and tells how frequently Mr. Potter makes speeches.)
TIME	Mr. Potter spoke <u>yesterday</u>. (*Yesterday* modifies *spoke* and tells when Mr. Potter spoke.)
PLACE	Mr. Potter spoke <u>here</u>. (*Here* modifies *spoke* and tells where Mr. Potter spoke.)
NEGATION	Mr. Potter <u>never</u> turns down a chance to speak. (*Never* modifies *turns down a chance to speak* and denies or negates that phrase.)
AFFIRMATION	Mr. Potter <u>certainly</u> likes to talk. (*Certainly* modifies *likes to talk* and affirms or reinforces that phrase.)
QUALIFICATION	<u>Perhaps</u> Mr. Potter forgot his watch. (*Perhaps* modifies *forgot his watch* and expresses a qualification of the degree of uncertainty or probability of that phrase.)

Because adverbs modify so many different elements, their positions within sentences are varied. In general, they appear near the words they modify, as in the preceding examples. See also 20c for a further discussion of adverbs.

6b CLASSES

Depending on their form and their function in the sentence, adverbs can be divided into several classes.

Adjectival.   The great majority of adverbs are **adjectival adverbs,** that is, adverbs made from adjectives.

> impressively, tightly, oddly, mistakenly, characteristically, finally

Some adverbs, called **plain adverbs,** have the same form as adjectives; that is, they have no additional derivational suffix to mark them as adverbs. There are two important varieties of plain adverbs: those from adjectives with no suffix and those from adjectives already ending in -*ly.*

NO SUFFIX	-LY SUFFIX
straight	early
hard	daily
right	weekly
far	hourly
late	deathly

Prepositional.   **Prepositional adverbs** are identical in form to prepositions. Note that most of these express spatial relationships of some kind.

out	up	outside	across	beyond
over	through	past	behind	near
down	in	around	by	
off	inside	on	below	

PREPOSITIONAL ADVERBS	Uncle George took his teeth *out.* Uncle George dropped *in* this morning.
PREPOSITIONS	Uncle George threw his teeth *out* the window. Uncle George dropped his teeth *in* the sink.

Interrogative and Relative.   The **interrogative** and **relative adverbs** are *where, when, why,* and *how.* Interrogative adverbs are used to ask questions, and relative adverbs are used to introduce relative clauses.

INTERROGATIVE ADVERBS	*How* does this latch work? *Why* is the sky blue?
RELATIVE ADVERBS	I left *when* the park closed. Bracken springs up *where* land has been overgrazed.

Conjunctive.   See 9b, "Adverbial Conjunctions."

Miscellaneous.   Many common adverbs are not derived from any other part of speech. We recognize these words as adverbs by their unique form and by their function in the sentence.

also	maybe	quite	then
always	never	rather	there
anyhow	not	seldom	thus
anyway	now	so	too
ever	often	somehow	very
indeed	perhaps	somewhat	

EXERCISES: Adverbs

List all the adverbs in the following sentences. Beside each adverb, write the word or words it modifies and the letter from the list below that defines what kind of adverb it is.

A. Adjectival   C. Interrogative   E. Miscellaneous
B. Prepositional   D. Relative

1. Walter became very nervous when he saw the man furtively motion to the three policemen.

2. The police, unfortunately, had already been called in.

3. All that could be seen of the two swimmers then were blond heads bobbing up and down.

4. Now, where did I put that book?

5. The senator never says publicly how he got the money so quickly or, indeed, precisely how much money is involved.

6. She launched into her usual round of meetings, firmly convinced that she would surely feel stronger if she worked harder.

7. How his father thought he should dress was certainly the very least of Paul's worries.

7 PRONOUNS

Pronouns are traditionally defined as words that substitute for nouns. Pronouns can also be defined by the positions they fill in sentences.

7a CHARACTERISTICS

Many pronouns have inflections for number, some for number and case, and some for number, case, person, and gender. Pronouns are also characterized by their function in a sentence as noun substitutes serving as subjects, objects, and complements.

Inflections and Derivational Suffixes. Only personal pronouns, the relative pronoun *who*, and the demonstrative pronouns are inflected. Pronouns in general have no derivational endings, although *-one*, *-body*, and *-thing* (as in *someone, nobody, everything*) might be considered derivational endings.

Function and Position. Pronouns are used instead of nouns or noun phrases and to avoid repetition of the noun or noun phrase.

>   N   Pron
> Let the <u>dog</u> in. <u>He</u> is scratching at the door. (*He* avoids repetition of the noun *dog*.)

>   N   N   Pron
> Ron wanted to take <u>botany</u> and <u>geology</u>, but <u>neither</u> was offered this semester. (*Neither* avoids repetition of *botany* and *geology*.)

Pronouns are also used when the appropriate noun is unknown or unspecified.

> Pron
> <u>Someone</u> has taken Yvonne's tennis racket. (It is not known who took the racket.)

> Pron
> I'm thinking of <u>something</u> old and brown. (You know what you are thinking of, but you do not care to specify it.)

Finally, pronouns are used when there is no appropriate noun but the sentence must have a subject.

> Pron
> <u>It</u> will probably snow tonight. (There is no suitable subject for the verb *snow*, but the sentence must have a subject.)

As substitutes for nouns, pronouns serve the same functions and take almost all the positions in a sentence that nouns do.

SUBJECT	<u>They</u> ate a whole watermelon.
SUBJECT COMPLEMENT	Determination is not <u>enough</u>.
OBJECT COMPLEMENT	We have to name the canary <u>something</u>.
DIRECT OBJECT	Uncle Sam wants <u>you</u>.
INDIRECT OBJECT	Alice showed <u>me</u> her appendectomy scar.
OBJECT OF PREPOSITION	Don't tread on <u>me</u>.
APPOSITIVE	Mother wants a new vacuum cleaner, <u>one</u> with a headlight.
DIRECT ADDRESS	<u>You</u> in the striped shirt! Get out of the way.
NOMINATIVE ABSOLUTE	<u>Nothing</u> having been planned beforehand, disaster was the result.

7b CLASSES

There are eight classes of pronouns: (1) personal pronouns, (2) reflexive and intensive pronouns, (3) demonstrative pronouns, (4) interrogative pronouns, (5) relative pronouns, (6) indefinite pronouns, (7) reciprocal pronouns, and (8) expletive pronouns.

Personal. **Personal pronouns** are called "personal" because they are inflected to indicate the grammatical category called **person.** Person distinguishes the individual who is speaking **(first person),** the individual being spoken to **(second person),** and the individual or thing being talked about **(third person).** Thus, *I* and *we* are first-person pronouns, *you* is a second-person pronoun, and *she, it, he,* and *they* are third-person pronouns.

Like nouns, personal pronouns are also inflected for case (see 3a). But, whereas nouns have just two cases (common and possessive), personal pronouns have three cases: subject, object, and possessive. The **subject case** is used for subjects and subject complements, the **object case** is used for objects of all kinds, and the **possessive case** is used to substitute for a possessive adjective and a noun.

CASE	FUNCTION	EXAMPLES
Subject	Subject	<u>I</u> took three aspirins and went to bed.
	Subject complement	It was <u>I</u> who called the police.
Object	Direct object	Mr. Dowling does not remember <u>me</u>.
	Indirect object	Betsy told <u>me</u> her tale of woe.
	Object of preposition	I brought a toothbrush with <u>me</u>.
Possessive	Substitute for possessive adjective and noun	Henry's bicycle is red and <u>mine</u> is yellow. (*Mine* substitutes for *my bicycle*.)

Also like nouns, personal pronouns are inflected for singular and plural number. Thus, *I* and *me* are first-person singular pronouns, and *we* and *us* are first-person plural pronouns.

The third-person singular personal pronoun is also inflected for gender. **Gender** indicates whether the person or thing being talked about is a male **(masculine gender)**, a female **(feminine gender)**, or neither **(neuter gender)**. *He* and *him* are masculine, *she* and *her* are feminine, and *it* is neuter.

All the possible inflections of the personal pronouns are summarized in the following table. The forms in parentheses are possessives used only as adjectives and not as pronouns.

PERSON	CASE		NUMBER	
			Singular	Plural
First	Subject		I	we
	Object		me	us
	Possessive		mine (my)	ours (our)
Second	Subject		you	you
	Object		you	you
	Possessive		yours (your)	yours (your)

PERSON	CASE	GENDER			
		Masc.	Fem.	Neut.	
Third	Subject	he	she	it	they
	Object	him	her	it	them
	Possessive	his (his)	hers (her)	its (its)	theirs (their)

Others. **Reflexive pronouns** indicate that the object of the verb is the same as the subject of the verb. **Intensive pronouns** emphasize the noun or pronoun they follow. **Demonstrative pronouns** point out or specify things as being "nearer to" or "farther from" the speaker. **Interrogative pronouns** introduce questions. **Relative pronouns** introduce subordinate clauses and serve as subjects or objects in those clauses. **Indefinite pronouns** refer to members or parts of a category without specifying which particular member or part. **Reciprocal pronouns** refer to interaction between two or more persons or things. **Expletive pronouns** serve as subjects of clauses and sentences when no other subject is appropriate or when the subject is a long clause.

TYPE OF PRONOUN	FORMS	EXAMPLES
Reflexive	myself, yourself, himself, herself, itself, oneself, ourselves, yourselves, themselves	Joanne cut <u>herself</u> on the glass. Did you enjoy <u>yourself</u>?
Intensive	same as reflexive	Joanne <u>herself</u> didn't break the glass. Dean went to Texas <u>himself</u>.
Demonstrative	this/these that/those	<u>These</u> must go back tomorrow. I will never believe <u>that</u>.
Interrogative	what, which, who, whose, whom, and forms in *-ever* (whoever, and so on)	<u>Who</u> invented the clothespin? <u>Whoever</u> could be calling at this hour?
Relative	same as interrogative; *that*	Gretchen is the one <u>who</u> dropped the tray. Did you see the coyote <u>that</u> I shot?
Indefinite	another, each, either, neither, many, few, more, enough, some, such, less, any, much, nothing, and so on	<u>Many</u> are called, but <u>few</u> are chosen. <u>Each</u> received a share; <u>neither</u> was disappointed.
Reciprocal	each other, one another	Clio and I congratulated <u>each other</u>. The children all play well with <u>one another</u>.
Expletive	it, there	<u>There</u> is no reason for despair. <u>It</u> is a mistake to argue with a judge.

gr

EXERCISES: Pronouns

List all pronouns in the following sentences. After each pronoun, write the letter from the list below that identifies its grammatical function and the number from the list that identifies the kind of pronoun it is.

A. Subject	1. Personal
B. Subject complement	2. Reflexive
C. Object complement	3. Intensive
D. Direct object	4. Demonstrative
E. Indirect object	5. Interrogative
F. Object of preposition	6. Relative
G. Appositive	7. Indefinite
H. Direct address	8. Reciprocal
I. Nominative absolute	9. Expletive

1. The parrot that the neighbors brought home from their vacation squawks day and night, and even though everyone has complained, nothing has been done about it.

2. "That's it!" Nancy squealed. "That's the one I've wanted for so long!"

3. George offered to give me some of them, but I refused to take any.

4. There was a real absence of love in that house, felt by all who entered it.

5. "But she stood there herself and told me I could eat anything in the refrigerator," Pablo argued.

6. What did they give each other on their anniversary?

7. No one having remained behind to guard the camp, the hikers were worried about their food supplies.

8. It is important that you do it yourself rather than relying on others.

9. I thoroughly enjoyed myself at the concert last night.

10. This employer considered her someone with a very promising future.

8 PREPOSITIONS

Prepositions are words used before nouns or pronouns to form phrases that modify some part of the sentence. Prepositions have no inflections or derivational suffixes. The combination of a preposition, its noun or pronoun object, and any modifiers of that object is called a **prepositional phrase**.

PREPOSITIONAL
PHRASES

The mice <u>in the attic</u> are driving me <u>out of my mind</u>. <u>Despite the traps</u> that I put <u>behind the chimney</u> and <u>by the door</u>, they seem to have multiplied <u>during the past two months</u>.

There are fewer than a hundred different prepositions in English, but they are used very frequently. Most prepositions have a basic meaning concerned with space (*above, beyond, from, through,* and so on) or time (*during, since, until,* and so on) or both space and time (*around, before, following, near,* and so on), but most of these have extended meanings that have little to do with actual time or space (for example, *beyond my comprehension, from my experience*). The remaining prepositions express many different kinds of relationships, including, for example, exclusion (*but, except*), cause (*because of, due to*), and focus (*concerning, with regard to*). A partial list of prepositions follows. Note that there are a number of phrasal prepositions, that is, prepositions consisting of more than one word. Note also that many of these words also serve as adverbs (see 6b).

about	below	for	regarding
above	beneath	from	since
according to	beside	in (into)	through
across	besides	in the	to
after	between	middle of	toward
against	beyond	in spite of	under
ahead of	but	including	underneath
amid(st)	by	like	until (till)
among	by means of	near	up
around	concerning	next to	versus
as	despite	of	via
as for	down	off	with
at	due to	on (upon)	with regard
away from	during	out	(respect)
because of	except	out of	to
before	except for	over	within
behind	following	past	without
		prior to	

EXERCISES: Prepositions

In the following sentences, underline each preposition, circle the object of the preposition, and enclose the entire prepositional phrase in parentheses.

1. Next to his uncle Fred, his cousin Gertrude had always been the subject of the most gossip among members of the family.

2. Looking around the room, Mrs. Badenoch found all but two of the kittens.

3. During the winter Cherokee is like a ghost town, deserted by the hordes of summer vacationers who come to see the Indians.

4. Prior to 1867, Alaska was owned by Russia, but in that year the United States purchased it for $7.2 million; it did not, however, become a state until almost a hundred years later.

5. Without her hat, the girl with the red hair reminded Mr. Pahlitzsch of an actress he had seen in a play in Washington.

6. The stunt pilot flew his plane under the bridge and, with a burst of speed, made three loops over the crowd watching from the riverbank.

7. Whirling about like spinning tops, the Cossack dancers spellbound the audience, ending the performance only at midnight.

9 CONJUNCTIONS

Conjunctions are words that link single words, phrases, and clauses. Like prepositions, they have no inflections or derivational suffixes. Many conjunctions are identical in form with prepositions (for example, *but, after, since, for*), and only their function in the sentence identifies them as conjunctions. There are three major classes of conjunctions: (1) coordinating conjunctions, (2) adverbial conjunctions, and (3) subordinating conjunctions.

9a COORDINATING CONJUNCTIONS

Coordinating conjunctions connect elements that serve the same grammatical function. The primary coordinating conjunctions are *and, but, or,* and *nor.*

> Daffodils <u>and</u> violets bloom early. (*And* connects *daffodils* and *violets,* both of which are nouns and both of which are subjects of the sentence.)
>
> We planted crocus <u>but</u> not lily of the valley. (*But* connects two nouns, both of which are direct objects.)
>
> Would you prefer to weed <u>or</u> to transplant? (*Or* connects two infinitives.)
>
> I cannot find the rake, <u>nor</u> is the trowel on the shelf. (*Nor* connects two independent clauses.)

The word *yet* is often used as an adverb but may also be used as a coordinating conjunction with approximately the same meaning as *but.* Even though they do not connect grammatically parallel elements, *for* and *so* are punctuated like coordinating conjunctions (see 27a). *For* introduces a clause expressing cause, and *so* a clause expressing result.

> She watered the hydrangea faithfully, <u>yet</u> it still died. (Note that *"but* it still died" would have the same meaning.)
>
> We sprayed the birch, <u>for</u> Japanese beetles were eating its leaves. (*For* introduces the clause that explains why we sprayed the birch.)
>
> The garden hose had a leak, <u>so</u> we patched it with tape. (*So* introduces the clause that explains the result of the fact that the garden hose leaked.)

Correlative coordinating conjunctions are special types of coordinating conjunctions that are used in pairs; that is, one part of the correlative conjunction appears in the first element being connected, and the second part of the correlative conjunction appears before the second element.

CORRELATIVE CONJUNCTION	EXAMPLE OF USE
both . . . and	Hemophilia is <u>both</u> hereditary <u>and</u> incurable.
either . . . or	Can you <u>either</u> type <u>or</u> take shorthand?

CORRELATIVE CONJUNCTION	EXAMPLE OF USE
neither . . . nor	I can <u>neither</u> type <u>nor</u> take shorthand.
not only . . . but (also)	Keys are made <u>not only</u> of steel <u>but also</u> of brass.
whether . . . or	Beulah didn't know <u>whether</u> to laugh <u>or</u> to cry.
the . . . the	<u>The</u> more I look at it, <u>the</u> less I like it.
as . . . as	Marie is <u>as</u> messy <u>as</u> Ruth is neat.
(just) as . . . so	<u>Just as</u> adjectives modify nouns, <u>so</u> adverbs modify verbs.
such . . . as	<u>Such</u> unsanitary conditions <u>as</u> these produce epidemics.
no (or not) . . . or	Ellen did <u>not</u> phone <u>or</u> write for a year.
not so much (that) . . . as	He was <u>not so much</u> evil <u>as</u> ill-advised.

9b ADVERBIAL CONJUNCTIONS

Like coordinating conjunctions, **adverbial conjunctions** (sometimes called **conjunctive adverbs**) connect independent clauses. Unlike coordinating conjunctions, which appear only at the beginning of a clause, many adverbial conjunctions may appear within the clause itself.

COORDINATING CONJUNCTION	Candy is dandy, <u>but</u> liquor is quicker.
ADVERBIAL CONJUNCTION	Candy is dandy; <u>however</u>, liquor is quicker. Candy is dandy. <u>However</u>, liquor is quicker. Candy is dandy; liquor, <u>however</u>, is quicker. Candy is dandy. Liquor is quicker, <u>however</u>.

Note: The punctuation of adverbial conjunctions also differs from that of coordinating conjunctions (see 28b for punctuation of adverbial conjunctions).

A further difference between adverbial conjunctions and coordinating conjunctions is that, whereas there are only seven words that serve as coordinating conjunctions, there are scores of adverbial conjunctions, and they express very diverse meanings.

ILLUSTRATION	for example, incidentally, namely, that is
ADDITION	after all, also, besides, further(more), likewise, moreover, second, similarly, what is more
CONTRAST	alternatively, however, in contrast, instead, nevertheless, on the other hand, otherwise, still
QUALIFICATION	certainly, indeed, in fact, perhaps, possibly, undoubtedly

RESULT	accordingly, as a result, consequently, hence, therefore, thus
ATTITUDE	frankly, happily, unfortunately, luckily
SUMMARY	in other words, in sum(mary), to conclude
TIME	at first, finally, meanwhile, now, then, thereafter

SUBORDINATING CONJUNCTIONS

Subordinating conjunctions connect clauses that are not grammatically equal. The relationship between the two clauses is indicated by the particular subordinating conjunction used. This relationship may be one of condition, cause, time, manner, or contrast.

CONDITION	Do not attempt this climb <u>unless</u> you are in top physical shape.
CAUSE	The Fords are inconsolable <u>because</u> their TV is broken.
TIME	<u>After</u> she had learned to drive, Alice felt independent.
MANNER	Do <u>as</u> I say.
CONTRAST	<u>Although</u> seldom entered in shows, Maine cats are beautiful.

The most important subordinating conjunctions are listed below.

after	if only	that
although (though)	inasmuch as	the day (minute,
as	in case	year, and so on)
as if	insofar as	unless
as long as	no matter how (no	until (till)
as though	matter when,	when
because	and so on)	whenever
before	once	where
even though	rather than	wherever
if	since	while

A rather large group of subordinating conjunctions end in *that*.

assuming that	in order that	provided (pro-
except that	in view of the fact	viding) that
for fear that	that	save that
given (granted) that	now that	seeing that
in the hope(s) that	on the grounds that	so that

Like coordinating conjunctions, subordinating conjunctions sometimes come in pairs. The most important of the **correlative subordinating conjunctions** are listed below.

if . . . then	<u>If</u> the ridgepole was removed, <u>then</u> the roof must have collapsed.
no sooner . . . than	<u>No sooner</u> had the rebellion been put down <u>than</u> a foreign invasion began.
scarcely . . . when	<u>Scarcely</u> had the rebellion been put down <u>when</u> a foreign invasion began.
so . . . that	The circuits were <u>so</u> overloaded <u>that</u> a fuse blew.
such . . . that	He is <u>such</u> a liar <u>that</u> no one trusts him.

EXERCISES: Conjunctions

List all conjunctions in the following sentences, including all elements of correlative conjunctions, and, next to each one, write the letter from the list below which identifies the kind of conjunction it is.

      A. Coordinating
      B. Correlative coordinating
      C. Adverbial
      D. Subordinating
      E. Correlative subordinating

1. Hal not only sloshed a pitcher of water in the waiter's face, but he also tore up the bill as the manager stood helplessly by.

2. After the Americans won at Saratoga, France was so impressed that she recognized the new nation; further, she gave General Washington both supplies and moral support.

3. The closer Mars gets to earth, the brighter Mars appears to be.

4. I know that Bobby Nichols is either a golfer or an actor.

5. The old man had been generous to her, for she was his only living relative; indeed, she seemed to be the only person to get any generosity from him.

6. No sooner had Hettie stepped into the bathtub than the telephone began to ring; nevertheless, she decided to tune out not only the telephone but any other obstacles to a quiet bubble bath.

7. When he began work on the newspaper's copy desk, John could neither change the ribbons on the Teletype machines nor put paper in the wirephoto transmitter; what is more, he considered these chores so menial that he did not want to learn how to do them.

8. Since the accident, Marty's father has forbidden her to ride the horse again; moreover, he is thinking of selling the horse if he can find someone who really likes horses as much as he and Marty do.

10 ISOLATES

The eighth part of speech is usually listed as the interjection, a grammatically independent word that expresses emotion. However, many words and phrases other than interjections are either used as separate utterances by themselves or are independent of (isolated from) the grammar of the sentences in which or with which they appear. Hence we use the term **isolate;** interjections are only one type of isolate.

    Most isolates take a set form or are highly conventional; that is, we cannot substitute synonyms for the words in them without changing the meaning completely. Even though *nice* is often used as a synonym for the adjective *good,* we cannot say *nice-bye* instead of *good-bye.* Some isolates are onomatopoetic; that is, they attempt to imitate sounds not used in normal speech. Examples include *eek!* to represent a scream or *brrr!* to represent the rapid vibration of our lips when we are indicating that we are cold. Many isolates have several different meanings, depending on the way in which they are spoken. For example, the word *well* spoken with a rising tone means that we are waiting for a response of some kind from our listener. *Well* spoken with heavy emphasis and a falling tone indicates indignation, and a drawled *well* with a level tone indicates doubt or hesitation.

Isolates can be classified into a number of standard types according to the situations in which they are used. The traditional category of interjections, or expressions of strong emotion, is included here as one kind of isolate.

USE AND MEANING	EXAMPLES
Meeting and parting	Hello, Hi, Good-bye, So long, How are you?, How do you do?, Fine, and you?, Nice to see you
Agreement and disagreement	Yes, No, Okay, Right, Sure, No way!, Uh-uh, Maybe
Asking and receiving	Please, Thank you, Thanks, You're welcome
Apology	Sorry, Excuse me, Whoops, Think nothing of it, That's all right
Direct address and name-calling	Dad, George, Good girl!, You idiot!
Alarm or attention-getting	Sssh! Look out! Help! Boo! Hey! Psst!
Special occasions	Happy birthday! Merry Christmas! Good luck! Here's to you! Congratulations!
Hesitation	Uh, You know, I mean, Of course, Well, Why
Physical comfort or discomfort	Whew! Mmmm! Ugh! Eek! Yum! Brrr!
Emotional reactions	Range from mild interjections such as *Wow!* and *Darn it!* to swear words (which usually involve religious terms) and taboo words (which usually refer to bodily functions)

11 PHRASES

A **phrase** is a sequence of words arranged grammatically but not containing a subject and a predicate. This definition can be expanded to include the fact that a phrase functions as a single component in a sentence. That is, a phrase serves as a subject, the main part of a predicate, a complement, an object of some kind, or a modifier.

Phrases can be classified into several different types according to the nature of the most important word in the phrase and the function of the phrase in the sentence. These include (1) noun phrases, (2) verb phrases, (3) verbal phrases, (4) prepositional phrases, and (5) absolute phrases.

11a NOUN PHRASES

A **noun phrase** consists of a noun and all of its modifiers. Noun phrases are used in the same positions as single nouns, that is, as subjects, objects, or complements.

SUBJECT	<u>The medium-sized vase with the star-burst design</u> was made in Czechoslovakia.
DIRECT OBJECT	Mrs. Prentice wore <u>sunglasses too large for her face</u>.
SUBJECT COMPLEMENT	The culprit was a <u>seedy-looking middle-aged man with a long, jagged scar over his right eyebrow</u>.

As these sentences illustrate, a noun phrase may itself include other types of phrases. For example, in the last sentence, the noun phrase includes two prepositional phrases, *with a long, jagged scar* and *over his right eyebrow*.

11b VERB PHRASES

Verb phrases consist of a main verb and all of its auxiliaries or semi-auxiliaries, if any. Verb phrases serve as the essential elements of predicates.

You <u>forgot</u> the mustard.
<u>Did</u> you <u>remember</u> a bottle-opener?
I <u>was supposed to bring</u> potato salad.
The dog <u>has eaten</u> all the olives.

11c VERBAL PHRASES

Verbal phrases are those whose main component is a nonfinite verb or gerund. Types of verbal phrases include (1) infinitive phrases, (2) participle phrases, and (3) gerund phrases.

Infinitive Phrases. **Infinitive phrases** consist of the infinitive (*to* followed by the base form of the verb) and any objects or modifiers of the infinitive or its object. Infinitive phrases serve as modifiers, subjects, objects, or complements.

MODIFIER	Sheila has errands <u>to run</u>. (*To run* modifies *errands*.)
MODIFIER	Napoleon was happy <u>to leave Elba</u>. (*To leave Elba* modifies *happy*.)
SUBJECT	<u>To own a motorcycle</u> is Kurt's only ambition.
SUBJECT COMPLEMENT	My summer project is <u>to brush up on my tennis</u>.

Participle Phrases. **Participle phrases** consist of the present participle or past participle of a verb along with any modifiers, objects, or complements of that participle. The phrase may contain a perfect participle (present participle plus past participle). Participle phrases modify subjects or objects.

PRESENT PARTICIPLE	The batter strode to the plate, <u>smiling confidently</u>.
PAST PARTICIPLE	<u>Alarmed by a wave of burglaries</u>, Mr. Leland put glasses of water on his windowsills.
PERFECT PARTICIPLE	<u>Having refueled at Lisbon</u>, the plane flew on to Rabat.

A special kind of participle phrase is the **nominative absolute,** or **absolute phrase,** which consists of a noun or pronoun plus a present or past participle phrase. Absolute phrases serve as modifiers; they modify, not just a single word or phrase, but an entire clause or sentence.

<u>All things considered</u>, I'd rather be rich than poor.
Clara and Henry separated, <u>she moving to Nashville</u> and <u>he staying in Chicago</u>.

Gerund Phrases.   **Gerund phrases** consist of a gerund and its modifiers and objects, if any. (A gerund is a kind of noun made from a verb by adding *-ing.*) **Perfect gerunds** consist of a gerund plus a past participle. Gerund phrases are used as subjects, objects, or complements.

SUBJECT	<u>Building the pyramids</u> took many years and many lives.
OBJECT OF PREPOSITION	The boss was worried about <u>my not having worked before</u>.
COMPLEMENT	Her hobby <u>is collecting buttons</u>, but her husband says it should be <u>sewing on buttons</u>.

11d PREPOSITIONAL PHRASES

A **prepositional phrase** consists of a preposition, its object, and any modifiers of that object. Prepositional phrases normally function as modifiers.

I bought the camera <u>with the carrying case</u>. (*With the carrying case* modifies *camera.*)
Classes were canceled <u>during the reading period</u>. (*During the reading period* modifies *were canceled.*)

EXERCISES: Phrases

Identify each of the underlined phrases in the following sentences by writing above each a letter from column one below to indicate its type and a number from column two to indicate its function. If the underscored phrase includes other phrases, classify only the larger phrase.

A. Noun	1. Main verb (with or without modifiers)
B. Prepositional	2. Subject (with or without modifiers)
C. Verb	3. Direct object
D. Infinitive	4. Indirect object
E. Participle	5. Subject complement
F. Gerund	6. Object complement
G. Absolute	7. Object of preposition
	8. Adjective
	9. Adverb
	10. Sentence modifier

1. <u>Weeding the strawberry plants</u> was a tiresome chore to Gary, who loved <u>to eat strawberries</u> but not <u>to tend them</u>.

2. <u>Purring softly</u>, the kitten snuggled <u>into the velvet cushions</u> on the sofa <u>to take its afternoon snooze</u>.

3. <u>The decision made at last</u>, the jurors <u>filed back into the courtroom</u> to give their verdict.

4. <u>The new sports car in the driveway</u> is a rather lavish graduation present <u>from Eileen's grandparents</u>.

5. For <u>getting a second F in French</u>, Doug <u>was put on academic probation</u>.

6. Francie checked <u>teaching swimming</u> as her first choice of the jobs <u>offered at the camp</u>.

7. Mr. Jonah is <u>the new supervisor</u> of the quality control department.

8. Surprisingly, most of those <u>questioned about personal values</u> gave <u>being happy</u> a much higher rank than they gave <u>being rich</u> or being successful <u>in their professions</u>.

---

12 CLAUSES

A **clause** is a sequence of grammatically arranged words that contains a subject and a predicate. The two most important types of clauses are independent clauses and dependent clauses.

12a INDEPENDENT CLAUSES

An **independent clause** (or a **main clause,** as it is often called) is capable of standing alone as a complete sentence. An independent clause may be part of a larger sentence, but if it is removed from the sentence in which it appears, it still forms a complete sentence by itself.

> When he pulled the shade, <u>it fell on his head</u>. (*It fell on his head* can stand as a complete sentence.)

> <u>Don't talk to Regina</u> until she has had a cup of coffee. (*Don't talk to Regina* can stand as a complete sentence.)

> <u>Jerry eats a pound of carrots a day</u>; <u>as a result, his skin has an orange tinge</u>. (*Jerry eats a pound of carrots a day* and *as a result, his skin has an orange tinge* are both independent clauses.)

12b DEPENDENT CLAUSES

A **dependent clause** is introduced by some kind of subordinating word and cannot stand alone as a complete sentence; in other words, a dependent clause requires an independent clause to complete it. Dependent clauses serve the same functions as nouns, adjectives, or adverbs.

Noun Clauses.   Dependent noun clauses fill the positions in a sentence that nouns may fill. They are typically introduced by *that, who, which, what, whom, whoever, whomever, whatever, whichever, whether, where, when, why,* and *how.*

> Whoever painted this room certainly likes purple and orange. (The noun clause is subject of the sentence.)
>
> I wonder whether he is color-blind. (The noun clause is the direct object.)
>
> The surprise is not that there are stripes but that the stripes run sideways. (The noun clauses are subject complements.)

Adjective Clauses.   **Adjective clauses** modify nouns, pronouns, or other groups of words serving as nouns. They follow the words they modify and are typically introduced by relative pronouns (*what, which, who, whom, that*) or relative adverbs (*where, when, why, how*).

> The desk that wouldn't fit through the door was sawn in half. (The clause modifies the subject *desk.*)
>
> That is an idea whose hour will never come. (The clause modifies the subject complement *idea.*)
>
> Can you think of any good reason why I should go to class today? (The adjective clause modifies the direct object *reason.*)
>
> Millie is still talking about the boy with whom she played Ping-Pong last week. (The clause modifies *boy,* the object of the preposition.)

Adverb Clauses.   **Adverb clauses** modify verbs, verb phrases, adjectives, adverbs, or entire clauses or sentences.

> Laurie began to speak Spanish when she was eight years old. (The adverb clause modifies the verb *began.*)
>
> Laurie speaks Spanish better than her mother does. (The clause modifies the adverb *better.*)
>
> Within two months, Laurie's Spanish was as fluent as her mother's had been after two years. (The clause modifies the adjective *fluent.*)
>
> Because she was so young, Laurie was not embarrassed by her mistakes in grammar. (The clause modifies the independent clause *Laurie was not embarrassed by her mistakes in grammar.*)

12c ELLIPTICAL CLAUSES

Sometimes clauses are hard to identify because part or all of the subject or the predicate has been omitted and is understood only from the context. Such clauses are called **elliptical clauses;** they may be either independent or dependent clauses.

INDEPENDENT	I will drive the car and <u>Jane the van</u>. (The verb phrase *will drive* has been omitted.)
DEPENDENT	Amy does not work well <u>when under pressure</u>. (The subject *she* and the verb *is* have been omitted.)
DEPENDENT	You don't explain irregular verbs <u>as well as he</u>. (The verb *explains* and the direct object *irregular verbs* have been omitted.)

EXERCISES: Clauses

Identify each underlined clause in the following sentences by writing the appropriate letter code beside it.

I	independent clause	IE	independent elliptical clause
D–NO	noun clause	DE	dependent elliptical clause
D–ADJ	adjective clause	NC	not a clause
D–ADV	adverb clause		

1. <u>Galloping across the meadow toward the stable</u>, the huge black horse seemed the most majestic animal <u>that Jeffrey had ever seen</u>.
2. <u>After the winter storm had subsided</u>, thousands of families found <u>that they were without electricity</u>.
3. <u>After following his career in the newspapers for many years</u>, Jorge was thrilled to be able to meet the great boxer.
4. Sven and Ingrid were <u>particularly fond of refinishing old furniture</u> for their apartment, and <u>they had found several pieces at local secondhand stores</u>.
5. <u>Because no one had been there to show the guests their quarters</u>, Kate had taken the blue room and <u>Will the downstairs bedroom</u>.
6. After dinner the men all congregated <u>in the den to watch football on television</u>, and <u>their wives decided to go to a movie</u>.
7. <u>Whichever flight Pedro takes</u> is always the one <u>that is delayed for one reason or another</u>.
8. Do not try to do handstands <u>while in the shower</u>.

13 RESTRICTIVE/ NONRESTRICTIVE PHRASES/CLAUSES

Phrases and clauses used as modifiers are either restrictive or non-restrictive. A **restrictive modifier** is essential to the meaning of the sentence or clause in which it appears. A **nonrestrictive modifier** provides additional information but is not essential to the basic meaning of the sentence or clause. Nonrestrictive modifiers are set off by commas in writing; restrictive modifiers are not set off by commas. (See 20d, 27e.)

RESTRICTIVE CLAUSE	The shells <u>that she sells by the seashore</u> are overpriced. (The restrictive clause limits the shells being discussed to those sold by the seashore.)
NONRESTRICTIVE CLAUSE	The shells, <u>which she sells by the seashore,</u> are overpriced. (All the shells being discussed are overpriced; the nonrestrictive clause simply gives additional information about the shells.)
RESTRICTIVE PHRASE	The car <u>parked in front of the bank</u> was ticketed. (The phrase *parked in front of the bank* identifies the specific car being discussed.)
NONRESTRICTIVE PHRASE	My car, <u>parked in front of the bank,</u> was ticketed. (The word *my* specifically identifies the car; the phrase *parked in front of the bank* simply gives additional information about it.)

EXERCISES: Restrictive and Nonrestrictive Phrases and Clauses

Write one sentence using each of the following phrases and clauses as a restrictive modifier and another sentence using it as a nonrestrictive modifier. Be sure that you punctuate correctly.

Example:

Restrictive	The woman *wearing a green jumpsuit* is my physics instructor.
Nonrestrictive	Ms. O'Leary, *wearing a green jumpsuit,* went out to milk her cow.

1. running through the crowd
2. with a mouthful of feathers
3. who had seen the entire incident
4. given two days extra vacation
5. which polluted the atmosphere
6. from a local department store

14 APPOSITIVES

Like a modifier, an **appositive** refers to the same thing as the word, phrase, or clause with which it is associated. However, unlike other modifiers, an appositive has the same grammatical function as the word or phrase with which it is associated. That is, an appositive to a subject could also serve as subject, and an appositive to a subject complement could also serve as complement, and so on. Appositives are most often nouns or noun substitutes, but appositives may also serve as adjectives, adverbs, or even predicates.

NOUN PHRASE APPOSITIVE TO SUBJECT	The manatee, <u>an aquatic mammal native to Florida</u>, is in danger of extinction. (*An aquatic mammal native to Florida* refers to *the manatee.*)

NOUN PHRASE APPOSITIVE TO SUBJECT	A few people were invited, <u>all close friends</u>. (*All close friends* refers to *a few people*.)
ADJECTIVES APPOSITIVE TO SUBJECT COMPLEMENT	Ferdinand I was a true Hapsburg, <u>shrewd and stubborn</u>. (*Shrewd and stubborn* refers to *a true Hapsburg*.)
PREPOSITIONAL PHRASE APPOSITIVE TO PREPOSITIONAL PHRASE	The train left on time, <u>at exactly 9:37 a.m.</u> (*At exactly 9:37 a.m.* refers to *on time*.)
PAST PARTICIPLE PHRASE APPOSITIVE TO PAST PARTICIPLE	Computer programs must be edited, that is, <u>checked for errors</u>, before being run. (*Checked for errors* refers to *edited*.)

Most appositives are nonrestrictive, but noun appositives are sometimes restrictive, particularly if the appositive is a proper noun.

| RESTRICTIVE | My son <u>Warren</u> broke his wrist. (The appositive *Warren* limits the meaning of *my son* to one specific son.) |
| NONRESTRICTIVE | My son, <u>a seventh-grader</u>, broke his wrist. (The appositive *a seventh-grader* merely gives further information about *my son*.) |

EXERCISES: Appositives

Underline all appositives in the following sentences, and punctuate the sentences correctly.

1. The new reporter was sent to the morgue that is the newspaper's library to find background information about the Public Service Commission hearings.
2. For late spring the ice storm was a freakish happening a trick of nature.
3. During the nineteenth century the period of the Industrial Revolution perhaps nothing stirred up so much controversy as did one invention namely the steam locomotive.
4. The dancer one of the great male ballet performers of the twentieth century refused to tour the United States.
5. In his painting the effect that Imre wanted to create the effect that his teacher encouraged him to create was an almost photographic rendering of the violence of modern society.
6. The colors lemon yellow, cantaloupe orange, and pagan purple made the room into a garish nightmare.

15 NOMINALS, ADJECTIVALS, ADVERBIALS

One of the distinguishing characteristics of English is the ability of a single word to serve in various functions without changing its form. For example, the word *here* is normally considered an adverb, and adverbs are normally modifiers. However, in the sentence "Khartoum is a long way from here," *here* serves as the object of a preposition, although we usually think of the object of a preposition as being a noun or a pronoun. In instances like this, where the form of a word conflicts with its function in the sentence, it is convenient to have a separate label for the function. Because *here* in this sentence is serving as a noun, we can call it a nominal.

Distinguishing labels are particularly useful for describing the function of phrases and clauses in a sentence. For example, in the sentence "Go to the dentist *before you get a toothache*," the dependent clause, "before you get a toothache," modifies the main clause. The entire clause is not an adverb, yet it is serving the same function as an adverb. We can call it an adverbial. Similarly, in the sentence "Pour the ink *in this bottle*," the prepositional phrase "in this bottle" is an adverbial modifying the verb *pour*. But in the sentence "The ink *in this bottle* had dried up," the phrase "in this bottle" functions as an adjective because it modifies the noun *ink;* it is an adjectival.

15a NOMINALS

Any word or group of words that serves the function of a noun is a **nominal**.

KIND OF NOMINAL	FUNCTION	EXAMPLE
Noun	Subject	My <u>brother</u> loves Mexican food.
Infinitive phrase	Direct object	He likes <u>to cook Mexican food</u>.
Gerund phrase	Subject	<u>Cooking with hot peppers</u> is his favorite pastime.
Participle phrase	Object of preposition	I am surprised at <u>his having survived his own cooking</u>.
Adjective	Subject	The <u>hottest</u> is not hot enough.
Dependent clause	Subject	<u>How his stomach can stand it</u> is a mystery to me.
Adverb	Object of preposition	I've had enough tamales for <u>now</u>.

15b ADJECTIVALS

A word or group of words that serves the function of an adjective is an **adjectival**.

KIND OF ADJECTIVAL	FUNCTION	EXAMPLE
Adjective	Modifies subject complement	There will be an <u>indefinite</u> delay.
Noun	Modifies subject	The <u>plane</u> ticket cost more than I had expected.

KIND OF ADJECTIVAL	FUNCTION	EXAMPLE
Infinitive	Modifies direct object	I have several complaints <u>to make</u>.
Participle	Modifies object of preposition	We had reservations on that <u>canceled</u> flight.
Adverb	Modifies subject	People <u>here</u> are suspicious of strangers.
Prepositional phrase	Modifies direct object	Will you cash an <u>out-of-town</u> check?
Dependent noun clause	Modifies object of preposition	When will I be paid for the luggage <u>that you lost</u>?

gr

15c ADVERBIALS

A word or group of words that serves the function of an adverb is an **adverbial**.

ADVERBIAL	FUNCTION	EXAMPLE
Adverb	Modifies past participle	The koala's body is <u>thickly</u> covered with fur.
Prepositional phrase	Modifies main clause	<u>Without eucalyptus leaves</u>, koalas will die.
Dependent clause	Modifies verb phrase	The infant koala remains in its mother's pouch <u>until it is three months old</u>.
Infinitive phrase	Modifies adjective	Koalas are difficult <u>to breed in zoos</u>.

EXERCISES: Isolates, Nominals, Adjectivals, and Adverbials

Write the identifying letter from the list below over each underlined word, phrase, or clause in the following sentences.

    A. Isolate   C. Adjectival
    B. Nominal   D. Adverbial

1. "<u>Yum</u>! <u>Smelling</u> that <u>baked</u> ham is making me hungry," said Ralph.

2. <u>To find out</u> won't be a problem; we can just call up the <u>reference</u> desk.

3. Professor Craig is always at his <u>worst</u> on Mondays, but <u>saying</u> when he is at his <u>best</u> is difficult.

4. "<u>On the front seat of the car</u> is where I last saw your <u>chemistry</u> book," Natalie told Tom <u>as he frantically scrambled through his books and notes</u>, "and your <u>calculus</u> text is over <u>there</u>."

5. We live <u>in two different worlds</u>, <u>yes</u>, but we must learn <u>to speak to each other</u> if either world is to survive <u>beyond the twentieth century</u>.

6. The <u>scowling</u> customer clutched a <u>trading-stamp</u> book <u>in his left hand</u> as he searched <u>in vain</u> for the floor manager.

7. <u>Where Agatha was last week</u> is a mystery <u>that we will perhaps never solve</u>.

16 CLASSIFICATION OF SENTENCES

In addition to describing sentences according to the elements of which they are composed (see 1), sentences can also be classified by the types of clauses they contain, by their function, and by whether they are affirmative or negative.

16a CLASSIFICATION BY TYPES OF CLAUSES

Sentences are made up of grammatically related phrases and clauses. One fundamental classification of sentences is according to the number and types of clauses contained in them. The four basic types of sentences are (1) simple sentences, (2) compound sentences, (3) complex sentences, and (4) compound-complex sentences.

Simple Sentences. **Simple sentences** consist of one independent clause and no dependent clauses. This independent clause may, however, have a compound subject or a compound predicate.

SIMPLE SENTENCE	Fiona ran away from home.
SIMPLE SENTENCE WITH COMPOUND SUBJECT	Fiona and Nigel ran away from home.
SIMPLE SENTENCE WITH COMPOUND SUBJECT AND COMPOUND PREDICATE	Fiona and Nigel ran away from home and joined the circus.

Compound Sentences. **Compound sentences** consist of two or more independent clauses and no dependent clauses.

Fiona joined the circus, and Nigel joined the navy.
Fiona ran away from home; she intended to join the circus.

Complex Sentences. **Complex sentences** consist of one independent clause and one or more dependent clauses. The dependent clauses may either precede or follow the independent clause.

After Fiona ran away from home, Nigel joined the navy.
Nigel joined the navy because Fiona had run away from home.

Compound-Complex Sentences. **Compound-complex sentences** contain at least two independent clauses and at least one dependent clause.

Fiona ran away from home, and, as soon as she had left, Nigel joined the navy.
Before Nigel joined the navy, Fiona ran away from home; she intended to join the circus.

16b CLASSIFICATION BY SYNTAX AND FUNCTION

Sentences are also classified according to their function or purpose. The usual classifications are (1) declarative sentences, (2) interrogative sentences, (3) imperative sentences, and (4) exclamatory sentences. Each kind has a typical word order.

Declarative Sentences.   **Declarative sentences** make statements of fact or opinion. Normally, the word order is subject + verb phrase + object (or complement), if the sentence contains an object or complement.

> Ms. Loomis borrowed a set of golf clubs.
> The mills of the gods grind slowly.

Occasionally, the word order of a declarative sentence is inverted for the sake of emphasis. The first sentence below has the order complement + subject + verb in both its independent clauses. The second sentence begins with an adverb, followed by the verb and then the subject.

> A Republican he is and a Republican he will always be.
> Down came the pile of boxes.

Interrogative Sentences.   **Interrogative sentences** ask questions. There are two types of interrogative sentences, those with a WH-word (*who, what, which, when, where, why,* and *how*) and yes-no questions (questions to which an answer of *yes* or *no* is expected). WH-questions normally begin with the WH-word followed by the verb. Yes-no questions usually begin with an auxiliary verb followed by the subject.

> WH   Why did he leave? How do you know? Where is Jean?
> YES-NO   Are you coming? Did they call? Have you heard yet?

Imperative Sentences.   **Imperative sentences** make a request or command. Typically, the implied subject is *you,* but *you* is omitted, and the sentence begins with the verb. Occasionally the subject is expressed.

> Take a left after two stop lights.
> Someone please tell me what is going on.

Exclamatory Sentences.   **Exclamatory sentences** usually express an attitude or strong emotion. They frequently begin with *what* or *how* and have inverted word order.

> How happy you must be!
> What a high price to pay for a ticket!

16c AFFIRMATIVE AND NEGATIVE SENTENCES

Sentences may be either affirmative or negative. An **affirmative sentence** makes an assertion; a **negative sentence** denies an assertion by means of a negating word such as *not, no,* or *never.* (For problems with double negatives, see 20b.)

AFFIRMATIVE   Seats are available.

NEGATIVE   Seats are not available. No seats are available.

EXERCISES: Classification of Sentences

Write the letter and number from the lists below in front of each of the following sentences to classify each sentence by the type of clauses it contains and by its function.

A. Simple sentence   1. Declarative sentence
B. Compound sentence   2. Interrogative sentence
C. Complex sentence   3. Imperative sentence
D. Compound-complex sentence 4. Exclamatory sentence

1. The aardvark and the ant attacked the other animals, but the antelope avoided the assault.
2. Don't let that lizard have much leeway until you've loosed the lightning bugs, llamas, and leopards.
3. Did the duck and the dugong drink together during the day, and was the weasel with the warthog when the walrus and the whippoorwill wrestled with the whale?
4. Did the baboons babble along with their babies about the battalion of bison bellowing below?
5. Tigers are terrifying!
6. Empty elephants are like vacuous vultures, and ravenous rabbits are like hollow hounds and hungry hyenas.
7. Catching a captivating kitten is like snaring a sleeping sloth, but snaring a sleeping sloth is sillier than catching a captivating kitten or than corralling a cuddly koala because a sleeping sloth is sitting still.
8. Make that mole go back into his hole before he catches a cold.

---

17 PROBLEMS WITH VERBS AND VERB PHRASES

Verbs are the source of a number of grammatical problems because verbs have more inflections than other parts of speech, because many common verbs are irregular, and because verbs and verb phrases must be changed to indicate changes in tense, mood, and voice.

17a FORMS OF VERBS / vbf

Problems involving the forms of verbs include using a present form when past meaning is intended, using an incorrect form of a past tense or past participle, and using incorrect auxiliary verbs.

Regular Verbs.   All **regular verbs** form both their past tense and their past participle by adding *-ed* or *-d* and form their third-person singular present tense by adding *-s* or *-es*. In speech, these endings are often said so rapidly as to be indistinct. In some dialects, they may be omitted entirely. In writing, however, never omit these *-s* and *-ed* endings.

INCORRECT	Yesterday we <u>ask</u> her to meet us at the pool.
CORRECT	Yesterday we <u>asked</u> her to meet us at the pool.
INCORRECT	I have never <u>walk</u> so far in my life.
CORRECT	I have never <u>walked</u> so far in my life.
INCORRECT	Joe always <u>act</u> silly when he is around girls.
CORRECT	Joe always <u>acts</u> silly when he is around girls.

The idioms *be supposed to* and *used to* are particularly troublesome because they can be confused with the verbs *to suppose* and *to use*. Remember that *supposed* in *be supposed to* (meaning "required to, obliged to") and *used* in *used to* (meaning "formerly accustomed to") always end in *-d*. In other words, in these idioms, *supposed* is always a past participle and *used* is always a past tense. Both are always followed by the infinitive form of the main verb.

Do you suppose we are <u>supposed</u> to call first?
The twins <u>used</u> to buy Ivory, but now they use another brand.

Irregular Verbs.   **Irregular verbs** are troublesome because their past tenses and past participles have different and unpredictable forms. Some irregular verbs have the same form in all three principal parts (*cut, cut, cut*), some have vowel changes but no inflectional endings (*sing, sang, sung*), still others have vowel changes and an *-n* in the past participle (*drive, drove, driven*), and some change the final *-d* of the infinitive to *-t* in the past tense and past participle (*build, built, built*). Your dictionary should be your guide; all good dictionaries list the principal parts of all irregular verbs.

If you are unsure which form of an irregular verb is required in a given kind of verb phrase, see 17b. In particular, avoid using a past tense form as a past participle or a past participle form as a past tense.

INCORRECT	The temperature this week has <u>broke</u> all records.
REVISED	The temperature this week has <u>broken</u> all records.
INCORRECT	David <u>run</u> in the Boston Marathon two years ago.
REVISED	David <u>ran</u> in the Boston Marathon two years ago.

Especially confusing are pairs of verbs that are similar in form and meaning. Of these, the chief offenders are the three pairs *lie/lay*, *sit/set*, and *rise/raise*. In each case, the first member of the pair is an irregular intransitive verb (takes no direct object), and the second is a transitive verb (takes a direct object). You may find it helpful to remember that the intransitive, verbs *lie, sit,* and *rise* always have a vowel change in the past tense and past participle, whereas the transitive verbs have no vowel change.

> I <u>lie</u> here every day. Yesterday I <u>lay</u> here. I have just <u>lain</u> down.
> I <u>lay</u> my books on my desk every day. Yesterday I <u>laid</u> my books on my desk. I have just <u>laid</u> my books on my desk.

> I <u>sit</u> here every day. Yesterday I <u>sat</u> here. I have just <u>sat</u> down.
> I <u>set</u> my mug on the shelf every day. Yesterday I <u>set</u> my mug on the shelf. I have just <u>set</u> my mug on the shelf.

> I <u>rise</u> at seven every morning. Yesterday I <u>rose</u> at seven. I have just <u>risen</u>.
> I <u>raise</u> the shade every morning. Yesterday I <u>raised</u> the shade. I have just <u>raised</u> the shade.

EXERCISES: Irregular Verbs

Fill in the blanks in the following sentences with the correct tense of the verb that is given in parentheses.

1. During the three years when he had lived alone, on Sunday mornings Luke always _____ (awake) an hour later than usual and _____ (lie) in bed while he _____ (drink) a pot of mint tea and leisurely _____ (read) the newspaper.

2. Marjorie _____ (wring) out her towel and her T-shirt, but before she could get away her three brothers _____ (come) along and _____ (throw) her into the pool again.

3. Chuck laughed heartily as he _____ (sit) down to enumerate all the delicacies he had neither _____ (eat) nor _____ (drink) in this first terrible week of his latest diet.

4. No matter what the soprano _____ (sing), the critics were always so kind that other members of the opera company _____ (become) jealous and _____ (do) everything possible to jeopardize her performances.

5. The prisoner, whom the authorities had _____ (forbid) to see either his wife or his lawyer, _____ (hang) himself just before dawn.

6. Although Sergei had _____ (lie) in bed sick for more than a week, an invitation to accompany his aunt to New York for three weeks miraculously cured him: he _____ (fling) back the covers, _____ (lay) aside his heating pad and pills, and _____ (spring) from his bed.

7. When the man had _____ (set) the basket down, everyone _____ (sit) around him on the ground, watching as he _____ (take) out the snakes and _____ (lay) them across his bare shoulders.

8. The sailor _____ (dive) from the deck of the ship and _____ (swim) straight to the fisherman, who _____ (cling) to an overturned lifeboat.

Auxiliary Verbs. The **auxiliary verbs** are *be, have, do,* and the modal auxiliaries. Most problems with auxiliary verbs occur in verb phrases with one of the modal auxiliaries (*will, would, shall, should, can, could, may, might, dare, need, ought, must*).

1. Shall-Will. The future tense is formed with *will* or *shall* plus the infinitive form of the main verb. Although some people believe that *shall* should be used for first-person subjects and *will* for second- and third-person subjects, this rule is seldom observed, especially in American English. Except for very formal writing, *will* is used for all persons. Use what seems natural to you; it is far better to stick to *will* than to use *shall* foolishly.

I <u>will</u> inform you of our decision.
I <u>shall</u> inform you of our decision.

Shall is, however, always used in asking for instructions in the first person.

<u>Shall</u> we leave now?
<u>Shall</u> I take this package to the post office?

2. Ought. No verb phrase should contain more than one modal auxiliary. Hence it is incorrect to write *should ought to* or *shouldn't ought to*. Use either *should* or *ought to*, but not both in one verb phrase.

INCORRECT	They <u>shouldn't ought to</u> treat us like children.
CORRECT	They <u>shouldn't</u> treat us like children.
CORRECT	They <u>ought not</u> treat us like children.

It is also incorrect to write *had ought to* or *hadn't ought to*; omit the *had* or *hadn't*.

INCORRECT	You <u>had ought to</u> write to Action Line.
CORRECT	You <u>ought to</u> write to Action Line.

3. Of for Have. In speech, *have* as an auxiliary verb is usually spoken so rapidly that it sounds like *of*. *Of* is not an auxiliary verb and should never be written as one.

INCORRECT	The table <u>might of been</u> scratched when we moved it.
CORRECT	The table <u>might have been scratched</u> when we moved it.
INCORRECT	He <u>wouldn't of sold</u> the textbook before the examination.
CORRECT	He <u>wouldn't have sold</u> the textbook before the examination.
INCORRECT	We <u>should of drained</u> the pipes last fall.
CORRECT	We <u>should have drained</u> the pipes last fall.

17b TENSE OF VERBS / t

Problems involving verb tenses include special and conventional uses of the present tense and the correct tense of verbs in subordinate clauses (the so-called sequence of tenses).

Special Uses of the Simple Present.   The simple present is used (1) in expressing universal truths, (2) in indicating future time with an adverbial of time, and (3) in discussing the contents of literary works.

1. **Universal truths.** The present tense is used when there is no limitation on the time to which the statement applies.

> Four plus three <u>equals</u> seven.
> Milk of magnesia <u>tastes</u> awful.
> All the stars visible from the earth <u>orbit</u> around the Milky Way.

2. **Future time.** The present tense is often used as an alternative to the future tense when there is an adverbial of time in the clause.

> The barbershop <u>opens</u> an hour from now.
> We <u>leave</u> for Toledo next week.

3. **Literary works.** The simple present is conventionally used in discussing the contents of literary works, even though these works were, of course, written in the past and even though the author may have used the past tense throughout his or her work.

> After betraying Miss Brodie, Sandy <u>becomes</u> a nun and <u>writes</u> a book on psychology.

However, when discussing the facts of writing and publication of a book, use the past tense.

> Muriel Spark's first novel, *The Comforters,* <u>was published</u> in 1957, and *The Prime of Miss Jean Brodie* <u>appeared</u> four years later.

Sequence of Tenses.   The term **sequence of tenses** refers to the relationship between the verb in the main clause of a sentence and the verb in a subordinate clause or phrase of that sentence.

1. **Main Clause in Present Tenses.** When the verb of the main clause is in any present tense (simple present, present progressive, present perfect, or present perfect progressive), the verb tense in the subordinate clause is determined by the meaning intended. That is, if you mean present time, use the present tense; if you mean future time, use the future tense, and so on.

> Jane <u>insists</u> that she <u>is</u> nervous. (Jane is nervous now.)
>
> Jane <u>insists</u> that she <u>was</u> nervous. (Jane was nervous in the past.)
>
> Jane <u>insists</u> that she <u>will be</u> nervous. (Jane will be nervous in the future.)
>
> Jane <u>is insisting</u> that she <u>is</u> nervous.
>
> Jane <u>has insisted</u> that she <u>is</u> nervous.
>
> Jane <u>has been insisting</u> that she <u>is</u> nervous.

2. **Main Clause in Past Tenses.** When the verb of the main clause is in any past tense (simple past, past perfect, past progressive, or past perfect progressive), the verb of the subordinate clause is also in a past tense, even though it may refer to present or future time.

He <u>told</u> me that his name <u>was</u> Cleasby. (His name is Cleasby.)

He <u>told</u> me his name <u>had been</u> Cleasby. (His name was Cleasby in the past.)

He <u>told</u> me that his name <u>would be</u> Cleasby. (His name will be Cleasby in the future.)

He <u>was telling</u> me that his name <u>was</u> Cleasby.

He <u>had told</u> me that his name <u>was</u> Cleasby.

He <u>had been telling</u> me that his name <u>was</u> Cleasby.

Note: Practice varies when the subordinate clause expresses a universal truth; either past tense or present tense is acceptable in the subordinate clause.

Glenn knew that a marimba <u>was</u> a musical instrument.

Glenn knew that a marimba <u>is</u> a musical instrument.

3. **Main Clause in Future Tenses.** When the verb of the main clause is in any future tense (simple future, future progressive, future perfect, or future perfect progressive) or when the verb of the main clause implies a future tense (as in an imperative or with *be going to*), the verb of the subordinate clause is in a present tense.

Melanie <u>will call</u> you when her plane <u>lands</u>. (Her plane will land in the future.)

Melanie <u>will call</u> you when her plane <u>has landed</u>.

Melanie <u>will be thinking</u> of you when her plane <u>lands</u>.

Melanie <u>will have traveled</u> for eight hours by the time her plane <u>lands</u>.

Melanie <u>will have been traveling</u> for eight hours by the time her plane <u>lands</u>.

<u>Call</u> me when your plane <u>lands</u>.

Melanie is <u>going to call</u> me when her plane <u>lands</u>.

4. **Tense in Participle Phrases.** The tenses of participle phrases used as modifiers vary according to their relationship to the main verb. Use a present participle to express action simultaneous with that of the main verb. Use a perfect participle to express action that precedes the action of the main verb.

<u>Eating</u> a radish, he <u>left</u> the dining room. (He ate the radish and left the dining room at the same time.)

<u>Having eaten</u> a radish, he <u>left</u> the dining room. (He ate the radish before he left the dining room.)

5. **Tense in Infinitive Phrases.** Use a present infinitive to express the same time as or a time later than the action of the main verb. Use a perfect infinitive to express time earlier than the action of the main verb.

We want <u>to see</u> that movie. (At present, we want to see that movie in the future.)

We wanted <u>to see</u> that movie. (In the past, we wanted to see that movie.)

We had wanted <u>to see</u> that movie. (In the more distant past, we had wanted to see that movie in the less distant past.)

We would like <u>to have seen</u> that movie. (At present, we wish that we had seen that movie in the past.)

6. **Tense in Indirect Discourse. Direct discourse** is the exact quotation of a speaker's or writer's words. Obviously, the tense of the verbs should be the same as that used by the speaker. **Indirect discourse** is a paraphrase, a report of what someone said rather than the exact words used. The same sequence-of-tense rules apply to indirect discourse as to other subordinate clauses.

DIRECT   She said, "It <u>is</u> raining here."

INDIRECT   She says (that) it <u>is</u> raining there. (It is raining while she is speaking.)

She said (that) it <u>was</u> raining there. (It was raining while she was speaking.)

EXERCISES: Sequence of Tenses

Alter the verb tense as is necessary in the following paragraph to make the sequence of tenses correct.

Because he considered himself out of touch with the scientific community when he died in 1955, Albert Einstein, who saw many of his theories lauded and many others ridiculed in the course of his seventy-six years, did not realize fully the great contributions his discoveries will make to modern life. Although he had never been a disciplined student, his lack of motivation to study subjects in which he had no interest caused him to fail the entrance exam at the prestigious Swiss Federal Institute of Technology, and later, after he has been admitted, to antagonize his teachers and to rely on his friends' notes and help in order to have graduated in 1900. Beginning in 1905, while he is employed as an examiner in the Swiss Patent Office, Einstein, who by this time married Mileva Maric, begins to shake the foundation of Newtonian physics with several theories: an explanation of the photoelectric effect, an explanation of the movements of particles in liquid, and, of course, his theory of relativity. Although his famous theory, $E = mc^2$, fathers the atomic age, Einstein is a pacifist and urged the end of all warfare. After the atomic bombs were dropped at Hiroshima and Nagasaki, in great remorse he has claimed that his motivation for working on the development of the bomb was fear that Germany, his native country, also developed it. Although he will die having seen the destructive force of his work (much of his work was done at Princeton, New Jersey, where he lives for twenty-two years), he did not realize the extent to which many of his theories opened up avenues to great discoveries that benefit our generation.

17c MOOD OF VERBS / mood

Of the three moods of English verbs (indicative, imperative, and subjunctive), normally only the subjunctive creates problems for the writer. The subjunctive is troublesome because it occurs so infrequently that we simply lack practice in using it. In modern English, the subjunctive is used only in (1) certain kinds of clauses introduced by *that*, (2) subordinate clauses expressing unreal conditions, and (3) certain idioms.

That Clauses.   In subordinate clauses beginning with *that*, the present subjunctive is required after many verbs of requesting, ordering, and recommending, such as *ask, demand, command, suggest, recommend, order*, and *insist*. The present subjunctive is also required in subordinate clauses after adjectives expressing urgency, such as *necessary, important, imperative, crucial, essential, urgent*, and after phrases such as *of great importance*. The present subjunctive has the same form as the infinitive of the verb.

> We asked only that she <u>be</u> careful.
>
> It is important that he <u>understand</u> how the timer works.

Unreal Conditions.   To express unreal conditions after the verb *wish* or in clauses beginning with *if*, the so-called past subjunctive is used. The past subjunctive has the same form as the plural past indicative of the verb (*were, had, saw*, and so on).

> I wish he <u>were</u> my father.
>
> I wish that I <u>had</u> more energy.
>
> If he <u>were</u> able, he would leave tomorrow.

In highly formal usage, *if* is omitted and the subjunctive verb precedes the subject.

> <u>Were</u> he able, he would leave tomorrow.

To express actual past time with the past subjunctive, use the past perfect form of the verb.

> I wish he <u>had been</u> my father. (Not *I wish he would have been my father*.)
>
> If he <u>had been</u> able, he would have left yesterday. (Not *If he would have been able*.)
>
> <u>Had</u> he <u>been</u> able, he would have left yesterday.

Idioms.   A few idioms take the present subjunctive in an independent clause.

God help us	far be it from me
suffice it to say	come what may
Heaven forbid	be that as it may
so be it	

The past subjunctive is used in the idiom *as it were* and as an alternative to an infinitive phrase after *it's time*.

> It's time we <u>went</u> home. (Compare *It's time for us to go home*.)
>
> Food faddists have, <u>as it were</u>, redefined the word *natural*.

17d VOICE OF VERBS / voice

Most writing problems involving the voice of verbs are really stylistic problems, not grammatical problems. That is, we may overuse the passive at the expense of the active voice, but we rarely have difficulty with the appropriate grammatical form of the passive. (See 4a.)

In speech or very informal writing, *get* is sometimes used instead of *be* as the auxiliary for the passive voice. Avoid *get* as an auxiliary in college writing.

ACTIVE	Someone <u>stole</u> Joshua's pacifier.
PASSIVE	Joshua's pacifier <u>was stolen</u>.
COLLOQUIAL PASSIVE	Joshua's pacifier <u>got stolen</u>.

17e INCOMPLETE VERB PHRASES

When a sentence has a compound verb phrase, we can often omit, in one of the verb phrases, those parts after the auxiliary that are identical to the other verb phrase.

The second game <u>was taped</u>, but the first <u>was</u> not. (The second occurrence of *taped* can be omitted because it is identical to the first; both are past participles.)

The players <u>wanted to</u>, but <u>could not leave</u> immediately after the game. (The first occurrence of *leave* can be omitted because it is identical to the second; both are infinitives.)

Do not, however, omit parts of a compound verb phrase that are not identical. The result will be an incomplete verb phrase.

INCORRECT	The players <u>have</u> not and <u>will</u> not <u>sign</u> the proposed contract. (The omitted verb *signed* is a past participle and not an infinitive.)
REVISED	The players <u>have</u> not <u>signed</u> and <u>will</u> not <u>sign</u> the proposed contract.

Similarly, it is best not to omit the verb *to be* in a compound predicate unless the omitted verb has exactly the same form in the two verb phrases.

QUESTIONABLE	The players <u>were</u> defiant and the manager indignant. (The omitted verb *was* is singular and the first verb is plural.)
REVISED	The players <u>were</u> defiant and the manager <u>was</u> indignant.
CORRECT	The players <u>were</u> defiant and the coaches indignant. (The omitted verb *were* is plural, as is the first verb.)

EXERCISES: Identifying Verb Problems

Write the correct letter or letters from the list below over each of the underlined verb phrases in the following sentences.

A. Correctly used
B. Wrong form of verb
C. Incorrect use of auxiliary verb

D. Violation of tense sequence
E. Incorrect mood
F. Incomplete verb phrase

1. The flea market—an American institution otherwise <u>known</u> as a garage sale, a bazaar, or a white elephant sale—<u>are</u> a stage where the adage "one man's trash is another man's treasure" <u>be enacted</u> each week to standing-room-only audiences across the nation.

2. Particularly in the spring, the urge <u>to have cleaned things out</u> fills the sellers' tables with varied goods—antique china dolls with <u>broke</u> heads, dusty books, and assorted bric-a-brac <u>laying</u> unused on shelves of its prior home.

3. Just as bizarre as the variety of goods <u>is</u> the motley collection of buyers who gather to dicker over the mountains of goods haphazardly <u>lain</u> around.

4. Usually, long before the hour when a sale is <u>suppose to begin</u>, a long line of hopeful buyers <u>agitates</u> for the sale doors <u>to have been opened</u>.

5. Once the sale officially begins, there is a stampede: two women argue over who <u>shall buy</u> a banged-up hassock, a mob <u>succeeds</u> in overturning a table and demolishing the merchandise that <u>might of</u> sold for ten dollars, and others remark that the sellers <u>shouldn't ought to of</u> let people run wild and <u>had ought to mark down</u> the prices if they really <u>wanted</u> to sell their goods.

6. One woman picks up a broken toaster, <u>sits</u> it back on the table, and quickly picks it up once again. Then she <u>demands</u> that she should get a money-back guarantee if she <u>will buy</u> it.

7. <u>Having double-checked the price</u>, two men are <u>wanting to buy</u> a set of golf clubs, although neither of the men <u>have ever or will ever play</u> golf.

8. Meanwhile, the sellers <u>are being relieved</u> of numerous unwanted items, and their cash boxes <u>have gotten fattened</u> with money to be used by their club, <u>to have been given</u> to a charity, or <u>to be enjoyed</u> personally.

agr/18 PROBLEMS WITH SUBJECT-VERB AGREEMENT

Agreement is the correspondence between grammatically related words whereby the use of one form of one word requires the use of a specific form of another word. For example, the use of *he* as a subject pronoun requires the use of *has* (as opposed to *have*). Except for the verb *to be*, the only kind of agreement required between subject and verb is number agreement for third-person singular subjects. Further, again except for the verb *to be*, number agreement appears only in the present tense. However, because all nouns and the majority of pronouns are third person and because so many verb phrases include a present-tense verb, subject-verb agreement is potentially a problem in almost all kinds of writing.

The verb *to be* has separate forms in the present tense for first-person singular *(am)*, third-person singular *(is)*, and all other persons and numbers *(are)*. In the past, *to be* has separate forms for first- and third-person singular *(was)* and all other persons and numbers *(were)*. These forms are, of course, required whether *to be* is used as a linking verb or as an auxiliary in verb phrases.

18a IDENTIFYING THE REAL SUBJECT

Confusion often occurs, not because we do not know whether the subject is singular or plural, but because we forget or do not recognize the real subject of a sentence.

Intervening Modifiers Between Subject and Verb.   Do not mistake a modifier for a subject. This error is most likely to occur when a modifier containing a plural noun comes between a singular subject and the verb or when a modifier with a singular noun comes between a plural subject and the verb.

> A collection of amateur paintings <u>is</u> on display. (The real subject is *collection*.)

> The members of the panel, one of whom is a student, <u>meet</u> every Thursday. (The real subject is *members*.)

Inverted Order of Subject and Verb.   When the verb precedes the real subject, be sure the verb and subject agree.

> After Thanksgiving <u>come</u> the winter holidays. (The real subject is *the winter holidays,* a plural subject requiring a plural verb.)

> <u>Has</u> any one of you done as much? (The real subject is *one;* compare *Any one of you has done as much.*)

Subject and Complement with Different Numbers. Singular subjects may have plural complements and vice versa. Regardless of the number of the complement, make the verb agree with the subject.

> Diamonds <u>are</u> a girl's best friend.

> A girl's best friend <u>is</u> diamonds.

> Our problem <u>was</u> too many chiefs and not enough Indians.

18b SPECIAL KINDS OF SUBJECTS

Sometimes we know what the real subject is but are uncertain whether it is singular or plural.

Collective Nouns.   **Collective nouns** (those that refer to groups, not individuals) normally take a singular verb but may take a plural verb if attention is being focused on the various individuals making up the group.

> The family <u>is</u> at the movies. (Focus on the family as a unit.)

> The family <u>are</u> all avid movie fans. (Focus on the individuals making up the group.)

Proper Nouns. The proper names of books, works of art, places, and the like, that are plural in form nonetheless take a singular verb because they are considered a single unit.

> Carlsbad Caverns is a popular tourist attraction.
> *Fathers and Sons* provides a picture of Russia in the 1860s.

Nouns with Special Forms. A few nouns look plural because they end in *-s*, but nonetheless always take a singular verb. Examples include *news, measles, billiards,* and *molasses.*

> Good news is always welcome.
> Molasses adds flavor to pecan pie.

Nouns ending in *-ics* take a singular verb when they refer to a field of study but a plural verb when they refer to individual practice or application. Examples of such nouns are *ethics, athletics, physics, ceramics, politics,* and *mathematics.*

> Ethics is a branch of philosophy.
> His ethics are questionable.

Some nouns have the same form in both singular and plural; the meaning of the sentence determines the form of the verb. Among such nouns are *means, barracks, series, gallows, sheep,* and *deer.*

> Four series of lectures were offered.
> A series of lectures was offered.

A fairly large number of nouns have no singular form and always take a plural verb. Examples include *people, clergy, clothes, fireworks, tongs, cattle, bowels, manners, remains, soapsuds, wages,* and *thanks.*

> The cost of living has gone up, but my wages have not.
> The soapsuds were flowing all over the bathroom floor.

Words as Words. Words being cited as words take a singular verb, regardless of their form.

> *Indices* is one of the plural forms of *index.*

Expressions of Quantity. In expressions of adding and multiplying, either a singular or a plural verb is correct.

> Three and five is (or *are*) eight.
> Three times five equals (or *equal*) fifteen.

In expressions of subtraction and division, a singular verb is correct.

> Four minus two is two.
> Four divided by two equals two.
> Two into four is two.

As a subject, the phrase *the number* takes a singular verb, but the phrase *a number* takes a plural verb.

The number of applicants <u>was</u> small.
A number of applicants <u>were</u> disqualified.

Plural expressions of quantity take either a singular or a plural verb, depending on whether the expression is considered a single unit or not.

Three days <u>is</u> too long to wait. (*Three days* is being treated as a single unit of time.)
Three days <u>remain</u> before the deadline. (Each day is considered as a separate unit.)

18c COMPOUND SUBJECTS

Compound subjects (those connected by a conjunction) take either a singular or a plural verb, depending on the conjunction.

Connected by And. Compound subjects connected by *and* always take a plural verb except in the rare instances when both subjects refer to the same (singular) individual or thing.

My sister and best friend <u>are</u> visiting me. (My sister and my best friend are not the same person.)
My sister and best friend <u>is</u> visiting me. (My sister is also my best friend.)

Some compound subjects are so closely associated that they are thought of as a single unit. In such instances, a singular verb is correct.

Apple pie and cheese <u>makes</u> a good dessert.
Law and order <u>was</u> the theme of his campaign.

Connected by Correlative Conjunctions.   In sentences with a compound subject connected by the correlative conjunctions (*either*) . . . *or, neither . . . nor, not only . . . but,* or *not . . . but,* the verb agrees with the subject nearest the verb.

<u>Are</u> the boys or their mother driving today?
<u>Is</u> either the mother or her sons driving today?
Neither the boys nor their mother <u>drives</u> to work.
Neither the mother nor her sons <u>drive</u> to work.

Connected by Along with, etc.   When a compound subject is accompanied by a phrase beginning with (*along*) *with, as well as, rather than, more than,* or *as much as,* the verb agrees with the first subject.

Mr. Menotti, along with his neighbors, <u>opposes</u> rezoning.
Insects, rather than drought, <u>are</u> responsible for the poor harvest.

18d PRONOUN SUBJECTS

When the subject of a clause or sentence is a pronoun, subject-verb agreement can be confusing because pronouns do not have an *-s* ending that clearly marks the plural forms.

Indefinite Pronouns.   The indefinite pronouns *either, neither, each, another, one,* and all pronouns ending in *-one, -body,* or *-thing* take a singular verb.

> She went to both offices, but neither <u>was</u> open.
> Each of these organisms <u>is</u> microscopic.

The pronouns *all, any, most, more, none,* and *some* take a singular verb if their antecedent is a mass noun (see 3b) but a plural verb if their antecedent is a plural noun.

> Sarah made a big pot of soup. <u>Is</u> any left? (The verb is singular because the antecedent of *any* is a mass noun, *soup.*)
> Sarah baked four dozen brownies. <u>Are</u> any left? (The verb is plural because the antecedent of *any* is a plural noun, *brownies.*)

Note: *None* may also take a singular verb, even with a plural antecedent.

> Sarah baked four dozen brownies. None <u>are</u> left.
> Sarah baked four dozen brownies. None <u>is</u> left.

Expletive Pronouns.   The **expletive pronouns** *it* and *there* differ from each other in their rules for subject-verb agreement. *It* always takes a singular verb, regardless of the following noun.

> It <u>was</u> Carmen who spilled the beans.
> Who <u>is</u> it? It <u>is</u> the Wristons and the Scotts.

The form of the verb after the expletive pronoun *there* is determined by the number of the following noun or pronoun.

> There <u>is</u> a letter to be typed. (*A letter* is singular, so the verb is singular.)
> There <u>are</u> letters to be typed. (*Letters* is plural, so the verb is plural.)

Relative Pronouns.   When a **relative pronoun** (*that, which, who*) is used as the subject of a clause, the verb agrees with the antecedent of the pronoun.

> She gave them a box of clothes that <u>were</u> too small for her. (*Clothes* is the antecedent of *that.*)
> She gave them the box of clothes that <u>was</u> in the back hall. (*Box* is the antecedent of *that.*)
> Gregory is one of the clerks who <u>work</u> late. (*Clerks* is the antecedent of *who;* the implication is that several clerks work late.)
> Gregory is the only one of the clerks who <u>works</u> late. (*One* is the antecedent of *who;* the meaning of the sentence would not be changed if *of the clerks* were omitted.)

18e PHRASES AND CLAUSES AS SUBJECTS

Phrases and clauses as subjects usually take a singular verb.

> Singing in the shower <u>is</u> an old American custom.
> Before lunch <u>is</u> too early for a martini.

How I learned that <u>is</u> none of your business.
That all of you disagree with me <u>comes</u> as a surprise.
To avoid a scene <u>was</u> very important to him.

Clauses beginning with *what* are generally treated like collective nouns. That is, if the complement of the clause is thought of as a single unit, a singular verb is used; if the complement is thought of as separate units, a plural verb is used. As a rule of thumb, use a singular verb if you can substitute *the thing that* for *what*, but use a plural verb if you can substitute *the things that* for *what*.

What I want <u>is</u> three square meals a day.
What once were beautiful rivers <u>are</u> now open sewers.

EXERCISES: Subject-Verb Agreement

Correct all errors in subject-verb agreement in the following sentences.

1. Neither Abe nor his friends is ever prompt in keeping appointments.
2. Dolores, along with Dave and Cecil, have taken up gliding this year.
3. *The Snows of Kilimanjaro* were shown on television last week.
4. Each of the boys are to bring a sleeping bag and warm clothing.
5. Mr. Hill is one of those fussy bosses who is never satisfied with anything that their employees do.
6. Six months are much too long for us to wait; none of us have enough money to remain here for that length of time.
7. On his bookshelf stands many rare editions bound in leather.
8. That the compromise annoyed both the men and the women were obvious.
9. Both the children and the dog is afraid of thunderstorms, but everyone else in the house, including the grandparents, actually enjoy them.
10. There is bacon and a couple of oranges in the refrigerator.
11. The number of motorcycles on the road this morning were unbelievable.

pron / 19 PROBLEMS WITH PRONOUNS

Pronouns are substitutes for nouns or nominals. The noun or nominal for which a pronoun substitutes is called its **antecedent,** and we say that a pronoun **refers** to its antecedent.

Little Miss Muffet was distressed when <u>she</u> saw a spider near <u>her</u>. (*She* and *her* are personal pronouns whose antecedent is *Little Miss Muffet*.)

Name the presidents <u>who</u> were in office during the eighteenth century. (*Who* is a relative pronoun whose antecedent is *presidents*.)

Pronouns should always agree with their antecedents in **gender** (masculine, feminine, or neuter), **number** (singular, mass, or plural), and **person** (first person, second person, or third person). However, the **case** of a pronoun (subject, object, or possessive) is determined by its function in its own clause, and a pronoun does not necessarily have the same case as its antecedent.

19a PRONOUN REFERENCE / ref

Whenever a pronoun is used, its form should be the appropriate one for its antecedent, and the antecedent of the pronoun should be clear to the reader.

Reference to Collective Nouns.   To refer to a collective noun, use the singular pronoun *it* if attention is being focused on the group as a unit. Use the plural pronoun *they* if attention is on the individuals making up the group.

> The army congratulated <u>itself</u> on <u>its</u> performance in the war games. (Focus is on the army as a unified group.)
>
> The Congress voted <u>themselves</u> an increase in salary. <u>They</u> must now explain this inflationary move to <u>their</u> constituents. (Focus is on the individual members who received the raise.)

Indefinite Reference: He and She.   Because English has no "sex-neutral" third-person singular pronoun, the plural pronoun *they* is often used in speech as a substitute for (1) indefinite pronouns such as *anyone* and *everybody*, (2) indefinite nouns such as *person* and *individual*, and (3) the many nouns that can refer to either a male or female such as *citizen, parent, bystander,* or *artist.* In writing, however, the use of a plural pronoun to refer to a singular antecedent is ordinarily not acceptable. Traditionally, the masculine pronoun *he* has been used to refer to such indefinite human beings. Today, however, some people feel that the exclusive use of the masculine pronoun is sexist and therefore offensive. *He* is still grammatically correct but may be resented by some readers. Unfortunately, there is as yet no universally acceptable alternative. Many writers use *he or she* instead of simply *he,* and this strategy often solves the problem.

> Every parent discovers that <u>he or she</u> cannot always be patient and sweet-tempered.

However, if a pronoun is used several times within one sentence, the result is likely to be cumbersome.

> Everyone had to decide for <u>himself or herself</u> whether <u>he or she</u> was willing to spend several years of <u>his or her</u> life mastering this new skill.

Sometimes you can avoid the problem by using a plural noun or pronoun as an antecedent.

> Participants had to decide for <u>themselves</u> whether <u>they</u> were willing to spend several years of <u>their</u> lives mastering this new skill.

Alternatively, you can often rewrite the entire sentence to avoid pronouns with gender.

ORIGINAL   No one will be accepted until he or she has passed a physical examination.

REVISED   No one who has not passed a physical examination will be accepted.

Indefinite Reference: You, They, We, It, and One. In speech, we often use *you, they, we,* and even *it* when we wish to refer to people in general or when the referent is unknown or irrelevant. In writing, however, the acceptable use of these pronouns is highly limited.

1. *You* is always appropriate when the reader is clearly being addressed personally. Hence *you* is correct in imperative sentences or in writing instructions, even if the writer does not know the reader.

IMPERATIVE   Before arranging a foreign trip, be sure <u>you</u> have a passport.

You is also appropriate as a kind of indefinite pronoun in quoting proverbs or fixed expressions.

<u>You</u> can always tell a Harvard man, but <u>you</u> cannot tell him much.

<u>You</u> shouldn't count <u>your</u> chickens before they are hatched.

In informal writing, *you* is acceptable as an indefinite pronoun for statements that apply to every human being. In formal writing, however, *one* is preferred.

INFORMAL   When <u>you</u> are born, <u>you</u> are toothless and hairless.

FORMAL   When <u>one</u> is born, <u>one</u> is toothless and hairless.

2. *They* is not appropriate as an indefinite pronoun in writing. Fortunately, it can be avoided by rewriting.

UNACCEPTABLE   They say it will be a hard winter.

REVISED   A hard winter has been predicted.
Forecasters predict a hard winter.

UNACCEPTABLE   In my high school, they made us take algebra.

REVISED   Algebra was a required subject in my high school.

3. *We* as an indefinite pronoun is somewhat less formal than *one*. It can be employed to avoid overuse of the passive or to include the writer in a general statement.

PASSIVE   Even greater delays can be expected in the future.

REVISED   We can expect even greater delays in the future.

WRITER
INCLUDED   We all know at least one or two handicapped persons.

4. The indefinite *it says* (with reference to printed matter) is not acceptable in formal writing. Further, it is usually wordy because the

true subject is also mentioned. Avoid *it says* by making the book, newspaper, or magazine being quoted the subject of the clause.

| UNACCEPTABLE | It says in the *Herald* that Robbins has been indicted. |
| REVISED | The *Herald* says that Robbins has been indicted. |

5. *One* is always correct as an indefinite personal pronoun, but it may sometimes seem stilted. In American usage, *he* or *he or she* can replace *one* after the first reference.

| FORMAL | One often faces situations that one would rather avoid. |
| ACCEPTABLE | One often faces situations that he or she would rather avoid. |

Ambiguous Reference.   Whenever a pronoun is used, its antecedent should be clear to the reader. Correct ambiguous reference by rewriting the sentence or by repeating one of the nouns.

AMBIGUOUS	When Jim attacked George in public, he was very angry. (Who was angry, Jim or George?)
REVISED	George was very angry when Jim attacked him in public.
REVISED	Jim was very angry when he attacked George in public.
AMBIGUOUS	There's a fly in your salad; do you want to eat it? (The salad or the fly?)
REVISED	There's a fly in your salad; do you want to ask for another salad?

Remote Reference.   When a pronoun is too far removed from its antecedent, the reader may be at least temporarily confused. Correct remote reference by repeating the noun or a synonym of that noun, or by rewriting the passage so that the pronoun is closer to its antecedent.

| REMOTE REFERENCE | Yesterday I bought a new toaster. The first slice of bread that I toasted turned to carbon. When I put in a second slice of bread, a fuse blew. I am beginning to suspect that it is defective. (What does *it* refer to?) |
| REVISED | Yesterday I bought a new toaster. The first slice of bread that I toasted turned to carbon. When I put in a second slice of bread, a fuse blew. I am beginning to suspect that the toaster is defective. |

Broad Reference.   In many sentences, the pronouns *this, that, it,* and *which* are used to refer to an entire preceding clause or sentence. This practice is natural in speech and is also acceptable in writing when the idea is completely clear to the reader.

The nation is overpopulated; this has led to unemployment and even famine.
It rained all day long, which prevented us from taking pictures.

Often, however, broad reference produces ambiguity, lack of clarity, or awkwardness. In such cases, rewrite the sentence to make the antecedent clear or to eliminate the pronoun completely.

UNCLEAR	He told me that he had been arrested for embezzlement, <u>which</u> surprised me. (What surprised you? That he had been arrested? Or that he told you?)
REVISED	I was surprised to learn that he had been arrested for embezzlement.
REVISED	I was surprised that he admitted to having been arrested for embezzlement.
UNCLEAR	Myron has proposed to Sue. <u>This</u> is not what she wants.
REVISED	Myron has proposed to Sue, but she doesn't want to get married.
REVISED	Myron has proposed to Sue, but she doesn't want to marry him.

Implied Reference.   The antecedents of pronouns should be either nominals or, occasionally, entire clauses or sentences. Avoid using pronouns that have no antecedents or that refer to words or structures that are not nominals.

INCORRECT	The house has oak floors. <u>This</u> is more expensive than pine. (The implied antecedent is *oak*, but *oak* is a modifier here, not a nominal.)
REVISED	The floors of the house are made of oak, which is more expensive than pine.
REVISED	The house has oak floors; oak is more expensive than pine.
INCORRECT	Tanya dog-paddled down the lane, <u>which</u> is not a recognized stroke in competition swimming. (The implied antecedent is *dog-paddled*, but *dog-paddled* is a verb, not a nominal.)
REVISED	Tanya dog-paddled down the lane; the dog-paddle is not a recognized stroke in competition swimming.

Unnecessary Reference.   Personal pronouns are substitutes for nouns. Therefore, a pronoun subject should not be used when a noun subject is already present in the phrase. Use either the noun subject alone or the pronoun alone.

INCORRECT	Those dogs <u>they</u> ought to be on leashes.
REVISED	Those dogs ought to be on leashes.
REVISED	They ought to be on leashes.

EXERCISES: Pronoun Reference

Correct faulty pronoun references in the following sentences.

1. Despite the recession, our firm had retail sales of $5 million last year and is planning to open a new branch in Toronto, which causes much concern among our competitors.

2. All children should receive measles shots because it is a highly contagious and often dangerous disease.

3. Laura was extremely annoyed because her friends were all late, but this did not seem to faze anyone in the group.

4. Everybody must decide for themselves what color hair they want to have.

5. After Frances insisted that Cora go home, she was very tactless and said some things that she will likely regret.

6. The party has told its members that you should vote early and often.

7. Bill's father bought the drill and some lumber, but it wasn't the kind he had wanted.

8. One should look before one leaps, and we should also make sure that no one is under us when we jump.

9. It says in the *Examiner* that Roberta was disqualified from the race.

10. Three competitors were disqualified in yesterday's race. Roberta was the only female; the other two were male. They should have been more careful.

11. Those race officials they were certainly watching carefully.

19b PRONOUN CASE / case

The proper case of a pronoun depends on its use in its own clause. Normally, this causes no problem; no one would say or write, for example, "I talked to she." As native speakers of English, we would automatically use the object case of the pronoun and say, "I talked to her." Problems with pronoun case usually arise only when other elements in the clause create confusion about the actual role of the pronoun. Ordinarily, problems with the appropriate case of pronouns occur in only a few types of constructions, including (1) compound constructions, (2) relative constructions, (3) appositive constructions, (4) constructions with *than, as,* and *but,* (5) after the verb *to be,* and (6) possessive constructions.

Compound Constructions. In compound constructions, use the form of the pronoun that would be correct if it were not part of a compound. When in doubt about the proper form of a pronoun after *and* or *or,* mentally omit the first part of the compound.

INCORRECT	Belle and <u>him</u> moved to St. Paul in 1974. (You would not write "Him moved to St. Paul.")
REVISED	Belle and he moved to St. Paul in 1974.
INCORRECT	Loud music annoys Frank and <u>I</u>. (You would not write "Loud music annoys I.")
REVISED	Loud music annoys Frank and me.
INCORRECT	This rule applies to both them and <u>we</u>. (You would not write, "This rule applies to we.")
REVISED	This rule applies to both them and us.
INCORRECT	Pat embarrassed both of us, Ellen and <u>I</u>. (You would not write, "Pat embarrassed I.")
REVISED	Pat embarrassed both of us, Ellen and me.

Similarly, do not use the reflexive pronouns ending in *-self* as subjects or objects. Again, confusion normally arises only in compound constructions.

INCORRECT   Edward and <u>myself</u> volunteered to work on Saturday. (You would not say, "Myself volunteered to work on Saturday.")

CORRECT   Edward and I volunteered to work on Saturday.

INCORRECT   This dispute is between Edward and <u>myself</u>.

CORRECT   This dispute is between Edward and me.

Relative and Interrogative Constructions.   Of the relative and interrogative pronouns (*who, which, what*), only *who* is inflected for case (*who/whom/whose*).

1. **Who and Whom.** The relative and interrogative pronouns *who* and *whom* probably cause more problems to writers than all the other pronouns put together. This is because, in speech, *whom* is virtually ignored except when it immediately follows a preposition. Further, clauses with *who* or *whom* often have an inverted word order, causing us to lose track of whether the pronoun is functioning as a subject or as an object. Although we can usually let the *who's* and *whom's* fall where they may in speech, formal writing reserves *who* for subjects and *whom* for objects. As always, the function of the pronoun in its own clause determines the correct form. When in doubt, find the subject and the verb in the clause. If there is no other subject for the verb, then the pronoun must be the subject, and *who* is the correct form. If there is another subject, then the pronoun is an object, and *whom* is correct.

<u>Who</u> put the Limburger cheese in my closet? (The only possible subject of *put* is *who.*)

<u>Whom</u> did Washington appoint ambassador to France? (*Washington* is the subject, so *whom* is an object.)

My curses on the scoundrel <u>who</u> put the Limburger cheese in my closet.

Monroe, <u>whom</u> Washington had appointed ambassador to France, became governor of Virginia in 1799.

Especially confusing are clauses that contain parenthetical phrases such as *they said, I think, we feel,* and the like. Here the parenthetical phrase is often misinterpreted as the subject and verb of the clause, and the object form *whom* is incorrectly used.

<u>Who</u> do you think I am? (That is, "Who am I?")

<u>Whom</u> did they say Ginny would marry? (That is, "Ginny would marry whom?")

Perry is the only person <u>who</u> we know is going to Fort Worth. (That is, "Perry is the only person <u>who</u> is going to Fort Worth.")

Perry is the only person <u>whom</u> we know in Fort Worth. (That is, "We know whom in Fort Worth?")

Confusion can also arise when a noun clause beginning with *who* or *whom* is the object of a preposition. The grammar of the following clause (*not* the preposition) determines the correct form of the pronoun.

> We are worried about <u>who</u> might get hurt. (*Who* is the subject of the verb phrase *might get hurt;* the entire clause is the object of the preposition.)

> We are worried about <u>whom</u> the new rules might hurt. (*Whom* is the object of the verb phrase *might hurt.*)

> Send an invitation to <u>whoever</u> is in town. (*Whoever* is the subject of *is in town;* the entire clause is the object of the preposition.)

> Send an invitation to <u>whomever</u> you like. (*Whomever* is the object of the verb *like.*)

2. **Whose.** *Whose* (never *who's*) is a correct possessive form for both persons and things, although some people prefer to use *of which* for things and *whose* for persons. Use *of which* when it does not seem awkward, but use *whose* if *of which* seems stilted and artificial.

> Taxes is a subject the mere mention <u>of which</u> upsets my uncle. (It would be awkward to write, "whose mere mention.")

> This town, <u>whose</u> taxes are the highest in the state, just approved another bond issue. (It would be awkward to write, "This town, the taxes of which are the highest.")

If both *whose* and *of which* seem awkward to you, you can usually rewrite the sentence to avoid the possessive entirely.

> The mere mention of the word *taxes* upsets my uncle.

> The taxes in this town are the highest in the state, but the voters have just approved another bond issue.

Appositive Constructions. A noun in apposition to a pronoun does not affect the case of the pronoun. Use the form of the pronoun that would be correct if the noun were not present.

INCORRECT	<u>Us</u> students are worried about the rising cost of books. (You would not write, "Us are worried.")
REVISED	<u>We</u> students are worried about the rising cost of books.
INCORRECT	The rising cost of books concerns <u>we</u> students. (You would not write, "The rising cost of books concerns we.")
CORRECT	The rising cost of books concerns <u>us</u> students.

After than, as, and but. Writers are often confused about the proper form of pronouns after *than*, *as*, and *but* because they are unsure whether these words are conjunctions or prepositions. Conjunctions introduce clauses, and the proper form of a pronoun depends on its function in the clause. Prepositions, on the other hand, always take the object form of the pronoun.

1. **Than.** *Than* is a conjunction and not a preposition, so the appropriate case of a pronoun after *than* depends on its function in the following clause. Confusion occurs when clauses introduced by *than* are elliptical, that is, when the verb and either the subject or the object of the clause are omitted. When in doubt, mentally supply the missing words to determine whether the pronoun should be in the subject case or the object case.

> Mr. Gregg has more faith in her than me. (Meaning: "Mr. Gregg has more faith in her than Mr. Gregg has faith in me.")
> Mr. Gregg has more faith in her than I. (Meaning: "Mr. Gregg has more faith in her than I have faith in her.")

2. **As.** In *as . . . as* constructions, the second *as* is a conjunction, and the following clause is often elliptical. Again, the case of the pronoun depends on its function in the elliptical clause.

> Clara argues with Geri as much as him. (Meaning: "Clara argues with Geri as much as Clara argues with him.")
>
> Clara argues with Geri as much as he. (Meaning: "Clara argues with Geri as much as he argues with Geri.")

3. **But.** In the meaning "except," the word *but* is usually considered a preposition and should therefore be followed by the object case of the pronoun.

> I know everyone here but him.

After the Verb to Be. Theoretically, the subject case of a pronoun should always be used as the complement of the verb *to be*. However, such sentences as *That was him* and *It's me* are universally used in speech, and many people find *It is I* uncomfortable even in writing. If the subject case seems stilted or awkward, rewrite the sentence to avoid the dilemma.

> AWKWARD   Ms. Harvey thought that Ross was I.
> REVISED   Ms. Harvey mistook Ross for me.
> CORRECT   It was I who chopped down the cherry tree.

EXERCISES: Pronoun Case

Correct errors in pronoun case in the following sentences.

1. Fred wanted to know who we had asked to be publicity director.
2. The new neighbors never spoke to anyone, but they seemed to go out of their way to avoid Dave and I.
3. Billings is the student who, as you should remember, the university's administrative officials tried to throw out of school because of his antiwar activities.
4. I can run longer than her, but she is as fast as me.
5. No one was willing to risk the president's wrath but she, although George and myself did abstain from voting.

6. This office will provide a letter of introduction for whomever may need one.

7. Angie was sure that the girl who waved to we three on the beach was her, that same girl who we had met at the disco two nights before.

8. Although he denies it, it was him who leaked the story to the newspapers.

9. Whom did he say is favored to win the tournament?

mod /20 PROBLEMS WITH MODIFIERS

Modifiers, words that describe or limit other words, are either adjectivals or adverbials (see 15). Modifiers may be single words, such as the adjective *heavy* or the adverb *then*, or groups of words, such as the phrase *in the midafternoon* or the clause *until I find my umbrella*. Grammatical problems with modifiers can occur with the form of the modifiers or with the placement of the modifiers.

20a SINGLE-WORD ADJECTIVALS / adj

The two most important problems with single-word adjectivals are (1) incorrectly using an adverb instead of an adjective and (2) using an incorrect form of a possessive adjective.

Predicate Adjectives.   Linking verbs (see 4b) are properly followed by adjectives rather than adverbs. Linking verbs include verbs of sensation and verbs expressing a state of existence or a change in a state of existence. The adjectives that follow linking verbs are called **predicate adjectives.**

VERBS OF SENSATION	VERBS OF EXISTENCE	
feel	act	prove
look	appear	remain
smell	be	seem
sound	become	sit
taste	continue	stand
	grow	turn

Confusion occurs because many linking verbs can also be used as ordinary verbs that take an adverbial modifier. However, there are differences in meaning: If the subject is being modified, use an adjective. If the verb is being modified, use an adverb.

Stephanie looked <u>angry</u> about the referee's decision. (*Angry* describes Stephanie.)

Stephanie looked <u>angrily</u> at the referee. (*Angrily* describes the way in which Stephanie looked at the referee.)

Bob grew <u>tall</u>. (*Tall* describes Bob.)

Bob grew <u>rapidly</u>. (*Rapidly* describes how Bob grew, not Bob himself.)

Possessives as Adjectivals.   All possessives are adjectivals. Problems involving possessives include selecting the correct form of the possessive and knowing when to use possessive forms.

1. **Indefinite Pronouns.** Some indefinite pronouns can be made into possessive adjectives by adding an apostrophe and -*s*.

another's	anyone's	anybody's	anybody else's
(the) other's	everyone's	everybody's	everybody else's
one's	no one's	nobody's	nobody else's
either's	someone's	somebody's	somebody else's
neither's			

Mrs. Rossoni questioned both Livia and Salvatore, but <u>neither's</u> answer satisfied her.
One can never predict <u>someone else's</u> tastes.

All other indefinite pronouns (*any, each, both, few, many, several, all, much,* and so on) form their possessives with *of.*

Mrs. Rossoni questioned Livia and Salvatore, and the answers <u>of both</u> satisfied her.
The interests <u>of some</u> are not the interests <u>of all</u>.

2. **The Group Possessive.** In spoken English, the -'*s* of the possessive does not always appear on the end of the noun that is the logical modifier. Instead, it often appears on the end of the last word of the entire noun phrase. It may even appear on a word that is not a noun or pronoun. Such possessive constructions are called **group possessives.** Except for possessives of a proper noun, such as *the Czar of Russia's death,* avoid the group possessive in writing. Instead, use a phrase with *of* or rewrite the sentence.

COLLOQUIAL	the man I talked to's opinion
FORMAL	the opinion of the man that I talked to
COLLOQUIAL	the girl in the corner apartment's dog
FORMAL	the dog owned by the girl in the corner apartment

3. **Possessives before Gerunds.** Like nouns, gerunds are modified by possessive forms of nouns and pronouns.

Dad objects to <u>Paul's</u> sleeping on the roof.

Were you surprised at <u>our</u> having won the lottery?

Because gerunds and participles both end in -*ing*, it is sometimes difficult to tell one from the other and to determine the proper form of a preceding noun or pronoun. If the -*ing* word is the subject or object, it is a gerund, and the preceding noun or pronoun should be possessive.

<u>Martin's</u> swimming amazed even the coach. (It was the swimming that amazed the coach.)
I watched <u>his</u> swimming with great envy. (You watched the *swimming: swimming* is a gerund and the possessive *his* is correct.)

If the noun or pronoun is the subject or object, the *-ing* word is a modifier, and the noun or pronoun should not be possessive.

> <u>Anyone</u> swimming after dark is endangering his or her life. (*Anyone,* not *swimming,* is the subject.)
> I watched <u>him</u> swimming in the surf. (You watched *him: swimming* is a participle modifying *him.*)

20b SINGLE-WORD ADVERBIALS / adv

Problems with single-word adverbials include the improper use of adjectives as adverbs, double negatives, and the improper use of *so, such,* and *too.*

Adjectives as Adverbials. Although such adjectives as *real, sure, awful, pretty, bad,* and *good* are frequently used to modify verbs in the spoken language, this practice should be avoided in writing. If you are in doubt about whether a word is an adjective or an adverb, consult your dictionary.

| INCORRECT | The new pencil sharpener works <u>good</u>. |
| CORRECT | The new pencil sharpener works <u>well</u>. |

Frequently the best solution to an incorrect use of an adjective as an adverbial is to omit the modifier completely.

INCORRECT	The Night Owl is a <u>real</u> fast train.
QUESTIONABLE	The Night Owl is a <u>really</u> fast train.
REVISED	The Night Owl is a fast train.

Double Negatives. The unacceptable double negative occurs when additional negative words in a clause are used merely to intensify the negative meaning. To correct a double negative, rewrite the sentence to eliminate all but one of the negative words.

INCORRECT	There <u>wasn't nobody</u> under the bed.
REVISED	There wasn't anybody under the bed.
REVISED	There was nobody under the bed.
REVISED	Nobody was under the bed.
INCORRECT	The parrot <u>didn't hardly</u> talk at all.
REVISED	The parrot hardly talked at all.
INCORRECT	Christmas <u>doesn't only</u> come <u>but</u> once a year.
REVISED	Christmas comes but once a year.
REVISED	Christmas comes only once a year.

So, Such, and Too. In speech, the words *so, such,* and *too* are often used simply to intensify the statement being made. In writing, do not use *so, such,* or *too* without a following clause or phrase that completes the statement.

COLLOQUIAL	It was so cold in the house!
REVISED	It was so cold in the house that the plumbing froze.
REVISED	It was unbearably cold in the house.
COLLOQUIAL	Alex Workes is such a good magician!
REVISED	Alex Workes is such a good magician that he fools even children.
REVISED	Alex Workes is an exceptionally good magician.
COLLOQUIAL	Your offer is too insulting.
REVISED	Your offer is too insulting to accept.
REVISED	Your offer is intolerably insulting.

20c PLACEMENT OF MODIFIERS / mm / dm

Except for a few fixed expressions like *court martial* or *attorney general*, single-word adjectives usually precede the words they modify, and adjectival phrases usually follow the words they modify. Adverbials are more flexible than adjectivals in their placement but, in general, should be placed as close as is grammatically possible to the words they modify.

Misplaced Modifiers.   A **misplaced modifier** is one that appears to modify the wrong word or words. Correct a misplaced modifier by rewriting the sentence to put the modifier closer to the word it is intended to modify.

MISPLACED	A fish was found in the Atlantic Ocean <u>that had been considered extinct.</u> (Had the Atlantic Ocean been considered extinct?)
REVISED	A fish that had been considered extinct was found in the Atlantic Ocean.
MISPLACED	He <u>almost</u> understood every word. (Did he almost, but not quite, understand?)
REVISED	He understood almost every word.
MISPLACED	Everyone was born in July <u>in this room.</u> (Were all the people born in this room?)
REVISED	Everyone in this room was born in July.

Dangling Modifiers.   A **dangling modifier** is one that either appears to modify the wrong words or that apparently has nothing to modify. The most common kinds of dangling modifiers are dangling participles, dangling infinitives, dangling gerund phrases, and dangling elliptical clauses. (An elliptical clause is one in which words have been omitted because they are understood from the context.) Correct a dangling modifier by rewriting the sentence.

| DANGLING PRESENT PARTICIPLE | <u>Budgeting his money carefully,</u> his debts were finally paid. (Who did the budgeting?) |
| REVISED | Budgeting his money carefully, he finally paid his debts. |

DANGLING PAST PARTICIPLE	<u>Confused by the complicated wording</u>, the contract made no sense. (Who was confused?)
REVISED	Confused by the complicated wording, I could make no sense of the contract.
DANGLING INFINITIVE	<u>To lose weight</u>, fatty foods should be avoided. (Who wants to lose weight?)
REVISED	To lose weight, one should avoid fatty foods.
DANGLING GERUND PHRASE	<u>By digging test wells</u>, new oil sources were located. (Who did the digging?)
REVISED	By digging test wells, the company located new oil sources.
DANGLING ELLIPTICAL CLAUSE	<u>A brilliant performer</u>, her concert was quickly sold out. (Who was a brilliant performer?)
REVISED	Because she was a brilliant performer, her concert was quickly sold out.

Squinting Modifiers. A **squinting modifier** is one that is ambiguous because it could refer either to what precedes it or to what follows it. Correct squinting modifiers by moving them so that they clearly modify only the intended words.

SQUINTING	Dentists remind children <u>regularly</u> to brush their teeth.
REVISED	Dentists regularly remind children to brush their teeth.
REVISED	Dentists remind children to brush their teeth regularly.

Split Infinitives. A **split infinitive** occurs when, and only when, a modifier comes between the word *to* and the infinitive form of a verb. Thus, *to carefully plan* is a split infinitive, but *to have carefully planned* is not. Strictly speaking, there is nothing ungrammatical about split infinitives, but they are often stylistically awkward, and consequently many people disapprove of them. Avoid a split infinitive if the meaning is clear without it, but don't hesitate to split an infinitive if avoiding it would lead to lack of clarity or awkwardness. In the following example, the adverb *really* cannot reasonably be placed anywhere except directly before *understand* because it modifies *understand* and only *understand*.

UNIDIOMATIC	<u>Really</u> to understand calculus, one must do the exercises.
UNIDIOMATIC	To understand calculus <u>really</u>, one must do the exercises.
PREFERABLE	To <u>really</u> understand calculus, one must do the exercises.

In the following sentence, on the other hand, a split infinitive is not necessary because the sentence is clear and idiomatic when the modifier is placed outside the infinitive.

| SPLIT | You ought to <u>carefully</u> weigh the alternatives. |
| PREFERABLE | You ought to weigh the alternatives <u>carefully</u>. |

In any case, avoid splitting an infinitive with a modifier several words long.

AWKWARD	The cat began to <u>slowly and with much hesitation</u> back down the tree.
REVISED	The cat began to back down the tree slowly and with much hesitation.
REVISED	Slowly and with much hesitation, the cat began to back down the tree.

Unidiomatic Modifiers.   Modifiers are unidiomatic when their placement and order of occurrence in the sentence is not natural to English. For example, adverbials of place normally precede adverbials of time, and both normally follow the rest of the predicate. Adverbials of manner most commonly appear either before the main verb or after the entire predicate. When these orders are violated, the resulting sentence is likely to be awkward and unidiomatic.

UNIDIOMATIC	Mary <u>on Wednesday</u> met me in Chapel Hill.
REVISED	Mary met me in Chapel Hill on Wednesday.
UNIDIOMATIC	You hurt <u>deliberately</u> her feelings.
REVISED	You deliberately hurt her feelings.
REVISED	You hurt her feelings deliberately.

Most native speakers of English have a natural feeling for what is idiomatic and what is not but sometimes become careless or forgetful in writing. Reading your sentences aloud will help you spot unidiomatic placement of modifiers.

20d RESTRICTIVE AND NONRESTRICTIVE MODIFIERS

When a modifier is essential to the identification of the word or group of words being modified, it is called a **restrictive modifier.** When a modifier merely provides additional information about the words it modifies and is not essential in identifying these words, it is called a **nonrestrictive modifier.** In writing, problems arise when restrictive and nonrestrictive modifiers follow the word or words they modify. Nonrestrictive modifiers should be set off by commas, but restrictive modifiers should not be set off by commas.

RESTRICTIVE	People <u>who are allergic to smoke</u> make poor firemen. (The restrictive modifier restricts the specific people being discussed to those who are allergic to smoke.)
NONRESTRICTIVE	Human beings, <u>who are among the larger animals</u>, are bipeds. (The nonrestrictive modifier merely supplies more information about all human beings. It does not restrict the kinds of human beings being discussed. If the nonrestrictive modifier is omitted, the meaning of the sentence is not greatly changed.)

The writer usually knows whether he or she intends a modifying phrase or clause to be restrictive or nonrestrictive, but often the only clue the reader has is the presence or absence of commas. If commas are omitted from a sentence with a nonrestrictive clause, or if commas are incorrectly used with a restrictive clause, the reader is given a false clue and is likely to misinterpret the sentence.

If you have difficulty in deciding whether a modifier is restrictive or nonrestrictive and hence cannot decide what the correct punctuation for the sentence is, check the modifier against the following list. (See also 27e.)

RESTRICTIVE MODIFIERS	NONRESTRICTIVE MODIFIERS
Restrictive modifiers are essential to the meaning.	Nonrestrictive modifiers are not essential to the meaning.
In speech, restrictive modifiers are not preceded by a pause.	In speech, nonrestrictive modifiers are preceded by a short pause.
Restrictive clauses can be introduced by *that: Irma does not like the poem that I wrote for her.*	Nonrestrictive clauses cannot be introduced by *that: Irma does not like the poem, which I wrote just for her.*
In a restrictive relative clause, the relative pronoun can be omitted if it is not the subject of the clause: *Irma does not like the poem I wrote for her.*	In a nonrestrictive relative clause, the relative pronoun cannot be omitted: *Irma does not like the poem, which I wrote just for her.*
Restrictive modifiers follow the words they modify: *The woman reading a comic book is Irma.* (We cannot write *Reading a comic book, the woman is Irma.*)	Nonrestrictive modifiers often may precede the words they modify: *Irma, smiling nervously, said she did not like my poem.* Or *Smiling nervously, Irma said she did not like my poem.*

EXERCISES: Modifiers

Correct all mistakes in modifiers in the following sentences.

1. Mr. Fitzgerald still looked badly when he returned to work after his operation.
2. Randy only wants to buy milk and bread.
3. Mrs. Allison's remarks at the convocation were really too irresponsible.
4. After doing calculus problems for six hours, John's foot went to sleep.
5. Both ACTH and cortisone are valuable drugs, but both's side effects can be dangerous.
6. The woman in the balcony's comments could not be heard from the podium.
7. We were amazed at the doctor being so understanding.
8. The piano teacher urges Donna often to practice.
9. Because my dog is old, he doesn't hear very good.
10. The war hadn't hardly begun when refugees started pouring into the capital.

11. People, who are mistreated as children, often become poor parents.

12. There was a wreck while the Davises were eating supper in the road in front of their house.

13. The bartender seemed to unfailingly and with deadly accuracy spot patrons under 21.

comp / 21 PROBLEMS WITH COMPARISONS

Comparisons are sometimes difficult for the writer because there are so many different rules for the different kinds of comparison. Further, what is acceptable comparison in speech is not always acceptable in writing. Among the problems that arise are those of (1) "double" comparison, (2) comparison of absolutes, (3) misuse of the superlative, (4) illogical comparisons, (5) ambiguous comparisons, (6) incomplete comparisons, and (7) the idiom of comparisons.

21a DOUBLE COMPARISONS

Do not use both *more* and *-er* to make a single adjective or adverb comparative. Do not use both *most* and *-est* to make a single adjective or adverb superlative.

INCORRECT	I am <u>more lonelier</u> here than I was in California.
REVISED	I am lonelier here than I was in California.
REVISED	I am more lonely here than I was in California.
INCORRECT	Joel kicked the pumpkin the <u>most farthest</u> of all.
REVISED	Joel kicked the pumpkin the farthest of all.

21b COMPARISON OF ABSOLUTES

Adjectives or adverbs such as *main, daily, prior, entire,* and *only* are inherently comparative or superlative in meaning, and we normally would never be tempted to add a comparative or superlative ending to them. Such words as *complete, dead,* and *round* present more of a problem. Logically, they are also absolute and cannot be compared. Practically, however, we often wish to express a comparison between two things that have qualities of completeness or deadness or roundness but that could never be perfectly complete or dead or round. For example, when we write, "Amy's face is rounder than Janet's," we know and our readers know that no one's face is a perfect circle; the expression "a round face" means only that the face resembles a circle more than it resembles a square or a triangle. It would be silly to write, "Amy's face resembles a circle more than Janet's face does."

Some people object to making absolute adjectives and adverbs comparative or superlative. To avoid offending them, we can use the formal *more nearly* instead of *more*, and *the most nearly* instead of *the most*.

INFORMAL	In order to form a <u>more perfect</u> union, we adopted a constitution.
FORMAL	In order to form a <u>more nearly perfect</u> union, we adopted a constitution.
INFORMAL	Hall's summary is <u>the most complete</u> of the three.
FORMAL	Hall's summary is <u>the most nearly complete</u> of the three.

Note: For the use of the word *unique*, see Appendix B, "Glossary of Usage."

21c MISUSE OF THE SUPERLATIVE

A superlative should not be used where a comparative is appropriate, nor should a superlative be used as an intensifying adverb.

Superlative with Two Items. Use the comparative when making a comparison between only two items; use the superlative when making a comparison among three or more items.

INCORRECT	Of the two wars, the Civil War was <u>the longest.</u>
CORRECT	Of the two wars, the Civil War was <u>the longer.</u>
CORRECT	Of the three wars, the Civil War was <u>the longest.</u>

Superlatives as Intensifying Adverbs. When speaking, we sometimes use a superlative as a kind of intensifier to emphasize the adjective without really intending any kind of comparison. Avoid this use of the superlative in writing; substitute an adverb for the superlative if necessary.

COLLOQUIAL	We saw the <u>funniest movie</u> last night.
REVISED	We saw a <u>very funny movie</u> last night.

21d ILLOGICAL COMPARISONS

Illogical comparisons are those that imply a comparison between two things that are not actually being compared or that cannot be compared. Illogical comparisons should be corrected by rewriting to make it clear what things are being compared.

ILLOGICAL	She has a car smaller than her brother. (Is her brother really bigger than a car?)
REVISED	She has a car smaller than her brother's.
ILLOGICAL	Mario's grades are better than last year. (*Grades* cannot be compared with *years*.)
REVISED	Mario's grades are better than they were last year.

| ILLOGICAL | New York's taxes are higher than California. (Is California high?) |
| REVISED | New York's taxes are higher than those of California. |

21e AMBIGUOUS COMPARISONS

The second part of a comparison of equality (for example, *as big as*) or a comparison of superiority (for example, *bigger than*) is often elliptical; that is, some words in the second part are omitted because they are understood from the context.

I dislike handball as much as squash. (That is, "I dislike handball as much as I dislike squash.")
Fran ate more macaroni than Christie. (That is, "Fran ate more macaroni than Christie ate macaroni.")

Such elliptical comparisons usually cause no problem because only one interpretation of the sentence is reasonable. In some instances, however, it may be unclear whether the second part of the comparison is intended as a subject or as an object. To avoid such ambiguity, fill in as many words as are necessary for clarity.

AMBIGUOUS	He likes Laura better than Nancy.
REVISED	He likes Laura better than he likes Nancy.
REVISED	He likes Laura better than Nancy does.

21f INCOMPLETE COMPARISONS

In general, do not make a comparison unless you state explicitly what the basis of the comparison is, that is, what two things or categories you are comparing.

INCOMPLETE	Smiladent gives you <u>whiter</u> teeth. (Whiter than you used to have? Whiter than anyone else's teeth? Whiter teeth than other toothpastes do?)
REVISED	Smiladent gives you whiter teeth than any other brand of toothpaste.
INCOMPLETE	Michael has <u>the worst</u> cold. (The worst cold he has ever had? The worst cold he has had this year? The worst cold of anyone in his family?)
REVISED	Michael has the worst cold he has had this year.

The basis of comparison may be omitted in common expressions or idioms.

I haven't <u>the faintest idea</u> where Kuala Lumpur is.

Mr. MacFuddy disapproves of <u>the younger generation</u>.

21g THE IDIOM OF COMPARISONS

One of the major difficulties in writing comparisons is that we must keep track, not only of the words being compared, but also of the prepositions, conjunctions, and articles that belong to each type of comparison.

Like and As. Introduce a comparative clause with *as* or *as if* and a comparative word or phrase with *like*.

CLAUSE	Helen's desk looks <u>as if</u> the Army Corps of Engineers had abandoned it.
WORD	Helen's desk looks <u>like</u> mine.
PHRASE	Helen's desk looks <u>like</u> a disaster area.

Other and Any. When comparing members of the same class, use *other* or *any other*. When comparing members of different classes, use *any*.

INCORRECT	A Honda gets better gas mileage than <u>any</u> Japanese cars.
CORRECT	A Honda gets better gas mileage than <u>other</u> Japanese cars. (*A Honda* is a member of the class of Japanese cars.)
CORRECT	A Honda gets better gas mileage than <u>any other</u> Japanese car.
INCORRECT	A Honda gets better gas mileage than <u>other</u> American cars.
CORRECT	A Honda gets better gas mileage than <u>any</u> American car. (*A Honda* is not a member of the class of American cars.)

More and Rather Than. If you use *more* (or *less*) in the first part of a comparison, do not use *rather than* to introduce the second part of the comparison.

INCORRECT	That symphony sounds <u>more</u> like Haydn <u>rather than</u> Mozart.
REVISED	That symphony sounds <u>more</u> like Haydn than Mozart.
REVISED	That symphony sounds like Haydn <u>rather than</u> Mozart.

Different From and Different Than. It is always correct to write *different from*, but *different than* is gaining in acceptance, particularly if the object of *than* is a clause. *Different to* is not acceptable.

INCORRECT	Why is your solution <u>different to</u> mine?
QUESTIONABLE	Why is your solution <u>different than</u> mine?
CORRECT	Why is your solution <u>different from</u> mine?
ACCEPTABLE	Hawaii was <u>different than</u> he had imagined it.
CORRECT	Hawaii was <u>different from</u> what he had imagined.

Fewer and Less. Use *fewer* in comparing plural nouns and *less* in comparing mass nouns.

| INCORRECT | India has <u>less</u> natural resources and land than China. |
| REVISED | India has <u>fewer</u> natural resources and <u>less</u> land than China. |

Equality and Superiority.   When using both a comparison of equality and a comparison of superiority (or inferiority) in the same clause, do not omit the *as* after the first adjective or adverb.

INCORRECT	Rubber cement holds <u>as well</u> or <u>better than</u> glue.
REVISED	Rubber cement holds <u>as well as</u> or <u>better than</u> glue.
INCORRECT	Hang-gliding is <u>as dangerous</u> or <u>more dangerous than</u> parachuting.
REVISED	Hang-gliding is <u>as dangerous as</u> or <u>more dangerous than</u> parachuting.

EXERCISES: Comparisons

Correct all faulty comparisons in the following sentences.

1. Camembert and Roquefort are both good, but we like Roquefort best.
2. Harvey has always loved fishing more than Amy.
3. People were much more friendlier than Mary had thought they would be.
4. When the twins had finished their baths, the bathroom looked like a tidal wave had struck it.
5. I will never be satisfied until I get a more perfect score.
6. The men both bought suits at the sale, but Joe's is different to Bill's in the way the jacket is cut.
7. Edinburgh, Scotland, has more stone buildings than any other American city.
8. Although she always looks like a fashion model, Marge has far less money and outfits than most of her friends have.
9. Ammonia cleans most floors as well or better than many higher-priced floor-cleaners.

prep/22 PROBLEMS WITH PREPOSITIONS

Prepositions and the rules for their use are highly idiomatic; indeed, foreign learners of English often feel that every expression involving a preposition is a separate idiom. Fortunately, as native speakers of English, we apply most of the rules for the use of prepositions automatically, and our questions concerning their use are limited to occasional doubts about where to put them, when to repeat them, and which one to use with a given word.

22a PLACEMENT OF PREPOSITIONS

Although we normally think of prepositions as preceding their objects, they often follow their objects and appear at the end of a clause or sentence.

What are you complaining <u>about</u>?

The streets are dangerous to walk <u>in</u>.

The house that the car stopped <u>at</u> had a For Sale sign on the lawn.

This kind of construction is natural in speech, but some people disapprove of it in writing. If, for some reason, highly formal writing is desirable or necessary, you can usually rewrite the sentence so that the preposition precedes its object.

<u>About</u> what are you complaining?

It is dangerous to walk <u>in</u> the streets.

The house <u>at</u> which the car stopped had a For Sale sign on the lawn.

However, if moving the preposition so that it precedes its object results in awkwardness, leave it where it was; it is not ungrammatical to end a sentence with a preposition.

AWKWARD	It was the worst accident <u>of</u> which I had ever heard.
NATURAL	It was the worst accident I had ever heard <u>of</u>.
AWKWARD	His answer will depend on that <u>for</u> which you ask.
NATURAL	His answer will depend on what you ask <u>for</u>.

22b REPETITION OF PREPOSITIONS

Do not repeat a preposition that has already appeared with its object earlier in the sentence.

INCORRECT	Marty could not find the man <u>with</u> whom he had been assigned to work <u>with</u>.
REVISED	Marty could not find the man <u>with</u> whom he had been assigned to work.
REVISED	Marty could not find the man whom he had been assigned to work <u>with</u>.
INCORRECT	<u>To</u> what devices could Sherman resort <u>to</u> now?
REVISED	<u>To</u> what devices could Sherman resort now?
REVISED	What devices could Sherman resort <u>to</u> now?

For the repetition of prepositions in parallel constructions, see 23f.

22c IDIOMATIC USE OF PREPOSITIONS

Many nouns, verbs, adjectives, and phrases are associated with specific prepositions, and the use of any other preposition is incorrect. Further, the correct preposition may vary, depending on the verb or the object of the preposition. For example, if you decide to use a pen instead of a pencil, you *substitute* the pen *for* the pencil, but you *replace* the pencil *with* the pen. You are *answerable to* a person or authority, but you are *answerable for* your own actions. There are so many such idiomatic prepositional combinations that it is impossible to list all of them here; only a few of the most troublesome are given in the following list.

according to	disapprove of
amazed at *or* by	eager for
annoyed at *or* by	familiar to (someone)
beware of	familiar with (something)
capable of	in accordance with
coincide with	in search of
conform to	inferior to
consist of	married to
consistent with	prior to
convince	refrain from
(someone) of	responsible to (someone) for (something)
(something)	result from (a cause)
critical of	result in (an effect)
differ with	speak to (someone) about (something)
(someone)	succeed in
about	surprised at
(something)	take charge of
differ from	
(something else)	

When in doubt about the appropriate preposition for a particular word or expression, consult your dictionary. Although dictionaries do not list the correct preposition for all nouns, adjectives, and verbs, good dictionaries do list many of the correct combinations.

EXERCISES: Prepositions

Rewrite the following sentences to correct problems caused by incorrectly placed or misused prepositions.

1. The second edition of the book differed greatly to the first edition.

2. His refusal was one of the meanest gestures of which I have ever heard.

3. I cannot understand why my professor was so critical with my term paper.

4. Until she was nearly thirty, Louisa always had to tell her parents with whom she went out with and where she was going to.

5. A large sign near the entrance warns visitors to beware about bears.

6. The young teacher's aide was terrified when Miss Abjornson asked her to take charge over the class during the arithmetic lesson.

7. To what ends could Smitty's boss expect him to go to to meet the deadline?

PROBLEMS WITH SENTENCE FORM

sen fm / 23

Among the most common problems of sentence form are (1) sentence fragments, (2) shifted constructions, (3) mixed constructions, (4) comma splices and fused sentences, (5) faulty complements and appositives, and (6) faulty and false parallelism.

23a SENTENCE FRAGMENTS / frag

Sentence fragments, or **incomplete sentences,** are constructions that have no independent clause. Sentence fragments are common in speech, especially as answers to questions or as afterthoughts to statements.

> "When did you go to the market?" "<u>This morning.</u>"

> "You're standing on my foot. <u>And blocking my view.</u>"

In writing, on the other hand, sentence fragments are rarely acceptable, except in writing dialogue to imitate speech. Most sentence fragments consist of (1) dependent clauses, (2) unfinished clauses, (3) detached predicates, (4) modifying phrases, or (5) explanatory phrases. Many, although not all, sentence fragments properly belong with the preceding sentence and can be corrected by changing only the punctuation and the capitalization.

Dependent Clauses.   Correct sentence fragments consisting of dependent clauses by joining the clause to the preceding sentence.

FRAGMENT	The Arabs contributed much to astronomy. <u>Which they considered a branch of mathematics.</u>
REVISED	The Arabs contributed much to astronomy, which they considered a branch of mathematics.
FRAGMENT	I didn't want Leslie to come home. <u>At least until I had had a chance to wash the dishes and make the beds.</u>
REVISED	I didn't want Leslie to come home—at least until I had had a chance to wash the dishes and make the beds.

Incomplete Clauses.   Sentence fragments consisting of incomplete clauses often occur in sentences with lengthy modifiers. By the time the writer has finished with all the modifiers, he or she has forgotten that the main clause has not been completed.

FRAGMENT	The term "down East," referring to the state of Maine and causing much confusion to people outside New England, who do not understand why going north is going "down East." (The subject, *The term "down East,"* has no predicate.)
REVISED	The term "down East" refers to the state of Maine. It causes much confusion to people outside New England, who do not understand why going north is going "down East."
FRAGMENT	Whenever Eddie had to answer the telephone, which was equipped with more buttons and red lights than the cockpit of a Boeing 707. (There are two dependent clauses but no independent clause.)
REVISED	Eddie panicked whenever he had to answer the telephone, which was equipped with more buttons and red lights than the cockpit of a Boeing 707.

Detached Compound Predicates.   Sentence fragments consisting of a detached compound predicate can be corrected by reattaching the second part of the predicate to the sentence in which its subject appears.

FRAGMENT	He went to the market to buy a sheep. <u>And came home fleeced</u>.
REVISED	He went to the market to buy a sheep and came home fleeced.
FRAGMENT	Esther has always loved needlework. <u>But hates mending</u>.
REVISED	Esther has always loved needlework but hates mending.

Modifying Phrases.   Sentence fragments consisting of modifying phrases include prepositional phrases, appositives, participle phrases, and infinitive phrases. Reattach the phrases to the preceding sentence, or rewrite the phrase to make a complete sentence.

PREPOSITIONAL PHRASE	George attended school for thirteen years. <u>Without missing a single day</u>.
REVISED	George attended school for thirteen years without missing a single day.
APPOSITIVE	The capital of Java is Jakarta. <u>Formerly called Batavia</u>.
REVISED	The capital of Java is Jakarta, formerly called Batavia.
PARTICIPLE PHRASE	We began to row furiously. <u>Our engine having died</u>.
REVISED	Our engine having died, we began to row furiously.
INFINITIVE PHRASE	After dieting for three weeks, Henry was pleasantly surprised when he weighed himself. <u>To discover that he had lost five pounds</u>.
REVISED	When he weighed himself after dieting for three weeks, Henry was pleasantly surprised to discover that he had lost five pounds.

Explanatory Phrases.   Sentence fragments consisting of explanatory phrases beginning with *such as, for example, namely*, and so on, can be corrected by incorporating the fragment into the preceding sentence.

FRAGMENT	The hijacking ring specializes in high-value merchandise. <u>Such as jewelry, furs, and Oriental rugs</u>.
REVISED	The hijacking ring specializes in high-value merchandise such as jewelry, furs, and Oriental rugs.
FRAGMENT	One legislative item was never voted out of committee. <u>Namely, the child-abuse bill</u>.
REVISED	One legislative item, the child-abuse bill, was never voted out of committee.

Deliberate Fragments.   You have probably noticed that some authors occasionally write deliberate sentence fragments, especially in descriptive passages where no action is taking place and the author is simply listing detail to convey a picture to the reader.

> It was a large square room. There was a double bed with a pink bedspread, a table with a green cloth, two wooden chairs and an armchair, a cupboard, two or three skimpy carpets. <u>Pale gray walls in need of painting, a photo of King Paul, an oleograph ikon over the bed</u>. Another door led into a bathroom.
> —John Fowles, THE MAGUS

Similarly, fragments are sometimes effective in answering rhetorical questions, in exclamations, in citing proverbs, and in reporting dialogue.

ANSWER	What does Professor Digger know about fossils? <u>Everything</u>.
EXCLAMATION	How depressing Poughkeepsie is on a raw November day!
PROVERB	Least said, soonest mended.
DIALOGUE	"Nice day," Jerry said. "Yeah, for ducks," replied Pamela.

Students sometimes deliberately write a sentence fragment, only to have their instructors mark it as an error. Instructors do this because they cannot be sure that their students know the difference between a fragment and a complete sentence or because the fragment, deliberate though it may be, simply is not effective. If you feel that a fragment is the most effective way of making a point, go ahead and use a fragment, but add a note to your instructor letting him or her know that you are deliberately using it for stylistic effect.

Sentences Beginning with a Conjunction.   Some people object to beginning sentences with coordinating conjunctions, regarding such constructions as sentence fragments. They are not fragments if there is a subject and a finite verb. Nevertheless, do not overuse such sentences, or the result will be choppy prose.

CHOPPY	Father praised my good grades. And mother sent her love. But they didn't enclose a check.
REVISED	Father praised my good grades and mother sent her love, but they didn't enclose a check.

EXERCISES: Sentence Fragments

Rewrite the following sentence fragments to make them complete sentences.

1. Dieters can be seen everywhere, clutching their Bibles. Better known as their calorie-counters.

2. The fisherman, settling down for a long, peaceful afternoon of casting, interspersed with catnaps and reeling in the fish.

3. The fraternity party finally ended at 3 a.m. The band having left at 2 a.m., and the police having arrived at 2:45 a.m. to quiet things down.

4. While one part of the TV screen carried the football game and another part showed the scores of other games being played and a storm warning was being flashed across the bottom of the screen.

5. When all of the family had finally gathered in grandmother's parlor, where mother had insisted that we meet to discuss the sale of the farm.

6. Businesses quickly sprang up along the new highway. Including fast-food restaurants, bowling alleys, used car lots, and a 24-hour launderette.

23b SHIFTED CONSTRUCTIONS / shift

Shifted constructions are unnecessary changes in such grammatical features as tense, voice, person, number, and mood. Obviously, some shifts are necessary in writing; for example, if we are contrasting past action with present action, we must shift the tense of the verb accordingly. Errors occur when the shift is unnecessary or illogical.

Shifted Tense. Do not shift the tense of the verb unless you intend to indicate a shift in the time of action.

SHIFTED TENSE	I <u>asked</u> the clerk where I <u>could appeal</u> the fine, and he <u>tells</u> me that I <u>will have</u> to go to court. (Shift from past to present tense)
REVISED	I <u>asked</u> the clerk where I <u>could appeal</u> the fine, and he told me that I <u>would have</u> to go to court.

Shifted Voice. Do not shift from active to passive voice or vice versa in the middle of a sentence.

SHIFTED VOICE	After she <u>pressed</u> the fabric and <u>laid</u> the pattern on it, the pattern <u>was pinned</u> to the fabric. (Shift from active to passive voice)
REVISED	After she <u>pressed</u> the fabric and <u>laid</u> the pattern on it, she <u>pinned</u> the pattern to the fabric.

Shifted Person or Number. Do not shift unnecessarily from one person to another or from singular to plural.

SHIFTED PERSON	When <u>one</u> wakes up with a terrible headache after a party, <u>you</u> shouldn't blame the pretzels. (Shift from third person to second person)
REVISED	When <u>one</u> wakes up with a terrible headache after a party, <u>he</u> (or <u>he or she</u> or <u>one</u>) shouldn't blame the pretzels.
SHIFTED NUMBER	When <u>someone</u> wakes up with a terrible headache after a party, <u>they</u> shouldn't blame the pretzels. (Shift from singular to plural)
REVISED	When <u>someone</u> wakes up with a terrible headache after a party, <u>he or she</u> shouldn't blame the pretzels.
REVISED	People who wake up with terrible headaches after a party shouldn't blame the pretzels.

Shifted Mood.   Do not shift from one mood to another in the middle of a sentence.

SHIFTED MOOD	The doctor suggested that he <u>get</u> more sleep and that he <u>should exercise</u> less strenuously. (Shift from subjunctive to indicative mood)
REVISED	The doctor suggested that he <u>get</u> more sleep and that he <u>exercise</u> less strenuously.
REVISED	The doctor told him that he <u>should get</u> more sleep and <u>should exercise</u> less strenuously.
SHIFTED MOOD	First, <u>take</u> the receiver off the hook; then you <u>should listen</u> for a dial tone. (Shift from imperative to indicative mood)
REVISED	First, <u>take</u> the receiver off the hook; then <u>listen</u> for a dial tone.

23c COMMA SPLICES AND FUSED SENTENCES / cs / fs

Comma splices (or **comma faults**) result from using only a comma to connect two main clauses. Fused sentences result from joining two main clauses with neither punctuation nor a coordinating conjunction. Because proper use of punctuation is the most important way of avoiding or correcting comma splices and fused sentences, these errors are discussed in the section on punctuation, 27a.

23d MIXED CONSTRUCTIONS / mix

Mixed constructions result from beginning a phrase, clause, or sentence with one type of construction and then changing to another type without completing the first construction. The possible types of mixed constructions are almost unlimited, but a few kinds are especially common.

Direct and Indirect Quotations.   Do not mix a direct and an indirect quotation.

MIXED	He assured the customer I know how to make change.
REVISED	He assured the customer that he knew how to make change.
REVISED	He assured the customer, "I know how to make change."

Direct and Indirect Questions.   Do not mix a direct and an indirect question.

MIXED	I wonder do ladybugs eat mosquitoes?
REVISED	I wonder if ladybugs eat mosquitoes.

Adverbials and Subjects or Complements.   Do not use an adverbial phrase or clause as a subject or complement. Many such problems arise from improperly using *when, why, where,* or *how* to introduce a complement after the verb *to be.*

MIXED	By turning to look at the dog was when I fell off the bicycle.
REVISED	I fell off the bicycle when I turned to look at the dog.
REVISED	Turning to look at the dog, I fell off the bicycle.
MIXED	Because Peter's window was open was how the bat came into his room.
REVISED	The bat came into Peter's room through his open window.
REVISED	Because Peter's window was open, the bat came into his room.

Subjects and Objects.   Do not make an object the apparent subject of a sentence. This error usually occurs when the object is the real topic and the focus of the writer's attention. The writer begins the sentence with this topic, then switches to a construction in which the topic is an object.

MIXED	<u>People who have bad backs</u>, doctors advise <u>them</u> to sleep on a hard mattress.
REVISED	Doctors advise people who have bad backs to sleep on a hard mattress.
MIXED	<u>The baby skunk we found in the barn</u>, we took <u>it</u> to the veterinarian to be de-scented.
REVISED	We took the baby skunk we found in the barn to the veterinarian to be de-scented.

Independent Clauses and Subjects.   Do not use an independent clause as the subject of a sentence. To correct this error, you can (1) change the independent clause to a noun phrase, (2) make the independent clause into a dependent clause and the predicate into an independent clause, or (3) completely rewrite the sentence.

MIXED	<u>The salesman's face looked very honest</u> was what persuaded me to buy the set of encyclopedias.
REVISED	The salesman's honest face persuaded me to buy the set of encyclopedias.
REVISED	Because the salesman's face looked very honest, I decided to buy the set of encyclopedias.
REVISED	It was the salesman's honest face that persuaded me to buy the set of encyclopedias.

23e FAULTY COMPLEMENTS AND APPOSITIVES

Sentences with linking verbs, especially the verb *to be*, are really like equations; the subject is the left side of the equation, the verb is the equal sign, and the complement (that is, the rest of the predicate) is the right side of the equation. When we say "Cats are mammals," we are, in effect, saying "Cats = mammals." But not all nouns can logically be equated with each other; we would not, for instance, say "Cats are a devotion" or "Cats are difference." These last two sentences are examples of faulty complements. Faulty complementation usually occurs when we are writing so rapidly that we concentrate only on the ideas we want to convey and not on the proper form for these ideas. Correct a faulty complement by rewriting the sentence to make the subject and the complement logically and grammatically equivalent.

FAULTY	In my philosophy class, the discussion is only a few students and the instructor. (*Students* or *instructor* is not *a discussion.*)
REVISED	In my philosophy class, the discussion is carried on by only a few students and the instructor.
FAULTY	One of the best antiseptics is by washing with soap and water. (*By washing* is not *an antiseptic.*)
REVISED	One of the best antiseptics is soap and water.

Faulty appositives are a type of faulty complementation in which the verb *to be* has been omitted.

FAULTY	Competition is intense for the higher-paid professions, such as doctors and lawyers. (*Doctors and lawyers* are not *professions.*)
REVISED	Competition is intense for the higher-paid professions, such as medicine and law.

EXERCISES: Mixed and Illogical Constructions

Correct mixed and illogical constructions in the following sentences.

1. Couples seen holding hands or kissing are indicators of affection.
2. Midway through the examination, Peter found his mind wandering and that his vision had become blurred.
3. The coach asked Sam how much sleep did he get last night.
4. His father suggested that he look around for a good used car and that he should see some agents about auto insurance.
5. While the girls went for a swim, Pat and Howard made the salad and set the table, and then the steaks were grilled by them.
6. Everyone has good intentions about filing their income tax returns early, but somehow you always end up staying up all night on April 14.
7. In running to catch the bus was how I twisted my ankle.
8. Sarah's painting is a work of art that never fails to elicit comments from visitors to her studio and which is the result of more than a year's hard work.

23f PARALLELISM / ||

Parallelism means using the same grammatical structure for all items that have the same function. Parallelism holds sentences together, adds emphasis, and provides a smooth, rhythmic flow to writing. Parallelism helps both writer and reader organize the thoughts being expressed. Parallelism usually is economical; that is, it takes fewer words to express ideas if they are grammatically parallel. Finally, parallelism seems to satisfy a basic human love for symmetry. We understand and remember sentences better if they are in parallel form. It is for this reason that so many proverbs and famous quotations use heavy parallelism.

> I came, I saw, I conquered.
>
> God send you more wit, and me more money.
>
> Whither thou goest, I will go; and where thou lodgest, I will lodge.

Grammatical problems with parallelism can involve either faulty parallelism or false parallelism.

Faulty Parallelism. Faulty parallelism occurs when ideas serving the same grammatical purpose do not have the same grammatical form; that is, when the second or successive items do not fit the pattern established by the first item. Correct faulty parallelism by putting all the related ideas into the same grammatical form. Faulty parallelism may involve almost any kind of grammatical construction but is especially common in series.

INCORRECT	Eating is time-consuming, expensive, and it makes you fat. (The first two items in the series are adjectives and the last item is an independent clause.)
REVISED	Eating is time-consuming, expensive, and fattening.

Faulty parallelism is also common in items connected by coordinating or correlative conjunctions.

INCORRECT	Mexico is overpopulated, but there are not enough people in Canada. (The first clause has a subject complement, whereas the second clause begins with an expletive pronoun.)
REVISED	Mexico is overpopulated, but Canada is underpopulated.
INCORRECT	It is easier said than it is to do it. (The first part of this comparison ends in a past participle, whereas the second part has an infinitive and a direct object.)
REVISED	It is easier said than done.
INCORRECT	Vitamin A is found not only in vegetables, but eggs and butter also have it. (The first clause has a passive verb and a prepositional phrase, whereas the second clause has an active verb and a direct object.)
REVISED	Vitamin A is found not only in vegetables but also in eggs and butter.

If all the related ideas in a series cannot be put into the same form, break the series up into two or more parallel series.

INCORRECT	The foundations of the house are sinking, it must have a new roof, the paint is peeling, and it doesn't have storm windows.
REVISED	The foundations of the house are sinking and the paint is peeling; furthermore, it needs storm windows and a new roof.

False Parallelism.   False parallelism occurs when ideas that are not parallel in grammatical function or meaning are put into parallel or seemingly parallel form. Correct false parallelism by rewriting to eliminate the parallelism. Common errors of false parallelism include (1) making a subordinate clause falsely parallel to a main clause;

INCORRECT	We spent hours doing crossword puzzles and playing word games, and which most people would find boring. (The coordinating conjunction *and* connects an independent clause and a subordinate clause introduced by *which*.)
REVISED	We spent hours doing crossword puzzles and playing word games, activities that most people would find boring.

(2) using the same word in two or more different ways;

INCORRECT	They will complete the repairs *by* the bridge *by* Wednesday *by* hiring extra workers.
REVISED	They will hire extra workers in order to complete the repairs near the bridge by Wednesday.

and (3) mixing words with different levels of generality or with clearly unrelated meanings.

INCORRECT	This wheelbarrow is available in red, orange, and bright colors. (*Bright colors* is a general term that includes *red* and *orange*.)
REVISED	This wheelbarrow is available in red, orange, and other bright colors.
INCORRECT	The judge was well-educated, liberal, and gray-eyed. (*Well-educated* and *liberal* are mental characteristics, but *gray-eyed* is a physical characteristic.)
REVISED	The judge was well-educated and liberal.

Parallelism and Repetition.   Parallel structures are frequently identified and clarified by the repetition of words common to all the parallel elements. Such parallelism often is optional; you may either omit the common word or repeat it, but be consistent. If you repeat, for example, a preposition before one item in a series, repeat it before all items in the series.

INCORRECT	He collected the information <u>from</u> letters, newspapers, <u>from</u> diaries, and city records.
REVISED	He collected the information <u>from</u> letters, newspapers, diaries, and city records.
REVISED	He collected the information <u>from</u> letters, <u>from</u> newspapers, <u>from</u> diaries, and <u>from</u> city records.
INCORRECT	Janice brought home <u>her</u> guitar, bicycle, <u>her</u> geology textbook, and <u>her</u> roommate.
REVISED	Janice brought home <u>her</u> guitar, <u>her</u> bicycle, <u>her</u> geology textbook, and <u>her</u> roommate.

EXERCISES: Parallelism

Correct faulty or false parallelism in the following sentences.

1. Madeleine is a woman with true compassion for stray animals, who tries to find their owners or getting them adopted.

2. All of this compassion means that she usually has quite a menagerie to care for while she makes phone calls, places ads in the newspapers, and she solicits help from the radio stations.

3. The animals not only require a lot of attention, but Madeleine finds that caring for them is expensive and she gets very tired.

4. At six each morning, Madeleine serves breakfast to her clientele, opening cans of food for the dogs and cats, crumbling up bread for the birds and ducks, and fresh vegetables are chopped up for the rabbits and raccoon.

5. Caring for her menagerie is important to Madeleine for two reasons: she deeply loves animals and to teach animals to trust people.

punctuation
and
mechanics

Much of the material discussed in this book is common to both the spoken and the written language. In both speech and writing, we have a message to convey. We must select words to convey this message and then arrange these words into phrases, clauses, and sentences. Whether we are speaking or writing, the logic and the organization of what we say is important.

Punctuation, spelling, and mechanics, however, are almost exclusively features of the written language. Punctuation, the use of special marks to group written words, phrases, and clauses, sometimes corresponds to pauses and changes of pitch in speaking but often is purely conventional—a mark is used in a particular place only because readers expect the mark to appear in that place. Spelling, the use of written symbols to represent words, is similarly a feature unique to writing. When we speak, we never have to worry about how a word is spelled. Further, while we accept varying pronunciations of a single word, any given word normally has only one acceptable spelling. Mechanics, a subdivision of spelling that includes capitalization, abbreviation, and the way in which numbers are expressed in writing, is even less closely related to speech: There is no difference whatsoever in speech between the sounds of the words *Frankfurter* and *frankfurter*, between *F.* and *Fahrenheit*, or between *15* and *fifteen*.

Punctuation, spelling, and mechanics also differ from other aspects of writing in their relative inflexibility; the writer simply has fewer options and almost no room for individuality. For example, we often can choose to write a subordinate clause instead of an independent clause, but once we have made that decision, we have very little choice about how we punctuate the resulting sentence. Although we may decide, for the sake of variety, to use the word *excuse* instead of *pardon*, we cannot decide to spell it *excuze* or *ekscuse* just to add variety to our spelling. Nor can we decide to display our originality by abbreviating *condescend* as *con.* or by writing *ante meridiem* instead of *a.m.*

The sole purpose of punctuation, spelling, and mechanics is to support the message conveyed by the words, sentences, and paragraphs. Punctuation in particular supports our writing by preventing misreading and assuring clarity. Correct punctuation is not of course a substitute for good writing, but incorrect punctuation detracts from and can even destroy what would otherwise be good writing. Correct punctuation does not convey a message in and of itself and does not attract attention to itself. Incorrect punctuation, on the other hand, often sends the reader a message that the writer does not intend to convey; it tells the reader that the writer is careless or even ignorant of the traditional rules of written English.

./24 PERIODS

USE A PERIOD
—At the end of most sentences
—After abbreviations and initials
—In dramatic, poetic, and Biblical citations

The **period** is the most important mark of punctuation in English because it separates one sentence from another, and sentences are the basic units of writing. In addition to its structural use as ending punctuation for sentences, the period has a number of conventional uses.

24a AS ENDING PUNCTUATION

Every sentence or deliberate sentence fragment should end with a mark of punctuation. The most common mark of punctuation for ending sentences is the period (or *stop* or *full stop*, as it is sometimes called).

After Complete Sentences.   Periods are used at the end of declarative sentences, indirect questions, and polite commands or requests, even though these commands may have the word order of a question.

DECLARATIVE SENTENCES	All cows eat grass.
	During the battle, General Wolfe was mortally wounded.
INDIRECT QUESTIONS	I asked when the movie would be over.
	People have often wondered whether there is life on other planets.
POLITE REQUESTS	Please turn down your radio.
	Would you kindly refund my money as guaranteed.

After Deliberate Sentence Fragments.   Periods are also used after deliberate or conventionally acceptable sentence fragments. (See 23a for a discussion of sentence fragments.)

Yes.	Better late than never.
Good night.	So much for rose petals.

Exception: Titles at the tops of pages or otherwise set off from the text are not followed by a period, even when they are complete sentences.

Mountain Climbing Is an Uphill Job

The Failure of Western Medicine

24b CONVENTIONAL USES

In addition to its use as a grammatical signal that a sentence has ended, the period has a number of conventional uses.

Abbreviations and Initials. Periods are used after most abbreviations and initials. (See 43 for the appropriate use of abbreviations.)

> Be here by 10 a.m.
> Mrs. Paulsen lived in Washington, D.C., for over three years.
> Will A. J. Foyt win the Indianapolis 500 again?

Usage has not yet been settled on the punctuation of the title *Ms.* However, because periods are used after *Mr.* and *Mrs.*, you will not be wrong if you use a period after *Ms.* too.

1. Periods are used after the traditional abbreviations of states, but not after the official post office abbreviations. Note that the two-letter post office abbreviations should be used only in addressing mail.

TRADITIONAL ABBREVIATION	POST OFFICE ABBREVIATION
Calif.	CA
Mass.	MA
N.Y.	NY

2. Periods are not used after shortened word forms that have become accepted as independent words. Nor are periods used with nicknames.

> She has an *exam* this afternoon.
> The school plans to build a new *gym* on that site.
> *Ed* and *Flo* send their love.

3. Many acronyms (words formed from the initial letters of a name several words long) do not use periods. However, because practice varies greatly, consult one dictionary and follow it consistently. Periods are never used with the call letters of radio and television stations and networks.

ACRONYMS		CALL LETTERS
YMCA	B.C.	WGBH
GNP	I.Q.	NBC
NASA	Q.E.D.	WOR

Dramatic, Poetic, and Biblical Citations. Periods separate act, scene, and line in citations from drama; separate chapter and verse in Biblical citations; and separate book and line in citations from long poetic works.

BIBLICAL CITATION	Psalm 23.3 or Psalm xxiii.3
DRAMATIC CITATION	*Othello* II.iii.24–27
POETIC CITATION	*The Faerie Queene* III.vii.1

?/25 QUESTION MARKS

USE A QUESTION MARK
—After direct questions
—After doubtful figures

Like a period, the **question mark** is used structurally as a mark of ending punctuation. Unlike a period, it is used only after direct questions.

25a DIRECT QUESTIONS

A question mark is used after a direct question.

> What is the difference between a duck and a goose?
>
> Do you have a good book on bricklaying?

Even if the word order of a sentence is that of a statement, use a question mark if a direct question is being asked; that is, if the voice would rise at the end when the sentence is spoken, a question mark should be used.

> The newspaper was late again this morning?
>
> You said you called the office and complained?

1. If a sentence contains a question within a question, use only one question mark.

> Who was it that asked, "Of what use is a baby?"

2. When a sentence contains a series of words, all of which are being questioned, a single question mark may be placed at the end of the entire sentence.

> What does he propose to do about rising taxes, crime in the cities, unemployment, the international situation, and inflation?

Less formally, you can place question marks after each separate question, even if the questions are not complete sentences.

> What does he propose to do about rising taxes? crime in the cities? unemployment? the international situation? inflation?

To add greater emphasis, you can capitalize the first word of each item being questioned.

> What does he propose to do about rising taxes? Crime in the cities? Unemployment? The international situation? Inflation?

25b CONVENTIONAL USE

A question mark is conventionally used to indicate a doubtful figure or date.

> John Chapman (1775?–1845) is better known as Johnny Appleseed.

25c SUPERFLUOUS USES

Question marks should not be used after exclamations, indirect questions, or requests. Nor should they be used to indicate humor or sarcasm.

Exclamations. Do not use a question mark after exclamations phrased as questions.

INCORRECT	Will you please leave immediately?
REVISED	Will you please leave immediately!

Indirect Questions and Requests. Do not use a question mark after an indirect question or a polite request phrased as a question. (See 23d for more information about indirect questions.)

INCORRECT	George asked Harriet where she got her hat?
REVISED	George asked Harriet where she got her hat.

Humor and Sarcasm. Avoid the use of question marks to indicate humor or sarcasm.

INAPPROPRIATE	Our expert (?) Maine guide led us directly into a swamp.
REVISED	Our supposedly expert Maine guide led us directly into a swamp.

! / 26 EXCLAMATION POINTS

USE AN EXCLAMATION POINT
—After emphatic or emotional statements

The **exclamation point** is the most dramatic mark of ending punctuation. Because it does convey such a strong feeling of excitement, it should be used sparingly; otherwise, the writer will appear somewhat hysterical.

26a DRAMATIC OR EMOTIONAL STATEMENTS

The exclamation point is appropriate after interjections, exclamatory words and phrases, and exceptionally strong commands.

Help!   Ouch! You're standing on my foot!
Look at him run!   There! That should do it.
Stop that!

The exclamation point is especially common after exclamations beginning with one of the question words *how, what,* and *who.*

Who would have thought it!
How wonderful!
What a job that will be!

In general, it is safest to reserve the exclamation point for reporting dialogue. But even in the reporting of dialogue, not every interjection requires an exclamation point.

Well! So this is what you do the minute my back is turned! (Genuine indignation is being expressed by the *Well!* and the following statement.)

Well, we'll just have to wait and see. (The *Well* is resigned and thoughtful, not excited.)

26b SUPERFLUOUS USES

1. Do not use an exclamation point to indicate humor or sarcasm.

INAPPROPRIATE   Our expert (!!) Maine guide led us directly into a swamp.

REVISED   Our supposedly expert Maine guide led us directly into a swamp.

2. Never use more than one exclamation point after a word or phrase, and never combine exclamation points with question marks.

OVEREMOTIONAL   You can't be serious?!!
REVISED   You can't be serious!

EXERCISES: Periods, Question Marks, and Exclamation Points

Correctly punctuate the following sentences with periods, question marks, and exclamation points.

1. On the exam Ms Jones asked us to comment on *Othello* I iii 377–391

2. An automatic page turner What on earth will they think of next

3. Dr L A Pettit of Washington, DC, chief authority on American Indian culture, told the audience, "We believe Indians came to America about 18,000 BC"

4. Did you see the interview CBS arranged with the top directors of the CIA

5. "Oh gosh" she shrieked "Did you really get the job with the FDA"

6. Mary wondered why Thomas Nast had chosen the elephant to represent the Republican Party in his famous 1872 cartoon that made the elephant the symbol of the GOP.

7. Goods for the garage sale poured into the headquarters of the Macon branch of the DAR in such abundance that the building was overflowing by 8 pm

8. The director bowed to the cast and exclaimed, "That was undoubtedly the most moving performance I have ever seen of *Who's Afraid of Virginia Woolf*"

9. Without looking up from his desk, Dr Morales said, "Miss, would you please sit down"

, / 27 COMMAS

USE A COMMA
—Between independent clauses
—Between items in a series
—After introductory elements
—Around nonrestrictive modifiers
—Around parenthetical elements
—Before direct quotations
—Between geographic units
—Between parts of dates
—Between names and titles or degrees
—Between units of thousands
—After salutations and complimentary closings
—For clarity

The **comma** is by far the most important mark of internal punctuation. Structurally, it functions as a separator—separating clauses and phrases from each other, separating items in a series, and separating nonessential elements from the rest of the sentence. The comma also has a number of conventional uses, both as a separator of words and numbers and simply as a mark that conventionally appears in certain places.

27a INDEPENDENT CLAUSES

Independent clauses are those that contain a subject and a finite verb and are not preceded by a subordinating word such as *that, until,* or *whenever.* (Finite verbs are those that can serve as complete verb phrases; see 4b.) When two or more independent clauses appear within one sentence, they must be separated by some mark of punctuation. If a coordinating conjunction connects the clauses, a comma is the appropriate mark of punctuation.

With Coordinating Conjunctions. Use a comma before a coordinating conjunction connecting two independent clauses. The coordinating conjunctions are *and, but, or,* and *nor.*

> The land has been worked for centuries, <u>and</u> no effort has been made to maintain the fertility of the soil.
>
> Ballads are found in the thirteenth century, <u>but</u> they did not become popular until much later.
>
> The architecture may have an English flavor, <u>or</u> it may display French influence.
>
> There are no photography courses offered at the local high school, <u>nor</u> are any planned in the future.

Note: The comma is often omitted if the two clauses are short. However, it is never wrong to use a comma, even between short clauses.

> The soil is poor and water is scarce.
>
> Her sins were scarlet but her books were read.
>
> I don't like rutabagas nor will I eat parsnips.

With yet, for, and so. For purposes of punctuation, *yet* in the meaning of "but," *for* in the meaning of "because," and *so* in the meaning of "therefore" are often treated like coordinating conjunctions and are preceded by commas.

> Mount Hood can often be seen in Portland, <u>for</u> this extinct volcano is only 52 miles away.
>
> He gets all A's, <u>yet</u> he never cracks a book.
>
> There is no public transportation, <u>so</u> most people drive to work.

Comma Splices. Using a comma to separate two main clauses that are *not* connected by a coordinating conjunction produces the very serious error called **comma splice** or **comma fault.**

> I made my husband a mince pie for Christmas, he ate it all by himself and didn't offer me one bite.

Comma splices can be corrected by any of the following four methods:

1. By adding a coordinating conjunction.

> I made my husband a mince pie for Christmas, but he ate it all by himself and didn't offer me one bite.

2. By using a semicolon instead of a comma.

> I made my husband a mince pie for Chistmas; he ate it all by himself and didn't offer me one bite.

3. By making two separate sentences.

I made my husband a mince pie for Christmas. He ate it all by himself and didn't offer me one bite.

4. By rewriting to make one of the clauses subordinate to the other.

When I made my husband a mince pie for Christmas, he ate it all by himself and didn't offer me one bite.

There are, however, "allowable" comma splices. Commas alone are sometimes used to separate a series of short parallel independent clauses, even though the clauses are not connected by coordinating conjunctions. In such cases, semicolons may also be used.

Life is a toil, love is a trouble.

I came, I saw, I conquered.

Church bells rang, sirens blew, people danced in the streets.

Church bells rang; sirens blew; people danced in the streets.

An adverbial conjunction such as *however, nevertheless, what is more,* or *incidentally* cannot substitute for a coordinating conjunction; a comma splice still results.

COMMA SPLICE	I made my husband a mince pie for Christmas, however, he ate it all by himself and didn't offer me one bite.
CORRECT	I made my husband a mince pie for Christmas. However, he ate it all by himself and didn't offer me one bite.
CORRECT	I made my husband a mince pie for Christmas; however, he ate it all by himself and didn't offer me one bite.

Fused sentences. Failure to use either coordinating conjunctions or punctuation between independent clauses results in the error called **fused sentences.**

Housing is scarce in Japan apartments are hard to find and very expensive.

Fused sentences can be corrected in the same ways as comma splices:

1. By adding a comma and coordinating conjunction.

Housing is scarce in Japan, and apartments are hard to find and very expensive.

2. By using a semicolon.

Housing is scarce in Japan; apartments are hard to find and very expensive.

3. By making two separate sentences.

Housing is scarce in Japan. Apartments are hard to find and very expensive.

4. By rewriting to make one of the clauses subordinate to the other.

Because housing is scarce in Japan, apartments are hard to find and very expensive.

Note: A fused sentence usually cannot be corrected by simply putting a comma between the two clauses. The result will be a comma splice.

Housing is scarce in Japan, apartments are hard to find and very expensive.

EXERCISES: Commas and Independent Clauses

Correctly punctuate the following sentences by inserting a comma wherever necessary between independent clauses. If the sentence is already correct, write C before the sentence. Write IC if the sentence lacks a comma before an independent clause. Write CS before sentences containing comma splices and FS before fused sentences.

1. For vacations Aubrey preferred the cool, soothing quiet of the mountains but Karen liked early morning sunrises over the ocean and hot, sunny days on the beach.

2. The play began at 8:30 p.m., however the theatre was only half full.

3. By applying an accounting trick, John saw that in copying the numbers he had transposed some figures for the differences in his total and that of the booklet was evenly divisible by nine.

4. The police car gave chase for two miles but then gave up on catching the speeder and returned to town.

5. Although it was past midnight, Dr. Williams was still out in his flood-lit back yard practicing his golf swing and hacking up the lawn and rose garden.

6. Do you want to picnic on that inviting lawn at the opera center or would you rather eat at the Golden Lion?

7. The handsome man flashed a smile at the new blonde teller and then he pushed the crispy-new counterfeit bills toward her.

8. Allen said he would come to the party, nonetheless he did not show up.

9. Lisa and her chubby fellow conspirator filled Joe's room with balloons they sprayed shaving cream all over both sides of the door.

10. In a bad mood for most of the day, Chuck would not answer the phone, nor did he go down to meals or attend class.

11. We should turn off a few lights wasting electricity is foolish.

27b ITEMS IN A SERIES

When words belonging to the same part of speech or serving exactly the same function in a sentence appear consecutively, we speak of a **series.** Series may consist of single words, phrases, or even clauses.

Three or More Items. Use commas to separate three or more items in a series.

> Adam Smith, Jeremy Bentham, and J. S. Mill all contributed to classical economic theory.
>
> The nose of mammals is a structure of flesh, bone, and cartilage.
>
> St. John Chrysostom was born in Antioch, lived in Constantinople, and died in Armenia.
>
> Your arguments are vigorous, appealing, well phrased, but wholly impractical.
>
> I did all the driving, Ellen navigated by reading the road maps, and Will maintained a running commentary on the scenery.

Although some writers prefer to omit the comma before the conjunction and final item in a series, it is safest always to use a comma in this position because its omission often leads to ambiguity.

> AMBIGUOUS The audience consisted primarily of sick people, old men and women.

Here, the reader cannot tell whether the words *old men and women* refer to the same thing as *sick people* or whether they are in addition to *sick people*. A comma eliminates this ambiguity.

> REVISED The audience consisted primarily of sick people, old men, and women.

If there is no conjunction before the last item, a comma *must* be used.

> Cockroaches were crawling in the sink, along the walls, over the floor.

A comma should never be used *after* the final item in a series.

> INCORRECT Lakes Superior, Michigan, and Huron, are all over a hundred miles wide.
>
> CORRECT Lakes Superior, Michigan, and Huron are all over a hundred miles wide.

No commas are used if all the items in the series are connected by coordinating conjunctions.

> To keep in shape, Evan jogs and swims and lifts weights.

Two Items. Except for independent clauses (see 27a for use of commas with independent clauses), do not use a comma between the members of a series of only two items connected by a coordinating conjunction. In other words, the two parts of a compound subject, object, predicate, or modifier should not be separated by commas.

> INCORRECT Bluejays, and starlings are often very noisy.
> CORRECT Bluejays and starlings are often very noisy.
>
> INCORRECT Egypt borders on Libya, and the Sudan.
> CORRECT Egypt borders on Libya and the Sudan.
>
> INCORRECT He does not drink, or smoke.
> CORRECT He does not drink or smoke.

Series of Adjectives.   Use a comma to separate a series of two or more adjectives not connected by a conjunction if the order of the adjectives can be reversed and still keep the same meaning.

> Your son is a clever, sensitive child.
> Your son is a sensitive, clever child.

If the order of the adjectives cannot be reversed, do not separate them by commas.

> INCORRECT   Old, stone fences are a familiar sight in Vermont.
>
> CORRECT   Old stone fences are a familiar sight in Vermont.

EXERCISES: Commas with Items in a Series

Correctly punctuate the following sentences by inserting a comma wherever necessary between items in a series.

1. Stamp collecting is an exciting educational hobby shared by young old rich and poor philatelists around the world.

2. From the very beginning, collectors have valued stamps that were printed in small quantities those that exhibited printing errors and those that had beautiful or peculiar designs.

3. Before they can think of specializing, however, enthusiastic serious beginners must first learn to view their tiny paper treasures with a magnifying glass to handle them with tweezers to store them carefully in pockets or paste them on with hinges in a moistureproof flat album and to revere them as amazingly detailed miniature works of art.

4. Some collectors accumulate only commemorative stamps of birds or reptiles or particular people some collect only stamps of a particular shape or color some specialize in surcharged or semipostal stamps and some want stamps from only one or two countries or decades.

5. Although regular postage stamps in hundreds of shapes and sizes and designs provide a large resource for collectors, philatelists also buy trade and save airmail parcel-post postage-due special-delivery personal-delivery postal-savings newspaper and provisional stamps of all kinds.

27c INTRODUCTORY ELEMENTS

Introductory elements include modifying words, phrases, and subordinate clauses.

Introductory Words and Phrases.   Use a comma to separate introductory phrases from the main part of the sentence.

> Unfortunately, money does not grow on trees.
>
> By the end of World War I, Europe was devastated.
>
> Having checked the punctuation, the careful writer proofreads for spelling errors.

If the introductory phrase is short, the comma is sometimes omitted.

> After lunch he took a nap.   In Ireland there are no snakes.

However, if the introductory phrase ends with a preposition, a comma is always used to avoid ambiguity.

> To sum up, the discussion was a waste of time.
> To begin with, the first page is missing.

Introductory Clauses.   If the order of two clauses in a sentence could be reversed, use a comma to separate them when the subordinate clause comes first.

> If the bowl is greasy, the egg whites will not stiffen.
> Because the lights were on, I knew that someone was home.

27d PARENTHETICAL ELEMENTS

Parenthetical elements are words or phrases that are not essential to the grammar of the sentences in which they appear, although they may alter the meaning of the sentences.

Adverbs and Adverbial Phrases.   Use commas to separate parenthetical adverbs and adverbial phrases from the rest of the sentence.

> Used-car dealers were, on the whole, regarded with some suspicion.
> The Etruscans, on the other hand, were not Indo-Europeans.
> Warts, however, are generally found on the hands and fingers.

Contradictory Phrases.   Use commas to separate contradictory phrases from the rest of the sentence.

> It was Erica, not Eric, who dropped the typewriter.
> Wash this garment with a mild soap, never a harsh detergent.

Direct Address and Other Isolates.   Use commas to separate names used in direct address or other isolates such as *yes, no,* and *thank you* from the rest of the sentence.

> Tell me, Miss Perkins, why you find grammar irrelevant.
> Yes, insurance is expensive, but a lawsuit is much more expensive.

Tag Questions.   Use commas to separate tag questions from the rest of the sentence. (Tag questions are added to a declarative sentence and consist of an auxiliary verb and a pronoun.)

> You did that on purpose, didn't you?
> It is true, is it not, that the United States imports all of its coffee?

Illustrative Words.   Use commas to separate words and abbreviations that introduce an example or a list of examples or illustrations, including *namely, that is, to wit, i.e., e.g., for example,* and *for instance.* Because the examples themselves are nonrestrictive appositives, they too are separated from the rest of the sentence by commas.

> Many Algonquian tribes, for example, the Pennacooks, the Cowesits, and the Wampanoags, practiced agriculture.
>
> The double bridle, that is, a snaffle and a curb bit, is standard for well-trained riding horses.

Exception: Do not use a comma immediately after *such as* or *such . . . as.*

> Our local company performs only popular operas such as *La Bohème, Madama Butterfly,* and *Carmen.*

> Left-handed people have trouble using such implements as can openers, scissors, and spatulas.

27e RESTRICTIVE AND NONRESTRICTIVE MODIFIERS

Nonrestrictive modifiers are not essential to the meaning of the sentence. **Restrictive modifiers** are essential to the meaning of the sentence. (For a detailed discussion of restrictive and nonrestrictive modifiers, see 20d.)

Nonrestrictive Modifiers. Use commas to separate nonrestrictive clauses, phrases, and appositives from the rest of the sentence. (See 14 for a discussion of appositives.)

NONRESTRICTIVE CLAUSES	Tamerlane, <u>who was a descendant of Genghis Khan</u>, united the Mongols.
	The tarantula, <u>which is a large and hairy spider,</u> can inflict a painful bite.
	The topic of conversation all evening was cattle breeding, <u>about which I know nothing</u>.
	He doesn't play golf, <u>unless you call chopping up the turf "playing golf."</u>
NONRESTRICTIVE PHRASES	The dessert, <u>soaked in brandy and served flambé</u>, was the high point of the meal.
	Joel's mittens, <u>dangling by a cord from his sleeves</u>, seemed to fascinate our cat.
	The scout leader, <u>overweight and out of shape,</u> trudged painfully up the slope.
NONRESTRICTIVE APPOSITIVES	Tamerlane, <u>a descendant of Genghis Khan,</u> united the Mongols.
	The choir sang an old hymn, "<u>Bringing in the Sheaves.</u>"
	He comes from Vernal, <u>a small town in Utah</u>.

Restrictive Modifiers. Do not use commas to separate restrictive clauses, phrases, or appositives from the rest of the sentence.

RESTRICTIVE CLAUSES	It was Tamerlane <u>who finally succeeded in uniting the Mongols</u>.
	A tarantula <u>that is fully grown</u> may have a leg spread of eight or nine inches.
	The cattle <u>that Mr. MacDougall sells</u> are all Aberdeen Angus.
	He won't play golf <u>unless he has a partner</u>.

RESTRICTIVE PHRASES	Not everything <u>soaked in brandy</u> is cherries jubilee.
	The cat's playful reaction was triggered by the mittens <u>dangling from a cord on Joel's sleeves.</u>
	I hate to see scout leaders <u>overweight and out of shape.</u>
RESTRICTIVE APPOSITIVES	The Oriental conqueror <u>Tamerlane</u> was a descendant of Genghis Khan.
	Andrew went to New York with his roommate <u>Jacques.</u>

EXERCISES: Commas with Introductory, Parenthetical, and Nonrestrictive Elements

Correctly punctuate the following sentences by inserting a comma where necessary after introductory components; parenthetical words, phrases, and clauses; and nonrestrictive words, phrases, and clauses.

1. Her neck on the other hand was loaded down with ornate chains that sparkled and glistened in the candlelight.

2. Mrs. Petrovitch who had lived in Iowa City all her life moved to Orlando when she retired.

3. After Gutenberg's invention of movable type in the fifteenth century printing was easier and more efficient.

4. Her brother Rob was the only one of six sons to finish college.

5. Isadora Duncan one of the founders of modern dance was a controversial woman who rebelled against classical ballet in favor of natural movement.

6. After the development of photography in 1839 and the discovery of the photoengraving process in 1852 newspapers were able to offer their readers pictures of news-making people and events.

7. As day dawned, the sunlight shimmering and glistening on the water was mirrored in the bow of the yacht that was moored at Mr. Kleindienst's dock.

8. His reluctance to accept the award really only a ploy on his part to get a larger grant irritated the members who had voted for him and made them determined to select someone who would seem more grateful than he.

9. We want to find the current address of the Mrs. Petrovitch who used to live in Iowa City.

10. Begun in 1702 by Elizabeth Mallett the first English daily newspaper was the London *Daily Courant.*

27f CONVENTIONAL USES

The comma has a number of conventional uses that are determined more by accepted current practice than by grammatical logic.

Direct Quotations. Use a comma to separate direct quotations from the phrase identifying the speaker.

As Samuel Butler said, " 'Tis better to have loved and lost than never to have lost at all."

"You must fill out the application in duplicate," the person at the desk told me.

"Well," she sighed, "we'll just have to wait and see."

Do not use a comma if *that* precedes a direct quotation.

Alexander Pope said that "an honest man's the noblest work of God," to which Samuel Butler replied, "An honest God's the noblest work of man."

Geographic Units.   Use commas to separate the names of smaller geographic units from the names of the larger units within which they are contained. Most writers prefer a comma after the name of the last geographic unit also, when this last unit appears in the middle of a sentence.

My summer address will be 77A Colinton Road, Edinburgh, Scotland.

The population of Portland, Oregon, is much larger than that of Portland, Maine.

Note: No comma is used between the name of the state and the ZIP code.

Missoula, Montana 59801

Dates.   In dates, if the order is month—day—year, use commas to separate the day from the year. If the date appears in the middle of the sentence, use another comma after the year.

Harry was born on July 17, 1946, in a small town in upstate New York.

If the order is day—month—year, no commas are used.

The installation officially closed on 17 July 1946.

If only the month and year are given, the comma is optional.

We visited Lima in December 1972.

We visited Lima in December, 1972.

Titles and Degrees.   Use commas to separate names from titles or degrees that follow the name.

Elizabeth II, queen of England

Cornelia Anderson, D.D.S.

Otto Kerner, former governor of Illinois

Arthur Schlesinger, Jr.

Use no comma if the title precedes the name. Use no punctuation before a Roman numeral or an ordinal numeral used to differentiate persons or vehicles with the same name.

Her Royal Highness Queen Elizabeth II

Pope John XXIII   *Mariner III*

James Parker IV   Henry the Eighth

Numbers. Use commas to separate digits by thousands when writing numbers over 1,000. Starting from the right, place a comma between every three numerals.

    7,519,453   72,735

Do not use commas to separate numbers in identification numbers, ZIP codes, telephone numbers, street addresses, or years. Do not use commas to separate numerals after a decimal point.

    Serial No. 863219677   19349 Crestwood Blvd.
    Providence, R.I. 02912   2500 B.C.
    Tele. 463–8750 π = 3.14159

Salutations and Complimentary Closings. Use a comma after the salutation in informal writing and after the complimentary closing of a letter. (In formal letters, a colon is often used instead of a comma after the salutation; see 29d.)

    Dear Ms. Peabody,   Sincerely,
    Dear Alice,   Love,
    Dear Ms. Olsen:

27g CLARITY

Use a comma to provide clarity and prevent misreading, even when none of the preceding rules applies.

> To the young, blood pudding may not be appealing food. (Without the comma, the reader may at first interpret this as *To the young blood, pudding. . . .)*
>
> We left him, assured that he would succeed. (*We* knew that he would succeed.)
>
> We left him assured that he would succeed. (*He* knew that he would succeed.)

Omitted Words. Commas are often used to mark allowable omissions of repeated words, especially verbs. Here the comma, like an apostrophe within a word, marks the point where the omission is made.

> Your analysis is superb; your execution, appalling.
>
> Marjorie was knitting a sweater; Paul, an afghan.

Consecutively Repeated Words. Commas are used to separate two or three consecutive occurrences of the same word within a sentence.

> And still I cried, cried until my eyes were swollen and my nose was red.
>
> What that is, is an anteater.
>
> Rain, rain, rain—doesn't the sun ever shine around here?

EXERCISES: Other Uses of Commas

Correctly punctuate the following sentences by inserting commas as needed.

1. "It was Jonas not Sam who made the error" Mr. Quarles snapped.
2. "If she is really my friend" said Juanita "she won't hesitate to lend me the money."
3. Most leafy green vegetables for example turnip and collard greens, kale, and spinach, have few calories but supply large amounts of iron and vitamins.
4. "As of June 1 1978 your company's assets totalled $30114940.88," the auditor said.
5. When his girlfriend came by, Fred asked her in in spite of his mother's objections.
6. Luigi your three favorite dishes are chop suey ham and eggs and lasagna aren't they?
7. The check was sent to Loren Robertson M.D., whose office address is 266½ Dresden Avenue Topeka Kansas 66031.
8. Some names of animals for instance *turkey, cat,* and *bull,* have enriched American slang.

27h SUPERFLUOUS COMMAS

The elements of a basic declarative sentence have the order adjective—subject—verb—complement (or direct object). This order represents the natural flow of an English sentence. The flow is interrupted if commas appear between any two of these elements.

Adjective and Noun or Pronoun. Do not use a comma to separate an adjective from the noun or pronoun it modifies.

INCORRECT	Solving differential equations can be a difficult and time-consuming, task.
CORRECT	Solving differential equations can be a difficult and time-consuming task.

Subject and Verb. Do not use a comma to separate a subject (unless it is followed by a nonrestrictive element) from its verb.

INCORRECT	Delegates and newspaper reporters, crowded into the hall.
CORRECT	Delegates and newspaper reporters crowded into the hall.
CORRECT	Delegates and newspaper reporters, who had been waiting an hour for the doors to open, crowded into the hall.
INCORRECT	Using gasoline to light the logs in a fireplace, is inadvisable.
CORRECT	Using gasoline to light the logs in a fireplace is inadvisable.

Verb and Complement or Direct Object. Do not use a comma to separate a verb from its complement or direct object.

INCORRECT	Brass is, an alloy made of copper and zinc.
CORRECT	Brass is an alloy made of copper and zinc.
INCORRECT	Charles Babbage set out to build, a calculating machine.
CORRECT	Charles Babbage set out to build a calculating machine.

Verb and Subordinate Clause. Do not use a comma to separate the verb from the subordinate clause in indirect quotations or indirect questions. In such cases, the following clause is actually the direct object of the verb. Thus, this rule is really only a variation of the preceding rule.

INCORRECT	Marianne said, that she wanted to live in Copenhagen.
CORRECT	Marianne said that she wanted to live in Copenhagen.
INCORRECT	The landlord asked, if the roof had stopped leaking.
CORRECT	The landlord asked if the roof had stopped leaking.

Correlative Conjunctions. Do not use a comma to separate sentence elements connected by the correlative conjunctions *so . . . that, as . . . as, more . . . than, both . . . and, either . . . or*, and *neither . . . nor*.

INCORRECT	Scott was so distracted, that he forgot to put the car in gear.
CORRECT	Scott was so distracted that he forgot to put the car in gear.
INCORRECT	Passengers receive neither gracious, nor competent service.
CORRECT	Passengers receive neither gracious nor competent service.

EXERCISES: Comma Review

Correctly punctuate the following sentences with commas.

1. As people gain experience in banking they become increasingly aware of the extent to which the lives of everyone not just those with bank accounts are affected by banks.

2. Banking is not however a modern innovation for records show that a crude sort of banking existed by 2000 B.C. In Babylon people deposited valuables in sacred temples which no one would have dared to rob.

3. In Greece in the fourth century B.C. temples were also depositories for valuables but in addition some private firms and public groups began to offer similar services.

4. Although these crude Greek banks gave rise to similar systems in Egypt and Rome it was only with the establishment of the Banco di Rialto in Venice in 1587 that modern banking really began.

5. The term *bank* derives from the Italian word *banco* a word meaning "bench" because the early bankers did their business at benches in the streets.

6. After 1500 something similar to the modern check appeared and in the seventeenth century English goldsmiths began to issue bank notes that came to be accepted almost universally as money.

7. The check and the bank note having been developed the first clearinghouse was established in London in 1670 and the Bank of England in 1694.

8. Chartered in 1781 the Bank of North America the first bank in the United States was begun with the aid of the Continental Congress which needed a bank to help finance the Revolution.

9. Developing quickly after the founding of the Bank of Massachusetts in 1784 and the Bank of New York in 1791 banks in the United States numbered about ninety by 1811.

10. Although the number of banks in the United States doubled from 1900 to 1920 a critical drop in agricultural prices caused about 16000 banks especially those in the Midwest to fail between 1921 and 1933.

11. On March 6 1933 President Franklin D. Roosevelt acting in a crisis brought about by poor bank management shortage of capital and general panic ordered the temporary closing of all banks in order to determine which were strong enough to reopen.

12. The banking crisis of 1933 resulted in the trend toward corporate branch banking establishment of federal insurance up to $10000 on each bank account expansion of the power of the Federal Reserve System and a reduction by half in the number of existing banks.

13. Today's modern commercial bank provides its customers with many services such as savings plans safe-deposit boxes loans and administration of trusts.

14. Everyone in a community is served by the banking system for the bank combines the money of all its depositors into large sums that it can lend to individuals businesses and governments so that the community can grow.

; / **28** SEMICOLONS

USE A SEMICOLON
—Between main clauses without a coordinating conjunction
—Between word groups already containing commas

The **semicolon** is a useful supplement to the comma and the period, intermediate in force between the weaker comma and the stronger period. The semicolon is, however, used only between elements of equal rank.

Often the choice among comma and conjunction, semicolon, or period and new sentence is determined by the desired pace. A comma and a conjunction provide the most rapid pace.

> Hopi women own the houses and fields, and Hopi men are the priests and leaders of the community.

A semicolon is slower.

> Hopi women own the houses and fields; Hopi men are the priests and leaders of the community.

A period together with a new sentence is slowest of all.

> Hopi women own the houses and fields. Hopi men are the priests and leaders of the community.

28a MAIN CLAUSES

Often two main clauses are so closely related that they should be included within one sentence. If no coordinating conjunction seems appropriate, or if the use of a coordinating conjunction would make the sentence seem to ramble, the semicolon is the proper mark of punctuation.

Note how the use of separate sentences produces a choppy, disjointed effect in the following two examples.

> The electrocardiograph records heartbeats and their variations. It can also be used to examine nerves and muscles.

> In his *Diary*, Samuel Pepys was extraordinarily frank about his personal and public affairs. John Evelyn's *Diary* is less intimate.

On the other hand, using simple coordination to connect the two parts of the sentences is also somewhat unsatisfactory. Because the two main clauses in the sentences are not parallel, simple coordination produces an overly loose, rambling effect.

> The electrocardiograph records heartbeats and their variations, and it can also be used to examine nerves and muscles.

> In his *Diary*, Samuel Pepys was extraordinarily frank about his personal and public affairs, but John Evelyn's *Diary* is less intimate.

But a semicolon connects the two closely related clauses of each sentence without creating either a choppy or a rambling effect. This use of the semicolon is also one of the most effective ways of avoiding a comma splice (see 27a).

> The electrocardiograph records heartbeats and their variations; it can also be used to examine nerves and muscles.

> In his *Diary*, Samuel Pepys was extraordinarily frank about his personal and public affairs; John Evelyn's *Diary* is less intimate.

28b ADVERBIAL CONJUNCTIONS

The exact relationship between two main clauses is often expressed by means of an adverbial conjunction such as *however, therefore, in addition, on the other hand, nevertheless,* and *fortunately.* (See the more extensive list in 9b.) When such conjunctions are used with a semicolon, the semicolon follows the first main clause. If the adverbial conjunction is the first word or phrase of the second clause, it is followed by a comma.

Father was cooking kidney stew; <u>therefore,</u> I decided to spend the day outdoors.

Father was cooking kidney stew; <u>in addition,</u> the drain in the upstairs bath had backed up.

Father was cooking kidney stew; <u>nevertheless,</u> I decided to hold a wine-tasting party that afternoon.

If the adverbial conjunction is located within the second clause, it is usually set off by commas.

Father was cooking kidney stew; Mother, <u>on the other hand,</u> was varnishing the front-hall floor.

Father was cooking kidney stew; Alan and I, <u>however,</u> could escape to the garage.

Do not confuse adverbial conjunctions with subordinating conjunctions. (See 9 for more information on conjunctions.) Note that, although subordinating conjunctions always precede the rest of the clause, adverbial conjunctions may appear within a main clause.

CONJUNCTIVE ADVERB	Father was cooking kidney stew; no one, <u>however</u>, was willing to eat it.
SUBORDINATING CONJUNCTION	Father was cooking kidney stew <u>even though</u> no one was willing to eat it.

28c COORDINATING CONJUNCTIONS

A semicolon is sometimes used before a coordinating conjunction if the first clause is very long and already contains commas as internal punctuation.

After driving for sixteen hours across Texas in the blistering sunshine, we started looking for a motel on Route 67 outside of San Angelo; but there were no rooms available, and we had to go all the way to Odessa to find a place to stay.

Short clauses connected by a coordinating conjunction should be separated by a comma, not a semicolon.

INCORRECT	Ask me no questions; and I'll tell you no lies.
REVISED	Ask me no questions, and I'll tell you no lies.

28d SEPARATING WORD GROUPS

Use a semicolon to separate word groups when the elements of each word group are already separated by commas or other marks of punctuation.

The most common home knitting yarns are worsted, a heavy four-ply yarn used for outer garments; sport yarn, an intermediate-weight yarn; and fingering yarn, a light yarn often used for infants' clothing.

Participating in the Third Crusade were Philip Augustus, king of France; Richard I (Richard the Lion-hearted), king of England; and Frederick Barbarossa, Holy Roman emperor.

28e SUPERFLUOUS SEMICOLONS

Once writers have discovered the semicolon, they may be tempted to use it at every opportunity—in other words, to overuse it or to misuse it. In general, avoid using the semicolon unless you are sure it is appropriate; unlike the comma, the semicolon can be successfully avoided by the uncertain writer. The most common errors in the use of semicolons involve using a semicolon where either a comma or a colon is appropriate.

With Elements of Unequal Rank. Do not use a semicolon between sentence elements of unequal rank (for example, between a dependent and an independent clause or between a modifier and the word or phrase it modifies).

INCORRECT	Although he was married to Hera; Zeus had many love affairs.
REVISED	Although he was married to Hera, Zeus had many love affairs.
INCORRECT	Vitamin C is unstable in solution; especially under alkaline conditions.
REVISED	Vitamin C is unstable in solution, especially under alkaline conditions.

With Direct Quotations. Do not use a semicolon before a direct quotation. (See 27f for puncutation of direct quotations.)

INCORRECT	My mother said; "Close your mouth when you're eating."
REVISED	My mother said, "Close your mouth when you're eating."

With Listings or Summaries. Do not use a semicolon before a listing or summary statement. (See 29b and 30b for punctuation of listings or summary statements.)

INCORRECT	Please bring the following; sleeping bag, tarpaulin, day pack, extra socks.
REVISED	Please bring the following: sleeping bag, tarpaulin, day pack, extra socks.
REVISED	Please bring a sleeping bag, day pack, and extra socks.
INCORRECT	Aching muscles, sore feet, insect bites; these are the pleasures of hiking.
REVISED	Aching muscles, sore feet, insect bites—these are the pleasures of hiking.

EXERCISES: Semicolons

Correctly punctuate the following sentences by replacing commas with semicolons wherever necessary.

1. George immediately introduced his crew of helpers: Caroline Serfis, a high-school student, Dan Rossi, an unemployed painter, Sam DeKay, a fireman, and Muriel Brun, a former discotheque owner.

2. Charles has only one interest in life, consequently, I sometimes get tired of listening to tall tales about fishing expeditions.

3. Although French became the official language in England in 1066, English was still spoken by the common people, therefore, many words for basic goods and services remained English, while most legal, political, and artistic terms were replaced with French words.

4. The anaconda, a snake that entwines and strangles birds and small mammals with its body, grows to at least twenty feet and often to thirty feet in length, in fact, it is the largest snake found in South America.

5. Golf developed in Scotland about 1100, nevertheless, it was banned in Scotland in the fifteenth century by James II because sportsmen preferred golf to archery, which was necessary to the defense of the country.

:/29 COLONS

USE A COLON
—Between general and specific main clauses
—Before listings and series
—Before long quotations
—In biblical citations
—In time expressions
—With rhymes and grammatical forms

The **colon** is a strong mark of punctuation, as strong as the period. However, whereas the period tends to cut off, to isolate one sentence from another, the colon is used only as internal punctuation to point forward and indicate that the following material is closely related to the preceding material.

29a MAIN CLAUSES

A colon may be used to separate two main clauses if the second clause develops, details, or amplifies the first clause. The first clause is usually general; the second, specific. When a colon is used this way, it substitutes for such words as *namely, for example, that is,* or for the abbreviations *e.g.* or *i.e.* Hence a colon should not be used with these terms. Capitalization of the first word of a complete sentence after a colon is optional.

> There is only one solution: Drunken drivers must go to jail.

> Marvin never forgot his manners: when his wife left him, he opened the door for her.

29b LISTINGS AND SERIES

A colon is often used to set off a listing or series of items, especially a listing introduced by the words *the following* or *as follows*.

> The poisonous species of the area are the following: scorpions, black widows, brown recluse spiders, tarantulas, conenose bugs, velvet ants, wasps, hornets, and bees.
>
> There are many kinds of needlework: knitting, crochet, embroidery, macramé, and so forth.

Note: A colon should be used only when the first clause is grammatically complete. Do not use a colon between a verb and its complement or its object, or between a preposition and its object.

INCORRECT	The most important monetary units of the world are: the dollar, pound, franc, mark, ruble, and yen.
CORRECT	The most important monetary units of the world are the dollar, pound, franc, mark, ruble, and yen.
INCORRECT	Jim is allergic to: feathers, dust, cat dander, and pollen.
CORRECT	Jim is allergic to feathers, dust, cat dander, and pollen.

29c LONG QUOTATIONS

Although short quotations and dialogue are normally introduced by commas, a colon is often used to introduce a long quotation if the clause preceding the quotation is grammatically complete.

> The preamble to the Constitution of the United States is written in lofty eighteenth-century prose: "We the People of the United States, in order to form a more perfect Union, establish justice, insure domestic tranquility. . . ."

29d CONVENTIONAL USES

In addition to its use as a grammatical signal indicating a close relationship between two elements of a sentence, the colon has a number of conventional uses.

Biblical Citations. Use a colon between chapter and verse in citations from the Bible. (Periods may also be used for this purpose.)

> John 3:16

Time Expressions. Use a colon between hours and minutes in expressions of time.

> 5:43 A.M.

Salutations. A colon is conventionally used (instead of a comma) after the salutation in formal letters.

> Gentlemen:
>
> Dear Dr. Ernst:

Rhymes and Grammatical Forms. Use a colon between rhymes or to indicate a relationship between grammatical forms. (The slash is also appropriate in these uses.)

> RHYMES   moon : June
> RELATED FORMS   go : went : gone

EXERCISES: Colons

Correctly punctuate the following sentences with colons, replacing commas and semicolons wherever necessary.

1. A beginning carpenter needs six basic tools, a hammer, a handsaw, a screw-driver, pliers, a T square, and a vise.
2. Without consulting his son, Jim's father had completely planned the future, Jim would attend Harvard Law School, marry a socialite, and become an influential and wealthy corporate lawyer.
3. The worst calamity in the town's history struck at 10 28 a.m., a tornado ripped through the downtown area killing 120 people and leveling 40 stores.
4. The answer to your problem is easy, get a better-paying job.

— / 30 DASHES

USE A DASH
—**Around parenthetical statements**
—**Before summary statements**
—**In dialogue for interrupted speech**

In most of its uses, the **dash** serves as an informal and usually more emphatic substitute for some other mark of punctuation—a comma, a colon, a semicolon, or parentheses. Properly used, the dash adds variety and lightness to writing; improperly used or overused, it gives the impression that the writer is flighty or disorganized. Use the dash, but sparingly and not as a substitute for clear thinking and well-constructed sentences.

If the material to be set off by a dash occurs at the end of a sentence, only one dash is used. But if the material occurs within the sentence, a dash is used both before and after the inserted material.

30a PARENTHETICAL STATEMENTS

Use a dash to mark a sharp break in thought or in the syntax of the sentence or to insert a parenthetical statement into a sentence. Sometimes the material set off by dashes is an appositive.

BREAK IN THOUGHT	We were asked—well, actually we were told—to pick up our belongings and leave.
	The Dark Ages—though the term is really a misnomer—lasted from the fall of Rome until the eleventh century.
APPOSITIVE	*The Cyclops*—a drama first produced about 44 B.C.—is a burlesque of Homer's story about Odysseus and Polyphemus.

The dash should not be treated as a mark of desperation to be used whenever the syntax of a sentence has gotten out of hand. In such cases, rewrite the entire sentence to untangle the syntax.

TANGLED SYNTAX	It is interesting to speculate that Americans may start a new life on another celestial body, but certain things need to be given priority—such as the lives of humans on earth and the conditions in which they live—before we allocate funds for planetary exploration and settlement.
IMPROVED	It is interesting to speculate that Americans may start a new life on another celestial body. However, in the allocation of funds, improvement of living conditions on earth should have priority over planetary exploration and settlement.

30b SUMMARY STATEMENTS

Before a summary statement and after an introductory list, the dash can be used as an informal substitute for a colon.

"Penny-wise and pound-foolish," "Better late than never," "The early bird gets the worm"—all of us have heard these proverbs.

Biology, chemistry, calculus—these courses are familiar to freshman premedical students.

30c DIALOGUE

In writing dialogue, use a dash to indicate hesitant or interrupted speech.

"To tell you the truth, I—we—aren't interested."

"He is a complete idi—uh—he's been acting rather foolishly."

( ) / 31 PARENTHESES

USE PARENTHESES
—**Around nonessential information**
—**Around numbers or letters of enumeration**

Parentheses (singular: parenthesis), commas, and dashes are all used to enclose nonessential elements. However, parentheses are normally used to set off material less relevant or essential than that set off by commas. Parentheses are more formal than dashes. Further, whereas dashes emphasize the point being made and attract the attention of the reader, parentheses deemphasize and minimize the importance of the enclosed material.

Parentheses, unlike commas and dashes, *always* occur in pairs. If the material enclosed within the parentheses forms a complete sentence and is not inserted within another sentence, the first word should be capitalized and final punctuation (period, question mark, exclamation point) should be placed before the closing parenthesis.

> Bake the chicken in a 350° oven for at least an hour. (Be sure to preheat the oven for fifteen minutes.)

Otherwise, the first word is not capitalized and final punctuation, if any, follows the closing parenthesis.

> If the drumstick moves easily in your hand (you can test either drumstick), the chicken is done.

31a NONESSENTIAL INFORMATION

Use parentheses to enclose nonessential information, "asides," minor digressions, amplifications, or explanations. If the parenthetical information is lengthy, consider putting it into a footnote instead of including it in the main text.

> Definitions are given in Part II (pp. 75–154).
>
> Frédéric Chopin spent a winter (1838–39) on the island of Majorca.
>
> Chisholm, Minnesota (pop. 6,000), has one of the deepest open-pit iron mines in the world.
>
> Endive (the word is ultimately Egyptian in origin) is a variety of chicory.
>
> In preparing this survey, the author interviewed over two hundred individuals. (Their names are listed in Appendix X.)

31b NUMERALS AND LETTERS

Use parentheses to enclose numerals or letters being employed to number the items in a series.

> Some common taboos involve names of (1) deities, (2) wild animals, (3) parts of the body, (4) relatives, (5) bodily functions, and (6) death.

[ ] / 32 BRACKETS

USE BRACKETS
—For editorial comments
—As parentheses within parentheses

The use of **brackets** is highly restricted, and brackets should be considered a supplement to parentheses, not a substitute for them.

32a EDITORIAL COMMENTS

Use brackets to enclose your own comments within a quotation from another writer. The two most common reasons for inserting your own editorial comments into a quotation are (1) to indicate that an error occurs in the original passage and (2) to fill in necessary information when the quotation might otherwise be unclear or misleading to the reader. The conventional way of indicating that an error occurs in the original is to insert the bracketed Latin word [*sic*] (meaning "thus") into the quotation directly after the error.

> "In the months that followed, the American army continued to raid New York City, making the British very uneasy. At one point they raided Staton [*sic*] Island with some 2,500 men."

Here, the use of [*sic*] shows that the misspelling of the name *Staten Island* appears in the original. Note that the word *sic* should be italicized (underlined).

To clarify a quotation for the reader, insert the necessary material in brackets at an appropriate place in the quotation. In the sentence below, the bracketed material indicates the referent of the pronoun *they*.

> "At one point they [the American forces] raided Staten Island with some 2,500 men."

32b PARENTHESES WITHIN PARENTHESES

Brackets serve as parentheses within parentheses. However, be sparing in such piling up of parentheses, because they tend to clutter up the sentence and distract the reader. The information enclosed in brackets can often be put into a footnote and the use of brackets avoided.

> Henri Bergson takes quite a different approach to the question (*Creative Evolution* [New York: Modern Library, 1944], chap. IV).

EXERCISES: Dashes, Parentheses, and Brackets

Correctly punctuate the following sentences with dashes, parentheses, and brackets.

1. The new hospital administration has called for 1 the expansion of the central facility to 400 beds it now has 290; 2 the addition of an emergency room; 3 the hiring of an additional 35 nurses; and 4 the purchase of new equipment.

2. The satisfaction of printing her name all by herself for the very first time, her first acquaintance with the seashore, the arrival of her baby brother, her first trip on an airplane these scenes were indelibly pressed into Matilda's mind.

3. The fearsome Attila the Hun A.D. 406?–453 first invaded the Eastern Roman Empire and then pushed into France.

4. Merle Miller's book *Plain Speaking: An Oral Biography of Harry S Truman* New York: Berkley Publishing Corp., 1974 was a best seller.

5. When he got home, Joe found Trip's toys six stuffed animals, a wagon, several cars, and what seemed like a million building blocks all over the living room.

6. A recent article in the local newspaper stated, "Central ranks first in the state in garft *sic* among town officials, and citizens who are aware of the corruption are too frightened to try to stop it."

7. Spiders, swinging bridges, snakes, and thunderstorms these have been objects of fear to Ivan since his childhood.

" " / 33 QUOTATION MARKS

USE QUOTATION MARKS
—**Around direct quotations**
—**Around titles of shorter works**
—**Around words used in a special sense**

Quotation marks are visual cues that isolate one group of words in a text from another group. The isolated groups may be the exact words of a speaker or writer, titles of various kinds, or words used in a special sense. Quotation marks always occur in pairs; do not forget to include the closing quotation marks when you quote directly.

33a DIRECT QUOTATIONS

Use quotation marks for direct quotation of the exact words of a speaker or writer. The name of the speaker or writer and the word *said* (or its equivalent) are an identification phrase and are not enclosed within the quotation marks.

> As Joel Chandler Harris said, "Licker talks mighty loud w'en it git loose fum de jug."

1. If the total quotation is split by the identification phrase, both parts are enclosed in quotation marks, and the first half of the quotation is followed by a comma.

"I'm ready whenever you are," said Martha, "but don't let me rush you."

2. If each part of the quotation forms a complete sentence, the identification phrase is followed by a period, and the second part of the quotation begins with a capital letter.

"Many hands make light work," declared Paul. "On the other hand, too many cooks spoil the broth."

3. In the recording of direct quotations, a question mark or an exclamation point is used directly after the question or exclamation to which it applies, even if the total sentence has not yet ended. No comma is used in such instances.

"Where have you hidden my sunglasses?" he asked irritably.
"The sky is falling!" cried Chicken Little.

4. In reporting the dialogue of more than one speaker, new quotation marks and a new paragraph are used every time the speaker changes.

"We'll reach Pittsburgh by tonight," Jim said.
"Pittsburgh!" exclaimed Sara. "We haven't even reached Kansas City."
"We'll make it if you don't insist on stopping every fifteen minutes."
"I'm not the one who wants to stop all the time."

5. If the words of a single speaker or writer involve more than one paragraph, opening quotation marks are placed at the beginning of each new paragraph, but closing quotation marks are used only at the end of the entire quotation.

"Simple. Here is your basic pantsuit. Take off the blouse, add a vest and you're ready for polo. Take off the slacks, put on the shorts and you're dressed for bicycling. Zip the lining into the shorts, add the halter and it's a bathing suit. Take the straps off the halter and it's a bra. Add a short skirt and you're ready for tennis.

"Now, turn the blouse inside out and it's a bathrobe. Turn down the cuffs on the slacks, take the belt off the overblouse and you're in your jammies."

—Erma Bombeck, *IF LIFE IS A BOWL OF CHERRIES— WHAT AM I DOING IN THE PITS?*

6. When it is necessary to have quotation marks within a quotation, single quotation marks are used. (On the typewriter, the apostrophe serves as a single quotation mark.)

Tylor reports, "the phrase 'raising the wind' now passes as humorous slang, but it once, in all seriousness, described one of the most dreaded of the sorcerer's arts."

33b LONG QUOTATIONS

For relatively long quotations (over four or five lines of prose or over three lines of poetry), the quoted material should be blocked, that is, separated from the main body of the text. Begin on a new line, indent the quoted material an extra paragraph indentation, and single-space the text of the quotation. (The *MLA Handbook* recommends double-spacing of indented quotations.) Do not enclose the quoted material in quotation marks; they are not needed because the material has been sufficiently set off by the indentation and single-spacing. Use a colon at the end of identifying phrases such as "The author says."

> In his essay, "The English Renaissance," L. M. Myers says:

> It is a very curious fact that we seem to regard the roots and prefixes of Greek and Latin as the natural building blocks of new words, to be used with complete freedom, but are extremely conservative about making any combination with their English equivalents that are not already authorized by the dictionary. In this respect English is in strong contrast with German, which still compounds native elements so freely that no dictionary pretends to list all the legitimate combinations.

> Not everyone would agree with Myers' conclusions, however, . . .

If the quotation is not preceded by such an identifying phrase, you can simply end the preceding sentence with a period.

> L. M. Myers believes that English no longer makes compounds out of native elements.
> It is a very curious fact that . . .

33c TITLES

Use quotation marks to enclose the titles of shorter works of art or of works that form part of a larger work. (A "shorter" poem is one that is not divided into numbered parts, books, cantos, or the like.)

ARTICLES	"The Blossoms of Spring"
ESSAYS	"Philosophic Ants"
SHORT STORIES	"Polikushka"
CHAPTERS OF BOOKS	"White Dwarfs and the Dying Sun"
SHORT POEMS	"To a Waterfowl"
SHORT MUSICAL PIECES	"Drink to Me Only with Thine Eyes"

The titles of motion pictures, radio or television programs, paintings, and sculptures are often enclosed in quotation marks. Some prefer, however, to italicize (underline) these titles. Whichever you choose, be consistent and never use both quotation marks and italics. (See also 36a for a discussion of the use of italics.)

MOTION PICTURES	"How the West Was Won" *or How the West Was Won*

RADIO OR TELEVISION PROGRAMS	"Meet the Press" *or Meet the Press*
PAINTINGS	"View of Delft" *or View of Delft*
STATUES	"Family Group" *or Family Group*

Titles of unpublished works, such as doctoral dissertations, are always enclosed in quotation marks, regardless of the length of the work.

33d SPECIAL USES OF WORDS

Use quotation marks with words being used in special ways, including

1. An unconventional context or unusual meaning.

To Edgar, an "ancient" author is one who wrote before 1960.

2. Potentially confusing technical terms.

Proofreaders may have to "slug" copy that has been corrected.

3. Coined words.

The children spent their summer in an extended "hikeathon."

4. Words used to refer to themselves. (Some writers prefer to italicize words used as words.)

The word "very" is often overused.

Some writers use quotation marks to enclose slang or colloquial expressions that are included in a piece of more formal writing.

His discussion is a little more than an intellectual "cop-out."

Contemporary practice, however, tends to regard such use of quotation marks as overly apologetic, and hence they are often omitted. Effective slang is part of an author's style, and quotation marks should not single the slang out for special attention. In any case, slang expressions and colloquialisms, with or without quotation marks, should be used sparingly, or they will lose their effectiveness. It is usually best to rewrite the sentence, substituting another word or term that is less slangy.

In his discussion, he fails to commit himself.

33e SUPERFLUOUS QUOTATION MARKS

By convention, quotation marks are not used with certain kinds of titles and quotations.

Titles. Do not use quotation marks to surround the name of the Bible or parts or all of any sacred works. Do not use quotation marks to enclose mottoes or signs. Do not use quotation marks around the names of catalogs, directories, or political documents. (See also 36e, "Superfluous Italics.")

SACRED WORKS	Bible, Ecclesiastes, Talmud, Upanishads, Hail Mary, The Lord's Prayer, Nicene Creed
MOTTOES	In God We Trust, Remember the Alamo
SIGNS	No Smoking, Right Turn on Red
CATALOGS AND DIRECTORIES	the Sears, Roebuck Catalog, the Detroit Telephone Directory
POLITICAL DOCUMENTS	Constitution of the United States, Monroe Doctrine, Magna Charta, Treaty of Utrecht, Gettysburg Address

Do not use quotation marks around the title at the top of a paper or on the title page. But do use quotation marks if the exact title appears within the text.

He wrote a paper entitled "Extinct Animal Species."

Do not use quotation marks to enclose the titles of longer written works or works of art. (See 36 on italics.)

INCORRECT	She claims to have read "Paradise Lost" four times.
CORRECT	She claims to have read *Paradise Lost* four times.

Indirect Quotations.   Do not use quotation marks to enclose indirect quotations.

INCORRECT	Elinor said that "she hated to sew on name tapes."
CORRECT	Elinor said that she hated to sew on name tapes.
CORRECT	Elinor said, "I hate to sew on name tapes."

Nicknames.   Do not use quotation marks to enclose familiar nicknames.

King Richard the Lion-hearted   my old friend Alex
the Great Emancipator

EXERCISES: Quotation Marks

Correctly punctuate the following sentences with quotation marks, adding periods, commas, question marks, and exclamation points where they are necessary. Adjust capitalization as necessary.

1. Don't you just love the songs from the musical *Oliver*, especially Where is Love Joyce asked Louise

2. What you say isn't necessarily true argued Ernest if you will read Wednesday's editorial in the *Times*, A New Strategy for the Middle East, I think you will see the errors in your reasoning

3. My teacher said we have to learn the Bill of Rights and all the stanzas of the Star-Spangled Banner by first period tomorrow José complained to his mother

4. All night long I kept dreaming about being in a dark forest Celeste told her roommate at breakfast and that song Who's Afraid of the Big Bad Wolf? kept running through my head

5. Just wait here, Sir said the receptionist Mr. Jenkins is with a client.

6. Looking at these beautiful Greek vases always makes me think of Keats's poem Ode on a Grecian Urn Gene said and I always go home from the museum and reread that poem

,34 APOSTROPHES

USE AN APOSTROPHE
—With possessives
—With contractions
—For special grammatical endings

The primary uses of the **apostrophe** are (1) to indicate the possessive forms of nouns and some pronouns and (2) to indicate missing letters or numbers. The apostrophe is also used to prevent misreading of special symbols being used as words.

34a POSSESSIVES

The apostrophe is used to indicate the possessive (genitive) form of both singular and plural nouns and of some singular pronouns. Even though you may see the apostrophe omitted from possessive nouns (on signs, in newspapers, etc.), do not omit it in your writing unless it is omitted in an official proper name, such as Farmers Home Administration or Adams Mills, Ohio.

Singular Nouns and Pronouns. Use the apostrophe, followed by s, to form the possessive of singular nouns and some indefinite pronouns.

dog's collar	Thailand's rice crop
policeman's badge	someone's hat
New York's taxes	nobody's business
Marge's handwriting	

Though practice varies with nouns that end in an -s or -z sound, it is never wrong to add -'s to these nouns. Always add -'s if you pronounce the possessive as a separate syllable. If the possessive does not form a separate syllable in speech or if the following word begins with an s sound, you can use just an apostrophe without an s.

the class's performance
Yeats's life *or* Yeats' life
Tacitus's description *or* Tacitus' description
for goodness' sake
Myers' study *or* Myers's study

Plural Nouns. Add just an apostrophe to form the possessive of regular plural nouns.

the students' complaints
the Browns' dog (More than one person named Brown is implied.)
the soldiers' uniforms
a mayors' conference (The conference is for several mayors.)

With irregular plural nouns (that is, those that do not add -*s* or -*es* to form their plurals), add -'*s* to form the possessive.

children's playground   women's rights
men's clothing   alumni's reunions

Joint Possession. To indicate joint possession, add -'*s* only to the last item.

Beaumont and Fletcher's comedies (They wrote them together.)
Janice and Larry's children (They have the same children.)

But to indicate individual possession, add -'*s* to each item.

Mozart's and Haydn's sonatas (Mozart and Haydn did not write the sonatas together.)
the men's and women's rooms (The men and women do not share the same rooms.)

Compound Nouns and Pronouns. With compound nouns and pronouns, add -'*s* to the last element.

attorney general's office
sister-in-law's recipes (recipes from one sister-in-law)
sisters-in-law's recipes (recipes from more than one sister-in-law)
nobody else's business

Gerunds. A gerund is a noun made from a verb by adding -*ing*. The possessive should be used before gerunds just as before other nouns. (See also 20a for a discussion of possessives with gerunds.)

Bob's quitting his job surprised everyone.
They resented the girls' getting all the prizes.

Double Possessives. The so-called double possessive involves both an *of* phrase and an -'*s*. It is normally used only when the possession being indicated is one among several such possessions, and it is used only when the possessor is human.

> Sloppiness was a fault of Harry's. (Harry had more than one fault.)
>
> The sloppiness was Harry's fault. (Only one fault is being mentioned.)

If in doubt about the use of a double possessive, test to see if you could rewrite the phrase using *one of;* if you can, the double possessive is appropriate.

> She wore an old dress of her sister's. (She wore one of her sister's old dresses.)
>
> Sloppiness was a fault of Harry's. (Sloppiness was one of Harry's faults.)
>
> The sloppiness was Harry's fault. (This does not mean the same as "The sloppiness was one of Harry's faults." Thus the double possessive should not be used.)

If you omit the double possessive when it is appropriate, your reader will probably misinterpret the sentence. For example, if you want to say that you took a picture that belongs to your mother, you will need to use the double possessive.

> AMBIGUOUS   I took my mother's picture.
>
> CORRECT   I took a picture of my mother's.

Personal and Relative Pronouns.   Do not use an apostrophe in forming the possessive of personal pronouns or relative pronouns. Be especially careful to distinguish *its* (belonging to *it*) from *it's (it is)* and *whose* (belonging to *whom*) from *who's (who is).*

INCORRECT POSSESSIVES	CORRECT POSSESSIVES
their's	theirs
our's	ours
who's	whose
it's	its
a friend of her's	a friend of hers

Titles.   Do not form the possessive of the titles of books, plays, and so on, by adding *-'s*. Instead, use an *of* phrase.

> AWKWARD   *Love's Labours Lost's* language
>
> PREFERABLE   the language of *Love's Labours Lost*

34b CONTRACTIONS

Apostrophes often replace missing letters in words and missing numbers in dates.

Missing Letters.   Use the apostrophe to replace the missing letters in accepted contractions. Be sure to place the apostrophe at the point where the missing letter or letters would have appeared. (See also 44 for a discussion of contractions.)

don't	let's	he'll
they've	o'clock	she's
ma'am	you'd	shouldn't
we're	I'm	jack-o'-lantern

Do not use the apostrophe before clipped or abbreviated words that have become accepted as complete words in their own right. If in doubt, consult your dictionary.

INCORRECT	CORRECT
'plane	plane
'flu	flu
'phone	phone
'cab	cab

Missing Numbers. In highly informal writing, the apostrophe is used to indicate the missing century in dates. In more formal writing, express the date in full.

INFORMAL	FORMAL
the class of '68	the class of 1968
the '54 hurricane	the 1954 hurricane
a '75 Chevy	a 1975 Chevrolet

Do not use the apostrophe with the hyphen in expressions of inclusive numbers (dates and pages).

INCORRECT	CORRECT
pp. 275–'76	pp. 271–76
1921–'24	1921–24

34c SPECIAL GRAMMATICAL ENDINGS

Use the apostrophe to avoid confusion or misreading of grammatical endings (plural, past tense, past participle) added to letters, figures, acronyms, or symbols being used as nouns or verbs.

CONFUSING	His *is* can be mistaken for 1s.
CLEAR	His *i*'s can be mistaken for 1's.

Similarly,

Mind your *p*'s and *q*'s.

This table omits the 0's before a decimal point.

There are more +'s than −'s.

He k.o.'d his opponent in the third round.

If there is no possibility of confusion, the apostrophe may be omitted.

Your 3s look like 5s.

Do not use the apostrophe in forming the plurals of regular nouns, proper names, or numbers that are spelled out.

INCORRECT PLURALS	CORRECT PLURALS
business's	businesses
Brown's	Browns
eleven's	elevens

EXERCISES: Apostrophes

Correctly rewrite each of the following sentences, replacing the italicized *of* phrase with a possessive noun or pronoun and adding other apostrophes where they are needed.

1. Because *the birthdays of Ralph, Andy, and Mark* are within three days of one another, its become a tradition *in the office of them* to celebrate *the birthdays of all the employees* that week with an elaborate dinner at *the finest restaurant of Miami.*

2. *The facial muscles of the coach* tightened as he watched *the top player of the team* fumble the ball for the second time, and *the deafening roar of the crowd* was a thunderous signal *of the disappointment of it.*

3. Dr. Ryan couldn't preside over *the homecoming festivities of the college* because *the farmhouse of his brother-in-law* burned down, and he had to fly to Iowa to help with *the resettlement of the family.*

4. "When you learn your ABCs," Kate prophesied to her three-year-old brother, "youll be *one of the favorite students of the teacher.*"

5. *Mama wouldnt even hear of Joan and Lindas going to New York for the summer even though theyd been promised work* in the firm of Uncle Peter.

—/35 HYPHENS

USE A HYPHEN
—For word division
—With certain prefixes and suffixes
—For clarity
—With certain compounds
—For inclusive dates and pages
—For spelled-out words

The most common functions of **hyphens** are to unite words divided between two lines and to bring together the separate words that make up compounds.

35a WORD DIVISION

Use a hyphen after the first part of a word divided between the end of one line and the beginning of the next line. Hyphenated words should be divided only between syllables. The dictionary is your guide to syllabication; the raised dot between letters in the dictionary entry indicates a syllable division. Because different dictionaries do not always agree on syllabication, choose one dictionary as your authority and stick with it.

Never divide words that have only one syllable when spoken, no matter how long the words may be. Do not isolate a single letter, even if it forms a separate syllable. If the word to be divided already has a hyphen in its spelling, break it only at that hyphen. Do not hyphenate the last word on a page or the last word of a paragraph.

Avoid hyphenating personal names. Do not use a hyphen to separate numerals, contractions, acronyms, or abbreviations used with numerals.

INCORRECT	CORRECT
Richard Bak- er	Richard Baker
have- n't	haven't
UNES- CO	UNESCO
200- B.C.	200 B.C.
$23,100- 000	$23,100,000

35b PREFIXES AND SUFFIXES

Use a hyphen after the prefixes *ex-*, *self-*, *all-*, *quasi-*, *half-*, and *quarter-*. Use a hyphen before the suffixes *-elect* and *-odd*, and between any prefix and a proper name.

ex-sailor	secretary-elect	pseudo-French
all-encompassing	sixty-odd	anti-American
half-drunk		trans-Siberian
self-propelling		

35c CLARITY

Use a hyphen within a word to prevent ambiguity or misreading and to avoid a double *i* or the same consonant three times in a row.

two-bit players (insignificant players)

two bit-players (two players with small roles)

re-cover ("to cover again"; used to avoid confusion with *recover* "to regain")

semi-industrial (not *semiindustrial)*

hull-less (not *hullless*)

35d COMPOUNDS

Accepted usage for the hyphenation of compound words tends to change fairly rapidly; the trend is toward writing formerly hyphenated compounds as single words. Choose one dictionary as your guide, use it faithfully, and be consistent.

Letters or Numerals.   Normally, a hyphen is used between the elements of a compound in which one element is a letter or numeral. However, practice varies, and some compounds of this type are often written without a hyphen. Check your dictionary for specific items.

A-line	DC-10
U-boat	E sharp
4-ply	U-turn *or* U turn

Compounds of Equal Weight.   Use a hyphen to connect compounds in which both or all of the elements of the compound are of equal grammatical weight.

city-state	yellow-green
Yankee-Red Sox game	Monday-Wednesday-Friday classes
soldier-statesman	

Compound Modifiers.   Use a hyphen to connect compound modifiers when these modifiers appear *before* nouns, but do not hyphenate them when they follow nouns or when they are used adverbially.

icy-cold water	*but*	The water was icy cold.
spur-of-the-moment decision	*but*	He decided on the spur of the moment.
across-the-board increases	*but*	Increases were granted across the board.

all-purpose cleanser   evil-smelling water
off-season rates   twice-told tales

Do not hyphenate a compound modifier if the first word is an adverb ending in -*ly*, even when the modifier precedes the noun.

sorely needed improvements
rapidly growing cities

Long Compounds.   If the compound is very long, quotation marks can be substituted for hyphens.

an I-told-you-so expression on his face
an "I told you so" expression on his face

Other Compound Words.   Do not hyphenate compound words that are properly written as single words or as two separate words. Check your dictionary if you are not certain whether a hyphen should be used.

INCORRECT	CORRECT
to-day	today
all-right	all right
out-side	outside

Compound Numbers.   Use a hyphen to connect the two parts of a written-out compound number up to ninety-nine, even when the compound is part of a larger number.

thirty-three   *but*   five thousand and six
sixty-eight   *but*   two hundred and sixty-eight

Some writers use hyphens to connect the parts of all written-out fractions unless either the numerator or the denominator already contains a hyphen.

one-half *but* a half   seven forty-fifths
seven-eighths   twenty-one twenty-seconds

Other writers prefer to hyphenate fractions used as modifiers but not to hyphenate fractions used as nouns.

Saunders has a two-thirds ownership in the company.
Saunders owns two thirds of the company.

Suspended Hyphen.   Use the so-called suspended hyphen when a series of compounds all have the same second element. Space after the hyphen and before the following word.

four- and five-year programs
pro- or anti-British

35e INCLUSIVE DATES AND PAGES

Use a hyphen to express inclusive dates and pages.

pp. 276–381   A.D. 56–84   1899–1906

35f SPELLED-OUT WORDS

Use hyphens to indicate the spelling-out of a word and to indicate stuttering.

t-h-e-i-r   "D-d-don't you know?"

EXERCISES: Hyphens

Correctly punctuate the following sentences by inserting hyphens to insure correct spelling and clarity. Consult your dictionary if necessary.

1. "I d d dunno what you mean!" shouted the dirty faced eight year old boy as he scurried to his room.

2. Forty two people applied for the six new government funded jobs in Clinton.

3. The two anti American speakers asked the crowd to help them overthrow the government.

4. Gene doesn't remember if the car had an eighteen or twenty four month warranty.

5. Although the restaurant had had an A rating for years, the inspector was appalled at its grease covered walls, dirty floor, improperly washed dishes, and insect infested kitchen.

6. The Yankee Red Sox game will be on television tonight.

7. Cleve placed his new laminated T square on the glass topped drafting table.

8. For four years (1954 58), we lived in a run down old house on Main Street.

---

ital / 36 ITALICS

USE ITALICS
—**For titles of longer works**
—**For heavy emphasis**
—**For words used as words**
—**For foreign words**

In printing, **italics** are special forms of letters that slant toward the right. (Regular, nonslanting letters are called roman letters.) Because italic letters are not available on standard typewriters, underlining is used instead. If your typewriter has an italic typeface, underline to indicate italics just as if the typeface were roman.

36a TITLES

Italicize the titles of books, newspapers, periodicals, plays, long poems, and long musical compositions. Italicize the names of individual ships, airplanes, and spacecraft. Many authorities prefer to italicize (rather than enclose in quotation marks) the titles of paintings, sculptures, radio or television programs, and motion pictures. Do not italicize the word *the* when it appears as the first word in the titles of newspapers and periodicals unless it is regarded as part of the title by the newspaper or periodical itself.

BOOKS	*Wuthering Heights, Of Time and the River*
NEWSPAPERS	the *Chicago Tribune, The New York Times*
PERIODICALS	*Time,* the *Reader's Digest, The New Yorker*
PLAYS	*Merchant of Venice, Oedipus Rex*
LONG MUSICAL COMPOSITIONS	*Madama Butterfly,* the *Messiah*
SHIPS AND AIRCRAFT	*Queen Elizabeth II, Spirit of St. Louis, Apollo II*
PAINTINGS	*View of Delft*
SCULPTURES	*Family Group*
RADIO OR TELEVISION PROGRAMS	*Meet the Press*
MOTION PICTURES	*How the West Was Won*

Note: The names of types or makes of ships or aircraft should be capitalized but not italicized: DC-10, Concorde, PT-boats. The abbreviations S.S., U.S.S., and H.M.S.S. should not be italicized, even when used with the name of an individual ship: S.S. *United States.*

36b EMPHASIS

Italicize words or phrases to indicate particularly heavy emphasis.

> I can, I think, best explain by avoiding hackneyed words which *seem* to convey the correct meaning but in fact fail to do so.
> —Bertrand Russell *"Moral Standards and Social Well-being"*

Italicization for emphasis should be used sparingly in expository prose. When italics are overused, they lose their effectiveness and create the impression that the writer is immature and easily excited.

36c WORDS AS WORDS

Italicize letters, words, or numerals being used to indicate the letters, words, or numerals themselves.

> *Technique* is spelled with a *q*, not a *g*.
> Your 3's look like your 5's.

Alternatively, words used as words may be enclosed in quotation marks. Use either italics or quotation marks, but be consistent. In any case, never use both quotation marks and italics with the same word.

36d FOREIGN WORDS

Italicize foreign words or phrases that have not become fully Anglicized. If in doubt, consult your dictionary; dictionaries have special symbols or labels to indicate such words. (See 48c.)

> The judge issued a writ of *capias* after the defendant failed to appear in court.

If the foreign word is translated into English, put the foreign word in italics, and enclose its translation in quotation marks. Single quotation marks are normally used for the translation if it immediately follows the foreign word.

> These latter subjects are still, for the most part, subsumed under what the Japanese called *kikenshiso* or "dangerous thoughts."
> —Karl Mannheim, *IDEOLOGY AND UTOPIA*

> The French word *orgue* 'organ' is masculine when singular and feminine when plural.

If the entire sentence is in a foreign language, do not italicize it. But do italicize foreign phrases that appear within an English sentence.

> "Pega, ladrão!" shouted the unfortunate peddler.

> "My *pièce de résistance* will be eel-and-octopus croquettes," announced the hostess.

36e SUPERFLUOUS ITALICS

Do not italicize the names of sacred books, political documents, and certain other titles and names. (See 33c for the use of quotation marks with titles.) Do not italicize the title of your own paper when it appears at the top of the first page. Do not italicize foreign proper names, either of persons or of places.

SACRED BOOKS	Ecclesiastes, the Talmud
POLITICAL DOCUMENTS	The Declaration of Independence
TITLES OF PAPERS	Belgium in the Hundred Years War
FOREIGN PROPER NAMES	Anwar Sadat, le massif Central

//37 SLASHES

USE SLASHES
—For alternatives
—In quoting poetry
—For fractions

The **slash** (also called *slant, diagonal, virgule, solidus,* or *oblique*) has more names than it has appropriate uses.

37a ALTERNATIVES

The slash is sometimes used to indicate alternatives; the term *and/or* is the most familiar example of this use. However, it is generally preferable to rephrase the sentence and avoid the use of the slash.

QUESTIONABLE	The office provides outright grants and/or loans.
PREFERABLE	The office provides outright grants or loans or both.

37b QUOTING POETRY

Use the slash to separate lines in short quotations of poetry being quoted in running text.

"Thy root is ever in its grave, / And thou must die."

37c FRACTIONS

When fractions written with numerals are included within the body of a sentence (not set off on a separate line), use a slash to separate the numerator from the denominator.

A kilometer is 31/50 of a mile.

... /38 ELLIPSES

USE ELLIPSES
—for omitted material

Ellipses are a series of three spaced dots used to indicate that material has been omitted from a quotation.

> Fourscore and seven years ago, our fathers brought forth . . . a new nation, conceived in liberty, and dedicated to the proposition that all men are created equal.

1. Use a regular period followed by three spaced dots to indicate that (a) the end of the sentence has been omitted, (b) the first part of the next sentence has been omitted, or (c) one or more entire sentences have been omitted.

> Any one who has kept his eyes open at the seaside will have seen the Herring Gulls congregate in soaring intersecting spirals. . . . But such flights are nothing compared with those of other birds. —Julian Huxley, *ESSAYS OF A BIOLOGIST*

2. Use an entire row of spaced dots to indicate that one or more lines of poetry have been omitted.

> Good friends, sweet friends, let me not stir you up
> To such a sudden flood of mutiny.
> . . . .
> I come not, friends, to steal away your hearts:
> I am no orator, as Brutus is; —William Shakespeare,
> *JULIUS CAESAR III.ii.214*

3. Do not use ellipses as a substitute for a dash or any other mark of punctuation.

INCORRECT	The air conditioner has two settings . . . high and low.
REVISED	The air conditioner has two settings: high and low.
REVISED	The air conditioner has two settings, high and low.
REVISED	The air conditioner has two settings—high and low.

dia /39 DIACRITICS

USE DIACRITICS
—In spelling foreign words

Diacritical marks are special symbols that indicate the pronunciation of particular letters. English uses no diacritics as a regular part of its spelling system, but all diacritical marks in foreign words should be carefully observed and copied. The most common diacritical marks are illustrated in the list that follows.

ACUTE ACCENT	cliché, idée fixe	TILDE	cañon, señor
GRAVE ACCENT	à la carte, crèche	UMLAUT	Fräulein
CEDILLA	façade, aperçu	HAČEK	Kučera
CIRCUMFLEX	château, bête noire		

The **dieresis** is a diacritical mark formed like the umlaut and occasionally used over a vowel in English to indicate that the vowel is to be pronounced separately from the preceding vowel. This use of the dieresis is, however, nearly obsolete in English and is normally seen only in older printed books (for example, in such words as *coördinate* or *preëminent).*

EXERCISES: Italics, Slashes, and Diacritics

Underline words that need to be italicized, and insert the slash wherever necessary. Circle diacritical marks, and identify them by name in the margin of the sentences where they occur.

1. When the Titanic hit an iceberg in 1912, 1,517 people lost their lives.

2. Toulouse-Lautrec reflected Parisian life in such paintings as The Laundress, At the Moulin Rouge, The Barmaid, M. Boileau in a Café, and The Ballet "Papa Chrysanthème."

3. In Book I of Paradise Lost, Milton explains that through his poem "I may assert Eternal Providence, And justify the ways of God to men."

4. The defendant, a stoop-shouldered, thin little man, entered a plea of nolo contendere.

5. Lunik II, launched by the Soviet Union in 1959, was the first man-made spacecraft to make physical contact with the moon.

6. The author writes fire but must mean file.

---

40 COMBINING MARKS OF PUNCTUATION

The marks of punctuation used to separate phrases, clauses, and sentences (commas, semicolons, colons, dashes, periods, question marks, and exclamation points) are mutually exclusive. In other words, a sentence, for example, should not end with both a period and a question mark, nor should a parenthetical statement be enclosed by both dashes and commas. Some marks of punctuation do occur together, but, by convention, appear only in a given order.

1. Question marks and exclamation points always take precedence over other marks and replace them.

> "But what will I tell my mother?" he asked. (Question mark replaces comma before identification of speaker.)
>
> Don't you ever do that again! (Exclamation point replaces period.)

2. Within a sentence, the period as a mark of abbreviation can be used with other marks of punctuation.

> Send it C.O.D.—I don't have enough money with me.
>
> Several of these plants, e.g., azaleas, asters, and primroses, are perennials in warmer climates.

If, however, the last word in a declarative sentence is an abbreviation, use only one period at the end of the sentence.

> In 1800, the capital of the United States was moved from Philadelphia to Washington, D.C.

3. Do not combine dashes with commas, semicolons, or parentheses.

INCORRECT   Before World War I,—but not afterwards,—Iceland was part of Denmark.

CORRECT   Before World War I—but not afterwards—Iceland was part of Denmark.

CORRECT   Before World War I, but not afterwards, Iceland was part of Denmark.

INCORRECT   Ariadne saves old pieces of string;—I can't imagine why.

CORRECT   Ariadne saves old pieces of string; I can't imagine why.

CORRECT   Ariadne saves old pieces of string—I can't imagine why.

4. Commas, semicolons, and colons never precede parentheses within a sentence. They may follow parentheses as required by the logic of the sentence.

INCORRECT   After the processing of common salt, (sodium chloride) the salt must be recrystallized.

CORRECT   After the processing of common salt (sodium chloride), the salt must be recrystallized.

5. Commas and periods *always* precede the ending quotation marks, regardless of the logic of the sentence.

> Joan could recite all of "A Visit from St. Nicholas," but did not know the Pledge of Allegiance. (Even though the comma applies to the entire first clause and not just the quoted material, it precedes the quotation marks.)

6. Colons and semicolons *always* follow quotation marks.

> Joan could recite all of "A Visit from St. Nicholas"; she did not, however, know the Pledge of Allegiance.

7. Exclamation points and question marks are combined with quotation marks according to the logic of the sentence.

What is meant by the term "exceptional children"? (The question mark follows the quotation marks because it refers to the entire sentence, not just to "exceptional children.")

We have just read Peter Taylor's "What You Hear from 'Em?" (The question mark is part of the title of the story and thus precedes the quotation marks. Note that no period is used at the end of the sentence.)

41 TYPING PUNCTUATION

All readers (including instructors) are favorably impressed by well-typed papers that follow the conventions for typewritten material. The rules listed here also apply to handwritten papers, although spacing will, of course, be less exact than with typewritten copy.

41a PERIODS

The spacing of periods varies according to whether the periods are used as ending punctuation or as marks of abbreviation.

Ending Punctuation. Type the period directly after the last word of the sentence with no intervening space. Leave two spaces after the period.

```
no intervening space.  Leave two spaces
```

Mark of Abbreviation. Type the period directly after the letter of abbreviation. Leave no space after a period within an abbreviation, *except* when the abbreviation is the initials of a person's name.

```
U.S.A.     U. S. Grant
```

Leave one space between the period of an abbreviation and the next word.

```
U.S. Post Office
```

If the abbreviation is the last word in a sentence, leave two spaces after the final period of abbreviation.

```
in Washington, D.C.  Many buildings
```

Mark of Separation. Do not space before or after a period used as a mark of separation (for example, when the period separates chapter from verse or act from scene). Do not space before or after a period used as a decimal point.

```
Genesis 1.1     87.67
```

41b COLONS, QUESTION MARKS, AND EXCLAMATION POINTS

Do not space before a colon, question mark, or exclamation point. Leave two spaces after all of these marks. (The *MLA Handbook* recommends one space after a colon.)

```
Study the following:  sociology, anthropology
Is there a solution?  Few would care to
What nonsense!  Even a child
```

41c COMMAS AND SEMICOLONS

Do not space before a comma or semicolon. Leave one space after both.

```
In sum, the function
citation; nevertheless, the council
```

41d QUOTATION MARKS

Do not space between quotation marks and the words or marks of punctuation that they enclose.

```
The word "elbow" is
"Oh, no," she said, "I was seasick."
```

41e HYPHENS AND DASHES

A hyphen is a single horizontal stroke. A dash is two consecutive hyphens with no space between them. Do not space before or after either a hyphen or a dash. Never begin a line of typing with a hyphen or a dash.

```
red-eyed       was red--not blue--and the
```

Try to avoid more than two consecutive hyphenated words at the ends of lines. By leaving a relatively wide margin on the right-hand side, you can fit in many words in full and not have to divide them.

41f PARENTHESES AND BRACKETS

Type parentheses and brackets flush to the words they enclose. Leave one space before opening parentheses and brackets and one space after closing parentheses and brackets. But if an entire sentence is contained within these marks, leave two spaces after the closing parentheses or brackets.

```
a winter (1838-1839) on the island
individuals.  (Their names are below.)  Some
```

If your typewriter has no brackets, leave an extra space for them when you type and insert them later by hand in black ink.

41g APOSTROPHES

Do not space before or after an apostrophe unless the apostrophe appears at the end of the word.

```
hasn't    a day's work    Mr. Jones' family
```

41h ITALICS

Use the underline key to indicate italics. When several consecutive words are underlined, some people prefer to underline the spaces between the words. Others prefer to underline each word separately. You can follow either rule; just be consistent in your practice throughout a single piece of writing.

```
be consistent in your practice
be consistent in your practice
```

41i ELLIPSES

Leave one space before, between, and after each period that forms part of an ellipsis, but do not space before an end-of-sentence period preceding the ellipsis.

```
When in the Course of human events, it becomes
necessary for one people to . . . assume the powers
```

41j SLASHES

When a slash is used to separate lines of poetry, leave one space before and one space after the slash. Otherwise, do not space before or after a slash.

```
What our contempts do often hurl from us / We wish

8/15    ft/sec
```

41k DIACRITICAL MARKS

Ordinary typewriters do not have keys for diacritical marks. Insert them by hand in black ink. If you make a light pencil mark in the margin as you type, you can easily locate the spot where the diacritics are to be added.

```
René Descartes    résumé
```

EXERCISES: Punctuation Review

Correctly punctuate the following sentences.

1. The barking of dogs the scraping of branches against the window the far-off echo of a train whistle all these sounds magnified Lucys uneasiness at being alone in the house

2. The leak was in a hard to get at pipe nevertheless the plumbers bill seemed exorbitant to Ms Schneider

3. Counselor if you will look up the case of Avakian v Johnson you will find a precedent for my clients petition the silver haired bespectacled lawyer said rapping his pen on the edge of the table

4. Sir Edmund P. Hillary who with Tensing Norkay reached the 29028 foot peak of Mount Everest on May 29 1953 recorded this pioneering climb in his book High Adventure

5. Grim faced Miss Taylor sternly asked the half frightened fifth graders Who said I only regret that I have but one life to lose for my country

6. Winslow Homer 1836 1910 born in Boston is famous for his paintings of coastal scenes e g The Gulf Stream Fog Warning and Eight Bells

7. The common pompano genus Trachinotus species carolinus sometimes called the butterfish is plentiful along the Atlantic coast of the United States

8. Edgar Allan Poe who wrote famous poems such as The Raven Annabel Lee and Ulalume and famous stories such as The Gold Bug and The Pit and the Pendulum was the inventor of the modern detective story

9. Too many cooks spoil the broth A bird in the hand is worth two in the bush Dont count your chickens before they hatch these sayings were always Jessicas fathers advice for every problem

10. Its never Christmas for me Bob said until Ive heard Bing Crosbys White Christmas

11. After the meeting had ended Al told the president that he was dissatisfied because many of the members werent present because two of the committee chairmen gave half prepared hard to follow reports and because the members had spent too much time socializing

12. The word fortissimo a musical direction meaning very loudly is derived from the Latin adjective fortissimus the strongest

---

cap/42 CAPITALIZATION

In general, the conventions of **capitalization** can be divided into two categories: capitalization of the first word only and capitalization of proper names. Capitalization of proper names includes the names of people, groups, religions, places, artistic works, official documents, and trade names. In addition, many single letters used as words are capitalized.

42a FIRST WORDS

Capitalize the first words of sentences, lines of poetry, parts of letters, resolutions, and entries in outlines.

1. Capitalize the first word of every sentence or deliberate sentence fragment.

Freddie likes big cars. In fact, the bigger the better.

Exception: Do not capitalize a sentence inserted *within* another sentence by means of dashes or parentheses.

> Yesterday—would you believe it?—he ordered a Cadillac.

Capitalization of the first word of a complete sentence after a colon is optional: if the material after the colon does not form a complete sentence, do not capitalize the first word.

> There's just one problem: He doesn't know how to drive.
> There's just one problem: he doesn't know how to drive.
> Please buy the following: bread, milk, lettuce, and cat food.

Do not capitalize the first word of the second part of a direct quotation divided by the words *he said* (or their equivalent) unless the second part begins a new sentence.

> "I'm lighting a candle to St. George," said Paula, "and another to the dragon."
> "I'm lighting a candle to St. George," said Paula. "Perhaps I should light one to the dragon, too."

2. Capitalize the first word of every line of poetry, provided that it was capitalized in the original.

> There is a pleasure in the pathless woods,
> There is a rapture on the lonely shore,
> There is society, where none intrudes,
> By the deep sea, and music in its roar:
> —Byron, *CHILDE HAROLD*, c.IV.clxxviii

42b PERSONAL NAMES AND TITLES

Capitalize the proper names, nicknames, and official titles or degrees of persons, as well as most adjectives derived from proper nouns.

1. Capitalize the names, nicknames, and epithets of persons. Capitalize a person's name after a prefix, *unless* the compound is listed in your dictionary without a hyphen.

> George Washington, Honest Abe, Alexander the Great, anti-Roosevelt, antichrist

Capitalization of personal names with prefixes (e.g., *von, van, de, de la*) and of names beginning with *Mac* varies. Capitalize such names as your dictionary lists them or as the individuals themselves capitalize them. Names beginning with *Mc* usually capitalize the first letter after the *Mc*.

> Arthur Vandenberg   *but*   Martin Van Buren
> Ferdinand Delacroix   *but*   Walter de la Mare, Agnes de Mille
> Bernarr Macfadden   *but*   Clifford MacFadden
> Cyrus McCormick, William McKinley, Edward McMillan

2. Capitalize words derived from proper nouns unless your dictionary spells them without a capital letter.

McCarthyism	the Doppler effect	sherry
Sam Browne belt	macadam	johnnycake
Melba toast	diesel engine	

3. Capitalize the titles of officials, nobility, and relatives when these titles precede the person's name or when they are used as a substitute for the name of a specific individual. Do not capitalize titles when they are used alone as a statement of the office or relationship.

General Eisenhower	*but*	the general
Lord Berners	*but*	a lord
Cardinal Spellman	*but*	the cardinal
Aunt Helena	*but*	his aunt
Senator John Pastore	*but*	a senator
Queen Alexandra	*but*	the queen
Mama	*but*	my mother

If the office or rank is a very high one, the title is sometimes capitalized even when used without a following name.

the President (of the United States) *but* the club's president
the Duke (of Windsor)   the Secretary of State

4. Capitalize the names or abbreviations of academic degrees or titles that appear after a person's name.

Clarence V. Holmes, Ph.D.   Charlene Fraser, Attorney at Law
Frederic Larssen, M.D.

5. Do not capitalize occupational titles that appear after the person's name.

John Pastore, senator from Rhode Island
General Eisenhower, commander in chief
Elton McNamme, president of the UNCO Corporation
Janet Rossi, our treasurer

6. Do not capitalize the generic (general) names of occupations or of social and academic classes.

She wants to become either a lawyer or an accountant.
Most Americans belong to the middle class.
Special preference will be given to seniors.

42c NAMES OF GROUPS

Capitalize the names of ethnic groups and the official names of organizations.

1. Capitalize the names of national, linguistic, and racial groups and of adjectives formed from these names.

English	Mongol	Afro-American	Melanesian
Turkish	Asian	Algonquian	Ainu
Nordic	French	Semitic	

2. Capitalize the names of officially organized groups of any kind but not of unofficial or loosely organized collections of people. Do not capitalize such general designations as *the army, the nation*.

League of Women Voters	Indiana University
New York Mets	United States Coast Guard
the Massachusetts Historical Society	Hanseatic League
	Internal Revenue Service
New York Philharmonic	House of Commons
Del Monte Corporation	

42d RELIGIOUS TERMS

Capitalize the names or epithets of deities, organized religious groups, sacred texts and ceremonies, and adjectives derived from these names.

God, Christ, Allah, Jehovah, the Messiah, the Virgin, Buddha, the Prophet

Judaism, Roman Catholic, Shinto, Islam, Latter-Day Saints, the Church of England, Zen, Sufism, St. Paul's Cathedral, Protestant

the Scriptures, the Bible, the Vulgate, Genesis, Revelation, the Pentateuch, Koran, Talmud, Upanishads, Book of the Dead

Hail Mary, the Ten Commandments, the Litany, Hegira, the Crucifixion, Holy Communion

Christian churches, Moslem leaders, Gospel writers, Biblical exegesis

It is not necessary to capitalize pronouns referring to deities unless the pronoun could otherwise seem to refer to someone else.

42e NAMES OF PLACES

Capitalize the names of political and geographical divisions and the names of individual structures or vehicles.

1. Capitalize the names of nations, states, provinces, counties, cities, towns, streets, highways, parks, mountains, rivers, lakes, and other recognized political and geographical divisions.

Thailand	the Grand Canyon
Nebraska	the Near East
the Province of Alberta	the Balkans
Dade County	the Black Forest
Schaffer Road	the Roman Empire
the Ohio Turnpike	the Loop
Glacier National Park	the Old World
Mount Whitney	the Ozarks
the St. Lawrence River	the Bay Area
Lake Huron	the Lake District (England)
Great Salt Lake	the Tropic of Capricorn
the Continental Divide	Mammoth Cave

2. Do not capitalize the names of the points of the compass unless these names refer to specific geographic regions.

> We drove east for about fifty miles and then turned south.

> The East is more heavily industrialized than the South. (Here, *East* and *South* refer to specific geographic areas of the United States.)

3. Capitalize the names of individual structures, buildings, monuments, ships, and aircraft.

> World Trade Center   *Apollo II*
> Lincoln Memorial   S.S. *France*
> the Cow Palace

42f TITLES OF WORKS

In the titles of essays, articles, chapters, books, periodicals, newspapers, films, television programs, musical compositions, and works of art, capitalize all the words except articles, conjunctions, and prepositions. If the article, conjunction, or preposition is the first word of the title, it is capitalized.

> "Moorish Influence on   "The Tonight Show"
> on Medieval Art"   *Tea and Sympathy*
> *Encyclopedia of History*   "The Stars and Stripes Forever"
> *Sports Illustrated*   *The Last Supper*
> *Boston Globe*   *Birth of a Nation*

If a work is divided into parts, the names of these parts should also be capitalized.

> Foreword   Book III   Act I   Index
> Part IX   Chapter 17   Volume II   Appendix B

42g OTHER NAMES

Conventions for the capitalization of other kinds of names are not always logical; some are capitalized, some are not. The most important conventions are the following.

1. Capitalize the names of the days of the week, months of the year, and official holidays. Capitalize the names of geological time divisions but not the words *era, period, epoch,* and so on.

> Thursday   Veterans Day   Paleozoic era   Pleistocene epoch
> February   the Fourth of July   Devonian period

2. Capitalize the names of treaties, laws, historical documents, historical epochs or events, and legal cases.

> Treaty of Versailles   Boston Tea Party
> Taft-Hartley Act   War of Jenkins' Ear
> Declaration of Independence   *N.L.R.B.* v. *Jones & Laughlin*
> Era of Good Feeling   *Steel Company*

3. Capitalize the names of flags, awards, and official brand names (but not the general name for a product).

Union Jack	the flag
Nobel Peace Prize	a grant from N.S.F.
Sprite	bubble gum
a Yamaha guitar	

4. Capitalize the official name of an academic course, but do not capitalize the general name of the subject matter unless it is a proper name in its own right (such as the name of a language).

Physics 102   *but*   My physics lab meets on Tuesday.
English 314   *and*   My English seminar meets on Tuesday.

5. Do not capitalize the names of the seasons of the year. Do not capitalize the words *world, sun, moon, universe,* or *star.* Capitalize the names of planets, but do not capitalize the word *earth* unless it is being used as the name of a planet in contrast with other planets in the solar system.

Two-thirds of the earth's surface is covered with water.
The atmosphere of Mars is thinner than that of Earth.

6. Do not capitalize the names of centuries or the designations of most general historical periods. Check your dictionary to be certain: there is more tradition than logic in the capitalization rules for historical periods.

the eighteenth century	the Middle Ages
the space age	the Age of Reason
the colonial period	

7. Do not capitalize the names for diseases, conditions, medical tests, and so on, unless the term contains a proper name.

tuberculosis	German measles
scratch test	Wassermann test
rubella	Hodgkin's disease
amblyopia	Pap smear

42h SINGLE LETTERS

Many—but not all—single letters used as words or as abbreviations for words are capitalized.

1. Capitalize the pronoun *I,* the interjection *O,* the letters used to designate grades in a course, letters used to describe or define a following noun, and letters used to designate musical notes. In designating musical keys, capitalize letters indicating major keys, but do not capitalize letters indicating minor keys.

A-frame	G-string	T square
I-bar	vitamin C	A major
V-neck	B-girl	a minor

2. Capitalize letters of abbreviation if the words for which they

stand would be capitalized when spelled out. Some abbreviations are always capitalized, even though the full words for which they stand are not capitalized. Always capitalize *A.D., B.C., R.S.V.P.,* and the abbreviations for time zones. Capitalize the first letter of abbreviations for chemical elements, whether the abbreviation stands for a single element (Na for sodium) or the elements within a compound (NaCl for sodium chloride). Capitalize the abbreviations for academic degrees, even if they do not follow names.

A.D. 24 (= anno Domini 24)
R.S.V.P. (= Répondez s'il vous plaît)
EST (= Eastern Standard Time)
a Ph.D. in history (= a doctorate in history)
$AgNO_3$ (= silver nitrate)

3. Capitalization of the abbreviation for the word *number* (*No.* or *no.*) is optional. (See 43a.)

No. 55   *or*   no. 55

EXERCISES: Capitalization

Place capital letters wherever they are necessary in the following sentences.

1. "of all my courses," eric explained to jane, "I most enjoy art history and anthropology, but my german class, which is filled with obnoxious juniors, is the most unpleasant class I've taken since english 101."

2. memorial day, which honors those who died in the civil war, the world wars, and other foreign wars, is commemorated in the north on may 30; but some southern states also celebrate confederate memorial day on one of several days: april 26 in alabama, georgia, florida, and mississippi; may 10 in north and south carolina; and june 3 in kentucky, louisiana, tennessee, and texas.

3. neatly taped below the diploma of ernest schwartz, ph.d., issued in 1948 by the univerity of california, was the well-known quotation from robert browning's "andrea del sarto": "ah, but a man's reach should exceed his grasp, / or what's a heaven for?"

4. edvard grieg, the first norwegian composer to use scandinavian folk themes in his music, is probably best known for his *concerto in a minor* and for his music written for ibsen's play *peer gynt.*

5. during the renaissance, copernicus challenged the ptolemaic philosophy of astronomy, which taught that the earth was a stationary body at the center of the universe.

6. the state comptroller was indicted by the richland county grand jury on twelve counts of larceny and embezzlement.

7. "have you got any aspirin or bufferin with you?" judge mcfadden asked his secretary. "believe it or not, i have to spend the rest of the afternoon hearing testimony in the *towndes* v. *roper* case."

8. "if the president does not quickly settle his differences with congressional leaders," the speaker continued, "he may very well be one of the least effective presidents the country has ever had."

9. seneca, who lived from 4 b.c. to a.d. 65, an essayist and dramatist, was one of the leading proponents of stoicism.

ab / 43 ABBREVIATIONS

Abbreviations, or shortened forms of words, are both useful and widely used in informal writing, note taking, and many kinds of technical writing. Abbreviations, however, are much less acceptable in nontechnical writing. With the exception of the few almost universally used abbreviations explained in the following sections, a safe rule to follow is "When in doubt, spell it out."

In American usage, most abbreviations are usually followed by a period. Do not space between periods *within* an abbreviation (Ph.D., A.D.) except when the abbreviation is the initials of a person's name (S. S. Stevens).

43a ABBREVIATIONS TO USE

In general, certain titles of address, expressions of time and temperature, and certain Latin terms should always be abbreviated.

Personal Titles.   Always abbreviate the following titles before personal names.

Mr. Francis	Ms. Francis	St. Francis
Mrs. Francis	Dr. Francis	

Always abbreviate *Junior* and *Senior* and titles of degrees when they immediately follow the full personal name. Separate the name from the abbreviation with a comma.

Peter Heath, Sr.	Peter Heath, Ph.D.
Peter Heath, Jr.	Peter Heath, S.T.B.

Time and Temperature.   Always use the following abbreviations in expressions of time and temperature that are accompanied by a numeral.

10:30 a.m. (or 10:30 A.M.)
8:16 p.m. (or 8:16 P.M.)

7:30 EST (Eastern Standard Time; no periods follow the abbreviation)

A.D. 734 (Note that A.D. precedes the year.)
in the eighth century A.D.
734 B.C.

20° C. (centigrade or Celsius)
20° F. (Fahrenheit)

When accompanied by a numeral, the word *number* may be abbreviated to either *No.* or *no.*

Train No. 504 will be leaving on Track No. 7.
Train no. 504 will be leaving on Track no. 7.

If the expression of time or temperature or the word *number* is not accompanied by a numeral, do not use the abbreviation in general writing.

INCORRECT	The hearing is scheduled for tomorrow a.m.
CORRECT	The hearing is scheduled for tomorrow morning.
CORRECT	The hearing is scheduled for 10:30 a.m.
INCORRECT	They have trouble converting temperatures from F. to C.
CORRECT	They have trouble converting temperatures from Fahrenheit to Celsius.
CORRECT	A temperature of 22° C. is approximately the same as 72° F.

Latin Expressions. Always abbreviate common Latin expressions such as *e.g.*, *i.e.*, and *etc.* Many writers now prefer the English equivalents of the Latin words and avoid the Latin expressions entirely.

43b ABBREVIATIONS TO AVOID

Aside from the universally used abbreviations just discussed, avoid most other abbreviations.

Names. Names of persons, names of geographical locations, and names of days, months, and holidays should not be abbreviated.

1. Do not abbreviate the first or last names of persons unless these persons are best known by their initials.

INCORRECT	Robt. Browning lived in Italy until his wife, Eliz. B. Browning, died in 1861.
CORRECT	Robert Browning lived in Italy until his wife, Elizabeth Barrett Browning, died in 1861.
CORRECT	O. J. Simpson has become a folk hero.

2. Do not abbreviate the names of countries, states, cities, towns or streets.

INCORRECT	One of the most extravagant Thanksgiving Day parades in the U.S. takes place on N.Y.C.'s Bdway.
CORRECT	One of the most extravagant Thanksgiving Day parades in the United States takes place on New York City's Broadway.

3. Do not abbreviate the names of the months of the year, the days of the week, or the names of holidays.

INCORRECT	Dec. 25 fell on Mon. in 1978, so we had a long Xmas weekend.
CORRECT	December 25 fell on Monday in 1978, so we had a long Christmas weekend.

Parts of Books.   Within the text of an essay, do not abbreviate the names of the parts of a written work.

INCORRECT   The author discusses the effect of television on children in Pt. I, Chap. 5.

CORRECT   The author discusses the effect of television on children in Part I, Chapter 5.

Measurements.   Do not abbreviate terms for measurements (*ft., yd., in., oz., lb., gal., mi., tsp.,* and so on) in general writing; such abbreviations are, however, often acceptable in technical writing.

INCORRECT   Her one-month-old baby is twenty-three in. long, weighs nine lbs., and drinks thirty oz. of milk a day.

CORRECT   Her one-month-old baby is twenty-three inches long, weighs nine pounds, and drinks thirty ounces of milk a day.

Symbols.   Do not use ampersand (the symbol for *and*) or the symbols %, ¢, =, +, @, or # in general writing. These symbols may be used in technical writing or in tables accompanying nontechnical writing.

INCORRECT   When Mr. & Mrs. Perry bought their Halloween candy, they found that prices had skyrocketed in the last year: a 10¢ candy bar was now 25¢, an increase of 150%.

CORRECT   When Mr. and Mrs. Perry bought their Halloween candy, they found that prices had skyrocketed in the last year: a 10-cent candy bar was now 25 cents, an increase of 150 percent.

Others.   Do not use such abbreviations as *gov't, cont., co.,* and *dept.* (But see 43c for the names of particular companies.)

INCORRECT   The president of the co., who was afraid that he could not pay his bills, applied for a small-business loan from the gov't.

CORRECT   The president of the company, who was afraid that he could not pay his bills, applied for a small-business loan from the government.

43c SPECIAL PROBLEMS

Exceptions to the general rules for abbreviation in nontechnical writing include many kinds of personal titles, company names, and a few special cases.

Titles Preceding Names.   Titles that precede names (other than those listed earlier, which are always abbreviated) should not be abbreviated unless the *full* name of the person follows.

INCORRECT   Rep. Youngman

CORRECT   Representative Youngman; Rep. John Youngman

INCORRECT	Rear Adm. Moore
CORRECT	Rear Admiral Moore; Rear Adm. Algernon Moore

Company Names. The official name of a company or other organization should be written exactly as the company itself writes it, including any abbreviations.

Sears, Roebuck and Co.
IBM Corp.
Harper & Row, Publishers

Others. Nicknames and short forms regularly used as full words are not treated as abbreviations. The abbreviations for certain geographical names follow special conventions.

1. Do not use a period after nicknames or after abbreviations that have become accepted words in their own right; check your dictionary when in doubt.

Chris, Al, Jo, Marge
gym, flu, taxi

2. The name *District of Columbia* is always abbreviated when it follows the city name *Washington* but is written in full when it occurs by itself.

Washington, D.C.; in the District of Columbia

43d ACRONYMS

An **acronym** is a special kind of abbreviation formed by the first letter or letters of each word of a multiword name or phrase. For example, *CIA* is an acronym for Central *I*ntelligence *A*gency, and *sonar* is an acronym for *so*und *na*vigation *r*anging. Some acronyms are pronounced as if they were independent words, that is, we pronounce *NATO* as if it were a word *nato;* we do not say *N-A-T-O.*

Common Acronyms. The use of acronyms has increased greatly during the twentieth century, and many acronyms are now acceptable even in formal writing. In general, use the acronym in writing if it is universally used in speech. Because no one says "deoxyribonucleic acid" or "The American Federation of Labor and Congress of Industrial Organizations," it is acceptable to write *DNA* and *AFL-CIO.* The most common acronyms are usually spelled without periods, but consult your dictionary to be sure.

CARE	UNICEF	scuba
SEATO	ACTH	radar
CBS	NAACP	

Less Familiar Acronyms. Even if an acronym is not universally known, it can be used if the name is to be repeated many times within a paper. In such cases, spell the name in full the first time it is used. Place the acronym in parentheses immediately after the full name. All future references can then use only the acronym.

> Raoul Monroe began working for Clark, Randall, and Oddfellow (CRO) in 1964. By 1971, Monroe was a junior vice-president of CRO.

44 CONTRACTIONS

A **contraction** is a special kind of abbreviation in which two words are spoken or written as one and in which one or more sounds or letters have been omitted. In written English, an apostrophe substitutes for the missing letter or letters.

We would not sound like native speakers of English if our speech did not include the most familiar contractions. In writing, however, contractions are best reserved for personal-experience papers and avoided in more formal writing such as research papers. When you do use contractions, be sure to spell them correctly and to put the apostrophe at the point where the letters have been omitted.

44a WITH NOT

Among the most common English contractions are those consisting of a verb and a following *not*. The word *not* is abbreviated; the verb never is. The accepted contractions of verbs with *not* are the following.

aren't	wouldn't	doesn't	mightn't	needn't
isn't	shan't	didn't	haven't	oughtn't
wasn't	shouldn't	can't	hasn't	mustn't
won't	don't	couldn't	hadn't	

44b WITH PRONOUNS

Another common type of contraction consists of a pronoun and a following auxiliary verb. The verb is abbreviated, but the pronoun never is.

BE	HAVE	HAD	WILL	WOULD
I'm	I've	I'd	I'll	I'd
you're	you've	you'd	you'll	you'd
he's	he's	he'd	he'll	he'd
she's	she's	she'd	she'll	she'd
it's	it's	it'd	it'll	it'd
we're	we've	we'd	we'll	we'd
they're	they've	they'd	they'll	they'd
who's, who're	who's, who've	who'd	who'll	who'd
there's, there're	there's, there've	there'd	there'll	there'd

44c IS, HAS, HAD, AND WOULD

Other pronouns and noun subjects also form contractions with *is* and *has*. The rule is the same: The full form of the subject is followed by -'s.

Someone's eaten all the brownies.	=	Someone has eaten all the brownies.
Edgar's going to Minnesota.	=	Edgar is going to Minnesota.
My dog's just a mongrel.	=	My dog is just a mongrel.

When spelling out contractions of pronouns and verbs, be sure to use the correct full form. This can sometimes be confusing because both *is* and *has* are contracted as -'s, and both *had* and *would* are contracted as -'d.

He's a good friend of mine.	=	He is a good friend of mine.
He's caught a bad cold.	=	He has caught a bad cold.
I'd like to come.	=	I would like to come.
I'd better come.	=	I had better come.

EXERCISES: Abbreviations and Contractions

In the following sentences, abbreviate words incorrectly spelled out, and spell out the forms for which abbreviations and contractions would be incorrect in formal essay writing.

1. Forgetting the change from EST to EDT, Chas. M. Anderson, Senior, president of Anderson Advertising Services, Inc., arrived, red-faced, almost an hour late for the annual stockholders' meeting at the corp. offices on Fifth Ave.

2. Because the temperature had risen to a sweltering 98° F. within the cabin of the newest spacecraft being developed by the U.S., scientists at the research ctr. estimated that they'd need at least three more months for tests both on the coast and at the Ariz. site.

3. Because he hadn't anticipated that the ERA would be an issue in his campaign for reelection, Rep. Hodgens was caught off guard by a top reporter from one of the leading D.C. newspapers, who asked him whether he had supported the amendment.

4. Doctor Rebecca M. Friedman, one of the best-known sociologists in the U.S., was asked to give the opening speech at the national convention of the NAACP on Aug. 22 in L.A.

5. Who'd have thought that the owner of sweepstakes ticket #4932 would've been Tracy Stevens, four yrs. old!

6. Who's going to support an increase in county taxes when the services provided by the county (e.g., police protection, garbage pickup, fire protection, recreational facilities) aren't approaching the superior quality of two yrs. ago when the taxes were 12% less than they are now?

7. Nancy Cook, sen. in the N.C. legislature, told the rep. from N.O.W. that unfortunately many women from rural areas of her state wouldn't attend organizational meetings of that group.

num /45 NUMBERS

The conventions for spelling out **numbers,** as opposed to using figures, vary from one kind of writing to another. In general, the more technical the writing, the greater the tendency to use figures rather than spelled-out forms. In any case, consistency of usage throughout a given paper is the most important rule.

Even in nontechnical writing, conventions for spelling out numbers vary. Some people and some publishing houses spell out all numbers that can be expressed in one or two words. Others spell out numbers one through twelve and use figures for numbers over twelve. Still others spell out the numbers one through nine and use figures for numbers over nine. (See 35d for the hyphenation of spelled-out numbers.) If you will be expressing only a few numbers, you can spell them all out. But if you have many numbers to express, you will save time and space by using figures. Whichever rule you decide to follow, follow it consistently. Do not write *seventy-six courses* in one sentence and *18 courses* in the next sentence.

INCORRECT	Lucille has 152 pairs of shoes and eight hats.
CORRECT	Lucille has one hundred and fifty-two pairs of shoes and eight hats.
CORRECT	Lucille has 152 pairs of shoes and 8 hats.

45a WHEN TO SPELL NUMBERS

In addition to the general rule that small numbers should be spelled out, there are certain conditions under which any number should be fully spelled out.

1. If a sentence begins with a number, the number should always be spelled out, regardless of its length or relationship to other numbers in the sentence. Often it is best to rephrase the sentence so that it does not begin with the number.

INCORRECT	125 years ago this area was virgin forest.
CORRECT	One hundred and twenty-five years ago this area was virgin forest.
CORRECT	This area was virgin forest 125 years ago.

2. Approximate or indefinite expressions of number should also always be spelled out.

There are roughly thirty-one centimeters in a foot.
That house was built over a century ago.

45b WHEN TO USE FIGURES

There are several exceptions to the general rules for spelling out numbers. Use figures in the following situations:

1. Except for extremely formal writing (such as wedding invitations), use figures to express street numbers, room or apartment numbers, telephone numbers, amounts of money, temperature, percentages, sports scores, Social Security and other identification numbers, air flight or train numbers, ZIP codes, and television channel numbers. Use figures for the pages of books or other written material and also for divisions such as chapters and volumes.

> His address is Apartment 6, 711 North Larch Street, Memphis, Tennessee 38115.
>
> Our mortgage is for $27,500 at 9½ percent interest.
>
> I heard on Channel 6 that the Mets had won by a score of 3-1.
>
> You will be responsible for all material in Chapters 1–6, pages 3–157.
>
> She booked a seat on Flight 36 from Kennedy Airport and charged her ticket to VISA Card No. 5266-140-323-158.

If the name of the street itself is a low number, it is often spelled out to avoid confusion with the building number: *220 Fourth Avenue.*

2. Use figures to express numbers before an abbreviation or symbol of any kind.

27°3′N	55 mph	3″ × 5″
6 g	35 mm film	f/1.8

3. Use figures to express mixed whole numbers and fractions, or numbers with a decimal point.

> The painters worked 6½ hours on Tuesday, 5 hours on Wednesday, and 7¼ hours on Thursday.
>
> Plat No. 53 is 2.66 times as large as Plat No. 52.

4. Use figures in tabular material and in numbering lists or series. In numbering a list, either place a period after the figure or enclose the figure in parentheses.

1. German	(1) German
2. Italian	(2) Italian
3. Russian	(3) Russian
4. Portuguese	(4) Portuguese

5. Use figures to distinguish one set of numbers from another set within the same sentence or group of sentences.

> You will need two 3-inch nails and four 2-inch nails.

6. In expressions of time, use figures before *a.m.* and *p.m.*, but spell out the number before *o'clock*. Spell out numbers not using decimals, such as *half past, a quarter till, twenty of, in the morning.*

10:00 a.m.	ten o'clock	a quarter till eleven
10:30 p.m.	half past ten	ten in the morning

7. Dates may be expressed in a number of different ways.

May 6, 1945
6 May 1945 (no comma if the day precedes the month)
May 6
May 6th (but preferably not *May 6th, 1945* or *May sixth, 1945*)
the sixth of May (but preferably not the *6th of May*)

45c INCLUSIVE NUMBERS

In writing inclusive numbers, that is, in indicating a series of continuous dates or pages, it is always correct to use the full figure for both the beginning and the ending numbers of the series:

the years 1917–1923   pages 554–558   numbers 503–509

If the number is over 110, those digits of the ending number that are identical to digits of the beginning number can be omitted when the inclusive numbers are connected by a hyphen. Always repeat the numbers in the units and tens positions, *except* when the number in the tens position is *0*. (The *MLA Handbook* recommends repeating a *0* in the tens position.)

the years 1917–23   pages 554–58   numbers 503–9

If the words *from* and *to* are used, the full figures should be written. Do not combine *from* with a hyphen.

INCORRECT	from 1923–1927
INCORRECT	from 1923–27
CORRECT	from 1923 to 1927

45d ORDINAL NUMBERS

Cardinal numbers indicate quantity but not order in a series.

The room had *five* rows of chairs.

Ordinal numbers indicate a specified position in a series of numbers.

I sat in the *fifth* row.

Spelling.   A suffix is added to the last element of a number to indicate that it is an ordinal number. The spelling of the ordinal numbers corresponding to *one*, *two*, and *three* is completely irregular, and the ordinals for *five*, *eight*, *nine*, and *twelve* have some irregularities. Other ordinal numbers simply add the suffix *-th*. When a cardinal number ends in *-y*, change the *-y* to *-i-* and add *-eth*.

CARDINAL	ORDINAL
one	first
two	second
three	third
four	fourth

CARDINAL	ORDINAL
five	fifth
six	sixth
seven	seventh
eight	eighth
nine	ninth
ten	tenth
eleven	eleventh
twelve	twelfth
thirteen	thirteenth
twenty	twentieth
seventy	seventieth
hundred	hundredth
thousand	thousandth
million	millionth

Abbreviating Ordinals. Most ordinal numbers are abbreviated by adding *-th* to the figures. The abbreviated forms of the ordinals for *one*, *two*, and *three* are irregular. No periods are used after the abbreviations for ordinals.

1	1st	3	3rd	12	12th
2	2nd	4	4th	29	29th

Ordinals as Parts of Speech. Ordinal numbers may be used as nouns, adjectives, or adverbs without any change in form, so there is no need to add *-ly* to ordinals when using them as adverbs.

INCORRECT   We came early because, <u>firstly</u>, we wanted to get a good parking place and, <u>secondly</u>, we had to buy our tickets before the performance.

CORRECT   We came early because, <u>first</u>, we wanted to get a good parking place and, <u>second</u>, we had to buy our tickets before the performance.

Spelling out Ordinals. In general, the rules for using figures or spelled-out forms of ordinal numbers are the same as those for cardinal numbers. However, the spelled-out forms of ordinals are used, even for large numbers, when designating governmental units, military groups, and religious organizations.

the Eighty-ninth Congress
Fifteenth Ward
First Presbyterian Church
Twenty-first Regiment
Sixth Fleet

45e ROMAN NUMERALS

The ordinary figures we use to express numbers (1, 2, 3, 47, 9,650) are called Arabic numerals. Roman numerals are letters used as numbers. Although Roman numerals are used relatively infrequently, everyone should be able to read them because failure to understand them leads to errors and confusion.

Only seven letters are used in writing Roman numerals. Depending upon the purpose, these letters may be expressed in either capital or small letters.

I (i)	=	1	C (c)	=	100
V (v)	=	5	D (d)	=	500
X (x)	=	10	M (m)	=	1,000
L (1)	=	50			

A line over any Roman numeral indicates that its value should be multiplied by 1,000.

D = 500 $\overline{D}$ = 500,000

Reading Roman Numerals. Use the following rules to read Roman numerals.

1. When numerals are repeated, add them together.

III = 1 + 1 + 1 = 3
XX = 10 + 10 = 20

2. When a smaller number follows a larger number, add the two.

VI   = 5 + 1 = 6
CLV = 100 + 50 + 5 = 155

3. Whenever any smaller number precedes a larger number, subtract the smaller number from the following larger number.

IV = 5 − 1 = 4
CM = 1,000 − 100 = 900

Hence

DXLI   = 500 + 50 − 10 + 1 = 541
MCMXLIII = 1,000 + 1,000 − 100 + 50 − 10 + 1 + 1 + 1 = 1,943
MDCCXXIV = 1,000 + 500 + 100 + 100 + 10 + 10 + 5 − 1 = 1,724

Conventional Uses. Although we use Arabic numerals on most occasions, Roman numerals are conventionally used for special purposes.

1. Capital Roman numerals are used to designate volumes, books, and parts of large works. Small Roman numerals are used as page numbers for the preliminary material (introduction, table of contents, acknowledgments, and the like) of a book or a very long paper, such as a dissertation.

Volume IV of the *Oxford English Dictionary*
Part VI, Chapter II
in the *Odyssey,* Book XVII
on page ix of the Introduction

2. Acts of plays are numbered with large Roman numerals and scenes of plays with small Roman numerals.

Twelfth Night, IV:ii

3. Capital Roman numerals are used for main headings of outlines. Small Roman numerals are used for fifth-level headings in outlines. (See 53a for a sample outline.)

4. Capital Roman numerals are occasionally used to indicate dates. In particular, they are often carved on public buildings to indicate the date of construction. Older books often have the date of publication expressed in capital Roman numerals.

MDCCCLIX = 1859

5. Ordinal numbers are used in speech to distinguish different persons or vehicles with the same name, but cardinal Roman numerals are normally used for this purpose in writing.

George VI	*Mariner III*
Pope John XXIII	Queen Elizabeth II
Bronston Jacobs III	

If the ordinal is used in writing, it is spelled out, not written in figures.

George the Third

EXERCISES: Numbers

Part A: Correct errors in the following sentences by changing figures to words or words to figures as necessary.

1. Flight three fifty seven was delayed for more than thirteen hours on March tenth, 1976, while 8 detectives questioned the two hundred and seven passengers and searched the plane.

2. Kim bought 3 8-foot 2″ × 4″ planks.

3. Although twenty-four percent of those interviewed said they favored Senator Burns, only three percent of them were registered to vote.

4. King Richard the 1st of England, known as Richard the Lion-hearted primarily for his exploits during the 3rd crusade, was in England only for 2 brief periods during his reign of 10 years.

5. "I must have told at least 100 people today that the warehouse is located at 351 Heywood Road, not at twenty-seven Rutherford Street," snapped the irate secretary to what must have been the one hundred and first customer.

6. Mike was negotiating a 2nd mortgage on his twenty-year-old home in order to finance a 3rd car for the family—a 2nd-hand Ford to be driven by his 17-year-old daughter, Beth.

7. In the 9th inning, when Joey Mason hit the ball 305 feet, the Giants scored 2 runs, tying the game 8 to 8.

Part B: Translate the following Roman numerals into figures and figures into Roman numerals as specified.

1. Translate the following Roman numerals into figures: CXLVI, DCCVII, MDLXXI, MCMXXXIV, MCCXLIII.

2. Write the following figures in Roman numerals: 1984, 954, 3,421, 2,008.

sp / 46 SPELLING

Some people seem to be natural-born spellers, but most of us have difficulty spelling at least some words or groups of words. **Spelling** is not necessarily related to intelligence or writing ability, yet spelling is one of the first things that readers notice about a piece of writing. If there are a number of misspelled words, the writer will probably be classified as ignorant or careless. Furthermore, misspellings often confuse readers, diverting their attention from the subject matter.

Even if you are a terrible speller, your difficulties are not as insolvable as you may think. You already spell better than you realize. Even if spelling has always been troublesome for you, you still spell most words correctly. You never spell a word entirely wrong; you miss only a letter or two. A little attention to spelling can lead to a great deal of improvement.

Keep a dictionary handy while you are writing, and refer to it whenever you have doubts about the correct spelling of a word. When you find a misspelling in your writing or when one is pointed out to you, check the correct spelling. Spell the entire word aloud and write it down. Try to fix the correct spelling in your mind, making a mental image of the written word. Write the word on a 3-by-5-inch card and keep a collection of such cards to be reviewed when you have a few minutes to spare.

Develop your own crutches for remembering the spelling of words that you misspell over and over again. It doesn't matter how silly the crutch is as long as it helps you remember the correct spelling. For example, many people have difficulty remembering whether a word ends in *-sede, -cede,* or *-ceed.* If you memorize the rather foolish sentence "The *proceeds succeeded* in *exceeding* estimates," you will have learned the only three words that end in *-ceed.* Then, if you remember that *supersede* is the only word that ends in *-sede,* you know that any other word with the same sound must end in *-cede (intercede, precede, recede, concede, accede, antecede, secede,* and all their derivatives, such as *procedure, antecedent,* and *conceded*).

Look for patterns in your spelling difficulties. For example, you may find it easier to remember that *pronounce* has an *o* that does not appear in *pronunciation* if you notice that other words have the same pattern: *denounce/denunciation; announce/annunciation; renounce/renunciation.* Some spelling problems, such as the confusion between *-ant* and *-ent (dominant, apparent)* are just historical accidents and cannot be resolved by memorizing a rule. Other problems, however, can be reduced greatly by applying a few basic rules. For example, the rule for adding the ending *-ly* is relatively simple (see 46d).

Be sure you have both the right spelling *and* the right word. In many so-called misspellings, the spelling is actually correct, but the wrong word has been chosen. This problem occurs most often when two words that are pronounced alike are confused. For example, in the sentence "Life is sometimes called a *veil* of tears," the word *veil* is spelled correctly, but the writer meant *vale* (valley) not *veil* (a piece of cloth worn over the face). See Appendix C for a list of frequently confused words.

46a SPELLING AND PRONUNCIATION

Everyone knows that, in many ways and for many words, there is a poor match between English spelling and English pronunciation. The reason for this poor match is historical: English spelling was fixed in all but minor details when printing was introduced in England at the end of the fifteenth century. But English pronunciation has been changing continually during the past five centuries. Hence today the same sound is often spelled several different ways (*go, grow, toe, though*), and different sounds are often spelled the same way (*good, food, blood*). But because we see the most common words in print nearly every day and because we constantly write them ourselves, we seldom misspell them. Regardless of how inconsistent the spellings are, the words are so familiar that we usually spell them correctly. The words most often misspelled are normally somewhat less familiar ones. Many spelling errors caused by the mismatch of pronunciation and spelling involve silent letters, omission of letters, addition of letters, wrong letters, and transposed letters.

Silent Letters.   Silent letters can occur in all positions of a word—at the beginning, in the middle, at the end. Words beginning with silent letters are especially frustrating because, if you do not know the first letter, you usually cannot find the word in a dictionary. Words with silent letters must be learned one by one. Try to form a mental picture of such words, concentrating on the position of the silent letter.

BEGINNING	gnaw, knapsack, psalm, pneumonia
MIDDLE	aisle, mortgage, handkerchief, silhouette
END	debris, depot, crumb, rendezvous

Omission of Letters.   Letters are often incorrectly omitted because the sounds they represent are dropped in rapid speech. Careful, even exaggerated, pronunciation will help you remember these neglected letters.

INCORRECT	CORRECT
enviroment	environment
libary	library
quanity	quantity
suprise	surprise

In words in which two letters stand for a single sound, try to concentrate on the two letters for the single sound.

INCORRECT	CORRECT
aquaint	acquaint
inteligent	intelligent
embarass	embarrass
tecnique	technique

Addition of Letters. Letters are often incorrectly added because the words are pronounced with an extra syllable or sound. Standard pronunciation will assist in correct spelling.

INCORRECT	CORRECT
drownded	drowned
hundered	hundred
atheletic	athletic
wonderous	wondrous

In other instances, letters are incorrectly added by analogy with related words or similar words. Here you must concentrate on remembering the individual word.

INCORRECT	CORRECT
explaination	explanation
fullfill	fulfill
passtime	pastime
fourty	forty

Wrong Letters. Probably the most common cause of wrong letters in spelling is the fact that all unstressed vowels in English tend to become one obscure vowel. Unfortunately, this obscure vowel is spelled in many different ways (compare *a*way, *e*ffect, *i*magine, *o*ccur, *u*pon). Again, focus your attention on the correct spelling of the obscure vowel in the given word. An exaggerated pronunciation is often helpful in remembering the spelling of obscure vowels. That is, as you write a word such as *separate*, sound it out as *see-pay-rate*.

INCORRECT	CORRECT
seperate	separate
catagory	category
analisis	analysis
contraversy	controversy

Even the same consonant sound may have various spellings; the sounds of *s* and *z* are especially troublesome.

INCORRECT	CORRECT
nesessary	necessary
fantacy	fantasy
disguize	disguise
suffitient	sufficient

Transposed Letters. Transposed (reversed) letters most often appear in words that are slurred in pronunciation, especially in the vicinity of an *r*. Careful pronunciation will aid correct spelling.

INCORRECT	CORRECT
childern	children
jewlery	jewelry
prespire	perspire
revelant	relevant

Words with silent letters also cause transposition problems when the writer knows there is a silent letter, knows what the letter is, but cannot remember exactly where it goes.

INCORRECT	CORRECT
fa<u>c</u>sinate	fa<u>s</u>cinate
su<u>tb</u>le	su<u>bt</u>le
dia<u>hrr</u>ea	dia<u>rrh</u>ea
ge<u>h</u>tto	g<u>h</u>etto

EXERCISES: Spelling and Pronunciation

Part A: Use your dictionary to help you identify which of the following words are misspelled. List the misspelled words, and write the correct spelling next to them.

1. familiar	7. alright	13. lavatories
2. temperment	8. grammar	14. alltogether
3. similiar	9. labratories	15. willful
4. perrogative	10. forrest	16. mathematics
5. knowledge	11. priviledge	17. nusance
6. peculiar	12. bizare	18. particular

Part B: Underline the misspelled words in the following sentences.

1. While dinning with his grandparents, the child spilled strawberry parfay and lasagnea down the front of his new kaki safarri suit.
2. Frederick, who had always thought he would remain a bachlor, found himself rehersing his proposal of marrage, ordering champaine, and ocassionally eyeing the two-carrat diamond with which he planned to suprise Marian.
3. Sitting in the dissorderly apartment and eating a sandwitch and vegtable soup, Beth began writting out a list of all the improvments necessary just to make her new quarters liveable.
4. Pedro had always been willfull, but as he grew older, he became so obstinate and tempermental that his friends' only cleu that anger was brewing and a firey arguement would ensue was his habit of twirling the ends of his moustashe when he was at the boiling point.

46b FOUR STANDARD SPELLING RULES

Unpredictable as much of English spelling is, there are a few helpful rules. All of the rules have exceptions, but they are, nonetheless, applicable much more often than not. The first rule uses pronunciation as a guide to spelling; the last three rules involve an automatic modification of the end of a word when a suffix is added.

ie and *ei.* If the sound is long *e* as in *me,* then *i* precedes *e* except after *c.* After *c,* the spelling is *ei.*

LONG *e*	achieve, belief, field, grief, niece, siege, yield
AFTER *c*	ceiling, conceit, deceive, perceive, receipt

Exceptions: *caffeine, codeine, protein, seize, weird, financier.*   The words *either, leisure,* and *neither* will also be exceptions for speakers who use a long *e* in these words.

If the sound is not long *e*, but is something else, especially long *a* as in *day*, then *e* precedes *i*.

LONG *a*	eight, feign, freight, neighbor, weigh, rein, veil, vein
LONG *i*	height, kaleidoscope, sleight, stein
SHORT *i* or *u*	counterfeit, forfeit, foreign, sovereign
SHORT *e*	heifer, heir, their

Exceptions: *friend, sieve, mischief.*

If the *i* and the *e* are pronounced as two separate vowels, the rule does not apply: *atheist, fiery, science, variety.* If the *c* is pronounced like the *sh* in *she*, then *i* precedes *e*: *conscience, efficient, species, sufficient.*

Final -*y* before a Suffix. When a word ends in -*y* preceded by a consonant, change the -*y* to -*i* before adding a suffix, unless the suffix begins with *i*-. If the suffix begins with *i*-, keep the -*y* except before the suffix -*ize*.

BEFORE -*I*		BEFORE -*IZE*
envy/envious, envies	copy/copyist	agony/agonize
forty/fortieth, forties	dirty/dirtyish	colony/colonize
likely/likelihood	study/studying	(also colonist)
plenty/plentiful		memory/memorize

If the -*y* is preceded by a vowel, -*y* does not change to -*i*.

joy/joyful
journey/journeying
toy/toyed
valley/valleys

Exceptions:

1. Proper names do not change -*y* to -*i* before a plural ending.

Averys, Stacys, Harrys, Martys

2. A few one-syllable words in which -*y* is preceded by a vowel change -*y* to -*i* before some endings.

pay/paid *but* payer, payment
say/said *but* says
lay/laid/lain/laity *but* layable, delayable
day/daily *but* days
gay/gaily *or* gayly; gaiety *or* gayety
slay/slain *but* slayer

3. Some one-syllable words in which -*y* is preceded by a consonant vary in their treatment before suffixes.

slyest *or* sliest
dryness *but* drier *or* dryer
wryness *not* wriness
shyly *not* shily

Final Silent -e. If a word ends in a consonant followed by a silent -e, drop the -e before endings beginning with a vowel, but keep -e before endings beginning with a consonant.

BEFORE A VOWEL		BEFORE A CONSONANT
excite	exciting	excitement
extreme	extremity	extremely
fate	fatal	fateful
shame	shaming	shameless

Exceptions:

1. The following words are exceptions to the general rule.

acre/acreage	nine/ninth
awe/awful	whole/wholly
mile/mileage	

Some exceptions are made to avoid confusion with another word.

dye/dyeing	(to avoid confusion with *dying* from *die*)
line/lineage	(to avoid confusion with *linage*)
singe/singeing	(to avoid confusion with *singing*)

2. The final -e is retained after *c* and *g* before suffixes beginning with *a-* and *o-* when the "soft" pronunciation of *c* and *g* remains.

notice/noticeable	courage/courageous
replace/replaceable	charge/chargeable
service/serviceable	disadvantage/disadvantageous
	outrage/outrageous

3. In American English, the final -e of words ending in -*dge* drops before -*ment*.

abridgment	acknowledgment
judgment	dislodgment

4. If the word ends in -*ue*, the final silent -e is usually dropped even before a consonant. If the word ends in -*oe*, the -e is retained before -*ing*.

argue/argument	true/truly	hoe/hoeing
due/duly	canoe/canoeing	shoe/shoeing
pursue/pursual		

Doubling of Consonants. If, after the suffix has been added, the stress is on the syllable before the suffix *and* if the last consonant is preceded by a single vowel, double the consonant before a suffix beginning with a vowel.

acquit	acquítted, acquítting, acquíttal
begin	begínning, begínner
occur	occúrred, occúrring, occúrrence

regret	regrétted, regrétting, regréttable
slip	slíppery, slípping, slípped, slíppage
refer	reférral, reférring (compare *réference* and *referée*, where the stress is not on the syllable before the suffix and where there is only one *r*)

Do not double the consonant before a suffix beginning with a consonant (*defer/deferment; sun/sunless*). Do not double the consonant if it is preceded by another consonant (*hurl/hurled; farm/farmer*). The letter *x* counts as two consonants and never doubles (*tax/taxable; fix/fixing*). Do not double the consonant if it is preceded by *two* vowels (*sour/soured; roam/roaming*).

Exceptions:

1. There is some variation when the final consonant is *-l*. Final *-l* may be doubled even though the stress is not on the syllable before the suffix: *éxcellence*. Some words have alternative spellings, either with or without a doubled *-l*: *quarreling* or *quarrelling; traveler* or *traveller*; in American usage, the single *-l* is usually preferred. Consult your dictionary when in doubt.

2. Except for *-ing* and *-ish*, suffixes beginning with *-i* normally do not double the preceding consonant even when the stress is on the syllable just before the suffix.

sit/sitting	rapid/rapidity	violin/violinist
top/topping	moral/morality	solid/solidify
sot/sottish	alcohol/alcoholic	Boston/Bostonian
snob/snobbish	atom/atomic	

EXERCISES: Four Standard Spelling Rules

Part A: List the words below that are misspelled. Write the correct spelling beside each.

1. recipeint	7. shriek	13. concieve
2. counterfiet	8. soveriegn	14. theif
3. forfeit	9. medeival	15. heist
4. resileince	10. wierd	16. beige
5. hygeine	11. preist	17. feind
6. releive	12. piety	18. sieze

Part B: Add the ending given in parentheses to each of the following words.

1. carry (er)	7. defy (ance)	13. tidy (ing)
2. essay (ist)	8. manly (ness)	14. February (s)
3. purvey (or)	9. sympathy (ize)	15. fantasy (ize)
4. cry (ing)	10. betray (al)	16. wary (ly)
5. cry (er)	11. employ (ment)	17. wry (er)
6. annoy (ance)	12. glory (ous)	18. convey (ance)

Part C: Add the ending given in parentheses to each of the following words.

1. note (able)	7. pressure (ize)	13. trace (ing)
2. tiptoe (ing)	8. blame (less)	14. guide (ance)
3. grace (less)	9. value (able)	15. appease (ing)
4. trace (able)	10. live (lihood)	16. appease (ment)
5. alternate (ly)	11. clue (ing)	17. confine (ing)
6. use (able)	12. salvage (able)	18. confine (ment)

46c NOUN PLURALS AND VERBS

The rules for forming noun plurals and those for the third-person singular present of verbs are identical in most cases. Nouns or verbs ending in -*y* follow the rules for final -*y* (see 46b). Some nouns, of course, have irregular plurals; these are discussed separately below.

Adding -*s*. The majority of nouns form their plurals and the majority of verbs form their third-person singular present by adding -*s*. This rule includes words ending in -*a*, -*i*, and -*u*.

cup/cups	banana/bananas
take/takes	ski/skis
inspection/inspections	guru/gurus
implant/implants	

Adding -*es*. Words ending in -*ch*, -*s*, -*sh*, or -*x* add -*es* to form the plural or the third-person singular if the ending makes an extra syllable.

watch/watches	rush/rushes
miss/misses	tax/taxes

One-syllable words ending in a single -*s* or a single -*z* preceded by a vowel may double the final consonant before adding -*es*, but practice varies. Check your dictionary when in doubt. Words of more than one syllable do not double the final consonant.

MONOSYLLABIC WORDS	POLYSYLLABIC WORDS
bus/buses *or* busses	trellis/trellises
gas/gases *or* gasses	callous/callouses
fez/fezzes	rumpus/rumpuses
quiz/quizzes	

Words Ending in -*f* or -*fe*.   Words ending in -*f* or -*fe* vary in the way they form their plurals. All *verbs* ending in -*f* or -*fe* take a regular third-person singular ending in -*s* (*knife/knifes; dwarf/dwarfs,* and so on). Some of the most common *nouns* drop the -*f* or -*fe* and add -*ves*. Some simply add -*s*. A few form their plural either way. Since no hard-and-fast rule can be made, check your dictionary when in doubt.

NOUNS IN -*VES*		NOUNS IN -*S* OR -*VES*
half/halves	shelf/shelves	dwarf/dwarfs *or* dwarves
knife/knives	thief/thieves	scarf/scarfs *or* scarves
leaf/leaves	wife/wives	

NOUNS IN -*S*	
belief/beliefs	roof/roofs
giraffe/giraffes	(and most other nouns)
proof/proofs	

Nouns ending in -*ff* form a regular plural in -*s*.

sheriffs, tariffs, stuffs, tiffs

Words ending in -*o*. Very few verbs end in -*o*; those that do form their endings like the corresponding nouns (*echo/echoes*, and so on). Nouns ending in -*o* preceded by a consonant vary in their formation of the plural. Some add -*es*, some add -*s*, and some may take either -*s* or -*es*. Even different dictionaries do not agree on every noun ending in -*o*, so choose one dictionary and follow its listings consistently. Almost all dictionaries agree on the following spellings.

-*ES*	-*S* or -*ES*	-*S*	
echoes	halos *or* haloes	altos	oratorios
embargoes	mementos *or*	bassos	photos
heroes	mementoes	cantos	pianos
Negroes	mosquitos *or*	dynamos	quartos
potatoes	mosquitoes	embryos	solos
tomatoes	mottos *or* mottoes	Eskimos	sopranos
torpedoes	volcanos *or*	Filipinos	
vetoes	volcanoes		
	zeros *or* zeroes		

Words ending in -*o* preceded by a vowel take a regular plural in -*s*.

cameos, stereos, patios, studios, kangaroos, zoos

Compound Words. Compound words normally form their endings according to the rules for the last element of the compound.

NOUNS		VERBS	
handfuls	court martials	freeze-dries	sidesteps
jack-in-the-pulpits	madmen	brainwashes	bypasses
merry-go-rounds	three-year-olds	water-skis	outdoes
cease-fires	sit-ins	shadowboxes	cold-shoulders

In a few compound nouns in which the first element is a noun and clearly the most important part of the compound, the first element takes the plural ending.

mothers-in-law	presidents-elect	commanders in chief
passersby	cousins-german	sums total
men-of-war	poets laureate	battles royal
rules-of-thumb	attorneys general	knights errant

In a very few combinations in which both elements are words for human beings, both elements take a plural.

menservants
women teachers
gentlemen farmers

Irregular English Plurals. In a very few words, the plurals are totally irregular.

child/children	foot/feet	tooth/teeth
ox/oxen	goose/geese	man/men
brother/brethren	louse/lice	woman/women
	mouse/mice	

Note: The plural *brethren* is restricted to religious contexts; otherwise, the regular plural *brothers* is used.

Irregular Foreign Plurals. Words borrowed from other languages, especially Latin and Greek, sometimes retain their foreign plurals. The tendency, however, is to regularize foreign words, and many have alternative English plurals. In general, if the singular of a foreign word ends in *-s*, the foreign plural is more likely to be used. A few common patterns are listed here. Check your dictionary when in doubt.

SINGULAR	PLURAL	MODEL	OTHER EXAMPLES
-us	-i	terminus/termini	alumnus, cactus, focus, fungus, locus, nucleus, radius, stimulus
-us	-era	genus/genera	corpus, opus
-is	-es	crisis/crises	analysis, axis, basis, diagnosis, hypothesis, neurosis, oasis, parenthesis, synthesis, thesis
-um	-a	memorandum/ memoranda	bacterium, curriculum, datum, medium, ovum, rostrum, stratum
-on	-a	criterion/criteria	automaton, ganglion, phenomenon
-eau	-eaux*	tableau/tableaux	beau, bureau, chateau, plateau, trousseau
-a	-ae	larva/larvae	alga, alumna, amoeba*, antenna*, formula*, nebula*
-ex	-ices*	index/indices	matrix, apex, appendix, vortex
-ma	-mata*	stigma/stigmata	enigma, stoma
No change in plural		species/species	apparatus, chamois, chassis, corps, hiatus, insignia, nexus, series, status

*These words may also take a regular English plural in *-s*.

No Separate Plural Forms. A few nouns have the same form in singular and plural. Many of these are the names of kinds of wild animals and fish. Tribal or national names from foreign languages often have the same form in singular and plural, but usage varies. In any case, if the name ends in *-ese*, no plural ending is added.

ANIMAL NAMES	TRIBAL NAMES	NAMES IN -ESE	OTHERS
cod	Swahili	Chinese	barracks
bass	Bantu	Burmese	(air) craft
trout	Bedouin	Portuguese	means
salmon	Sioux		gross
mackerel	Algonquian		bellows
pike			
fish			
deer			
moose			
mink			
sheep			
swine			
wildfowl			

Irregular Plurals of Titles.   The plurals of *Mr.* and *Mrs.* are irregular.

Mr. White	Messrs. White and Redd
Mrs. Tanner	Mmes. Tanner and Puce

EXERCISES: Noun Plurals and Verbs

Write the plural forms of the nouns and the third-person singular forms of the verbs in the following list. If the plural form or verb form is the same as the form given, write *correct.* If there are two correct forms, give both.

1. charwoman	11. oasis	21. member-at-large
2. tablespoonful	12. fiasco	22. taco
3. bonus	13. hobo	23. ghetto
4. menu	14. pliers	24. plateau
5. study	15. curriculum	25. lady-in-waiting
6. couch	16. Javanese	26. poncho
7. blitz	17. stepchild	27. shelf
8. leash	18. laundress	28. whiz
9. thief	19. shrimp	29. sheep
10. wish	20. cactus	30. basis

46d PREFIXES AND SUFFIXES

Few people have trouble spelling the most common everyday words such as *eye, thought,* or *one,* regardless of how mismatched the spelling is to the pronunciation. A glance at any list of the words most frequently misspelled by college students (see Appendix F) will quickly reveal that the majority of them are more learned words, most of them borrowed from other languages, especially Latin. Most of them consist of a prefix, a stem (or base, to which prefixes and suffixes are attached), and a suffix.

Spelling words with prefixes and suffixes is difficult for several reasons. First, as we have just noted, many of them are words that we use relatively infrequently. Second, we often do not recognize the various elements of the words for what they are. We do not realize that they consist of a prefix and a stem, and hence we do not associate them and their spelling with other words that contain the same prefix or the same stem. Third, the same prefix, stem, or suffix may be spelled in different ways in different words.

You need not be a Latin scholar to analyze words into prefix—stem—suffix. You already know the meanings of many prefixes and suffixes, even if you have not consciously memorized them. For example, you know that *pre-* means "before, in advance" because you know the meaning of such words as *prejudge, preheat,* and *prepay.* You also know that it is almost a sure bet that any word ending in *-ion* is a noun. You may not recognize the stem *-dict-;* but if you think for a moment, you can recall several words with this stem, such as *dictate, diction,* or *dictionary,* and will conclude that *-dict-* must mean something like "speak, pronounce, say." Thus, the word *prediction* consists of a prefix *pre-* meaning "before," a stem *-dict-* meaning "to speak," and a suffix *-ion* meaning "noun." So the word *prediction* means "something that is spoken in advance."

Cultivating the habit of analyzing words into prefix—stem—suffix will not only help you spell correctly but will also help you develop your vocabulary. Because you already knew the meaning of *prediction,* analyzing it into its parts did not increase your vocabulary. But let us assume that you encounter the word *premonition* in your reading and do not know its meaning. Because you know the meaning of the prefix *pre-* and of the suffix *-ion,* you remove these from the word, leaving a stem *-monit-.* You surely know the word *monitor* and probably also the word *admonish.* A *monitor* is someone or something that gives a warning, and the verb *admonish* means "to warn, to scold." Hence the word *premonition* must mean something like "a warning in advance." This would probably be sufficient information for you to understand the word in the context of a written passage. If you were considering using the word *premonition* in your own writing, you would want to check the dictionary for a more precise definition. In any case, if you take the time to break the word down into its parts, you will probably not forget the meaning of that word, and you will also add a new word to your vocabulary. Further, if you associate the word *premonition* with the word *monitor,* you will be less likely to misspell it as, for example, *premenition.*

Although, as was noted earlier, there are numerous pitfalls and inconsistencies in spelling words with prefixes and suffixes, there are also a few rules that always apply and a number of other rules that apply in most instances.

Words with Prefixes.   The spelling of the root word or stem is *never* changed by the addition of a prefix.

    mis + spell = misspell
    trans + plant = transplant
    un + necessary = unnecessary

```
counter + revolution = counterrevolution
a + rouse = arouse
de + fuse = defuse
inter + act = interact
uni + cycle = unicycle
```

Many prefixes also keep the same form, regardless of the stem to which they are attached.

PREFIX	MEANING	EXAMPLES
be-	all over, around	bedeck, befriend, belabor, belittle
counter-	against	counterintelligence, counterpart
dis-	reverse, not	disinherit, displace, distrust
for-	away, off	forbid, forsake, forswear
fore-	ahead, before	forearm, forecastle, foresaid
hyper-	over, beyond	hyperactive, hypercritical, hypersensitive
inter-	between, during	interchange, interlocking, interrelate
mis-	wrong	mislabel, misstate, misunderstand
out-	beyond	outcry, outpost, outthrust
over-	excessive, complete	overeat, overhaul, overstuffed
poly-	many	polychrome, polysyllabic, polytechnical
post-	after	postgraduate, postnatal, postwar
pre-	before	predate, prehistoric, premedical
semi-	half	semicircle, semidetached, semifinal
trans-	across	transaction, transform, transmigration
tri-	three	triangle, tricolor, tripod
ultra-	excessive	ultramodern, ultrared, ultrasonic
un-	not	unflattering, uninteresting, unreliable
under-	beneath, below	undercoating, underrate, underestimate
uni-	one, single	uniform, unilateral, unisex

Other prefixes assimilate to (become similar to) the first letter of the stem to which they are attached.

PREFIX	MEANING	EXAMPLES
ad-	to, toward	admit, adjunct, accept, affect, aggression, allocate, announce, apply, aspire
com-	together, with	compare, commit, cooperate, cohere, contain, collect, correct
en-	in, on	engrave, enlace, embrace, empower
in-	not	inorganic, indecision, illiterate, impossible, irregular
ob-	against	obtain, obligation, omit, occur, offer, oppose
sub-	under, beneath	submarine, subdivide, suspect, suffer, suggest, summon, support, sustain
syn-	together, with	synthesis, synchronize, symmetry, syllable, system

Among the most troublesome prefixes are those that are pronounced alike or nearly alike but are spelled differently. Sometimes the meaning of such prefixes is the same; sometimes it is different. Often changes in meaning of the words have made the meaning of the prefix obscure. A few of the most commonly confused groups are listed below.

PREFIX	MEANING	EXAMPLES
ante-	before	antedate, antecedent, antechamber
anti-	against	anticlimax, antibody, antiwar
en-	make, put into	encase, enslave, enlarge, endanger
in-	(1) in, toward	inaugurate, influx, inscribe, incisive
	(2) not	inactive, incorrect, infinite, insane
un-	not, reverse	unborn, undo, unfold, unutterable
enter-	variant of *inter-*	entertain, enterprise
inter-	between, among	interpret, interrupt, intermural, intersperse
intra-	within, inside	intracity, intramural, intravenous
intro-	in, into	introduce, introspect, introvert
hyper-	over, excessive	hyperactive, hyperthyroid, hyperbola, hypercritical
hypo-	under, insufficient	hypodermic, hypotenuse, hypochondria, hypothesis
for-	completely, off	forbid, forever, forgo, forget, forlorn, forsake
fore-	before	forebode, forecast, forego, forehead, foresee
per-	through, completely	percolate, perennial, perfect, persist, pertain
pre-	earlier, before	precede, predict, prefer, preclude, premature
pro-	forward; in favor of	proclaim, procreate, procure, profess, program
pur-	variant of *pro-*	purchase, pursuit, purloin, purport, purpose

Words beginning with *de-* and *di-* are particularly difficult to spell because the pronunciation is often of no assistance and because the prefixes themselves have so many different meanings. In a few instances, the *di-* is part of the stem and not a prefix at all. The proper spelling of *de-* and *di-* words must be learned for each individual word.

DE-	*DE-*	*DI-*	*DI-*
despair	degree	divide	dimension
destroy	deliver	divine	direct
describe	demand	dilemma	divulge
device	descend	divorce	diversion
decide	design		

Stems of Words. Stems that are independent words cause few spelling problems because we recognize the stem, because the stem usually keeps the same form when prefixes or suffixes are added, and because the meaning of the stem remains fairly clear even when prefixes or suffixes are attached to it. For example, the stem *class* keeps its form and meaning even with prefixes or suffixes, as in *subclass, classify, classifiable,* and *unclassified.*

Bound stems, those that do not occur as independent words, create more of a problem. Because they are bound, we may not realize that the words in which they appear consist of a stem with prefixes or suffixes. Even if we recognize the stem, its meaning may be unclear to us, both because it is likely to be Latin (or Greek) in origin and because the meanings of many bound stems are rather vague. For example, the bound stem *-doc-* comes from a Latin verb meaning "to teach," yet this meaning is not at all obvious in such English words as *docile, document, doctor,* or even *indoctrinate.* Finally, bound stems often change their forms when different suffixes are added. For example, a Latin stem meaning "touch" takes the form *tang-* in the words *intangible* and *tangent,* but the form *tac-* in the words *contact* and *tactile.*

Although there are thousands of bound stems, only a few hundred of them appear over and over in common words. Furthermore, these common stems tend to appear with the most common prefixes and suffixes. Many words form patterns that can be grouped and learned together. In the verb *conceive,* for example, the stem has the form *-ceive,* but in the noun *conception* the stem has the form *-cept.* This variation, though it may seem unnecessary, does at least have the advantage of being consistent; that is, once you have recognized the relationship between *conceive* and *conception,* you have also learned *receive/reception* and *deceive/deception.* We do not have space here to list the scores of such patterns that occur with bound stems. However, the examples below of the spelling patterns of verbs and related nouns with bound stems illustrate how identifying the variant forms of bound stems can help you spell not just one but several pairs of related words.

VERB	NOUN	VERB	NOUN	VERB	NOUN
ad*mit*	ad*mission*	sub*scribe*	sub*scription*	pro*pel*	pro*pulsion*
com*mit*	com*mission*	de*scribe*	de*scription*	com*pel*	com*pulsion*
re*mit*	re*mission*	in*scribe*	in*scription*	ex*pel*	ex*pulsion*
sub*mit*	sub*mission*	pre*scribe*	pre*scription*	re*pel*	re*pulsion*

EXERCISES: Prefixes and Stems

Circle the prefix of each word given below, and underline the stem. Referring to the list of prefixes in the preceding section, make a new word using one of those prefixes and the stem that you have underlined. Try to use a different prefix for each of your new words.

1. forbid	6. propose	11. inverse
2. submission	7. interject	12. postnatal
3. purport	8. subtract	13. commit
4. pertain	9. transform	14. enact
5. introduce	10. divert	

Words with Suffixes. With the exception of inflectional suffixes (see 2a), suffixes usually change a word from one part of speech to another. The pattern is normally clear and consistent for such suffixes as *-ful*, which makes an adjective out of a noun: *masterful, beautiful, thoughtful*. Once you remember that the suffix is spelled *-ful* and not *-full*, you should have no problem with this suffix.

Unfortunately, not all suffixes are as straightforward as *-ful*. When a suffix is attached to a bound form, we may not recognize it as a suffix. For example, the adjective-making suffix *-ite* is not particularly obvious in such words as *opposite, infinite,* and *erudite*. In addition, English is notorious for **functional shift,** that is, for using what was originally one part of speech as another part of speech. The word *precipitate,* for example, with the suffix *-ate,* was first used in English as a verb but today may be a noun, an adjective, or a verb. Hence we often cannot associate a particular suffix with a particular part of speech. Finally, and most troublesome of all, the same suffix may have different spellings for no reason at all other than an accident of history. There is no logical pattern behind *independent* versus *pleasant* or *falsify* versus *liquefy*. In sum, the spelling of most words with suffixes must be learned individually. There are, however, reliable rules for a few of the most common suffixes.

Words Ending in -ly. The last two letters are always *-ly, never -ley*. Add *-ly* to the word, unless the word ends in *-ll* or *-le* preceded by a consonant. If the word ends in *-ll,* add only *-y*. If the word ends in *-le* preceded by a consonant, drop the *-e,* and add *-y*.

actual/actually	WORDS IN *-LL*
adequate/adequately	full/fully
cool/coolly	dull/dully
home/homely	shrill/shrilly
sole/solely	WORDS IN CONSONANT + *-LE*
love/lovely	capable/capably
	humble/humbly
	subtle/subtly

Exception: *whole/wholly*

If the word ends in *-y,* the regular rule for changing *-y* to *-i-* before an ending applies (see 46b).

hearty/heartily   ready/readily   coy/coyly

Exceptions: *sly/slyly; wry/wryly; day/daily; gay/gayly* or *gaily*

Adjectives ending in *-ic* always take the suffix *-ally*. Many such adjectives have an alternative form in *-ical,* and thus the *-al-* can actually be considered part of the adjective.

basic/basically	fanatic(al)/fanatically
classic(al)/classically	historic(al)/historically

Exception: *public/publicly*

Words Ending in -ble. The suffix -able is used after common nouns and verbs and for newly coined adjectives. The suffix -ible is most often used with bound stems and with stems that have a corresponding noun ending in -ion.

COMMON NOUNS AND VERBS	NEWLY COINED ADJECTIVES
comfortable	patchable
fashionable	swallowable
reasonable	typable
livable	
sinkable	STEMS WITH NOUNS IN -ION
washable	corruption/corruptible
	digestion/digestible
BOUND STEMS	division/divisible
compatible	permission/permissible
edible	
incredible	
plausible	

If the stem ends in "hard" c or g, the suffix is always -able.

applicable	indefatigable
despicable	navigable

If the stem ends in "soft" -ce or -ge, -e is retained before -able but dropped before -ible.

-ABLE	-IBLE
charge/chargeable	deduce/deducible (cf. deductible)
notice/noticeable	force/forcible
place/placeable	tangible

Words Ending in -izé, -ise, or -yze. If the word is a verb, the most common ending is -ize. If the word is a noun or can be used as a noun, it ends in -ise. (Note that, in many of the words ending in -ise, the -ise is actually not a suffix but part of the stem.)

VERBS	NOUNS
apologize	compromise
characterize	demise
dramatize	disguise
emphasize	enterprise
legalize	exercise
realize	franchise
recognize	paradise
stylize	surprise

Exceptions: Two common verbs end in -yze: analyze and paralyze. A few verbs end in -ise. In all of these, the -ise is actually part of the stem of the word.

advise	apprise	rise	exorcise	despise
devise	comprise	arise	incise	surmise
improvise	reprise	uprise	advertise	
revise			chastise	
supervise				

The *z* in the endings *-ize* and *-yze* is replaced by *s* when a word ending in *-ist*, *-istic*, *-ism*, or *-is* is made from the verb.

apologize/apologist	emphasize/emphasis
dramatize/dramatist	hypnotize/hypnosis
characterize/characteristic	analyze/analysis
stylize/stylistic	*but* analyst
baptize/baptism	
criticize/criticism	

Words Ending in an *l* sound. Most adjectives end in *-al*. Nouns made from verbs usually end in *-al*. Verbs with the meaning of repeated action usually end in *-le*.

ADJECTIVES		NOUNS	VERBS	
beneficial	intellectual	approval	babble	rustle
brutal	moral	arrival	dazzle	sniffle
colloquial	occasional	denial	garble	sprinkle
controversial	personal	dismissal	mumble	startle
dual	presidential	refusal	nuzzle	tickle
ethical	principal	trial	ogle	tousle
financial	several	withdrawal	ripple	wrestle

Words Ending in *-ous*. The most common ending is *-ous*. If the ending is *-uous*, the *u* can be heard clearly in pronunciation. In words ending in *-ious*, either (1) an *e* sound can be heard in pronunciation, or (2) a preceding *c*, *t*, or *x* is pronounced as *sh*, or (3) there is a preceding "soft" *g*.

ADJECTIVES IN *-OUS*		ADJECTIVES IN *-UOUS*	
anonymous	mischievous	ambiguous	sensuous
barbarous	ridiculous	arduous	strenuous
grievous	synonymous	deciduous	vacuous
jealous	unanimous	innocuous	virtuous

ADJECTIVES IN *-IOUS*

e-sound	preceding *sh*-sound	preceding "soft" *g*
copious	conscious	prestigious
ingenious	gracious	religious
various	precious	sacrilegious
	ambitious	
	conscientious	
	fictitious	
	anxious	

When *-ous* is added to words ending in *-er*, the *e* is sometimes lost. For a few words, either spelling is acceptable.

disaster/disastrous	dextrous *or* dexterous
leper/leprous	thundrous *or* thunderous
luster/lustrous	
wonder/wondrous	
monster/monstrous	

Instead of *-ious*, some adjectives are spelled with *-eous*.

advantageous	miscellaneous
courageous	nauseous
erroneous	outrageous

Words Ending in *-ic* and *-ac*. Before a suffix beginning with *-i*, *-e*, or *-y*, add *k*.

panic/panicking/panicked

This rule applies also to *frolic, mimic, picnic, politic, shellac, traffic.*

EXERCISES: Words with Suffixes

Part A: Use the endings given in parentheses to transform these verbs into other parts of speech.

1. terrorize (-ist)	6. moralize (-istic)	11. realize (-istic)
2. modernize (-istic)	7. mesmerize (-ism)	12. organize (-ism)
3. idealize (-ism)	8. finalize (-ist)	13. paralyze (-is)
4. parenthesize (-s)	9. formalize (-ism)	14. analyze (-ist)
5. revolutionize (-ist)	10. synthesize (-is)	15. exorcise (-ism)

Part B: Circle the misspelled words in the following list and write the correct spelling for each.

1. scandel	7. mammel	13. vivacous
2. mimicing	8. councel	14. avaricous
3. advantagous	9. mendacous	15. wonderous
4. strenuous	10. vigel	16. picniced
5. channal	11. gorgous	17. fossel
6. marvle	12. kennal	18. prestigous

46e VARIANT SPELLINGS

Many words have two (or even more) acceptable spellings. This is especially true of words borrowed from languages that do not use the Latin alphabet. For example, the *Random House College Dictionary* lists as alternatives of the Arabic word *caliph* the spellings *calif, kalif,* and *khalif;* other dictionaries list still other alternatives. More familiar words usually have no more than two alternative spellings (*usable/useable; sulfur/sulphur; controller/comptroller; labeled/labelled; luster/lustre*).

The first spelling listed in the dictionary is either the most common spelling or is as common as subsequent spellings. Unless your instructor advises you differently, use the most common spelling. If you do use a variant spelling, use it consistently throughout an entire paper.

diction

d

"In the beginning was the word. . . ." And words are truly the beginning of language. Long before children speak in sentences, they use words to communicate with others. When we are learning a foreign language, we ask, not "What is the grammar of this?" but "What is the word for this?" Words are the fundamental unit of human communication; they are our way of interpreting our experience in the world and of conveying this experience to others.

The words we use tell our audience a great deal about us: our education, our attitudes, our ways of thinking, our sensitivity, even our age. We respond differently to different words, primarily because of the meanings we associate with those words, but also because words in and of themselves can delight or dismay. For example, *gazebo* is to me a very funny word and amuses me in a way that *summerhouse* does not. I find *espadrilles* much more elegant than *sandals*, *drunk* a more powerful word than *inebriated*, *gossamer* a happier word than *cobweb*.

Our **vocabulary** is the total number of words we know; all of us have vocabularies of many thousands of words. **Diction** is the choices we make from this vocabulary in order to express ourselves. Choice is the distinguishing feature of diction. Earlier sections of this handbook have concentrated on aspects of language about which writers have little choice—grammar, punctuation, mechanics, and spelling. The spelling of a word, for instance, is either correct or incorrect, and that's all there is to it. On the other hand, while the words we select are sometimes just plain wrong, more often they are not completely wrong; rather, they are fuzzy, or tired, or inadequate, or slightly off-center. Hence we do not speak of "standard" diction the way we speak of "standard" grammar. Instead, we speak of appropriate diction, exact diction, economical diction, and fresh diction.

Writers attain pleasing diction, not by memorizing dictionaries, but by wide reading, by careful attention to words, and by a love and respect for words. Nonetheless, your dictionary is an invaluable tool for improving your diction. Many people are not aware of how much guidance and information about words dictionaries provide. Although they know they must use a dictionary to check the spelling and meaning of words, they often do not realize that dictionaries give the histories of words, distinguish between closely related words, and even provide a great deal of fascinating information about the world. From a dictionary, you can learn that *pingpong* was originally a trade name, that *gallop* and *wallop* come from the same source, or that the violet is the state flower of Wisconsin. Dictionaries are both informative and fun. Time spent browsing through a good college dictionary is time well spent.

47 CHOOSING THE RIGHT WORDS

Whether we are speaking or writing, we use words to convey our message. But choosing the right word is more crucial in writing than in speech. When we speak to a live audience, we can use gestures, facial expressions, tone of voice, and often the physical setting itself to clarify our meaning. If a friend and I were restoring a piece of old furniture, I might say, with perfect clarity for that particular situation, "Hand me that curvy thing." On the other hand, if I were writing instructions on how to refinish wood, I could not say, "For finishing details, you will need a curvy thing." Instead, I would have to be much more precise and say something like "For finishing details, you will need a bent riffler." When our audience is present, sometimes no words at all are needed: a raised hand or a raised eyebrow can often communicate more effectively than a dozen words. But when we write, we have nothing to point to, so we must use words, and we must choose the words more carefully than we usually do in speech.

Which words? There are thousands of words to choose from. English has a huge vocabulary, the largest of any language in the world. Just to express the notion of "lack of size of physical objects relative to other physical objects of the same class," we have

> small, little, petite, runty, wee, diminutive, tiny, puny, elfin, minuscule, itsy-bitsy, stunted, minute, shrimpy, Lilliputian, microscopic, minikin, pigmy, infinitesimal

All of these words mean "not big, not large," but they are not interchangeable. The choice you make should depend on the context. In the context of describing a person, for example, you could say *tiny* but not *minute.* If you wanted to convey a favorable impression, you could say *diminutive, elfin,* or *petite* but not *stunted, runty, shrimpy,* or *puny.* You can apply the word *small* to almost any object, but you cannot use the word *elfin* to describe a potato, a pickup truck, or a prism. If you were writing a research paper on insects, you could describe some insects as *microscopic* but not as *itsy-bitsy.*

The right word at one time or place may not be the right word at another time or place. For example, a *puny* nobleman in earlier centuries was inferior in rank, but a *puny* nobleman today is undersized. Or, in Scotland today, you can call a young child a *wee* boy, but in America, *wee* sounds affected or humorous. Indeed, the very decision to use any word meaning "not big" depends on what you are describing and the total context in which you are describing it: A small meal for a football player is not a small meal for a dieter; a small lake is a very large puddle.

The use of words, or **diction,** is more subtle than just "good" words and "bad" words; the same word may be good in one context and bad in another. For example, the words you use to describe your reaction to a low grade on an examination will differ, depending on whether you are talking to your roommate or to your instructor. It is completely appropriate to tell your roommate that you are really *ripped* about that grade and to tell your instructor that you are *distressed* about that grade. It is less appropriate to tell your roommate that you are *distressed* and your instructor that you are *ripped*.

Thus, the definition of the "right" word is very complex. It depends on the medium (speech or writing), the topic, the level of formality, the audience, and even the time and the place. All of this may seem very confusing, and you may feel that it is impossible to keep track of so many different variables simultaneously. Don't despair. As a native speaker of English, you already know intuitively a great deal about choosing the right words. If you do have occasional problems with diction, they probably involve appropriateness, exactness, economy, or freshness.

47a USING APPROPRIATE WORDS / app

Appropriate means "suitable for the occasion." There are various types of appropriateness: grammatical appropriateness, geographic appropriateness, temporal appropriateness, and stylistic appropriateness.

Grammatical Appropriateness. What is grammatically appropriate in speech is not always appropriate in writing. For example, many, perhaps most, well-educated speakers regularly use *like* as a conjunction.

It seemed <u>like</u> we would never be finished.

But, in writing, *like* is not acceptable as a conjunction before a clause: *as if* should be used instead.

It seemed <u>as if</u> we would never be finished.

See sections 1–23 for extensive discussions of grammatical appropriateness in writing.

Geographic Appropriateness. Writing is geographically appropriate when the words used are suitable for, and familiar to, the audience. If you were writing in Britain for a British audience, for example, you would use the British term *lift* instead of the American term *elevator*. In America, the term *lift* would be inappropriate.

Fortunately, geographic appropriateness is rarely a serious problem for the American writer, because written English in the United States is highly homogeneous. Regional differences in pronunciation are hidden by our uniform spelling system. There are a few differences in acceptable grammar from one part of the country to another; for example, *wait on* (rather than *wait for*) is acceptable in the meaning "await" in the Midwest but not in the East. Avoid such regionalisms if you are aware of them; if you are not aware of them, chances are good that your audience will not be aware of them either.

Differences in vocabulary are somewhat more extensive. For example, what is a *green pepper* in most of the United States is called a *mango* in parts of the Midwest; this difference could create a misunderstanding because, to many Americans, a *mango* is a large, peach-like fruit. Similarly, *tonic* is a general term for carbonated beverages in much of New England but a specific term for quinine water in the rest of the country. Luckily for the writer, most regional differences in vocabulary involve homely, everyday items such as food products and farm implements, items that are seldom mentioned in essays.

Temporal Appropriateness.   Temporal appropriateness means using words appropriate both to the time *at* which one is writing and to the time *about* which one is writing. To ensure that your writing is temporally appropriate, you should avoid archaisms, obsolete words, and anachronisms.

Archaisms are words or constructions no longer in general use and normally found only in old texts, religious works, and poetry. For example, *forsooth*, an adverb meaning "indeed," is an archaism. **Obsolete words** are words that have passed out of use entirely and are not used even in special contexts: *gnarl* as a synonym for "snarl, growl" is obsolete. Although some writers do employ them for humorous purposes, archaisms and obsolete words usually strike the reader as affected or even downright ridiculous. Avoid them.

Anachronisms are errors that place persons, events, objects, or customs out of their proper time. Thus, anachronisms are words that are inappropriate for the time about which one is writing. To say that Hamlet "had been dating Ophelia" is an anachronism because dating is a twentieth-century social institution completely unknown in Shakespeare's—or Hamlet's—day. Similarly, although Queen Elizabeth II still has attendants, calling them *courtiers* is anachronistic because the former conventions of royal courts are not observed today. Unless you have an excellent sense of history, you will not always be certain whether a word or expression is anachronistic. You can, however, avoid such obvious anachronisms as calling a seventeenth-century person who cares for someone else's child a *baby-sitter*.

Stylistic Appropriateness.   Stylistic appropriateness in general means writing in a manner that is suitable for both the subject matter and the audience. Stylistic appropriateness involves sentence structure as well as diction. But as sentence structure is discussed elsewhere (see 49), we will concentrate here on choice of words. There are many terms that refer to various aspects of stylistic appropriateness, some of them overlapping, some of them often misunderstood, some of them with more than one meaning. A few definitions may be helpful.

1. **Idiom.** The term **idiom** has several slightly different meanings. In one use, *idiom* means simply the normal language of a particular area or group of people. More often the term *idiom* is used to designate accepted phrases that do not follow the regular patterns of the language or whose meanings cannot be predicted from the meanings of the separate words of which they are composed. For example,

give someone a hand is an idiom because it does not mean that you remove your hand and give it away. *Stand a chance* is an idiom because *stand* normally means "be in an upright position" and does not take a direct object.

The adjective *idiomatic* can have a slightly different meaning from the noun *idiom;* it refers simply to the usual and grammatical way of expressing things. For example, both *I bought my dog a collar* and *I bought a collar for my dog* are idiomatic, whereas *I bought for my dog a collar* is unidiomatic because English normally does not put the prepositional phrase that substitutes for an indirect object before the direct object. Good writing may or may not use many idioms, but it is always idiomatic.

2. **Slang. Slang** is the most casual type of vocabulary. It may consist of coined words (*twerp* for "silly person") or of extended meanings of existing words or phrases (*on the rocks* for "moving toward an unhappy ending"). Slang almost always expresses an irreverent or exaggerated attitude toward the subject matter. Most slang expressions have a short life: a few years ago, *heavy* was an all-purpose expression of approval, but today it is less often heard. Effectively handled, slang adds vividness to your writing, but slang should never be used only because you cannot immediately recall a more formal word. If you use slang in writing, use it deliberately, not carelessly or accidentally.

The word *slang* also sometimes refers to the specialized vocabularies of particular occupations or social groups. For example, in the terminology of computer scientists, a computer *crashes* when it ceases operating because of a malfunction, and a *loop* is a sequence of repeated steps. In the language of printers, a *widow* is a single incomplete line of type ending a paragraph at the top of a page, and *to put to bed* is to lock printing plates into place and put them on a printing press. Such specialized vocabulary may also be called **technical terminology** (if one approves of it), **jargon** (if one feels neutral about it), or **cant** (if one disapproves of it). Occupational slang is longer-lived than more generally used slang.

3. **Formal English. Formal English** is the language in its Sunday best. It is the language of scholarly and technical writing, found in academic journals, textbooks, some essays, and many research papers and themes. In speech, formal English is used for sermons and public addresses. It is dignified, precise, serious, and attempts to be highly objective. It may use many polysyllabic words, but it does not have to; indeed, the best formal English avoids overuse of big words. The term *formal English* is a stylistic label, not a value judgment: there can be bad formal English as well as good formal English.

FORMAL ENGLISH

The great and simple appeal of fiction is that it enables us to share imaginatively in the fortunes of these created beings [fictional characters] without paying the price in time or defeat for their triumphs and frustrations. One moves with them in lands where one has never been, experiences loves one has never known. And this entrance into lives wider and more various than our own in turn enables us more nicely to appreciate and more intensely to live the lives we do know. It is impossible to say how much novelists teach us to look at our fellow beings, at "their tragic divining of life upon their ways."

—Irwin Edman, *ARTS AND THE MAN*

Typical characteristics of formal English illustrated by the preceding passage include the following:

a. Avoidance of the first-person singular (*I, me*) and the second person (*you*) and use of the more impersonal first-person plural (*we, us*) and *one* (*One moves with them. . . .* rather than *You move with them. . . .*)

b. Avoidance of contractions (*It is impossible. . . .* rather than *It's impossible. . . .*)

c. Avoidance of colloquial terms

d. Precise and conservative use of words (The author uses *nicely* in its more formal meaning of "accurately, precisely," as opposed to its more frequently heard meaning of "pleasantly." He uses *various* in its less common meaning of "having different qualities" rather than in its more familiar meaning of "several, many.")

e. Inclusion of learned quotations

f. Fairly long and carefully constructed sentences, often with parallelism

The following passage illustrates the formal English of scientific writing.

FORMAL ENGLISH

Nutrient procurement by animals usually involves much more activity than it does in plants. Animals must often resort to elaborate methods of locating and trapping their food. Their incredibly varied feeding habits may be classified in any number of ways. We have already mentioned one possible classification, which distinguishes carnivores, herbivores, and omnivores, depending on whether the diet consists primarily of animals, plants, or both. Another possible criterion for classification is the size of the food. Thus we can recognize microphagous feeders, which strain microscopic organic materials from the surrounding water by an array of cilia, bristles, legs, nets, etc. And we can recognize macrophagous feeders, which subdivide larger masses of food by teeth, jaws, pincers, or gizzards, or solely by the action of enzymes.

—William T. Keeton, *BIOLOGICAL SCIENCE*

Like Edman, this author avoids the use of *I* and *you* and uses no contractions or colloquial expressions. The vocabulary includes a number of technical words from Latin and Greek, not because the author is trying to parade his learning, but because he wants to be as specific and precise as possible. For example, the term *microphagous*, imposing as it may look, is actually much more economical than *feeding on small particles*. Similarly, *nutrient* is more precise than *food*. Where scientific exactness is not essential, the author uses familiar words such as *trapping, size, dirt*, and *legs*.

4. Informal English. Informal English is more casual and usually more subjective than formal English. The writer is often more concerned about conveying an overall impression than about absolute, impersonal precision. Informal English is typically the language of magazine articles, newspaper editorials, many essays, and well-written personal letters. In speech, it is the language of most classroom lectures.

INFORMAL ENGLISH

In the primitive days of 1959, when I worked at a playground in Flushing, Queens, and carried Faulkner in my pocket, lived on "The Adventures of Augie March" and "The Viking Portable James Joyce," I wouldn't have considered touching any women writers. Who were Doris Lessing and Muriel Spark? I was both an idiot and a snob. Then I discovered something in a barrel outside a Fourth Avenue book shop. It was an old reviewer's copy of "The Little Disturbances of Man." I was witless for the next 24 hours.   —Jerome Charyn, Review of *MARA* by Tova Reich,
in *The New York Times Book Review*

Like the passage of formal English from Edman, this selection concerns literature, but it is a more casual discussion. The author uses the first-person singular (*I*) and contractions (*I wouldn't have considered*). Although there are no words or phrases that are exclusively informal, a number of the words are used less precisely than they would be in formal English. In particular, the author tends to exaggerate: strictly speaking, he was of course not an *idiot* nor was he ever *witless*. In the first sentence, *primitive* is an exaggerated term for a period less than twenty years before. Sentences are shorter and looser in construction than in the corresponding passage of formal English.

Like the selection of formal English by Keeton, the subject of the next passage is food. But it is a highly subjective and personal discussion.

INFORMAL ENGLISH

"A cold potato at midnight . . ." [about] the turn of our century, a Midwestern writer put this haunting phrase in one of her forgotten essays, although I can find no reference to it. I remember it clearly from when I first heard it in about 1940. She was lonely. She felt comforted, or perhaps merely revived, when she could sneak down to the silent family kitchen and pull out a boiled potato from a bowl of them in the icebox. As I see it now, she ate it standing up in the shadows, without salt, but voluptuously, like a cat taking one mouseling from a nest and leaving the rest to fatten for another night.   —M. F. K. Fisher, *"The Midnight Egg And
Other Revivers," Bon Appétit*

Typical of informal English are the first-person singular and the colloquial expressions such as *sneak down* and *pull out*. The simile at the end of the paragraph (*like a cat taking one mouseling . . .*) is intended, not to analyze or classify the experience in any objective sense, but to create a mood.

5. **Colloquial English. Colloquial English** is natural conversational English, our everyday speech. It is not substandard or disreputable in any way. Indeed, it would be highly inappropriate to use formal English in discussing, say, your vacation plans with a friend. It is, however, the language of speech and not of writing, and many words and phrases that are completely acceptable in speech are not suitable in most types of writing. Examples include such "fillers" as *you know* and *I mean* or vague classifiers such as *kind of* and *sort of.* Other colloquialisms include *funny* in the meaning of "strange," *guy* in the meaning of "man or person," and *dumb* in the meaning of "stupid."

Closely related to the term *colloquial* is the term **vernacular,** which refers to the spoken as opposed to the written language. The term dates from times when all serious writing was done in Latin but when people usually spoke other languages such as English, French, or German. Since people almost never write in Latin today, *vernacular* has come to mean a common term for which there is a corresponding technical term. For example, *buttercup* is the vernacular equivalent of *Ranunculus acris,* and *leprosy* is the vernacular term for *Hansen's disease.*

The three levels of formal English, informal English, and colloquial English form a continuum; there is no sharp dividing line between formal and informal English or between informal and colloquial English. The vocabularies of all three levels overlap to a large extent. Most of the words we know and use are appropriate for all three levels.

6. **College Writing.** What is the appropriate stylistic level for college writing? Appropriateness depends on what you are writing about and the audience for whom you are writing. In general, most college writing is expected to range between high-informal and low-formal. Use colloquialisms sparingly and only when a more neutral word is not available. Avoid slang except for special purposes such as dialogue and humor. Even in dialogue, be sure that the slang is suitable for the person to whom it is attributed. Thus, do not put phrases such as "Yeah, that really bugs me" into the mouth of a judge in a courtroom. Similarly, slang expressions are usually out of place in formal writing.

| INAPPROPRIATE | Dr. Wickens and two other members of the panel have submitted a report that is really a gasser. |
| IMPROVED | Dr. Wickens and two other members of the panel have submitted an extraordinary report. |

Be particularly careful to avoid careless inconsistency of diction, that is, mixing words that clearly belong to extreme ends of the stylistic spectrum. For example, the word *sibling* is appropriate only for formal, technical English, but the words *brother* and *sister* are appropriate at all levels. If you were writing a term paper on the sociology of family life, it might be appropriate to say, "Disputes among siblings are not uncommon." But if you were writing a brief paper about an incident in your childhood, it would be inappropriate to say, "When I was little, I often fought with my female sibling."

The jarring effect of inconsistency of diction is well illustrated in the following passage.

> One of my last runs during the 1974–75 season was a lulu. After the industry trade shows in Las Vegas, a bunch of us had gone over to Sun Valley for the Lange Cup, and naturally spent most of the time on the Warm Springs side of Baldy, where the races were held. Then one morning, Ray Pinella, a retailer from Pennsylvania, challenged me to ski with him on the River Run side.
>
> Ray and I had had our differences over ski safety, aired somewhat acrimoniously at ASTM meetings, and I suspect he wanted to ski me into the turf as another way of proving I didn't know beans about safe shop practices.
>
> —Al Greenberg, "Sun Valley: The Compleat Resort," Skiing

The author obviously intends to establish a casual tone and uses such occupational slang as *runs* and *ski me into the turf* in addition to other general slang expressions and colloquialisms like *lulu, a bunch of us,* and *didn't know beans about.* Some would argue that these terms are overly slangy, even for an extremely casual article. But in the first sentence of the second paragraph, the author abruptly inserts the phrase *aired somewhat acrimoniously,* a highly formal way of saying that they had had some big fights. This sudden and apparently unmotivated shift in the stylistic level of the passage can be as disturbing to a reader as the heavy use of slang.

EXERCISES: Using Appropriate Words

Part A: In the following sentences, underline the words and phrases that would be inappropriate in formal written English. Classify each inappropriate word by the letter that corresponds to the violation of formal English that applies.

    A. Grammatically inappropriate
    B. Archaic or anachronistic
    C. Too informal (excluding slang but including such characteristics as the use of the first and second person pronouns, contractions, and imprecise words)
    D. Unidiomatic
    E. Slang
    F. Colloquial (excluding D and E)

1. One of the most famous tapestries in the world is the Bayeux Tapestry, which is concocted of red, green, blue, and yellow wool on white canvas. The tapestry illustrates how in 1066 William the Conqueror hustled over from France, lowered the boom on Harold, and grabbed the English throne for himself. William's wife, Matilda, may have whipped up the tapestry herself as a gift to Odo, the bishop of Bayeux, to spruce up the cathedral there.

2. Although in 1869 in the United States Susan B. Anthony and Elisabeth Stanton had got the women's suffrage movement off the ground, it was not until 1920, when the pressures of World War I had booted many women into public positions of authority, that the Nineteenth Amendment became law, guaranteeing all women a slice of the political pie.

3. The Prohibition movement in the United States didn't really get rolling until the founding of the Prohibition party in 1869. It was not until 1920, however,

that Prohibition made the entire United States as dry as a bone through the Eighteenth Amendment to the Constitution, an amendment that put the cap on erstwhile congressional acts to prohibit the manufacture, shipment, and sale of beer, wine, and liquor. In 1933, on the other hand, when an amendment to put the kibosh on Prohibition was introduced, the necessary thirty-six states ratified it quick as a wink, taking less than a year.

4. Al Smith, whom Franklin D. Roosevelt gave the moniker the "Happy Warrior" to, ran into a brick wall in his 1928 race for the United States presidency, particularly in the rural South, because he opposed Prohibition and because he was Catholic. A grade-school dropout, he hung in there and pulled himself up by his bootstraps from his job as a clerk in a New York City fish market to the governorship of New York, a position which he held for four terms before he hit the jackpot as the Democratic party's nominee for president.

Part B: Choose one of the following general topics and write two or three good sentences about it in (1) colloquial English, (2) informal English, and (3) formal English.

EXAMPLE: One sentence at each stylistic level on the topic of eye and hair color.

COLLOQUIAL: You're stuck with the eye color your old man and your old lady gave you, but the blah color of your hair is something you don't have to put up with.

INFORMAL: We can't do much about the color of our eyes, but we can change the color of our hair if we don't like it.

FORMAL: Heredity determines both the color of one's eyes and the color of one's hair. However, although it is difficult to change the color of one's eyes, it is relatively easy to alter the color of one's hair.

1. Embarrassment: How to Cope
2. The Computer: Friend or Foe?
3. Coincidence Shrinks the World
4. "You Cannot Judge a Book by Its Cover"
5. Spring: Herald of Hope

47b USING EXACT WORDS / exac

Exact means "accurate, precise, correct, not approximate." Exactness in writing means selecting words with the proper denotations and connotations. It also implies the proper use of abstract and concrete words and of general and specific words.

Denotation and Connotation. Words have both denotations and connotations. The **denotation** of a word is what it refers to, its direct, literal meaning, its dictionary meaning. The **connotation** of a word is its emotional meaning, the associations we make with that word.

Improper denotations can result either from confusion of similar referents (the things words refer to) or from confusion of similar words. If you speak of *bacteria* as *viruses,* you have confused the referents of these words: bacteria are one-celled microorganisms, and viruses are submicroscopic protein molecules. On the other hand, if you call a *diary* a *dairy*, you have confused the two words; you know perfectly well the difference between the referents, that is, between a written record of events and a place where milk and milk products are kept. A ridiculous confusion of similar words is called a **malapropism**.

Ida Tarbell wrote about the business practices of American typhoons.

This sentence contains a malapropism because *typhoons* means "tropical cyclones or hurricanes." The writer should have used the word *tycoons*, meaning "wealthy and powerful business people." Avoid wrong denotations and malapropisms by checking your dictionary for the definitions of words with which you are not thoroughly comfortable and familiar.

The connotations of a word are its implications, the meanings that the word suggests beyond its literal, dictionary meaning. For example, the denotations of the words *authoritative* and *dictatorial* are similar; some dictionaries even list one as a synonym of the other. The connotations, however, are not the same. People who are *authoritative* are often admired, but people who are *dictatorial* are not.

The connotations of words may vary along a number of dimensions, for example, from "colorful" to "colorless," from "weak" to "strong," from "optimistic" to "pessimistic," or from "interesting" to "boring." Perhaps the most common dimension is from "favorable" to "unfavorable."

FAVORABLE	NEUTRAL	UNFAVORABLE
famous	well-known	notorious
nourishing	rich	fattening
summer home	cottage	shack
aroma	smell	stench

Connotations may be conveyed by all parts of speech. The sentence *Betsy is lively and strong-willed* uses adjectives to convey a favorable connotation, whereas the sentence *Betsy is a brat* uses a single noun to convey a correspondingly unfavorable connotation. In the sentence *Grant was supposedly a great general*, the adverb *supposedly* suggests that Grant was not, in fact, a great general. Unfavorable connotations are often created by using colloquial or slang expressions with reference to a serious subject: *Economists are always fooling around with figures* has unfavorable connotations because of the colloquial verb phrase *fooling around with*. Changing this to *working with* creates a neutral connotation: *Economists are always working with figures*.

Improper and unintended connotations in writing often result from carelessness. Writers cannot easily think of the exact words they want, so they use words with similar denotations but different connotations. If you are uncertain of the connotations of a word you want to use, check your dictionary. Sometimes words are specifically labeled as favorable or unfavorable. More often, you can get a general idea of the connotations of a word from the synonyms used to define it. (See also 48c.)

EXERCISES: Denotation and Connotation

For each of the following relatively neutral words, list another word or phrase that has a similar denotation but an unfavorable connotation. Then list a word that has a similar denotation but a favorable connotation

EXAMPLE:	NEUTRAL	legislator
	UNFAVORABLE	politician
	FAVORABLE	statesman

1. thin		4. thrifty		7. unusual	
2. to talk		5. old		8. steadfast	
3. simplicity		6. criticism		9. argument	

Euphemism. A **euphemism** is a word or phrase with pleasant or neutral connotations that is used to avoid a word with distasteful connotations. Euphemisms often reflect a society's fears and feelings of guilt. In America today, the three subjects about which most euphemisms have developed are death, bodily functions and malfunctions, and social problems. The following list enumerates only a few common euphemisms; you can easily add to the list. As a rule, euphemisms should be avoided in college writing.

AREA	EUPHEMISM	MEANING
death	pass away	die
	funeral director	undertaker
	remains	corpse
	memorial park	burial ground
bodily functions or malfunctions	dentures	false teeth
	bathroom tissue	toilet paper
	matter	pus
	irregularity	constipation
social problems	inner city	slum
	correctional officer	prison guard
	senior citizens	old people
	poorly motivated	lazy

Doublespeak. **Doublespeak** is a kind of euphemism that is used to cover up one's own faults and to deceive others. A fairly recent example of doublespeak is "That statement is no longer operative," meaning "I lied to you before." Military and governmental spokespersons use doublespeak when they, for example, call bombs designed to kill people "antipersonnel devices." Manufacturers who label used wool as "reconstituted fibers" are doublespeaking. Euphemisms have at least the marginal justification that they are often used to avoid offending others: after all, some people really are embarrassed by the word *toilet* and prefer to hear *lavatory* or *bathroom*. But there is no excuse for doublespeak.

EXERCISES: Euphemism and Doublespeak

Underline all examples of euphemism and doublespeak in the following sentences. Rewrite each sentence to eliminate them.

1. Because his family was of a low socioeconomic profile, Sam qualified for several substantial grants for college.

2. "It's your decision," the boss told his disgruntled employee. "Either you will accept the downward adjustment in your salary or the duration of your relationship with this company will be sharply curtailed."

3. When we went into the powder room, Addie said that dancing so vigorously had given her underarm wetness.

4. Many of the youthful offenders in that neighborhood had grown up in broken homes, but most had lived in state-operated children's homes.

5. The general announced that prisoners who did not willingly participate in the reeducation process would be terminated at once.

Slanting.   The conscious use throughout a piece of writing of words with particularly favorable or unfavorable connotations is called **slanting** or **slanted writing.**

> Nixon is a man of some intelligence—not of a high order, but enough to manage his survival. One would suppose that from his experience at the center of so many storms he could provide some kind of insight into the political process in his time. But there is nothing worthy of being called an idea in this four-pound ego trip. Nixon is incapable of reflection. He can't stand back and take a hard look at anything or anybody, least of all himself. . . . As for truth, who knows? When he is scoring against others, he relies heavily on his diaries. They seem a bit too pat, too accurate in prophecy.
> —Richard Rovere, Review of *RN: THE MEMOIRS OF RICHARD NIXON*,
> *The New Yorker*

One does not have to admire Richard Nixon to realize that Rovere has attacked him in this passage but has given almost no real information about Nixon's book. For example, the phrase *to manage his survival* is heavily slanted because, after all, even insects have enough intelligence to manage their own survival. The description of the book as a *four-pound ego trip* is also deliberately insulting. Perhaps the best demonstration of the slanting in this review is a rewritten version with essentially the same denotations but slanted as favorably as Rovere's review is slanted unfavorably.

> Nixon is not one of your eggheads; he is a man of practical intelligence. Although he has been at the center of many storms, he does not waste time philosophizing about the political process in his day. His book is not full of dreary abstract theorizing, nor does he pass judgment on himself or on others. No one can, of course, know the truth, but Nixon does use diaries to substantiate his statements. These diaries are highly precise and accurate in their prophecies.

Absolute objectivity in writing is impossible—and not even necessarily desirable. But deliberate slanting is irresponsible. Further, it is often so annoying that the reader rejects completely the author's point of view.

EXERCISES: Slanting

Read the following opinionated selections carefully. Underline the figures of speech and words that slant each selection. For each identified figure of speech or heavily connotative word, substitute one of your own with the opposite connotation.

1. Educational television has had two crosses to bear, its dedicated supporters and its dedicated foes. Frantic overselling of television as a pedagogical panacea merely stiffened the backs of those who view any outside source of instruction as a threat to education's workhorse, the teacher. But for several reasons, not the least of them the modern child's early conditioning, educational television today is closer than ever to defeating its opposition. Changes in technology almost assure its victory.

   The enemies of Instructional Television (ITV) march in a mixed army of diverse interests and views. Among intellectuals, hostility to the "boob tube" is an article of faith, and teachers are, or pretend to be, intellectuals. Some teachers also see ITV as a threat to their job security, and such fears were bolstered by the medium's early supporters, who portrayed the screen as a replacement for live instruction.

   A mixed bag of psychologists and reformers seized on overindulgence in TV to explain all the youth troubles they could not cure. They like to say, as did nearly half of all educators in a recent survey, that "children watch enough TV at home; they don't need to watch more in school."

   —Fred M. Hechinger, *"Learning On The Tube
   Has Finally Arrived," The New York Times*

2. The peculiar inertness of Axelrod's book stems from its refusal to face up to any of these questions. Lip service is paid, but in superficial ways, to Lowell's compositional powers. Imagery is doggedly pursued. Absurd ambiguities are "found" where none exist. The semblance of literary criticism is maintained while, to my mind, all that is essential goes unremarked.

   —Helen Vendler, Review of *PUDDING STONE*
   by Steven Gould Axelrod in *The New York Review of Books*

Concrete, Abstract, General, and Specific Words.   **Concrete** words refer to tangible, material things that can be experienced with the senses. **Abstract** words refer to qualities or conditions rather than to specific objects or examples. **General** words refer to entire groups or classes; **specific** words refer to explicit, particular, limited examples of a group or class. Abstract words are often general but are not necessarily so. Similarly, concrete words may be either general or specific.

ABSTRACT AND GENERAL	old age	authority	amusement
ABSTRACT AND SPECIFIC	senility	dictatorship	the game of football
CONCRETE AND GENERAL	old people	rulers	football games
CONCRETE AND SPECIFIC	my grand-father	Czar Nicholas I	the Indiana-Purdue game today

One of the chief causes of vagueness in diction is the overuse of abstract and general words. It is a good practice, therefore, to select concrete words and examples whenever possible. This is not to say that you should never use abstract or general words: effective writing employs both abstract and concrete words and both general and specific words. Abstract and general words are often essential for introducing a topic and for summarizing. A problem arises, not because abstract and general words have no meaning, but rather because they have too much meaning or too many meanings. Further, abstract and general words often mean different things to different people. Hence, when using abstract and general words, be sure you make your intended meaning clear to your reader by defining the words or by giving concrete and specific illustrations.

General words are needed in classification and definition. We could not classify a *zebra* without mentioning that it is an *animal* or define *mauve* without noting that it is a *color*. Even in description and narration, general words are occasionally as suitable as specific words. For example, if you were describing your experiences in obtaining a driver's license, it would be appropriate to say, "After having my picture taken, I *went* upstairs to pay the fee." Whether you sauntered or walked briskly or stumbled up the stairs or took the elevator is irrelevant to the main point of your story. The general verb *go* is all that is required if the focus of your narration is not your physical motions but the process of getting a license.

On the other hand, when you are discussing or describing something crucial to your central topic, be as specific as possible.

OVERLY GENERAL

The White Mountains, although not especially high, are very dangerous because the weather is severe and unpredictable, because there are high winds above tree line, and because the area is heavily wooded. For these reasons, the mountains are used as a training ground for mountaineers.

MORE SPECIFIC

The tallest peak in the White Mountains, Mount Washington, is only 6,288 feet high, and most of the peaks are under 5,000 feet. Yet brilliant sunshine can suddenly change to freezing fog, snow has fallen in every month of the year, and the highest wind velocity ever recorded on earth—231 m.p.h.—was recorded on top of Mount Washington. Dense evergreen forests make bushwhacking extremely difficult and perilous. The U.S. government trains its Antarctic crews in the White Mountains, and Rocky Mountain rescue teams often learn their profession here.

The first paragraph is not inaccurate, but it lacks interest and conveys little real information because it is too general. The second paragraph replaces the general *not especially high* with specific figures. The first paragraph's description of the weather as *severe and unpredictable* is so unspecific that it could apply just as well to the Mojave Desert as to the White Mountains; the second paragraph gives specific examples of the severity and unpredictability. Instead of the first paragraph's *heavily wooded,* the second paragraph states what kind of woods there are (*evergreen forests*) and then explains why they are dangerous. The reader is not likely to be impressed by the final sentence of the first paragraph but should be highly impressed by the final sentence of the second paragraph, which explicitly puts the White Mountains into the same category as Antarctica and the Rocky Mountains.

Abstract words are also an essential part of language, but writing about abstractions is full of pitfalls if you do not define the abstract words. For example, consider the question, "Is faith in democracy justified?" This short question contains two dangerous abstract words, *faith* and *democracy.* What does *faith* mean? A dictionary will tell you that it means "unquestioning belief; belief that is not based on proof." Do you want to accept any form of government unquestioningly? Do you assume that democracy has no faults? Are you willing to accept democracy without any consideration of the alternatives? Will you demand no proof, no evidence of the superiority of democracy?

What does *democracy* mean? Again, a dictionary will inform you that it means "government by the people, either directly or through elected representatives." By this definition, the Soviet Union is a democracy because the governing officials are elected by the people. Indeed, a far higher percentage of the people vote for their representatives in the Soviet Union than in the United States. Does this mean that the Soviet Union has "more" democracy than the United States? Many of the restrictions and controls to which we are subject are placed upon us by officials who are not elected—by regulatory agencies, by judges, by police. Do we then not have a democracy after all? This brief example illustrates another problem with abstractions: dictionary definitions often do not capture the entire meaning of abstract words.

In summary, good writing requires both abstract and concrete words and both general and specific words. But do not try to hide fuzzy ideas behind all-purpose abstract words, and do not use general words as a substitute for specific information.

EXERCISES: Concrete, Abstract, General, and Specific Words

Each of the following sentences is dull because the language is too abstract and general. Rewrite each, substituting concrete, specific information for the generalities and abstractions.

1. The day was typical of early spring: the birds were singing, the grass was green, a breeze was blowing, and everything seemed fresh and new.

2. The restaurant was ugly on both the outside and the inside, and the food that we ordered was just like the surroundings—poor.

3. Very unattractive physically, Professor Adamson was equally unattractive as a lecturer because of his voice and mannerisms.

4. Seeing the Grand Canyon for the first time is really impressive because of its great size, lovely colors, and varied terrain.

47c USING WORDS ECONOMICALLY / econ

Economical means "thrifty, sparing, frugal, avoiding waste or extravagance." Economical writing is concise and uses as few words as possible to convey its message clearly. Uneconomical writing is repetitious and verbose. To keep your writing economical, do not use more words than you need, and do not use big complicated words when little, simple words can say the same thing.

Deadwood. Unnecessary words are called **deadwood.** Deadwood is insidious; it can creep in and take over entire sentences and paragraphs without the writer's being aware of its presence. To combat deadwood, reread your first drafts, eliminating every word or phrase that does not contribute something essential.

> In my opinion, ~~I think that~~ clairvoyance, ~~which is~~ the perception of physical events ~~that take place~~ without the use of the five senses ~~of sight, hearing, smell, taste, or touch,~~ ~~actually exists because it~~ has been well demonstrated ~~as a fact~~ by ~~scientific~~ psychological research.

In the sentence above, *I think that* is unnecessary because it merely repeats the meaning of *In my opinion.* The relative pronoun *which* and the verb *is* can be omitted because the word *perception* contains their meaning. Everyone knows what the five senses are, so it is unnecessary to specify them. The words *actually exists because it* add nothing that is not implied by the following verb phrase. *As a fact* can be omitted because the meaning is implied by *demonstrated.* *Scientific* can be eliminated because psychological research is usually scientific. Some would argue that even the introductory phrase *In my opinion* should be deleted. Its inclusion is justified here because it tells the reader that the writer realizes that there are differences of opinion on the subject.

When the deadwood is eliminated, the sentence is actually clearer than the original, yet contains fewer than half the words.

> In my opinion, clairvoyance, the perception of physical events without the use of the five senses, has been well demonstrated by psychological research.

One common source of deadwood is the overuse of the expletives *there* and *it.* Examine all sentences and clauses beginning with these words to see if rewriting can eliminate them without changing your intended meaning and emphasis.

DEADWOOD	It is lamentable that Hamlet is so indecisive.
IMPROVED	Hamlet's indecision is lamentable.
DEADWOOD	There are various uses of shale, such as in the manufacture of cement, bricks, and tile.
IMPROVED	Shale is used in the manufacture of cement, bricks, and tile.

Omnibus Words. Many examples of deadwood involve a relatively small number of **omnibus words,** which are sometimes both abstract and general and which add little or no information to the sentence. Omnibus words may be nouns, adjectives, verbs, or adverbs. The following list contains some of the most common omnibus nouns.

aspect	factor	line	quality	state
case	feature	manner	situation	thing
character	field	matter	sort	type
fact	kind	problem		

Omnibus nouns usually detract from the effectiveness of a sentence.

WEAK	One of Clara's <u>problems</u> was her family <u>situation</u>.
IMPROVED	Clara was self-conscious because her husband was an alcoholic.
WEAK	A surprising <u>aspect</u> of the Easter Island sculptures is their solemn <u>quality</u>.
IMPROVED	The Easter Island sculptures are surprisingly solemn.

Common omnibus adjectives are *bad, crucial, fine, good, great, important, nice,* and *significant.* Sometimes the adjective should be eliminated entirely.

WEAK	His falling asleep at the dinner table is a <u>good</u> indication of how tired he is.
IMPROVED	His falling asleep at the dinner table is an indication of how tired he is.

Sometimes a more exact adjective is needed.

WEAK	She was saving her money to buy a <u>good</u> car.
IMPROVED	She was saving her money to buy a <u>reliable</u> car.

Among the omnibus verbs are *appear, be, do, exist, get, happen, have, occur,* and *seem.*

WEAK	What <u>occurred</u> was that the wind blew the door shut.
IMPROVED	The wind blew the door shut.
WEAK	The noise level that presently <u>exists</u> is intolerable.
IMPROVED	The present noise level is intolerable.

Omnibus adverbs include empty intensifiers and qualifiers such as *basically, completely, definitely, quite, rather, somewhat,* and *very.* These omnibus adverbs usually weaken rather than strengthen the sentences in which they appear, yet sometimes two or three clutter up a single sentence.

WEAK	She was <u>basically quite</u> interested in politics.
IMPROVED	She was interested in politics.
WEAK	Summer was <u>definitely</u> over, but the weather remained <u>somewhat</u> warm.
IMPROVED	Summer was over, but the weather remained warm.

Circumlocution. Another variety of deadwood is **circumlocution,** the use of big words or long phrases instead of more common and shorter words and phrases. (See also 47b).

WEAK	It came to my attention that the post office was not always to be relied upon.
IMPROVED	I learned that the post office was not always reliable.
WEAK	As far as the children were concerned, they considered that the purpose of the driveway was to enable them to skateboard.
IMPROVED	The children thought that the driveway was for skateboarding.

Tautology. **Tautology,** or the unnecessary repetition of a concept, is a particularly irritating source of deadwood. One of the most common forms of tautology is the modification of a noun by an adjective that means the same thing as the noun: *free gift, predicted forecast, necessary essentials, forthcoming future.* Other parts of speech may also be involved. For example, in the sentence "The convalescent was recovering from a heart attack," the verb *recovering* unnecessarily repeats the meaning of the word *convalescent.* In the tautology *repeat again,* the verb *repeat* contains all the meaning of the adverb *again.* Eliminate tautology by paying close attention to the denotations of words.

EXERCISES: Using Words Economically

Rewrite the following sentences to eliminate deadwood, circumlocution, and tautology. Where it is possible, eliminate omnibus words, or, if not possible, replace them with specific expressions.

1. These days, many segments of the American population—investors who are trying to make a profit, collectors who enjoy acquiring the rare, people who appreciate aesthetic beauty in and of itself—are buying up Oriental rugs made in several regions of Asia.

2. There are basically six kinds of Oriental rugs—Chinese, Indian, Caucasian, Turkmen, Turkish, and Persian—and within each of the six kinds there are many subdivisions, usually names that indicate where the rug was originally made.

3. It is a true fact that people who know a lot about Oriental rugs can usually identify where a rug was made by looking at the weave of it and its design.

4. Until only recently these splendid rugs, which are greatly varied in size, color, and design, were the gorgeous showpieces of only royal palaces and religious temples and not at all within the reach of the ordinary person, who was neither rich enough to buy them nor noble enough to receive them as free gifts.

5. The ornamental design of rugs includes such features as geometric patterns (at least as background), garden scenes, figures of animals or people, hunting scenes, and verses or slogans.

6. Learning enough about the complexities of Oriental rugs to become an expert takes many years, and the would-be investor or collector makes the very wisest decision when he or she decides to solicit the help of a respected dealer who has built up a good, solid reputation for dealing in rugs.

47d USING FRESH WORDS / fresh

The word **fresh** can mean "novel," "different," "original," but freshness of diction does not mean that you should try to invent new words. Instead, it means avoiding overfamiliar words and expressions. In fact, very often it is not the individual words that have gone stale, but combinations of words. For example, both *lining* and *silver* are perfectly healthy English words, but their combination in the phrase *silver lining* has deteriorated through overuse.

The greatest enemies of freshness of diction are clichés, vogue words, nonce words, fine writing, and overuse of particular words and phrases.

Clichés.   **Clichés** are trite, overworked, automatic phrases—the TV dinners of writing, and just as unappealing to the reader as TV dinners are to the eater. The person who first said or wrote *ice water in his veins* or *truth is stranger than fiction* was imaginative, but constant repetition of such phrases over the years has worn them out. Many clichés are overfamiliar metaphors, similes, and proverbial expressions.

avoid like the plague	bite the dust
sell like hot cakes	burn the midnight oil
spread like wildfire	face the music
stick out like a sore thumb	meet the eye
work like a dog	pave the way
down but not out	cool as a cucumber
gone but not forgotten	light as a feather
last but not least	neat as a pin
sadder but wiser	quick as a wink
slow but sure	sharp as a tack
dyed in the wool	better late than never
method in your madness	easier said than done
nip in the bud	hotter than hell
skeleton in the closet	more sinned against than sinning
soft place in my heart	no sooner said than done
all work and no play	bitter end
few and far between	broad daylight
hustle and bustle	fatal flaw
pride and joy	happy medium
short and sweet	vicious circle
crack of dawn	
facts of life	
sigh of relief	
twinkling of an eye	
walks of life	

How can you be sure whether an expression is a cliché? If, when you think of one word, an entire phrase comes to mind, that phrase is probably a cliché. If you then ask a friend to complete the expression and he or she comes up with the same phrase that you did, it is certainly a cliché. For example, if you say *fresh as a . . .*, you automatically complete the phrase with . . . *daisy*. *Fresh as a daisy* is anything but fresh. Try again for a comparison that is not so familiar.

The following passage is an example, admittedly exaggerated, of cliché-ridden prose.

> When I first crossed the <u>portals of learning</u>, I was <u>as innocent as a newborn babe</u>, but I had a <u>sneaking suspicion</u> that I would have to <u>toe the line</u> or my education would come to a <u>tragic end</u>. I soon learned that I was not the <u>center of attention</u> on campus, but just one of the <u>rank and file</u> of students. However, although it was <u>easier said than done</u>, I <u>burned the midnight oil</u> until the <u>wee hours</u> and <u>walked the straight and narrow</u> amidst all <u>the hustle and bustle</u> of life in the <u>halls of academe</u>. I stayed <u>sober as a judge</u> while my roommates were out <u>painting the town red</u>. My <u>untiring efforts</u> allowed me to <u>weather the storms</u> of papers and examinations. After four years of <u>honest toil</u>, I left college as the <u>proud possessor</u> of a diploma and many <u>fond memories</u>.

Even the careful writer who shuns such clichés as *commune with nature* and *doomed to disappointment* often succumbs to expository clichés, especially as transitional devices.

as a matter of fact	in the final analysis
believe it or not	it goes without saying
consensus of opinion	it is interesting to note
first and foremost	last but not least
in a nutshell	needless to say
in a very real sense	to all intents and purposes

It is almost impossible to avoid an occasional expository cliché, but weed out the most obvious of them. Such weeding also eliminates deadwood.

WEAK	<u>It is interesting to note</u> that <u>the consensus of opinion</u> in New England was <u>to all intents and purposes</u> against the War of 1812.
IMPROVED	Most New Englanders opposed the War of 1812.

Vogue Words. **Vogue words** (sometimes called **buzzwords**) are words or terms that become very popular, are used and overused for a brief period of time, and then drop back into relative obscurity. For example, as I write this, the terms *syndrome, low-profile, bottom line, ball-park figure, life-style, parameters,* and *game plan* can be seen and heard everywhere. Three years from now, there will be a new set of vogue words, and such expressions as *bottom line* will seem out-of-date. In their overuse and normally brief life, vogue words resemble slang. Unlike most slang, vogue words are often scholarly words (for example, *syndrome* and *parameters*). Further, vogue words are used by a wider range of people than slang and often appear in quite formal writing. Avoid vogue words because they give the impression that you are mindlessly repeating whatever you hear around you.

Nonce Words.   **Nonce words,** or **neologisms,** are words made up on the spur of the moment. There is nothing wrong with inventing a word if there is no other appropriate word. However, it is not acceptable to invent a word such as *elasticness* when the word *elasticity* already exists. Most nonce words result from making one word or part of speech from another word by adding suffixes such as *-ize, -ish, -ment, -tion, -y,* and so on.

NONCE WORD	Despite all the <u>publicization</u>, few people voted in the primary.
CORRECT	Despite all the <u>publicity</u>, few people voted in the primary.
NONCE WORD	All the bearings were recently <u>lubricized</u>.
CORRECT	All the bearings were recently <u>lubricated</u>.
NONCE WORD	Napoleon found himself in a <u>tightish</u> situation.
CORRECT	Napoleon found himself in a <u>rather tight</u> situation.

Check your dictionary if a word that you want to use does not seem completely familiar to you. If the word is not listed in a good college dictionary, it is probably a nonce word. Find the accepted form of the word in the dictionary and use it instead. If you cannot find an accepted form in the dictionary, try to rewrite the sentence so as to avoid having to use a nonce word. For example, you might want to describe a piece of paper so old and fragile that it could not be picked up. Instead of using the awkward nonce word *unhandleable,* you could write *too fragile to be handled.*

EXERCISES: Clichés, Vogue Words, and Nonce Words

Underline and identify by letter each of the clichés (C), vogue words (V), and nonce words (N) in the following sentences.

1. It is crystal clear that if we don't get a hedge against inflation, the unprofitability of continuing to fight for the program will be political suicide.

2. "You tell me that it's all his fault that they fight like cats and dogs," Mr. Thaxton said, "but let me remind you that it takes two to tango!"

3. The government's threat of wage and price controls has brought forth a lot of constructive input from the private sector, especially with regard to the government's efforts to create a viable program for reducing unemployment.

4. I believe our survivability depends on our maintaining a low profile during the decision-making process, but once we see how the man on the street reacts to the policy, we can support the popular faction and milk the publicity for all it's worth.

5. "You are optimizing when you say that the power outages will be under control by early morning," the shop steward said, "but I suppose only time will tell."

6. I know that the fat's in the fire as far as Greta is concerned, but getting out of this hot water is merely a question of time and of mind over matter.

Fine Writing. **Fine writing,** or **flowery writing,** as it is sometimes called, is the unnecessary use of descriptive adjectives and adverbs, of polysyllabic and foreign words, of artificial or "poetic" expressions, and of rhetorical devices. Fine writing, despite its label, is not good writing; it is affected writing. Although fine writing is usually motivated by the writer's desire to sound dignified and learned, the reader is more annoyed than impressed. Avoid the artificiality of fine writing.

WEAK	Undesirable waste material is removed on a semiweekly basis by municipal employees specifically assigned to such activity.
IMPROVED	City collectors pick up garbage twice a week.
WEAK	*À propos* apprehensions, my *bête noire* has ever been altitude, albeit of late I have acquired a certain *sangfroid* with respect to the same.
IMPROVED	I have a fear of heights, but I'm conquering it.
WEAK	The heavy, dull, leaden *cumuli mammati* amassed menacingly and released upon the eager earth their life-sustaining burden, thereby effectively destroying our well-laid plans for a sylvan outing accompanied by comestibles.
IMPROVED	It began to rain, spoiling our picnic in the woods.

EXERCISES: Fine Writing

Translate the following examples of fine writing into good, plain English.

1. It is beyond the capacity of mortal mind to elucidate the tendency of domestic felines to express vocally their discontent with others of their species.
2. The woman's *Weltanschauung*, a combination of grim foreboding and massive insecurity, is patently evident whenever she encounters another solitary wanderer on this our earth.
3. It was with decided alacrity that I hastened to respond to the reverberations of the signalling device at my portals.
4. He remains wedded to his books, still in the infancy of his cerebral *Wanderjahr*, clothing himself in the weeds of learning in preparation for launching himself on the great sea of life.
5. An imprudent man rarely, if ever, has the innate capacity and intellectual wherewithal to retain for a sustained period of time the profusion of currency that Fate has, in all of her bountiful generosity, heaped upon him.

Overuse of Words or Phrases. Perhaps you have recently learned the word *cogent* and enjoy using it as often as possible. Your reader, however, may not share your enthusiasm. If you have written *cogent* five times in a three-page paper, substitute *compelling, convincing,* or *forcible* for three or four of these uses.

A related problem is that of repeating one noun over and over again. It may be the correct noun, but excessive repetition is annoying to the reader. If there is no danger of ambiguity or improper connotations, substitute a pronoun or a synonym now and then to break the monotony.

REPETITIVE | When I was a sophomore in high school, I came down with <u>chicken pox</u>. <u>Chicken pox</u> is a childhood disease, and I was embarrassed to have to admit to my friends that I had <u>chicken pox</u> as an adult of fifteen. Although my younger sister had <u>chicken pox</u> at the same time, she didn't get as many spots as I did. Apparently, the older people are, the worse <u>chicken pox</u> affects them.

IMPROVED | When I was a sophomore in high school, I came down with <u>chicken pox</u>. <u>This</u> is a childhood disease, and I was embarrassed to have to admit to my friends that I had <u>it</u> as an adult of fifteen. Although my younger sister had <u>chicken pox</u> at the same time, she didn't get as many spots as I did. Apparently, the older people are, the worse the <u>disease</u> affects them.

Eliminating excessive repetition does not mean that you should eliminate every repeated word. If a word has no good synonyms or if pronouns or synonyms would be ambiguous, repeat it as often as is necessary for clarity. Deliberate and parallel repetition can even be an effective rhetorical device for achieving emphasis (see 49c).

EXERCISE: Overuse of Words or Phrases

The following paragraph suffers greatly from overuse of certain words. Rewrite it, retaining the sentence structure as much as possible but substituting synonyms or pronouns to break the monotony.

The man and the woman seated themselves on opposite ends of the park bench. They exchanged covert glances, and each inched from the opposite direction to a position a little nearer the middle of the bench. Each pretended to read—she a magazine, and he the newspaper—but all the while each peeked covertly at the other. Almost simultaneously each coughed and pretended to adjust his or her shoe, but each seized the opportunity to bend over as a covert opportunity for a second move closer to the center of the bench. Now each was only inches from the other. The woman covertly blushed behind her magazine; the man smiled. Almost at once each moved almost into the lap of the other, a move that sent both jumping to their feet. "I arrest you," he shouted, waving a police ID covertly slipped from his pocket, but before he could finish his statement, she countered, "I hereby arrest you," displaying her police badge. Each looked at the other in amazement, both covertly pocketed their IDs, and both walked away in wonder that they could have been so wrong as all that.

47e FIGURES OF SPEECH

Figures of speech are expressions in which words are used, not to convey a literal meaning but to add freshness and vividness to writing.

Metaphors and Similes.   The most familiar figures of speech are **metaphors** and **similes**. Both metaphors and similes compare two

unlike things that have something in common. The difference between the two is primarily in their grammar. A simile makes an explicit
comparison by means of such words as *like, as,* or *as if.*

> The impatient tapping of her fingers on the table was like corn popping.
>
> Myra's acceptance was as hesitant as one's first bite of squid.

A metaphor makes an implicit comparison or identification,
often of the form *X is Y.*

> My hometown is a culinary desert; however, the traveler will find no
> oases, only the waterholes of Burger King and Kentucky Fried Chicken.
>
> His memoirs provide not so much a window on the past as a keyhole
> through which we may guiltily peep.

Both metaphors and similes are especially common in proverbs
and proverbial expressions. *There's many a slip 'twixt the cup and the
lip, Great oaks from little acorns grow,* and *The early bird gets the worm* are
all metaphors, whereas *as big as a barn, as welcome as water in your
shoes,* and *like a bolt out of the blue* are all similes. Many of these
expressions are so common that they have become "dead" metaphors
or similes; that is, we use them without being aware that they are
actually figures of speech. In fact, it is almost impossible to write
without using an occasional dead metaphor.

Rather than trying to rid your writing of all dead metaphors,
concentrate on becoming more aware of their presence and on not
letting them come back to life unexpectedly. For example, *to have a
frog in one's throat* is a common dead metaphor for hoarseness, and,
in most contexts, no one would take it literally. But in any context
that includes animals, it is potentially dangerous.

> Professor Hawkins' lecture on amphibians was difficult to understand
> because he had a frog in his throat.

In the context of *amphibians,* the word *frog* suddenly takes on literal
and not figurative meaning and the resulting sentence is ludicrous.
On the other hand, the skillful writer may occasionally resurrect a
dead metaphor to good effect.

> Unfortunately, Fred is an alarmist and cannot tell the difference between
> the handwriting on the wall and simple graffiti.
>
> I had finally found a man after my own heart; only later did I discover
> that he was also after my money.

A **mixed metaphor** is the use of several different and incom-
patible comparisons in one construction. Mixed metaphors usually
occur because the writer has unknowingly employed several dead
metaphors.

> Deborah shot straight from the hip and didn't pull any punches.
>
> Although old MacAdoo had one foot in the grave, he kept his ear to
> the ground and always knew which end was up.

Strained similes and metaphors result from comparing two things that do not have enough common characteristics or from making comparisons that suggest the wrong connotations.

STRAINED
SIMILE

All my faith in technology has scattered like papers in a breeze.

STRAINED
METAPHOR

Her mind was a veritable garbage truck; it picked up vast amounts of loose information, compressed it, and spewed it out again in compact form.

In the first sentence, *faith* does not *scatter*, nor can one imagine how it possibly could scatter; the simile just does not work. In the second sentence, the writer apparently intends the comparison between a *mind* and a *garbage truck* to be complimentary, but the connotations of the term *garbage truck* are so unfavorable that the metaphor is not effective.

In sum, metaphors and similes are an important means of adding freshness and vividness to writing. Like most good things, they have some built-in traps and should not be misused or overused.

Irony.   Irony is saying one thing and meaning something else—often just the opposite. Well-handled, irony is neither so obvious that the reader is annoyed ("heavy" irony) nor so subtle that the reader does not realize that irony is intended.

> The apartment was adequate: six flights of stairs to keep me in shape, no closets to be cleaned or windows to be washed, and plenty of living creatures for company.

This sentence is ironic because the writer says *adequate* but means *inadequate*. The reader knows that a seventh-floor walk-up is *not* a desirable apartment, that good apartments have both closets and windows, and that the *living creatures* are vermin such as cockroaches and rats.

One of the dangers of employing irony is its tendency to become sarcastic. Although sarcasm and irony are closely related, irony is relatively restrained, good-natured, light-hearted, and gentle, while sarcasm is more sneering, more vicious, and more personal; it is intended to hurt. Readers usually respond with pleasure to well-handled irony but are likely to turn against the author of sarcasm. The distinction between the two is fairly easy to maintain in speech, where facial expressions and tone of voice reveal the speaker's intentions. In writing, only the words reveal the speaker's intentions, and words are easily misinterpreted.

EXERCISES: Figures of Speech

Part A: Use similes, metaphors, or irony to make the following sentences more specific and vivid. Avoid using mixed or strained metaphors, and avoid using those which have become clichés.

1. When Inga got up and saw the cold rain outside, she felt really depressed—especially when she saw her undone homework on the desk and all of her dirty laundry scattered around the room.

2. At the school for handicapped children where Bob is a tutor, one of the children brought him a paper daisy she had made for him. He was very touched by this present. He felt like crying.

3. When the cop pulled us over and gave us a speeding ticket, we were really angry because he was so mean and nasty about it.

4. The owner of the store yelled a lot, but he didn't really mean it, and no one was scared of him.

Part B: Identify and label the strained and mixed metaphors and similes and the poorly used irony in the following sentences. Then rewrite the sentences, using more suitable figures of speech.

1. My first (and last) date with Jay was nothing short of heaven: he was fashionably late; his impeccable attire was punctuated with a brown shoe on one foot and a black one on the other; he took me to a lovely, intimate restaurant down in the boondocks; he delighted me to the brink of insanity with his elephant jokes; and then he allowed me to pay the check!

2. The old man's agile body ticks along like a fine Swiss watch that never misses a beat and rarely needs rewinding.

3. "Hilda is," John remarked, "a woman with all the discretion of a full-blown sandstorm that knows no boundaries and respects no restraints."

47f TONE AND POINT OF VIEW

Tone is the attitude we express toward our subject, our reader, and even ourselves. Tone determines to a large extent both the emotional and the intellectual effect of our writing on our reader. Tone may be formal or informal, tragic or comic, angry or cheerful, kindly or cruel, personal or impersonal. It can be bitter, hopeless, ironic, or sympathetic—in other words, tone can reflect the entire range of human emotions. Choice of words is one of the most important components of tone, although choice of grammatical constructions and even content—what is included and what is omitted—also contribute to tone.

SYMPATHETIC TONE	Omar tends to be frustrated by mental tasks.
CRUEL TONE	Omar is too stupid to do anything calling for even a minimum of intellectual ability.
HUMOROUS TONE	Omar wasn't behind the door when they passed out the brains—he wasn't even in the house.

Point of view is closely related to tone. It is the position from which we see our subject as we write. We may be emotionally moved, or we may be dispassionate observers. Point of view is revealed by the words selected and by what facts are included or excluded.

As the following descriptions of the Battle of Wounded Knee

illustrate, changing the tone and point of view also changes the message the reader receives.

> Following the Custer massacre, columns under General Crook, John Gibbon, and Alfred Sully marched into the Sioux country and by January 1877 most of the Indians had surrendered. This ended large-scale Sioux hostilities in this region, until the "Ghost Dance" craze of 1890–1891 again set them on the war path. The so-called battle of Wounded Knee, S.D., Dec. 29, 1890, and subsequent mopping-up operations ended this final Sioux uprising.
>
> —*COLLIER'S ENCYCLOPEDIA*

> The fighting tribes did not give in easily. There were uprisings, raids of hunger and desperation. Briefly they had known a wonderful life and started a culture that might have evolved greatly had it been given time. They tried to hold to that life against hopeless odds. When everything seemed darkest, the new Ghost Dance religion . . . gave them a flicker of new hope. . . . On December 22nd, a band of Sioux, all Ghost Dance followers, under a chief named Big Foot, returning to their reservation, camped under a strong cavalry guard at Wounded Knee. A battery of quick-firing Hotchkiss cannons was trained on the camp. The next day, the soldiers started to disarm the Indians and someone—probably a Sioux, but it is not sure—started shooting. The cannons opened rapid fire with explosive shells, the soldiers moved in. Sixty soldiers, two hundred Sioux men, women, and children were killed or wounded in a few moments. That was the Battle of Wounded Knee and the end of everything.
>
> —Oliver La Farge, *THE AMERICAN INDIAN*

The tone of the first passage, taken from an encyclopedia, is intended to be objective. Most of the words are neutral, although slanting appears in *war path* and *craze*. The author concentrates on relating facts such as dates and names. However, the point of view, that of a white author, is revealed by the mention of white officers but not of Indian leaders and the description of Indian activities as *massacres* and *hostilities*.

The tone of the second passage, which was written by a noted friend of Indians, is more openly subjective, as is revealed by such words and phrases as *wonderful life, hopeless odds, everything seemed darkest, flicker of new hope,* and *the end of everything.* (Note that the Ghost Dance is described by the white author as a *craze* and by the Indian author as *a flicker of new hope.*) The author adds emotion and pathos to his description by citing the number of people killed or wounded. The point of view is clearly more sympathetic to the Indians than to the whites; the author identifies himself with the Indian cause.

Objectivity is not an automatic virtue, nor is subjectivity necessarily a fault. Research papers should be as objective as possible; their purpose is to convey factual information. But a personal-experience paper may quite properly be highly subjective because its chief purpose is to convey impressions and emotions, not factual information. The important things are that your readers understand your approach to your topic and that you not try to pass off opinions as facts.

Both tone and point of view should be established in the opening sentences of a paper and should be maintained consistently throughout the paper. Otherwise, the readers will be confused about how they are supposed to respond to the writing. Excesses of tone should be avoided. A pompous tone will bore the reader, a flippant tone applied to a serious subject will annoy the reader, and an overly sentimental tone will embarrass the reader. Tone should also be determined by the intended audience. For example, your description of a class that you are taking might have a humorous (or, for that matter, poisonous) tone in a letter to a friend, but should be serious and objective in an official course evaluation.

EXERCISES: Tone and Point of View

The following two problems require several brief, well-written paragraphs of three to four sentences each. Write each paragraph from a different point of view and in a distinctly different tone. Use the same general information within each paragraph. Do not try to resolve the problem, but concentrate on point of view and tone.

1. Problem—Jeff Meyerson has discovered that the new car that he has owned for one week has a slightly warped chassis.
   a. Write the first paragraph of Jeff's letter to the dealer from whom he bought the car.
   b. Write the first paragraph of the dealer's letter to the regional headquarters of the automobile manufacturer.
   c. Write the first paragraph of the letter from the president of the regional headquarters to Jeff.

2. Problem—Susan and Miriam were roommates during the previous semester and therefore shared a telephone. When she left school, Susan did not pay her share of the telephone bill. The telephone company has disconnected the service, and Miriam cannot get service reinstated unless she pays the $112.82 that Susan owes.
   a. Write the first paragraph of Miriam's letter to the telephone company.
   b. Write the beginning of the telephone company's response to Miriam.
   c. Write part of Miriam's letter to Susan.
   e. Write part of Susan's response to Miriam.

---

dict / 48 THE DICTIONARY

Your dictionary is the most valuable reference book you will ever own. What is more, dictionaries are real bargains; you get a well-bound, well-printed book with from 1,200 to 1,800 pages for less than the price of most hard-cover textbooks. Because dictionaries are so valuable and because they are relatively inexpensive, every writer should own a good hard-cover edition. Paperback editions have only about one-half as many entries as hard-cover editions, and their bindings are not sturdy enough to withstand heavy use. A paperback edition is, however, very convenient as a second dictionary to carry with you to class or to the library.

There are numerous misconceptions about dictionaries. The first and perhaps major misconception is that all dictionaries are alike. There are many differences among dictionaries. A second misconception is that dictionaries are infallible. Nothing is infallible, and if two dictionaries disagree on a point, obviously both cannot be "right." A third misconception is that, if a word is not in the dictionary, it is not a word. Even the largest, so-called unabridged dictionaries do not and cannot include every new technical term, every ephemeral slang expression, every slight change in meaning of existing words. Still another misconception is that the first definition listed under a main entry is the "preferred" definition. This is not so; the first definition listed is either the historically earliest meaning (and may even be archaic today) or the meaning in most frequent use (not necessarily the best use).

Your dictionary should be up-to-date; if it is over ten years old, keep it for cross-referencing and double-checking, but buy a new edition of another dictionary. Every printing of good dictionaries includes many changes from the previous printing, so the edition number itself is not enough to ensure that you have the most recent version. Check the date of printing on the back of the title page.

48a COLLEGE DICTIONARIES

When buying a dictionary, be sure you have the exact title you want. The name *Webster* itself is not copyrighted, and many inadequate dictionaries include the word *Webster* in their titles. You may be required to buy a particular dictionary. If you are not, you can choose the one most suited to your own interests and tastes. All of the following are excellent college dictionaries.

> *The American Heritage Dictionary of the English Language* (Boston: Houghton Mifflin Company)
>
> *Funk & Wagnalls Standard College Dictionary* (New York: Funk & Wagnalls)
>
> *The Random House College Dictionary* (New York: Random House, Inc.)
>
> *Webster's New Collegiate Dictionary* (Springfield, Mass.: G. & C. Merriam Company, Publishers)
>
> *Webster's New World Dictionary of the American Language* (Cleveland and New York: The World Publishing Company)

The American Heritage Dictionary is available in both a standard size and in a version with a larger typeface. It has an exceptionally attractive format and many illustrations, including photographs. It provides much information on usage, and, with its 155,000 entries, it has slightly more than the average number of entries. For the person interested in the origins of words, its index of Indo-European roots is invaluable.

Funk & Wagnalls Standard College Dictionary has an adequate type size but relatively few illustrations. It has many notes on usage. Its 150,000 entries make its coverage about average among college dictionaries.

The Random House College Dictionary has an exceptionally large number of entries (around 170,000). To achieve this while keeping the overall physical size of the dictionary relatively compact, the publishers use a small typeface. The number of illustrations is about average.

Webster's New Collegiate Dictionary has a clear and easily readable typeface but relatively few illustrations. It has many fewer notes on usage than the other dictionaries, but the brief contexts provided for a large number of words partially compensate for the absence of usage labels. The pronunciation guides may be slightly more difficult to interpret than those of the other dictionaries. The number of entries (about 150,000) is about average. It is the only one of the five dictionaries listed to include an index.

Webster's New World Dictionary is in the middle of the range in physical size, clarity of format, and discussion of usage. Although it has fewer entries than the other dictionaries (140,000), the publishers have emphasized simple and easily understood definitions, and it is a good dictionary for the nonspecialist. On the other hand, it does not include, for example, the Latin names for plants and animals, and the specialist in any one particular area may prefer the more technical definitions of the other dictionaries.

48b USING THE DICTIONARY

Unfortunately, many people use a dictionary only for information on spelling, definitions, and pronunciation. To get the most out of your dictionary, you should be familiar with the front and back matter, which includes explanatory notes on how the dictionary is organized, lists of abbreviations used, a statement of the editors' goals, and brief articles on the history of the language and on dialects and usage. Make a mental note of where the list of abbreviations is located so that you can refer to it easily when you encounter an unfamiliar abbreviation.

Unless you have no idea how to spell it, finding a word in the dictionary should not take you longer than from twenty to thirty seconds. Open the dictionary to the general location, and then use the guides at the tops of the pages; do not waste time scanning the page itself. If you are using the dictionary to check spelling, read the definition to be sure you have the right word: *discrete* and *discreet* are both English adjectives, but their meanings are different.

48c THE DICTIONARY ENTRY

Within each dictionary entry, the information appears in a given order. This order varies slightly from dictionary to dictionary, but a typical order is (1) main entry, (2) pronunciation, (3) part of speech,

(4) spelling of inflected forms, (5) etymology, (6) definitions. Following these may be additional information, such as synonyms and antonyms, information on usage, derived forms, alternative spellings, and idioms in which the word is used. A typical dictionary entry is reproduced at the bottom of this page.

The Main Entry. The **main entry** gives the proper spelling of the word; some dictionaries also list acceptable variant spellings at this point. Dictionaries usually agree on the first spelling of words but differ in the extent of their listings of variant spellings. The greatest difference among dictionaries is in their treatment of compound words. For example, *New World* lists the spelling *home-bred,* whereas all the others list *homebred. Webster's New Collegiate* lists *home brew,* but the others have *home-brew.* All five agree on *home run.*

The main entry also gives the appropriate word division; the raised dot between letters corresponds to a hyphen in writing or typing. All dictionaries agree on the division of the great majority of words, but occasionally they differ here too. For example, *Webster's New Collegiate, Heritage,* and *Random House* divide the word *flunky* as *flun·ky,* but *New World* and *Funk & Wagnalls* divide it as *flunk·y.*

If the main entry is capitalized in the dictionary, the word should be capitalized in writing.

Pronunciation. The **pronunciation,** including stress or accent, is indicated between parentheses (between diagonal slashes in *Webster's*

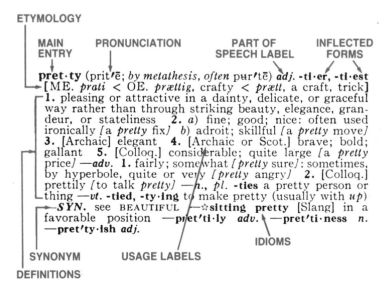

ETYMOLOGY

MAIN ENTRY   PRONUNCIATION   PART OF SPEECH LABEL   INFLECTED FORMS

pret·ty (prit′ē; *by metathesis, often* pur′tē) *adj.* **-ti·er, -ti·est** [ME. *prati* < OE. *prættig,* crafty < *prætt,* a craft, trick] **1.** pleasing or attractive in a dainty, delicate, or graceful way rather than through striking beauty, elegance, grandeur, or stateliness **2.** *a)* fine; good; nice: often used ironically [a *pretty* fix] *b)* adroit; skillful [a *pretty* move] **3.** [Archaic] elegant **4.** [Archaic or Scot.] brave; bold; gallant **5.** [Colloq.] considerable; quite large [a *pretty* price] —*adv.* **1.** fairly; somewhat [*pretty* sure]: sometimes, by hyperbole, quite or very [*pretty* angry] **2.** [Colloq.] prettily [to talk *pretty*] —*n., pl.* **-ties** a pretty person or thing —*vt.* **-tied, -ty·ing** to make pretty (usually with *up*) —*SYN.* see BEAUTIFUL —☆**sitting pretty** [Slang] in a favorable position —**pret′ti·ly** *adv.* —**pret′ti·ness** *n.* —**pret′ty·ish** *adj.*

IDIOMS

SYNONYM   USAGE LABELS

DEFINITIONS

New Collegiate). A pronunciation guide appears at the bottom of every right-hand page in *Webster's New Collegiate, Random House, New World,* and *Funk & Wagnalls. Heritage* runs the pronunciation guide across the bottom of both the left-hand and right-hand pages. Acceptable alternative pronunciations follow the pronunciation that the editors judge to be most common. If no pronunciation is listed beside a word, it is pronounced like a preceding entry with the same root.

Part of Speech.   The **part-of-speech** category to which the word belongs is abbreviated in all dictionaries. If a single word can be more than one part of speech, most dictionaries include other parts of speech under the main entry, with a new part-of-speech label preceding the definition. *Webster's New Collegiate,* however, usually makes a new main entry for every different part-of-speech designation.

Our sample entry indicates that *pretty* is used not only as an adjective but also as an adverb, a noun, and a transitive verb.

Inflected Forms.   If the spelling of **inflected forms** of words is irregular, the inflected forms are listed. In our example, the comparative and superlative forms of *pretty* are spelled out in full because the final *-y* changes to *-i-* when these endings are added.

Etymology.   The **etymology** of a word is its history; the entry will note whether it existed in Old English, was borrowed from another language, or has an unknown origin. In addition, the etymologies listed in dictionaries give, as far as possible, the original components of the word and earlier spellings and meanings. For obvious compounds such as *lampshade,* no etymology is listed because the etymology is that of the two parts of the compound.

Our sample shows us that the word *pretty* has been in the language since Anglo-Saxon (Old English) times but that its spelling and especially its meaning have changed a great deal over the years.

Definitions.   **Definitions** typically consist of explanations or synonyms or both. Brief examples of words in context are sometimes provided. Even though dictionaries concentrate on the denotative and not connotative meanings of words, the usage labels (see page 219) and synonyms give some information about connotations. For example, *Heritage* lists *frugal, thrifty,* and *economical* as synonyms of *sparing* but *close, niggardly, parsimonious, miserly,* and *penny-pinching* as synonyms of *stingy,* thus clearly indicating that the connotations of *sparing* are more favorable than those of *stingy.*

Most dictionaries list what the editors feel is the most common or general meaning of a word first, followed by more restricted meanings. *Webster's New Collegiate* orders definitions by historical occurrence, with the earliest meanings first.

New World makes a special effort to provide clear and simple definitions. Suppose, for example, you had encountered the word *plasmodium* in your reading and did not know its meaning. Compare the basic definitions you would find in *New World* and *Random House*. (The definitions in *Heritage, Funk & Wagnalls,* and *Webster's New Collegiate* resemble those of *Random House.*)

NEW WORLD	"a mass of protoplasm with many nuclei, formed by the fusion of one-celled organisms"
RANDOM HOUSE	"an amoeboid, multinucleate mass or sheet of protoplasm characteristic of some stages of organisms, as a myxomycete or slime mold"

New World does not assume that you already know that *amoeboid* organisms have one cell or that *multinucleate* means "with many nuclei." On the other hand, *Random House* give you more information and more detailed information about plasmodium.

Nearly every dictionary entry contains the basic information just discussed. Many entries also provide information about usage, idioms, and synonyms and antonyms.

Usage Information.   Information on **usage** takes two forms, brief labels before a definition and longer notes following a definition. If neither a label nor a note appears, the word is considered universally acceptable. Every dictionary has its own system for marking usage; this system is explained in the material at the beginning of the dictionary. In general, there are four broad categories of usage labels: occupational, geographic, currency, and status.

1. **Occupational labels** indicate that the word is limited in the given meaning to a specific occupational or intellectual field. Typical occupational labels include *Mathematics, Chemistry, Poetic,* and *Military.* For example, *Heritage* labels the word *conic* as a mathematical term when it is used as a noun. (Note that the label applies only to its use as a noun; the adjective *conic* is considered to be in general use.)

2. **Geographic labels** indicate that the word is limited in the given meaning to a specific geographical area of the English-speaking world. Typical geographic labels include *New England, British, Southern,* and *Scottish.* For example, *Funk & Wagnalls* labels the noun *roundabout* as British in the meanings of "a merry-go-round" and "a traffic circle."

3. **Currency labels** refer to how commonly the word is used in modern English. **Rare** means that the word is uncommon. **Archaic** means that the word is still seen in books but seldom used; for example, *Webster's New Collegiate* labels *odor* in the meaning of "something that emits a sweet or pleasant scent; perfume" archaic. **Obsolete** means that the word in the given meaning is never used today and that it is not familiar to the average educated person.

4. **Status labels** indicate the social acceptability of words or phrases. Dictionaries vary rather widely in the particular labels used and in the extent to which they apply status labels. But in general, seven categories of status labels can be identified.

a. **No label.** The word or meaning is universally acceptable.
b. **Informal** or **Colloquial.** The word is widely used in conversation but not in formal writing. For example, the noun *takeoff* in the meaning "a burlesque imitation of someone" is colloquial.
c. **Slang.** The word is widely used but is extremely informal and usually expresses an irreverent or exaggerated attitude. For example, the use of the word *dog* to refer to an unattractive person is slang.
d. **Nonstandard.** The word is widely current, even among educated people, but is usually disapproved of. Examples of nonstandard usage would include *irregardless* (instead of *regardless*) or *like* as a conjunction.
e. **Substandard** or **Illiterate.** The word or form is widely used but only by the least well educated people and not by prestige groups. It is considered incorrect, usually even by the people who regularly use it. An example of substandard usage would be *he ain't* (instead of *he isn't*).
f. **Dialectal** or **Regional.** Dialectal or regional labels are similar to geographic labels but are normally restricted to small geographic areas. Forms labeled dialectal are acceptable within the particular region but are considered incorrect or at least old-fashioned outside of that region. An example of dialectal usage would be *het* as the past tense or past participle of *heat*, especially in the expression *all het up*.
g. **Vulgar.** The label of vulgar means that there is a social taboo attached to the word; many people consider it impolite or offensive. An example is the word *snot*. If the taboo is very strong, the word may be labeled **obscene** or **taboo.** Included in the general category of vulgar words are **derogatory** terms (such as *wop*) and **profane** terms (such as *goddamn*).

Usage notes at the end of an entry discuss the usage of words in more detail. Dictionaries differ rather widely in their employment of usage notes and in their "permissiveness." *Heritage* is probably the most prescriptive; that is, it provides the greatest number of explicit rules and statements about usage. *Webster's New Collegiate* has a policy of employing usage notes very sparingly. For example, *Heritage* carefully distinguishes *disinterested* and *uninterested* and notes that 93 percent of their usage panel disapprove of using the two synonymously. *Random House* notes that *disinterested* and *uninterested* are not properly synonyms. *New World* labels the meaning "uninterested" for *disinterested* colloquial. *Funk & Wagnalls* carefully distinguishes the two words but has no usage note about using them interchangeably. *Webster's New Collegiate* lists *uninterested* as a synonym for *disinterested*. Writers who feel somewhat shaky about their own usage will probably prefer one of the more prescriptive dictionaries.

Foreign Words. Dictionaries also specially indicate foreign words that have not become fully assimilated into English. (Foreign words should be underlined in writing.) *New World* uses the symbol ‡ before the main entry; *Random House* puts the main entry in italics; *Webster's New Collegiate* and *Heritage* put the language of origin and the meaning in that language in square brackets after the pronunciation. *Funk & Wagnalls* puts the language of origin in italics before the definition. For example, the expression *sine qua non,* meaning "something that is essential," is treated as a foreign expression by all the dictionaries.

Idioms.   All the dictionaries list some common idioms under main entries. *Random House* and *New World* probably have the most complete coverage, followed by *Heritage* and *Funk & Wagnalls*. *Webster's New Collegiate* lists the fewest idioms; many of the idioms in *Webster's New Collegiate* have separate main entries and are not listed under the key word. For example, *Random House* lists eighteen idioms with the word *play, New World* lists sixteen, *Heritage* and *Funk & Wagnalls* each list ten, and *Webster's New Collegiate* lists seven (including those under separate main entries).

Synonyms and Antonyms.   At the end of many main entries, dictionaries provide a list of synonyms and sometimes antonyms. Often a brief paragraph explains the differences in shades of meaning among the synonyms. For example, under the main entry for the noun *associate, Funk & Wagnalls* discusses the differences among the words *associate, companion, comrade, partner, mate, colleague,* and *ally* and also lists the antonyms *opponent* and *rival.* Dictionaries also cross-reference many entries, referring the reader to other entries.

48d SPECIAL FEATURES OF DICTIONARIES

Besides their regular entries, dictionaries provide a great deal of other useful information. Nearly all dictionaries give, either in the main text or as separate sections at the end, biographical and geographical information, tables of weights and measures, signs and symbols, abbreviations, colleges and universities in the United States and Canada, chemical elements, proofreaders' marks, and various alphabets. Some dictionaries have currency tables, forms of address, brief manuals of style, rhyming dictionaries, lists of common given names, and tables of Greek and Latin prefixes, suffixes, and roots used in English.

48e UNABRIDGED DICTIONARIES

The college dictionaries discussed here are sufficient for most needs, but occasionally you may wish to refer to a so-called unabridged dictionary. These are usually located in the reference section of a library. There are four unabridged dictionaries in current use.

> *Funk & Wagnalls New Standard Dictionary of the English Language* (the basis of *Funk & Wagnalls Standard College Dictionary*)

The Random House Dictionary of the English Language (the basis of the *Random House College Dictionary*)

Webster's Third New International Dictionary (the basis of *Webster's New Collegiate Dictionary*)

The Oxford English Dictionary (12 volumes plus supplements; unique in its extensive historical information about words)

EXERCISES: The Dictionary

1. Compare the formats and levels of specialization of at least three of the following standard college dictionaries.

   The American Heritage Dictionary of the English Language (Boston: Houghton Mifflin Company)

   Funk & Wagnalls Standard College Dictionary (New York: Funk & Wagnalls)

   The Random House College Dictionary (New York: Random House, Inc.)

   Webster's New Collegiate Dictionary (Springfield, Mass.: G. & C. Merriam Company, Publishers)

   Webster's New World Dictionary of the American Language (Cleveland and New York: The World Publishing Company)

   Borrow the latest editions from your friends, or check the reference desk in your library (almost every library has all five). If you have a dictionary not listed above, add it to the list. Quickly familiarize yourself with the abbreviations and symbols each dictionary uses—this information is in the introductory material—and then read each dictionary's treatment of the following words.

a. Bible Belt	d. yin (the Chinese, not	f. Morris Chair
b. cliché	the Scottish, word)	g. cool
c. yahoo	e. accessory	

   Make notes on basic differences among the dictionaries in the entries for each word. Consider such things as capitalization, pronunciation aids and variations, and the definitions themselves. How detailed are they? Are they basic, or do they assume some knowledge of the field? Do they contain phrases or sentences illustrating proper usage? Are they labeled according to usage level (slang, colloquial, dialectal, archaic, literary, Biblical, and so on)? Are there grammatical explanations? Are synonyms and antonyms listed? How detailed is the etymology? Are related words formed from the same root listed? Are there drawings or pictures? Using your notes made on each word, write from two to three paragraphs explaining which dictionary you think is best for you. Be sure to include concrete examples to support your observations.

2. Acquaint yourself with the *Oxford English Dictionary* (it will be in the library). Look up the following two words and write a brief paragraph on the history of each. Are there meanings that you did not know? Are they still in use?
   a. enclosure   b. kind

3. Write your own brief dictionary (ten to twelve items) of slang expressions that you encounter among one particular group of people or in one place (for example, the pool hall, the dorm, a disco, the stables; black slang, Chinese slang, Jewish slang, and so on). Use terms peculiar to the chosen place or group as much as possible. Make as specific a definition of each as you can and guess at etymologies by looking up the words in a standard dictionary and comparing those meanings with definitions of the words found in the slang dictionaries.

rhetoric

The word *rhetoric*, a word always invoked in discussions of effective writing, is itself somewhat ineffective because it can have so many different meanings. Historically, the term *rhetoric* referred only to speech, and especially to oratory intended to persuade. Today, in its broadest meaning, *rhetoric* refers to both spoken and written communication. It is sometimes more narrowly defined as the study—as opposed to the practice—of the devices used in communication. More narrowly still, it can mean the art of prose as opposed to the art of poetry. It can be used with positive connotations to mean the power of pleasing or persuading by speech or writing. Or it may be used with negative connotations to refer to artificial and ornate language. With even more strongly negative connotations, it can refer to language that is deliberately dishonest and intended to deceive.

In the following sections, we shall use the word *rhetoric* to mean the art of effective prose writing, including the construction of sentences, paragraphs, and entire papers. We will also use it with some of its historical meaning of the art of making a persuasive argument. Rhetoric is our means of focusing our readers' attention on what we want to emphasize and of persuading them to think or act as we believe they should.

The most natural way of expressing ideas is by stringing one idea after the other with no particular concern for their arrangement or relative importance. This is the way we think and this is the way we normally speak. However, our language offers us a great variety of ways to express even very simple ideas, and, within a given context, some ways are usually preferable to others. In writing, we select a certain arrangement, not because there is an inherent virtue in that arrangement, but because it makes the greatest contribution to the entire piece.

In the following pages, various aspects of rhetoric—sentences, paragraphs, entire papers, logic—are discussed separately. The process of composition is not as straightforward or as simple as these divisions might imply. We do not take a handful of words and juggle them around until a sentence appears, then shuffle sentences until we have a paragraph, then move paragraphs here and there until a paper comes into being, and then finally go back and put logic into the sentences, the paragraphs, and the paper as a whole. Instead, we consider the entire paper as we write paragraphs, we think of groups of paragraphs as we write individual sentences, and we try to keep our reasoning clear and logical at every stage of composition. The divisions presented here are necessary for purposes of explanation, but the actual process of writing a paper is an integrated one, not easily divisible into discrete steps.

49 WORDS INTO SENTENCES

The essentials of good sentences are clarity, emphasis, and variety. Clarity is the universal requirement—if the reader doesn't understand what we intend to say, the entire sentence is a failure. Emphasis and variety are relative matters. Everything we say should be clear, but we do not want to emphasize every single word that we use, nor is there much value in variety just for the sake of variety. In other words, proper emphasis and variety depend on the context in which we are writing. This context includes more than just the sentences before and after the sentence we are writing; it includes also the subject matter, the audience, the type of writing, and the purpose of the paper.

As an illustration of how different contexts demand different arrangements, assume that you have the following ideas to express.

> Fumes kill things. Some fumes come from automobiles. These automobile fumes have killed maple trees. These maple trees are along the boulevard.

All these ideas can easily be combined into one simple, "neutral" sentence.

> Automobile fumes have killed the maple trees along the boulevard.

If you had been discussing the different kinds of fumes that damage the environment, you might make fumes the subject of the sentence.

> Fumes from automobiles have killed the maple trees along the boulevard.

If you were stressing the different kinds of vegetation harmed by pollution, you could begin the sentence by stating a particular kind of vegetation.

> The maple trees along the boulevard have been killed by automobile fumes.

If your focus were on the various areas of the city where pollution damage has occurred, you might mention the particular area first.

> Along the boulevard, automobile fumes have killed the maple trees.

If you wished to correct an erroneous impression that it was old age or vandalism that killed the maple trees, you could write the sentence to stress that idea.

> It was automobile fumes that killed the maple trees along the boulevard.

All of these sentences are clear. The order has been changed to provide different kinds of emphasis suitable for different contexts.

rh

These sentences also illustrate the importance of position in a sentence. In most English sentences, we expect the topic, or what we are focusing our attention on, to come early in the sentence, followed by the comment, or what we have to say about that topic. Thus, in the first of the rewritten sentences above, the topic is automobile fumes, whereas in the third sentence, the topic is maple trees. Effective sentences fulfill the reader's expectations about topic and comment; weak sentences do not meet the reader's expectations. For example, if the third sentence were used in a context focusing on types of harmful fumes, our expectations would be frustrated because the early position of the phrase *the maple trees* (and its use as subject of the sentence) leads us to think that it is the focus of attention. A composition teacher would probably write "Weak Passive" beside that sentence, not because the passive is wrong as such, but because its use in such a context gives the reader false expectations.

49a RHETORICAL TYPES OF SENTENCES

In addition to the types of sentences (simple, compound, complex, and compound-complex) discussed in 16a, there are two basic stylistic forms of sentence arrangement—*cumulative* (or *loose*) sentences, and *periodic* sentences—as well as sentences that represent a mixture of the two. Cumulative, periodic, and mixed sentences may be simple, compound, complex, or compound-complex. It is not the type of grammatical construction that determines whether a sentence is cumulative, periodic, or mixed; rather, it is the placement of the elements that contain the most important ideas.

Cumulative Sentences. **Cumulative sentences** follow a natural, or "neutral," sentence structure. Topic and comment are stated first, followed by amplifying detail.

> He had large white hands like those in pictures of King David in the Bible. —John Gardner, THE SUNLIGHT DIALOGUES

> But the story of Assyria lies outside the story of Greece, since the Greeks, except in one outlying corner, came into no immediate contact with the lords of Nineveh.
> —J. B. Bury, A HISTORY OF GREECE

Periodic Sentences. In **periodic sentences,** the main idea is not completed until near the end, after amplifying detail has already been stated. Because the main idea is delayed, a certain amount of suspense is built up.

> But in the same rush of clear-headed detachment he had recognized, like Jacob of old when he found he'd got Leah, whose arms were like sticks and whose mouth was as flat as a salamander's, that he'd have to be a monster to tell her the truth.
> —John Gardner, THE SUNLIGHT DIALOGUES

> While the Greeks were sailing their own seas, and working out in their city-states the institutions of law and freedom, untroubled

by any catastrophe beyond the shores of the Mediterranean, <u>great despotic kingdoms were waxing and waning in the east</u>.
—J. B. Bury, *A HISTORY OF GREECE*

The main statement is usually made in the independent clause of a periodic sentence. However, it may occur in a subordinate clause, as in the first sentence above. Occasionally, for special effect, the most important part is put into a modifying phrase.

The place was crawling with cockroaches as big as your fist, <u>like the one on your collar</u>.

Virtually any cumulative sentence can be rewritten as a periodic sentence, and vice versa. The decision as to which sentence type to use depends on the amount of emphasis desired. A periodic sentence is nearly always more emphatic than a cumulative sentence.

CUMULATIVE
<u>But the story of Assyria lies outside the story of Greece</u>, since the Greeks, except in one outlying corner, came into no immediate contact with the lords of Nineveh.
—J. B. Bury, *A HISTORY OF GREECE*

REWRITTEN AS PERIODIC
Since the Greeks, except in one outlying corner, came into no immediate contact with the lords of Nineveh, <u>the story of Assyria lies outside the story of Greece</u>.

PERIODIC
While the Greeks were sailing their own seas, and working out in their city-states the institutions of law and freedom, untroubled by any catastrophe beyond the shores of the Mediterranean, <u>great despotic kingdoms were waxing and waning in the east</u>.
—J. B. Bury, *A HISTORY OF GREECE*

REWRITTEN AS CUMULATIVE
<u>Great despotic kingdoms were waxing and waning in the east</u> while the Greeks were sailing their own seas and working out in their city-states the institutions of law and freedom, untroubled by any catastrophe beyond the shores of the Mediterranean.

Mixed Sentences. Although good writers use both purely cumulative and purely periodic sentences, a mixture of the two is probably more common than either. **Mixed sentences** begin with some amplifying detail, continue with the main statement, and end with more amplifying detail.

Even with their lights on, <u>the houses looked abandoned</u>, like habitations depopulated by plague.
—John Gardner, *THE SUNLIGHT DIALOGUES*

In the seventh century, <u>the mighty empire of Assyria was verging to its end</u>; the power destined to overthrow it had arisen.
—J. B. Bury, *A HISTORY OF GREECE*

Mixed sentences are especially useful when several modifying phrases are to be included in the sentence. In such cases, a periodic structure would result in a long string of introductory material, leaving the reader wondering if the writer will ever get to the point. A cumulative structure would pile all the modifiers at the end, weakening the end of the sentence. Notice how much weaker a mixed sentence can become when it is rewritten either as a periodic or a cumulative sentence.

MIXED	Even with their lights on, <u>the houses looked abandoned</u>, like habitations depopulated by plague. —John Gardner, *THE SUNLIGHT DIALOGUES*
PERIODIC	Like habitations depopulated by plague, even with their lights on, <u>the houses looked abandoned</u>.
CUMULATIVE	<u>The houses looked abandoned</u>, even with their lights on, like habitations depopulated by plague.

EXERCISES: Rhetorical Types of Sentences

Part A: Identify each of the following sentences as cumulative (C), periodic (P), or mixed (M). Underline the part of the sentence that contains the core meaning.

> EXAMPLE: When the car sputtered to a halt, <u>Monique put on the emergency signal and climbed out</u>, hoping that a passing motorist would stop to help.

1. Returning to their hotel room after spending the morning sight-seeing, Jim and Marie found that they had been robbed of everything.

2. It was not until the thunder and lightning became fierce and the air grew steamy that the farmers knew the inevitable: a tornado would soon twist its gyrating blackness across the plains.

3. Unimpressed by the D that he had received on the chemistry exam, Dave cut the three chemistry classes after the test, finding out too late that those people who had attended class that week had been allowed to retake the exam.

4. The old woman glowered at the children and they glowered back at her, pitiless and unyielding in their defiance.

5. Greg was fired after only one night's work in the supermarket because he stamped a whole case of cans with the wrong price, unwittingly destroyed four cartons of eggs with the handle of a mop, and almost ran down a customer with a train of shopping carts he was returning to the front of the store.

6. To the delight of the cheering crowds who had lined the shore to marvel at these old vessels, the tall ships made their way into Boston harbor—their sails flapping like great white sheets hung out to dry, their crews climbing like circus entertainers about the rigging.

Part B: Write one cumulative, one periodic, and one mixed sentence for *each* of the following bits of information. The main idea is given in the first sentence, and ideas to be subordinated are given in sentences within parentheses.

1. Our beach house had survived the storm. (It was protected by an enormous sand dune. All the neighboring houses lay in ruins. The contents of these houses were strewn about the beach like playthings.)

2. The giraffe's problem was finally diagnosed as a sore throat. (The giraffe had not eaten for several days. She had seemed listless. She had been avoiding the zoo attendants and the other giraffes.)

49b CLARITY / cl

The three qualities of good sentences are clarity, emphasis, and variety. Of these, clarity is the most important. If the reader does not understand what you are saying, no amount of tinkering to achieve emphasis or variety can salvage the writing. The first essential of clarity is having something to say and then saying it in an organized fashion. If a piece of writing has no focus, even clear sentences will not save it.

However, many writers who do have something to say and who arrange what they have to say logically still have difficulty in making their individual sentences clear to their readers. Among the most common causes of unclear sentences are errors in grammar and usage, improper punctuation, improper transitions, overuse of nouns as modifiers, awkward placement of modifiers, irrelevant details, overuse of long, complicated sentences, and overreliance on speech patterns.

Grammatical Errors.   Almost all grammatical and usage errors detract from clarity. Typical errors include (1) incorrect or vague pronoun reference, (2) improper agreement, (3) dangling, misplaced, and squinting modifiers, (4) improper or illogical comparison, (5) omission of necessary articles or prepositions, (6) lack of parallelism, (7) careless adverb placement, (8) improper use of subordination and coordination, and (9) shifted constructions. (See sections 1–23.)

Improper Punctuation.   One of the chief purposes of punctuation is to signal which of two possible grammatical relationships the writer intends. Good punctuation contributes to clarity by preventing ambiguity. Clarity may be destroyed either by errors of omission (failing to put punctuation where it is needed) or by errors of commission (putting punctuation where it does not belong). In the following example, the lack of a comma after *short* makes the reader think that *short* modifies *autobiographies.* Not until the reader gets to the verb *are* does it become apparent that, because there is no subject for *are, in short* must be an introductory phrase.

| UNCLEAR | In short autobiographies of famous people are often self-serving. |
| CLEAR | In short, autobiographies of famous people are often self-serving. |

In the following sentence, the comma after *that* leads the reader to believe that the clause has ended (rather than just begun).

| UNCLEAR | Roberts knew that, he wouldn't have the courage to say no. |
| CLEAR | Roberts knew that he wouldn't have the courage to say no. |

See sections 24–40 for a review of punctuation.

Improper Transitions.   We use various kinds of **transitional words** to relate what we have said previously to what we are going to say later. Readers, often unconsciously, rely heavily on transitional words to establish the logic of sentences and groups of sentences. For example, *the* often signals that its following noun is familiar or has already been mentioned. Personal pronouns serve the same purpose. An improper transitional word sends a false or ambiguous signal to the reader, resulting in loss of clarity.

Of particular importance in transitions are subordinating conjunctions, coordinating conjunctions, and conjunctive adverbs. The first sentence below is ambiguous because the subordinating conjunction *while* can mean either "although" or "during the time that." (See also 9c.)

AMBIGUOUS	While he was only a child, he could name twenty kinds of dinosaurs.
CLEAR	When he was only a child, he could name twenty kinds of dinosaurs.
CLEAR	Although he was only a child, he could name twenty kinds of dinosaurs.

Careless use of the coordinating conjunctions *and* and *but* also detracts from clarity. *And* means simply "in addition to." *But* always implies some kind of contrast or something contrary to expectation.

> I brought binoculars, *and* Dean brought a small telescope.
>
> I brought binoculars, *but* Dean brought a small telescope.

The *and* in the first sentence implies that we had two optical instruments with us. The *but* in the second sentence implies that Dean was not expected to bring a telescope or that a telescope was somehow more suitable or less suitable than binoculars. Choose the coordinating conjunction that conveys the exact meaning you intend (see also 9a).

Improper use of conjunctive adverbs frequently leads to unclear transitions.

> I have always been a poor speller; <u>nevertheless</u>, I look up every word whose spelling I am uncertain of.

Here, *nevertheless* leads the reader to expect that what follows will be a contradiction of or an exception to what has preceded. But the writer really wants to express a cause-effect idea and should have used *therefore* or *consequently* instead of *nevertheless*.

> I have always been a poor speller; <u>therefore</u>, I look up every word whose spelling I am uncertain of.

Overuse of Nouns as Modifiers.   **Noun adjuncts,** or the use of nouns to modify other nouns, are a familiar and often convenient feature of English. Noun adjuncts can, however, easily become too much of a good thing. One noun adjunct per noun phrase is rarely a problem (*traffic control, oil refinery, shotgun pellet*). Lack of clarity begins when three or more nouns appear in succession. For example, the phrase *city hospital planning committee,* in addition to being ungraceful, is also unclear. Does it mean a committee to make plans for a city hospital? A planning committee established by the city hospital? A city committee for hospital planning? To avoid excessive use of nouns as modifiers, substitute prepositional phrases for some of the nouns. Sometimes you can rewrite the phrase, replacing one of the nouns with a verb.

UNCLEAR	neighborhood traffic control regulations
PREPOSITIONAL PHRASE	regulations for the control of neighborhood traffic
UNCLEAR	There has been no citizen revaluation dispute participation.
VERB	The citizens have not participated in the revaluation dispute.

Awkward Placement of Modifiers.   When a writer inserts modifiers as they come into his or her mind and without concern for the most effective placement, the result is lack of clarity. Probably the most distracting interruptions are long modifiers that split up a verb phrase or that separate a verb from its object or complement. Correct this fault by moving the modifying phrase to another position in the sentence; the beginning of the sentence is usually the best position (see also 20c).

AWKWARD	A retail store may, through a special division established for the purpose, also conduct a mail-order business.
IMPROVED	Through a special division established for the purpose, a retail store may also conduct a mail-order business.
AWKWARD	Mendel was able to formulate, as a result of his long years of experimentation, three basic laws of heredity.
IMPROVED	As a result of his long years of experimentation, Mendel was able to formulate three basic laws of heredity.

Irrelevant Detail.   Irrelevant detail not only clutters up the sentence but may confuse readers by leading them to think that there is a relationship between the detail and the main statement that they do not understand.

In 1502, Leonardo da Vinci, <u>who was left-handed</u>, became Cesare Borgia's military engineer. (His left-handedness is irrelevant to his job as a military engineer.)

Context determines whether detail is relevant or not. In the following sentence, the clause *who was left-handed* is appropriate because left-handed people often smear their writing when they write from left to right and hence are more likely to want to do mirror writing.

Leonardo da Vinci, <u>who was left-handed</u>, left notebooks in mirror writing, writing which must be viewed in a mirror in order to be read.

Overuse of Long Sentences.   In the eighteenth and nineteenth centuries, the sentences of good writers were as long as sixty or seventy words. Today, readers are accustomed to shorter sentences and find long, involved sentences tiresome and difficult to decipher, especially if these sentences contain a great deal of subordination. To avoid lack of clarity caused by extraordinarily long sentences (over thirty or forty words), break them up into two or three shorter sentences.

TOO LONG	It was not so much that I resented my father's advice—after all, I had often asked him for advice—as that I resented his giving it at that time, when I was having difficulty accepting authority from any source, whether it were that of a parent I knew loved me or an outsider who I felt was hostile to me, and therefore any advice offered was open to my suspicion, which I could not easily conceal.
IMPROVED	I could not resent my father's advice because I had often asked him for it. However, at that time I was having difficulty accepting authority from any source, whether from a loving parent or from a hostile outsider. Therefore, I was suspicious of all advice, and I could not easily conceal this suspicion.

Overreliance on Speech Patterns.   Sentences that are technically grammatical and that are completely clear when spoken may be confusing when written. The following example, although exaggerated, can be made comprehensible if spoken with the proper intonation but is virtually indecipherable when written.

I know that that that that that that refers to is wrong.

A more typical example of confusion resulting from overreliance on speech patterns is the following.

UNCLEAR	With the decrease in epidemics, heart disease and cancer have become the leading causes of death. (The reader may at first think that epidemics, heart disease, and cancer have all decreased.)
IMPROVED	Now that epidemics have decreased, heart disease and cancer have become leading causes of death.

EXERCISE: Clarity

Rewrite the following paragraph to make it clear. Decide what the focal point is and state it clearly. Correct any errors in grammar and punctuation. Use proper transitions and concrete diction. Avoid overuse of nouns as modifiers, irrelevant detail, too many long sentences, wordiness, and overreliance on speech patterns. Maintain *one* level of English throughout.

The mountain of success is very much like the life of a common person. Many people are continuously seeking for that mountain to conquer. To many people this mountain may mean different things. Money is one of the utmost goals man has ever striven for. The mountain along with fame is success. Much of the world today is run on this success. Trees, rocks, cliffs, and the never-ending inclines. All of these are obstacles we must oppose and overcome. It is there and in great numbers for all men. And just as surely as that mountain exists, man today is confronted with work that must be conquered and put to the test. To finish college or pass that exam or to get a good job just sets you higher on the mountain toward the top. And still there is much competition among people to get to the top, whether by physical or mental activity. The top is success and an abundant life.

49c EMPHASIS / emph

Emphasis is stress on or prominence of certain ideas. Appropriate emphasis adds to clarity by drawing the reader's attention to the most important points and keeping the less important ones in the background. Inappropriate emphasis confuses the reader. Appropriate emphasis is easy to achieve in speech by means of facial expressions, tone of voice, loudness of voice, pauses, and gestures. Writing does not offer these methods for creating emphasis, and the writer is limited to choice of words, arrangement of these words in the sentence, and, occasionally, punctuation and other graphic devices.

Do not feel that every sentence you write should be dramatically emphatic. Emphasis is effective only when it contributes to the whole paper, and the context determines what should be emphasized. If you try to emphasize every clause, every sentence, you will, like the boy who cried "Wolf!" find that your audience no longer believes you.

Graphic Devices. When we hear the word *emphasis*, we may first think of underlining, capital letters, and exclamation points. And indeed, some writers rely heavily on these graphic devices to achieve emphasis. Although such devices are occasionally justified, overreliance on them tends to make the writer appear somewhat hysterical. The best writers achieve emphasis through a judicious choice of words and careful sentence construction.

UNSUITABLE	There is *absolutely no* excuse for such behavior!
IMPROVED	Such behavior is inexcusable.
UNSUITABLE	In 1890, leg-of-mutton sleeves were THE THING in fashion.
IMPROVED	In 1890, leg-of-mutton sleeves were highly fashionable.

Position. By far the most important method of achieving emphasis in writing is careful placement of the elements of the sentence. The end of a clause or sentence is usually the most emphatic position. Hence, a periodic sentence is usually more emphatic than a cumulative sentence because it allows a certain amount of suspense to build up and leaves readers with the main idea foremost in their minds. The beginning of a clause or sentence is also a strong position because it is usually the place where the topic is introduced.

You can take advantage of these naturally strong positions by placing those elements that you wish to emphasize either at the end or at the beginning of a sentence. Conversely, you should avoid placing weak elements in a strong position.

    1. **Periodic Structure.** Short, simple sentences are usually periodic in effect because the topic is introduced first, and the rest of the sentence contains the main idea or the comment on that topic.

> Speed kills.
> Many plants reproduce by means of spores.
> The leadership of Europe fell into the hands of Prince Metternich.

In longer, complex sentences, you can achieve the more emphatic periodic sentence structure by placing subordinate clauses early in the sentence and leaving the end of the sentence for the main clause.

LESS EMPHATIC	It is disturbing to realize that we destroy several million brain cells whenever we sneeze.
MORE EMPHATIC	It is disturbing to realize that, whenever we sneeze, we destroy several million brain cells.

    2. **Adverbial Phrases at the Beginning.** You can often move adverbial phrases to the beginning of the sentence, leaving the subject or direct object in the emphatic position at the end of the sentence.

LESS EMPHATIC	A vicious-looking whip was in his hand.
MORE EMPHATIC	In his hand was a vicious-looking whip.
LESS EMPHATIC	The prospector struck gold after ten years of searching.
MORE EMPHATIC	After ten years of searching, the prospector struck gold.

    3. **Conjunctive Adverbs at or near the Beginning.** Like subordinate clauses, clauses with conjunctive adverbs qualify a preceding clause or sentence. Sentences are more emphatic if conjunctive adverbs appear at or near the beginning of their clauses. Such placement also adds to clarity because it informs the reader at once about the relationship of the sentence or clause to the preceding material.

UNEMPHATIC	Smoking is bad for one's health; many people ignore this fact, however.
EMPHATIC	Smoking is bad for one's health; however, many people ignore this fact.

    4. **Inversion.** The expected word order of declarative clauses and sentences is subject + verb + object or complement. Consequently, when this word order is violated, the reader's attention is drawn to the inverted words, and greater emphasis is the result. We are not free to make just any kind of inversion in English: obviously, inverting *John builds gliders* to *Builds John gliders* is not emphatic—it is ungrammatical. However, we can often place a direct object or complement before the subject and verb, thus lending emphasis to that object or complement.

LESS EMPHATIC	Steven has asked for trouble and he will get trouble.
MORE EMPHATIC	Trouble Steven has asked for and trouble he will get.
LESS EMPHATIC	Though Marie was poor, she was always generous.
MORE EMPHATIC	Poor though Marie was, she was always generous.

When you use position to achieve emphasis, be sure that the emphasis is appropriate to the context. False emphasis is a greater stylistic flaw than weak emphasis. For example, the sentence above (*Trouble Steven has asked for and trouble he will get*) would be appropriate when the context concerned Steven's behavior, lack of cooperation, or the like.

> Steven has always refused to cooperate, and now he has insulted everyone. Trouble he has asked for and trouble he will get.

However, if the context concerned a contrast between Steven's behavior and the behavior of others, the main focus would be on Steven, and the inverted word order would not be appropriate.

> Everyone else has been cooperative. Trouble Steven has asked for and trouble he will get.

Climactic Order.   Emphasis can also be gained by putting words, phrases, and clauses in an ascending order of importance, saving the strongest points for last.

| UNEMPHATIC | For her birthday, Jeffrey bought his wife a cashmere sweater, a Jaguar, and a jigsaw puzzle. |
| EMPHATIC | For her birthday, Jeffrey bought his wife a jigsaw puzzle, a cashmere sweater, and a Jaguar. |

Sometimes climactic order is deliberately reversed for a humorous effect.

> During her college years, Karen learned to think critically, question perceptively, write clearly, and play a mean game of gin rummy.

Careless anticlimax, however, simply destroys emphasis.

> The Soviet Union is the largest nation in the world, the richest country in natural resources, and the world's leading exporter of caviar.

Context determines what is climactic and what is anticlimactic. Taken in isolation, the following sentence might appear anticlimactic, but in a narrative about a search for a missing hairbrush, it would be highly climactic and emphatic.

> I came down from the attic, carrying an antique doll's head, some love letters written by my grandfather, and my long-lost hairbrush.

Coordination and Subordination.   Proper use of coordination and subordination is essential for appropriate emphasis. As a general rule, put important ideas in main clauses and less important ideas in subordinate clauses. Simple coordination is usually not especially emphatic because the reader expects coordination to connect ideas of equal importance. In the following sentence, the focus is on Eleanor's accent. Her trip to Atlanta merely explains where the accent came from. Therefore, we stress the fact of the accent by putting it in the main clause and subordinating the origin of the accent.

UNEMPHATIC	Eleanor returned from Atlanta, and we were amazed by the change in her accent.
EMPHATIC	When Eleanor returned from Atlanta, we were amazed by the change in her accent.

We frequently wish to emphasize two ideas equally. In such cases, coordination (a compound sentence) is the appropriate means of connecting the two ideas. Subordination (a complex sentence) would give false emphasis to the idea in the main clause.

FALSE EMPHASIS	Although the walls were green, the rug was white.
APPROPRIATE EMPHASIS	The walls were green and the rug was white.

Again, context and intended meaning should determine whether to use coordination or subordination. If you are simply describing the appearance of a room, the compound sentence above is appropriate. On the other hand, if you were discussing practical colors for rooms and room furnishings, the complex sentence would be better because it would imply the impracticality of a white rug. (See 9 for a more extensive discussion of coordinating and subordinating conjunctions.)

Passive Voice. Some writers seem to feel that the passive voice adds authority and dignity to a sentence. This is rarely the case, and overuse of the passive makes for dull, wordy writing and detracts from proper emphasis.

WORDY PASSIVE	It is argued by the author that the cease-fire agreement was violated by the Egyptians.
IMPROVED	The author argues that the Egyptians violated the cease-fire agreement.

There are four conditions under which the passive voice is normally preferable to the active voice and when its use adds to, rather than detracts from, proper emphasis.

1. **Focus on Receiver or Result of Action.** Use the passive when the focus of attention is on the receiver of the action. Ordinarily, the sentence "A child was hit by a car this afternoon" would be preferable to "A car hit a child this afternoon" because we would normally be more concerned about the child than about the car. Context is the determining factor here. If the topic of discussion were state laws, the first sentence in the following example would provide the appropriate emphasis. But if the topic were advertising, the second sentence, with the passive, would be more appropriate.

Most states have laws regulating advertising.
Advertising is regulated by law in most states.

Similarly, if you want to create a picture of the *results* of action rather than to emphasize the action itself, the passive is appropriate. For example, if you were focusing on how hard an individual worked to make a good appearance, you might stress his or her activities by using only active verbs.

Bruce got a haircut, cleaned his nails, shined his shoes, and pressed his best suit carefully.

On the other hand, if you wanted to emphasize how the individual appeared to someone else, you could create an effective static picture by using the passive voice.

Bruce's hair was neatly trimmed, his nails clean, his shoes shined, and his suit carefully pressed.

2. **Doer of Action Unknown.** Use the passive when the doer of the action is unknown or irrelevant. The sentence "The meeting was adjourned at 3:30" is appropriate because it is unimportant—and probably unknown—who made the motion to adjourn and which people voted for adjournment.

3. **Long Clause as Subject.** Use the passive when a lengthy clause would otherwise be the subject of the sentence. Lengthy clauses make awkward and unemphatic subjects.

LESS EMPHATIC | To hear that the city plans to repair our street delighted me.

MORE EMPHATIC | I was delighted to hear that the city plans to repair our street.

4. **Avoidance of First Person.** Use the passive when convention demands it. In many kinds of technical writing, it is conventional to avoid the use of the first person, and frequently the only alternative is the passive voice.

INAPPROPRIATE | I placed four mice in the maze.

IMPROVED | Four mice were placed in the maze.

Balance and Parallelism. Balanced sentences are especially useful for emphasizing complementary or contradictory ideas. Parallelism, or using the same grammatical structure for all items that have the same function, is the chief component of balanced sentences (see also 23f).

Do not let us speak of darker days; let us rather speak of sterner days. —Winston Churchill, *Speech*

The race is not to the swift, nor the battle to the strong.

A man of sense only trifles with them [women], plays with them, humours and flatters them, as he does with a sprightly and forward child; but he neither consults them about, nor trusts them with, serious matters. —Lord Chesterfield, *Letter To His Son*

In these sentences, the clauses are parallel. For example, in the first sentence above, both clauses begin with an imperative and end in a prepositional phrase. The last sentence is a good example of how effective and emphatic even long sentences can be if they are balanced.

The sentences above also illustrate that **repetition** reinforces parallelism and balance. The amount of repetition may vary according to the content. The Churchill quotation repeats the words *let, us, speak, of,* and *days.* The second sentence repeats only *take, the,* and *road.* But repetition alone does not create emphasis. The repetition must be parallel; careless, nonparallel repetition is annoying to the reader. For example, consider how ineffective Lincoln's famous lines "government of the people, by the people, and for the people" would have been if he had worded them differently.

> [we here highly resolve] that the government of the *people* shall not perish from this earth, that the *people* should control the government, and that the purpose of government is to serve the *people's* needs.

In Lincoln's original lines, *people* appears three times, each time as the object of a preposition. In the ineffective paraphrase, the repetition of *people* is not parallel; *people* is first an object of a preposition, then a subject, and finally a modifier of a noun.

Change in Sentence Length. A short sentence before or after a series of longer sentences is an effective way of adding emphasis by providing a change of pace.

> There is always a surprise during Derby week. This year, it came in the Kentucky Oaks, for three-year-old fillies, which was run the day before the big race. Neither Lakeville Miss nor Caesar's Wish finished in the first three. The winner was the Newstead Farm's undefeated White Star Line, a filly who is noted for beginning slowly and finishing with a great rush, and that is just what she did in the Oaks.
> —Audax Minor, "The Race Track: Affirmed's Kentucky Derby,"
> The New Yorker

> Brothers may separate and quarrel, especially when each is created with a separate, personal soul that he retains through all eternity. The lofty Hindu declares that 'one should love his neighbor as himself because he *is* his neighbor.' All selves are one.
> —Herbert J. Muller, THE USES OF THE PAST

In both these examples, the emphasis arises from the *contrast* between the short sentence and the long sentences, not from the short sentence in and of itself. Notice how much emphasis is lost from the first example if it is rewritten so that all the sentences are short.

UNEMPHATIC   There is always a surprise during Derby Week. This year, it came in the Kentucky Oaks. This is a race for three-year-old fillies. It was run the day before the big race. Neither Lakeville Miss nor Caesar's Wish finished in the first three. The winner was the Newstead Farm's undefeated White Star Line. This filly is noted for beginning slowly and finishing with a great rush. That is just what she did in the Oaks.

EXERCISES: Emphasis

Part A: To get practice in achieving emphasis in a number of ways, write sentences according to the following specifications.

1. Using periodic structure to achieve emphasis, write a sentence about a moment when you were very frightened.

2. Using inversion to achieve emphasis, write two sentences about your least favorite teacher in elementary school.

3. Using climactic order to achieve emphasis, write a sentence about events during an industrial strike.

4. Write two simple sentences that describe a beautiful natural setting. Then combine the two into one sentence, emphasizing one idea by subordinating the other.

5. Use the passive voice to focus attention on the subject of a sentence about an experience in a department store.

6. Using balance and parallelism to achieve emphasis, write a sentence about the difference between selfishness and selflessness.

Part B: Read the following two passages carefully. Then choose the device or devices from the list below that the authors have used to achieve emphasis. Indicate beside the name of the device the number of the sentence that contains it.

Graphic device	Subordination/coordination
Periodic structure	Passive voice
Climactic order	Balance and parallelism
Inversion	Change in sentence length

1. Medieval Englishmen were not, like stereotype modern Englishmen, calm and sensible people: they were as passionate, as affectionate, as quick to change moods, and as easily stirred to violence as, say, the stereotype modern Italian.[1] When greeting each other, they hugged and kissed like modern Frenchmen; when insulted or injured they snatched at their daggers without thinking.[2] The younger Henry of Lancaster once, in a fit of pique, forgot and drew his sword on the king himself.[3] To show just how little such things meant in that age, nothing came of it.[4] Without inhibition they showered their affection on their children and whenever possible, took them with them wherever they went, especially to church, to general fairs, to holy-day outings (which averaged one a week), and to Friday horse fairs.[5] On those days when all England got off work, London and the countryside surrounding became tumultuous with games—noisy, often dangerous games, frequent cause of riots.[6] Even those noble games tennis and chess were illegal inside London, though often played—the one because of the riots tennis regularly incited (this was "real" or "royal" tennis, fast and ferocious), the other because chess, a gamblers' game, had a name for provoking murders.

—John Gardner, THE LIFE AND TIMES OF CHAUCER

2. A few hours ago I discharged my last duty as King and Emperor, and now that I have been succeeded by my brother, the Duke of York, my first words must be to declare my allegiance to him.[1] This I do with all my heart.[2] You all know the reasons which have impelled me to renounce the Throne, but I want you to understand that in making up my mind I did not forget the Country or the Empire, which as Prince of Wales and lately as King, I have for twenty-five years tried to serve.[3]

> But you must believe me when I tell you that I have found it impossible to carry the heavy burden of responsibility and to discharge my duties as King, as I wish to do, without the help and support of the woman I love, and I want you to know that the decision I have made has been mine, and mine alone.
>
> —*From the abdication speech of King Edward VIII of England*

49d VARIETY / var

The purpose of using a variety of sentence types in writing is to avoid monotony, which bores and distracts the reader. Although too much of anything results in lack of variety—too many short sentences, too many long sentences, too much subordination, too many periodic sentences—the most common problem of variety in student writing is an excess of short, choppy sentences. If the writing consists only of a series of short declarative sentences, the reader is likely to assume that the writer's thoughts are immature; that is, the constant use of short sentences suggests that the writer can think only in terms of simple statements and cannot see their interrelationships.

Variety is not a virtue in and of itself but only as it contributes to clarity and emphasis. Indeed, if you pay careful attention to clarity and especially to emphasis, you will probably find that variety results automatically. When revising for variety, always keep an eye on how your revisions affect clarity and emphasis.

Variety by Sentence-Combining.   One of the most basic and most obvious ways of achieving variety is to vary sentence length. This implies a variety of sentence types because simple declarative sentences tend to be short—there is a limit to the number of adjectives you can stick in front of nouns to stretch out the length of a sentence. So, to avoid an excess of short simple sentences, you can combine some of them into longer sentences. Sentence combination may take the form of (1) coordination, or making a single compound sentence out of two or more simple sentences; (2) subordination, or making a single complex sentence out of two simple sentences; or (3) embedding, or making one of the simple sentences into an adjectival or adverbial modifier or an absolute construction (see 11c) within the other simple sentence. The same set of simple sentences can often be combined in a number of different ways.

SIMPLE SENTENCES	Jeremiah prophesied the defeat of Judah. He was condemned as a traitor.
COORDINATION	Jeremiah prophesied the defeat of Judah, and he was condemned as a traitor.
SUBORDINATION	After Jeremiah prophesied the defeat of Judah, he was condemned as a traitor.
	Jeremiah was condemned as a traitor because he prophesied the defeat of Judah.
EMBEDDING	Jeremiah, having prophesied the defeat of Judah, was condemned as a traitor.

> Jeremiah, who prophesied the defeat of Judah, was condemned as a traitor.
>
> Having prophesied the defeat of Judah, Jeremiah was condemned as a traitor.

Note: When the subject (or the predicate) of the two sentences to be combined is the same, it can be omitted in the second clause. The result is technically a simple sentence with a compound subject (or predicate), but the principle is the same as that of a compound sentence.

> Jeremiah prophesied the defeat of Judah and was condemned as a traitor.

To illustrate how sentence-combining adds variety to a series of sentences or paragraphs, let us assume that you were writing a paper on the *Titanic* disaster of 1912. As an introduction to the paper, you have decided to give some information about icebergs. You have consulted an encyclopedia, have discovered the following facts, and have written down all these facts in simple sentences.

> Icebergs are frozen fresh water.[1] Ice floes are frozen salt water.[2] Pack ice is also frozen salt water.[3] Icebergs rise up to 200 feet above the waterline.[4] Icebergs reach below the waterline for seven to nine times their height.[5] The direction of drift of an iceberg depends on the wind.[6] Icebergs do not move into the wind.[7]
>
> Most icebergs come from the glaciers of Greenland or from the shelf ice of Antarctica.[8] South Pacific icebergs come up almost to southern Australia.[9] North Pacific icebergs occur only in the Bering Strait.[10] There are many icebergs in the North Atlantic.[11] About 10,000 to 15,000 icebergs a year break off from western Greenland alone.[12] Other icebergs break off from eastern Greenland.[13] North Atlantic icebergs appear in shipping lanes.[14] Icebergs appear as far south as the Azores.[15]

These sentences are all short, and the result is clearly too choppy. Many of the sentences are related to each other and can be combined. By using coordination alone, you might produce the following.

> Ice floes and pack ice are frozen salt water, but icebergs are frozen fresh water. (**1, 2** and **3** combined) Icebergs rise up to 200 feet above the waterline and reach below the waterline for seven to nine times their height. (**4** and **5** combined) The direction of drift of icebergs depends on the wind, and icebergs do not move into the wind. (**6** and **7** combined)
>
> Most icebergs come from the glaciers of Greenland or from the shelf ice of Antarctica. South Pacific icebergs come up almost to southern Australia, but North Pacific icebergs occur only in the Bering Strait. (**9** and **10** combined) There are many icebergs in the North Atlantic. About 10,000 to 15,000 icebergs a year break off from western Greenland alone, and others break off from eastern Greenland. (**12** and **13** combined) North Atlantic icebergs appear in shipping lanes; they appear as far south as the Azores. (**14** and **15** combined)

By using subordination only, you could combine several of the original sentences, making complex sentences.

> Although ice floes and pack ice are frozen salt water, icebergs are frozen fresh water. (**1, 2,** and **3** combined) Icebergs rise up to 200 feet above the waterline. Icebergs reach below the waterline for seven to nine times their height. Because their direction of drift depends on the wind, icebergs do not move into the wind. (**6** and **7** combined)
>
> Most icebergs come from the glaciers of Greenland or from the shelf ice of Antarctica. Although South Pacific icebergs come up almost to southern Australia, North Pacific icebergs occur only in the Bering Strait. (**9** and **10** combined) There are many icebergs in the North Atlantic. About 10,000 to 15,000 icebergs a year break off from western Greenland alone. Other icebergs break off from eastern Greenland. North Atlantic icebergs appear in shipping lanes. Icebergs appear as far south as the Azores.

By changing some of the original sentences into adverbial modifiers or absolute constructions, you might produce the following.

> Icebergs are frozen fresh water. Ice floes are frozen salt water. Pack ice is also frozen salt water. Rising up to 200 feet above the waterline, icebergs reach below the waterline for seven to nine times their height. (**4** and **5** combined) The direction of drift of an iceberg depends on the wind. Icebergs do not move into the wind.
>
> Most icebergs come from the glaciers of Greenland or from the shelf ice of Antarctica. South Pacific icebergs come up almost to southern Australia. North Pacific icebergs occur only in the Bering Strait. Of the many icebergs in the North Atlantic, about 10,000 to 15,000 a year break off from western Greenland alone. (**11** and **12** combined) Other icebergs break off from eastern Greenland. North Atlantic icebergs appear in the shipping lanes as far south as the Azores. (**14** and **15** combined)

None of these revisions is completely satisfactory because a passage consisting primarily of coordination or subordination or embedded modifiers is almost as monotonous as a passage consisting solely of short, simple sentences. Therefore, you would want to select a mixture of various sentence types. The result might be the following.

> Although ice floes and pack ice are frozen salt water, icebergs are frozen fresh water.[1] Rising up to 200 feet above the water line, icebergs reach below the waterline for seven to nine times their height.[2] The direction of drift of icebergs depends on the wind, and they do not move into the wind.[3]
>
> Most icebergs come from the glaciers of Greenland or from the shelf ice of Antarctica.[4] Although South Pacific icebergs come up almost to southern Australia, North Pacific icebergs occur only in the Bering Strait.[5] Of the many icebergs in the North Atlantic, about 10,000 to 15,000 a year break off from western Greenland alone; others break off from eastern Greenland.[6] North Atlantic icebergs appear in shipping lanes as far south as the Azores.[7]

In this final version, three simple sentences (2, 4, 7), two compound sentences (3, 6), and two complex sentences (1, 5) provide a good variety of sentence types. Sentence length varies from thirteen words (7) to twenty-six words (6), and there is a rough alternation of short and long sentences.

Using coordination to combine sentences usually does not greatly affect emphasis. Subordination, however, almost always results in at least a slight change of emphasis. When combining sentences by means of subordination, be sure that the resulting emphasis is appropriate. In the first sentence of the final version above—*Although ice floes and pack ice are frozen salt water, icebergs are frozen fresh water*—the emphasis is correct because ice floes and pack ice, which are introduced only to distinguish them from icebergs, are relegated to the subordinate clause. The real topic of the paragraph—icebergs—is placed in the stronger position, in the main clause and at the end of the sentence. If this position were reversed to read, "Although icebergs are frozen fresh water, ice floes and pack ice are frozen salt water," the reader would at first think that the topic of discussion was going to be ice floes and pack ice, not icebergs, and the emphasis would be inappropriate.

Combining sentences by means of embedding also affects emphasis. Making the sentence about the height of the icebergs—*Rising up to 200 feet above the waterline, icebergs reach below the waterline for seven to nine times their height*—into an adjective absolute phrase tends to de-emphasize it and to stress the importance of how far below the waterline icebergs reach. As always, the context determines where the emphasis should be.

Variety by Other Means.   Sentence combination is by far the most important means of achieving a variety of sentence structures. However, for a bit of spice now and then, you might try a rhetorical question, inversion, or a short sentence fragment. Since these are all rather dramatic devices, however, they should be used very sparingly.

1. **Rhetorical Questions.** A rhetorical question is one used just for emphasis, one to which no answer is expected.

SIMPLE SENTENCES	Everyone has heard of Davy Crockett. Most people do not know that he was a congressman.
RHETORICAL QUESTION	Who has not heard of Davy Crockett? But few people know that he was a congressman.

2. **Inversion.** Put an occasional complement or direct object before the subject and verb.

SIMPLE SENTENCES	The boy at the door was selling potato-peelers. I do not need potato-peelers.
INVERSION	The boy at the door was selling potato-peelers. Potato-peelers I do not need.

3. **Short Sentence Fragments.** Although sentence fragments are usually unacceptable (see 23a), short fragments can be an effective means of achieving emphasis, humorous anticlimax, or transition, provided you deliberately use them for these purposes and are fully aware of what you are doing.

EMPHASIS	My father told me I needed a haircut. A haircut!
ANTICLIMAX	At last, he had mastered the rules of cricket. Well, almost.
TRANSITION	We have enumerated the many advantages of organic gardening. Now for the disadvantages.

EXERCISES: Variety

Write the following paragraph according to the specifications listed. The result will be, of course, somewhat artificial, but the practice will help you to explore some techniques that you can use to improve your own style.

Write a description of your room. Avoid mentioning the obvious—bed(s), dresser(s), desk(s)—and concentrate on something unique—the giant spider web in your window, for instance. Do not begin any sentences with *there, it, this* or *the.* Try to entertain your reader.

The eight sentences of your paragraph should be structured as follows:

1. Begins with a present participle, has at least one main clause and one subordinate clause, and has between fifteen and thirty words
2. Begins with the subject and has no more than ten words
3. Begins with a prepositional phrase, has at least two main clauses, and has from fifteen to twenty-five words
4. Begins with a subordinate clause, has at least one main clause, and has from twelve to seventeen words
5. Has no more than four words
6. Begins with the subject, has two main clauses, and has fifteen to twenty words
7. Begins with an adverb and has from ten to fifteen words
8. Begins with a subordinate clause and has fifteen to twenty words

¶/50 PARAGRAPHS

Everyone understands, at least implicitly, what a sentence is because we all speak in sentences. Regardless of how long and rambling or how short and incomplete the sentences may be, changes in the speaker's voice tell us when one sentence has ended and another has begun. Paragraph changes are not as obvious; we may realize that a speaker has changed the subject, but we normally do not hear the point at which he or she made the switch. Nor does it disturb us that we do not hear paragraphs because paragraphs are not an essential part of most kinds of speech.

Paragraphs are, however, conventional and essential in writing. Because we are accustomed to seeing paragraph divisions, we are uneasy when they do not appear or even when they appear only infrequently. All of us are familiar with the sense of despair that comes from turning a page and discovering that the next page does not contain a single new paragraph. Paragraphs are both a physical and a mental convenience for readers. Physically, they provide a break and allow readers to keep their places on the page more easily. Mentally, they signal that one unit of thought has been completed and another is about to begin. Paragraphs are a convenience for writers too because they help them organize their ideas into manageable blocks.

A common definition of a **paragraph** is ''a group of related sentences developing one idea.'' It often includes a topic sentence that summarizes that idea, followed by additional sentences that expand, qualify, analyze, or explain the idea. Ideas, however, are not like automobiles; they are not clearly distinct units with standardized parts that can be easily counted and classified. Ideas may be as simple as ''I am eating a Reese's Peanut Butter Cup'' or as complex as ''the role of technology in the universe.'' One idea may blend into another with no sharp division between the two. Yet if we are to deal with ideas at all, we must have ways of segmenting them—we cannot comprehend or express complex ideas all in one breath or all in one sentence. In writing, we use the paragraph to handle one segment at a time. Because ideas are so diverse in their content and complexity and because the possible ways of segmenting them vary greatly, we cannot state hard-and-fast rules for what constitutes a good paragraph. Rather, we can only talk about ''typical'' paragraphs.

There is no absolute rule governing the length of a paragraph. Sometimes (though rarely) only a one-sentence paragraph is needed to make a transition between sections of a paper or to add dramatic emphasis. Sometimes a full typewritten page is appropriate if the paragraph treats an especially complex and closely knit argument. More typically, a paragraph has from one hundred to two hundred words, or from three to ten sentences, and fills from one-third to two-thirds of a double-spaced typewritten page. (Newspapers should not be taken as models because the conventions of newspaper paragraphs depend on typographical appearances and differ greatly from those of other kinds of writing.)

Despite great differences in content, organization, and length, all good paragraphs are unified, complete, and coherent. Unity means that the paragraph has a single focus. Completeness means that the subject of the paragraph is adequately developed so that the reader is satisified and not left with vague impressions and unanswered questions. Coherence means that all of the sentences in the paragraph are related to one another.

50a UNITY

Unity is oneness, the combination of all elements to form a single whole. A unified paragraph is internally consistent and has a single focus. In a well-unified paragraph, every sentence contributes to this focus by exemplifying it, explaining it, or expanding on it in some way. A unified paragraph may contain more than one simple idea, but all of the ideas expressed should be related to the same theme.

The biggest enemy of unity in paragraphs is our own thinking processes. We tend to think associatively rather than logically. If our free associations are not curbed and controlled in our writing, irrelevancies creep in, and the resulting paragraph is an unfocused series of sentences. To test whether a paragraph is unified, ask yourself first, "What is the main idea?" and then, "Is every sentence clearly related to this main idea?"

UNIFIED PARAGRAPH

The punishment of criminals has always been a problem for society.[1] Citizens have had to decide whether offenders such as first-degree murderers should be killed in a gas chamber, imprisoned for life, or rehabilitated and given a second chance in society.[2] Many citizens argue that serious criminals should be executed.[3] They believe that killing criminals will set an example for others and also rid society of a cumbersome burden.[4] Other citizens say that no one has the right to take a life and that capital punishment is not a deterrent to crime.[5] They believe that society as well as the criminal is responsible for the crimes and that killing the criminal does not solve the problems of either society or the criminal.[6]
                                                              —Student paper

The writer of this paragraph has stated the main idea in the first sentence. Sentence 2 then specifies the exact nature of the problem by listing the choices the society has. Sentence 3 breaks the topic down still further by stating the viewpoint of one group of citizens, and sentence 4 gives the reasons for this viewpoint. Sentence 5 states the opposing viewpoint. Sentence 6 lists the reasons for the opposing viewpoint. The paragraph as a whole has a unified and logical structure that follows a clear pattern of development.

POORLY UNIFIED PARAGRAPH

It is a fact that capital punishment is not a deterrent to crime.[1] Statistics show that in states with capital punishment, murder rates are the same or almost the same as in states without capital punishment.[2] It is also true that it is more expensive to put a person on death row than in life imprisonment because of the costs of maximum security.[3] Unfortunately, capital punishment has been used unjustly.[4] Statistics show that every execution is of a man and that nine out of ten are black.[5] So prejudice shows right through.
                                                              —Student paper

This paragraph has a promising beginning; like that of the unified paragraph above, its first sentence makes a general statement, and its second sentence expands on the first by offering evidence to support it. But sentence 3 changes the subject from capital punishment as a deterrent to crime to the costs of capital punishment. Sentence

4 once again changes the subject—this time to the justice of capital punishment. Sentences 5 and 6 are related to sentence 4 if one agrees that executing men and blacks is evidence of injustice and prejudice, but the injustice of capital punishment is quite a different matter from the effectiveness of capital punishment as a deterrent to crime. The paragraph lacks unity because it contains not one but three main ideas: (a) capital punishment is not a deterrent, (b) capital punishment is expensive, and (c) capital punishment is unfair.

EXERCISES: Paragraph Unity

Indicate which of the following paragraphs are good examples of unity and which are poor examples, and explain how the poor examples lack unity.

1.   Dance is one of the oldest and most beautiful art forms. Figures of human dancers are recorded in paintings and on pottery made in northern Africa as early as 2500 B.C. Ballet, a very stylized dance form, flowered in Italy in the fifteenth century. In its early years it was very much a part of the opera, dancers performing during the acts or intermissions. During the eighteenth century, Russian ballet became world renowned, remaining so today, but it was not until the twentieth century that the United States had a ballet company or indeed any interest in supporting this art form. Learning to be a ballet dancer takes many years, and the student should begin training by at least age six. The training, as grueling as that of any athlete, requires determination, constant self-discipline, and a special sensitivity toward this old and beautiful form of art.

2.   Efforts by the president and congressional leaders to remove the trucking industry from governmental regulation should be halted. Deregulation of the trucking industry would, in effect, create the very monopolistic, cutthroat practices that the government seeks to prevent by removing the industry from the watchful eye of the Interstate Commerce Commission, which currently regulates its prices, routes, and safety standards. If the industry were deregulated, the fierce competition among large firms would force small, regional trucking companies out of the market. Swallowing up the smaller companies, larger firms would have little incentive to serve small communities that could offer little volume and little profit to their national conglomerates. In addition, increased profit-making incentives would probably result in increased efforts to economize by cutting out some of the costly safety standards currently imposed by government regulation. The trucking industry, which hauls 55 percent of the nation's freight, must continue to be regulated if prices are to remain fair, if the entire nation is to be served, and if high standards of safety are to be maintained.

3.   The twentieth century, with all its computer wizardry and electronic gadgetry, seems to be ringing the death knell for liberal arts education. A few students in every decade have defied trends toward technical training so that they could "find themselves" by tracing their intellectual and spiritual insights back through the humanism of the Renaissance and further back through the medieval teachings of the seven liberal arts to the roots of liberal education in ancient Greece and Rome. In Rome, the term *liberal education* meant education befitting a liberal, or free, person. The subjects taught were grammar, rhetoric, logic, arithmetic, geometry, astronomy, and music, subjects that continued to make up liberal arts curricula through the Middle Ages and Renaissance.

The Topic Sentence.   In the earlier unified paragraph about capital punishment, the first sentence is a **topic sentence**, one that summarizes the entire paragraph. For writers who have difficulty in keeping paragraphs unified, topic sentences are useful in helping them stick to the point as they write. Topic sentences also help readers by letting them know what the main idea of the paragraph is.

The most common position for a topic sentence is at the beginning of the paragraph.

TOPIC SENTENCE AT BEGINNING OF PARAGRAPH

<u>Never before have the English people been so vocal on so many issues at the same time.</u>[1] Public participation has been encouraged to the point where the only contribution of which some are capable is a display of incoherence.[2] The fields of dissent are boundless.[3] Government measures, social injustices, financial policy, industrial relations, classical and modern literature, new trends in music, the causes of England's defeats in international sport—all these and a host of others are vigorously argued about.[4] Nothing is taken for granted.[5] No serious book can appear without at once stimulating a counterview.[6] Britain is indeed an isle full of noises.[7] The impression given abroad is of a bitterly divided, atrabilious, quarreling society.[8] What is actually happening is that a healthily skeptical English democracy is seeking to establish new foundations.[9]

—William Haley, "*Will There Always Be An England?,*" *The American Scholar*

Here the author introduces the main idea—that the English are very vocal today—in the first sentence. Sentence 2 says that this speaking out has been encouraged. Sentences 3 through 6 list the many subjects of dispute. Sentence 7 stresses the resulting noise, and sentence 8 notes the foreign impressions of the British wrangling. Finally, sentence 9 says that all this vocal reaction is actually healthy. Note that every sentence after the topic sentence expands in some way on it.

Topic sentences sometimes appear in the middle of paragraphs, either following a transition from preceding paragraphs or, as in the next example, following introductory descriptive details. All these details are clearly related to the topic sentence. The example below also shows that you need not restrict the topic sentence to a bare statement of the topic. Particularly in a lengthy sentence, you may include material that develops the topic. Here the simple statement of the topic is "The Battle of Bennington was celebrating its 200th birthday"; the rest of the sentence—"and some 1,400 'soldiers,' from states as far away as New Jersey, had come to celebrate"—helps to describe the celebration.

TOPIC SENTENCE IN MIDDLE OF PARAGRAPH

One hazy Saturday last August 13th, 10,000 American fans swarmed over the highways and meadows of Bennington. Thousands of cups of coke were consumed. Thousands of feet ached. Thousands upon thousands of rolls of Kodak film clicked through Instamatics and Nikons, Brownies and Hasselblads. Fast food counters in downtown Bennington took an hour to fill a chili dog order. The free food line in the V.A. park stretched for many hundreds of yards, and moved like a tank in mud. TV crews, the press, the curious, bus loads of school-age children, all crowded to the front edges of roped off areas. Bennington was under siege. <u>The Battle of Bennington was celebrating its 200th birthday, and some 1,400 "soldiers," from states as far away as New Jersey, had come to celebrate.</u> The soldiers represented various Revolutionary companies whose members have been travelling the path of the Revolution, and will be doing so until 1981, refighting, reliving and redying the moments of each major Revolutionary battle. —Marjorie Ryerson, "They're Battling Again At Bennington," Vermont Life

Occasionally the topic sentence appears as the last sentence in the paragraph. This is one effective method of handling an introductory paragraph because a certain amount of suspense is built up and the reader is teased into reading to the end to find out what the point is. You can also put the topic sentence at the end of a closing paragraph to summarize the entire argument. In the paragraph below, the author first states the exceptions to his point (that a few writers can afford to break the rules), then explains his point (that most writers cannot break the rules), and finally summarizes with a topic sentence (that anarchy in language is as bad as anarchy in society).

TOPIC SENTENCE AT END OF PARAGRAPH

If you are writing literature under your own name, you can afford to be a maverick with words. If you are good, like Jan Morris, you use words instinctively, as an artist, with no conscious need for rules or regulations. Those of us who work for corporate word-factories such as *The Times* or a Department of State cannot afford such licence. If all we everyday hacks used words and grammar to mean exactly what we chose them to mean, neither more or less, a Babel would issue from New Printing House Square, and we should lose all but our most patient readers: the ones who buy it not to read, but to carry under their arms to demonstrate that they can afford it. <u>Anarchy in language is as nasty, brutish, and short-tempered as anarchy in society.</u>
—Philip Howard, "On Using Words," Encounter

When you have a paragraph with a fairly complicated argument, you may wish to state the topic sentence twice, once at the beginning to introduce the argument and again at the end to summarize it. (Obviously, you would not word the two topic sentences exactly the same.) In the next example, the author first states his topic in the negative—meteorites are not hot when they hit the ground. He then explains that they are initially cold, then are heated on the outside, then are cooled again. Finally, he summarizes by stating his point in the affirmative—meteorites are cold when they hit the ground.

TOPIC SENTENCE AT BOTH BEGINNING
AND END OF PARAGRAPH

<u>It is a widely held but erroneous belief that meteorites arrive at ground level in a very hot condition.</u> In space meteorites are extremely cold and their temperature on entering the Earth's atmosphere is well below zero. During the brief few seconds of their blazing fireball flight the outer layers of a meteorite are

melted and sprayed aside at a faster rate than heat penetrates inwards, so that any heating effect is confined to just a few millimetres below the surface. After slowing to free fall at around 20km height, the meteorite spends a minute and a half falling at about 200 km/hour through some of the coldest layers of the Earth's atmosphere and this cools the outer skin rapidly. <u>The meteorite arrives cold—usually very cold indeed.</u>

—Keith Hindley, *"Meteorite Photography,"* London News

The purpose of a topic sentence is to let the reader know what the main point of the paragraph is, but it is usually not necessary to tell the reader overtly what you are going to do next. Try to avoid such sentences as "Now I am going to discuss . . ." or "In this section we will explain . . ." It is not exactly wrong to tell the reader openly what you plan to do before you do it, but it is wordy and inelegant. The topic sentence should be clear enough to let the reader know what is going on without your having to put up signposts.

Although topic sentences are an aid to unity, many well-unified paragraphs have no single topic sentence or only an implied one. This is especially true of descriptive and narrative writing, where a topic sentence is normally unnecessary because, if there were to be one sentence that summarized the entire paragraph, it could only be something like "This is what it looked like" or "This is what happened." Consider the following description by Charles Dickens of a nineteenth-century American railroad car.

NO TOPIC SENTENCE IN PARAGRAPH

The cars are like shabby omnibuses, but larger: holding thirty, forty, fifty, people. The seats, instead of stretching from end to end, are placed crosswise. Each seat holds two persons. There is a long row of them on each side of the caravan, a narrow passage up the middle, and a door at both ends. In the centre of the carriage there is usually a stove, fed with charcoal or anthracite coal; which is for the most part red-hot. It is insufferably close; and you see the hot air fluttering between yourself and any other object you may happen to look at, like the ghost of smoke.

—Charles Dickens, AMERICAN NOTES

EXERCISES: Topic Sentences

Underline the topic sentences in each of the following paragraphs.

1.   Such neglected opportunities would hardly seem to recommend me as one to give advice on buying and selling antiques. But those were far from being my only mistakes. At the first show in which Betty and I sold antiques I took $10 for a $600 Steuben glass bowl. At an auction, much more recently than I can comfortably admit, I paid a ridiculously high price for a figural urn that, on delivery, I discovered to be marked "Deenie's Ceramics Studio." I once lost a $10,000 painting to a competitor who took it with a winning bid of $60. At a flea market I wasted half a day waiting for a dealer to show me a promised "art glass vase" that turned out to be worthless, while my neighbor casually strolled to the next table and picked up a fine Mettlach stein for $25.

—Michael De Forrest, ANTIQUING FROM A TO Z: BUYING
AND SELLING COLLECTIBLES AND OTHER OLD THINGS

2. All dogs came from two common ancestors millions of years ago. Even though they have changed in shape and size through the centuries, some breeds claim the wolf as their ancestor, while the rest claim the jackal. Collies, with their weather-resistant coats and their endurance and cleverness, were selected to be bred as herd dogs. The northern dogs, such as the husky, chowchow, and Samoyed, all with their heavy coats and curled tails to protect their noses while sleeping in the cold and their powerful build, were bred to be sled and draft animals. Terrier dogs, powerful little animals, were bred to catch rats and badgers, by farmers and hunters in the British Isles. The guard dogs, on the other hand, come from the Greek and Roman arenas, and the bull mastiffs are their ancestors. They were large and stouthearted and often had to fight lions in the arenas.

—Louis L. Vine, *YOUR DOG: HIS HEALTH AND HAPPINESS*

3. Rock. Hard rock. Live. That unmistakable driving, pulsating rock beat. Amplifiers way up. A kid in a leather jacket works the dials and periodically dashes half way up the aisle to check the decibels. Tall, lanky Valery Vernigor belts out *Evil Woman* and *Spinning Wheel,* hits made famous by the American group Blood, Sweat and Tears. He sings with feeling. In English. It could be the original except for sharp brassy riffs from trumpets and trombones. At the electronic organ, throbbing with rhythm, is a goateed dandy in a flaming red shirt. The drummer, lean and intense, is developing a handlebar mustache. A bank of electric guitarmen in neck-length hair give out with the vacant-eyed look and rolling body motion that go with rock. At center stage Lyosha Kozlov, with stringy beatnik hair and a full Solzhenitsyn beard, works over a wild, rippling alto sax. The room swims in sound. Then, sharp enthusiastic applause all around me. And Makhurdad Badi, a Moscow-born Persian lad with a high wavering tenor and kinky hair falling to his shoulders, joins in a medley from *Jesus Christ, Superstar.*   —Hedrick Smith, *THE RUSSIANS*

4. The writing of graffiti, perhaps because its practitioners are so elusive, is one human activity not given serious consideration or study by behavioral scientists—the historians, philosophers, sociologists, psychologists, psychiatrists, columnists. I consider this a grave oversight. Graffiti, too, are revelatory of developments, trends, and attitudes in man's history. Man is a natural communicator. A thought occurs to someone suddenly, or something is experienced during the day, and there is a compulsion to express it, if not to another person, then to whatever is close at hand: paper, wall, rock, tree, door. Graffiti, then, are little insights, little peepholes into the minds of individuals who are spokesmen not only for themselves but for others like them.

— Robert Reisner, *GRAFFITI: TWO THOUSAND YEARS OF WALL WRITING*

Other Kinds of Unity.   In addition to unity of ideas within the paragraph and the use of topic sentences as an aid to unity, grammatical unity and unity of diction are also important. Grammatical unity is achieved by correct agreement, consistency of tenses, proper placement of modifiers, and appropriate use of coordination and subordination. (See 17–23.) Unity of diction means that the words are compatible with the subject matter and the purpose of the paragraph. Slang, for example, has no place in the description of a laboratory experiment. Fairytale diction ("Once upon a time") is not suitable for historical narration. (See 47 for a discussion of choosing the right words.)

Finally, what adds to unity in one context may detract from it in another context. For example, extensive detail contributes to unity in descriptive writing but may detract from it in the summary of an argument.

EXERCISES: Review: Paragraph Unity

The following paragraphs lack unity. Explain what is wrong with each paragraph and rewrite *one* of the three, making it into a well-developed, unified paragraph.

1. Modern London, a swarming, sprawling city, is a city of great paradox. In every corner, ghosts of the past rise up to remind the visitor that this city is built on pageantry and splendor, suffering and deprivation, revolution and bloodshed, creativity and the unconquerable will of the human spirit. Samuel Johnson is almost afoot in Fleet Street; Admiral Nelson's ship is almost visible on the Thames; throngs of Londoners mass outside the Tower of London, eager for the next public execution of a nobleman; Queen Victoria's carriage seems to rumble through the narrow streets.

2. The modern consumer movement, which has brought about sweeping changes in the public's awareness of the political influence of its buying power, was largely spearheaded by the efforts of one man—Ralph Nader. Pressure by American buyers who have learned effective lobbying has forced stringent new safety standards on the automobile industry, more complete labeling of products in the food industry, new honesty in advertising, and new antipollution laws in industry.

3. Rising gasoline prices and the shortage of energy have forced most cities to put more emphasis on the development of mass-transit systems. Local governments are creating new kinds of transit systems and renovating old ones. Some of these are bus systems, subways, and commuter trains. Many of these changes are being subsidized by the federal government. These forms of mass transit were once considered the domain of the lower socio-economic strata, but as the energy crisis escalates, more and more people in the middle- and high-income brackets are jumping on the bandwagon of mass transit.

50b COMPLETENESS

Completeness in a paragraph means that the topic of the paragraph is adequately developed by details, explanations, definitions, evidence, and the like, so that the reader is not left with only a fuzzy idea of what the writer means. How much development is "adequate"? Unfortunately, there is no formula for completeness; we cannot say, for example, that three examples or two pieces of evidence make a complete paragraph. The amount of development necessary for any given paragraph will vary widely according to the topic, the audience, and the purpose of the paper of which the paragraph is a part. However, completeness does not mean simply that you should keep writing until you have 200 or 250 words and then start a new paragraph. Every sentence should be clearly related to the topic and to other sentences in the paragraph, or the result will lack both unity and coherence.

COMPLETE PARAGRAPH

Railroad travel in Spain is a nightmare which tourists should know about before embarking on a voyage.[1] Each compartment holds eight people, which usually results in a conglomeration of soldiers, tourists, farmers, and villagers.[2] Within minutes after the train pulls out of the station, the compartments become saturated with the mixed odor of wine, urine, and sweat.[3] Chickens and dogs casually stroll the narrow passageways.[4] Drunkards and perverts roam through the cars shouting obscenities and pinching the oversized rear-ends of standing or passing females.[5] Travelers suffer silently, passing the dreary hours by playing tic-tac-toe and poker.[6]

—Student paper

In the paragraph above, the writer begins by stating the topic: Railroad travel in Spain is a nightmare. This statement is followed by a description of the size of the compartments and the different kinds of travelers. Sentence 3 states the results of the crowded conditions. Sentences 4 and 5 give details about the passageways of the cars. Finally, the writer describes how travelers respond to all these conditions. The reader is left with a vivid picture of why the writer called railroad travel in Spain a nightmare. All this detail is necessary because railroad travel in Spain is the topic of the paragraph. If, on the other hand, the topic of the paragraph were the more general one of the problems of vacationing in Spain, the details of railroad travel might be limited to those in the underlined sentence below.

Vacationing in Spain is not all bullfights and flamenco guitars. Potential tourists should know that they may find few people who speak English. Hotel accommodations often bear little resemblance to the pictures of rooms in travel brochures. The water is frequently unsafe to drink. Railroad travel is a nightmare because of overcrowded cars and unsanitary conditions. An encounter with the Spanish police can be, at best, a traumatic experience.

Here, only a few details about railroad travel are provided because the topic is more general than in the first paragraph on railroad travel in Spain. In fact, if all the details given in the first paragraph were included here, the resulting paragraph would be badly out of proportion.

A paragraph may actually contain a fair amount of information but still be incomplete if this information is not developed.

INCOMPLETE PARAGRAPH

New filming techniques and new methods of creating special effects contribute to the influence a film will have on the industry. This influence is one aspect of whether or not a film is considered a classic. *King Kong* was one of the most important films in history and had a profound effect on the technical aspects of the film industry.

—Student paper

The passage above is really more an outline than a paragraph. The reader is left wondering about the nature of new filming techniques and special effects. What is the exact relationship between a film's influence on the industry and whether or not it is considered a classic? What were some of the new techniques of *King Kong*? What films did *King Kong* directly influence? This potentially good paragraph is ineffective because of lack of completeness.

Paragraph Development. One of the most serious and persistent problems in many student papers is underdeveloped paragraphs, paragraphs consisting of only one to three short sentences. What is more, underdeveloped paragraphs often lead indirectly to a lack of unity and coherence: The writer sees that a preceding paragraph is too short, and so, rather than begin a new paragraph when taking up a new point, he or she simply adds that point to the preceding paragraph to bring it up to a respectable length. Hence, solving the problem of underdevelopment can also help solve problems with unity and coherence.

Most writers have enough information—know enough about their subject—to write complete paragraphs. Their difficulty is that they do not know how to develop their information logically and interestingly. There are many possible methods for developing a paragraph. Further, there are both types of development and sequences of development. The **type of development** is the way in which the main idea is supported—by details, definitions, statements of cause and effect, and so on. The **sequence of development** is the order in which supporting sentences are presented—from the general to the particular, chronologically, by order of importance, and so on.

Among the most important types of paragraph development are development by (1) detail, (2) comparison and contrast, (3) analogy, (4) process, (5) classification and partition, (6) cause and effect, (7) definition, and (8) mixed development.

1. **Development by Detail.** Development by detail is one of the most common and most useful types of development. Typically, the paragraph begins with a topic sentence or general statement that is then expanded by specific illustrations or examples.

DEVELOPMENT BY DETAIL

There are some fifty square blocks of pre-World War II apartment buildings in what used to be one of the most genteel neighborhoods of New York City, near Columbia University, where things have gone slightly, delicately, to seed.[1] The area is called Morningside Heights, and many old ladies live there.[2] Inside the front hallways, the polished tables are scratched and the Tiffany lampshades have a panel or two of their stained glass missing.[3] On the outside, the cream-white stones have graffiti on them and the wrought-iron railings of the buildings are surrounded by weeds.[4] —Paul Malamud, *"Rented Rooms,"* Atlantic

In the descriptive paragraph above, the author first makes the general point that an area in New York City is deteriorating. Sentence 2 supplies details: the name of the neighborhood and the kind of people who live there. Sentence 3 gives details about the interior of the houses in the area, and sentence 4 gives details about their exteriors.

DEVELOPMENT BY DETAIL

The Pueblos do not understand self-torture.[1] Every man's hand has its five fingers, and unless they have been tortured to secure a sorcery confession they are unscarred.[2] There are no cicatrices upon their backs, no marks where strips of skin have been taken off.[3] They have no rites in which they sacrifice their own blood, or use it for fertility.[4] They used to hurt themselves to a certain extent in a few initiations at the moments of greatest excitement, but in such cases the whole matter was almost an affair of collegiate exuberance.[5] In the Cactus Society, a warrior cult, they dashed about striking themselves and each other with cactus-blade whips; in the Fire Society they tossed fire about like confetti.[6] Neither psychic danger nor abnormal experience is sought in either case.[7] Certainly in the observed fire tricks of the Pueblos—as also in the fire tricks of the Plains—it is not self-torture that is sought.[8] In the Fire Walk, whatever the means employed, feet are not burned, and when the fire is taken into the mouth the tongue is not blistered.[9]   —Ruth Benedict, *PATTERNS OF CULTURE*

Like the paragraph by Malamud, this paragraph begins with a topic sentence and follows that sentence with details. Here, however, the details are used, not to fill in a picture, but to support an argument. Sentences 2, 3, and 4 support the argument by noting that the Pueblos do not maim themselves in any specific way. Sentence 5 notes situations in which Pueblo ceremonies may have led to accidental, but not deliberate, injury. Sentences 6 and 7 list ceremonies that are potentially dangerous but not intended to cause physical or mental damage. Details of fire ceremonies that do not involve self-torture are provided in sentences 8 and 9.

EXERCISES: Development by Detail

Use detail to develop a paragraph on one of the following subjects.

1. An event that impressed you at an early age (for example, a parade, circus, wedding, funeral)·

2. The atmosphere of a particular place that you go to frequently (for example, a theater, a disco, a library, a restaurant, or a shop)

3. The behavior of an eccentric person (real or imaginary)

---

2. **Development by Comparison and Contrast.** Strictly speaking, a comparison shows how two or more things are alike, and a contrast shows how they are different. In practice, comparison and contrast often appear together because two things that have everything in common and no differences are the same things, not two different things. Similarly, there is no point in grouping two things (say an eggshell and an earthmover) if they have nothing in common. Usually, the things being compared share a number of features and belong to a common and easily identifiable class such as types of human behavior, diseases, warlike situations, or kinds of games. If the similarities between the things being compared are so obvious that they need not be mentioned, the discussion may focus on the

differences alone. For example, in the following paragraph, the author does not mention that poets, dramatists, novelists, and historians are all human beings and are all writers because any reader will know this.

DEVELOPMENT BY COMPARISON AND CONTRAST

The poet, the dramatist, the novelist are free to exercise their imagination as widely as they choose.[1] But the historian may not be allowed so long a tether.[2] He must fulfill his function as a creative artist only within very rigid limits.[3] He cannot invent what went on in the mind of St. Thomas of Canterbury.[4] The poet can.[5] He cannot suppress inconvenient minor characters and invent others who more significantly underline the significance of his theme.[6] The novelist can.[7] The dramatist can.[8] The historian, as Sir Philip Sidney has said, "is captive to the truth of a foolish world."[9] Not only is he captive to the truth of a foolish world, but he is captive to a truth he can never fully discover, and yet he is forbidden by his conscience and his training from inventing it.[10]
—C. V. Wedgwood, *THE SENSE OF THE PAST*

The above paragraph is an example of almost pure contrast. Essentially, Wedgwood lists some of the many things that poets, dramatists, and novelists can do that historians cannot do. Note that sentences 9 and 10 do not overtly state a contrast, but, by their presence in this paragraph, they imply still another contrast: that poets, dramatists, and novelists are *not* "captive to the truth of a foolish world" as historians are.

DEVELOPMENT BY COMPARISON AND CONTRAST

D. H. Lawrence and Katherine Mansfield had a good deal in common.[1] Both were outsiders in English society: Lawrence because of his working-class background, Katherine because of her colonial origins.[2] Though they left their birthplace, they were strongly influenced by it and frequently recreated it in their work.[3] They revolted against the conventional values of the time; and had considerable sexual experience in early life, though Lawrence had been strengthened and Katherine hurt by it.[4] They spent many impoverished years on the Continent and maintained a European rather than an insular outlook.[5] They had intuitive and volatile personalities, experienced life with a feverish intensity, were highly creative and passionately committed to their art, and achieved a posthumous fame far greater than their contemporary reputations.[6] Most important of all, they were seriously ill for a great part of their adult lives, and made their pilgrimage from country to country in search of a warm climate and good health.[7] They were subject to sudden fits of black rage, suffered the constant pain of disease and the fearful threat of death, and died of tuberculosis at an early age.[8]
—Jeffrey Meyers, *"D. H. Lawrence: Katherine Mansfield and 'Women In Love',"* London Magazine

Meyers' paragraph illustrates almost pure comparison; only the last part of sentence 4 provides a contrast. Again, the author does not state the obvious contrasts—for example, that Lawrence was a man and Mansfield was a woman.

As the two preceding paragraphs show, comparisons and contrasts may be handled point by point (for example, "X is big and Y is little. X is expensive and Y is cheap."). Alternatively, the features of one subject may be discussed first, followed by the features of the second subject. In the latter type of development, a separate paragraph is often begun when the second subject is introduced, as in the following selection.

DEVELOPMENT BY COMPARISON AND CONTRAST

Choosing between the two [vinyl and aluminum], which are remarkably similar in panel sizes and shapes, mounting techniques and durability, is mostly a matter of taste and availability.[1] Vinyl is a bit easier to work, does not dent or show scratches and resists heat and cold better than aluminum.[2] But it can crack when struck in cold weather and cannot be repainted.[3]

Aluminum is usually less costly than vinyl, and comes in a brighter palette of factory-baked enamel finishes.[1] But it is easily dented and scratched, and some codes require electrical grounding.[2]

—Time-Life Books, *ROOFS AND SIDING*

Here, sentence 1 of the first paragraph compares vinyl and aluminum siding. Sentences 2 and 3 contrast the two by stating the characteristics of vinyl that are different from the characteristics of aluminum. The second paragraph then states the distinguishing characteristics of aluminum.

EXERCISES: Development by Comparison and Contrast

Use comparison and contrast to develop a paragraph on one of the following topics.

1. The relative effectiveness of news presented in a newspaper or magazine as compared to that presented on the radio or television
2. The merits of two rock groups or two solo vocalists or instrumentalists
3. The characteristics of two elderly people of the same sex, people whom you know
4. Your tastes in clothes compared with those of an older person of the same sex as you

3. **Development by Analogy.** Development by analogy is similar to development by comparison and contrast in that both compare two different things. In analogy, however, the comparison is between things that do not belong to the same class. In the next example, by Helen Keller, a ship is not a living creature as is a blind person; in the paragraph by James Michener, porridge is not related to lava.

Another difference between comparison and contrast and analogy lies in the purposes for which each is used. Comparison and contrast are used to classify and differentiate similar things, and in the process both things are explained. The purpose of analogy is to explain the unfamiliar in terms of the familiar: most people have some notion of what it is like to be caught in a fog, but sighted people do not understand what it is like to be blind (Keller's paragraph). Similarly, porridge (oatmeal) is generally familiar, but the material beneath the earth's crust is not (Michener's paragraph). (See 52d for a discussion of the proper uses of analogy.)

DEVELOPMENT BY ANALOGY

Have you ever been at sea in a dense fog, when it seemed as if a tangible white darkness shut you in, and the great ship, tense and anxious, groped her way toward the shore with plummet and sounding-line, and you waited with beating heart for something to happen?[1] I was like that ship before my education began, only I was without compass or sounding-line, and had no way of knowing how near the harbour was.[2] "Light! give me light!" was the wordless cry of my soul, and the light of love shone on me in that very hour.[3]   —Helen Keller, *THE STORY OF MY LIFE*

Here Keller states the familiar (a ship in a fog) in her first sentence. Sentence 2 then begins the analogy to the unfamiliar (the confusion of blindness) with the words "I was like that ship."

DEVELOPMENT BY ANALOGY

At the top of the mantle, only twenty-seven miles from the surface, rested the earth's crust, where life would develop.[1] What was it like?[2] It can be described as the hard scum that forms at the top of a pot of boiling porridge.[3] From the fire at the center of the pot, heat radiates not only upward, but in all directions.[4] The porridge bubbles freely at first when it is thin, and its motion seems to be always upward, but as it thickens, one can see that for every slow bubble that rises at the center of the pan, part of the porridge is drawn downward at the edges; it is this slow reciprocal rise and fall which constitutes cooking.[5] In time, when enough of this convection has taken place, the porridge exposed to air begins to thicken perceptibly, and the moment the internal heat stops or diminishes, it hardens into a crust.[6]

—James A. Michener, *CENTENNIAL*

In this paragraph, Michener reverses the order used by Keller. Sentences 1 and 2 introduce the unfamiliar (the area beneath the earth), and sentence 3 begins the analogy with the familiar (porridge) with the words "It can be described as . . ." Sentences 4, 5, and 6 continue the analogy by describing what happens to porridge as it cooks.

EXERCISES: Development by Analogy

Help your readers understand something unusual you know or do by making an analogy between it and something familiar to most people. For example, a sky-diver might explain the thrills of sky-diving through analogy with the sensations experienced on rides in an amusement park. Or a computer programmer might make an analogy between the process of writing programs and the process of writing a composition. The following are some suggested topics for analogies.

1. Being in a tornado (or landslide, hurricane, earthquake, blizzard, or other violent natural phenomenon)
2. Coming out of the anesthetic after an operation
3. The appearance of a newly born animal
4. Preparing a meal for twenty or more people
5. Being in a country or area where you do not speak or understand the language
6. Being arrested for a crime you did not commit

4. **Development by Process.** Development by process is a step-by-step description of how something is done. Because the steps of a process must occur one after the other, this method of development usually follows a chronological sequence. If the purpose of the process statement is simply to give readers a general understanding of how something is done, as in the first paragraph below, fewer explicit details are needed. If, as in the second paragraph below, the process statement is intended to teach the readers how to perform the task or activity themselves, more details are needed, the exact order in which operations should take place is crucial, and supplementary comments about why an operation must be carried out may be necessary to reassure readers that they are following the instructions properly.

DEVELOPMENT BY PROCESS

In the lost wax (*cire perdue*) technique of casting objects in metal, the object is first modeled in wax. The wax object is then coated in clay and baked, with vents being left through which the molten wax escapes. Then liquid metal is poured in through the vents to fill the cavity left by the wax. After the metal has cooled, the baked clay covering is broken. The resulting metal casting is an exact copy of the original wax object.

Because the paragraph above is intended only as a general description for the reader's information, specific details such as the kind of metal used, the location of the vents, and the temperature at which the object is baked are not given. Nonetheless, the order of steps of the process is carefully indicated by the order of the sentences and by the use of such words as *then*, *after*, and *resulting*.

DEVELOPMENT BY PROCESS

There are several ways of stopping, and it is wise to learn at least one (other than falling) early in your skating career.[1] If you are a skier, you are familiar with the *snowplow* move, which slows you down.[2] It works on ice as well as snow.[3] Skate in a glide, with your feet parallel but slightly apart; then push your heels apart farther, keeping your hands out at your sides for balance and your knees bent.[4] Your weight should be back.[5] The act of pushing your heels apart while your toes keep together makes you stop.[6] There also is a *one-foot snowplow* in which the heel and hip on one side are pushed forward strongly, causing the corresponding blade to skid.[7] With more pressure, this brings you to a stop.[8] This can be done with either foot acting as the brake.[9]

—Tina Noyes with Freda Alexander,
I CAN TEACH YOU TO FIGURE SKATE

In this paragraph, the author intends the readers actually to carry out the process themselves, so she gives specific details (sentence 5 for example) and even provides helpful hints not directly related to stopping on ice (the comparison with skiing in sentence 2). Note how crucial the order of presentation is; for example, if you first pushed your heels apart and then tried to skate in a glide, the tips of your blades would cross and you would fall on your face on the ice.

EXERCISES: Development by Process

Use development by process to explain the techniques or steps involved in one of the following situations.

1. Learning an athletic skill or game (for example, how to punt a football, how to hold and swing a golf club, how to learn beginning chess)
2. Changing a tire on a car
3. Repotting houseplants
4. Avoiding obnoxious acquaintances: the art of self-defense
5. Giving a pill to a cat or dog

5. **Development by Classification and Partition.** Classification is the process of grouping individual items on the basis of their similarities and differences; classification collects individuals and fits them into a larger pattern. Partition, or analysis, is the reverse process: It divides larger wholes into smaller component parts. In other words, classification puts things together and partition takes them apart. In practice, classification and partition are often not easily distinguished—classification usually includes partitioning, and partitioning implies classification. For example, in the following paragraph, the author first partitions the great apes into four groups. In the last two sentences, he then classifies all the great apes according to the characteristics they have in common.

DEVELOPMENT BY CLASSIFICATION AND PARTITION

The living great apes (Pongidae) fall into four groups: gibbons, orangutans, gorillas, and chimpanzees. All are fairly large animals that have no tail, a relatively large skull and brain, and very long arms. All have a tendency, when on the ground, to walk semi-erect. —William Keeton, *BIOLOGICAL SCIENCE*

Both classification and partition are forms of definition, and both frequently appear in a single definition. Classification and partition are also similar to comparison and contrast in that the very acts of classifying and partitioning usually involve some comparison.

DEVELOPMENT BY CLASSIFICATION AND PARTITION

The gibbons, of which several species are found in southeast Asia, represent a lineage that probably split from the others soon after the pongid line itself arose.[1] They are the smallest of the apes (about 3 feet tall when standing).[2] Their arms are exceedingly long, reaching the ground even when the animal is standing erect.[3] The gibbons are amazing arboreal acrobats and spend almost all their time in trees.[4] —William Keeton, *BIOLOGICAL SCIENCE*

This paragraph is primarily one of partition: Keeton is distinguishing the gibbons from the other apes according to their habitat, lineage, size, proportions, and acrobatic ability. This very distinction implies a contrast with the other great apes, and Keeton uses an overt comparison ("the smallest of the apes") in sentence 2. Note also that the distinctions help define the gibbon.

In development by classification and partition, as in comparison and contrast, separate paragraphs are often used to develop each of the items being classified or partitioned.

DEVELOPMENT BY CLASSIFICATION AND PARTITION

There are two kinds of late-snack invitations. One is the sort that a cheerful husband proffers the whole dance floor while the band plays "Good Night Ladies." "Lesh all come over t'our housh for shcrambled eggsh!" (His wife is the feverish-looking lady by the door, with the armful of coats. She knows there are five eggs in the refrigerator, every one of them spoken for.) These occasions are seldom outstandingly successful.

The second kind is the invitation you issue yourself because these things are a community habit and it's your turn. If you can't move out of the community, you should make the first move—as part of your community endeavor—and suggest that everyone stop eating so much. But until you get around to this, the following late-snack ideas may be helpful. They are all easy and they take very little last-minute doing.

—Peg Bracken, THE I HATE TO COOK BOOK

Here Bracken states the classification in the first sentence of the first paragraph and uses the rest of the paragraph to describe one kind of late-snack invitation. She devotes the next paragraph to the description of the second kind of invitation.

EXERCISES: Development by Classification and Partition

Develop by classification and/or partition one or two paragraphs on one of the following subjects:

1. Varieties of secretaries or receptionists
2. Types of public restrooms
3. Types of fashion magazines (or sports or news magazines)
4. Varieties of salesmanship
5. Breeds of college professors

---

6. **Development by Cause and Effect.** The basic purpose of a cause-and-effect paragraph is to explain why a condition or conditions exist or existed. Although some causes and effects are so complex that they require an entire paper to explain, simpler cause-and-effect relationships can often be explained within a single paragraph. Normally, the effect is stated first and its cause follows.

DEVELOPMENT BY CAUSE AND EFFECT

An enduring problem among the Scotch was that of personal nomenclature. As I have noted, a certain number of the clans transported themselves to Canada in bulk, or, in any case, re-formed their ranks quickly on arrival. McCallums, Campbells, Grahams and McKillops were exceptionally numerous. That so many had the same surname would not have been serious had they not so often had the same Christian names as well. To call a son something other than John was to combine mild eccentricity with unusual imagination. And even an unusual imagination did

> not normally extend beyond Dan, Jim, Angus, Duncan or Malcolm. A fair proportion of the people we knew were called John McCallum. The John Grahams and the John Campbells were almost equally numerous.   —John Kenneth Galbraith, *THE SCOTCH*

In this paragraph, the effect (the problem of personal names) is stated first. Galbraith then explains in the following sentences what caused this problem (so many entire clans, all with the same surnames, came to Canada and all the people tended to name their sons John).

DEVELOPMENT BY CAUSE AND EFFECT

> There are three fundamental problems that have caused the current dilemma of environmentalism. First, there is the myth, which environmentalists have fashioned, of an ideal, preindustrial, prepesticide past, when crops were good, living was easy, and insects were few. This is a complete fantasy. Second, there is the false distinction between "natural" and "unnatural" chemicals, and the implicit assumption that chemicals like pesticides never occur in nature. Third, there is the myth that these "unnatural" chemicals are causing an equally mythical "epidemic" increase in cancer. Unfortunately, the genesis of all three of these ideas can be traced directly to *Silent Spring.*
> —William Tucker, *"Of Mites and Men," Harper's*

Like Galbraith, Tucker states the effect (the dilemma of environmentalism) in the first sentence. He then explicitly spells out three causes of this dilemma. Finally, the last sentence states that all three of these causes were brought about by the publication of Rachel Carson's *Silent Spring.* Although they are not reprinted here, later paragraphs in the article expand on each of these three causes. This device of summarizing all the causes or effects in one paragraph and then using following paragraphs to explain each cause or effect in detail is an especially clear and useful method for handling fairly complicated cause-and-effect relationships.

EXERCISES: Development by Cause and Effect

Use cause and effect to develop a paragraph. Make one of the following topics *either* the cause *or* the effect of something else.

1. The high cost of paperback books
2. Increased interest in gymnastics in the United States
3. The trend toward small automobiles
4. An important change in your life, such as the loss of a friendship
5. Increased dependence on nuclear energy

---

7. **Development by Definition.** In a broad sense, almost any kind of writing is definition—whatever we say about something helps to define it. In a narrower sense, a definition is an explicit statement of what a term means. Such definitions may be as simple as a synonym or a two- or three-word explanation or as elaborate as a full-length paper.

When a paragraph has definition as its means of development, the definition should be more than a simple sentence or phrase. It may include examples or negative examples (what the term does *not* mean), analogies, and comparisons and contrasts. Extended definitions often include classification, partition, and statements of cause and effect.

DEVELOPMENT BY DEFINITION

> *Hue,* a term often used interchangeably with color, is the quality or characteristic by which we distinguish one color from another. The *primary* hues—red, yellow, and blue—are the basic building blocks of color from which all others are blended. The *secondary* hues, produced by mixing two primaries, are orange, green, and violet (purple). The *tertiary* hues (often called intermediates) stem from various combinations of the basic six; they are the "double-name" colors, such as yellow-green and blue-violet.
>
> —*THE VOGUE SEWING BOOK*

The simple, nontechnical definition of hue in this paragraph first gives a one-sentence general statement of what hue means. The next three sentences use partition to define different kinds of hues.

Definitions are particularly important for limiting the intended meaning of abstract or technical terms. If you use a familiar term in an unusual or technical sense, a definition explaining exactly what you mean by that term is essential. In the paragraph below, Francis must state exactly what he means by *literary dialect* because both *literary* and *dialect* can mean different things to different people.

DEVELOPMENT BY DEFINITION

> One more type of standard dialect should be recognized at this point.[1] That is the *literary dialect.*[2] Any dialect may be a medium for literature, of course, as anyone knows who has read *Huckleberry Finn, Uncle Remus,* or the poems of Robert Burns.[3] But it often happens that a single dialect is considered the appropriate one for artistic and scholarly composition.[4] It may, of course, be the same as the standard spoken dialect, as is the case with most modern European languages.[5] This is likely to be true when literacy is widespread and many people engage in literature, whether it be reciting and listening to epic poems or writing and reading novels.[6] On the other hand, when literacy is restricted to a rather small and sometimes exclusive group—a scholar class—this group may use a special dialect for its writing.[7] Often this is an older form of the language, as it appears in literary classics which the scholar class is intimately familiar with.[8] Sanskrit is such an archaic literary dialect.[9] The extreme is reached when a literary dialect is actually another language, as was the case with classical Latin in Western Europe during the Renaissance.[10] —W. Nelson Francis, *THE STRUCTURE OF AMERICAN ENGLISH*

EXERCISES: Development by Definition

Use definition to develop a paragraph on one of the following subjects. You may check a dictionary first, but do not simply quote the dictionary's definition.

1. Ragtime 2. Eyeglasses 3. Boredom 4. A pet 5. Childhood disease

8. **Development by a Mixture of Types.** As we have seen, a single paragraph often contains more than one type of development. In the paragraph by Francis above, for instance, a brief analogy forms part of the definition. Almost any kind of paragraph may include examples or illustrations. The important thing is to avoid switching abruptly and apparently without reason from one kind of development to another in the middle of a paragraph. For example, you might be describing how to knit a sock and suddenly realize that the reader does not know what *stockinette* means. Rather than stop in the middle of your instructions and say, "Oh, by the way, stockinette means that you knit odd-numbered rows and purl even-numbered rows," you should include the definition in an earlier paragraph where you have defined such technical terms as *purl, yarn over,* and *fisherman's stitch.*

The following paragraph is a good illustration of the mixture of definition and analogy. The first six sentences are devoted to straight definition. Sentences 7 and 8 switch to an analogy between the devotee of culture and a lover of games. Notice how much this analogy contributes to the definition.

DEVELOPMENT BY A MIXTURE OF TYPES

The devotee of culture is, as a person, worth much more than the status seeker.[1] He reads as he also visits art galleries and concert rooms, not to make himself acceptable, but to improve himself, to develop his potentialities, to become a more complete man.[2] He is sincere and may be modest.[3] Far from trotting along obediently with the fashion, he is more likely to stick too exclusively to the 'established authors' of all periods and nations, 'the best that has been thought and said in the world'.[4] He makes few experiments and has few favourites.[5] Yet this worthy man may be, in the sense I am concerned with, no true lover of literature at all.[6] He may be as far from that as a man who does exercises with dumb-bells every morning may be from being a lover of games.[7] The playing of games will ordinarily contribute to a man's bodily perfection; but if that becomes the sole or chief reason for playing them they cease to be games and become 'exercise'.[8]

—C. S. Lewis, *AN EXPERIMENT IN CRITICISM*

EXERCISES: Development by a Mixture of Types

Combine two or more of the methods of paragraph development to write a well-developed paragraph on one of the following topics.

1. Nonverbal communication
2. Grade inflation
3. Religion in America in the 1970s
4. The most memorable place I have visited
5. Annoying habits of my friends

Sequences of Paragraph Development. As was noted earlier, methods of paragraph development can be divided into types of development and sequences of development. Sequences of development are not independent of types of development; that is, every type of development will follow some kind of sequence. Some sequences, such as general to particular, may be used with virtually any type of development. Other sequences are much more limited. For example, a spatial sequence would not appear in a paragraph whose basic type of development was cause and effect. The most important sequences of development are (1) general to particular, (2) particular to general, (3) climactic, (4) chronological, and (5) spatial.

1. **General-to-Particular Sequence.** A general-to-particular sequence is the most common type of sequence in nonfiction writing. A general statement, usually the topic sentence, introduces the paragraph and is followed by specific details that expand, explain, or illustrate the topic sentence. The sequence is easy for readers to follow because they are told at once what the main point is and so have this main point in mind as they read the rest of the paragraph.

The following selection illustrates a general-to-particular sequence in a paragraph with development by detail.

GENERAL-TO-PARTICULAR SEQUENCE

Most tropical animals are more sensitive to change—especially toward higher temperatures—than northern ones, and this is probably because the water in which they live normally varies by only a few degrees throughout the year.[1] Some tropical sea urchins, keyhole limpets, and brittle stars die when the shallow waters heat to about 99° F.[2] The arctic jellyfish Cyanea, on the other hand, is so hardy that it continues to pulsate when half its bell is imprisoned in ice, and may revive even after being solidly frozen for hours.[3] The horseshoe crab is an example of an animal that is very tolerant of temperature change.[4] It has a wide range as a species, and its northern forms can survive being frozen into ice in New England, while its southern representatives thrive in tropical waters of Florida and southward to Yucatan.[5]

—Rachel Carson, THE EDGE OF THE SEA

In this paragraph, the first sentence states the general point—tropical animals are more sensitive to temperature change than northern animals. All of the examples that follow list particular details: sentence 2 gives examples of tropical animals that die in overheated water, sentence 3 gives an example of a hardy northern animal, and sentences 4 and 5 modify slightly the general statement by mentioning a particular species that can survive in both cold and warm waters.

The following paragraph shows a general-to-particular sequence used for a slightly different purpose.

GENERAL-TO-PARTICULAR SEQUENCE

Then again, there would be the millions of acre feet of water permanently sequestered in dead storage.[1] Glen Canyon Dam, for instance, must impound 6,100,000 acre feet before it could generate one kilowatt of electricity.[2] These 6,100,000 acre feet would run no turbines, water no fields, supply no towns with drinking water.[3] Their sole purpose would be to raise the level of the lake to the point where additional water flowing into the reservoir would pass into the intake conduits at the dam.[4] Between them, Marble Gorge and Bridge Canyon dams would hoard another 4,073,000 acre feet in dead storage.[5] Together with Lake Powell, they would permanently store away, like money in a mattress, almost a year's average flow of the Colorado River— a year's flow of water, which, allowed to run down to Lake Mead, could not only generate power at Hoover Dam but could subsequently be used for irrigation or diverted to municipal water supply systems.[6]   —François Leydet, *TIME AND THE RIVER FLOWING*

Here the author is arguing against the building of additional dams on the Colorado River. One of his reasons for opposing dams is that they contain much water that could be better used elsewhere, as he states in sentence 1. In sentence 2, he supports this reasoning by citing the amount of water a specific dam would store. Sentence 3 notes particular uses to which the water could otherwise be put. Sentence 4 notes that the water behind Glen Canyon Dam would serve no good purpose. In sentence 5, two other examples of water-hoarding dams are listed. The final sentence notes the great amount of water stored away ("a year's flow") and repeats some of the uses to which it could be better put.

2. **Particular-to-General Sequence.** A particular-to-general sequence begins with a series of particular details and ends with a general statement (usually the topic sentence). This general statement is normally a conclusion reached by considering all the details. The particular-to-general sequence is much less common than the general-to-particular sequence, in part because it places a greater burden on readers, who are not told the rationale for all the specific facts until they reach the end of the paragraph.

PARTICULAR-TO-GENERAL SEQUENCE

As I have noted, the revenues [from communications satellites] now exceed $140 million per year.[1] The total revenues received for all traffic routed by satellite, however, a figure no one tallies, is a much larger one, undoubtedly now exceeding $1 billion per year.[2] Intelsat pays its member countries a 14 percent return on their investment.[3] This, plus the profits on earth-station operations, enables overseas telecommunications agencies in most countries to operate well in the black.[4] The global system seems profitable on all counts.[5]

—Burton I. Edelson, *GLOBAL SATELLITE COMMUNICATIONS*

In the paragraph above, sentences 1 through 4 present details about revenues. Sentence 5 concludes that the global satellite system is highly profitable.

PARTICULAR-TO-GENERAL SEQUENCE

From distant events—a potato famine in Ireland, revolution in Germany, a pogrom in Russia—have come shock waves carrying new words and speechways to our shores.[1] When, in the 1840's, starving Irish streamed toward the land of plenty; when, in the same period, troubled Germans sought escape from violent political turmoil in their land; and when, little more than a generation later, persecuted Jews fled eastern Europe in an exodus of Biblical proportions, they brought with them their living languages.[2] As their descendants gradually left old words and ways behind, they retained in their speech elements of these ancestral tongues; and the American language, ever hospitable, reached out to take them in.[3] —Mary Helen Dohan, *OUR OWN WORDS*

This paragraph is a somewhat more complicated example of a particular-to-general sequence. Sentence 1 cites three details (potato famine, revolutions, pogrom) and their result (new words to America). Sentence 2 expands on the details given in sentence 1. Finally, sentence 3 states the general point of the paragraph—that the immigrants' native languages have had a permanent effect on the American vocabulary.

3. **Climactic Sequence.** In a climactic sequence, the most intense or highest point of interest is saved for the final sentence, which may be, but is not necessarily, the topic sentence. For example, in the following paragraph, the first sentence is the topic sentence and the remaining sentences provide detail. The paragraph has a climactic sequence, however, because the final sentence both states the result of the narrative and provides a shock for the reader.

CLIMACTIC SEQUENCE

The Horse, 'Cobham's heroes' according to Enoch Bradshaw, did most of the murdering. They went hurrahing after every human being between Drummossie Moor and Inverness. Close by Barnhill, outside the town, some of them came up with 'a very honest old gentlemen [sic] of the name of MacLeod' who had nothing to do with wars in general and the Rebels in particular. He had come to see the battle. He ran before the horsemen until he could run no further, and then he turned, going down on his knees with a cry for mercy. The dragoons swore at him and pistolled him through the head. —John Prebble, *CULLODEN*

The next paragraph, which uses process (how Florida got its name) as its type of development, also has a climactic sequence of development. The author tells us that a land was to be named and describes in detail the process of making the decision. After a great deal of suspense has been built up, he finally tells us that the land was named Florida.

CLIMACTIC SEQUENCE

Since he had not yet landed, he could not know what the Indians called that country, and in his impatience he wanted a name at once. Doubtless then he thought of many names, as a man does at such times. He might have called it for some place in Spain, perhaps New León after his own province; or he might have thought of honoring the King, or some saint. So, it would seem, as he hesitated in his own mind, or talked with his captains, he saw that one particular name was twice suitable. For, he remembered, the season was still that of Our Lord's Resurrection, only six days after the Easter of Flowers. At the same time, he thought that the green land toward which he now looked was at this season a flowered land. That there might be no doubt in the future, Herrera later wrote in plain words that Juan Ponce de León gave the name "for these two reasons." Thus they named it Florida. —George R. Stewart, *NAMES ON THE LAND*

4. **Chronological Sequence.** A chronological sequence is one in which earlier things precede later things; items are listed in the order in which they occur in time. The most obvious use of a chronological sequence is in telling a story, as in the following paragraph, where the events of several years are narrated.

CHRONOLOGICAL SEQUENCE

In the wintry February of 1846, Brigham Young led the Great Trek toward Utah.[1] This brilliant example of the westward movement by groups was one of the great triumphs of organization in all American history.[2] For the long march across Iowa, the Mormons built their own roads and bridges, and even planted crops to be harvested by those who came after them the next season.[3] By August 2, 1847, Brigham Young was laying out the new Zion which would be Salt Lake City. Again he used Joseph Smith's geometric plan.[4] Young's meticulous and effective organization brought party after party across the plains.[5] One group which finally reached Utah in early October had brought 1540 Mormon emigrants in 540 wagons, with 124 horses, 9 mules, 2213 oxen, 887 cows, 358 sheep, 35 hogs, and 716 chickens.[6] When another group of nearly twenty-five hundred arrived under Young's personal leadership a year later, they found a flourishing capital "city" and ten other settlements, already operating two gristmills and four sawmills.[7] The Mormon epic was again about to be re-enacted—this time on a wider stage, for larger stakes, and with decisive results.[8]

—Daniel J. Boorstin, *THE AMERICANS: THE NATIONAL EXPERIENCE*

Notice here that Boorstin carefully maintains a chronological sequence—sentence 1 refers to the year 1846; sentence 4 refers to August, 1847; sentence 6 to October, 1847; and sentence 7 to "a year later." However, Boorstin explains or amplifies these chronological statements as he proceeds. Sentence 2 states the importance of the Great Trek, and sentence 3 tells what the Mormons did as they traveled across the country. Sentence 5 explains how this great migration was possible, and sentence 8 emphasizes the results of the Great Trek.

Chronological sequence may be used not only for the narration of events but also for development by process. Woody Allen's humorous description of an imaginary dramatic production could justifiably be classified as either narration or process statement.

CHRONOLOGICAL SEQUENCE

A melodic prelude recounts man's relation to the earth and why he always seems to wind up buried in it. The curtain rises on a vast primitive wasteland, not unlike certain parts of New Jersey. Men and women sit in separate groups and then begin to dance, but they have no idea why and soon sit down again. Presently a young male in the prime of life enters and dances a hymn to fire. Suddenly it is discovered he is *on* fire, and after being put out he slinks off. Now the stage becomes dark, and Man challenges Nature—a stirring encounter during which Nature is bitten on the hip, with the result that for the next six months the temperature never rises above thirteen degrees.

—Woody Allen, *WITHOUT FEATHERS*

5. **Spatial Sequence.** A spatial sequence is used in descriptions of various types. It starts the reader at a particular point and then moves logically in some direction.

SPATIAL SEQUENCE

He followed her up the stairs, to find she had entered a room that faced north, over the large gardens below. It was an artist's studio. On a table near the door lay a litter of drawings; on an easel a barely begun oil, the mere groundlines, a hint of a young woman looking sadly down, foliage sketched faint behind her head; other turned canvases by the wall; by another wall, a row of hooks, from which hung a multi-colored array of female dresses, scarves, shawls; a large pottery jar; tables of impedimenta—tubes, brushes, color-pots. A *bas-relief,* small sculptures, an urn with bulrushes. There seemed hardly a square foot without its object. —John Fowles, THE FRENCH LIEUTENANT'S WOMAN

In the paragraph above, the reader can follow the character up the stairs and into the room and then follow his eyes around the room.

SPATIAL SEQUENCE

We went on, up a marvelously eroded road, like a deep trench in the red clay; on both sides of the road were deep canyons of erosion, in the clefts of which tall century plants bloomed like huge asparagus.[1] The banks of these canyons are full of burrows, and these are inhabited by small parrots; at our approach the parrots tumbled out and went squalling away down the canyon.[2] From the top of the road, one could look back on Orizona, nestled in the broad fronds of its banana trees, under its yellow spires.[3] Around it and beyond lay the green, rolling open range of Goiás.[4]
—Peter Matthiessen, THE CLOUD FOREST

In this paragraph, Matthiessen uses a familiar and logical spatial sequence: The rider in the car first notices the road itself, then the sides of the road (sentence 1). Sentence 2 extends the vision to the banks beyond the sides of the road. In sentence 3, the rider looks back over the town he has just left, and in sentence 4, his gaze extends to the entire area behind him.

EXERCISES: Sequences of Development

Part A: Read the following paragraphs carefully. Then identify which sequence of development is used in each and explain why the sequence of development is appropriate for that paragraph.

   A. General-to-particular sequence
   B. Particular-to-general sequence
   C. Climactic sequence
   D. Chronological sequence
   E. Spatial sequence

1.   What I saw was a small man so short in the thighs that when he stood up he seemed smaller than when he was sitting down. He had a plum pudding of a body and a square head stuck on it with no intervening neck. His brown hair was parted exactly in the middle, and the two cowlicks touched his eyebrows. He had very light blue eyes small enough to show the whites above the irises, which gave him the earnestness of a gas jet when he talked, an

air of resigned incredulity when he listened, and a merry acceptance of the human race and all its foibles when he grinned. He was dressed like the owner of a country hardware store. (On ceremonial occasions, I saw later, he dressed like a plumber got up for church.) For all his seeming squatness, his movements were precise, and his hands in particular were small and sinewy. —Alistair Cooke, *SIX MEN*

2.   Along with our overriding anxieties about the state of the world and our own country we are resentfully aware of shoddiness in cars, foods, services, in almost everything except the language we use. While an aroused public applauds the exposure of civic corruption and environmental pollution, neither the public at large nor officialdom has any concern with the corruption and pollution of language except to contribute to it. And this kind of corruption is quite as disastrous as any other, if not more so, partly because common violation of traditional usage is an ugly debasement of our great heritage, partly because sloppy English is a symptom and agent of sloppy thinking and feeling and of sloppy communication and confusion. To the famous question, "How do I know what I think till I hear what I say?" the answer might be "Do you and I know then?" —Douglas Bush, *POLLUTING OUR LANGUAGE*

3.   A good watering schedule is to water plants once a week in early spring, twice a week in full spring, and three times a week in summer, which is when plants are in active growth. In fall, start tapering off water to twice a week, then once a week, to only occasional watering in winter—besides a rest from high temperatures, as we said, plants need a rest from watering. If you do water too much in the winter, your plants will bear abnormal growth, be susceptible to rot, and not bloom in summer. (Exceptions are Christmas and Easter cacti and hybrids, and Epiphyllums, which have leaflike stems and need winter watering.) Plants will give you hints as to when to resume your watering schedule: new growth and a perkier appearance. So adjust your watering schedule to the seasons; your plants will excel.
—Jack Kramer, *CACTI AND OTHER SUCCULENTS*

4.   Estimates place the Indian population of what is now the United States at 846,000 at the close of the fifteenth century. It is not likely that there was any considerable increase during the next 125 years, although some authorities place the number of Indians in 1600 at 1,300,000. These million Indians spoke something like 350 languages belonging to some twenty-five families, which at the least were probably as different as the Germanic and Slavic, or the Celtic and Romance tongues. This means that the total number of speakers of many of the languages was relatively small, and also that the English-speaking settlers came into contact with a large number of different languages.
—Albert H. Marckwardt, *AMERICAN ENGLISH*

5.   The next day we, the defendants, saw each other for the last time before the announcement of the individual sentences. We met in the basement of the Palace of Justice. One after the other we entered a small elevator and did not return. In the courtroom above the sentence was announced. Finally it was my turn. Accompanied by an American soldier, I rode up in the elevator. A door opened, and I stood alone on a small platform in the courtroom, facing the judges. Earphones were handed to me. In my ears the words reverberated: "Albert Speer, to twenty years imprisonment."
—Albert Speer, *INSIDE THE THIRD REICH*

Part B: Choose two of the following subjects, and develop each into one good paragraph. Use the specified sequence and type of paragraph development.

1. Movies as registers of society's needs (classification type, general-to-particular sequence)

2. Integrity (definition type, particular-to-general sequence)
3. The struggle between technology and humanism (comparison and contrast type, general-to-particular sequence)
4. A memorable childhood triumph (details type, climactic sequence)
5. The first day at your first job (details type, chronological sequence)

50c Coherence / coh

Coherence is connection and consistency. A coherent paragraph is one in which all the sentences are related logically and grammatically to make a whole that allows the reader to follow the writer's train of thought step by step. A paragraph may be unified (all the sentences related to one topic) and complete (enough is said about that topic), but it will still fail as a paragraph if it lacks coherence.

COHERENT PARAGRAPH

The personal element is tremendously important in climbing.[1] It is one of the freest of sports in that it is entirely up to you and your colleagues on the rope to make your own decisions in the light of your judgement of the situation at the time.[2] To take responsibility in this way when the rewards and the penalties are both high is one of the most satisfying of the attractions of climbing.[3] At the same time the fact that things can so easily go badly wrong means that you must prepare yourself thoroughly in experience, in techniques, and physically, and that you must exercise a good deal of judgement and self-discipline when you are on the mountain, so that you always keep within your safety margin.[4] —Alan Blackshaw, *MOUNTAINEERING*

This paragraph achieves coherence by several means. The author announces his topic in the first sentence. Sentence 2 is an expansion of sentence 1, explaining that the personal element of sentence 1 means that the climber must make his or her own decision and use his or her own judgment. Sentence 3 stresses the satisfaction of being responsible for one's own decisions. Sentence 4 expands on the penalties mentioned in sentence 3 and states how one avoids these penalties. Transitional devices that help relate one sentence to another include the pronoun *It* beginning sentence 2, which ties sentence 2 to sentence 1 by referring to the word *climbing* in sentence 1. In sentence 3, *in this way* refers to the decision-making discussed in sentence 2. The words *At the same time* link sentences 3 and 4 and show that the ideas expressed in sentence 4 restrict or contrast with the ideas of sentence 3.

INCOHERENT PARAGRAPH

In mountain-climbing, one must concentrate on each move he is to make during the ascent.[1] A person must know his own limits and learn that his moves will affect the entire group of climbers.[2] Therefore, when a climber endangers himself, he endangers his comrades as well.[3] Many times during the climb you will find yourself being supported by the tips of your fingers and toes,

and you are aware that one thin rope may at any time be called upon to save you from death.[4] All the equipment from the smallest piton to the longest stretch of rope must be meticulously inspected and packed, because in this sport, mistakes may prove fatal.[5]
                                                                  —Student paper

Although this paragraph lacks an obvious topic sentence, it is not totally lacking in unity because the reader can see that the writer's main point is the great caution required in mountain-climbing. But the paragraph does lack coherence. Sentences 1 and 2 stick together well enough, but the word *therefore* that begins sentence 3 leads the reader to expect a following statement of result. Instead, an amplification of sentence 2 follows; that is, endangering one's comrades is an *example* of how one person's moves affect the entire group. Instead of continuing the discussion of the entire group, sentence 4 stresses the personal danger. Sentence 5 then switches abruptly from the personal danger discussed in sentence 4 to the importance of checking one's equipment. The switch in voice from third person to second person in sentence 4 is jarring, as is the switch from future to present tense. Finally, sentence 5 is chronologically incoherent because preparations for climbing are discussed after the climb itself has been discussed; one expects preparations for an event to precede the event itself.

Transition.   As already noted, proper transition is necessary for coherence. There should be transitions between paragraphs, between sentences, and even within long sentences. The best transitional device is a logical presentation; there is no substitute for getting ideas into their proper order in the first place and for avoiding interruptions and irrelevant details. In addition to logical presentation, a number of specific devices aid transition. These include pronouns and pronominal adjectives, synonyms for or the repetition of important words and phrases, parallel sentence structure, consistent point of view, and transitional words, especially conjunctions and adverbs.

The following selection, containing two consecutive paragraphs and a third paragraph taken from a later section of the same essay, illustrates all of these transitional devices.

TRANSITION WITHIN AND AMONG PARAGRAPHS

Cell membranes are not, it turns out, just featureless, efficient, smooth sheets—a kind of smart cellophane.[1] <u>They</u> are studded with surface features that render the membrane as recognizable as a United States Marine in full-dress uniform.[2] Recognition, <u>however</u>, depends not on any visual process but rather on contact.[3] Another <u>cell</u> must bump up against the brass buttons, so to speak, to know that they are there.[4] <u>And</u> one kind of <u>cell</u> is usually capable of identifying only a limited number of other types.[5]

<u>Nonetheless</u>, the process of identifying one another by coming into contact is ubiquitous among <u>cells</u> and all-important to countless processes required to coordinate <u>them</u> into communities—as when <u>they</u> form large organisms.[6] Such recognition-by-contact serves a variety of purposes.[7] In some cases, one <u>cell</u> uses another

to find its way to the proper location; as it brushes by, it reads a message that says, "Keep going."[8] Or two cells, as they touch each other, may be triggered to settle down and begin to specialize: "You be skin, I'll be muscle."[9]

· ·

What is this remarkable object on which life so critically depends?[10] Think for a moment what has to be achieved in designing a cell membrane.[11] It must accommodate the most extraordinary changes in size and shape of cells—and therefore must be both flexible and easily augmented or diminished as the occasion arises.[12] It must be reasonably tough (though not perfectly so; many cells utilize some kind of supplementary structural material to protect themselves from hard knocks).[13] It must be capable of performing an array of chemical tricks, and in higher organisms this repertoire changes during development.[14] It must carry distinctive features on its outer surface—and have a way to get them from the inside, where presumably they are made, to their final location on the exterior.[15] And it must always separate outside water from inside; passage of water and substances dissolved in water must be forever under strict control.[16]

—William Bennett, "Brass Buttons, Fingertips, And The Fluid Mosaic,"
Harvard Magazine

1. Pronouns and Pronominal Adjectives. In sentence 2, Bennett uses the pronoun *they* to refer to the *cell membranes* in sentence 1. In sentence 6, *they* and *them* refer to *cells*, and in sentence 8, *its* and *it* refer to *cell*. In sentence 7, *Such* ties sentence 7 to sentence 6. In sentences 12 through 16, *it* refers to *cell membrane*.

2. Synonyms and Repetition. Bennett repeats the key word *cell* several times throughout the paragraphs. In sentence 10, *this remarkable object* is used as a synonym for *cell membrane*.

3. Parallel Sentence Structure. Parallel structure is illustrated by the last five sentences of the third paragraph, all of which begin with *It must*.

4. Consistent Point of View. Bennett uses the present tense and the third person consistently throughout the three paragraphs.

5. Transitional Words. Specific transitional words include *however* in sentence 3, where it indicates that the analogy just made is not complete. In sentence 5, *And* indicates that Bennett is continuing the contrast. *Nonetheless* at the beginning of the second paragraph is also contrastive; in addition, it ties the second paragraph to the first paragraph.

Of the various ways of achieving clear transitions and hence coherence, transitional conjunctions and adverbs are both among the most important and among the most troublesome for insecure writers. The problem lies in choosing the word appropriate for the kind of relationship you want to express.

She owns three cats and a gerbil, *although* her apartment is already crowded.

She owns three cats and a gerbil. *Consequently,* her apartment is crowded.

She owns three cats and a gerbil. *In other words,* her apartment is crowded.

In the first example, the relationship between the two clauses is one of *concession*; that is, in light of the condition stated in the second clause, the fact stated in the first clause is surprising. In other words, one wouldn't expect her to own so many pets because her apartment is already crowded. In the second example, the relationship between the two sentences is one of *result*; that is, the fact stated in the second sentence is the result of the fact stated in the first sentence: Her crowded conditions result from her having so many pets. In the third example, the second sentence is a *summary* of the first. In effect, it implies *three cats and a gerbil = crowded apartment.*

These examples show how important it is that the transitional words you choose be appropriate for the kind of relationship you want to indicate. Possible types of relationships and some of the transitional words that can be used to express them are listed below.

TIME	afterward, before, meanwhile, later, until, soon, during
PLACE	here, there, elsewhere, beyond, opposite, behind, in the background
RESULT	consequently, hence, therefore, accordingly, as a result, thus
COMPARISON	likewise, similarly, also, too, in like manner
CONTRAST	however, yet, nevertheless, on the other hand, but
EXAMPLE *or* ILLUSTRATION	for example, for instance, that is, such as, specifically, as an illustration
ADDITION	furthermore, and, next, besides, first, second, in addition, also, moreover
CONCLUSION	in conclusion, to conclude, finally
SUMMARY	to sum up, in other words, in brief, in short
CONCESSION	although, of course, admittedly, true, granted that
EMPHASIS	in particular, most important, indeed, chiefly, note that

Important as transitional conjunctions and adverbs are, they should not be used at the beginning of every sentence, or the result will be as painfully obvious as electrical wiring on the outside of walls. Try to avoid attracting the reader's overt attention to your connections and transitions. If you find that your paragraphs are cluttered with *therefores, howevers,* and *furthermores,* check to see whether your logic is clear without some of them. If it is, simply eliminate the unnecessary transitional words, or bury a few of them within their sentences instead of having all of them at the beginning of sentences. For instance, instead of writing "However, many people do object to lengthy paragraphs," try "Many people, however, object to lengthy paragraphs."

EXERCISES: Coherence

Part A: Analyze the following coherent paragraph. List the logical, grammatical, and transitional devices that make it coherent.

Analogy would lead me one step further, namely, to the belief that all animals and plants have descended from some one prototype. But analogy may be a deceitful guide. Nevertheless all living things have much in common, in their chemical composition, their germinal vesicles, their cellular structure, and their laws of growth and reproduction. We see this even in so trifling a circumstance as that the same poison often similarly affects plants and animals; or that the poison secreted by the gall-fly produces monstrous growths on the wild rose or oak-tree. Therefore I should infer from analogy that probably all the organic beings which have ever lived on this earth have descended from some one primordial form, into which life was first breathed by the Creator.
—Charles Darwin, *ON THE ORIGIN OF SPECIES*

Part B: Rewrite the following two paragraphs, which lack adequate subordination, coordination and transition. Use grammatical and transitional devices to develop the simple sentences into well-unified paragraphs.

1. Dr. Warder was unusually jittery. Dr. Warder turned around too quickly. Dr. Warder's lab coat caught on the rack of test tubes. The test tubes were full of blood samples taken from people suffering from a rare disease. The test tubes fell to the floor and broke. The search for the cause of the disease would be delayed. More samples would have to be taken from the patients.

2. Leaving his apartment for work, Edwin felt lucky. A black cat ran across the road directly in front of his car just as he pulled onto the expressway. Edwin had only thirteen minutes in which to get to work. Edwin speeded up. Edwin was stopped by a policeman. Edwin got a ticket for speeding. The ticket cost twenty-five dollars. Edwin was now late for work. Edwin felt himself growing irritable. Edwin drove into his parking garage. The attendant looked at Edwin in an odd way. Edwin walked to his office. Edwin walked under a ladder where a painter was working furiously on a store-front sign. Edwin pushed the door of his office building. The door did not open. Edwin tried once more. Then it dawned on Edwin: today was Saturday—Edwin's day off.

50d SPECIAL-PURPOSE PARAGRAPHS

There are certain occasions when special-purpose paragraphs are called for. These include beginning and concluding paragraphs, transitional paragraphs, and dialogue. Beginning and concluding paragraphs are discussed in 51h.

Transitional Paragraphs. Important as transition is for coherence, it is generally best to avoid devoting an entire paragraph to transition, especially in short papers. A very long paper, such as a research paper, may sometimes need a transitional paragraph between sections. If a transitional paragraph is used, it is normally brief—only a sentence or two. In the following example, Bergen Evans completes a series of sixteen paragraphs on popular misconceptions about animal behavior by describing the notion that animals can be buried for years and later revive when exposed to air. He then uses a short one-sentence paragraph as a transition between his discussion of land animals and the six following paragraphs on erroneous ideas about sea animals.

TRANSITIONAL PARAGRAPH

. . . In the classic version—one often sees it in the paper, date-lined from some place inaccessible to inquiry—the creature is at first seemingly lifeless. But he revives in the open air, and, to the astonishment of the excavator, hops away apparently none the worse for his strange experience. Unfortunately for the veracity of the anecdotes, a toad must have air to survive; and, even with all the air, food, and water that he can desire, he will not survive many years.

<u>Of creatures that live in the sea, the whale, the shark, and the octopus appear most frequently in vulgar lore.</u>

Although all that comes out of a whale's blowhole is his breath, he is commonly represented as spouting a jet of water into the air. If the artist is unusually naïve or unusually playful he some-times puts a few small fish on top of the column . . .

—Bergen Evans, *THE NATURAL HISTORY OF NONSENSE*

Although Evans uses a separate paragraph for the transition from land animals to sea animals, he could have made that transitional sentence the first sentence of the following paragraph.

Dialogue.   In the paragraphing of **dialogue** (conversation), each di-rect quotation, along with the rest of the sentence of which it is part, requires a separate paragraph. Every time there is a change of speaker, there is a new paragraph indentation. If the conversation involves only two speakers, or if what is said makes it clear who is speaking, an identifying phrase like "she said" is not necessary for each change of speaker. However, an identifying phrase should be included every now and then to help the reader keep track of which character is speaking.

DIALOGUE

Honoria Waynflete flinched a little at the crudity of the lan-guage. She said, "I don't feel at all happy about her death. Not at all happy. The whole thing is profoundly unsatisfactory, in my opinion."[1]

Luke said patiently, "But you don't think her death was a natural one?"[2]

"No."[3]

"You don't believe it was an accident?"[4]

"It seems to me most improbable. There are so many—"[5]

Luke cut her short, "You don't think it was suicide?"[6]

"Emphatically not."[7]

"Then," said Luke gently, "you do think it was murder?"[8]

—Agatha Christie, *EASY TO KILL*

Notice here that, whenever the speaker changes, a new paragraph is made. Note also that, although paragraphs 3, 4, and 5 do not explicitly identify the speaker, Christie adds "Luke cut her short" in paragraph 6 and "said Luke gently" in paragraph 8 to help the reader remember who is speaking.

51 THE WHOLE PAPER

All of the details of grammar, punctuation, words, sentence construction, and the like are ultimately useful only as they contribute to a whole. In a composition course, this whole is typically nonfiction, relatively short (less than ten pages), and relatively formal. It is known by several names: essay, theme, composition, or, simply, paper. Whatever it is called, it is the basic unit of writing courses.

Writing is hard work. It is hard for everyone, including the most experienced and polished writers. So do not feel that you are incompetent if you find writing slow and tiring work. There are no gimmicks to make good writing easy for everyone—or anyone. There are, however, ways of making the task of writing less agonizing and of ensuring that the final result is something more than an incoherent muddle of words.

51a CHOOSING A TOPIC

Many students spend more time trying to decide on a topic than they do on the actual writing. If the topic is assigned, there is, of course, no problem. You may not care for it, but there it is, and you have no choice. Even if you do not like the topic, do not change it without permission. It was assigned for a reason. Actually, most of the writing you will do for the rest of your life will be on assigned topics. When your boss tells you to do an analysis of the available labor force for jewelry manufacturing in southern New Jersey, you cannot say, "But I just don't feel inspired by that topic." If your editor tells you to cover the Elks Club watermelon-eating contest, he will not be pleased if you write up the local golf tournament instead. When you are told to prepare a survey of the use of traffic signals in towns with a population under 50,000, you will not substitute a report on the history of hoof-and-mouth disease in Texas—or, if you do, you will soon be looking for a new job.

Even if an assigned topic distresses you initially, you will probably find your interest in it increasing as you learn more about it and work with it. And even with assigned topics, you normally have many options with respect to type of development, details to be included, and conclusions to be reached.

Finding an Appropriate Topic.   If the writing assignment is "open-ended," that is, if you are allowed to select your own topic, the problem is more serious. You may feel that you have nothing interesting or new to say about any subject at all. This is not true; every individual has had unique experiences, and almost everyone has some special skill or interest.

1. **Personal Experiences.** Perhaps you grew up in a rural area

and know a great deal about edible wild plants such as milkweed, dandelions, wintergreen, and wild blackberries and raspberries. You may not think that your expertise in this area is of much interest, but such knowledge is by no means universal and will fascinate many readers. You can write about the types of plants, how they are distinguished from nonedible plants, where they are found, or how they are prepared for eating.

But you need not have spent your childhood in the country—let alone in some exotic spot such as Nepal or Mozambique—to have had unique and interesting experiences. How did the residents of your neighborhood react to a crisis such as a major blizzard or a public-service strike? What are the problems of owning a pet in the city? How is the game of street hockey played? What was your reaction when you bumped into a glass door and swallowed the cap on your front tooth? (It is usually best, however, to avoid such topics as a trip to a ball game or an amusement park because, although you may have found it very exciting, most of your readers will have had a similar experience and will not be especially interested in your description unless something unusual happened during your trip.)

2. **Hobbies.** Hobbies are a rich source of topics for papers. Even if you are not an expert, you know more about the subject than most people do. What are the differences between a classical guitar and a bluegrass guitar? Should motorcyclists be required to wear helmets? How can chess players read for hours about opening moves? What sorts of people enjoy solving crossword puzzles? Perhaps your hobby is an unusual one. I once read an excellent essay written by a popcorn buff. But maybe you prefer to spend your leisure hours in front of the television set: Television programs and advertisements can provide a virtually unlimited number of topics. For example, you might discuss euphemism in advertisements for over-the-counter drugs, the portrayal of teen-agers in two different situation comedies, or the disadvantages of using former athletes as sports announcers.

3. **Reading.** Another source of topics is the reading that you have done for other courses or on your own. Perhaps you have read about conditioning in a course in psychology and have suddenly realized that the kitten you had when you were eleven had conditioned you instead of your conditioning the kitten. You have here the nucleus of an entertaining narrative paper. Or, based on your own past experience, you may disagree with one of the principles set forth in your education textbook. Are you a science fiction fan? Compare the typical villains of Bradbury, Asimov, and Young.

If you have recently read a book that you found particularly interesting, you might consider a book review. A book review should provide a summary of the contents detailed enough to give the reader a clear idea of what the book is about but not so detailed that the reader might feel that it is unnecessary to read the book. However, a good review includes more than just a synopsis of the contents. You should discuss the type of book (for example, fiction, history, travel), the intended audience, and your opinion of the value of the book. Include a few details or a quotation or two to give the reader an idea of the flavor of the book. Be sure to state whether you think the book is good, bad, or mediocre, and give the reasons for your opinion.

4. **Current Issues.** Current issues provide excellent paper topics: Is a national speed limit of 55 mph really a practical way of conserving energy? Or should there be different speed limits for, say, Connecticut and Idaho? Pick a current issue about which you have thought carefully or with which you have had direct experience—if you tend to get Idaho confused with Ohio, this topic is not for you. If a close friend or a family member works in a hospital, you may have some inside knowledge of the pros and cons of national health insurance. If you live in a town that manufactures shoes, you probably can say something about free trade versus protection.

5. **Likes and Dislikes.** Do you have likes or dislikes that run counter to popular tastes? Explain why you hate movies or enjoy going to the dentist. Or describe your own quirks and strange habits. Perhaps your total lack of a sense of direction has led to some embarrassing situations. Tell how you got lost coming back from your local supermarket. Maybe you find the letter z fascinating and will read anything that contains words like *guzzle, cozen, ooze, zephyr,* and *marzipan,* even when you do not know what the words mean. No topic is intrinsically boring—it is only made boring by a bored writer and dull writing.

6. **Character Sketches.** When you are gloomily pondering an assignment of "four pages on any topic at all," consider the character sketch or profile. Everyone knows interesting people because all people are interesting. If your family has an eccentric, as most families do, so much the better. But conventional people are interesting, too. Even those who seem to be perfect examples of "types" have many apparent contradictions in their behavior. For example, you may think of an aunt who appears to be the classic liberated woman. She works in the advertising department of a weekly magazine, discusses the stock market with authority, and hates to cook. But then you remember that she irons dish towels, puts down newspapers on freshly mopped floors, and does not know where the gas tank on her car is.

7. **Descriptions.** Instead of describing a person, you might describe a familiar place. What is your neighborhood like? What kind of architecture does it have? What kind of people live there? What do you see in the street? Has the neighborhood changed within your memory? Try to stand back and view it as a stranger seeing it for the first time. What impression does it make?

Or you might describe how to do something. Have you a favorite recipe for lasagna? How do you repair a faulty electrical plug? How do you determine your position at sea using dead reckoning? What is involved in using a wood-turning lathe? A good description of even a common activity such as operating a self-service gasoline pump can be entertaining and informative.

Topics to Avoid.   As a general rule, avoid very broad or highly abstract topics. Even if you know quite a bit about the subject matter, it cannot be handled adequately within three to five pages. The following topics are far too broad for a short paper.

> The Lumbering Industry in America
> The Development of Opera
> The Concept of Evil
> Changing Attitudes toward Child Rearing
> The Pros and Cons of City Planning
> The War of 1812
> The Novel and the Middle Class

The subject area of any of these topics could be suitable for a short paper, but the topic of the paper itself would have to be narrowed to one particular, small facet of the larger subject. For example, rather than trying to encompass all of the lumbering industry in five pages, you might write on the use of hemlock in the building trade (assuming you know something about hemlock). Or, instead of a paper on the concept of evil, you might describe your earliest memory of having done something wrong and your subsequent feelings of guilt.

If you are given a choice, avoid such overused topics as "My High School Graduation," "Why I Came to College," "First Impressions of State University," "The Values of a Liberal Arts Education," and "Why I Want to be a Veterinarian." The problem with such topics is that either your experiences are likely to have been nearly identical to everyone else's ("My High School Graduation") or you really do not know why you came to college (nor should you feel guilty that you do not). That oldest of chestnuts, "My Summer Vacation," is not as bad a topic as it sounds, particularly if you did something unusual during your summer vacation. Just do not entitle the paper "My Summer Vacation." Call it "Eight Weeks on a Coca-Cola Truck" or "House-Painting as an Art Form" or "Memoirs of a Tomato-Picker."

Finally, avoid topics about which you know little or nothing. If you cannot tell a prayer rug from a doormat, do not tackle "Buying an Oriental Rug." Do not write about the trials of motorcycle racing if you have never been on a motorcycle. Steer clear of the problems of old age unless you have always been surrounded by old people or have worked in a rest home. If you are hopelessly ignorant about a subject but still fascinated by it, consider saving that topic for a research paper, when you will have a chance to investigate the subject thoroughly.

EXERCISES: Choosing A Topic

Which of the following topics would *not* be suitable choices—as they are stated—for a three-to-five-page essay? For each one that you consider too general or abstract, write a more specific topic that would be appropriate for a short essay.

1. Making Hand Puppets from Papier-Mâché
2. *Superman, Star Wars,* and *Close Encounters of the Third Kind:* Why They Were Sellouts
3. The Benefits of Space Exploration

4. Golda Meir: Her Rise to Political Power
5. Cooking with Wine
6. How to Build a Simple Wooden Plant Stand
7. Violence in the Public Schools
8. The Development of Cubism
9. Wiring a House
10. Albert Einstein's Antiwar Stand

51b NARROWING THE TOPIC

Whether you are assigned a topic or have selected the subject area yourself, you will always have to narrow it considerably before it is appropriate for a paper of only a few pages. This is true whether you know a good deal about the topic or know very little about it. Indeed, the necessity of narrowing the topic is often greater in the latter case because, when you do not know very much about a subject area, your temptation is likely to be to write vague generalizations about it.

How do you know when you have sufficiently narrowed your topic? The answer will depend on the topic, the length of the final paper, and the level of generalization at which you discuss the topic. However, writing anything meaningful and interesting on a highly general level is very difficult, even for the expert writer, so you should plan to be as specific as possible.

Do not plan to write down everything you know first and then try to cut the result down to size. The result will be a choppy series of disconnected paragraphs lacking coherence and unity. Instead, first consider what you can tell your reader in, say, five hundred words. You will probably need one hundred or so of these words to introduce and define your topic. For example, if you were planning to write about purebred cats, you would have to introduce your subject and then tell the reader exactly what is meant by the term *purebred*. You would be left with only four hundred words in which to say everything else you have in mind about purebred cats. You cannot cover all the different breeds, the problems of breeding, the most popular breeds, the advantages and disadvantages of each breed, and the conventions of cat shows in just four hundred words. Clearly, you must subdivide your topic before you can begin writing.

Narrowing a topic is not simply a mechanical process of chipping away at a subject until it fits predetermined limits. The very process of narrowing the topic forces you to focus your own thoughts about the topic and gives you specific ideas about what you are going to say in the final paper.

Narrowing an Unfamiliar Topic.   Perhaps you have read Thoreau's "Civil Disobedience" as a class assignment and your instructor has told you to write a paper about taxation. You realize, first, that you do not know very much about taxation and, second, that the topic is so broad that it must be cut down to size before you can say anything about it at all. A good way to begin the narrowing process is simply to jot down things that come to mind when you think of taxes. Do not worry about the order of the items at this point; just put them down as you think of them. Your list might look like the one that follows.

1. Income tax
2. Purpose of taxation
3. Everybody hates taxes
4. Complicated system—nobody can figure it out
5. Many kinds of taxes—sales, property, income, hidden, on special products (cigarettes, gasoline), capital gains, import duties
6. Who decides on taxes?
7. What do taxes buy? Schools, fire and police, highways, defense, social programs
8. Alternatives to taxes—lotteries, legalized gambling
9. Fairness of taxes: progressive income tax
10. Should people vote on taxes? Proposition 13

When you cannot think of anything else to list, stop and look at what you have written down. As you scan the list, you see that No. 1, "Income tax," is really a subdivision of No. 5, "Many kinds of taxes." So you cross off No. 1. No. 2, "Purpose of taxation," looks like a subdivision of No. 7, "What do taxes buy?" Then you vaguely remember having heard that taxes are also sometimes used to curb inflation, but you do not understand the details of that, so you decide to omit No. 2 also. No. 3 looks promising—you certainly have heard many different people complain about taxes. But then you cannot think of anything else to say, and you decide you cannot expand the simple statement "Everyone hates taxes" into a five-page paper. Cross out No. 3.

No. 4 looks discouraging at first; you know you do not understand the taxation system yourself. On the other hand, you remember several specific instances when you confronted the complexities of taxation. You decide to leave No. 4 on the list. No. 5 looks promising because you have already listed a number of different kinds of taxes. You leave No. 5 on the list, at least temporarily. You see that No. 6, "Who decides on taxes?" is related to No. 10, "Should people vote on taxes?" but you decide that you do not know enough about Proposition 13 to write about it, so you eliminate both No. 6 and No. 10 from the list.

No. 7, "What do taxes buy?" also has a number of entries after it, so perhaps you have a good start on the subject. You leave No. 7 on the list. No. 8, "Alternatives to taxes," looks interesting, so you leave it on the list. You cross out No. 9 because you have already decided not to talk about income taxes in particular. Your list is now considerably shorter.

4. Complicated system—nobody can figure it out
5. Many kinds of taxes—sales, property, income, hidden, on special products (cigarettes, gasoline), capital gains, import duties
7. What do taxes buy? Schools, fire and police, highways, defense, social programs
8. Alternatives to taxes—lotteries, legalized gambling

As you look at your revised list, you decide that you are not especially interested in No. 7, so you eliminate it. You like the idea of writing on No. 8, "Alternatives to taxation," but you realize that you would have to do library research on the subject because you know little about lotteries and legalized gambling. The assignment was not a library paper, so you cross No. 8 from the list. You are now down to two items.

4. Complicated system—nobody can figure it out
5. Many kinds of taxes—sales, property, income, hidden, on special products (cigarettes, gasoline), capital gains, import duties

You see that you could add even more kinds of taxes to No. 5—excess profits taxes, one-time taxes, taxes marked for special purposes. Then you realize that explaining just one of these kinds of taxes would require an entire paper and involve research besides. You look at No. 4 again. You remember all the tax forms you had to fill out when you had a part-time job. You recall having had to pay customs on a bottle of perfume that you thought was tax-free. You know your father hires an accountant to fill out his federal and state income-tax forms for him. You remember that your hometown newspaper published a series of articles on the complexities of the property assessment. You have seen the tax charts that retail clerks have to consult every time they ring up a sale.

Finally, you decide to write about the complexities of the tax system, arguing that the tax system in the United States is too complicated. You can use the very fact that you do not understand it as part of the argument that the system is overly complex. The supporting evidence for your argument will be the confusing experiences you have had or have heard about. You can even salvage part of No. 5 from your earlier list ("Many kinds of taxes") by simply listing them and noting that the many different kinds of taxes add to the complexity of the system.

Narrowing a Familiar Topic.   When you are narrowing a topic that you know little about, your first task is to find some aspect of that topic about which you do have enough information to make an intelligent statement. When the topic is one about which you are relatively knowledgeable, your problem is that you have too much information and you cannot possibly include all of it in a brief paper. There are many broad subject areas about which you probably know a great deal (more than you realize).

the family	law	recreation	transportation
food	health	literature	history
education	television		

Suppose you wanted to write a paper on recreation. Clearly "Recreation" will not do as the title for a five-page paper. You can quickly subdivide the topic into kinds of recreation, purposes of recreation, attitudes toward recreation, and the history of recreation. You decide that you would like to write about specific kinds of recreation. As you think about this, you see that there are a number of ways of subdividing kinds of recreation.

1. Team sports versus individual sports
2. Participatory sports versus spectator sports
3. Popular recreation versus unusual recreation
4. Strenuous recreation versus nonstrenuous recreation
5. Physical recreation versus mental recreation

You are not especially interested in the distinction between team sports and individual sports, and too much has already been written about participatory versus spectator sports. You decide that it would be hard to draw the line between strenuous and nonstrenuous recreation, so it would be best to avoid that subdivision. You do not want to talk about mental recreation, so you eliminate the fifth item on the list. This leaves you with popular recreation versus unusual recreation. Unusual types of recreation sounds interesting, but you enjoy popular sports yourself. Further, you had originally had a hazy notion that you might write something about baseball. But, again, so much has been written about baseball that you are not sure you have anything new to say about it. Then you remember that your seventy-two-year-old grandmother is a dedicated Mets fan who watches every televised game, knows the names and statistics of every player, and makes several excursions a season to Shea Stadium to see the Mets play. At last you have a topic narrow enough to be handled in a short paper: "My Grandmother and the Mets."

Any broad subject area can be similarly narrowed by the process of subdividing.

BROAD TOPIC	NARROWED TOPIC
The family	The perfect baby-sitter
Food	Baking bread in a reflector oven
Education	My two days as a teacher's aide
Law	Right turns on red should be outlawed
Health	Hay fever isn't funny
Television	Local versus national news reporting
Literature	I love to read trash
Transportation	Taking Amtrak across the United States
History	Why the Mennonites settled in Indiana

EXERCISES: Narrowing the Topic

Assume that your instructor has assigned essays on each of these general subjects: football and birds. You have made the following lists of all your ideas on each subject. Now go over each list, striking off what you do not really know much about or what does not really interest you. Combine ideas that overlap. Most of what you will have left will still be too broad and general. From these leftover general ideas, distill one good, specific theme topic for each subject.

A. Football
1. Spectators at football games
2. Differences between professional football and college football

51c APPROACHING THE TOPIC

Once you have selected a topic and narrowed it to what seems to be reasonable proportions, you have to decide how you are going to approach the topic; that is, are you going to tell a story, explain something, try to persuade the reader that you are right, or describe what something is like? Traditionally, there are four types of approach to a topic, or four **rhetorical types,** as they are called. These are *exposition, argument and persuasion, description,* and *narration.*

Exposition. The purpose of **exposition** is to explain something. Exposition answers questions such as What is it? What does it do? How does it work? Why is it important? Expository papers convey facts and help the reader understand something he or she did not understand before. An expository paper about the perfect baby-sitter would explain what a good baby-sitter does and why it is important that the baby-sitter do these things. The paper might include such information as the facts that perfect baby-sitters are rare, that there are organizations of trained baby-sitters, that baby-sitters are most often teenagers, and so on. Or, if you were writing an expository paper about cross-country skiing, you would want to explain how cross-country skiing differs from downhill skiing, where cross-country skiing is done, and what the techniques are for turning and stopping on cross-country skis. In your paper, you might include such information as the following.

> Changing wax or rewaxing in the open air is at best a tedious chore and at worst a horror. Consequently, various types of waxless touring skis have been developed. Of these, the two most popular types are those with a plastic "fish-scale" bottom and those with strips of mohair on the bottom surface. Fish-scales are slower than other kinds of skis and tend to "hum" loudly as they glide. Mohair skis are quieter but lose their grip if they become too wet or if they freeze. Both fish-scale and mohair skis are excellent for climbing. . . .

Argument and Persuasion. The purpose of **argument and persuasion** is to persuade the reader, by a logical reasoning process, to accept the writer's point of view. An argument-and-persuasion paper on the perfect baby-sitter might assert that there is no perfect baby-sitter because there is no substitute for a child's mother. Alternatively, it might argue that mothers are seldom the best baby-sitters. In either case, evidence would be provided to support the point of view and to persuade the reader to accept it (see 52d). If you wanted to convince your readers that cross-country skiing was preferable to downhill skiing, your evidence might include the fact that cross-country equipment is much less expensive and cumbersome than downhill equipment. You would note that cross-country skiing provides better exercise, gives the skier more freedom and flexibility, and does not involve high tow fees or long hours of waiting in line at tows.

> Strong winds will blow the powder from the surface of downhill slopes, making skiing treacherous or even impossible. When the wind-chill factor reaches $-50°$ or colder, downhill slopes often are closed because of the danger of exposure to skiers. Cross-country skiers, on the other hand, can simply plan a tour along more wooded trails where the trees provide protection from the wind. Furthermore, the strenuous exercise of cross-country skiing keeps skiers warm under virtually any weather conditions, and they rarely need worry about frostbite or hypothermia. . . .

Description. The purpose of **description** is to convey a sensory impression, especially a visual impression. Exposition explains what it is; description tells the reader what it looks like, feels like, sounds like. A descriptive paper on the perfect baby-sitter might describe in detail the appearance of a baby-sitter that you once had. If you were describing the scene as you started down a mountain on cross-country skis, you might include a passage such as the following.

> Behind us was the weathered summit building, the roar of the machinery that controlled the gondola, and a few curious downhill skiers who openly stared at people crazy enough to ski down Wildcat Mountain on cross-country skis—and down the wrong side of Wildcat at that. Ahead of us was a terrifyingly steep, narrow, and sharply curving trail, little more than a path. Stunted though they were by the altitude and harsh climate, the twisted evergreen branches that hung over the trail were a menace to exposed faces or poorly controlled ski poles. Several hundred feet straight down, a sign with a red arrow pointed right, but the trail beyond was invisible. . . .

Narration.   The purpose of **narration** is to tell a story, fictional or true. Narration is concerned with events and actions, usually in the past. Narration answers the question "What happened?" A narrative paper on the perfect baby-sitter might, for example, relate an incident in which a baby-sitter handled a crisis with great skill. The narration of a cross-country ski tour might include an incident such as the following.

> The extent of their foolishness was revealed when they began to descend. With no edges on their light touring skis, they had no control whatsoever on the thick icy crust. At first, they simply schussed until their speed became terrifying, and then they deliberately fell to brake themselves. When the trail became more winding, schussing was impossible, and Ginny and Bert both resorted to sitting down on their skis, trying to guide the tips with their hands. But when Bert tore his knickers on a root, he decided to stand up again, regardless of the consequences. As he rocketed down the slope, he saw a large boulder directly in the middle of the trail. Attempting a quick step turn, he lost his balance, fell, and watched in dismay as his right ski continued down the mountain ahead of him. . . .

The four rhetorical types—exposition, argument and persuasion, description, and narration—are not, of course, completely independent of each other. In fact, most papers will contain elements of two or more types. For example, you may need to relate a sequence of events (narration) in order to explain something (exposition). At least some exposition is required in argument and persuasion. Description is frequently part of narration. However, the *primary* approach of any one paper should be identifiable as one of the four expository types.

EXERCISES: Approaching the Topic

Indicate which of the four rhetorical types in the list below you would use as the primary approach in developing the following topics. Be prepared to justify your answer.

A. Exposition   C. Description
B. Argument and persuasion   D. Narration

1. My triumphs in the state backgammon contest
2. State and federal tax benefits for the aged
3. The summer my grandmother lived with us
4. Learning the basic strategy of backgammon
5. Mrs. Laneau: my eighty-three-year-old fishing partner
6. Why backgammon is a game for everyone
7. Nursing homes: why they need more regulation by state and federal authorities
8. A firsthand look at the Sunny Slopes Retirement Home

51d FINDING A THESIS

One of the chief reasons that papers fail is for the lack of a clear **thesis.** The thesis of a paper is its main point, its central idea. It is the reason you are writing the paper (aside from the fact that your instructor told you to write it). A thesis statement sums up in one sentence what you want to convey to your readers.

It is crucial that you formulate your thesis *before* you start the actual writing. A good thesis statement helps you focus your thoughts about your topic before you start to write, and it helps you stick to your thesis as you write. It is much harder to revise an already written paper to provide a clear thesis than it is to begin writing with a thesis in mind.

Narrowing the topic and deciding on the rhetorical type to be used are steps in formulating a thesis, but they are not the thesis itself. For example, suppose you have been assigned an argument-and-persuasion paper on interpersonal relationships, and you have narrowed that broad topic to "the generation gap." What precisely do you want to persuade your readers to believe about the generation gap? There are many possible thesis statements for this topic.

> The generation gap is a fiction invented by sociologists and perpetuated by the media.
> The generation gap in America has resulted from the breakup of family life.
> There will always be a generation gap because parents will always be reluctant to allow children to make their own decisions.

Or, to take another example, if you were writing an expository paper on the topic "I love to read trash," your thesis statement might be "Because I have read trash all my life, I can read eight hundred words a minute and have an immense vocabulary." Or it might be "I love to read trash, not in spite of the fact that it presents a romantic, unreal world, but because it presents an unreal world."

A good thesis statement is specific and unified and is not self-evident. "Specific" means that the statement not only indicates exactly what the main point of the paper is, but also avoids vague generalities.

OVERLY GENERAL	IMPROVED
Teaching is a noble profession.	The first-grade teacher is responsible for the most important skill we possess: reading.
The United States should not be so wasteful.	Nearly every American wastes hundreds of pounds of paper each year.
You don't have to be rich to be happy.	A vacation in a state park can be both delightful and inexpensive.

A unified statement is one that includes only one idea or perhaps one main idea and one or two closely related subsidiary ideas. Consider the statement "There are many desirable professions for the college graduate, but some people choose the Peace Corps because economic conditions are so bad that they cannot find a job in the United States." This statement contains at least three ideas: (1) there are many desirable jobs for college graduates, (2) when economic conditions are bad, college graduates often cannot find good jobs, and (3) some people go into the Peace Corps only because they cannot find a good job in the United States. Any of these is a potential thesis statement, but it would be impossible to relate and develop all of them within the limits of a short paper.

NOT UNIFIED	IMPROVED
I like watching sports events on television, and I also like to participate in sports.	My love of spectator sports does not prevent me from participating in sports myself.
Many students do not like to read Chaucer, and they prefer Shakespeare, whose language is easier to understand.	Many students do not like to read Chaucer only because his language is hard to understand.
Even though we do not have much political terrorism in the United States, it is an inexcusable way of trying to get one's demands.	Political terrorism is never excusable.

Self-evident statements are those that need not be said at all because everyone agrees with them; there is no point in writing a paper arguing that horses are bigger than rabbits.

SELF-EVIDENT	IMPROVED
Automobile accidents cause many injuries and deaths.	Playground equipment causes many injuries and deaths.
Poor people have less money to spend than rich people.	In some instances, the poor may receive better medical care than the rich.

Although you should strive for a thesis statement that is specific, unified, and not self-evident, you need not try to make the thesis statement as dramatic or as shocking as possible. Do not claim more in your thesis statement than you can justify in the paper itself.

OVERLY DRAMATIC	IMPROVED
Overpermissive parents are the cause of juvenile crime.	Overpermissive parents are one cause of juvenile crime.
Napoleon was an incompetent general whose victories were due to luck alone.	Napoleon's victory at Wagram can be attributed more to his luck than to his military genius.

When you actually start writing the paper, include the statement of the thesis near the beginning. You may be able to use exactly the same sentence in your paper as your original thesis statement, or you may have to reword it to make it fit in with your introductory material. If, after you have started writing, you find that your paper cannot be developed exactly along the lines of your thesis statement, restate or revise your thesis rather than ignoring it or trying to justify an unworkable thesis. Even though you may have to revise your thesis after further thought and writing, formulating a thesis statement before you begin will help you focus your thinking as you write.

EXERCISES: Finding a Thesis

Label each of the following theses with the appropriate letter from the list below. Then, for each, write a specific, focused thesis statement that you could develop into an interesting paper.

A. Overly general   C. Self-evident
B. Not unified   D. Overly dramatic

1. Television breeds crime.
2. The rise in the number of working mothers has caused an increase in the number of child-care facilities, and it has contributed substantially to the phenomenal growth of the fast-food industry.
3. Sex education is necessary for adolescents.
4. Government deregulation of the airlines has led to competitive fares.
5. Dogs are great pets.
6. The electronic media are fostering illiteracy.
7. Baseball is one of the most popular American sports.
8. Chess and crossword puzzles are stimulating.

51e PREPARING TO WRITE

Once you have selected a topic and know the rhetorical type you will be using, you face the question "But exactly what am I going to say about it?" Actually, you probably have a number of good ideas already, or you would not have picked the topic in the first place. Begin by jotting these ideas down. Do not worry about order at this stage; just write ideas down as they come to you.

If you have the time to wait several days before you have to begin writing, use the time to mull over the topic as you stand in line, wait for a bus, clean your room, or do other tasks that do not require any great amount of mental effort. If you have the topic in the back of your mind as you go about your daily activities, you will be surprised how often you will encounter something that relates to it and that gives you a new perspective on it. For example, you may be planning to write about the frustrations of city life. On your way to class you see a pigeon on the sidewalk walking rapidly around and around in tight circles. You do not understand why the pigeon is doing this, but it seems symbolic to you of the haste and aimlessness of the lives of many city-dwellers. You can incorporate this observation into your paper; such concrete examples add interest to an essay. Write it down as soon as possible so that you do not forget it—nothing is more annoying than to have forgotten what you know was an excellent idea.

Regardless of the rhetorical type that you plan to follow, you can make notes of relevant quotations to be used, anecdotes to make your point more forceful, and specific facts that should be included. Specific facts are very important because lack of detail in a paper makes it boring. If you need to check a fact, make a note to do the checking before you start writing; incorrect detail destroys the reader's confidence in you. For example, you may be planning to write a paper on women as athletes and want to mention Gertrude Ederle. You think she was the first person to swim the English Channel. Or was she just the first woman to swim the Channel? Or did she just break a previous record? The correct answers to these questions may determine the turn your final arguments will take.

If you are writing an expository paper, consider the definitions you may need to formulate and the explanations that should be presented. What details can you include and what details should be omitted? For a paper on Quakerism, you might want to describe the origin of the term *Quaker*. You might have a note that you should explain the relationship between the structure of the church and the beliefs held by its members. Another note might say, "History of Quakers too complicated to include." Still another note might read, "Who are some famous Quakers?"

For an argument-and-persuasion paper, your preliminary notes should include at least the evidence you plan to use to support your argument and the counterarguments that you must refute. Think of who your audience is (even if it is a fictional audience). That is, if you were arguing that Americans eat too much sugar, the main thrust of your argument would differ, depending on whether your audience consisted of dentists, college students, or parents of small children.

Narrative papers require a great deal of detail; jot down the essential details. Decide on the order your narrative should take. Should you start at the beginning and plow steadily through to the end? Or should you state the outcome first and then give the events that led up to it? Or are you skillful enough to start in the middle, go back to the beginning, and then relate the outcome? Consider the questions "What if it *had not* happened?" or "What if it had not happened the way it did?"

If you are writing a descriptive paper, it will consist primarily of details. But if you are describing, for example, your sister's appearance, do not restrict yourself to a head-to-toe description of the sort one might make from looking at a snapshot. Describe her gestures and mannerisms. What is her walk like? How does she look when she eats, falls asleep in front of the television set, gets caught looking in the mirror? If you are describing an object or a scene, what comparisons can you make? Do not restrict your comparisons to vision alone—what does the object smell like, feel like, taste like, sound like? What does it remind you of? A good thesis sentence will provide a focus for your description. For example, the thesis sentence *"I could tell that Clyde was a man who marched to a different drummer when I saw that he wore hiking boots with a three-piece suit"* would allow you to focus your description on the contradictions in or eccentricities of Clyde's behavior.

EXERCISES: Preparing to Write

Choose one of the following general subjects. For it, write a narrowed topic and a thesis statement you could develop into an interesting paper. State the primary rhetorical approach you would use (exposition, argument and persuasion, narration, or description). Then list ideas, anecdotes, arguments, quotations, statistics, and details you could use in writing the paper.

1. Black entertainers
2. Soap operas
3. Early childhood development
4. Urban life
5. Advertising
6. Black holes in space
7. Solar energy

51f ORGANIZING THE PAPER

Once you have gathered your materials, you can start organizing the paper itself. Collect all your notes and lay them out before you. Eliminate material that is clearly irrelevant or that goes beyond the limits of your thesis statement.

Finding an Appropriate Organization. You have a topic, have narrowed that topic, and have formulated a thesis statement. You know what rhetorical type you plan to use in your paper. Now you must organize the material in the way most suitable for your thesis and your rhetorical design. In other words, you must decide on the order, or sequence, in which you will present your ideas. Appropriate organization helps you catch and hold the reader's interest and allows the reader to follow your train of thought as he or she reads the paper.

1. **Expository Papers.** Expository papers lend themselves to a variety of different sequences of organization. You can proceed from the general to the particular by stating general principles first and

then giving examples and details that support and illustrate these principles. For example, if you were writing a paper to explain the basic components of a computer, you might first note that computers have six main units—input, control, internal memory, arithmetic, output, and storage. You would then discuss each of these units in some detail.

Organization by cause-to-effect is a variation on general-to-particular organization. Here you would list the cause of something first and then detail the specific effects. For example, suppose you were explaining how the ecology of entire regions of the earth has been affected by man's attempts to alter the environment. You might first explain that people have often casually introduced animals or insects into areas where they previously did not exist (cause). You could then show how this practice has sometimes led to changes in the ecology of these areas (effect), listing as specific examples the introduction of the gypsy moth into New England, the English sparrow into New York City, and the rabbit into Australia.

You can sometimes organize an expository paper by proceeding from the particular to the general. For example, if you planned a paper on defense mechanisms in insects, you could first describe blister beetles that exude an oily substance that raises blisters on the skin, spider wasps that have a painful sting, and walking sticks that strongly resemble small twigs. From these examples, you could proceed to a general statement that all insects have some means of insuring their survival and perhaps continue with a general classification of the kinds of protective devices, such as coloration, stings or bites, and inaccessible habitats.

Another variety of the particular-to-general organization is organization by effect-to-cause. Here you first state a number of effects or results and then discuss their cause. In a paper about home accidents, you might first describe a family in which the teen-age daughter ran a sewing-machine needle through her finger, the father mangled his hand on a power mower, the mother received a severe burn from an electric skillet, and the son got a bad electrical shock when he dropped a hair dryer and reached into the sink to pick it up. After detailing these effects, you would explain that the cause of all these accidents was careless or improper use of home appliances.

If you were explaining something unfamiliar in an expository paper, you would probably want to proceed from the familiar to the unfamiliar. If, for instance, you wanted to discuss the various media used in painting, you might start with water and oil because these are likely to be familiar to everyone. You would then discuss less familiar media such as egg white, gum, and wax, perhaps comparing the characteristics of these less familiar media with those of the more familiar water and oil.

Similarly, in an expository paper intended to describe a process, you would use a simple-to-difficult organization. If you were describing how to tie various kinds of knots, you would begin with the simple half hitch because it is easy to tie and is the basis of many other knots. You would then proceed to the more difficult sailor's hitch and clove hitch, saving complicated knots like the two-leaf drag-onfly for the end of your paper.

2. **Argument-and-Persuasion Papers.** The most common type of organization for an argument-and-persuasion paper is the general-to-particular arrangement. You state your argument first and then support it with detailed evidence. The evidence itself is normally arranged in the order of most important to least important.

Early in the paper, you show your awareness of opposing views by refuting counterarguments or, if you cannot refute them, by con-ceding the points. For instance, if you were trying to persuade your readers that intercollegiate athletics should be banned, you would first state this as your argument. You might then concede that com-petitive athletics often do ensure badly needed financial contributions from alumni and provide enjoyment for many people both within and outside of the college community. You might refute the argument that physical exercise is essential to health by noting that intercolle-giate athletics provides exercise for only a very few athletes and that there are alternative ways for getting exercise. You would then cite the main evidence for your argument—that all the excitement over intermural sports draws attention away from the real purpose of a college, that the college's desire to get star athletes means that stu-dents may be admitted on the basis of their athletic rather than their academic qualifications, and that intercollegiate athletics is actually very expensive, siphoning away money for equipment, facilities, and scholarships that might better be used for academic purposes. Less important evidence such as the erroneous public image of colleges as athletic businesses, the normally heavy emphasis on contact sports, and the corruption that sometimes occurs would follow your main evidence. (See also 52.)

3. **Descriptive Papers.** Because the purpose of descriptive pa-pers is to convey a physical impression, the most logical organization is according to the dominant impression that you wish to convey. For example, if you were describing a policeman testifying before an in-vestigating committee, it would be impossible (and very boring for the reader) to itemize every single feature that could be observed. Instead, you might concentrate on a dominant impression of, say, nervousness. You might begin by describing his creased fore-head, his habit of blinking, his way of continually licking his lips. You could then note that he constantly rubbed his forefingers and thumbs together, crossed and uncrossed his legs, and sat forward tensely in his chair. After this more or less general description, you could continue by noting exactly how he replied to particular ques-tions, how he addressed his questioners, and so forth.

Organization by dominant impression can also be combined with an orderly spatial description. In a description of the interior of a Quaker meetinghouse, you might wish to give the reader an impres-sion of starkness and simplicity. You could simultaneously give a spatially ordered description by beginning your description from a single seat within the meetinghouse and gradually moving outward from this seat. Thus, you might first describe the straight-backed cane-bottomed chairs, then the uncarpeted wooden floor, and then the plain ceiling with its single light fixture. From there you could move to the white walls without pictures and to the windows with small panes and no curtains, perhaps finally noting that even the tree branches visible through the windows are bare, without the ornamentation of leaves.

4. **Narrative Papers.** The most natural organization for a narrative paper is the chronological arrangement. The first events are narrated at the beginning and subsequent events later, following the natural order of time. You may occasionally need to deviate briefly from a strictly chronological presentation in order to explain why a particular event is relevant or why it occurred, but in general the order is from earlier to later.

For many narratives, the end of the narrative will simply be the last event; when the final occurrence takes place, the story is over. This would be true if, for example, you were narrating a typical day in the life of a steelworker, a trip on a bus, or a riot in a state prison. Other kinds of narrative are more effective if they have a climactic order, that is, an order that proceeds up to a dramatic occurrence and then stops, even if the entire story has not been completed. For example, if you were narrating an automobile accident, you might wish to end your paper with a sentence describing the moment of impact. To continue the story by relating the arrival of the police and tow trucks would be anticlimactic and would detract from the effectiveness of the story.

EXERCISES: Organizing the Paper

For the topic you defined in the exercise "Preparing to Write," plan the organization of a paper, using the rhetorical method you chose and the general ideas you have listed. Write out a rough thesis and a rough statement of the sequence you would use to develop the topic.

Making a Preliminary Outline. Suppose you have decided to write an expository paper about travel. You have narrowed the topic to a three-day stop you made in Iceland when you were en route to Belgium as a representative to an international youth conference. You have further restricted the topic to those things that impressed you most about Iceland. As you thought about the topic, you realized that you were actually more impressed by little things not mentioned in travel brochures than you were by the volcanoes and glaciers. You have formulated a thesis statement: "In a foreign country, it is the seemingly insignificant things, not the exotic things, that most impress me."

Your rough notes for the paper might include the following items.

> Farming—sheep, hay, flax, cows in harnesses
> Sheep get out of road
> People—friendly, blond, good-looking
> Newsboys wear rubber boots in summer

Glaciers, volcanoes, lava fields, hot springs, geysers
Arctic skuas, golden plovers, puffins
Hot springs heat—water always hot in rest rooms
Bananas growing in greenhouses
Whaling—meat looks like corned beef
Not much difficulty with language
Hotels and food very expensive
Plane crowded
Food—fish, carrots and peas, *skyr*
What travel brochures lead you to expect
Treeless or stunted trees
Corrugated tin roofs and siding
Cleanliness of Reykjavik—no dogs in city
Small bridges or no bridges at all
Near Arctic Circle, but mild climate

As you look at the list of ideas, you see that it has virtually no organization. Because your thesis statement makes a basic division between insignificant things and exotic things, you start organizing by dividing the list into "Exotic" and "Insignificant," with a third column for those items that do not seem to fit into either category.

EXOTIC	INSIGNIFICANT	OTHER
1. Glaciers, volcanoes, lava fields, hot springs, geysers	9. Flax fields in bloom	20. Farming—sheep, hay
2. Arctic skuas, golden plovers, puffins	10. Cows in harnesses	21. People—friendly, blond, good-looking
3. Hot springs heat	11. Sheep get out of road	22. Not much difficulty with language
4. Bananas growing in greenhouses	12. Newsboys wear rubber boots	23. Hotels and food very expensive
5. Whaling industry	13. Water always hot in rest rooms	24. Plane crowded
6. *Skyr* (like yogurt)	14. Whale meat looks like corned beef	25. What travel brochures lead you to expect
7. Treeless	15. Carrots and peas	26. Cleanliness of Reykjavik
8. Near Arctic Circle, but mild climate	16. Corrugated tin roofs	
	17. No dogs in Reykjavik	
	18. Small bridges or no bridges at all	
	19. Stunted trees	

When you examine your "Other" column, you decide that most of the items in it are not related to your thesis statement, so you cross items 20, 22, 23, and 24 off that list. You cannot decide about items 21 and 26, so you leave them on the list for the time being.

Your thesis statement implies a comparison and contrast, and your two columns "Exotic" and "Insignificant" are also contrasting lists. Clearly, you will need several comparison-and-contrast paragraphs in your final paper. (See 50b.) But how should the comparison and contrast be organized? One possibility is by categories.

Geography: (1) (7) (8) vs. (19)   Food: (6) vs. (15)
Animal life: (2) vs. (10) (11) (17)   Everyday living: (3) vs. (12) (13) (16)
Plant life: (4) vs. (9)   Industry and technology: (5) vs. (14) (18)

This division looks a little unbalanced—some categories have four entries, some only two. Probably some categories need to be combined or split up. However, you decide to leave the division as it is for the moment and consider the rest of the paper. How are you going to lead into the comparison? You decide to make a rough outline of the entire paper. At this point, the outline is for your own use only, and there is no need to fuss about proper outline form.

I. People often disappointed by great sights—Stonehenge, Grand Canyon
II. Travel brochures—I expected to be impressed with Iceland
III. Specific examples
   A. Geography
   B. Animal life
   C. Plant life
   D. Food
   E. Everyday living
   F. Industry and technology
IV. "Insignificant" things may actually be more important

When you examine this rough outline, you see that Items I, II, and IV will probably each take a single paragraph. Item II, however, is far too large to fit into one paragraph. On the other hand, some of the subdivisions, such as III.C., "Plant life," seem too small for a separate paragraph of their own. Perhaps you can combine some of these entries and end up with only four or five paragraphs under "Specific Examples."

Item III.C., "Plant life," is rather skimpy. Further, as you think about it, the growing of bananas in greenhouses does not seem especially exotic. So you decide to eliminate the bananas and include the flax fields under II.A., "Geography." You can also put the present entries under "Food" in III.E., "Everyday Living," eliminating another category. You see that most of what you have to say under III.F., "Industry and Technology," really has to do with whales, and you have just recalled some more impressions of whaling. So you change the label of this subhead to "Whaling industry." But bridges are not related to the whaling industry, so you decide to move them to III.A., "Geography." Bridges are not really geography either, so you change the heading III.A. to "The countryside." Corrugated tin roofs are part of the countryside scene, so you move this entry from III.E., "Everyday living," to II.A., "The countryside." By this time, Item III in your outline is so marked up that you recopy it so that you can read it easily. As you recopy, you remember a few more details and include them in the outline.

III. Specific Examples
   A. The countryside
      1. Exotic
         a. Glaciers, volcanoes, lava fields, hot springs, geysers
         b. Treeless
         c. Near Arctic Circle, but mild climate

  2. Insignificant
   a. Stunted trees
   b. Small bridges or none at all
   c. Corrugated tin roofs and siding
 B. Animal life
  1. Exotic
   a. Arctic skuas, golden plovers, puffins
   b. Seals
  2. Insignificant
   a. Cows in harnesses
   b. Sheep stay out of road
   c. No dogs in Reykjavik
 C. Everyday living
  1. Exotic
   a. Hot springs heat
   b. Outdoor swimming all year round
   c. *Skyr*—national food
  2. Insignificant
   a. Newsboys wear rubber boots
   b. Water always hot in rest rooms
   c. Peas and carrots
 D. The whaling industry
  1. Exotic
   a. Small boats but big whales
   b. Processing stations
  2. Insignificant
   a. Whale meat looks like corned beef
   b. Strong odor of whale
   c. Sea birds all around dead whale

You can see that there are still some inconsistencies in your outline, but since this is to be a fairly short paper, you decide not to make a formal outline at this stage. If required to do so, you will make a formal outline after you have written the paper itself.

EXERCISES: Making a Preliminary Outline

Take the topic you chose in the exercise "Preparing to Write." Consult the list of ideas you made in that exercise, and review the rough plan you made for organizing your paper in the exercise "Organizing the Paper." Go over the list of ideas, eliminating those that do not fit anywhere, combining those that overlap, and subdividing those that are too general into specific facts and details. Now write a rough outline for an essay not to exceed 1,000 words.

51g WRITING THE FIRST DRAFT

In reality, getting an idea, narrowing the topic, formulating a thesis, and deciding on the rhetorical type and organization of a paper are overlapping processes. You will probably find that, by the time you have decided on a topic, you already have some notion of your thesis and the approach you will take. You may even become so interested in your paper that you start writing before you have completed all these other steps.

Some people, however, develop a kind of writer's paralysis when they reach the stage at which they must start composing sentences and paragraphs. If you have made an outline beforehand, paralysis is less likely to strike because you at least know what you are going to say and approximately where you are going to say it, even if you do not know exactly how you are going to say it. Knowing that your first attempt is only a rough draft can also help you overcome a block.

Try to begin writing when your mind is fresh. Whether you work better in the early morning, at midday, or late at night, do not wait for inspiration to strike: It will not. Reserve a fairly long, continuous period of time for writing the first draft; if possible, write the entire draft at one sitting. Such a procedure helps you maintain a uniform tone throughout the paper; moreover, trying to write a draft in several sittings requires a warm-up period for each session. If you do write the rough draft in several sittings, refresh your memory by rereading what you have written previously.

If you are a fairly good typist, you may prefer to compose on the typewriter because typing is faster than handwriting. On the other hand, even good typists are often more comfortable writing rough drafts in longhand because crossing out and inserting are easier with a pen or pencil.

Refer to your preliminary outline as you write. You will probably find that your paragraph divisions generally correspond to the headings in your outline. But do not be enslaved by your outline; if a heading requires two or more paragraphs, so be it. Conversely, you may find that two or more headings should be combined in one paragraph. If your outline is a good one, you will usually find that the order of points in your rough draft corresponds fairly closely to their order in the outline.

In general, try to avoid digressions that occur to you as you write. For example, as you are writing about your trip to Iceland, you may remember that your grandfather was stationed in Iceland during World War II. Or you may recall hearing a Japanese tourist in a cafeteria in Iceland ask for "a piece of Coca-Cola." These are interesting anecdotes, perhaps, but they are not related to your thesis statement and so should be omitted.

EXERCISES: Writing the First Draft

Write the first draft of an essay, using the preliminary outline you made in the exercise on "Making a Preliminary Outline." Your essay should not exceed 1,000 words.

51h INTRODUCTORY AND CONCLUDING PARAGRAPHS

The essential part of a paper is the middle, the body of the paper. But all papers have to begin and end in some way, although not every paper requires separate introductory and concluding sections. Whether or not you write a separate introduction or conclusion, the beginning and the end of a paper are important because these are emphatic positions. The beginning rouses—or fails to rouse—the reader's interest, and the ending strongly influences the reader's final impression of the paper.

Introductory Paragraphs.   At some time or another, you have probably had a good idea for a paper and a fairly detailed plan for developing the body of the paper. But when you sat down to write, you could get nothing down because you could not think of how to begin. When this happens, you may want to start in the middle; you will often find that after you have written a few paragraphs—or perhaps most of the paper—you will get a good idea for the beginning. Alternatively, you can put anything at all down just to get started and plan to revise it later. The problem with this second approach is that, by the time you have finished, you may be tired and tempted to leave the weak beginning as it is.

The purpose of a beginning paragraph is to launch the subject in such a way as to set the tone for what will follow and to attract the reader's interest. Although you can begin a paper by plunging headlong into the topic, a more effective approach is to introduce the topic less directly, using the first paragraph to narrow the subject and to entice the reader to continue. There is no single way to begin a paper on any topic; almost any topic lends itself to several possible approaches.

Suppose you were writing a short history paper on the Franco-Prussian War of 1870–1871. There are many possible ways of introducing this paper (or almost any paper).

1. **Begin with a quotation.** It may be obviously relevant to the subject or it may be only indirectly relevant, requiring further explanation. Since it is often very difficult to find an appropriate quotation, do not insist on using one unless you have one in mind beforehand. Rather than force an unsuitable quotation into place, select another kind of beginning.

> "The great questions of the day will not be decided by speeches and resolution of majorities—that was the blunder of 1848 and 1849—but by blood and iron." So spoke Otto von Bismarck to the German parliament in 1862. Within a decade, the German states were to be involved in three European wars.

2. **Begin with a concessive statement.** Start with a statement recognizing an opinion or approach different from the one you plan to take in the paper.

> Many scholars attribute the Franco-Prussian War to the machinations of a single power-hungry man, Otto von Bismarck, and particularly to his editing and publication of the Ems Telegram. This may have been the immediate cause, but wars do not have simple causes based on a single incident.

3. **Begin with an interesting fact or statistic.**

Today we call them guerrillas. In 1869 they were called *franc-tireurs* "sharpshooters." They were not part of the French army, they had no uniforms, and when they were captured by the Prussians they were immediately shot.

4. **Begin with a short anecdote or narrative.** A short narrative is particularly effective for adding a touch of variety to an expository paper.

On July 30, 1898, the Iron Chancellor died in Friedrichsruh at the age of 83. The headstone on his grave has only one word: Bismarck.

5. **Begin with a question or several questions.**

How could France, seemingly at a peak of strength and prosperity, be so swiftly and so thoroughly defeated? How could the secret diplomacy of one man, a man who faced serious opposition in his own country, succeed in taunting France into war?

6. **Begin with a paradox.**

The Germans crushed the French army at Wörth and Gravelotte and Sedan—and the French Empire expanded in North Africa and Indochina. The Germans humiliated France in the Hall of Mirrors at Versailles—and all the world looked up to France for culture and beauty and spirit.

7. **Begin with relevant background material.** Such background material should, however, be presented concisely and should be clearly related to your thesis. A long, rambling discussion of material only remotely related to your main point will bewilder and bore your reader.

Although the population was neither French nor German, Alsace had for centuries passed from French to German control and back again. But France had held it since the Treaty of Westphalia in 1648.

8. **Begin by stating a long-term effect or effects without immediately stating the cause.**

It brought about the Third Republic, one of the stormiest yet longest-lasting governments in France's history. Indirectly, it led to the Dreyfus affair. It was a test run for Germany's attack on France in 1914. Today it is called the Franco-Prussian War.

9. **Begin with an analogy.**

Before contractors begin constructing a new shopping center, architects draw up plans and build mock-ups on a miniature scale. In this way, they can identify potential problems, test controversial innovations, predict traffic flow, and get an idea of the overall appearance of the completed center. The Franco-Prussian War was a mock-up for World War I, and Otto von Bismarck was the chief architect.

10. **Begin with a definition of a term that is important to your topic.** This should not be a simple dictionary definition but an explanation of the term as it applies to your topic.

> Nineteenth-century armies could no longer be persuaded that they would win because God was on their side. France had substituted a new mystique: *élan. Élan* was dash, fervor, impetuousness, ardor, and spirit, and, for the French, it was much more. It was a will to win that could triumph over antiquated matériel, poor leadership, and obsolete battle strategy and tactics. Or so they thought.

There are several ways of introducing a paper that are guaranteed *not* to attract the reader's interest.

1. Do not merely paraphrase your title, overtly telling the reader what you are going to say next. If your paper is entitled "The Franco-Prussian War," you will have made no real beginning if you start out by writing "In this paper, I will discuss the Franco-Prussian War of 1870–1871." But you will have succeeded in boring the reader, who already knows what the topic of the paper is from the title.

2. Do not begin with sweeping generalities or platitudes. "Wars cause much destruction and devastation" is so obvious a statement that it should not be made at all.

3. Do not apologize for your incompetence or lack of knowledge. A beginning sentence such as "Although I am no authority on wars or on the Franco-Prussian War . . ." will only convince the reader that it would be a waste of time to continue reading.

Concluding Paragraphs. The purpose of a concluding paragraph is to strengthen the message conveyed by the whole paper and to leave the reader with a feeling of completion. Not every paper requires a separate concluding paragraph. This is especially true of short papers, where the reader can easily remember everything that you have said. Short narrative and descriptive papers in particular frequently require no concluding paragraph. Even a fairly lengthy process paper can end when the description of the process has been completed. If you have written all the rest of the paper and can think of nothing that does not seem repetitious or otherwise unnecessary, you probably do not need a separate concluding paragraph.

Concluding paragraphs are more likely to be necessary in expository or argument-and-persuasion papers, but even here a strong final sentence can often replace a separate paragraph. If your entire paper is organized climactically, your most important points will come at the end, and the reader will be left with a sense of finality.

When you do write a concluding paragraph, avoid the following common problems.

1. Do not merely summarize what you have just finished saying. If a summary statement is needed because the paper is long or the argument rather complex, do not overtly inform the reader that a summary is coming by such sentences as "Now I will summarize. . . ." or "I have just shown that. . . ."

2. Do not apologize for your poor performance or lack of knowledge.

3. Do not throw your entire thesis into doubt by making a major concession to an opposing point of view. If concessions are necessary, they belong at the beginning of the paper, not at the end.

4. Do not trail off feebly with a row of dots after your final sentence.

5. Do not introduce a new idea that is really the subject of another paper.

6. Do not use the final paragraph as a catchall to include details or points that you forgot to include in the main body of your paper.

If you feel that a paper needs rounding off with a separate concluding paragraph, most of the devices suggested for introductory paragraphs are also suitable for concluding paragraphs. For example, a relevant quotation or anecdote might be used. If the argument has been complex, your thesis can be summarized, not step by step, but by restating only the key points and the conclusion. You may want to end by suggesting that, now that you have advanced the question one more step, it is up to the reader to take action on it.

A concluding paragraph may suggest implications or ramifications of your findings that go beyond the limits of your own paper. But do not confuse implications of your own presentation with the introduction of an entirely new idea. That is, if you have written a paper arguing that wind power is a feasible alternative to fossil fuels, your last paragraph might note that one implication of this conclusion is that the United States will have to switch from giant, centralized power plants to small, decentralized units. This is an acceptable concluding statement. What you should *not* do is conclude your paper on wind power by changing the subject and saying, "But, of course, we should also consider solar power and water power."

EXERCISES: Introductory and Concluding Paragraphs

Part A: Choose two of the following subjects, select a specific topic based on each, and write a thesis sentence for each topic. Then for each of the two topics write three different kinds of introductions.

1. Women artists
2. Country music
3. Jogging
4. The family in America
5. Nuclear energy
6. The Jazz Age
7. Hispanic-Americans
8. Imagination

Part B: For the two topics you selected in Part A, list the various types of conclusions you believe would be appropriate. For each type of conclusion, indicate the kinds of information you might conceivably use in it. If you do not believe that a concluding paragraph is necessary for your topics, explain why.

51i TITLES

Every paper should have a title, which should specify or at least suggest the contents of the paper. A good title is more specific than simply a description of the general subject area of the paper. That is, if your instructor has assigned a paper on cheating in college, your title should not be simply "Cheating in College." To avoid overly general titles, it is best to postpone deciding on a title until after you have formulated a thesis statement or, even better, until after you have written your first draft.

Titles should not be too long; as a rule of thumb, if your title takes up more than one line on the page, try to shorten it. For example, "A Description of the Open-Air Market in Hopkinton" can easily be shortened to "Hopkinton's Open-Air Market." Catchy titles are appealing to the reader, but are more appropriate for informal or humorous topics than for serious topics. In any case, don't spend a great deal of time trying to think of a catchy title; a straightforward descriptive title is always acceptable.

Although the title is an essential part of a paper, it should be completely independent of the text. Do not begin your paper by referring to the title with vague words like *this, that, such,* or *it.*

UNACCEPTABLE	IMPROVED
Stamp-Collecting as a Hobby	Stamp-Collecting as a Hobby
Many people think of this as a hobby of fussy old men, but . . .	Many people think of stamp-collecting as a hobby of fussy old men, but . . .

Although a good title does not necessarily reveal the rhetorical type of a paper, it does provides an indication of it. Listed below are three broad subject areas. Possible titles are given for papers in each subject area and for each rhetorical type.

SUBJECT AREA	RHETORICAL TYPE	PAPER TITLE
tobacco	exposition	How to Roll Your Own Cigarettes
	argument	Why Snuff Should Replace Cigarettes
	description	The Paraphernalia of a Pipe-Smoker
	narration	My First Encounter with Chewing Tobacco
automobiles	exposition	Developing a Nonpolluting Engine
	argument	Teen-agers Make the Best Drivers
	description	My New Datsun 810
	narration	Tragedy on Route I-80
fires	exposition	Arson: Our No. 1 Crime
	argument	Smoke Detectors Are Worthless
	description	Our House After the Fire
	narration	The Peshtigo, Wisconsin, Fire of 1871

51j REVISING THE FIRST DRAFT

While you are writing the first draft, the most important thing is to get your ideas into words and the words onto paper. Once those words are on paper, you are probably proud of your act of creation and not a little relieved to have it completed. But unless you are a rare individual, the product is not yet ready for public viewing. You have been so wrapped up in the process of composition that you have not seen the flaws. Although most writers do at least some revising as they write, this is not enough. No first draft is perfect; errors and inconsistencies are unavoidable. Hence all writers must revise their work. The first draft of a paper is for the writer; the revisions are for the reader.

If possible, wait at least a few hours before starting to revise—a day or two is even better. This time lapse will give you a perspective on what you have written because you will not be so involved with the topic that you overlook many of the problems. If you simply do not have the time to wait even a few hours before beginning your revision, try to gain a little distance by rereading the paper aloud, rather than silently. As you reread, make brief notes about anything that strikes you as particularly in need of revision or correction. Then methodically check, point by point, all aspects of the paper, consulting the following checklist.

A. Content
   1. Does the paper as a whole develop your thesis statement?
   2. Have you unintentionally omitted something important from your outline?
   3. Is there irrelevant material that should be removed?
   4. Are all your statements accurate?
   5. Is your logic sound? Are there gaps in your logic? (See 52.)
   6. Are more details or more explanation necessary? Have you fully supported all your statements with facts?
   7. Have you anticipated counterarguments and responded to them?

B. Organization
   1. Is the organization logical and easy to follow? Or do you jump back and forth from one point to another?
   2. Are there clear transitions from one section to another? Are the transitions between paragraphs and between sentences easy to follow?
   3. Is the paper well-proportioned? Or is one section greatly under-developed or overdeveloped?
   4. Are the paragraph divisions logical? (See 50.)
   5. Is emphasis placed on the points you want to emphasize?
   6. Is the pace brisk enough to carry the reader along?
   7. Does the introductory paragraph lead logically and entertainingly into the main point of the paper?
   8. Does the concluding material leave the reader with the impression you intend?

C. Sentences (See 49.)
   1. Is there a variety of sentence types?
   2. Are sentences wordy and redundant?
   3. Are there completely unnecessary sentences?
   4. Is the syntax awkward or overinvolved?
   5. Are there failures in balance and parallelism?
   6. Are there unintentional sentence fragments or run-on sentences? (See 23.)

D. Use of Words (Diction) (See 47.)
   1. Is the language appropriate for the audience? Do you talk over the heads of your audience? Do you insult your audience by talking down to them?

rh

2. Do you use too many general or abstract words?
3. Are words used precisely? Or are there incorrect denotations and improper connotations?
4. Have you defined all necessary terms?
5. Do you overuse the passive?
6. Are there too many clichés?
7. Are there mixed or inappropriate metaphors or similes?
8. Is there "fine" writing?
9. Will your reader believe what you say, or have you destroyed credibility by exaggeration or sarcasm?

E. Grammar (See 1–23.)
   1. Do you use standard grammar throughout?
   2. Are there unidiomatic phrases or expressions?

F. Mechanics (See 24–46)
   Do spelling, punctuation, capitalization, hyphenation, and abbreviation all follow the conventions?

G. Euphony
   Does the paper *sound* good? Read the entire paper aloud to check for awkward phrasing, clumps of indigestible consonants, excessive alliteration, and poor rhythm.

H. Acknowledgments
   1. Have you acknowledged any outside sources you may have used?
   2. If you have footnotes, are they in proper footnote form? (See 56a.)

I. Title
   Is the title accurate and appropriate?

J. Your Own Weaknesses
   Have you double-checked for particular weaknesses that have given you trouble in the past?

EXERCISES: Revising the First Draft

Part A: Use the "Checklist for Revision" as a guide for revising the rough draft of the paper you have written in the exercise "Writing the First Draft." Be sure that your introduction and conclusion are effective.

Part B: Using the "Checklist for Revision" as your guide, revise the following first draft of a student essay.

Love is a rare phenomenon in our society. There are all kinds of relationships which are called love. There are the dominating themes that appear in the romantic songs and in the movies of sentimental impulses. No word is used with more meanings than this term, most of the meanings being dishonest in that they cover up the real motives in the relationship. But there are many other sound and honest relationships called love such as parental care for children, sexual passion, or the sharing of loneliness. The reality often discovered in when one looks underneath the surface of the individual in our lonely and conformist society, is how little love is actually involved in these relationships.

Our society is, as we have seen, thriving with competitive individualism, with power over others as a dominant motivation. Our particular generation is full of isolation and personal emptiness, which is not a good preparation for learning how to love. The capacity to love presupposes self-awareness, because love requires the ability to apreciate the potentialities of the other person. Love also presupposes freedom; because love which is not freely given is not love. To love someone because you are not free to love someone else is not love.

The error so common in our society is resorting to hypocrisy in trying to persuade himself that all of the emotions he feels are love. Learning to love will procede if we stop trying to persuade ourselves that to love is easy. And if we give up the disgiuses for love in a society which is always talking about love but has so little of it.

51k PREPARING A FORMAL OUTLINE

Although a rough or informal outline is important in organizing a paper, you need not prepare a formal outline unless you are required to do so. If your instructor asks for an outline, prepare it from the completed paper, not from your rough outline because you probably did not follow your rough outline exactly as you wrote. An outline submitted with a paper should observe all the conventions of formal outlines. See 53a for instructions on preparing formal outlines.

51l REVISING A GRADED PAPER

Even if you have methodically checked your paper for all the problems in the checklist, you will probably find that your instructor has made a number of corrections and comments on the paper before returning it to you. It is, of course, depressing to see a paper on which you have worked hard marked up with red pencil. But that is what the instructor is for—to help you locate and correct writing problems that you yourself do not identify.

Whether or not you are required to submit a revised version of the paper to the instructor, read all the comments and corrections very carefully. Be sure you are familiar with the grading symbols used; if you are not, refer to the correction chart inside the front cover of this handbook. If there are comments that you do not understand, ask your instructor to explain them to you. Pay particular attention to general comments your instructor may make, such as "You seem to have difficulty with sentence structure" or "Paragraphs are under-developed." Refer to the appropriate sections of this handbook for guidance on these general problems.

rh

51m MANUSCRIPT FORM

In preparing the final version of a paper to be submitted, follow carefully all specifications that your instructor may have given you beforehand. Make a carbon or photocopy of every paper that you submit in case you or your instructor should mislay the original. If possible, final copies should be typed (unless, of course, the paper has been written in class). Even if you find typing slow and painful, you still probably type nearly as fast as you write in longhand, and instructors are invariably predisposed toward typewritten papers because they are easier to read and correct.

Unless you have received directions to the contrary, follow the conventions listed here in preparing the final version of typewritten papers. (For the most part, the conventions given here agree with those recommended by the *MLA Handbook;* they differ somewhat in the instructions for single- and double-spacing.)

1. Use 8½-by-11-inch unruled white paper of fairly heavy stock, and type on one side of the paper only. Do not use colored paper or onionskin. Many readers object to the so-called erasable bond papers because they smudge very easily, are hard to make corrections on with a pen or pencil, and produce an unpleasant glare under most lighting conditions. (Erasable paper is also expensive.)

2. Double-space the text of the paper; do not use one and a half spaces because there will not be enough room for corrections and comments. Single-space only lengthy quotations that are set off from the text and notes that appear at the bottom of the page.

3. Use a black typewriter ribbon. Keep your typewriter keys clean to avoid blurred copy. Be sure that your ribbon is fresh enough to make a clear impression; the dim copy produced by a worn-out ribbon is unattractive and difficult to read.

4. Leave generous margins on all sides of the sheet. Margins should be at least one inch to one and a half inches wide. (On the other hand, do not try to stretch what is really a two-page paper to the required four pages by leaving three-inch margins all around— you will fool nobody.)

5. Center the title of the paper at the top of the first page, about two or three inches from the top edge. It may be typed either with all capital letters or with capital letters beginning all important words. (See 42.) Do not enclose the title in quotation marks. Do not underline the title. Do not put a period after the title, even if it is a complete sentence. The title may be followed by a question mark or an exclamation point if the grammar requires one (but consider carefully whether you really need an exclamation point).

If your title is unavoidably so long that it does not fit on one line, single-space and center the second line below the first line. Break the title at a logical place; that is, a long title such as *The Influence of Edmund Burke's Writing on the Revolutionary Fervor in the American Colonies* might be divided after *Writings* or *Fervor* but should not be broken after *Edmund, the,* or *Revolutionary.* Leave a triple space between the title and the first line of the text itself.

Your instructor may request that you type a separate title page. If so, follow his or her directions for doing so. If your instructor does not ask for a separate title page, there is no need to use one.

6. Indent five spaces for each new paragraph.

7. The first page of a paper may be left without a page number, or you may center the page number just above the bottom margin of the page. Number all subsequent pages in the top right corner, about one inch from the top and one inch from the right edge. Use only Arabic, not Roman, numerals. It is a good idea to type your name just before the page number so that, if the pages should become separated, your instructor can easily find and replace them.

8. Many instructors prefer that all notes be grouped together on a separate page following the text (endnotes). If you do have notes

at the bottom of the page, remember to leave enough room for them as you type. Separate footnotes from the text of the paper by a double space, then a one-inch line (ten units on a pica typewriter, twelve units on an elite typewriter) typed flush with the left margin. Then double-space again, make a paragraph indentation, and single-space the footnote itself. Double-space between two footnotes on the same page.

9. Your instructor may give you directions for endorsing (identifying) your papers. If you do not receive such directions, the following is an acceptable form of endorsement.

```
Marie Estes
English 108, Section 4
Paper No. 5
November 22, 1981
```

Type the endorsement in the top left corner of the first page.

10. Proofread your paper carefully after you have finished typing it. Watch especially for words that have been inadvertently repeated or omitted in the typing or writing process and for transposed (reversed) letters within words. Do not try to correct by striking over letters. Minor corrections may be made in black ink.

To correct a misspelled or otherwise incorrect word, draw a line through it, and write the correct form neatly above the crossed-out word. Do not put parentheses around words that are to be omitted.

```
     melancholy
a  meloncoly state
```

To correct transposed letters, use a curved line.

```
ratinoal
```

To indicate that a word or words should be added, put a caret (∧) at the point where the word should appear, and write the word above the line.

```
              exact
put a caret at the point
             ∧
```

To indicate that a word or words should be deleted, draw a single line through the word or words.

```
draw a single solitary line
```

To indicate that there should be no space where a space appears, close up the space with curved lines.

```
close up the space with cur͜ved lines
```

To indicate that there should be a space between two words, draw a vertical line between the words.

between|the words

To indicate a paragraph division where one does not appear, use the symbol ¶.

within the year.¶ At last,

To indicate that there should be no paragraph division, write "No ¶" to the left of the indentation.

before the sentence.
***No*¶ To indicate that**

If a page is exceptionally messy and contains many corrections, retype it if possible. A neat paper makes a much better impression on the reader.

Use black ink to insert by hand any necessary symbols such as brackets, accent marks, or mathematical and scientific symbols that your typewriter keyboard does not have. Be sure to leave ample space for such symbols as you type. If you make a light checkmark in the margin with a pencil as you type the line, you can easily find the spot later where the insertion is to be made.

11. Fasten the pages of the paper with a paper clip before you hand the paper in. Do not staple it unless your instructor tells you to. There is no need to waste money on fancy plastic or paper binders for short papers. The reader usually has to remove the binder in order to grade the paper, and you may lose your binder in the process. Binders are appropriate for long papers that are too thick to secure with a paper clip.

Handwritten papers are prepared in the same way as type-written ones, with a few exceptions.

1. Use 8½-by-11-inch *ruled* white paper. This may be either loose-leaf notebook paper or special theme paper designed specifically for handwritten themes. Write on one side only. Do not use paper torn from a spiral-bound notebook; the ragged edges tend to stick together and to shed scraps of paper.

Your instructor may ask you to write on every line or on every other line. If you use wide-ruled paper (lines three-eighths of an inch apart) and have reasonably small handwriting, writing on every line will probably be acceptable. If you use narrow-ruled paper (lines one-quarter of an inch apart) or have large handwriting, writing on every other line is preferable.

2. Write in black, blue-black, or blue ink. Do not use inks of other colors, such as red, violet, or green. Write as neatly and legibly as possible, avoiding ornate flourishes. Carefully distinguish capital letters from small letters, *a* from *o*, *n* from *u*, *v* from *r*, *g* from *q*. Cross all *t*'s and dot all *i*'s and *j*'s. Leave a definite space between individual

words. If your handwriting is really terrible, print instead of using script. (And consider improving your handwriting—it can be done.)

3. Margins should be the same as for typewritten papers. Do not write outside of the line marking the left margin.

log/52 MAKING A GOOD ARGUMENT

It is sometimes said that truth is that which can be proved. However, few things that we wish to accept as true can be proved in the demonstrable way that we can prove that fire burns dry paper. Truth is also defined as that which can be perceived by the senses, but we believe—and rightly so—many things that we cannot perceive directly with our senses. For example, if we see a dog run into a long pipe and then, a few seconds later, see a dog run out of the opposite end of that same pipe, none of our five senses tells us that this is the same dog that ran into the pipe—our eyes cannot follow the dog while it is in the pipe. Even if the dog that comes out is the same size and has the same markings, we cannot, strictly speaking, be absolutely sure that there was not another dog in the pipe. Furthermore, our senses can be mistaken. We "hear" nonexistent noises, we "smell" non-existent smoke, we "feel" nonexistent drafts, and we "see" non-existent ghosts.

Another definition of truth is that it is fact; it is what actually happens. But we constantly acquire new ways of interpreting previously known facts. The correlation between insects and decaying matter is a fact that has been known for centuries. Until the seventeenth century, this fact was interpreted as meaning that insects had no biological parents and were produced by spontaneous generation from the decaying matter itself. Today we know that all insects have parents and that these parents must have previously laid eggs in the decaying material. The fact of the correlation between insects and decaying matter remains, but its interpretation has changed.

Perhaps the best definition of truth is that truth is that which seems most probable to the most people who know all of the available facts. Unfortunately, we seldom have all of the facts. Few things are so clearly "true" or "false" that all reasonable and informed people agree about them. Most of what we believe is opinion, not truth. Quite naturally, we feel that our own opinions are better than those of people who do not agree with us, and quite naturally we want to persuade others to our point of view.

Although the words *argument* and *persuasion* are frequently lumped together, they do not mean the same thing. *Persuasion* is winning people over to a course of action or a way of thinking by appealing to their reason and understanding. *Argument* is the use of language to achieve this persuasion. The term *argument* includes both the question itself and the evidence brought forth to support or refute a point of view with respect to the question. Although some people will not be persuaded even by the most logical argument, no one will be persuaded by shouting and verbal abuse. The more logical the argument, the more likely we are to persuade others. There are six basic rules for making a good argument.

1. Define the argument clearly.
2. Define all terms used in the argument.
3. Limit the argument to the question at hand.
4. Present adequate evidence to support the argument.
5. Reason clearly and logically.
6. Anticipate contrary arguments and evidence.

52a DEFINING THE ARGUMENT

The first step in defining an argument is to make sure that you really have an argument. An argument requires a statement about which there can be disagreement. Statements such as "Water is necessary for life" or "Most people resent being insulted" are not statements of arguments because no one would disagree with them. Second, the statement must be one for which evidence for and against can be offered. "I have a bad headache" is not a statement of an argument because, even if you are lying, there is no way to refute it. Nor is "I dislike polka-dot ties" the statement of an argument because likes and dislikes are matters of taste, not of fact. On the other hand, the sentence "Most people like mashed potatoes better than mashed turnips" could be the statement of an argument because you could present evidence for or against it—evidence in the form of the results of a poll, statistics on the sale of potatoes and turnips, the number of restaurant menus listing mashed potatoes and turnips, and so forth.

Stating the Argument. When you have determined that you really have an argument, the next step is to state the argument clearly and fairly. In particular, avoid the fallacy of the **false dilemma,** which implies that there are only two alternatives when there may actually be several alternatives. The false dilemma frequently takes the form of an *if . . . then* statement or an *either . . . or* statement. The person who writes, "If these malcontents don't like the way things are run in this country, they should go to Russia" is guilty of setting up a false dilemma because he or she refuses to consider the alternative possibility of changing the society within this country. Similarly, the statement "Either we must agree that the pilgrimage of Chaucer's *Canterbury Tales* is an allegory of man's life on earth or we must assume that Chaucer had no overall theme in this work" is a false dilemma because it does not allow for alternative themes. A clearer and fairer statement of this argument would be "The pilgrimage of Chaucer's *Canterbury Tales* is an allegory of man's life on earth." (Of course, evidence would have to be presented to support this statement.)

EXERCISES: Defining the Argument

Identify which of the following topics could be the basis for an argumentative paragraph or essay and which could not. For those that are arguable, explain what kinds of evidence and support you would use in making the argument. For those that are not arguable, explain why they are not.

1. Solar energy is superior to all other kinds of energy.
2. Integrity is one of the most admirable human qualities.
3. The freedom of the press should never be restricted.
4. In spite of its complexities, life in the twentieth century is not much different from life in the Middle Ages or Renaissance.
5. A liberal arts education is the best foundation one could have as preparation for living in the modern world.

52b DEFINING ALL TERMS

Words are slippery customers. They often have multiple meanings, and the same word may have very different meanings for different people. Many an apparent disagreement turns out to be no disagreement at all when the speakers or writers realize that they have been using the same word in different meanings. Conversely, all of us agree that we want "the good life," but our definitions of "good life" will vary greatly. The error of **undefined terms,** or failure to limit the definition of the words used in an argument, often leads to unacceptable conclusions. For example, before making the argument that parents should control their children, we should define the word *control.* Does *control* include corporal punishment? Does it include selecting a husband or wife for the child? Is it limited to physical behavior or does it include verbal behavior?

The use of the same word in two different meanings is called **equivocation.** An absurd example will illustrate the point: "Chicken makes good soup, and John is chicken. Therefore, John must make good soup." Obviously, the words *chicken* and *make* are being used in two different meanings. Advertisements frequently employ equivocation to mislead the reader. If a pair of shoes is advertised as being made of *genuine vinyl,* the word *genuine* is equivocal because, in one sense, it means actual or real—and the advertiser could claim that "real vinyl" is all that is meant. On the other hand, the adjective *genuine* also has, to many people, the meaning of "high quality." High-quality shoes are usually made of leather, not vinyl; so, by using the word *genuine,* the advertiser is trying to convey the impression that the shoes are made of high-quality material, that is, leather.

Most cases of equivocation are not so obvious; abstract words in particular tend to have several closely related meanings, and it is not always easy to see when the same word is being used in more than one meaning. For example, in the statement "She must not know French because she doesn't know the word *bêche-de-mer,*" the word *know* is used equivocally. In the phrase "know French," it means "to have a practical understanding of''; in the phrase ''know the word *bêche-de mer*,'' it means ''to be sure of the meaning of.'' One can of course have a practical understanding of a language without being familiar with every word in that language.

52c LIMITING THE ARGUMENT

When we feel that our argument is somewhat shaky, we may be tempted to try to divert attention from the argument itself by launching into a discussion of a side issue. **Evading the issue** is a type of faulty argument that occurs when we ignore the real argument and attack something irrelevant to the main issue. One way in which an issue is often evaded is by setting up a **straw man.** Here, you pretend that your opponent means something that he or she does not, or you take the weakest portion of your opponent's argument and attack that, evading the main point. For example, your opponent might be arguing that manufacturers should put lead in exterior house paints because lead makes the paint last much longer. You then respond by saying that many small children have been poisoned by lead. You have set up a straw man because your opponent has not suggested that lead be used in interior house paints or in the paint on children's toys. Indeed, it has not even been proved that most of the cases of lead poisoning in children come from eating paint.

Whereas the straw man sets up an easy target by pretending that your opponent's argument is something other than it really is, the **red herring** deliberately tries to change the subject of the argument by concentrating on an irrelevant issue: ''You say it's too expensive, but just look at how well it fits.'' If, in response to the argument that Mussolini's government was very oppressive, you write, ''Mussolini's government may have been a bit oppressive, but he finally got the Italian society organized and he made the trains run on time,'' you have introduced a red herring—the argument concerns oppression, not efficiency.

Another common way of evading the issue is by an **ad hominem** argument. Here, instead of attacking issues, you attack personalities. ''How can you elect a person president who couldn't even keep a clothing store from going bankrupt?'' Or ''I don't see how you can call anyone who's had six husbands a great actress.'' Of course, sometimes a person's character may be relevant to an argument; you might quite reasonably hesitate to hire a person as cashier of a bank who had had four convictions for embezzlement. But the character flaw being attacked should be relevant to the issue under consideration.

Somewhat similar to the argument *ad hominem* is the **genetic fallacy,** which evaluates persons or things in terms of their origins: ''How can anyone born and bred in Montana understand the problems of the city?'' Or ''The money to set up that foundation was made through corrupt business practices, so you shouldn't accept a grant from it.'' Again, origins are not necessarily irrelevant, but they are not necessarily relevant either.

The **ad populum** argument evades the issue by playing on people's prejudices and emotions. Terms with strong connotations such as *radical, reactionary, grass roots, American way of life,* and *family* are used to make the audience respond emotionally rather than intellectually. For example, an *ad populum* argument against X-rated films might take a form such as "Do you decent, law-abiding citizens want to see innocent and helpless children exposed to this filthy vice and perversion?" A variant of the *ad populum* argument is the **bandwagon** approach, in which the appeal is to people's desire to be accepted as members of the group and their fear of being different or their mistrust of people who are different. The bandwagon approach is common in adverstising: "Are you the only person on your block who still uses a hand mower?" But we can find the bandwagon approach even in serious writing: "Dr. Miller concentrates primarily on classifying and describing the languages of Southeast Asia, despite the fact that most scholarly interest today focuses on theory and not on description."

The *tu quoque* error is still another way in which issues are evaded. **Tu quoque** (Latin for "you too") accuses your opponent of doing or being whatever he or she criticizes others of doing or being. We are all familiar with the less subtle forms of *tu quoque* as used by young children: "You can't tie your own shoes!" "Neither can you. So there!" But the adult who responds to a statement that he or she should get more exercise with the retort, "I don't see you out jogging at 6:00 a.m." is also using a *tu quoque* argument. If you respond to the argument that young people do not take their responsibilities as voters seriously enough by writing "Older people often fail to acquaint themselves with the candidates' records, and many do not even bother going to the polls," you are using *tu quoque* to evade the issue.

The best way to avoid the error of evading the issue is to define the question at hand clearly and carefully. Then you can ask yourself at each step in your argument if you are really addressing the issue or if you have allowed yourself to be sidetracked.

EXERCISES: Defining Terms and Limiting the Argument

Identify the logical fallacies in the following sentences by writing beside each sentence the name of the fallacy from the list below.

Equivocation	Bandwagon	Genetic fallacy
Red herring	False dilemma	*Ad hominem*

1. How on earth can you bring yourself to vote for Jacobs? He divorced his wife of twenty-five years to marry a woman he had all but stolen from his best friend.

2. We should have been much tougher on our prisoners of war. Just look at the way the Communists have treated American prisoners!

3. Drink Burpsa Cola! More Americans drink Burpsa Cola than all the other soft drinks put together.

4. I don't think you should hire Sam for that job. You know his father is a terrible alcoholic.

5. If you don't support me all the way, then I'll know you're my enemy.

6. Edward broke three ribs and an arm when he fell off the face of Stone Mountain. He's always trying to defy the law of gravity and now he's paying the penalty for being a law-breaker.

52d PRESENTING ADEQUATE EVIDENCE

In the long run, adequate evidence is the only way of proving an argument. Adequate evidence is reliable, sufficient, and verifiable. Evidence is reliable if it comes from a trustworthy and informed source. Evidence is sufficient if there is enough of it to represent all the points at issue. Evidence is verifiable if it is based on fact and not merely opinion. Facts can always, at least in theory, be tested; opinion cannot. For example, the argument that Unidentified Flying Objects from outer space have visited the earth cannot be proved—or disproved—because we have inadequate evidence. We lack reliable evidence because the trustworthiness of the people (although not necessarily their honesty or good intentions) who claim to have sighted UFOs is open to question. We lack sufficient evidence because "sightings" are few, unpredictable, and often explainable as being due to other causes. We lack verifiable evidence because we have no UFOs to be examined.

We all rely heavily on informed opinion in making judgments. Many of our beliefs about the world are based, and properly so, on the opinions of others. Such **appeal to authority** (or **argumentum ad verecundiam**) can be a legitimate form of evidence. Faulty reasoning occurs when we cite as an authority someone who is not really an authority on the particular subject under discussion. Just because someone is a famous athlete or TV star, he or she is not necessarily an expert on the quality of orange juice or political candidates. Further, yesterday's authorities are not necessarily today's authorities: Edward Gibbon was a great historian in his day, but many of his interpretations of history are unacceptable today.

Authority can be used to support an argument, but be sure that the authority really is a reliable authority and that the appeal is based on the specialized knowledge of that authority and not on emotion—a cherubic child is very appealing but is no expert on the quality of breakfast cereal. Finally, beware of using the authority cited as your sole evidence; authority should be used as one support of an argument, not as the only support.

Improper evaluation of statistics is still another source of faulty arguments. For example, suppose a business firm's gross income was $1 million last year and is $2 million this year. Before jumping to the conclusion that the firm's profits had increased by 100 percent, you should take into account expenses such as labor and production costs, capital investment, and the effect of inflation during the year. Statistics is a highly sophisticated and technical subject whose methodology is not intuitive to the untrained reader. Be very cautious in citing statistics and particularly in drawing conclusions from raw (unanalyzed) statistical data.

Biased evidence is another form of unreliable evidence. If you argued that the American people are in favor of cutting timber in national forests on the basis of a poll taken among Oregon lumberjacks, your evidence would be biased.

One common way of deliberately biasing evidence is to take a statement out of context. Advertising blurbs for books and movies are notorious offenders here. Consider the following possible advertisement for a book:

> "action . . . mystery . . . bright and bantering dialogue"

The complete statement from which this excerpt was taken gives a very different picture.

> "The action moves at a shuffle, the mystery is anything but mystifying, and the usually bright and bantering dialogue is exhausting."
>
> —Unsigned review of Dick Francis, *IN THE FRAME* in *The New Yorker*

Such quotation out of context is deliberate and inexcusable. However, people sometimes unintentionally use biased evidence because they do not thoroughly understand the source of their information or the way in which it was collected. Insofar as possible, use information from sources that are generally considered highly respectable and disinterested.

Insufficient evidence weakens an argument. For example, we often hear or read such statements as "This book isn't any good—my brother read it and he didn't like it." Is your brother representative of all possible readers? Is whether a reader enjoys a book the only criterion of its value? To take a more obvious example, if someone concluded that February was warmer than May because the temperature on February 16 was 60° and the temperature on May 16 was 55°, he or she would clearly have based the conclusion on insufficient evidence.

Inadequate evidence leads to **hasty generalization,** or the assumption that what is true in some situations is true in all similar situations. For example, the statement that health care in America is the most advanced in the world fails to take into account the fact that, in many parts of the United States, health care is very poor indeed. Or the hasty generalization that women are not as good scholars as men because so few women have won Rhodes Scholarships ignores the fact that, until recently, women were not even allowed to apply for Rhodes Scholarships. In other words, this generalization wrongly assumes that men and women have always had equal opportunity to prove themselves as scholars.

To avoid errors in reasoning caused by hasty generalization, try to consider all possible aspects of the question. Ask yourself if you have ignored or forgotten conditions that may influence the situation.

The error of **post hoc, ergo propter hoc** (Latin for "after this, therefore, because of this") results from treating something as evidence that is not evidence at all. A clearly absurd example of *post hoc* reasoning would be: "Every year the trees lose their leaves before winter comes. Therefore, falling leaves cause winter." A more typical example of *post hoc* reasoning would be the belief, held for centuries, that night air is poisonous. People had observed that they developed fevers after they had been exposed to night air and concluded that it was the night air that caused the fever. It was not until the nineteenth century that it was conclusively established that mosquitoes (which are especially prevalent at night) carried the organisms that produced the fevers. Effects do, of course, have causes, but beware of assuming that events are causally related just because they are related in time.

Analogy involves a comparison of two different things that have some characteristics in common. Analogy can be useful in illustrating and clarifying unfamiliar objects or concepts, and a good analogy can be very persuasive to the reader. However, in analogies, there should be basic similarities between the things being compared. Important details should be shared, and the details that are not shared should be irrelevant to the point under discussion and should not be included in the discussion. When we call streets and roads *arteries*, we are making an analogy between a highway system and the circulatory system of a living organism. If we are trying to explain a highway *system*, *artery* is a good analogy because both arteries and highways connect various points of a system and both are routes for carrying things from one point to another. However, if we are focusing on the *costs of building and repairing* a highway, *artery* is not a good analogy because the creation and repair of organic circulatory systems is in no way similar to the creation and repair of highways.

We use analogies constantly in our daily life, and we are often justified in doing so, but even excellent analogies may break down. For example, by analogy with words like *schedule*, *scheme*, *scholar*, and *school*, we may assume that other words beginning with *sch-* are pronounced as if they were spelled with *sk-*. The analogy works with the word *scherzo*, but fails with the word *schist*. Analogies are dangerous because "like" does not mean "the same," and, therefore, we can never actually prove anything by analogy. Argument by analogy is really no argument at all, though analogy can be helpful in clarifying what the argument is.

A **faulty analogy** assumes that just because two things are similar in one or two ways, they are also similar in other important ways. Faulty, or at least questionable, analogies are particularly common in arguments about history, when it is often assumed that because something happened in the past, it will happen in the future. For example, it is sometimes said that the United States is doomed to fall as the Roman Empire fell because, like the Roman Empire, the United States devotes a high percentage of its national income to military spending and public welfare. Among many other things, this analogy fails to take into account the fact that the United States has an extensive commercial and industrial base, whereas the Roman Empire had relatively little commerce or industry and relied heavily on booty or tribute from conquered nations for its national income.

EXERCISES: Presenting Adequate Evidence

Identify the logical fallacies in the following sentences by writing beside each sentence the name of the fallacy from the list below.

Appeal to unqualified authority   *Post hoc, ergo propter hoc*
Hasty generalization   Faulty analogy

1. It is ridiculous to say that private planes should be restricted or even banned because of the potential hazard to commercial jets. We don't make private motorists get off the roads just because they might get involved in an accident with a commercial bus, do we?

2. My priest said Sunday that a restructuring of the tax system in this country is imperative if its citizens are to prosper. Since the Reverend Donahue is so well-educated, he must know what he's talking about.

3. We had an especially cold January and February this year, and the cold must have really hurt local business. All of the merchants complained that their sales for the two-month period were lower than they were at the same time last year.

4. Ninety-five percent of all fatal accidents occur within 25 miles of the victims' homes. Most fast-speed driving is done on long trips, farther from home. Fast driving must be safer than slow driving.

52e REASONING CLEARLY AND LOGICALLY

No matter how good your intentions, you will not be persuasive if the reader cannot follow the steps in your reasoning or if the reasoning is faulty. This is not to say that every single step in an argument must always be explicitly stated. For example, the sentence "If we don't get rain, the crops will die" does not state that crops need rain to survive, but we can safely assume that everyone knows and accepts this fact and that it is unnecessary to state it explicitly. On the other hand, the sentence "The United States government should subsidize farm prices because the world's population is still increasing" has so many unstated assumptions that the reader may have difficulty in following the steps in the logic.

1. Farmers produce food.
2. People need food to live.
3. As the world's population increases, more people will need food.
4. It is desirable to produce enough food to feed all people.
5. Subsidies of farm prices will make farmers produce more food.
6. If the United States produces more food, there will be more food for all the world.

Of these unstated assumptions, numbers 1, 2, and 3 are common knowledge and need not be stated. However, assumptions 4, 5, and 6 are less obvious. Some people might actually argue that it is not especially desirable to produce enough food to feed all people. Not everyone will agree that subsidies of farm prices will automatically make farmers produce more food. And increased production of food in the United States will not lead to more food for all the world if distribution of this food is not adequate. The original statement can be expanded to include all the essential assumptions.

> The world's population is still increasing, and this population must be fed. The United States is capable of producing more food than it presently does and of distributing this additional food to the rest of the world. However, farmers need to be encouraged in some way to produce more food. One way of doing this is by having the U.S. government subsidize farm prices.

Although it is possible that not all readers will agree with all the assumptions, they will at least know what the assumptions are and can see how you arrived at your final statement.

Conditional, qualifying, and concluding words are very important in making a clear and logical argument. Overuse of *if, when,* and *unless* can lead to the fallacy of the false dilemma (see 52a). Qualifying words like *every, all, no, always, never,* and *probably* should be used with caution to avoid exaggerated claims. For example, the statement "Many politicians are corrupt" can be substantiated with evidence, but the statement "All politicians are corrupt" cannot be proved. Use concluding words like *thus, therefore, so, consequently,* and *as a result* only when the following statement is actually "as a result" of what has previously been said.

Be sure the conclusions you state are justified by the evidence you have presented. When the evidence does not justify the conclusion, the argument is called a **non sequitur** (Latin for "it does not follow"). One common form of *non sequitur* argument is **guilt by association.** Suppose you argue that all Mafia members live in the East End of town, that John lives in the East End, and that John must, therefore, be a Mafia member. Your conclusion does not follow from the premises stated because you have not considered the possibility that many people who live in the East End are not Mafia members. You have made John "guilty" of being a Mafia member by assuming that, just because he is like Mafia members in one way, he must be like them in other ways. The error of such conclusions can be more vividly illustrated by a ridiculous example: Someone could argue that all Mafia members like money, that John likes money, and that therefore John is a Mafia member. Clearly, this *non sequitur* argument is unacceptable.

The error of **begging the question** (or **circular argument**) is that of assuming that a point which is under dispute has already been proved. The statement "This essential legislation should be passed" begs the question because the word *essential* in this context means the same thing as *should be passed*. Similarly, "This harmless drug couldn't hurt anyone" begs the question because you have assumed that it couldn't hurt anyone when you call it "harmless."

Begging the question frequently takes the form of a **compound question.** A compound question is one that really has two parts; it begs the question by assuming the answer to one of them. The classic example of the compound question is "When did you stop beating your wife?" Here the questioner assumes that the man being questioned has at least on one occasion beaten his wife. The victim of this compound question cannot reply without agreeing to this assumption.

Advertisements and sales pitches frequently use or imply the compound question: "Will you have the pecan pie or the cheesecake for dessert?" (Perhaps you do not want any dessert at all.) Compound questions of the sort "Why did the mayor lie to us?" contain unstated assumptions (the unstated assumption here is "The mayor lied to us"). Although unstated assumptions are not necessarily wrong, the writer and the reader should be alert to their presence and decide whether they are acceptable. For example, the statement "Don't bother reading that; it won't be on the exam" contains two questionable unstated assumptions: (1) "I know what will be on the exam" and (2) "Anything that won't be on the exam is not worth reading."

52f ANTICIPATING CONTRARY ARGUMENTS

For any real argument, there will be opposing points of view and contrary evidence. To make a good argument, recognize these contrary points, and refute them as well as possible within the bounds of the evidence available to you. The most effective arguments usually follow the dictum of the good bridge player: "Take your losers first." In other words, anticipate and respond to your opponent's probable arguments early in the presentation of your own argument. If you cannot refute a point, concede it rather than trying to ignore it.

For example, suppose you are arguing that deer hunting should be banned as a cruel and unnecessary sport. You are aware that your opponents may claim that (1) such hunting channels hostile instincts and that it is better for people to kill wild animals than to kill each other, (2) such a ban would curtail still another of our freedoms, (3) people have always killed wild animals, (4) without controlled hunting, the population of deer would become too large for their habitats to support them, and (5) the fees for hunting licenses help support the protection of all wildlife. You might answer these counterarguments as follows:

> Some may argue that deer hunting channels hostile instincts and that it is better that people kill wild animals than that they kill each other. However, there is no evidence that deer hunters are potential murderers or that murder rates are higher in areas where hunting is prohibited. Banning deer hunting is a curtailment of individual freedom, but so are the laws against theft, murder, or destruction of public property. We must all give up freedoms in a highly complex society. Nor is the argument that men have always killed wild animals acceptable. Until the last century or so, men killed wild animals for food, for their own survival. Today we have ample food for everyone, and no one needs venison in order to survive. Indeed, many hunters do not even eat the deer they kill.

> The contention that, without controlled hunting, the population of deer would become too large is also weak. We have much evidence that natural forces do an adequate job of controlling

most wildlife populations without the intervention of man. Although the fees from hunting licenses do help support the protection of all wildlife, this source of income is minuscule compared to the total costs of conservation and preservation, and other sources of income could easily be found.

You have openly and fairly recognized that there are contrary arguments to your point of view, but you have carefully and reasonably responded to each opposing point, refuting some of them and partially conceding others. You can now proceed with your own arguments in favor of banning deer hunting. By answering the opposition at the outset, you reserve the rest of your presentation for your own arguments and evidence, leaving the reader with an impression of the strength of your point of view. Further, when you acknowledge opposing points of view without being abusive to your opponents, your readers are more likely to be persuaded to accept your point of view because you appear to be fair and reasonable.

EXERCISES: Review of Making a Good Argument

Part A: Write one example for each of the following fallacies.

1. Faulty analogy
2. Hasty generalization
3. Evading the issue (use any of the kinds discussed in this section)
4. Guilt by association
5. False dilemma
6. Begging the question

Part B: Identify the fallacious arguments in the following passages—both are letters to the editor sent to a daily newspaper. Most passages have several fallacies.

1. I am the father of three children. I try to do what I say I will do. This causes me to think about Taiwan. We signed a treaty with them over twenty years ago. If we, the United States, do not keep this treaty, what will our word mean to our other allies? Is expediency morally right? How will the American textile industry be affected? How will other industries fare twenty years from now? I am concerned about our honor! And I am concerned about our economy—in the long run.

2. Mrs. Simpson's interests concern us women. She is a member of many influential women's groups and she has introduced legislation which led to a shelter for battered wives and children in our county.

   I am sure that if last Tuesday all the women in our county had gone out to vote while their husbands were at work, Mrs. Simpson could have been elected. She has worked hard for us, and I believe that women have really let her down.

   When a woman as fine, as intelligent, and as well educated as Mrs. Simpson puts forth an effort, using her time and money, to improve the lives and rights of women, the least we can do is to support her. Let's face it—women's salaries still do not equal those of men doing the same jobs!

53 SPECIAL TYPES OF WRITING

The principles of good writing apply to all kinds of writing, not just to themes assigned in English classes. Most of the rules and suggestions presented elsewhere in this handbook are also applicable to letter-writing, technical reports, essay examinations, and even to outlines. These other types of writing, however, have their own characteristics and their own special conventions.

53a OUTLINES

All of us use **outlines** of one kind or another, even if we don't always think of them as outlines. The notes in our pocket calendars are an outline—however incomplete—of our day's activities. The list we take to the supermarket or stationery store is an outline of our intended purchases. When we write a letter to a friend, we have at least a mental outline of what we intend to say before we start writing. All of these are informal outlines, used to help us organize our thoughts and activities.

For many kinds of writing, an informal outline, either mental or written in the form of sketchy notes, is adequate. However, for long papers or for papers with complex arguments or ideas, a more formal outline is usually necessary because we cannot keep a mental picture of all the important points and their relationships. A written outline helps provide coherence to the final paper and reveals imbalances, logical gaps, and inadequate development of our thesis before we start writing. A well-developed outline also helps us estimate the length of the final paper and provides us with a guide as we write. Finally, an outline is actually a stimulus to thought and ideas; seeing ideas written down makes us think of other ideas and of interrelationships among ideas.

In addition to their usefulness in writing papers, outlines are helpful in taking notes from material that has already been written; the outline reveals the structure of the author's argument more clearly and more quickly than several rereadings can. An outline of an unsatisfactory paper of one's own can show what went wrong with it. In writing essay examinations, an informal outline made before the question is answered helps ensure that all important points are covered, and covered in a logical order. Some classroom lectures lend themselves to note-taking in at least rough outline form. If not, putting the notes into outline form after the class is over provides a more organized, coherent picture of what the instructor considers important.

To be useful in writing, your outline should be a good one; a poor outline will be a hindrance, not a help, to the writing process. In particular, the outline should be logical, and its logic should reflect the type of development and sequence of development that you intend to follow in the paper. For example, if you were writing an argument-and-persuasion paper, the major headings of your outline should be the major points and conclusions of your argument, and the subheadings should be details that support your argument. On the other hand, if you were writing a paper on how to recondition an old bicycle, your major headings would probably be the most important systems of the bicycle (brakes, gear system, frame, and wheels), and your subheadings would be the component parts of each major system (cables, levers, and calipers as components of the brake system).

In preparing an outline for a paper that is yet to be written, do not try to put it in formal shape the first time around. Begin by jotting down all the ideas you think might be included in the paper. Do not worry about their order at this stage; just write points down as they occur to you. When you have run out of ideas, look over your list and label with the same letter all items that seem to belong together. Then examine all the items that are labeled with the same letter to get a rough idea of the level of importance of each item. For example, you might be outlining a paper on the pros and cons of buying one's own house and put the letter B beside all the items dealing with financial matters, including "interest on the mortgage," "financial disadvantages," "taxes," "fee for title search," "maintenance," and "down payment." Clearly, the item "financial disadvantages" is at a higher or more general level than any of the others. Further, some of the expenses listed are paid only once, whereas others are paid over and over again. In the final outline, the above examples might appear in the following form.

A. Financial considerations
  1. Initial expenses
    a. Down payment
    b. Fee for title search
  2. Continuing expenses
    a. Interest on the mortgage
    b. Maintenance
    c. Taxes

As you put your rough notes into final form, you will probably discard some of your original items because they are not directly relevant to your topic. You will add new items that come to mind as you organize. Finally, you will probably continue to revise the outline as you write. Do not assume that once a formal outline has been prepared it must be followed slavishly and cannot be altered. If it does not work, revise it. If you are required to submit an outline along with a completed theme, it should be an outline of the actual paper submitted, not an earlier outline of what you had once thought the paper might be.

Informal Outlines. An informal outline consists of rough notes jotted down in no particular order but labeled either mentally or physically with letters (or some other such device) as a guide to the order of the final paper. Such an informal outline is suitable for a short paper or for the answer to an essay question on an examination. Although informal outlines are personal and only for the use of the writer, they are the basis of formal outlines. Informal outlines are normally used much more frequently than formal outlines, so familiarity with their preparation is important. For a discussion of the process of making an informal outline and an example of a rough outline, see 51f.

Formal Outlines.   Formal outlines are suitable for long papers or for taking careful notes on written material. Formal outlines are more carefully constructed than informal outlines and, unlike informal outlines, should be comprehensible to readers other than the author. Types of formal outlines include the paragraph outline, the topic outline, and the sentence outline.

1. **Paragraph Outlines.** Paragraph outlines summarize each paragraph with a single complete sentence. They are normally used for taking notes on written material. One disadvantage of a paragraph outline in taking notes is that not every paragraph is necessarily important enough to need a summary sentence. Further, a paragraph outline is really only a list of topics in the order they have been discussed; it does not reveal the relative importance of the topics. A paragraph outline of the first five paragraphs of this section on outlines might take the following form.

> I. All of us use outlines of some kind.
> II. Long papers require a formal outline.
> III. Outlines are also helpful in taking notes and writing essay examinations.
> IV. Outlines should reflect the logic of the material being outlined.
> V. Outlines should be revised as necessary.

Paragraph outlines may also be used in preparing very short papers for which you know beforehand the number of paragraphs. Here, each entry is in effect a topic sentence for the paragraph it represents. For longer papers, you probably cannot—and should not try to—predict the exact number of paragraphs, and a topic or sentence outline is more suitable.

EXERCISES: Paragraph Outlines

Part A: Write a paragraph outline of the first four pages of Appendix A, "A Brief History of English" in this book.

Part B: Write a paragraph outline for two of the following subjects, giving the thesis sentences for a five-paragraph paper on each.

1. How to get a job.

2. Gifted elementary-school students should (should not) be sent to special public schools for bright children.

3. A person definitely should (should not) bother to vote.

4. The government should (should not) have some control over religious cults.

---

2. **Topic Outlines.** The most common type of formal outline is the topic outline. Points are listed in the form of words or phrases, and the outline is preceded by a thesis sentence that serves as summary and title of the entire outline. The greatest advantage of the topic outline is that it reveals not only the subjects to be covered but also the logic (or illogic) of the organization of the entire paper.

Points are labeled with numbers and letters that indicate the order and relative importance of each point. From most to least important, the order is large Roman numerals, capital letters, Arabic numerals, small letters, and, if necessary, small Roman numerals. Parallel headings are indented the same distance from the left margin. A period follows each number or letter, but there are no periods at the end of the entries themselves. The first word of every entry is capitalized.

Thesis sentence: The potential homeowner should be aware of both the disadvantages and advantages of owning a house.

I. Disadvantages
    A. Financial considerations
        1. Initial expenses
            a. Down payment
            b. Fee for title search
        2. Continuing expenses
            a. Interest on the mortgage
            b. Maintenance
                i. Repairs
                ii. Improvements
            c. Taxes
            d. Capital all tied up in house
    B. Personal considerations
        1. Limited mobility of home-owner
        2. Responsibility of home-owner for upkeep
II. Advantages
    A. Financial considerations
        1. Profitable long-term investment
        2. Income-tax benefits
        3. Improved credit rating
    B. Personal considerations
        1. Satisfaction of owning property
        2. Freedom to remodel and redecorate
        3. No problem of living in house with strangers

To assure a logical, coherent structure for an outline—and for the paper based on the outline—the following conventions should be observed.

a. Put items of equal importance in parallel form. In the example above, both "Disadvantages" and "Advantages" are labeled with large Roman numerals, and the different types of continuing expenses are labeled with small letters. Grammatical structures within a given level should also be parallel. For example, prepositional phrases should not be mixed with noun phrases, nor should declarative statements be mixed with imperative statements. (Normally, complete sentences are not used at all in topic outlines.)

INCORRECT OUTLINE FORM

2. Continuing expenses
   a. Pay interest on the mortgage
   b. Maintenance
   c. Taxes
   d. Your capital is all tied up in your house

b. Make every subdivision a logical part of the topic under which it appears. In our example, "Down payment" and "Fee for title search" are part of the general category "Initial expenses."

c. Avoid single subdivisions under a heading. If you have only one point to make under a heading, incorporate it in the heading itself. For example, in the outline above, item II.A.2., "Income-tax benefits," is made a single subdivision instead of two subdivisions, one of them a single item.

INCORRECT OUTLINE FORM

2. Tax benefits
   a. Income tax
3. Improved credit rating

d. Insofar as possible, let each item in a topic outline deal with one concept and one concept only. Hence, it would have been improper to include both "Maintenance" and "Taxes" in one entry.

e. Make each item as specific as possible. Avoid vague, overly general headings and subheadings such as "Conclusions," "Reasons," "Objections," and the like.

f. Avoid long series of parallel items under a single subdivision. Usually, lengthy subdivisions need further breaking down. For example, under II., "Advantages," the six points labeled with Arabic numbers are properly subdivided into financial and personal considerations rather than being lumped together as six consecutive items.

g. Do not overlap headings and subheadings. For example, if, under "Disadvantages," there had been two subpoints, "Expenses" and "Problems," the second subpoint would have overlapped with both "Disadvantages" and "Expenses."

h. Do not include in the outline introductory material that serves merely to lead into the topic. For example, if you were planning to begin your paper with an anecdote about life in the suburbs, you would not need to make a special heading for this anecdote. On the other hand, if the beginning material is an integral part of the paper, it should be included. If you plan to define an important term or state the problem in your first paragraph, you should include this term or statement in the outline. For example, an expository paper on the various kinds of motorcycle racing might begin with an explanation of how racing motorcycles are classified. The major points of the outline might take the following form.

Motorcycle Racing: Not for the Timid
Introduction: Motorcycles classed by engine size: 100cc, 125cc, 175cc, 250cc, open class

    I. Motocross
    II. Desert racing
    III. Cow-trailing
    IV. Café racing
    V. Speedway racing

EXERCISE: Topic Outlines

Rewrite the following topic outline, arranging the elements in a logical order, making the elements grammatically parallel, and punctuating, capitalizing, and spacing correctly. Add, delete, or combine elements as is necessary.

Thesis: Television and magazine advertising is a psychological game.

  I. Use of color.
    A. Suggests mood.
      1. conditioned responses awakened
  II. Catching the eye
    A. Combination of colors attracts attention.
    B. Importance of intensity of color
  III. Language of ad
    A. Message's length
      1. Jingles can be effective.
      2. detailed, factual copy
  IV. Targeting the language.
      1. How formal is the language?
        a. class appeal
        b. appeal to age.
        c. sex appeal.
    A. Using people in ads.
        a. Why celebrities are used.
      1. To transfer the appeal of celebrity to product.
      2. For transferring the glamour of the celebrity to the reader or viewer.
    B. The "beautiful" people
        a. appeal to vanity of reader or viewer.
        b. sex appeal
        c. appeal to health
    C. Average people.
      1. Easy identification with the viewer or reader.
      2. Lends a sense of normalcy to product.
  IV. How the product is displayed
    A. setting
      1. Fantasy setting
      2. Setting is true to life.
    B. How prominently the product is displayed in the ad makes a psychological difference.
        a. Subtle treatment
        b. product is the central visual effect.

---

3. **Sentence Outlines.** The sentence outline is a variant of the topic outline. It has the same format and the same logic, but complete sentences are used instead of single words or phrases. Making a

sentence outline has the advantage of forcing writers to consider the specific things they want to say and not just the general topic they are going to discuss. Further, a sentence outline is easier for other readers to follow. The first part of the topic outline presented on page 328 is rewritten below as a sentence outline.

I. There are numerous disadvantages to owning one's own house.
   A. Home ownership is very expensive today.
      1. The initial expenses of buying a house are high.
         a. The down payment may be as much as one-third of the cost of the house.
         b. The title-search can cost several hundred dollars.

      2. The continuing expenses of home ownership are also high.
         a. The interest on one's mortgage may be as much as 90 percent of the total mortgage payment each month.
         b. Maintenance costs, such as exterior painting, gutters, landscaping, roof repairs, plumbing, and the like can cost an average of several thousand dollars a year.
         c. Real-estate taxes will vary according to the neighborhood, the value of the house, and the city in which the house is located.
         d. The homeowner has thousands of dollars tied up in the property, money that is not available to be used in other ways.

When you have completed an outline of any type, check it carefully to be sure you have not omitted anything important. Before finishing your rough draft of a paper, check your outline to be sure you have included everything you intended from the outline.

EXERCISES: Sentence Outlines

Make the outline in the exercise on topic outlines (page 330) into a logical sentence outline that is correctly capitalized, spaced, and punctuated.

53b LETTERS

Even if you never write an essay after leaving college, you will write many letters in your lifetime. The recipients of these letters will not put grades on them, but you will nonetheless be judged on the basis of your letters. Obviously, it is to your advantage to be able to write a good, clear letter that observes the conventions of letter writing.

Business Letters. A century ago, such phrases as "Yours of the 21st received" or "I remain, your faithful servant" were common in business letters. Fortunately, such artificial language is totally out of place today. The style of a business letter should be objective, direct, courteous, and relatively impersonal. The language should not be stilted or flowery. Only essential information should be included.

Business letters should be typewritten on 8½-by-11-inch white, unruled paper. Use only one side of the paper. The entire business letter is single-spaced, with double-spacing only between sections and between paragraphs. (The body of a very short letter of only two or three lines may be double-spaced.) If a second page is necessary, it should contain at least three or four lines of the text of the letter.

A business letter has six parts, as illustrated by the sample letter below. These parts are (1) return address and date, (2) inside address, (3) salutation, (4) body, (5) complimentary close, and (6) signature.

1. **Return Address and Date.** Type the return address in the upper right corner of the page with the date below it. If you use a printed letterhead containing the return address, give only the date here. Such abbreviations as *St.* and *Ave.* are usually acceptable, but you will never be wrong if you spell these words out. No comma separates the name of the state from the ZIP code, although there is at least one (often two) spaces between the name of the state and the ZIP code. There is no punctuation at the ends of the lines.

RETURN ADDRESS
468 Luzon Street
Tiverton, New Mexico 88516
June 25, 1980

Martha Shippey
Hermes Travel Agency
14 Larch Avenue
Wayland, New Mexico 88503

INSIDE ADDRESS

Dear Ms. Shippey: **SALUTATION**

BODY

Thank you for inquiring about arrangements for a flight to San Francisco prior to my trip to Hawaii.   Because I will be driving to San Francisco with a friend, I will not need flight reservations.   However, I appreciate your foresight in thinking about all parts of my trip.

Unless I hear otherwise from you, I will pick up my plane tickets and hotel reservations on July 9 as originally planned.

Sincerely,   **COMPLIMENTARY CLOSE**

Warren Jovin   **SIGNATURE**

Warren Jovin

---

2. **Inside Address.** Type the inside address flush left and four to six spaces below the return address. You can adjust the space between the inside address and the return address in order to balance the letter on the page. Note that the inside address includes the name of the addressee. There is no punctuation at the ends of the lines.

3. **Salutation.** Type the salutation flush left, two spaces below the inside address, and follow it with a colon. The salutation includes

such titles as *Mr., Mrs., Ms., Miss,* and *Dr.* (For the appropriate forms of address for government or church officials, see the appendix of *Webster's New World Dictionary, Funk & Wagnalls Standard College Dictionary,* or *Webster's New Collegiate Dictionary.*) If you are on a first-name basis with the addressee, you may use his or her first name instead of last name (*Dear Martha,*) and a comma instead of a colon at the end. When you know the title but not the name of the recipient, you can use just the title (*Dear Personnel Manager:, Dear Admissions Officer:*). If you know neither the name nor the title of the recipient, you can use *Dear Sir:* or *Dear Sir or Madam:* for a letter addressed to an individual, and *Gentlemen:* or *Gentlemen or Ladies:* for a letter addressed to a company or other institution.

4. **Body.** Single-space the body of the letter with double spaces between paragraphs. You may type the entire body flush left, or you may indent five spaces at the beginning of every paragraph. If the letter is more than one page long, put the addressee's name, the date, and the page number at the top of all pages after the first one. This information may all be on one line, separated by commas, or may be typed flush left in three lines at the top left corner.

5. **Complimentary Close.** Type the complimentary close either flush left or in the center of the page, and follow it with a comma. The conventional forms for a complimentary close are, in order of descending formality, *Very truly yours (Yours truly, Yours very truly), Sincerely yours (Sincerely, Yours sincerely),* and *Cordially yours (Cordially, Yours cordially).* For high-ranking church, government, or academic officials, the complimentary close *Respectfully yours* is appropriate.

6. **Signature.** Type the name of the sender four spaces below the complimentary close, and sign the letter by hand in the space between the complimentary close and the typed name. No title appears with the handwritten signature, but a title does precede the typed signature (except that the titles *Mr., Mrs., Miss,* and *Ms.* are not used here). A married woman should sign her own given and last names, not her husband's given name. She may, if she wishes, indicate her marital status in parentheses, as in the example below.

Joyce Storey
Joyce Storey
(Mrs. Allan Storey)

If the letter includes an enclosure, such as a check, indicate this by typing *Enc.* flush left and two spaces below the typed signature.

Enc.: check

If copies of the letter are to be sent to persons other than the addressee, indicate this by typing *cc.* flush left and two spaces below the typed signature:

cc.: Walter French

If it is impossible to type a business letter, handwrite it on unruled paper, following the same format as for typewritten letters.

For a one-page letter, either a small business-size envelope (3⅝ by 6 ½ inches) or a large envelope (4⅛ by 9½ inches) is appropriate. For letters of more than one page or letters with enclosures, use a large envelope. To fold a letter for a small envelope, fold the bottom up to within a half-inch or so from the top, and then fold it in thirds from left to right. For a large envelope, fold the letter in thirds from bottom to top.

The address on the envelope should be the same as the inside address. Addresses are single-spaced, except for two-line addresses, which are double-spaced. Type your return address in the upper left corner of the envelope. Special instructions such as "Attn: Credit Department" or "Personal" are typed in the lower left corner.

EXERCISES: Business Letters

Choose one of the following problems and write a suitable business letter to the addressee indicated. Type or handwrite it in correct letter form.

1. You ordered three different leather-craft kits, one for making a belt, one for making a purse, and one for making a backgammon case. You sent payment in full with the order. The company has sent you three identical kits for making backgammon cases and has billed you for an additional $28.43. Write to Paul N. Saunders in the Customer Service Department of the N. F. Casbon Company at 1943 Mohawk Trail in Portland, Oregon (the ZIP code is 97222).

2. You live alone in an apartment. Your water bill, which you have always paid on time, has increased by 50 percent during the last three months. Your repeated calls to the water company have been ignored. You suspect that there is a leak or that someone else has tapped into your water line and is using the water that you are paying for. Write to Anna M. Prentiss in the Consumer Complaint Department of the Wichita, Kansas, Water and Sewer Authority at Post Office Box 434 in Wichita (ZIP code is 67219). Explain your predicament, and include exactly what you expect to have done about it.

Letters of Application. Perhaps the most important business letters you will ever write will be letters of application for jobs. Whether it be for a summer job or for a full-time position after you have left school, your future can depend on the reaction to your letter, and you obviously want to make the best possible impression.

Begin your letter of application by telling how you heard of the position for which you are applying—through a newspaper advertisement, an agency, or a friend. If you are responding to an advertisement, the recipient will appreciate your mentioning the name of the newspaper and the date of the issue in which you saw the advertisement. Be as specific as possible about the position for which you are applying. If you are responding to no specific source but rather are "just checking," indicate why you are interested in working for that particular company or institution.

State your qualifications clearly and concisely, pointing out any special skills you may have gained from education or prior experience. If you have any potentially disqualifying handicaps or deficiencies, mention these too—they will soon be discovered anyway. On the

Vaille Hall
University of Vermont
Burlington, Vermont 05401
April 15, 1979

The Everest Store
19 Summit Street
Johnston, New Hampshire 03836

Gentlemen:

One of your former employees, Brian Moore, told me that
you often hire extra clerks during the summer months. If
you will be needing additional help for the coming
summer, I would like to apply for a job with you.

I am at present a sophomore at the University of
Vermont, and will be available for work from June 15 to
September 10.   Although I have had no previous clerking
experience, I am an experienced climber and am familiar
with most kinds of climbing equipment.   In addition to
several years' experience with climbing and backpacking
in New Hampshire, I spent eight weeks during the
summer of 1977 climbing in the Olympic, Sierra, and
Cascade Mountains.   During my senior year in high
school, I taught mountaineering skills in a special
program and advised the school's purchasing officer about
the type of equipment to buy.   I am an avid climber and
would like very much to have the opportunity to share my
enthusiasm with others.

I can come for an interview on any Thursday or
Saturday.   If you would like further information, please
let me know.

Sincerely,

Andrew Mac Intyre

Andrew MacIntyre

rh

other hand, do not apologize for lack of experience or training; instead, try to neutralize your deficiencies by expressing an interest in
the company and an eagerness to learn.

If you have a great deal of objective information to convey in
a letter of application, it should be summarized in a separate résumé
or data sheet. (See 53c for information on preparing a résumé.) One
advantage of a separate résumé is that it can be duplicated and en-

closed in all letters of application, saving you the trouble and time of repeating the information in each letter.

If you include names and addresses of references in a letter of application, be sure to ask these people beforehand for permission to use their names.

You will probably want to end your letter of application with a request for an interview. State clearly any times or dates at which you will not be available for an interview. If at all possible, express a willingness to appear for an interview at any time convenient to the recipient of the letter. Enclosing a stamped, self-addressed envelope is a courtesy that will not pass unnoticed.

Letters of application follow all the conventions of regular business letters, as illustrated in the sample letter of application on page 335. Take particular care in proofreading a letter of application, and retype it rather than send it off with messy corrections.

EXERCISES: Letters of Application

Write a letter of application for one of the following jobs. Because this letter will not include a résumé, include all the pertinent information in the letter itself.

1. A summer job as an assistant to a park ranger at Mammoth Cave National Park in Mammoth Cave, Kentucky. Write to Walter R. Carpenter, director of the park (ZIP code is 42259).

2. A permanent job in the data-processing department of Fairbanks Chemical Corporation at 1892 Port Royal Drive, Virginia Beach, Virginia (ZIP code is 23405). Write to Kenneth M. Parsons, personnel director.

53c RÉSUMÉS

The **résumé,** also called a **vita,** is a fact sheet that summarizes your experience and education for prospective employers. Clarity and ease of reading are particularly important because the prospective employer will want to find specific information quickly. If the résumé is confusing or difficult to read, the recipient may simply not bother trying to decipher it, and you will not be considered for the job.

Résumés are presented in tabular form. Use headings to guide the reader's eye. Name, address, and other vital statistics normally appear first, followed by experience and education (in *reverse* chronological order). References come last. If you have no honors or special interests and skills worth mentioning, omit these categories from your résumé. Be specific as to the nature of your previous jobs, stating the title of the job or the exact nature of your responsibilities. If you have a skill that makes you stand out a bit from others of your age and education, do not hestiate to include it, even if it seems only remotely relevant to the position for which you are applying. Employers are impressed by people who have accomplished more than their peers, regardless of the nature of the accomplishment. On the other hand, do not claim achievements or experience that you do not have.

RÉSUMÉ

NAME: Kathryn Anne Bullis

ADDRESS: 4615 S. Eleventh Street,
Batesville, Louisiana 70256

BIRTH DATE: August 6, 1958

WORK EXPERIENCE: Clerk-typist, part time, Mellon
College Admissions Office, 1978-80
Programmer, First State Bank, Batesville, La., sum-
mers, 1977-79
Camp counselor, Cragged Mt. Farm, Freedom, N.H.,
summers, 1974-76

EDUCATION: A.B., Mellon College, Olympus, N.C. Major
in political science and minor in French. Graduated
<u>cum laude</u>, June, 1980
Batesville High School, Batesville, Louisiana. Graduated
June, 1976

HONORS: Tuition scholarship, Mellon College, 1976-80

SPECIAL INTERESTS AND SKILLS: I speak fluent
Spanish. I am a licensed pilot.

REFERENCES: Professor Donald Piper
Department of Political Science
Mellon College
Olympus, N.C. 28901

Paul Arenz
Personnel Manager
First State Bank
Vine and Rockland Sts.
Batesville, La. 70256

Ms. Stacey Albers
Assistant Director, Admissions
Mellon College
Olympus, N.C. 28901

EXERCISES: Résumés

Prepare a résumé that you could enclose with a letter of application for one of the following jobs. Use imaginary information if you like, but be sure the résumé is a believable one.

1. A position as an artist in the advertising department of a department store
2. A position as a congressional aide
3. A position as a laboratory assistant for a drug company
4. A position as truck driver for a logging company
5. A position as a proofreader for a daily newspaper

53d PARAPHRASES AND SUMMARIES

Most students, at some point in their careers, have to write paraphrases and summaries, either of their own work or of the work of others. Both paraphrases and summaries are forms of rewriting, but they are quite different forms and serve quite different purposes.

Paraphrases.   A **paraphrase** is a restatement of the original in words different from those used in the original. The purpose of a paraphrase is to help either the writer of the paraphrase or someone else understand difficult material. Paraphrases are especially useful for clarifying highly technical writing for the general reader; here, the paraphrase often substitutes more familiar terms for specialized technical terms. Paraphrases of poetry restate the content of the poem in prose. Paraphrases of older texts "translate" these texts into modern English.

A paraphrase is not an evaluation, interpretation, or analysis of the original, but simply a rephrasing. It adds no new material and should preserve the tone of the original insofar as possible. Paraphrases are normally about the same length as their originals but may be longer if the original is exceptionally difficult or concise.

In writing a paraphrase, first read the original carefully two or three times or until you are sure that you thoroughly understand it. Then put the original aside and restate it in your own words. Avoid, whenever possible, using the original phrasing. After you have written the paraphrase, go back to the original to make sure that you have not left anything out or misstated anything. Note that even a complete paraphrase of someone else's writing must be footnoted if it is included in a paper of your own.

The following is a paraphrase of relatively technical writing, a paragraph discussing the organism that causes malaria. The paraphrase follows the original fairly closely but substitutes synonyms for some words and varies word order somewhat. It is approximately the same length as the original.

ORIGINAL

The malarial plasmodium, for instance, is probably among the oldest of human (and pre-human) parasites; yet it continues to

SPECIAL TYPES OF WRITING 339

inflict severe and debilitating fevers upon its human hosts. At least four different forms of the plasmodium infect human beings, and one of these, *Plasmodium falciparum*, is far more virulent than the others. Conceivably, *Plasmodium falciparum* entered human bloodstreams more recently, and has not had time to adjust as well to human hosts as the other forms of malarial infection. In this case, however, evolutionary adjustment between host and parasite is complicated by the diversity of hosts to which the infectious organism must accommodate itself to complete its life cycle. Accommodation that would allow the malarial plasmodium to live indefinitely within the red blood corpuscles of a human being would make no provision for successful transmission from host to host. —William H. McNeill, *PLAGUES AND PEOPLES*

PARAPHRASE

Probably one of the oldest parasites to afflict human beings is the plasmodium, the organism that causes malaria. Despite its long association with human beings, it still produces serious fevers. There are at least four types of plasmodium that affect human beings, but *Plasmodium falciparum* is the most virulent by far. The explanation for its virulence may be that it has come to afflict human beings more recently. If so, it has perhaps had less time to adjust to life in the human bloodstream than have the other types of plasmodium. Further, because the plasmodium adapts itself to a number of different hosts in order to complete its life cycle, more time is required for its evolutionary adjustment. However, these different hosts are necessary; if the plasmodium lived indefinitely in one host, such as the human bloodstream, it could not reproduce or "spread" by going from host to host.

The following is the text of I Corinthians 13:1–3 from the King James version of the Bible, followed by a paraphrase of this text. The paraphrase modernizes the older language of the original and explains in simple words the meaning of the metaphors and similes in the original.

ORIGINAL

Though I speak with the tongues of men and of angels, and have not charity, I am become as sounding brass, or a tinkling cymbal. And though I have the gift of prophesy, and understand all mysteries, and all knowledge; and though I have all faith, so that I could remove mountains, and have not charity, I am nothing. And though I bestow all my goods to feed the poor, and though I give my body to be burned, and have not charity, it profiteth me nothing.

PARAPHRASE

Even though I may speak very eloquently, everything I say is just noise if I do not have love. Even though I may be able to foretell the future and may know everything, and even though I may have enough faith to make mountains move, I am nothing without love. I can give everything I own to the poor and can even allow myself to be martyred by being burned, but it will do me no good if I do not have love.

EXERCISES: Paraphrases

Write a paraphrase of the following passage.

So cheap in fact were all provisions, which one had any chance of meeting with in a labouring man's house, that I found it difficult under such a roof to spend sixpence-a-day. Tea or coffee there was none: and I did not at that period very much care for either. Milk, with bread (coarse, but more agreeable by much than the insipid *whity-grey* bread of towns), potatoes if one wished, and also a little goat's, or kid's, flesh—these composed the cottager's choice of viands; not luxurious, but palatable enough to a person who took much exercise. And, if one wished, fresh-water fish could be had cheap enough; especially trout of the very finest quality. In these circumstances, I never found it easy to spend even five shillings (no, not three shillings, unless whortleberries or fish had been bought) in one week. And thus it was easy enough to create funds for my periodical transmigrations back into the character of gentleman-tourist. Even the half of five shillings I could not always find means to spend: for in some families, raised above dependence upon daily wages, when I performed any services in the way of letter-writing, I found it impossible at times to force any money at all upon them.   —Thomas De Quincey, *CONFESSIONS OF AN ENGLISH OPIUM EATER*

Summaries. A **summary,** also called a **précis** or a **synopsis,** is an abridgment or condensation of its original. A summary is not an explanation of or a substitute for the original. Rather, its purpose is to refresh the writer's memory about what the original said or to give others enough information about the original to let them decide whether they want to read the original. Like a paraphrase, a summary adds no interpretation or evaluation and retains the approach and tone of the original. A summary normally follows the same organization as its original, omitting minor details, illustrations, quotations, anecdotes, and other material that is not absolutely essential. Unlike a paraphrase, a summary may include some of the same wording as the original, especially important terms and definitions. A summary is usually only about one-fourth to one-third the length of the original, but preserves the general proportions of the original.

In writing a summary, read the original carefully two or three times, noting the author's main ideas and organization. Try to reduce entire paragraphs to a topic sentence, either of your own composition or by the original author. Check the original carefully to be sure you have not omitted crucial points. Check your summary to see if it can be further condensed. A good summary will, of course, be abbreviated but should nevertheless be smooth and fluent and without confusing gaps in logic.

The following selection is a summary of the tenth and eleventh paragraphs of Appendix A, "A Brief History of the English Language."

> Old English as a separate language began about the sixth century A.D. At first, the only writing in English was short inscriptions written in the runic alphabet called the futhorc. After England was Christianized in the sixth and seventh centuries, the Latin alphabet was used, but a few letters from the old runic alphabet were retained for indicating particular English sounds for which there were no symbols in the Latin alphabet.

EXERCISES: Summaries

Write a summary of the following passage.

Tying one's self-worth to performance standards leads to excessive concern about other people's opinions. It results in fearful, alert looking to the reactions of others for clues as to where one stands in life or how one measures up in their eyes. Such concern, of course, is a sure recipe for stress. Other people often do not know what they really value or believe. Their standards and preferences are often inconsistent and therefore unattainable. Pleasing others, by itself, even when possible, is always a hollow victory. One may escape censure or disapproval. But one achieves nothing in terms of increased self-esteem. That can come only from pleasing yourself, which has nothing to do with external standards of self-worth.

—Robert L. Woolfolk and Frank C. Richardson, *STRESS, SANITY, AND SURVIVAL*

53e ESSAY EXAMINATIONS

Essay examinations are an important part of nearly every college student's experience. In large classes, the instructor may be forced to judge a student's ability and knowledge solely on the basis of his or her performance on one or two essay examinations. Obviously, the first requisite for good performance is knowledge of the subject matter, and no amount of strategy or verbal skill can substitute for studying the content of a course. On the other hand, many students who know the subject matter well receive lower grades than they otherwise might because they do not know how to take essay examinations.

Studying for the Examination. When the examination is announced, listen carefully to what the instructor says about the examination and plan your studying accordingly. If the instructor says the examination will cover only four chapters, do not try to digest the entire book. If the instructor stresses the knowledge of factual material such as definitions, names, dates, or formulas, concentrate on learning this factual information.

If the instructor says that the examination will consist primarily of "thought" questions, consider the larger principles that have been emphasized in the class, try to formulate sample essay questions for yourself, and consider how you might answer them. Learn as many supporting details as possible, but focus on explanations, structure, and implications rather than on small details. For example, assume that in an anthropology class you have been studying the culture of Eskimos, and your instructor has told you that your examination will consist of "thought" questions. In lectures, the instructor has gone into detail about the building of houses; the making of tools, weapons, and boats; religious beliefs and ceremonies; child-rearing; and social organization. In an essay examination, the instructor will want you to make generalizations and draw conclusions from this detailed information. (You will, of course, be expected to support your generalizations with specific facts.) Typical "thought" questions might be something like the following examples.

> How are the religious beliefs of the polar Eskimos reflected in their social organizations?
>
> How is the Eskimo way of life influenced by the physical environment?
>
> Discuss the roles of the sexes among the polar Eskimos.
>
> Compare child-rearing among the Eskimos with that in contemporary America.

Taking the Examination. Get to the examination early or at least on time so that you will not have the handicap of walking in late and seeing all your classmates busily writing before you have even sat down. Take several pens with you to the examination. Bring a watch so that you will not have to rely on the instructor to tell you the time.

Before you start writing, scan the examination sheet to get a perspective on the entire examination. If percentages or expected times are indicated, mentally note these so that you can budget your time accordingly. Check carefully to see if a choice of questions is allowed. If so, plan to answer only the required number of questions. You will not receive credit for the extra answers, and you will waste time that would be better spent on improving the answers to required questions.

Start with the questions about which you know the most and feel most confident. They can serve as a warm-up and ensure that you are at your best when you get to the more difficult questions. Further, if you should find yourself running out of time at the end of the period, you will have answered those questions for which you expect to get full or nearly full credit. If possible, keep the order of your answers in the examination booklet the same as the order of the questions on the examination sheet. In any case, always number your answers according to the numbers of the questions on the examination sheet, not according to the order in which you answer the questions. Improbable as it may seem, instructors sometimes cannot tell from the answer alone which question is being answered.

Read each question very carefully; many students lose credit for not having read the question correctly. In particular, note whether a short answer or a full-length essay is asked for. If it is a short answer, restrict your answer to a sentence or two. You will not receive extra credit for a lengthy answer; you will waste time needed for other questions; and you will probably annoy the instructor, who does not want to do all that unnecessary reading.

Note the language of each question. *Why* does not mean *what*, and if the instructor asks *why* a certain sequence of events occurred, do not give a description of *what* those events were. Similarly, pay particular attention to such instruction words as *discuss, evaluate, describe, compare, identify, explain, list, outline, summarize,* and *define*. For example, *evaluate* means that you are to make a value judgment, supporting this judgment with specific details, whereas *describe* asks only that you present the facts, not that you evaluate them. *Summarize* means that you should list the most important facts or conclusions, not that you should go into great detail about one or two aspects of the question. *Define* asks you to state the meaning of something, not merely to give one or two examples of it.

As an example, assume that one of the questions on a psychology examination is "Write a short paragraph defining classical conditioning." Possible poor, fair, and good answers to this question follow.

POOR

Classical conditioning is when you make a dog salivate to a bell without any food. Pavlov discovered that this happens. He strapped his dogs into frames so that they couldn't move. Sometimes he used lights instead of bells. He thought that this was like telephone systems.

FAIR

Pavlov showed his dogs food and then gave it to them. This made them salivate. Then he sounded a bell before he gave them the food. After a while, the dogs salivated when they heard the bell even though they didn't get any food. This salivation without the presence of food is an example of classical conditioning.

GOOD

An unconditioned stimulus produces an inborn response (e.g., a dog automatically salivates when shown food). A neutral stimulus produces no such response (a dog does not salivate when it hears a bell). Classical conditioning occurs when a neutral stimulus (bell) is repeatedly paired with an unconditioned stimulus (food). The neutral stimulus eventually becomes a conditioned stimulus when it produces a response similar to that of the unconditioned stimulus, even when the unconditioned stimulus is not present.

The first answer is poor because, instead of defining classical conditioning, it gives a sketchy and disorganized description of the first experiments with classical conditioning. The information about strapping the dogs into frames is irrelevant. The writer does not say in what way Pavlov thought classical conditioning was like telephone systems. Even the sentence construction is weak.

The second answer is fair because, although it does not provide a good general definition of classical conditioning, it does give a straightforward description of the process of classical conditioning and then notes that this description is an example, not a general definition.

The third answer is good because, in addition to providing a general definition of classical conditioning, it also defines other terms (*unconditioned stimulus, neutral stimulus*) essential to a thorough understanding of the principle of classical conditioning.

When you are ready to answer a specific essay question, do not plunge right in, putting down all the points you can think of in the order they occur to you. Make a rough outline in the margin or on the back cover of the examination booklet. Examine these rough notes, and indicate the order in which points should appear by numbering them. Try to formulate a thesis sentence that will summarize your entire answer. If this thesis sentence rephrases the question as a statement, you can refer to it constantly as you write to be sure that you do not digress and that you direct the rest of your answer to this thesis sentence. In your answer, give as many specific illustrations, details, technical terms, names, and the like as you can think of, provided they are all relevant to the question and provided time allows. Avoid overgeneralizations that are not supported by details. Avoid digressions. Avoid repeating yourself and contradicting yourself. Do not try to put down everything you know about the subject; stick to what is asked for in the question. Be as economical as possible; the best answer is often not the longest answer. Above all, do not try to pad your answer or to bluff—your instructor will not be fooled.

Stop writing when you become uncertain of your answer. This is especially important with short-answer questions, where students frequently lose credit by not stopping when they run out of solid information.

If you are required to write on a question to which you have forgotten or simply do not know the answer, spend a few moments thinking of all that you do know about the area. The answer may come to you. Depending on the subject matter, you may be able to work out an answer by common sense and logic.

Instructors understand that students are under pressure when they take examinations and do not expect them to write elegant prose. On the other hand, the more polished your writing, the better off you are. Regardless of how hurried you feel, do not dash off disconnected words and phrases—if the instructor cannot understand what you are saying, you certainly will not get credit for it. Try to compose each sentence mentally before you write it.

Keep your handwriting as legible as possible. You will save very little time by scribbling, but you will lose a great deal of credit if the instructor cannot read what you have scribbled. Deletions and inter-linear or marginal insertions are acceptable but should of course be clear.

Normally, you should use all the time allowed for an essay examination. When you have finished writing, read over both the questions and your answers. Make necessary corrections in grammar and spelling, and add or delete material as seems appropriate.

If you find that you consistently do poorly on essay examinations even though you feel that you know the subject matter well, consult your instructor about your problems. Make it clear to the instructor that you are not complaining about your grade but, instead, would like advice about how to improve your performance in the future. You might also ask a good student if you may compare his or her examination with your own in an effort to see exactly what constituted a good set of answers.

research

res

Because of our modern emphasis on technology, the word "research" may conjure up images of white-coated people in laboratories gazing solemnly into test tubes. We may feel that unless we can discover a new chemical element—or at least a cure for dandruff—we are not really researchers. But research is much more than startling new scientific discoveries. Research is the deliberate and systematic investigation of *any* subject. The toddler who bumps against the radiator, burns himself, and then goes to each room in the house carefully touching every radiator is doing research—not significant research by adult standards, to be sure, but significant for his interpretation of his world. When you pore over consumer magazines and advertising material and talk to salespersons and friends before you decide what kind of cassette recorder to buy, you are doing research.

A distinction is often made between *primary* and *secondary* research. Strictly speaking, primary researchers are the first people to investigate a particular problem, and secondary researchers analyze the results of earlier researchers and draw their own conclusions. In practice, most research is a combination of primary and secondary research. Even the so-called pure scientist in the laboratory or the field must do a great deal of secondary research before he or she undertakes primary research, if only to avoid repeating work that has already been done. If you were investigating the language of advertising, you would be doing primary research when you examined advertisements to see how often they used superlatives or rhymes, and secondary research when you read articles or books about advertising.

Most college research papers are based on secondary research. This does not mean that the research paper is simply a summary of what others have done and said. A good research paper has its own problem to investigate. It organizes information in a way that gives the reader a new insight into the subject, and it presents its own conclusions.

Because college research papers do rely so heavily on secondary research, the student writing a research paper must be familiar with sources of written information and with the conventions for acknowledging the information he or she has obtained from outside sources. In other words, knowing how to write a research paper implies knowing how to use a library and how to document the material found in the library and used in the paper.

54 THE RESEARCH PAPER

The research paper goes by many different names: term paper, source paper, library paper, reference paper, documented paper, investigative paper. Whatever the name, the use of sources outside the writer's own experience is implied. Of course, any paper, no matter how short or how long, may use outside sources, if only to verify a date or provide a quotation. Research papers, however, use at least several outside sources. Research papers are also normally much longer than other papers, typically ranging from 1,500 to 5,000 words in length. Because of their length, they require particular attention to organization. Some people may be able to write a 500-word paper without making an outline beforehand, but most of us need an outline for a paper that is to be 8–15 pages long.

The preparation of a research paper gives you practice in critical reading and weighing evidence, practice that is valuable not only in college courses but in whatever you may do outside of and after college. It gives you a chance to learn how to use libraries and provides experience in the use of documentation. It gives you practice valuable for writing long papers in other courses, where the instructor usually assumes that you already know how to write a research paper. Finally, it gives you a chance to learn something new yourself. We learn more about a subject and learn it more thoroughly if we must sift evidence, organize various kinds of material, and then explain it to others by means of written exposition. It is always pleasant to discover that we have become somewhat expert on a subject about which we had previously known little.

54a CHOOSING A TOPIC

If, by chance, you are assigned a specific topic for a research paper, you may as well grin and bear it—at least, you have been spared the agony of trying to decide what to write about. More typically, instructors allow students a fair amount of freedom in their choice of topic. You may be given a list of topics from which to choose, or the assignment may be completely open-ended, allowing you to write on any topic you like. The following is a guide to the kinds of topics that are most appropriate for research papers.

1. Pick a topic in which you are interested, potentially interested, or that you are at least curious about. If you already know a little about the topic, so much the better. For example, if you were taking a religion course, you might be interested in investigating the history of Biblical translation, or Martin Luther's anti-Semitism, or the appeal of cult religions.

2. Pick a topic that can be understood by a general audience. In other words, your topic should be one that can be made compre-

hensible and interesting to the average adult. People do not have to be animal psychologists to understand and enjoy a paper about the language of dolphins and whales.

3. Pick a topic that can be treated objectively. Most topics can be so treated, but you should avoid topics about which final judgments will be primarily subjective. For example, a topic such as "Which was the greater composer, Mozart or Beethoven?" is unsuitable for a research paper because your conclusions will ultimately be subjective; there is no objective way of defining the greatness of outstanding composers. On the other hand, for the musically knowledgeable student, a topic such as the influence of literature on Beethoven's music could be treated objectively.

4. Pick a topic within the range of your abilities. No matter how fascinated you may be about the concept of black holes in the universe, you will not be able to make intelligent conclusions about them if you lack the background in physics, mathematics, and astronomy necessary to evaluate the opinions expressed in your sources.

5. Do not pick a topic that can be developed from your personal experience alone. The purpose of a research paper is to summarize and draw conclusions from a variety of sources outside your own experience and prior knowledge. Hence the topic "My impressions of Disneyland" is not appropriate for a research paper.

6. Do not pick a topic that can be developed from a single outside source. An example would be "Lenin's student days," the information about which could be drawn from any one biography of Lenin.

7. Do not pick a topic that is too controversial or about which you yourself have extremely strong prejudices. A topic such as "Which is the true Christian faith, Catholicism or Protestantism?" is not suitable for a research paper.

8. Do not pick a topic for which research materials are unlikely to be available. For example, libraries in Alabama will probably not have much material on the history of mining towns in Wyoming. For many topics, of course, you will not know whether sources are available until you actually start searching. However, you can be fairly certain in advance that topics that have just emerged in news stories of the past few weeks or months will have little or nothing about them in book form. Although your references should include periodicals, they normally should not be restricted to periodicals.

54b GETTING STARTED

Once you have decided on a general topic for a research paper, the next step is a trip to the library to start collecting source material. If your topic is still rather broad and if you need more general background information, you may want to read an article or two on the subject in a good, up-to-date encyclopedia, such as the *Encyclopaedia Britannica*. Encyclopedias also provide brief bibliographies for many of their entries.

Other possible general sources include almanacs, yearbooks, Who's Whos, and handbooks. Browse for a while in the reference room; you will probably discover sources of information that you did not know existed. Consult periodical indexes for magazine and journal articles on your subject. (For a discussion of types of reference works and lists of standard references in specific areas, see 55d.) Finally, do not hesitate to ask reference librarians for help—they are specially trained to help library users locate sources of information.

Even at this early stage in your research, you should have a thesis statement—or perhaps several alternative thesis statements— in mind. Even a tentative thesis statement will help you focus your search for additional information and will save you a great deal of unnecessary hunting and reading.

The Card Catalog and the Stacks.   The next step is the card catalog. (See 55a for a detailed description of card catalogs.) If you already have the names of several authors or books on your topic, you can simply locate the cards for these books in the card catalog. You will need to use the subject index to find other books. If you get your books from the stacks yourself, browse along the shelves where your books are located. You will probably find other relevant books for which you had no previous references.

The Preliminary Bibliography.   As you locate potential sources of information, you will need to compile a preliminary bibliography. The simplest way to do this is to use a separate 3-by-5-inch card for each reference. Put the call number of the reference at the top of the card, and include on the card all the information you will need for the final bibliography (author, title, place and date of publication, and so on). Use standard bibliographical form (see 56b) so that, when you prepare your final bibliography, you can simply copy the necessary information directly from your preliminary bibliography without having to reorganize the material. Two sample bibliography cards, one for a book and one for an article, are reproduced on page 350.

Taking Notes.   Everyone develops his or her own method for recording notes. The exact method used is not important; what is important is that the method be efficient, flexible, systematic, and relatively easy to use. Most people prefer to take notes on 4-by-6-inch or 5-by-8-inch index cards. Cards can be easily rearranged and are sturdy enough to withstand the shuffling. Lined cards help keep the notes neat and easy to read.

On the top line of each note card, write down enough information to identify the source. Use a separate card for each reference. If you are making notes on more than one point from a single reference, use a separate card for each point. Do not write on the backs of the cards because you may forget to turn the card over later. When you have more information than will fit on the front of a single card, use additional cards, identifying the source on each card and numbering the additional cards consecutively. Every card should include the specific page reference(s) for the information on it.

res

Periodicals
Room

Fowler, Mary Janet, Michael J.
Sullivan, and Bruce K. Ekstrand.
"Sleep and Memory." <u>Science</u>,
19, Jan. 1973, pp. 302-304.

QP
.D44
1974

Dement, William C. <u>Some Must
Watch While Some Must Sleep</u>.
San Francisco: W. H. Freeman
& Co., 1974.

Before actually writing down notes from a reference, skim the book or article. If the source is a book, glance at the table of contents, the preface, the introduction, and the index. Scan the various sections to get an idea of what the book contains and where the desired information is located. You may find that the book contains nothing useful to you at all. If so, make a note of this on the bibliography card for that book so that you will not needlessly come back to the book later. How closely you examine any particular source will depend on the stage of your research. If you still lack a clear thesis statement, you will not reject many possible references. If you are at an advanced stage in your research, you will know exactly what kind of information you need and can ignore irrelevant references more easily.

As you read, try to evaluate the quality of your source. You can often judge from the tone and style of a reference whether the author is writing a scholarly or a popularized report. Does the author seem biased? Does he or she support the arguments with evidence? Is the book out of date? If you have doubts about the quality of a book, you may want to read reviews of it. (See 55d for a list of book review indexes.)

When you take notes, summarize the information in your own words. (Of course, even summaries must be footnoted in your paper.) Try to avoid lengthy direct quotations. When you do make a direct quotation, put quotation marks around it so that you can properly credit it as a quotation and avoid plagiarism (see 54e). Double-check quotations for accuracy, including spelling and punctuation. If you omit material from a quotation, use ellipses to indicate the point of omission (see 38). Write down the numbers of *all* the pages from which you get information so that these page numbers will be available for your footnotes.

Purpose of Sleep

Webb, pp. 162-63

Webb believes that the problem with viewing sleep as a state that restores our worn-out, diminished energies is less preferable than the adaptive theory because " 'what' is being diminished and, in turn, 'restored' has been so elusive that it has not been specifiable."

Put your own reactions to your reading in square brackets or, even better, in a different color ink so that you can easily distinguish your own ideas and opinions from those of your source. Distinguish opinion from fact in your sources by prefacing statements of opinion with "The author believes that . . ." or "The author concludes that . . . ." A sample note card is reproduced above.

If you find material that contains many facts, figures, important but lengthy quotations, charts, or helpful illustrations, you can have these pages photocopied to ensure accuracy and to save time in copying. Be sure to write the sources on the photocopied pages so that you can identify them later. Do not, however, photocopy everything you find that you think may be relevant. Read the material carefully first, digest it, and then decide whether it is worth photocopying.

Review your notes occasionally as you read to see the direction in which your topic is developing and to determine what additional information you will need. As you read, you will probably get a clearer idea of how your topic can be narrowed and focused. Try to formulate a thesis or several alternative theses and a mental outline of your final paper while you are still reading your outside sources.

Organizing Notes. By the time you have consulted several references, you should be able to put headings on your note cards to indicate subdivisions of your topic. For example, if you were planning a research paper on archaeology in Colorado, headings on your note cards might include "History," "Methodology," "Specific Sites," "Findings," "Current Status." Additional reading will allow you to subdivide these headings further. The heading "Findings," for example, might be divided into "Pottery," "Architecture," "Tools," and so on. These headings and subheadings will be a guide for further research and for the final organization of your paper.

When you feel that you have a fairly clear idea about how you will develop your topic and when you have either exhausted your references or find that all additional references are merely repeating information that you already have, it is time to stop reading and start planning your paper. (When you actually start writing, you may of course discover that you need to do additional reading.)

54c PLANNING AND OUTLINING THE PAPER

Before you have finished taking notes from sources, you should have a clear thesis statement and a rough notion of what the structure of your final research paper will be. Read through all your notes to refresh your memory. Then, with your thesis statement in mind, sort your note cards into piles corresponding to the headings on the cards.

Next, make a rough written outline. You may find that you have some gaps in your sources; if so, plan to return to the library to do more reading. You will almost certainly find that you have some information that does not fit into a reasonable outline. Do not feel that you must force it into the paper; instead, make a discard pile of notes—far better to have taken a few unnecessary notes than to have a good research paper marred by material that is irrelevant. You will also probably discover that a number of your sources contain the same information. Select the best sources and discard the others. As you revise your rough outline, you will be able to narrow your topic further and focus it more sharply.

When your rough outline seems generally satisfactory, you are ready to make a detailed outline. You can use either a topic outline or a sentence outline, according to your own preference or the instructions of your teacher. (See 53a for the preparation of topic and sentence outlines.) The organization of the final outline will depend to a large extent on the topic you have chosen and the approach you plan to take.

54d WRITING THE FIRST DRAFT

Once you are ready to start the actual writing of your research paper, try to write as much as possible at one sitting to ensure continuity in your train of thought and consistency in your style. Most research papers are too long for the writer to complete the first draft in a single session, but you should plan to write each major section without interruption. Whether you compose the first draft in longhand or use a typewriter, leave ample space on each page for later corrections, insertions, and notes to yourself.

In general, the process of writing a research paper is similar to that of writing any other paper. There are, however, some differences in style, and there are greater problems in organization and transitions. Finally, there are conventional ways of handling citations and quotations.

Style. The style of a research paper should be objective, impersonal, and more formal than that of short essays. Research papers are usually written in the third person, although the first person is sometimes acceptable to avoid excessive use of the passive. Even if you are accustomed to using contractions in your shorter, more informal papers, avoid them in a research paper. Slang is definitely out of place, as are emotionalism and gushing, extravagant language. Impersonality of style does not mean, however, that a research paper must be boring. The sample research paper on pages 360–377 is written in an impersonal, objective style, yet is entertaining because the author has selected a topic of universal interest and has captured the reader's attention at the very outset by relating three case histories.

Organization. If you have a good outline to begin with, the overall organization of your research paper should not present a serious problem. Avoiding irrelevancies and repetition may cause greater difficulty because you may be tempted to include every bit of information from your notes. However, if you have previously discarded notes that contained repetitious and unnecessary material, you should have few problems with redundancy and irrelevancy.

As you write each section, be sure it is clearly related to the main idea and to preceding and following sections. Transition from one section to another is more difficult in research papers than in short papers because the greater length of a research paper makes it harder to keep all the parts in mind simultaneously. You will probably find that you need to write some transitional sentences or paragraphs. In the sample paper (page 11 of the research paper), notice how the author uses a question to make the transition from the discussion of the chemistry of sleep to the discussion of the effects of total deprivation of sleep. Most research papers need a separate concluding section or, at the very least, a concluding paragraph.

Presenting the Arguments. Few research papers are so complete or so definitive that there is no room for disagreement with their conclusions. Let the reader know what you are certain of and what you are uncertain of. When you find disagreement among your sources, note this and give both sides of the argument as well as your own opinion. Distinguish clearly between fact and opinion. You can usually indicate your own opinion without having to say directly, "I think that . . ." or "I disagree with . . ."

POOR Peters attributes the interlace design to Celtic influence. I disagree. I think it can just as well be explained by native tradition.

REVISED Although Peters attributes the interlace design to Celtic influence, it can just as well be explained by native tradition.

Handling Source Material. Although one purpose of a research paper is to use outside references, the paper itself should not be simply a patchwork of unrelated facts and quotations from your sources, strung together one after the other. Be sure that there is a good reason for every quotation—a reason other than proving to the reader that you consulted outside sources. Use quotations to fill in and support your own presentation, rather than using your own writing merely to tie the quotations together. When you are quoting or paraphrasing several different sources on one point, do not feel that you must have a separate paragraph for each source. Each source used, however, must have a separate footnote.

Avoid large numbers of long quotations; most source material should be paraphrased or summarized instead of being quoted in full. If a particular sentence or phrase from one of your sources is especially appropriate or well stated, try to work the quotation into the grammar of your own sentence. For example, if you were writing a paper on Mohammedanism, you might have read the following passage:

> Yet amongst the very earliest generations of Muslims, in all parts of the Islamic world, there were many men who brought the spirit of devotion into their daily activities, and to whom Islam was a discipline of the soul and not merely a collection of external rituals. Their creed was a stern ascetic creed, which bade every man go about his work with the fear of eternal punishment ever before his eyes, remembering that this world is but a temporary habitation, and that every gift it has to offer, power, riches, pleasure, learning, the joy of parenthood, is vanity and temptation—not indeed to be rejected or avoided, but to be used with a deep sense of the awful responsibilities which they entail.
> —H. A. R. Gibb, *MOHAMMEDANISM*

Instead of quoting this entire passage verbatim, you could summarize most of it and include a small part of it as a direct quotation.

> For many early Muslims, Islam was a stern religion emphasizing the transitoriness and responsibility of life on earth, a creed "which bade every man go about his work with the fear of eternal punishment ever before his eyes."[6]

Copy out all the quotations you plan to use in full from your first draft on; this allows you to see if the quotations fit smoothly and logically into your text and also helps you keep down the number of overly long quotations. Put an abbreviated reference (author's name and a page number) in your text as you write to ensure that you do not forget to credit your sources. Remember that summaries and paraphrases, as well as direct quotations, require footnotes.

54e   AVOIDING PLAGIARISM

Plagiarism is taking the writings, ideas, or thoughts of others and passing them off as one's own original work. Plagiarism is not restricted to published material: if you submit an old paper written by your roommate, if you buy a paper from a so-called "service," or even if you base a paper on a lecture you heard in a course without acknowledging that lecture, you are still guilty of plagiarism. Plagiarism is not restricted to long quotations; if you quote a sentence or even a memorable phrase without acknowledging it, you are plagiarizing. You can plagiarize without even using the exact words of the original author; if you paraphrase a passage without crediting its author, you are plagiarizing.

Plagiarism is dishonest, stupid, and dangerous. It is dishonest because it involves both stealing (taking the work of someone else) and lying (pretending that it is one's own work). It is stupid because people who plagiarize lose the opportunity to learn for themselves. It is dangerous because it is illegal; penalties for plagiarism range from an F on the individual paper, to an F for the entire course, to probation, to explusion from the college. Even if the immediate penalty is relatively light, the plagiarist has irretrievably lost the respect and trust of his or her instructor.

Although plagiarism is always an offense, not every plagiarist is intentionally cheating. Students sometimes do not know exactly what kind of information must be footnoted and what need not be. Or a student may have been allowed by his or her high-school teachers to use outside sources without acknowledging them and thus may not understand that even material which is clearly obtained from a specific outside source must be credited to that source. Sometimes writers unintentionally plagiarize through carelessness; they do not take notes properly and do not remember when they are quoting and when they are not. Or they may simply forget to footnote a passage or paraphrase that they had intended to acknowledge.

Deliberate plagiarism may result from fear; students may be so terrified of receiving a low grade or may feel that they do not have enough time to complete an assignment satisfactorily that they deliberately plagiarize out of panic. On the other hand, anyone who intentionally plagiarizes out of sheer dishonesty and an attempt to get a higher grade than he or she would otherwise receive deserves whatever penalties may result from the plagiarism.

To avoid plagiarism, follow the rule that *all outside information must be acknowledged.* The only exception to this rule is "common knowledge." That is, you need not footnote (1) information that everyone knows, (2) common proverbs and expressions, (3) information that is given in every source on the subject, and (4) general conclusions that anyone could reach. For example, you need not cite a source for the facts that Columbus discovered America, that "A penny saved is a penny earned," that Franklin Roosevelt died in 1945, or that watching television is a popular American pastime.

What is sufficient acknowledgment and what are the proper uses of source materials? Perhaps some examples will best illustrate proper and improper acknowledgment.

> Most of organized religion opposed McCarthy vigorously. Despite the inroads he made among working people, organized labor never ceased to criticize him. Here and there a college or a school board did something absurd in response to the atmospheric pressures generated by McCarthyism, but by and large American education resisted. Powerful sections of the press were always hostile. The New York *Times,* the New York *Herald Tribune,* the Washington *Post,* the Cowles newspapers, the Knight news-

papers, the Luce publications—all were anti-McCarthy. And so were many influential journalists with readers in all parts of the country: Walter Lippmann, Joseph and Stewart Alsop, Doris Fleeson, Marquis Childs, Drew Pearson, Thomas L. Stokes. And on radio and television there were, in the ranks of his critics, Edward R. Murrow, the late Elmer Davis, Quincy Howe, Martin Agronsky, Edward P. Morgan.   —Richard H. Rovere, SENATOR JOE McCARTHY

This quotation is too long to be included in most papers. There should be no need to quote it in full because the material can easily be paraphrased or condensed. There is little that is especially striking about the language of the original, nor is the original so well known that it would be an injustice to the author to change the wording. If you wanted to include most of the information in a paper of your own, you could paraphrase the passage, using a footnote to acknowledge the source. The paraphrase should, however, be a complete paraphrase, not simply a slight rewording that merely substitutes a few synonyms and changes the order of a few phrases or clauses.

PLAGIARISM

Most of organized religion opposed McCarthy strongly. Although he made inroads among working people, organized labor never stopped criticizing him. Occasionally a college or a school board did something absurd in responses to the atmospheric pressures generated by McCarthyism, but for the most part American education resisted. Powerful sections of the press were always hostile to McCarthy, for example, the New York *Times*, the New York *Herald Tribune*, the Washington *Post*, the Cowles and Knight newspapers, and the Luce publications. Many influential journalists with a national readership were hostile: Walter Lippmann, Joseph and Stewart Alsop, Doris Fleeson, Marquis Childs, Drew Pearson, Thomas L. Stokes. In the ranks of his critics on radio and television were Edward R. Murrow, Elmer Davis, Quincy Howe, Martin Agronsky, and Edward P. Morgan.[4]

Even with a footnote, and even though the wording is not identical to the original, this rewriting would be plagiarism if it were used as a part of the text of a student paper because the implication would be that most of the wording was that of the student author.

ACCEPTABLE PARAPHRASE

Among the institutions that opposed McCarthy were organized religion and organized labor (although McCarthy did have some support from working people). With a few exceptions, educational institutions usually resisted the pressures of McCarthyism. The nation's most influential newspapers, such as the *New York Times*, the *Washington Post*, and the Cowles and Knight newspapers were anti-McCarthy. The Luce publications were anti-McCarthy. Prominent national journalists like Walter Lippmann, the Alsop brothers, and Drew Pearson were anti-McCarthy. Finally, many important radio and television commentators, including, for example, Edward R. Murrow, Elmer Davis, and Quincy Howe, were anti-McCarthy.[4]

The footnote here is still necessary, but the passage has been so thoroughly rewritten that it would not be considered plagiarized.

If you do not need all the details from an original source, you can summarize it. Although the language of the summary below is almost completely different from the original, it still must be footnoted because the information it contains came from an outside source.

ACCEPTABLE SUMMARY

Large segments of the society opposed McCarthy, including organized religion, organized labor, most educational institutions, some of the most influential newspapers and magazines, and many prominent journalists and radio and television commentators.[4]

Sometimes you may wish to use only a single fact or two from a source. Again, a footnote is necessary.

ACCEPTABLE USE OF FACT

Walter Lippmann and Drew Pearson were always hostile to McCarthy.[4]

If you borrow a metaphor, other figure of speech, or any kind of striking language from a source, it should be placed in quotation marks and footnoted.

ACCEPTABLE QUOTATION

Many other institutions, however, were unable to resist the "atmospheric pressures generated by McCarthyism."[4]

The best way to avoid plagiarism or charges of plagiarism is to take careful notes and to religiously acknowledge all your sources. Whenever you have any doubt whatsoever about whether a footnote is required, it is best to err on the generous side and use a footnote.

54f REVISING THE PAPER

In planning a research paper, try to allow enough time so that you can wait at least two or three days between the completion of the first draft and the beginning of revision. If you begin revision immediately after completing the first draft, you will still be so close to that draft that you will tend to lack perspective and will fail to see where revision is necessary.

Revision does not mean that every single sentence must be rewritten and the entire draft recopied. You can usually make the changes for a second draft on the copy of your first draft, although you may need to do some cutting and pasting if paragraphs or sections have to be rearranged. Recopy the entire paper only when the draft becomes so marked up with changes that it is difficult to read.

When reading the first draft for possible revisions, check the larger matters of organization, proportion, clarity, and emphasis first.

When you are satisfied that these larger matters are in order, reread the paper sentence by sentence, following the "Checklist for Revision" in 51j.

After you have made the necessary revisions, compare the new draft of the paper with your topic or sentence outline, making sure that you have not inadvertently omitted any of the important points in the outline. If you have added material, changed focus, or reorganized the paper, make a new outline from the latest draft and check this new outline for logic, organization, and consistency. If you are required to turn in an outline along with your research paper, submit the revised outline, not the earlier version.

54g   THE FINAL DRAFT

Prior to typing or writing the final draft, reread the entire paper carefully. Check all footnotes to be sure they are in numerical order. Make sure that every reference has a corresponding footnote and every footnote a reference number in the text. (See 56a for proper footnote form.) Prepare your bibliography by listing in alphabetical order all the sources you have cited in your footnotes. (See 56b for the proper form for bibliographies.) Check the title of your paper to be sure it is accurate but as brief as possible.

In its final form, the research paper has four parts: (1) title page, (2) outline (if required), (3) text and footnotes, and (4) bibliography.

Title Page.   Follow the directions of your instructor in preparing the title page. If you receive no directions, the format described here will be acceptable. Use a separate sheet of paper for the title page. Center the title itself, either in all capital letters or with capital letters beginning all important words, in the upper half of the sheet. Center your name, in capital and small letters, two or three spaces below the title. On the lower third of the sheet and to the right side, list on separate lines the name and number of the course, the section number, the instructor's name, and the date. The title page is not numbered, nor is it counted in the page numbering of the paper. See page 360 for a sample title page.

Outline.   Do not submit your outline with your paper unless you are told to do so. If the outline is included, it comes immediately after the title page. Type the word *OUTLINE* in all capitals, and center it at the top of the page. Skip three spaces and type the thesis sentence. Skip three more spaces and type the outline, using the format described in 53a. The outline is not counted in the page numbering of the paper, but if the outline is more than one page long, you can number pages after the first page in small Roman numerals. See page 361 for a sample outline.

Text and Footnotes.   Follow the instructions given in 51m for typing or handwriting the text of the research paper. Follow the instructions in 56a for format of footnote reference numbers and footnotes. If you put all your footnotes on separate pages at the end of the paper, continue numbering these pages as if they were part of the text.

Bibliography. Type the word *Bibliography* (or *References* or *List of References* or *References Consulted*) at the top of a separate sheet of paper. Follow the instructions in 56b for the format of the bibliographical entries. Include the bibliography in the numbering of the text. See the sample bibliography on page 377.

Finishing Touches. After the paper has been typed or handwritten, proofread it carefully from title page through bibliography for typographical errors or any other errors that you may have missed in previous readings. Make minor corrections and changes in black ink, using the conventions and symbols given in 51j.

Unless you are instructed to do so by your teacher, do not staple the pages of your research paper. Instead, use a large paper clip so that the reader can easily separate the pages to compare sections or read notes at the end. Again, unless you are instructed to do so, there is no need to invest in fancy covers or binders for your research paper.

Before turning in your research paper, be sure you have a good copy of it for yourself, preferably a photocopy or carbon copy of the final version. Instructors have been known to mislay papers.

SLEEP: THE UNCONQUERED REALM

Carol Andrews

English 101
Mr. Griffin
November 14,1980

OUTLINE

THESIS: Sleep, seemingly one of the simplest of human activities, is
actually a very complex and still poorly understood phenomenon.

I.   Reasons for sleep

        A. Adaptive theory

        B. Restorative theory

II.   Quantity of sleep

        A. Variations in sleep length

        B. Average amounts of sleep

III.   Components of sleep

        A. Non-REM states of sleep

        B. The REM stage of sleep

            1. Memory-consolidation theory

            2. Stress-assimilation theory

            3. Brain-development theory

        C. Chemistry of sleep

            1. The prior-sleep effect

            2. Neurochemicals and sedatives

IV.   Loss of sleep

        A. Loss of all sleep

        B. Loss of selected stages of sleep

V.   The importance of continued research

It is 4 a.m., and for the fourth consecutive night Matthew Schneider, business executive, has been lying in his bed counting sheep, trying frantically for five hours to fall asleep. Matthew, who has become grouchy and moody, has begun to fear that his loss of sleep will drastically affect his on-the-job performance.

Mary Smith, a first-year elementary school teacher, works hard all day with her thirty-two children, and in the evening she plays tennis and swims. Mary, however, never goes to bed until at least 2 a.m., always rising sharply at 6 a.m. She feels healthy and happy, but lately friends have told her that her irreverence for a proper night's sleep is shortening her life and dulling her mind. No matter how hard she tries, though, after four hours of sleep--even on the weekends--Mary simply has to get out of bed.

Mr. and Mrs. Abe Kleitmann are the parents of a lively three-year-old daughter, Jessica, who will not sleep more than five hours at night. Repeatedly told that children must have a lot of sleep, the Kleitmanns are beginning to fear that Jessica is not normal.

These hypothetical cases, typical of those that are flowing into sleep clinics springing up across the country, are like experiences we all have had or like those we have heard others describe. Sleep, in short, affects us all. Most of us give up seven or eight hours a day--roughly a third of our lives--to sleep, and we think very little about it unless it becomes a problem. Sleep is, however, a major problem for about 14 percent of the population, or about one

Carol Andrews   -2-

in seven people.[1] This large block of our population suffers numerous
sleep disorders, but available treatment is handicapped by the riddles
of sleep research, a study that has flourished only in the last twenty
years. Although the sheer abundance of current information conveys
the impression that science is standing on the threshold of discoveries
that would affect millions of lives, sleep research is still a giant
maze of conflicting hypotheses and speculations. Indeed, understanding sleep remains one of man's most challenging frontiers.

There are two central theories that attempt to explain why man
sleeps: the adaptive theory and the restorative theory. The adaptive
theory claims that man's need for sleep results from evolution. Wilse
Webb, one of the foremost sleep researchers, believes that over millions of years each species evolved the sleep pattern that best enabled
it to survive. His hypothesis is simply that "sleep...evolved in each
species as a form of 'nonbehavior' when not responding in the environment would increase survival chances."[2] The differences between the
sleep patterns of various species do not seem to depend on physiological

---

[1] Wilse B. Webb, Sleep: The Gentle Tyrant (Englewood Cliffs, N.J.:
Prentice-Hall, Inc., 1975), pp. 114-15. A slightly more recent statistic
claims that 30 million people in the United States suffer sleep problems
(Wanda Lesley, "Forty Winks Puts Psyche in Gear," The Greenville
[S.C.] News and Greenville Piedmont, 22 January 1978, sec. C, p. 1).
Also, of 1,645 people surveyed in Gainesville, Florida, more than a
third, particularly "blacks, women, poor people, the elderly, and
those who were divorced, widowed, or separated" suffered sleep dis-
orders (Jody Gaylin, "Sleep: Tracking the Elusive Sandman," Social
Science and Medicine, 10; rpt. Psychology Today, 10 [April 1977], 101.

[2] Webb, Sleep: The Gentle Tyrant, pp. 158-59.

processes but reflect the species' needs for safety. Prehistoric
man would have found it safer to sleep, particularly in the dark
nights not lighted up with electric bulbs and neon signs, than to
prowl in harm's way. A lion, which does not fear many other animals,
may sleep soundly sixteen hours a day, but a gazelle, prey for many
beasts, is a short, light sleeper.[3]

The adaptive theory is interesting and convincing in many ways,
but it does not explain adequately why people today with their
twenty-four-hour lighting and sophisticated methods of obtaining
food and fighting off predators have not evolved a sleep pattern of
one or two hours per night. If sleep is not restorative but is
simply an evolutionary result, why does modern man need to sleep at
all? Will our descendants, continuing the evolutionary process,
need less sleep than we?

Ernest Hartmann, on the other hand, believes that "sleep
basically has a restorative function, in accordance with our own
commonsense notions."[4] He believes that sleep consolidates disrup-
tive, stressful events of the day into a person's normal emotional and
learning systems, especially since it is clear that most people do

---

[3]Maggie Scarf, "Oh, For a Decent Night's Sleep!" The New York
Times Magazine, 21 October 1973, p. 86.

[4]Ernest L. Hartmann, The Functions of Sleep (New Haven: Yale
Univ. Press, 1973), p. 145.

Carol Andrews   -4-

require more deep sleep and dream-sleep after stressful experiences or strenuous learning experiences. [5]   Although tests with sleep deprivation bear out some of Hartmann's theories, the hypothesis that sleep is basically restorative is problematic because, as Webb states, " 'what' is being diminished and, in turn, 'restored' has been so elusive that it has not been specifiable."[6]   The only clear observation is that the reasons why we sleep are enormously complex.

A good deal of sleep research has been concerned with pin-pointing the amount of sleep a person needs. Although most young adults seem to need or believe that they need six to eight hours of sleep per night, scientists have found a great variation in the quantity of sleep required by adults. For example, a husband worried about his wife's habitual four-hour-per-night sleeping pattern took her to a sleep clinic, where doctors found her sleep "remarkably efficient" and pronounced her very healthy. Doctors at the same clinic examined a physics professor about fifty years old who was concerned because he believed he needed to sleep at least fourteen hours a night. They found that he was absolutely correct in his assessment: he slept in normal patterns that stretched out

_____

[5]Hartmann, p. 147.

[6]Webb, pp. 162-63.

over fourteen hours. Cutting his sleep by even two hours left him

tired.[7] And, although older people generally do not require as

much sleep as young adults, some astounding cases have been found of

very old people who hardly sleep at all, for example, a seventy-

year-old physically sound woman who sleeps only one hour per night.[8]

The story is also told--though it has not been scientifically veri-

fied--of the artist Salvador Dali's famous method of sleep. Dali

reportedly sits in a chair, holding a spoon over a tin plate that

he has situated beside the chair. He relaxes. As he falls asleep,

the spoon drops from his hand, banging against the tin plate and

waking him. He says that the sleep he gets in the very tiny interval

that passes between the time the spoon falls and the time it strikes

the tin is enough for him.[9]

How much sleep is normal? The amount of time a human being

needs to sleep may well be hereditary, although such factors as pre-

natal care, illness, nutrition, and environment play a role in

determining the necessary quantity of sleep.[10] Even though most

---

[7]Scarf, p. 70.

[8]Wilse B. Webb, "On Sleep: The Long and the Short of It,"
The New York Times, 22 August 1975, p. 31.

[9]William C. Dement, Some Must Watch While Some Must Sleep
(San Francisco: W. H. Freeman & Co., 1974), p. 5.

[10]Webb, Sleep: The Gentle Tyrant, p. 66.

Carol Andrews   -6-

people seem to require about the same amount of sleep (something close to the proverbial eight hours), scientists agree that each person's requirements for sleep are individual. What they do not agree on is whether great variations in the quantity of sleep reflect basic differences in personality and intelligence.

On the basis of two studies in his laboratories, Webb believes that sleep length shows "no more difference in people than big or little ears," that it shows no basic differences in intelligence or personality or physical well-being.[11] Dr. Hartmann maintains, however, that there are basic differences between short and long sleepers. Those who need more sleep tend to be more neurotic and depressed and under greater stress than the shorter sleepers, who seem more vivacious, self-confident, and aggressive. The longer sleepers, though worriers, tend to be more creative, less conventional thinkers than short sleepers. However, Hartmann admits that it is not clear whether the sleep pattern produces the personality or whether the personality requires the particular sleep pattern. He is convinced only that there is a correlation between the quantity of sleep and certain traits.[12]

How we sleep--that is, the individual phases that make up a night's sleep--is one of the few noncontroversial areas of sleep

_____

[11]Webb, "On Sleep," p. 31.

[12]Hartmann, pp. 65-68.

research, but scientists do not know exactly why or when or how a person falls asleep. Even the electroencephalogram (EEG), which is used to chart the brain waves that reveal sleep patterns, cannot show the precise instant when sleep begins.[13] Once it has begun, however, normal sleep is made up of five distinct stages, which recur during the night in cycles of about ninety minutes. The normal sleeper passes fairly quickly through Stage-1 and Stage-2 sleep (light sleep phases differing in the kinds of brain waves) into the transitional Stage-3 sleep and into the intense, deep sleep of Stage 4. From Stage 4, or Deep Sleep as it is often called, the sleeper passes again through Stage-1, Stage-2, and Stage-3 sleep into Stage 4, rarely skipping a stage but changing stages about thirty-five times.[14] After he or she has passed through the sleep stages once, however, this sequence is interrupted regularly--often at the end of Stage 2--by a separate and very puzzling stage called Rapid Eye Movement Sleep, or REM Sleep, so called because it is characterized by bursts of eye movements along with brain waves somewhat like those of Stage-1 sleep. Until this REM sleep was first observed in 1952 by Nathanial Kleitman and Eugene Aserinsky, sleep

---

[13]Dement, p. 27.

[14]Webb, Sleep: The Gentle Tyrant, p. 26.

Carol Andrews   -8-

was thought to be a process from waking to intense, deep sleep and
back to waking. Now, however, it is obvious that sleep is cyclic.[15]
Most people follow this basic sequence of stages, but no two people
sleep in exactly the same pattern.

The discovery of REM sleep revolutionized sleep research. Studying the correlation of REM sleep and dreaming has led to numerous
hypotheses about the significance and function of both REM sleep and
dreaming. Many of the theories that attempt to explain the function
of REM sleep claim that it is a necessary tool for the consolidation
of new material into long-term memory. Dr. Peter Hauri, director of
the Dartmouth Sleep Laboratory at Hanover, New Hampshire, and Boston
researchers Chester Pearlman and Ramon Greenberg are among the
scientists who claim that REM sleep not only aids memory but also
allows the individual to absorb the stressful experiences suffered
during the day.[16]

On the other hand, Webb and William C. Dement, among others, find
that REM sleep does not seem to aid memory at all. Webb finds that
extreme deprivation of REM sleep has little effect on the individual.[17]
Dement, whose first (and now largely disproved) theory about REM

---

[15]Hartmann, p. 23.

[16]See "Sleep for the Memory," Time, 108 (23 August 1976),
39; and Scarf, pp. 81, 84.

[17]Webb, Sleep: The Gentle Tyrant, p. 154

sleep was that it was a psychological stabilizer the loss of which caused emotional disturbances,[18] has recently speculated that "perhaps REM sleep is necessary for the normal pre- and post-natal maturation of the brain" and that its real function is served long before we become adults.[19] In short, the precise function of REM--like so many other questions about sleep--continues to baffle researchers.

One particularly interesting recent discovery with regard to sleep and memory is the Prior-Sleep Effect, a phenomenon that suggests that certain sleep is detrimental to the memory. The Prior-Sleep Effect has shown that up to four hours of sleep just before learning has a detrimental effect on long-term memory. Even as little as one-half hour of sleep just before hitting the books is harmful to a student's memory. If the student sleeps as much as six hours before attempting to study, he or she will be more successful at remembering. Bruce Ekstrand and his co-workers, although convinced that "sleep facilitates memory,"[20] have found that "four hours' sleep prior to learning resulted in more forgetting than no

---

[18]Scarf, p. 81.

[19]Dement, p. 31.

[20]Bruce R. Ekstrand et al., "The Effect of Sleep on Human Long-Term Memory," Neurobiology of Sleep and Memory, ed. René R. Drucker-Colen and James L. McGaugh (New York: Academic Press, 1977), p. 419.

Carol Andrews   -10-

sleep prior to learning."[21]   The Prior-Sleep Effect does not,
however, affect short-term memory. Thus a student may be able to
learn enough information after three hours' sleep to pass a midterm
test, but when final exams roll around in a couple of months, he or
she will have to rememorize the information.

Ekstrand and his team speculated that the Prior-Sleep Effect is
caused by the gradual buildup in the brain of a chemical that blocks
the integration of information from the short-term memory into the
long-term memory. They believed that the chemical subsides when a
person wakes, gradually diminishing to allow the memory to function.[22]
This chemical, a hormone called somatotrophin, has recently been
found to increase in the sleeper's body, beginning within a half-hour
after he or she falls asleep. Though the hormone level diminishes
toward the end of the night, it is high during the first four hours
of sleep.[23]

Somatotrophin, which may account for the Prior-Sleep Effect, is
not the only body chemical that plays an important role in sleep.
The neurochemical sensoronin is now believed to be somewhat responsible both for the onset of sleep and for Stage-4 sleep, and the

_____

[21]Ekstrand et al., p. 431.

[22]Ekstrand et al., p. 435.

[23]Eric Hoddes, "Does Sleep Help You Study?" Psychology Today,
11 (June 1977), 69.

chemical norepinephrine may help to bring about REM sleep. Sleeping pills of all kinds, though they do produce some phases of sleep,
interfere with these chemicals and other brain chemistry, upsetting
regular sleep stages.[24] There is, however, a natural sedative built
into certain foods, a sedative that is compatible with these neuro-
chemicals. This sedative, tryptaphane, is found in milk, eggs, and
meat. Its presence accounts for the sleepiness we often feel after
a big meal or after the glass of warm milk that we may drink to help
us sleep.[25]

But what happens to a person who is deprived of all sleep or
deprived of all REM sleep or all Stage-4 sleep? Experimenters have
found some surprising data about the effects of sleep deprivation.
Though we always feel terrible--and irritable--when we do not get
what we believe to be our proper amount of sleep, a lot of our tired,
grouchy attitudes may result from our own expectations, for

> total wakefulness over a two- or three-day period
> has no known harmful effects. . . . Attention span,
> reaction time, and complex decision making may be
> somewhat impaired, but the major debilitating
> factor is related to worry about not having slept.[26]

---

[24]Scarf, p. 77.

[25]Scarf, p. 72; and "Nature's Sleeping Pill?" Newsweek, 86
(13 October 1975), 69.

[26]Sidney Cohen, "Sleep and Insomnia," Journal of the American
Medical Association (16 August 1976), p. 875.

Carol Andrews   -12-

Early sleep researchers doubtless believed that the loss of sleep was physically harmful because in the first sleep deprivation experiment conducted in 1894 by Marie de Manaceine, puppies deprived of all sleep died after four to six days.[27] Not only do human beings not die when deprived of sleep, but the physiological changes in a sleep-deprived person are few and fairly insignificant, though after five days of sleep loss, emotional changes are noted.[28] A sleep-deprived person can do well at almost any brief laboratory test, although motivation is a crucial problem, and performance on more complicated tasks may be impaired.

> . . . the general conclusion about performance seems
> to be that highly motivated subjects can perform
> almost any task that requires a short-term effort.
> On the other hand, sustained periods of performance
> will typically show deterioration, particularly if
> they are routine or 'dull.' Two major exceptions
> seem to be tasks that require rapid and complex
> reaction time and short-term memory tasks. These
> latter involve such things as listening to a series
> of digits and immediately recalling them.[29]

If we are reasonably efficient when we do not sleep and if our bodies do not suffer serious harm when deprived of sleep, why then do we feel sleepy? Why do we waste a third of our lives sleeping?

---

[27]Dement, p. 5.

[28]Webb, Sleep: The Gentle Tyrant, pp. 123, 133.

[29]Webb, Sleep: The Gentle Tyrant, pp. 126-27.

Dement believes that the time man spends in sleep is "the depressed phase of his circaian rhythm," that is, the cyclic, rhythmic movement that permeates all things--the planets, the tides, the seasons, and all of life.[30] This theory may account for the poorer performance of nonsleep-deprived persons who carry out tasks during periods when they normally would sleep. Outside the laboratory, this decreased efficiency during the individual's normal sleeping time is evidenced in industry's need to provide more intensive quality control and more safety checks for those workers who rotate to the odd-hour shifts.[31]

Understanding how we sleep and why is obviously an enormously complex challenge that cuts across physiological, psychological, and biochemical research. Scientists are turning up more and more questions about the extent to which sleep affects everyone. Can sleep deprivation be used to treat mental disorders?[32] To what degree are physical illnesses responsible for sleep disorders, and vice versa? Do sleep problems cause mental disorders? Sleep research has even entered the realm of the law. In 1961 after a British case in which an American soldier was acquitted of the

---

[30]Dement, pp. 18-19.

[31]Webb, Sleep: The Gentle Tyrant, pp. 47, 134.

[32]S. Bhanji, "Treatment of Depression by Sleep Deprivation," Nursing Times, 73 (14 April 1977), 540-41.

Carol Andrews -14-

murder of his girl friend on the grounds that he was asleep when he killed her, the House of Lords debated whether the verdict in such cases should henceforth be "guilty, but asleep."[33]

To most of humanity sleep seems a simple thing. In 335 B.C. Aristotle wrote, "When they are asleep you cannot tell a good man from a bad one, whence the saying that for half their lives there is no difference between the happy and the miserable."[34] On the one hand, sleep is the great equalizer of men, a common denominator in a world of expanding diversity and complexity. On the other hand, however, even though sleep universally demands our time and respect, we are only beginning to understand--in a way that Aristotle did not--that sleep exacts its due with incredible variety and intricacy among people, a variety and intricacy that make sleep one of the great puzzles of science.

---

[33]Margie Casady, "The Sleepy Murderers," Psychology Today, 9 (January 1976), 83.

[34]Quoted in "Sleep and Dreams: Where Are You When the Lights Go Out?" Harper's, 249 (December 1974), 6.

Carol Andrews -15-

BIBLIOGRAPHY

Bhanji, S. "Treatment of Depression by Sleep Deprivation."
    Nursing Times, 73 (14 April 1977), 540-41.

Casady, Margie. "The Sleepy Murderers." Psychology Today,
    9 (January 1976), 79, 83.

Cohen, Sidney. "Sleep and Insomnia." Journal of the American
    Medical Association, 16 August 1976, pp. 875-76.

Dement, William C. Some Must Watch While Some Must Sleep. San
    Francisco: W. H. Freeman & Co., 1974.

Ekstrand, Bruce R. et al. "The Effect of Sleep on Human Long-Term
    Memory." Neurobiology of Sleep and Memory. Ed. René R.
    Drucker-Colén and James L. McGaugh. New York: Academic Press,
    1977.

Gaylin, Jody. "Sleep: Tracking the Elusive Sandman." Social
    Science and Medicine, 10; rpt. Psychology Today, 10 (April 1977),
    101.

Hartmann, Ernest L. The Functions of Sleep. New Haven: Yale Univ.
    Press, 1973.

Hoddes, Eric. "Does Sleep Help You Study?" Psychology Today,
    11 (June 1977), 69.

Lesley, Wanda. "Forty Winks Puts Psyche in Gear." The Greenville
    [S. C.] News and Greenville Piedmont, 22 January 1978, sec. C,
    p. 1.

"Nature's Sleeping Pill?" Newsweek, 86 (13 October 1975), 69.

Scarf, Maggie. "Oh, For a Decent Night's Sleep!" The New York Times
    Magazine, 21 October 1973, pp. 36-37, 67, 70, 72, 77-78, 81,
    84, 86.

Carol Andrews   -16-

"Sleep and Dreams: Where Are You When the Lights Go Out?" Harper's,
    249 (December 1974), 5-12, 109-13.

"Sleep for the Memory." Time, 108 (23 August 1976), 39.

Webb, Wilse B. "On Sleep: The Long and the Short of It." The New
    York Times, 22 August 1975, p. 31.

_____. Sleep: The Gentle Tyrant. Englewood Cliffs, N.J.: Prentice-
    Hall, Inc., 1975.

Webb, Wilse B., and H. W. Agnew, Jr. Sleep and Dreams. Dubuque, Iowa:
    Wm. C. Brown Co., 1973.

55 THE LIBRARY

Because people have accumulated so much information of so many
different types over the past few thousand years, libraries are necessarily complex. Further, no two libraries are exactly alike in their
holdings, in their physical layout, or in their regulations and procedures. Consequently, people are often frightened by the thought of
using a library. When they finally do venture inside, they sometimes
waste their time wandering aimlessly around because they do not
know how to get the information they want. This fear of the library
is not unreasonable—after all, libraries *are* intimidating places. But
they are really not as confusing as they seem at first glance. There
are standardized procedures for storing and retrieving information
that are common to almost all libraries, and once you have learned
how to use one library, you will know how to use other libraries as
well.

   Familiarize yourself with the library system as soon as possible
after your arrival at college; do not wait until you are forced to use
its resources to write a paper. Many libraries offer guided tours to
acquaint users with the library's layout and procedures. Free maps
of and pamphlets about the library are often available. If you cannot
go on an official tour, take your own informal tour, and locate the

card catalog, the stacks, and the various reading rooms. Ask an attendant about the borrowing rules and the hours during which the circulation desk and the library as a whole are open (they may not be the same). Find out where the reference room and the reference librarian are located. Ask whether there are also branch libraries and, if there are, where they are located.

The library has much to offer you in addition to the books and periodicals you need to write a research paper for an English class. For example, most libraries have quiet reading rooms to which you can escape from a boisterous roommate. If you find your textbook for a course incomplete or confusing, the library will have books on the same subject to supplement your own texts. Many libraries contain such facilities as typing rooms, copying machines, listening rooms for records, and special displays.

Almost every library has a card catalog, usually located on the main floor, and stacks, the area where most of the books are stored. The card catalog consists of rows of filing drawers that contain 3-by-5-inch cards listing all the books owned by the library. Some libraries have open stacks, and users locate their own books; other libraries have closed stacks, and users request books they want by giving the necessary information to an attendant, who then finds the books and delivers them to the user.

The stacks normally contain books that circulate, that is, that can be taken out of the library. In addition, some of the library's holdings have restricted circulation. For example, current periodicals, books placed on reserve by instructors, reference books, special collections, and rare books usually must be read in the library. Libraries normally have special rooms in which to use materials with limited circulation.

Once you have a general idea of the layout of your library, return to the card catalog. The card catalog is the "brain" of the library, and an understanding of it is essential.

55a THE CARD CATALOG

Cards in the **card catalog** may be printed, typewritten, or, occasionally, handwritten. Every card will have a call number, usually at the top left corner of the card. All cards for the same book have the same call number, and this call number also appears on the spine of the book. In the United States, most libraries use one of two major cataloguing systems: the Dewey Decimal System or the Library of Congress System. (Many libraries have changed or are changing from the Dewey Decimal System to the Library of Congress System.) Both systems classify books by their subject matter.

Dewey Decimal System. The **Dewey Decimal System** first classifies works into ten broad categories, each identified by the number in the hundreds position. Further subclassification is indicated by the number in the tens position, then by the units position. Still further subdivisions are indicated by decimals. The ten major classes are as follows.

000–099	General (communication, library science, bibliography, and so on)
100–199	Philosophy and psychology
200–299	Religion and mythology
300–399	Social sciences (economics, education, sociology, government, and so on)
400–499	Language
500–599	Pure sciences (biology, botany, chemistry, mathematics, physics, and so on)
600–699	Technology (agriculture, aviation, engineering, medicine, and so on)
700–799	Fine arts
800–899	Literature
900–999	History (including biography, geography, and travel)

Information about subject classifications under the Dewey Decimal System can be found in *Sears List of Subject Headings*, which most libraries using the Dewey Decimal System will own.

Library of Congress System. The **Library of Congress System** uses a combination of letters and numbers for cataloguing. There are twenty-one major categories.

A	General (reference works, collections of essays, pamphlets, and so on)
B	Philosophy, religion, and psychology
C	Sciences related to history
D	Foreign history and topography
E	American history
F	Local American history
G	Geography, anthropology, sport and games
H	Social sciences
J	Political science
K	Law
L	Education
M	Music
N	Fine arts
P	Language and literature
Q	Science
R	Medicine
S	Agriculture and forestry
T	Engineering and technology
U	Military science
V	Naval science
Z	Bibliography and library science

An additional letter and the numbers after the first letter indicate further subdivisions of the categories. The letters *I, O, W, X,* and *Y* are not used in the Library of Congress System, but some libraries employ these letters to designate books held in special collections. Further information about the Library of Congress Classification System can be found in *Subject Headings Used in Dictionary Catalogs of the Library of Congress.*

When two different libraries both use cards printed by the Library of Congress, the call numbers for the same books will be the same. However, if the library does its own numbering, either by the Dewey Decimal System or the Library of Congress System, numbers may vary slightly from one library to another. This is especially true for older books. Books are occasionally misclassified because they have misleading titles, so the call number of a book is not always a reliable indicator of its contents. Finally, the contents of many books include two or more categories. You should not assume, for example, that every single book with geographical information will have a Library of Congress number beginning with G; it may have been classified as being primarily a book on history and therefore be catalogued under C, D, E, or F.

Author, Title, and Subject Cards.   In most libraries, every book owned by the library will have an **author card,** a **title card,** and one or more **subject cards.** If the book has more than one author or has been translated, edited, or compiled by someone other than the original author, there will also be cards for these other authors, translators, editors, or compilers. The author card is the main card and the other cards are duplicates of it, but with the additional information added at the top of the card. As a means of avoiding confusion between subject cards and title cards, title-card information is usually typed in black and subject-card information is typed in red.

Some libraries have a separate catalog for subject cards, but most libraries put author, title, and subject cards together in one large file. Every card is filed alphabetically according to the first line of written information on the card. That is, an author card is filed by the last name of the author, a title card by the first words of the title of the book, and a subject card by the name of the subject.

Because card catalogs contain so many thousands of cards and because author, title, and subject cards are usually all filed together, locating a specific card can sometimes be a problem if you do not understand the principles of alphabetization used by the library. Libraries vary somewhat in the details of their alphabetization rules, but the following principles are the most common.

1. Articles (*A, The*) at the beginning of a title and the foreign equivalents of articles (French *Le,* German *Der*) are ignored in alphabetizing. Thus, the title card for the book *A History of Greece* will be filed under *History.* The words *von* and *de* as parts of personal names are also ignored if they are written as separate words from the rest of the name but are included if the name is written as one word. Hence, you would look for Karl von Clausewitz under *C,* but for Cornelius Vanderbilt under *V.*

2. *Mc* is treated as if it were spelled *Mac.* Hence, *McIntosh, Angus* would precede *MacIntosh, Charles,* and both would precede *Mack, Laurence.* Other abbreviations are filed as if they were spelled out. For example, *U.N.* and *Dr.* are treated as if they were *United Nations* and *Doctor,* respectively.

3. Identical words have the order of (a) person, (b) place, and (c) title. Thus *Paris, Matthew* would precede *Paris, France,* which in turn would precede the card for the play *Paris Bound.*

4. When one author has many works, the titles of collected works come before the titles of individual works. Several editions of the same work are filed in chronological order. Books about an author follow books by an author.

5. Within a main subject heading, cards are filed alphabetically by author. For example, under the subject heading *Mythology—Greek,* Thomas Bulfinch's *Mythology* would come before Robert Graves' *The Greek Myths.*

6. Within subject headings, historical subdivisions are arranged chronologically.

U.S.—History—Colonial Period
U.S.—History—King William's War, 1689–1697
U.S.—History—King George's War, 1744–1748
U.S.—History—French and Indian War, 1755–1763

7. In most libraries, all alphabetization is word by word or "short words before long words" and hyphenated words are treated as two (or more) separate words. For example, *Con Man* would come before *Concise,* and *Mouth-to-Mouth* would come before *Mouthpiece* but after *Mouth Organ.*

When using the card catalog, read all the information printed on the card. The list of subject cards for the book may reveal that the book does not contain the kind of information you want. The date may tell you that the book is too old for your purposes. The title may reveal that the book is not in English. If the card indicates that the book has a bibliography, you may find it useful in locating other sources of information on the same subject. The author card reproduced below illustrates the different types of information that can be found on a card in the card catalog. Unfortunately, library cards, and especially subject cards, are often incomplete and cannot substitute for an examination of the book itself.

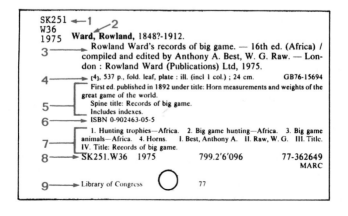

The numbers in the following list correspond to those on the sample card on page 381.

1. The call number of the book according to the Library of Congress System. In many libraries, special symbols or abbreviations below the call number indicate that the book is in a branch library or a special collection. Other symbols may be used to indicate an oversized book that is on special large shelves. If the library has more than one copy of the book, the number of copies owned may be indicated here.

2. The author's name, last name first. The author may be an organization or governmental agency. On many cards, the author's name is followed by the author's date of birth and death (if the author is not alive). On the sample card, the question mark after *1848* indicates that the date of Ward's birth is uncertain.

3. The title of the book and publication facts. The card tells us that the title is *Rowland Ward's Records of Big Game*, that it is the sixteenth edition of this book, that this edition was compiled and edited by Anthony A. Best and W. G. Raw, and that the book was published in London by Rowland Ward Publications Ltd. in 1975. The word *Publications* is in parentheses because, although it is part of the official name of the publisher, it does not appear on the book itself.

4. The collation or physical characteristics of the book. The collation includes such information as the number of pages, maps, illustrations, and the height of the book. If the book is one of a numbered series, the series name and number is listed here. On the sample card, [4] means that there are four preliminary pages; the brackets mean that these pages are not numbered. More typically, preliminary pages are numbered with small Roman numerals. The words *fold. leaf, plate* mean that the book contains a folded page which is a photograph. The entry *ill. (incl. 1 col.)* means that the book has illustrations, one of which is in color. *24 cm.* means that the book is 24 centimeters high (approximately 9½ inches).

The *GB76-15694* at the end of the line is the National Bibliography number of the book in Great Britain. It appears here because the description of the book is taken from the British card. If the book had been published in France, the letters *FR* would precede the numbers; if it had been published in Germany, *GE* would precede, and so on.

5. Notes giving other information about the book. If the book is a reprint, a first edition, or a facsimile, this information is included. The notes also indicate whether the book has an index or a bibliography. The sample card tells us that the first edition had a different title from the current edition, that the title on the spine of the book is slightly different from the official title, and that the book has indexes.

6. The International Standard Book Number. Books published within the past few years will have an ISBN printed in the book. This code number uniquely identifies the book and its publisher. For example, the second series of numbers identifies the publisher; all books published by Holt, Rinehart and Winston will have -03- as the second

series of numbers in the ISBN. The sample book has a very long second series because it is published by a private publisher.

7. The tracings or additional entries under which the same book is catalogued. Arabic numbers list subject cards for the book, and Roman numerals list second authors, sponsoring organizations, translators, the series name if the book is a member of a series, and so on. Roman numerals also indicate whether there is a title card for the book. The sample card lists two title cards, one for the official title and one for the title on the spine of the book.

8. Librarians' information. The first number is the Library of Congress number, the second the Dewey Decimal number. The third number in this row is the order number for librarians to use when ordering additional cards from the Library of Congress.

9. Librarians' information. *Library of Congress* means that the book is in the Library of Congress. *77* means simply that the card was printed in 1977.

If your library has an open-stack system, it is a good idea to practice using the stacks by locating a book whose call number you have identified in the card catalog. When you are looking for books on a specific subject for a research paper, you will of course use the card catalog, but you should also go to the area of the stacks in which books on that subject are shelved. By browsing in the area, you will probably find several useful books on the subject that you previously had not known about.

Occasionally, you will need a book that your library does not own. If you are in a city with public libraries, check them for the book. Or you might ask the reference librarian to order the book for you from another library through the interlibrary loan service. Many libraries have a copy of the *National Union Catalog,* which lists titles of books held in other libraries. Similarly, if you need to read an article in a periodical that is not listed in your library's card catalog, the *Union Lists of Serials in Libraries of the United States and Canada* will tell you which libraries have this periodical. Periodicals normally cannot be borrowed through interlibrary loan, but you usually can obtain photocopies of particular articles through this service. If you plan to use interlibrary loan, be sure to make your request early; it will take a minimum of several days for the material to reach your library.

55b PERIODICAL INDEXES

If you are writing a paper on a current topic, you will want to consult recent magazine articles on the subject. Magazine articles cannot be located in the card catalog because card catalogs list only the titles of periodicals and not the authors and titles of specific articles. Instead, you will need to consult a **periodical index.**

Periodical indexes are listings of articles published in newspapers, magazines, and journals. They appear on a regular schedule, for example, monthly, bimonthly, or annually. Indexes often list articles within only a few weeks after publication. Most indexes are cumulated into larger quarterly, annual, or biannual volumes for easier use.

Periodical indexes are usually organized by subject areas and authors. Within the subject areas, articles are listed alphabetically by title. Entries are heavily abbreviated to save space, so you will probably need to consult the material at the beginning of the index for an explanation of the abbreviations and of the method of organization. When you do not find a subject entry for the particular word you have in mind, try a synonym for that word. For instance, if you were looking for articles on roads and found no entry under "Roads," you should look under "Highways." If you cannot find an entry for a topic on which you are certain there have been recent articles, check other volumes of the periodical index; in fact, you will probably want to look at several volumes anyway to be sure you have located all the articles written over a period of several years.

After you have located the subject area in which you are interested, copy the information for the articles that seem promising. Then go to the card catalog to see if your library has the periodicals. If it does, write down the call number of the periodical, including the number of the volume that you want. Current issues of periodicals are usually shelved by call numbers in a periodicals reading room. Older issues are bound into volumes and shelved in the stacks.

Most libraries restrict the circulation of periodicals. Current issues normally can be used only in the periodicals reading room. Back issues may have a limited circulation, such as one week, or may have to be read in the library.

The best-known periodical index is the *Readers' Guide to Periodical Literature*, which indexes over 150 popular, nontechnical magazines like *Time, Fortune, Saturday Review, The New Yorker,* and *Seventeen*. It appears once in February, July, and August, and twice in the other months. In addition, it is regularly cumulated into large volumes.

Suppose you were writing a paper on federal aid to highway construction in the United States and wanted to read recent articles on the subject. If you checked *Readers' Guide* under "Highways," you might find the following information.

> **HIGHWATER, Jamake**
> In search of Indian America. il Ret Liv 18:21-7
> Ap; 38-41 My; 23-5 Je '78
> Indian peacepaint: canvas of a culture. il Sat R
> 5:30-1 N 25 '78
> PW interviews; ed by S. Crichton. por Pub W
> 214:6-8 N 6 '78
> **HIGHWAY accidents.** See Traffic accidents
> **HIGHWAY patrols.** See Traffic police
> **HIGHWAY safety.** See Traffic safety
> **HIGHWAY safety laws.** See Traffic regulations
> → **HIGHWAY Trust Fund.** See Express highways—
> Federal aid
> → **HIGHWAYS.** See Express highways; Roads
> **HIGLEY, Brewster, 7th**
> He made the prairie sing. South Liv 13:61
> Je '78 •

You would then turn to "Express highways," and find the following information.

EXPRESS highways
America's highways: going to pot. W. Frailey.
il U.S. News 85:36-8 Jl 24 '78
Our crumbling interstates: a national dilemma.
E. D. Fales, Jr. il Pop Mech 150:66-9+ Jl '78

Environmental aspects

Expressway interrupts. D. Thomas. Macleans
91:25 N 27 '78
How to fight a freeway—and win! M. A. Rock.
il por Nat Parks & Con Mag 52:12-16 Ag '78
PRP representative helps preserve park; Interstate 40. E. M. Leeper. BioScience 28:610 S
'78

Federal aid

Federal Highway Trust Fund. D. Allen. Sierra
63:12 F '78
Ploughing the highways: truckers blitz the
interstate; Highway Trust Fund. R. Sherrill.
Nation 226:498-502 Ap 29 '78
R.I.P.: Highway Trust Fund. Forbes 121:34 Ja
23 '78

Because you are not interested in environmental aspects of highways,
you restrict your search to the articles listed under "Federal aid."
When you consult the list of abbreviations at the beginning of this
issue of *Readers' Guide,* you find that the first entry means that D.
Allen is the author of an article entitled "Federal Highway Trust
Fund," which appeared in *Sierra,* Volume 63, page 12 of the February,
1978 issue.

If you had previously found a reference to an article by D. Allen
on the subject of highways, you could have looked in *Readers' Guide*
under "Allen" and have found the same information as above, but
with the author's full name.

ALLEN, Bonnie
Advertising for the small business: when, where
and how much? il Black Enterprise 8:25-7+
My '78
Even cowgirls get the black-and-blues. Essence
9:14+ Ja '79
Face to face. il por Essence 9:30-2 D '78
Movies/theater (title varies) Essence 9:19+ N;
43-4+ D '78; 27 Ja '79
Music makers. il por Essence 9:28+ Ag; 35 N
'78
Spotlight on Starletta Dupois. por Essence 9:36
N '78
Spotlight on the International Afrikan-Amer-
ican Ballet Company. Essence 9:12 S '78
ALLEN, Casey
(ed) See Szarkowski, J. Photography people
ALLEN, Charles, Jr
Hollywood's Wall Street connection. L. K.
Truscott, 4th. il pors N Y Times Mag p 18-22+
F 26 '78 •
More unpleasant encounters. il Time 111:64 Mr 6
'78 •
→ ALLEN, David
Federal Highway Trust Fund. Sierra 63:12 F '78
ALLEN, David F. and Allen, V. S.
What's so bad about a low I.Q.? pors Chr To-
day 22:24-6 F 10 '78
ALLEN, Debbie
Debbie Allen swings on a star. M. St John. il
pors Encore 7:26-9 O 2 '78 •

At the beginning of the issue, *Readers' Guide* lists all the periodicals indexed, including cost of subscriptions and publishers' addresses. The entry for *Sierra* appears as follows.

res

*Seventeen—$10.50. m Seventeen, Radnor, Pa. 19088

⟶ **Sierra; the Sierra Club Bulletin**—$8. bi-m Sierra Club Bulletin, Box 7959, Rincon Annex, San Francisco, Calif. 94120

Skeptic. See Politics Today

Readers' Guide also indexes current book reviews at the end of each issue, after the main author and subject index. This book review index is alphabetized by the last name of the author of the book being reviewed; the last item in the entry is the name of the reviewer.

> Bataille, G. Story of the eye; tr. by J. Neugroschel
> N Y Times Bk R 83:13 F 12 '78. P. Brooks
> Newsweek 91:88+ Mr 27 '78. P. S. Prescott
> Batchelor, D. Ferrari: the Gran turismo and competition Berlinettas
> Road & Track 30:25 S '78. D. Simanait
> Bate, W. J. Samuel Johnson
> Am Schol 47:277-81 Spr '78. D. Greene
> America 138:215-16 Mr 18 '78. G. Cronin, jr
> N Y Times Bk R 83:3+ F 26 '78. R. Locke
> Nat R 30:102-3 Ja 20 '78. M. J. Sobran, jr
> Progressive 42:57-8 Ap '78. W. McCann

Useful as *Readers' Guide* is, it indexes only popular articles. Because these are usually not written by experts in the field, you will often want to consult more specialized indexes. (Many of these more specialized indexes are listed by categories at the end of this chapter.) The general format and the abbreviations used by most specialized indexes are similar to those of *Readers' Guide.* Suppose, for example, that you were writing a paper for an art history course on the architecture of Corinth, Greece. You would find no entry for this in *Readers' Guide,* but if you consulted *Art Index,* you might find the following article by H. S. Robinson about the temple of Apollo Pythios in Corinth.

> **CORINTH, Greece**
> **Antiquities**
> Archaeology in Greece, 1975-76; Corinthia and Argolis. Corinth. H. W. Catling. il plan Archaeol Rep no22:5-10 '75-76
> Attic red figure of the late 5th and 4th centuries from Corinth. I. D. McPhee. bibl f il Hesperia 45:380-96 O '76
> Corinth, 1975: forum southwest [with catalogs] C. K. Williams, 2d; J. E. Fisher. bibl f il plans diags Hesperia 45:99-162 Ap '76
> Corinth 1976: forum southwest [with catalog] C. K. Williams, 2d. bibl f il plans diags Hesperia 46:40-81 Ja '77
> Corinthian inscription recording honors at Elis for Corinthian judges. N. Robertson. bibl f il Hesperia 45:253-66 Jl '76
> Excavations at Corinth: Temple hill. 1968-1972. H. S. Robinson. bibl f il plans diags Hesperia 45:203-39 Jl '76
>
> **Temple of Apollo Pythios**
> ⟶ Excavations at Corinth: Temple hill. 1968-1972. H. S. Robinson. bibl f il plans diags Hesperia 45:203-39 Jl '76

This entry tells you that the title of the article is "Excavations at Corinth: Temple Hill, 1968–1972." It appeared on pages 203 through 239 of *Hesperia* in the July 1976 issue. The entry also tells you that the article has bibliographical footnotes (which will list other sources of information), illustrations, plans, and diagrams.

55c SPECIAL RESOURCES

Because of lack of space for storing printed materials, today's libraries are relying more and more on microfilm and microfiche. Especially for older works, printed copies are often not available, so if the library is to contain these works at all, they must be on film. Each library has its own procedures for the use of materials stored on microfilm and microfiche. If you need to use these materials, ask an attendant to explain the procedure to you.

Most libraries also have special ways of classifying and storing government documents. Again, if you need access to government documents, check with a librarian.

55d REFERENCE BOOKS

The reference room of the library is a good starting point for a library paper, particularly if you know little about your subject when you begin your research. Most reference books do not circulate, so plan to use reference works in the reference room.

Listed below are a number of general and specialized reference works. The list is not complete because there are so many reference works available, and new ones are being published every year. To save space, no publishers are listed. Dates of publication have been omitted because many of these sources are revised regularly, and it is assumed that you will consult the latest edition available in your library. (Occasionally, you may wish to use earlier editions for special purposes. For example, the *Encyclopaedia Britannica* is now in its fifteenth edition, but scholars still consult the eleventh edition now and then because of the thoroughness and high quality of its articles on many subjects.)

All of the sources below are in English. Libraries usually have many reference works in languages other than English, and if you read a foreign language, you can also consult works in that language. Even if you do not read the language, you may find illustrations or tables helpful. For example, the seven-volume Italian *Enciclopedia dell'arte antica, classica e orientale* has very good illustrations.

GENERAL REFERENCES

Guides to Library Use and Research
Barton, Mary N. and Marion V. Bell. *Reference Books: A Brief Guide.*

Downs, Robert B. *How to Do Library Research.*

Gates, Jean Key. *Guide to the Use of Books and Libraries.*

Sheehy, Eugene P. *Guide to Reference Books*. (Earlier editions are by Constance Winchell.)

Periodical and Newspaper Indexes

Annual Bibliography of the Modern Humanities Research Association, 1924–.

Humanities Index, 1974–.

International Index to Periodicals, 1907–74. Replaced by *Humanities Index* and *Social Sciences Index* after 1974.

The New York Times Index, 1913–.

Poole's Index to Periodical Literature, 1802–1906. Replaced by *Readers' Guide to Periodical Literature*.

Readers' Guide to Periodical Literature, 1900–.

Ulrich's International Periodicals Directory, 1932–.

Note: There are also highly specialized indexes for many fields. Examples include *Cumulative Index of Mining Publications of the Society of Mining Engineers of the American Institute of Mining, Metallurgical, and Petroleum Engineers* and *Index to Learned Chinese Periodicals*. Your reference librarian can tell you whether such an index exists for the particular field in which you are interested.

General Encyclopedias

Chambers's Encyclopaedia. 15 vols. and supps. (British)

Collier's Encyclopedia. 24 vols.

Encyclopedia Americana. 30 vols.

New Encyclopaedia Britannica. 30 vols.

New International Encyclopedia. 23 vols. and supps.

Note: *Americana, Britannica, Chambers's,* and *Collier's* also publish yearbooks annually.

General Catalogs and Bibliographies

The Bibliographic Index: A Cumulative Bibliography of Bibliographies, 1937–.

Cumulative Book Index, 1928/32–.

The National Union Catalog. (All books known to exist in U.S. libraries. It includes titles of motion pictures, recordings, and film strips.)

The Publishers' Trade List Annual. Published by the same organization are (1) *Books in Print*, 1948–, (2) *Forthcoming Books*, (3) *Paperbound Books in Print*, 1955–, (4) *Subject Guide to Books in Print*, 1957–.

A World Bibliography of Bibliographies.

General Yearbooks and Almanacs

Facts on File, 1940–.

Information Please Almanac, Atlas and Yearbook, 1947–.

The New York Times Encyclopedic Almanac, 1970–72. Replaced by *Official Associated Press Almanac*, 1973–.

Statesman's Year-book, 1864–.

Statistical Abstract of the United States, 1878–.

World Almanac and Book of Facts, 1868–.

Atlases and Gazetteers

Encyclopaedia Britannica World Atlas.

Goode, John P. *Goode's World Atlas.*

National Geographic Atlas of the World.

Webster's New Geographical Dictionary.

Pamphlets and Other Media

Boyd, Anne M. *United States Government Publications.*

Limbacher's Reference Guide to Audiovisual Information.

Schmeckebier, Laurence F. and Roy B. Eastin. *Government Publications and Their Use.*

United Nations Documents Index, 1950–.

Book Review Indexes

Book Review Digest, 1905–.

Book Review Index, 1965–.

An Index to Book Reviews in the Humanities, 1960–.

Technical Book Review Index, 1917–29; 1935–40.

Dictionaries of Quotations

Bartlett, John and Emily M. Beck, eds. *Familiar Quotations.*

Bohle, Bruce, comp. *The Home Book of American Quotations.*

The Oxford Dictionary of Quotations.

Dictionaries of Usage, Dialect, Etc.

Bryant, Margaret M., ed. *Current American Usage.*

Craigie, Sir William A. and James R. Hulbert, eds. *A Dictionary of American English on Historical Principles.* 4 vols.

Evans, Bergen and Cornelia Evans. *A Dictionary of Contemporary American Usage.*

Major, Clarence. *Dictionary of Afro-American Slang.*

Mathews, Mitford M. *Dictionary of Americanisms.*

Partridge, Eric. *Dictionary of Slang and Unconventional English.*

Note: There are scores of specialized dictionaries in various fields. Examples include *A Dictionary of Chivalry, The Dictionary of Costume,* and *A Dictionary of Entomology.* To find out whether there is a specialized dictionary in a particular field in which you are interested, scan the card catalog under "Dictionary," check the subject index for that field, or ask your reference librarian.

Biography

Biography Index: A Cumulative Index to Biographical Material in Books and Magazines, 1946/47–.

Current Biography Yearbook, 1940–.

International Who's Who, 1935–. (Living people)

The McGraw-Hill Encyclopedia of World Biography.

Webster's Biographical Dictionary.

Who's Who, 1849–. (Primarily living British citizens)

Who's Who in America, 1899–. (Living citizens of the United States. There are also regional editions of *Who's Who*.)

Who's Who of American Women, 1958–.

HUMANITIES

Classics, Folklore, and Mythology

Gray, Louis H. et al., eds. *The Mythology of All Races*. 13 vols.

Hammond, N. G. L. and H. H. Scullard, eds. *Oxford Classical Dictionary*.

Harvey, Paul, ed. *Oxford Companion to Classical Literature*.

Sandys, John E., ed. *A Companion to Latin Studies*.

Sykes, Egerton. *Everyman's Dictionary of Non-Classical Mythology*.

Whibley, Leonard, ed. *Companion to Greek Studies*.

English and American Literature

Abstracts of English Studies.

Baugh, Albert C. et al., eds. *A Literary History of England*.

Bond, Donald F. *A Reference Guide to English Studies*.

Cambridge History of American Literature.

Fiction Catalog, 1908–.

Granger, Edith. *Granger's Index to Poetry*.

Hart, James D. *The Oxford Companion to American Literature*.

Harvey, Sir Paul, ed. *The Oxford Companion to English Literature*.

Modern Humanities Research Association. *Annual Bibliography of English Language and Literature*, 1920–.

MLA International Bibliography, 1921–.

New Cambridge Bibliography of English Literature, 1969–.

Short Story Index.

Spiller, Robert E. et al., eds. *Literary History of the United States*. 2 vols.

Ward, A. W. and A. R. Waller, eds. *The Cambridge History of English Literature*. 15 vols.

Wilson, Frank P. and Bonamy Dobrée, eds. *The Oxford History of English Literature*. 12 vols.

World Literature—General

Buchanan-Brown, J., ed. *Cassell's Encyclopaedia of World Literature*. 3 vols.

Fleischmann, Wolfgang B., ed. *Encyclopedia of World Literature in the 20th Century*. 3 vols.

Kunitz, Stanley J. and Vineta Colby. *European Authors, 1000–1900*.

Magill, Frank N. et al., eds. *Cyclopedia of World Authors*. 3 vols.

MLA International Bibliography, 1921–.

Yearbook of Comparative and General Literature, 1949–.

The Year's Work in Modern Language Studies, 1929/30–.

Philosophy

Copleston, Frederick C. *A History of Philosophy*. 9 vols.

Edwards, Paul, ed. *The Encyclopedia of Philosophy*. 8 vols.

The Great Ideas: A Syntopticon (vols. 2 and 3 of *Great Books of the Western World*).

The Philosopher's Index, 1967–.

Religion

The Cambridge History of the Bible. 3 vols.

The Catholic Periodical and Literature Index, 1930/33–.

Cross, Frank L. *The Oxford Dictionary of the Christian Church.*

Encyclopaedia of Islam. (In progress)

Hastings, James, ed. *Encyclopaedia of Religion and Ethics.* 13 vols in 7.

Index to Jewish Periodicals, 1963–.

Index to Religious Periodical Literature, 1952–.

Jackson, Samuel M. et al., eds. *The New Schaff-Herzog Encyclopedia of Religious Knowledge.* 13 vols.

Landman, Isaac et al., eds. *The Universal Jewish Encyclopedia.* 10 vols.

New Catholic Encyclopedia. 16 vols.

Sacred Books of the East. 50 vols.

SOCIAL SCIENCES

Social Sciences—General

Clarke, Jack A. *Research Materials in the Social Sciences.*

Hoselitz, Berthold F., ed. *A Reader's Guide to the Social Sciences.*

Mason, John B. *Research Resources: Annotated Guide to the Social Sciences,* 1968–71.

Seligman, Edwin R. A. and Alvin Johnson, eds. *Encyclopaedia of the Social Sciences.*

Sills, David L., ed. *International Encyclopedia of the Social Sciences.* 17 vols.

Social Sciences and Humanities Index, 1907–74.

The Social Sciences Index, 1974–.

White, Carl M. et al. *Sources of Information in the Social Sciences: A Guide to the Literature.*

Anthropology, Sociology, and Psychology

Biennial Review of Anthropology, 1959–.

Goldenson, Robert M. *The Encylopedia of Human Behavior: Psychology, Psychiatry, and Mental Health.* 2 vols.

Harriman, Philip L., ed. *Encyclopedia of Psychology.*

The Harvard List of Books in Psychology.

International Bibliography of Social and Cultural Anthropology, 1955–.

International Bibliography of Sociology, 1951–.

Social Work Year Book, 1929–60. Replaced by *Encyclopedia of Social Work*, 1965–.

Warren, Howard C. *Dictionary of Psychology.*

Economics, Business, and Political Science

Bulletin of the Public Affairs Information Service, 1915–.

Coman, Edwin T., Jr. *Sources of Business Information.*

Graham, Irvin. *Encyclopedia of Advertising*.

Greenwald, Douglas et al. *The McGraw-Hill Dictionary of Modern Economics*.

International Bibliography of Economics, 1952–.

International Bibliography of Political Science, 1953–.

Munn, Glenn G. *Encyclopedia of Banking and Finance*.

Plano, Jack C. and Milton Greenberg. *The American Political Dictionary*.

Universal Reference System. *Political Science, Government, & Public Policy Series*, 1965–69.

Education

Complete Guide and Index to ERIC Reports thru December 1969.

Deighton, Lee C., ed. *Encyclopedia of Education*. 10 vols.

Ebel, Robert L. et al. *Encyclopedia of Educational Research*.

Education Index, 1929–.

Good, Carter V., ed. *Dictionary of Education*.

International Yearbook of Education, 1948–.

History

Beers, Henry P. *Bibliographies in American History: Guide to Materials for Research*.

Bury, John B. et al., eds. *The Cambridge Ancient History*. 12 vols. (In progress)

Gwatkin, Henry M. et al., eds. *The Cambridge Medieval History*.

Howe, George F. et al., eds. *Guide to Historical Literature*.

International Bibliography of Historical Sciences, 1926–.

Johnson, Thomas H. *The Oxford Companion to American History*.

Lossung, B. J., ed. *Harper's Encyclopedia of United States History from 458 A.D. to 1912*. 10 vols.

The New Cambridge Modern History. 14 vols.

Poulton, Helen J. *The Historian's Handbook: A Descriptive Guide to Reference Works*.

U.S. Library of Congress. *A Guide to the Study of the United States of America: Representative Books Reflecting the Development of American Life and Thought*.

SCIENCE AND MATHEMATICS

Science—General

American Men and Women of Science, 1906–.

Applied Science and Technology Index, 1958–. This replaces *Industrial Arts Index*, 1913–57.

Jenkins, Frances B. *Science Reference Sources*.

McGraw-Hill Encyclopedia of Science and Technology. 15 vols. and supps.

Newman, James R. et al. *Harper Encyclopedia of Science*. 4 vols.

Science Books and Films, 1975–.

Agriculture, Biology, and Medicine

Bibliography of Agriculture, 1942–.

Biological Abstracts, 1926–. Replaces *Botanical Abstracts*, 1918–27 and *Abstracts of Bacteriology*, 1917–26.

Excerpta Medica, 1947–.

Gray, Peter, ed. *The Encyclopedia of the Biological Sciences.*

Kerker, Ann E. and Henry T. Murphy. *Biological and Biomedical Resource Literature.*

Quartlerly Cumulative Index Medicus, 1927–1956. Replaces *Index Medicus*, 1879–1926.

Smith, Roger C. and W. Malcolm Reid, eds. *Guide to the Literature of the Life Sciences.*

Astronomy and Space

Astronomy and Astrophysics Abstracts, 1969–.

Gentle, Ernest J. et al., eds. *Aviation and Space Dictionary.*

The McGraw-Hill Encyclopedia of Space.

The Space Encyclopedia: A Guide to Astronomy and Space Research.

Chemistry and Geology

Crane, Evan J. et al. *A Guide to the Literature of Chemistry.*

Encyclopedia of Chemical Technology. 22 vols.

Handbook of Chemistry and Physics.

Larousse Encyclopedia of the Earth.

Thorpe, J. I. and M. A. Whitely. *Thorpe's Dictionary of Applied Chemistry.* 12 vols.

U.S. Geological Survey, *Bibliography of North American Geology*, 1732–.

Physics, Engineering, and Mathematics

Besançon, Robert M., ed. *Encyclopedia of Physics.*

Encyclopaedic Dictionary of Physics. 9 vols. and supps.

Michels, Walter C., ed. *The International Dictionary of Physics and Electronics.*

Parke, Nathan G. *Guide to the Literature of Mathematics and Physics Including Related Works on Engineering Science.*

Universal Encyclopedia of Mathematics.

Whitford, Robert H. *Physics Literature: A Reference Manual.*

FINE ARTS

Art and Architecture

American Art Directory, 1898–.

Art Index, 1929–.

Chamberlin, Mary W. *Guide to Art Reference Books.*

Fielding, Mantle. *Dictionary of American Painters, Sculptors, and Engravers.*

Fletcher, Sir Banister F. *A History of Architecture on the Comparative Method.*

Focal Encyclopedia of Photography. 2 vols.

Harris, John and Jill Lever. *Illustrated Glossary of Architecture, 850–1830.*

Myers, Bernard S., ed. *Encyclopedia of Painting.*

Osborne, Harold. *The Oxford Companion to Art.*

Drama, Film, Dance, and Television

Baker, Blanch. *Theatre and Allied Arts: A Guide to Books Dealing with the History, Criticism, and Technic of the Drama and Theatre, and Related Arts and Crafts.*

Bawden, Liz-Anne, ed. *The Oxford Companion to Film.*

Beaumont, Cyril W., comp. *A Bibliography of Dancing.*

Chujoy, Anatole and P. W. Manchester, eds. *The Dance Encyclopedia.*

Dramatic Index, 1909–1949. Continued in *Bulletin of Bibliography & Magazine Notes,* 1950–.

Fidell, Estelle A. and D. M. Peake, eds. *Play Index,* 1949–67.

Firkins, Ina Ten Eyck, comp. *Index to Plays, 1800–1926.* Supp. to 1934.

The Focal Encyclopedia of Film & Television Techniques.

Hartnoll, Phyllis, ed. *The Oxford Companion to the Theatre.*

Music

Apel, Willi. *Harvard Dictionary of Music.*

Duckles, Vincent H. *Music Reference and Research Materials: An Annotated Bibliography.*

Ewen, David. *Encyclopedia of the Opera.*

Feather, Leonard G. *Encyclopedia of Jazz.*

Grove, Sir George. *Grove's Dictionary of Music and Musicians.* 10 vols.

Scholes, Percy A. *The Oxford Companion to Music.*

Sears, Minnie E. *Song Index.*

Thompson, Oscar, ed. *The International Cyclopedia of Music and Musicians.*

Watanabe, Ruth. *Introduction to Music Research.*

Westrup, J. A. et al., eds. *The New Oxford History of Music.* 10 vols.

Who's Who in Music and Musicians' International Directory, 1969–.

56 DOCUMENTATION

Documentation is the written acknowledgment of the sources of information used in the preparation of a paper. These are usually written sources but may also include oral sources such as recordings, interviews, or television programs. Careful, complete, and accurate documentation is essential to avoid taking the ideas and words of others and representing them as one's own. Documentation also shows the reader that you have investigated the topic thoroughly, allows the reader to evaluate your sources of information, and, indirectly, reveals your own original contribution to the topic.

56a FOOTNOTES

Footnotes are used for four purposes: (1) to cite sources of information, (2) to provide additional information or comments not suitable for inclusion in the text, (3) to direct the attention of the reader to other opinions, and (4) to refer the reader to other pages or sections of the text. Most students have occasion to use only the first two types of footnotes, source (or reference) notes, and, less often, comment (or substantive) notes.

When to Use Footnotes.   Comment or substantive notes are used when the writer wishes to add information not directly relevant to the text. This information may be further amplification, additional examples, or simply a digressive comment. Substantive notes should be used sparingly; if the information is important enough to be included at all, it probably should be incorporated into the text.

Reference notes should be used whenever information is borrowed from another source. All direct quotations must, of course, be acknowledged with a footnote, but indirect quotations, paraphrases, and summaries must also be footnoted. Even if you take only an isolated fact or a general idea from a source, that source must be documented. (See 54e, "Avoiding Plagiarism.") Whenever you quote directly from another source, even if it is only a few words, the quoted material should be enclosed in quotation marks. See 38 for the use of ellipses in omitting material from direct quotations; see 32 for the use of brackets to incorporate your own explanations into direct quotations.

Where to Put Footnotes.   All footnotes should be numbered consecutively throughout a paper, beginning with the number 1. Within the text of the paper, the footnote reference is a raised number placed at the *end* of the relevant words or sentence (or at the end of the quotation if you are quoting directly). Footnote reference numbers come after all punctuation except dashes. See footnotes 1, 2, 18, and 20 of the sample research paper (pp. 360–377) for illustrations of placement of footnotes.

The footnote itself should include the author's full name, the title of the publication, the facts of publication, and the relevant page number or numbers. Do not, however, repeat information already provided in the text of the paper. For example, if you give the author's full name in the text, it need not be repeated in the footnote.

Each footnote may be placed at the bottom of the page on which its reference number appears, or all notes may be put on one page at the end of the text. (Strictly speaking, notes that appear at the end are endnotes and not footnotes, but the term *footnote* is used to refer to both kinds of notes.) Either system has its advantages and disadvantages. Placing all the notes together at the end is easier for the typist but harder for readers, who must constantly shuffle pages if they want to consult the notes. Placing the notes at the bottom of the pages of text is easier for readers but presents spacing problems for

res

the typist. Check with your instructor to find out which method of placement he or she prefers.

If you do place your footnotes at the bottom of the page, they should be separated from the text by a double space, then a one-inch line (use the underscore key), then another double space. Each footnote should appear on the same page as its reference number, but the last footnote on a page may be continued on the following page if necessary. See the sample research paper on pages 360–377 for an illustration of pages with footnotes at the bottom.

The first line of each footnote is indented five spaces. The footnote number is raised slightly (like the footnote reference number). Do not space between the footnote number and the first word of the footnote. Footnotes are single-spaced, with a double space between footnotes.

Form of Footnotes. Different disciplines have slightly different conventions for the format of footnotes and bibliographies. For example, some sciences combine footnotes and bibliography into one numbered list and use only numbers in parentheses within the text to refer to the reference list at the end of the text. The format presented here usually follows that of the *MLA Handbook,* a guide widely used by writers in the humanities, though it differs from the *MLA Handbook* in a few details. Follow the directions for documentation given by your instructor; if you receive no specific directions, the rules presented here will be acceptable. Completeness, clarity, and consistency are more important than specific details of format.

Books. Always use the title page of a book as your source of footnote information because the information on book covers is often incomplete. If the date of publication is not on the title page, it can usually be found on the back of the title page. If the information on the title page is incomplete, you can often find it on the library card for the book, where the missing information will be enclosed in square brackets.

The basic information that every footnote reference to a book should include and the order in which it should appear are as follows:

1. **Author's Name.** The author's name is listed, first name first. The name is followed by a comma. If there are multiple authors, their names appear in the order in which they are listed on the title page, regardless of whether they are in alphabetical order. Degrees, titles, or affiliations that appear with the author's name on the title page are omitted in footnotes and bibliographies. Note that groups and organizations, as well as individuals, may be authors.

2. **Title of the Book.** The first word and all important words of the title are capitalized. The entire title is underlined. No punctuation follows the title if it is followed by parentheses. If the book has a subtitle, it is separated from the main title by a colon. Long subtitles may be omitted from footnotes but should be included in the bibliography. Short subtitles or subtitles that clarify the meaning of a vague main title should be included in both footnotes and bibliographies.

3. **Facts of Publication.** Facts of publication are in parentheses. The city of publication is followed by a colon, then the name of the publisher, a comma, and the year of publication. If the publisher's name has been changed since the publication of the book, use the name as it appears in the book, not the current form of the name. Some writers prefer to shorten the name of the publisher (for example, Scott, Foresman instead of Scott, Foresman and Company). But it is not wrong to include the full name and, by doing so, you avoid having to decide what an appropriate shortened form would be. Full forms of publishers' names are given in the examples presented here. If the city of publication is not a familiar large city or if it could be confused with another city of the same name, add the name of the state or country of publication (for example, Hillsdale, N.J.). The date of publication should be that of the latest edition, not that of the latest printing of the book.

4. **Relevant Page Numbers.** The word *page* is abbreviated as *p.* (*pp.* for *pages*), and the page numbers are followed by a period. For inclusive page numbers up through 99, write both numbers in full (for example, pp. 27–29). For numbers over 99, only the last two digits need be given if the preceding digits are the same in the two numbers. (For example, to indicate page 324 through page 359, write pp. 324–59, but to indicate page 324 through page 417, write pp. 324–417.)

The footnotes reproduced here provide models for documenting nearly any kind of reference that students are likely to encounter in preparing a research paper. If your teacher prefers a different format, follow his or her instructions.

1. Single Author

[1]Richard Foster Jones, The Triumph of the English Language (Stanford: Stanford Univ. Press, 1953), p. 94.

2. Corporate Author

[2]Inter-Territorial Language Committee of the East African Dependencies, A Standard Swahili-English Dictionary (Oxford: Oxford Univ. Press, 1939), pp. 408–09.

3. Two Authors

[3]Alexander Fol and Ivan Marazov, Thrace and the Thracians (New York: St. Martin's Press, 1977), p. 40.

4. Three Authors

[4]Charles T. Brusaw, Gerald J. Alred, and Walter E. Olin, Handbook of Technical Writing (New York: St. Martin's Press, 1976), pp. 206–16.

5. More Than Three Authors

[5]Merrill E. Shanks et al., Pre-Calculus Mathematics (Menlo Park, Calif.: Addison-Wesley Publishing Company, 1976), p. 338.

6. Books with a Translator

[6]Conrad Ferdinand Meyer, <u>The Saint</u>, trans. W. F. Twaddell (Providence, R.I.: Brown Univ. Press, 1977), pp. 63–64.

7. Books with an Editor

[7]David Hume, <u>Dialogues Concerning Natural Religion</u>, ed. Henry D. Aiken (New York: Hafner Publishing Company, 1951), p. 58.

8. Collections by One Author

[8]Randolph Quirk, "Langland's Use of <u>kind wit and inwit</u>," in <u>Essays on the English Language: Medieval and Modern</u> (Bloomington, Ind.: Indiana Univ. Press, 1968), pp. 20–26.

9. Collections by More Than One Author

[9]Dun Li, "The Taiping Rebellion," <u>in China Yesterday and Today</u>, ed. Molly Joel Coye and Jon Livingston (New York: Bantam Books, Inc., 1975), p. 189.

10. Books in Several Volumes

[10]Daniel N. Osherson, <u>Logical Abilities in Children</u>, 4 vols. (Hillsdale, N.J.: Lawrence Erlbaum Associates, Publishers, 1974–76), IV: 154–55.

If a single book appears in several volumes, it is a courtesy to the reader to include the total number of volumes in the footnote. (The *MLA Handbook* recommends doing this only if all volumes are relevant.) If the various volumes were printed in different years, the inclusive dates of publication are listed. The number of the volume actually being cited is then listed after the facts of publication, followed by a colon and the page number or numbers from which the quotation is taken. The abbreviation *pp.* is not used if the volume number is given.

11. Books in a Series

[11]C. L. Barber et al., <u>Contributions to English Syntax and Philology</u>, Gothenburg Studies in English No. 14 (Gothenburg: Univ. of Gothenburg, 1962), p. 7.

If a book is published in a foreign city, use the English spelling of the foreign city's name. In the example above, the Swedish spelling of the city is Göteborg, but the English spelling Gothenburg is used in the reference note. If you do not know the English spelling, look up the foreign spelling in a college dictionary; the entry will list the English spelling.

12. Reprinted Books

[12]Famous Stories of Code and Cipher, ed. Raymond T. Bond (1947; rpt. New York: Collier Books, 1965), p. 40.

Many paperback books are reprints of hardcover editions. The date of the hardcover edition is listed first, followed by a semicolon and the abbreviation *rpt*. Then the publication facts for the reprinted edition are given in regular form.

13. Subsequent Editions

[13]W. A. Poucher, The Scottish Peaks, 3rd ed. (London: Constable & Co., Ltd, 1971), pp. 370–78.

14. Foreword, Preface, Introduction, and so on

[14]George Barker, Foreword, Idylls of the King, by Alfred Tennyson (New York: The New American Library, 1961), pp. vii, ix.

15. Reference Works

[15]"Takuma School," McGraw-Hill Dictionary of Art (1969).

[16]E. C. H[elmreich], "Imperialism," Collier's Encyclopedia, 1957 ed.

If no author is listed, the first item in the footnote is the title of the article. Do not use the abbreviation *anon*. If the article is signed by the author's initials, the full name of the author can usually be found at the beginning of the volume. The rest of the name is placed in square brackets in the footnote, as in the example above.

Periodicals. The format for documenting periodicals differs from that for documenting books in that (1) the title of the article as well as the title of the periodical is included, (2) no place of publication is listed, (3) month and even day of publication are given, and (4) for some types of periodicals, a volume number is included. The order of items and the punctuation of the note are similar to that for books.

16. Weekly Magazines

[17]Robert Shaplin, "Letter from Indonesia," The New Yorker, 12 Dec. 1977, p. 153.

17. Monthly Magazines

[18]David Morris, "Solar Cells Find Their Niche in Everyday Life on Earth," Smithsonian, Oct. 1977, pp. 38–44.

18. Scholarly Journals

[19]Frederic L. Wightman and David M. Green, "The Perception of Pitch," American Scientist, 62 (1974), 208–15.

Scholarly journals usually have clearly displayed volume numbers, and pagination is continuous throughout all the issues of one volume. Even though the volume number is sufficient to identify the year of publication, the year is placed in parentheses after the volume number as a convenience to the reader. Note that the abbreviation *pp.* is not used when the volume number is given.

19. Signed Newspaper Articles

[20]Richard D. Lyons, "Pesticide: Boon and Possible Bane," The New York Times, 11 Dec. 1977, pp. 1, 83.

20. Unsigned Newspaper Articles

[21]"Nation's Farmers Hope to Meet with Carter," Providence Journal, City Ed., 13 Dec. 1977, p. A–10, col. 2.

If the newspaper being quoted identifies the particular edition (for example, Late Edition, City Edition, Suburban Edition), this information should be included in the footnote because the contents of the various editions for one day's newspaper may vary. Inclusion of the column number for a short article will help the reader find the story more easily.

21. Reviews

[22]Thomas L. Haskell, "Power to the Experts," rev. of The Culture of Professionalism, by Burton J. Bledstein, The New York Review of Books, 13 Oct. 1977, pp. 28–33.

Unsigned reviews are treated exactly like signed reviews, except that the note begins with the title of the review.

22. Letters to the Editor

[23]Andrew F. Fisher, Letter, Harvard Magazine, Sept.–Oct. 1977, p. 8.

23. Editorials

[24]Arlyn Powell, "Overview," Editorial, Appalachia, Nov. 1977, p. 5.

Other Sources of Information. Most of the information used in a research paper is normally taken from books or periodicals. You may, however, occasionally use other sources, including dissertations, pamphlets, governmental publications, conference proceedings, recordings, or legal references.

24. Unpublished Dissertations

[25]Ruth Cameron, "The Prose Style of Addison and Steele in the Periodical Essay," Diss. Boston Univ. 1972, p. 46.

A published dissertation is treated like any other book.

25. Interviews and Other Personal Communications

[26]Personal interview with Helen MacDonald, 4 Feb. 1978.

[27]Letter received from Helen MacDonald, 4 Feb. 1978.

26. Pamphlets

[28]Gilbert S. Maxwell, <u>Navajo Rugs: Past, Present and Future</u> (Palm Desert, Calif.: Best-West Publications, 1963), pp. 59–60.

As this example shows, pamphlets are treated like books.

27. Governmental Publications

[29]U.S. Post Office Dept., Bureau of Operations, <u>Directory of Post Offices</u>, POD Publication 26 (Washington, D.C.: Govt. Printing Office, July 1968), p. 33.

The citation of governmental publications is complicated because so much information is involved. In general, the name of the general division comes first, followed by subdivisions in descending order of size. The title of the publication is then given, followed by information such as the series number of the publication. Note that most federal publications are printed by the Government Printing Office. For more detailed information on handling governmental publications, see *A Manual of Style,* published by the University of Chicago Press and available in most libraries.

28. Conference and Symposium Proceedings

[30]George Mandler, "Consciousness: Respectable, Useful, and Probably Necessary," <u>Information Processing and Cognition</u>, Proc. of the Third Loyola Symposium on Cognitive Psychology, 30 Apr. and 1 May 1974, ed. Robert L. Solso (Hillsdale, N.J.: Lawrence Erlbaum Associates, Inc., Publishers, 1975), pp. 303–04.

[31]James H. Sledd, "Prufrock Among the Syntacticians," <u>Third Texas Conference on Problems of Linguistic Analysis in English, May 9–12, 1958</u> (Austin, Tex.: Univ. of Texas Press, 1962), pp. 1–21.

When a proceedings has no separate title the name on the title page is treated as the title.

29. Recordings

[32]Dylan Thomas, "Fern Hill," <u>Dylan Thomas Reading a Child's Christmas in Wales and Five Poems,</u> Caedmon, TC 1002, Vol. I, n.d.

Legal References.   The conventions for legal references are very complex and differ greatly from those for citations of other published material. If you should need to use a legal reference, consult *A Uniform System of Citation*, published by the Harvard Law Review Association and available in most libraries.

Special problems in documentation include the format to be used when reference information is not available, ways of handling repeated references to the same source, citations from secondary sources, and multiple places of publication or multiple publishers.

Missing Information. Especially if you consult older publications or special-purpose publications such as brochures and pamphlets, you may encounter sources that do not include all the standard information. Check the library card; it may have the missing information. If it does not, there are conventional ways of footnoting missing information.

1. **No Author.** If the author's name is not given, simply omit it and begin the footnote with the title of the book or article. Do not use the abbreviation *anon.*

> [33]Treasures of Britain, 2nd ed. (London: Drive Publications Limited, 1972), p. 201.

2. **No Date.** Use the abbreviation *n.d.* in the position where the date would normally appear.

> [34]Rudolf Koch, The Book of Signs (New York: Dover Publications, Inc., n.d.), p. 43.

3. **No Publisher or Place of Publication.** The abbreviation for both no publisher and no place of publication is *n.p.*

> [35]American Youth Hostels Handbook (n.p.: n.p., 1977), pp. 32–33.

4. **No Pagination.** If the pages of a publication are not numbered, use the abbreviation *n. pag.* in the position where the page numbers would normally appear.

> [36]Richard Reece, Iona: Its History and Archeology (Glasgow: Iona Community Publishing Dept., n.d.), n. pag.

Occasionally, you may wish to cite a publication that contains almost no publishing information. List all the information available, but indicate that the remaining information is missing so that the reader will not think that you are guilty of sloppy documentation.

> [37]The Great Hurricane and Tidal Wave: Rhode Island, September 21, 1938 (n.p.: n.p., n.d.), n. pag. This book contains 128 pages of text and photographs.

Sometimes information missing from the publication itself is available on the library card for that publication. The card will have the information in square brackets, and the footnote should also put the information in brackets.

[38]Francisco Rodrígues Adrados, <u>Festival, Comedy and Tragedy</u>, [trans. Christopher Holme] (Leiden: Brill, 1975), p. 412.

Quoting from Secondary Sources.   Whenever possible, original sources should be used in preference to secondary sources. If the original publication is simply not available, give as much information about it as your secondary source lists, and also provide full information about your secondary source.

[39]Francis Bacon, <u>Novum Organum</u>, as quoted in Edward Burnett Tylor, <u>The Origins of Culture</u> (New York: Harper & Row, Publishers, 1958), p. 136.

Multiple Places of Publication or Multiple Publishers.   If the title page of a book lists several places of publication, only one need be listed in footnotes or bibliographies. In general, choose the large city over the small one, and choose an American city over a foreign one.

If a book is simultaneously published by two different publishers, only one need be listed. It is, however, not wrong to include both publishers. (The *MLA Handbook* asks that both publishers always be listed.)

[40]R. W. Zandvoort, <u>A Handbook of English Grammar</u>, 3rd ed. (London: Longmans, Green and Co.; Englewood Cliffs, N.J.: Prentice-Hall, Inc., 1966), pp. 117–18.

Subsequent References.   Subsequent footnote references to the same work are shortened by omitting at least the information on publication. Practice varies with respect to the amount of information given in shortened references. The easiest form of shortened reference includes only the author's last name and the appropriate page number or numbers. If the references include works by two authors with the same surname, use the full name of each author in subsequent references.

FULL FORM

[1]Richard Foster Jones, <u>The Triumph of the English Language</u> (Stanford: Stanford Univ. Press, 1953), p. 94.

SHORTENED FORM

[41]Jones, p. 126.

If the work has more than one author, the last names of all authors listed in the first reference are included in subsequent references.

FULL FORM

[19]Frederic L. Wightman and David M. Green, "The Perception of Pitch," <u>American Scientist</u>, 62 (1974), 208–15.

SHORTENED FORM

[42]Wightman and Green, p. 214.

An alternative form of shortened reference includes both the author's name and the title of the book or article. This form must be used if the references contain two or more works by the same author. If the title is over five or six words long, it may be shortened, provided that the word order of the original is not changed.

FULL FORM

[25]Ruth Cameron, "The Prose Style of Addison and Steele in the Periodical Essay," Diss. Boston Univ. 1972, p. 46.

SHORTENED FORM

[43]Cameron, "Prose Style of Addison and Steele," p. 121.

If you will be quoting one work extensively throughout a paper, the first reference may note this fact, and subsequent references to page numbers may be made in the text itself without a footnote.

FIRST REFERENCE

[44]Thomas Mann, <u>Doctor Faustus</u>, trans. H. T. Lowe-Porter (New York: Alfred Knopf, 1948), p. 86. All future references to this work appear in the text.

SUBSEQUENT REFERENCE WITHIN TEXT

Mann felt that orthodoxy "itself committed the blunder of letting reason into the field of religion" (p. 89).

The Latin abbreviations *ibid., loc. cit.,* and *op. cit.* are still often found in footnotes, although current practice favors the types of shortened references just discussed.

Ibid. (Latin *ibidem* "in the same place") refers to an *immediately* preceding footnote. Neither the author's name nor the title of the work is given. The page number is given only if it differs from that of the preceding reference.

EARLIER REFERENCE

[3]Alexander Fol and Ivan Marazov, <u>Thrace and the Thracians</u> (New York: St. Martin's Press, 1977), p. 40.

NEXT FOOTNOTE

[4]<u>Ibid.</u>, p. 47.

Op. cit. (Latin *opere citato,* "in the work cited") is used with the author's name and substitutes for the title of the work.

FIRST REFERENCE

[28]Gilbert S. Maxwell, <u>Navajo Rugs: Past, Present and Future</u> (Palm Desert, Calif.: Best-West Publications, 1963), pp. 59–60.

SUBSEQUENT REFERENCE

[45]Maxwell, <u>op. cit.</u>, p. 64.

Loc. cit. (Latin *loco citato,* "in the place cited") is used only when referring to the same passage. It is also used with the author's name, but normally no page number is included.

FIRST REFERENCE

⁹Dun Li, "The Taiping Rebellion," in China Yesterday and Today, ed. Molly Joel Coye and Jon Livingston (New York: Bantam Books, Inc., 1975), p. 189.

SUBSEQUENT REFERENCE

⁴⁶Dun Li, loc. cit.

Unless you are specifically asked to use these Latin abbreviations, it is best to avoid them. First, not all readers know their meanings. Second, if you change the order of footnotes during revision, the Latin abbreviations *ibid.* and *loc. cit.* may no longer be correct. Third, if there are several pages between footnote references, the reader will have to shuffle back through the manuscript to find out what work an *ibid.* refers to.

56b BIBLIOGRAPHIES

The **bibliography** (or **list of references**) comes at the end of a work and is, as a minimum, an alphabetical listing of all of the works referred to in the footnotes. A bibliography often includes, not only works cited in footnotes, but also other works consulted but not directly used in the preparation of the paper. Bibliographies are sometimes annotated; that is, they include after each entry a brief statement about the contents and the value of the work. For very long research papers, the bibliography may be subdivided into primary and secondary sources. For example, the bibliography of a literary paper would include the works of the author under primary sources and criticism of those works under secondary sources. When a great many works have been consulted, the bibliography may be subdivided into separate lists for books and periodicals. For student research papers, one alphabetical list of all the works consulted, whether cited in footnotes or not, is usually sufficient.

The bibliography should be typed on a separate page or pages and placed at the end of the text of a paper. If the footnotes also appear at the end of the paper, the bibliography follows the footnotes. The title "Bibliography" (or "List of References") is centered at the top of the page. Entries in the bibliography appear in alphabetical order by the last name of the author; the items are not numbered. If there is no known author, the entry is alphabetized by the first words of the title (excluding *A* and *The*). If the bibliography includes more than one work by the same author, the author's name is not repeated. Instead, the name of the author is replaced by a long dash made by typing five to seven consecutive hyphens.

When a work is being prepared for publication, bibliographical entries are double-spaced, but for student papers, single-spacing with double spaces between entries is usually acceptable. Unlike footnotes, which have a paragraph indention, bibliographical entries traditionally have hanging indention; that is, the first line of the entry is at the left margin and subsequent lines of the same entry are indented three to five spaces.

A bibliographical entry includes the same information as a first footnote, but the format is slightly different. The major differences are (1) the last name of the first author is listed before his or her given names, (2) periods separate the major parts of the entry, and (3) publication information is not enclosed in parentheses. Page numbers are not included for entire books, but the page numbers for entire shorter pieces (periodical articles or articles in a collection) are included.

The examples provided earlier for footnotes are presented below in appropriate bibliographical form. See page 376 for an illustration of a complete bibliography for a typed research paper.

1. Single Author

Jones, Richard Foster. <u>The Triumph of the English Language</u>. Stanford: Stanford Univ. Press, 1953.

2. Corporate Author

Inter-Territorial Language Committee of the East African Dependencies. <u>A Standard Swahili-English Dictionary</u>. Oxford: Oxford Univ. Press, 1939.

3. Two Authors

Fol, Alexander, and Ivan Marazov. <u>Thrace and the Thracians</u>. New York: St. Martin's Press, 1977.

4. Three Authors

Brusaw, Charles T., Gerald J. Alred, and Walter E. Olin. <u>Handbook of Technical Writing</u>. New York: St. Martin's Press, 1976.

5. More than Three Authors

Shanks, Merrill E. et al. <u>Pre-Calculus Mathematics</u>. Menlo Park, Calif.: Addison-Wesley Publishing Company, 1976.

6. Books with a Translator

Meyer, Conrad Ferdinand. <u>The Saint</u>. Trans. W. F. Twaddell. Providence, R.I.: Brown Univ. Press, 1977.

7. Books with One or More Editors

Hume, David. <u>Dialogues Concerning Natural Religion</u>. Ed. Henry D. Aiken. New York: Hafner Publishing Company, 1951.

8. Collections by One Author

Quirk, Randolph. "Langland's Use of kind wit and inwit." In
Essays on the English Language: Medieval and Modern.
Bloomington, Ind.: Indiana Univ. Press, 1968, pp. 20–26.

9. Collections by More Than One Author

Li, Dun. "The Taiping Rebellion." In China Yesterday and
Today. Ed. Molly Joel Coye and Jon Livingston. New York:
Bantam Books, Inc., 1975, pp. 189–93.

10. Books in Several Volumes

Osherson, Daniel N. Logical Abilities in Children. Hillsdale,
N.J.: Lawrence Erlbaum Associates, Publishers, 1976. Vol.
IV.

11. Books in a Series

Barber, C. L., et al. Contributions to English Syntax and Phil-
ology. Gothenburg Studies in English No. 14. Gothenburg:
Univ. of Gothenburg, 1962.

12. Reprinted Books

Famous Stories of Code and Cipher. Ed. Raymond T. Bond.
1947; rpt. New York: Collier Books, 1965.

13. Subsequent Editions

Poucher, W. A. The Scottish Peaks. 3rd ed. London: Constable
& Co., Ltd, 1971.

14. Foreword, Preface, Introduction, and so on

Barber, George. Foreword. Idylls of the King. By Alfred Tennyson. New York: The New American Library, 1961.

15. Reference Works

"Takuma School." McGraw-Hill Dictionary of Art (1969).

H[elmreich], E. C. "Imperialism." Collier's Encyclopedia.
1957 ed.

16. Weekly Magazines

Shaplin, Robert. "Letter from Indonesia." The New Yorker,
12 Dec. 1977, pp. 153–80.

17. Monthly Magazines

Morris, David. "Solar Cells Find Their Niche in Everyday Life
on Earth." Smithsonian, Oct. 1977, pp. 38–44.

18. Scholarly Journals

Wightman, Frederic L., and David M. Green. "The Perception of Pitch." <u>American Scientist</u>, 62 (1974), 208–15.

19. Signed Newspaper Articles

Lyons, Richard D. "Pesticide: Boon and Possible Bane." <u>The New York Times</u>, 11 Dec. 1977, pp. 1, 83.

20. Unsigned Newspaper Articles

"Nation's Farmers Hope to Meet with Carter." <u>Providence Journal</u>, City Ed., 13 Dec. 1977, p. A–10, col. 2.

21. Reviews

Haskell, Thomas L. "Power to the Experts." Rev. of <u>The Culture of Professionalism</u>, by Burton J. Bledstein. <u>The New York Review of Books</u>, 13 Oct. 1977, pp. 28–33.

22. Letters to the Editor

Fisher, Andrew F. Letter. <u>Harvard Magazine</u>, Sept.–Oct. 1977, p. 8.

23. Editorials

Powell, Arlyn. "Overview." Editorial. <u>Appalachia</u>, Nov. 1977, p. 5.

EXERCISES: Footnotes and Bibliographies

Part A: Correct all errors (spacing, punctuation, order, abbreviations, and so on) in the following footnotes and bibliography entries. Circle the number of any correct examples.

1. Footnote
   [13]Coles, J. M., and E. S. Higgs, The Archaeology of Early Man, Frederick A. Praeger; New York, 1969, pg. 49.
2. Bibliography entry
   [2]Alderson, Brian, "Tracts, Rewards and Fairies: the Victorian Contributions to Children's Literature." In Essays in the History of Publishing: In Celebration of the 250th Anniversary of the House of Longman 1724–1974. Briggs, Asa, editor. New York: Longman, Incorporated, 1974, pgs. 245–282.
3. Bibliography entry
   Kleinberg, Harry. *How You Can Learn to Live with Computers.* Philadelphia: J.B. Lippincott Co., 1977.
4. Footnote
   [7]Jerome M. Roscow, "The Problems of the Blue-Collar Worker," in *Overcoming Middle Class Rage.* Edited by Murray Friedman, (Philadelphia, The Westminster Press, 1971) p. 28.
5. Footnote
   [14]Lynch, Rose Marie, "Reliving the Past," *College English,* 39, (September 1977), p. 43.

6. Bibliography entry
   Lynch, Rose Marie. "Reliving the Past." *College English,* 39 (September 1977), 42–44.
7. Footnote
   [4]Gary Ford, "Shakespeare's Mountain Home," *Southern Living,* July 1978, p. 78.

Part B: For each corrected footnote in Part A (ignore the bibliography entries), write an example of a subsequent reference to the source, making up a different page number for each. Do not use Latin abbreviations in this exercise.

Part C: For each of the following quotations, assume that you are writing a research paper and wish to include some of the information contained in the quotation.

a. Compose a sentence or two incorporating the information that you want to use. If you use direct quotations, be sure to enclose them in quotations marks. Put the footnote reference number in the appropriate place.

b. Write a correct footnote for each passage, using the information given in brackets at the end of the quotation.

c. Write a correct bibliography entry for each passage.

d. If you feel that any quotation is "common knowledge" and could be used without a footnote, state exactly why it need not be documented.

1. "Perhaps the most compelling reason for the widespread interest is that black holes seem to mark the point where astrophysics intersects metaphysics and science finally converges with religion. Indeed, black holes seem to have universal implications, for the gravitational collapse of stars suggests that the universe, too, can begin falling back in on itself. If that happens, its billions of galaxies will eventually crush together and could form a super black hole. And then what? Nothing? Or would a new process of creation somehow begin?" [pp. 53–54, *Time,* "Those Baffling Black Holes," volume 112, September 4, 1978, total article pp. 50–59.]

2. "The Nile is the only river to flow northwards across the Sahara, and only along its banks could an agricultural community survive the absence of rainfall. The Ancient Egyptians called their land 'Kemet,' the Black Land, because of the black silt which used to be deposited on the soil by the annual flood, caused by the rising waters of the Blue Nile when the river is swollen by the rainfall in Ethiopia. This silt is rich and fertile, and with careful irrigation enabled the Egyptians to produce two crops per year in some areas." [p. 11, Cornell University Press at Ithaca, N.Y., *The Egyptians: An Introduction to Egyptian Archaeology* by John Ruffle, 1977.]

3. "Moreover, feeding Mexico today is literally only half the job that it will soon become. Already the 10th largest in the world, Mexico's population is expected to double by the year 2000. This surge—due to a high birth rate coupled with a relatively low death rate—is perhaps Mexico's worst problem, and the one least solvable by oil money." [p. 26, *The Wall Street Journal,* by John Huey, Wednesday, August 30, 1978, "Despite Rising Wealth in Oil, Mexico Battles Intractable Problems," total pages of article: 1 and 26.]

4. "Although we do not realize it, the people we most want to impress are our fellow family members, and they are also the people from whom we most fear criticism." [p. 4, 1970, Delacorte Press, New York, by Barry Bricklin and Patricia M. Bricklin, *Strong Family Strong Child: The Art of Working Together to Develop A Healthy Child.*]

5. "Public sector strikes . . . are damaging in two general ways. They disrupt the flow of essential public services, often jeopardizing public health, safety, and welfare. Also, public sector strikes distort the normal democratic political process." [p. 19, 1978, third edition of a pamphlet entitled *Public Sector Bargaining and Strikes*, published by the Public Service Research Council, Vienna, Virginia.]

6. "One hundred and forty-three pieces of jewelry of various kinds were discovered inside the mummy's bindings. Of the thirty-three pages that Carter uses to describe the examination of the mummy, more than half are given over exclusively to listing precious articles found wrapped in the cerements. The eighteen-year-old Pharoah was literally wrapped in several layers of gold and precious stones." [p. 203, second edition, *Gods, Graves and Scholars: The Story of Archaeology* by C. W. Ceram, published in 1967 in New York by Alfred A. Knopf, translated by E. B. Garside and Sophie Wilkins.]

7. "The effort is already far enough along that energy experts consider Brazil the world leader in using alcohol as a motor fuel. This year alone, Brazil's alcohol program will result in the consumption of 635 million gallons of ethel alcohol either as a gasoline substitute or supplement." [The *Washington Post*, "Gas Guzzlers Becoming Alcoholics in Brazil," by Larry Rohter, Wednesday, August 30, 1978, p. A17, article only on one page.]

8. "Isadora Duncan was the greatest performing artist that the United States ever produced. Beyond that, she had gifts as an artistic creator that amounted to genius—in fact, she invented an art form of profound significance, in which, save for her six adopted pupils, she has had no successful direct heirs though she was to influence generations of later dancers." [p. 13, *The Real Isadora,* by Victor Seroff, published in 1971 by The Dial Press in New York.]

9. "The word 'Buccaneer,' so often used to describe pirates, had its origin in the West Indies. Originally the name was applied to runaway Frenchmen, often political or religious refugees, or escaped criminals. Somehow they had reached the West Indies, where they lived among the native Carib Indians. A large number gathered on the western part of the Island of Hispaniola (present-day Haiti) which was otherwise thinly settled but well stocked with cattle and pigs. From the natives they learned a process of curing the meat of the animals over a fire on a wooden frame called a 'boucan.' As a result they gradually became known as buccaneers, a name often applied to all pirates in general." [p. 16, *The Pirates of Colonial North Carolina,* by Hugh F. Rankin, 1976, published by the Department of Cultural Resources of the Division of Archives and History at Raleigh, N.C.]

appendices

A BRIEF HISTORY OF THE ENGLISH LANGUAGE

Appendix A

One of the basic facts about human languages is that they are constantly, though gradually, changing. Such change is most obvious with vocabulary. When a new product is introduced, it is given a name that enters the language as a new word. Fifty years ago no one ever spoke of *Xerox* machines. Or, for various reasons, the name of an existing product may be changed: within the past few years, the term *dye* as a name for a product to change the color of people's hair has been replaced by *hair coloring,* although the word *dye* of course survives in other contexts. Words are also lost from the language, though writing tends to preserve them for a long time even when they are no longer used in daily speech. For example, modern scientific knowledge has completely altered the nature of medicine and, with it, the vocabulary of medicine. You will be able to find the word *mithridate* in a large dictionary, but you probably have never heard the word before, and you certainly wouldn't ask a druggist for it as a remedy against poison.

These may seem like insignificant changes beside the vast number of words in English, but they are only three of thousands of such changes that are constantly taking place in the English vocabulary, changes that make the vocabulary of English today quite different from the vocabulary of English as recently as fifty years ago.

Although vocabulary changes are most easily detected, changes are also constantly occurring in other aspects of language—in pronunciation, in word order, in meaning. If your grandfather is a native speaker of English, you have perhaps noticed that he doesn't pronounce all words in exactly the same way that you do, even if you both have lived in the same area all your lives. He may, for example, pronounce the middle consonant in *latter* and *matter* as a clear *t,* whereas your pronunciation of these same words may be identical or nearly identical to that of *ladder* and *madder.* This sound change of *t* to *d* between a stressed vowel and an unstressed vowel is a characteristic of recent American, though not of British, English.

The history of English began about six thousand years ago, when a group of nomadic tribes lived somewhere in east central Europe. We do not know whether these tribes were racially related, but we do know that they spoke a common language. Because the language of these tribes would eventually spread all over Europe and as far east as India, we today call this parent language Indo-European.

We have no surviving texts from Indo-European because writing had not yet been invented. However, by examining the descendent languages of Indo-European, scholars have been able to learn a great deal about the parent language. We know that it was a highly inflected language, using suffixes and vowel changes to indicate such grammatical features as number, gender, tense, mood, and grammatical functions such as subject, object, direction, agent, and the like. We know that it had a basic vocabulary of kinship terms, words for natural phenomena, numbers, parts of the body, and so forth. This vocabulary still survives, though often with great changes, in the Indo-European languages today. For example, from the Indo-European stem *nokwt-*, we have the following words meaning "night" in various Indo-European languages.

English	night	Modern Greek	núkta
German	Nacht	Russian	noch'
French	nuit	Irish	-nočt
Italian	notte	Spanish	noche

Such related words descending from a common source are called **cognates;** hence, we say that Italian *notte* is a cognate of English *night.* (*Cognate* does not mean that one word "comes from" another word. That is, English *night* and Italian *notte* do not have a "mother-daughter" relationship. Rather, they have what could be called a "sister-sister" relationship.)

By the first century A.D., the original group of Indo-Europeans had dispersed widely, and the various subgroups had become isolated from one another. So many changes had taken place in the language of each of these subgroups that their speech was often mutually incomprehensible. We can now speak of individual members of the Indo-European family. The Hellenic branch had moved down into the Balkan peninsula, where it would become the ancestor of modern Greek. The Italic branch was in Italy, speaking various dialects, one of which—Latin—was to be the parent of all the Romance languages today (French, Italian, Spanish, Portuguese, Roumanian). The Baltic branch remained closer to its original homeland; its descendants are modern Lithuanian and Latvian. Very similar in many ways to the Baltic languages were the Slavic languages of eastern Europe, represented today by Russian, Polish, Czech, and Slovak. The Albanian group moved to the west coast of the Adriatic, and the Armenian group into the area south of the Caucasus Mountains. The Indic branch migrated to the subcontinent of India, and the Iranian branch into modern Iran and Afghanistan. The Celtic branch was for centuries spread all over Europe, but today survives only marginally in parts of Great Britain and northern France, where Irish, Welsh, Scots Gaelic, and Breton are still spoken by a few people. The Germanic branch moved into northern Europe and Scandanavia.

By about the fourth or fifth century A.D., Germanic itself had split into three further subdivisions—North Germanic, East Germanic, and West Germanic. North Germanic developed into modern Danish, Swedish, Norwegian, and Icelandic. East Germanic became extinct by the eighteenth century, although the name of one of its dialects, Gothic, is familiar to us today in other contexts. The modern descendants of West Germanic are German, Yiddish, Dutch, Flemish, and English.

English was not the first Indo-European language to be used in England. Celtic speakers had been there for some time before the beginning of the Christian era, and after the Romans took over part of the island in the middle of the first century A.D., Latin was also spoken there. During the fifth and sixth centuries A.D., however, waves of Germanic-speaking invaders began to raid and then to settle in what is today England. These invaders were the Angles, the Saxons, and the Jutes, tribes originally located near the shores of the North Sea on the continent of Europe. As the Angles, Saxons, and Jutes settled down, the Celts were either assimilated by them or were pushed to the extremities of the island, to Cornwall, Wales, and Scotland. Because the Celts were pushed out or assimilated, we have few loanwords from Celtic in English.

By the sixth century A.D., we are justified in speaking of an English language, or of Old English, although the language already— or still—was divided into several dialects. At the time of the invasions, the language that was to become English was rarely written down. The only alphabet was the Germanic *runic alphabet*, or *futhorc*, used primarily for inscriptions on monuments and weapons. This runic alphabet was ultimately based on the Greek alphabet, but it had been modified to facilitate carving on wood and stone, so that most of the letters, or runes, were sharply angled with few curves. Written in the runic alphabet, the word *futhorc* would look like the diagram below. (The symbol þ stands for the sound of *th*.)

The Angles, Saxons, and Jutes were pagans, but during the latter part of the sixth century and the seventh century, England was Christianized by missionaries from Ireland and Scotland and from Rome. With Christianity came the Latin alphabet, the alphabet that, of course, we still use today. Because Latin did not have some of the sounds used in English speech, two Latin letters were modified to represent these sounds. The symbol æ stood for the vowel sound in *man*, and ð (a crossed *d*) for the *th* sound of *the* or *with*. Two other symbols were adapted from the runic alphabet: þ (called "thorn") also represented the *th* sound, and a runic character, (called "wen") represented the sound of *w*.

The period from about A.D. 450 to about A.D. 1100 is called **Old English.** During this period, many different kinds of texts were written down. We have surviving today various kinds of poetry, history, sermons, Biblical translations, laws and other legal documents, charms, riddles, and even medical recipes.

Beginning in the latter part of the eighth century and continuing for the next 200 years or so, England was attacked by new waves of Germanic invaders. These were the Vikings, primarily from Denmark and Norway. Like their predecessors, these new invaders soon began to settle in the areas they raided. England thus acquired speakers of a closely related but nonetheless different Germanic dialect called Old Norse.

Within a few years, Old Norse words began appearing in English, and Norse words continued to infiltrate English until well after the Norman Conquest. Because the cultural level of the Viking invaders was not very high, we do not find many learned words in English from Norse. Rather, most of the borrowings were homely, everyday words such as *get, leg, egg,* and *call.* Often the Norse word drove out the native word completely, but sometimes both the English and the Norse words have survived, usually with a slight difference in meaning. Thus today we still have both the native *shin* and the Norse loan *skin.* Norse even influenced the grammar of English to some extent. The plural pronouns *they, them,* and *their* are from Norse, and our fondness for two-part verbs like *pick up, run off,* and *take over* is probably at least partly due to Norse influence because such formations were common in Norse before they became common in English.

By the eleventh century, the English and the Norse had achieved an uneasy peace, and the Norse settlers were becoming assimilated into English society. But in 1066, another invasion occurred that was to have a great effect on the history of English. Taking advantage of a somewhat dubious claim to the throne of England, William of Normandy (William the Conqueror) successfully invaded and then took over England. William and most of his followers were racially Germanic, but their ancestors had abandoned their original language for French when they settled in Normandy during the ninth and tenth centuries A.D. Hence the language brought to England by William was French. French became the official language of the court, of law, and of administration for the next 300 to 350 years. However, there were many more English people than French people in England, and the conquered English continued to speak their native tongue. Many natives surely learned to speak French, but the French also had to learn at least some English in order to be able to speak to their English servants. The English spoken and written from about 1100 (that is, shortly after the Conquest) until about 1500 is called **Middle English.**

As the years passed, the French rulers of England lost many of their possessions in France. The dialect of French that they spoke, Anglo-Norman French, became more and more different from the prestigious French of Paris. The Normans married English women, and their children grew up speaking English at least as fluently as French. And there continued to be many more native speakers of English in England than there were native speakers of French. For all of these reasons, French continually lost ground, even as an official language. In 1363 Parliament began to be conducted in English. English had once again become the national language of England.

For the first two centuries after the Norman Conquest, little writing was done in English. Because the language was seldom being written down, there was no written standard to act as a conservative and regularizing influence on it. When people did once again begin to write in English, it was evident that the language had changed a great deal since the Conquest. Many of the inflections that characterized Old English had been lost. Many French words had entered the language. Words such as *government, court, crime, religion, prince,* and *treason* reflected the superior political position of the French in England. The cultural superiority of the French was revealed by loans like *beef, broil, fashion, satin, mansion, furniture, ornament, music, art, college, tournament,* and *surgery.* But English had also borrowed such ordinary words as *carry, easy,* and *face* from French.

The various dialects of English had flourished in the interim between 1066 and the resurgence of English as the national language. People from one part of England had difficulty understanding speakers from other parts. However, at the same time, forces were counteracting the effects of this dialectal variation. Because London was the governmental and commercial center of the nation and the chief seaport, its dialect obviously was in a position of prominence. London was located at a dialect boundary and shared features of a number of other dialects; hence it was a good "compromise" dialect. Gradually, a spoken and written version of English based on the London dialect came to be accepted as a standard. Chaucer wrote in this dialect, and the standard English of both Britain and America today is the descendant of this late Middle English London dialect.

In 1476 a retired textile merchant named William Caxton established the first printing press in England and immediately began to print books in English. Printing had many effects on the language. Prior to mass-production printing, all books had to be copied by hand. This was, of course, a very expensive process, and few people could afford to own books. Printed books were much cheaper, and, as books became more accessible, more people became interested in learning to read. Thus education and widespread literacy were also encouraged by printing. As a mass-production industry, printing tended to produce a standardized writing system and act as a brake on language changes. Indeed, despite the fact that some rather drastic sound changes have occurred in English in the past 500 years, our modern spelling system remains, in its essential details, that established by the printers around the year 1500.

During the early sixteenth century, the Renaissance came to England, and the classics and classical languages were studied extensively. Important English authors often wrote their major works in Latin, but English was never seriously challenged as the language of the nation. Indeed, with the works of Spenser, Shakespeare, and Milton, English became one of the most important literary languages of the world. As a result of the interest in the classics, many books previously available only in Latin or Greek were translated into English. One by-product of these translations was the introduction into the English vocabulary of thousands of new loanwords, primarily from Latin. Often such borrowings were made deliberately in an effort to enrich the English vocabulary. Not surprisingly, there were those who opposed extensive borrowing from other languages; such opponents of borrowing spoke disparagingly of "ink-horn terms," and insisted that necessary new words should be made up from English roots. But the borrowing continued—and has continued to the present day. We might agree with the opponents of borrowing that the words *progredient* ("going forward, advancing") and *conquadrate* "to bring together in a square") were really not necessary, but what would we do without *education* or *progress*, both of which also entered English from Latin during the Renaissance?

The great period of English discoveries coincided with the latter part of the English Renaissance. As English speakers encountered exotic new plants, animals, geographic features, activities, and products from hitherto unknown parts of the world, they often borrowed the local terms for these phenomena, further enriching the vocabulary of English. Such borrowings have also continued to the present day, but form a much smaller proportion of the total vocabulary of English than do loanwords from Latin or French.

The grammar of English has been changing gradually but steadily ever since Old English, although there have been no dramatic grammatical changes since the **Early Modern English** period (1500–1650). In general, English has changed from a highly inflected (or *synthetic*) language in which word endings indicate grammatical function to an *analytic* language in which there are few inflectional endings and word order is the primary indicator of grammatical function.

Prior to the eighteenth century, few people concerned themselves with English grammar beyond, perhaps, considering it a simplified form of Latin grammar or feeling that it was so simple as to be practically no grammar at all. During the eighteenth century, however, many scholars were distressed over what they considered the degenerate state of English grammar and attempted to regularize English and to prevent further change. For the most part, their specific recommendations had little effect, but it is to this period that we owe, for example, the rule against the double negative and the distinction still taught but little observed between *shall* and *will*. Many of our present attitudes about grammar as a moral rather than a practical matter date from the eighteenth century.

By the nineteenth century, English was the national language not only of Britain but also of the United States, Canada, and Australia. With the rise of the British Empire, English became the most important second language of India and large areas of Africa. Today there are nearly 350 million native speakers of English. Furthermore, most of these speakers are in the economically advanced nations, so the influence of English in the world is even greater than the number of its native speakers might imply.

With the post-World War II decline of the British Empire and the continued increase in the influence of the United States in the world, American English has become the most important national variety of English. In addition, because about two-thirds of the world's native speakers of English live in the United States, American English is the predominant dialect in terms of sheer numbers. Although British English still enjoys great prestige, standard American English is today recognized as a "separate but equal" dialect of English.

The following texts from four different stages in the history of

English are included to illustrate the extent to which, and some of the ways in which, written English has changed over the centuries. As a means of making comparisons easier, all four passages are from the same text, Genesis 11, the Biblical story of the Tower of Babel.

1. Old English: from Ælfric's *Heptateuch,* c. 1000.

Soðlice ealle menn spræcon   ða ane spræce.   ða ða   hi
Truly   all   men   spoke   then/one/language.   When   they

ferdon   fram eastdæle,   hi   fundon   ænne   feld   on
went   from/eastern/area,   they   found   a   field   in

Senaarlande,   and wunodon   ðæron   ða   cwædon   hi
Shinar   and/dwelled   there.   Then   said   they

him betwynan: Vton   wyrcean us tigelan and ælan   hi   on
them   between: Let us   make   us   tiles   and   burn   them in

fyre. Witodlice   hi   hæfdon tigelan for   stan   and tyrwan
fire.   Indeed   they   had   tiles   for   stone   and   tar

for weall-lim. And   cwædon: Vton   timbrian us ceastre and
for   mortar.   And   said: Let us   build   us   city   and

stypel oð   heofon heahne, and   uton   wyrðian   urne   naman
tower   up to heaven,   high   and let us   honor   our   name

ær   ðam ðe   we   synd todælede   geond   ealle eorðan.
before   we   are   separated   through   all   earth.

To the reader totally unfamiliar with Old English, this text may appear very strange indeed. Some of the strangeness will disappear if you mentally substitute *th* for ð, and *a* for *æ*. (This particular text happens not to use þ, another Old English symbol for *th*, and *w* has been written instead of the Old English letter.)

A closer look at the Old English text and the translation will reveal that many of the words are still used today and in the same meaning, though the spelling has been changed. Examples from just the first sentence include *ealle* "all," *menn* "men," and *ane* "one." Other words still survive, but have undergone changes of meaning and usage as well as spelling. The first word of the passage, *soðlice,* consists of an adjective *soð,* plus an adverbial ending, *-lice.* English still has the adjective in the word *soothsayer* and in the archaic expression *forsooth.* The ending *-lice* survives in shortened form as the regular adverbial ending *-ly.* One of the most striking facts about this Old English vocabulary is its "purity"; all the words except place names are native words even though the text is a translation from Latin.

Pronunciation has also changed greatly. To take just one small example, the vowel of the word *stan* "stone" (l.5) has changed from a sound similar to that of the first vowel in the word *father* to the long-*o* sound used today.

Old English was a highly inflected language, and nouns and adjectives took different endings depending, for example, on whether they were being used as subjects, direct objects, or objects of prepositions. Like modern European languages such as French or German, every noun in Old English had a gender associated with it, and the forms of the articles and adjectives varied according to the gender of the noun they modified.

The basic word order of Old English prose resembled that of Modern English in many ways. However, it was in generally freer. For example, pronoun objects sometimes followed their verbs and sometimes preceded their verbs.

2. Middle English: from the Wycliffe Bible, c. 1395.

Forsothe the lond was of o langage, and of the same speche.
Truly   *one*   *speech*

And whanne thei ʒeden forth fro the eest, thei fonden a
      when   *went*   *from*   *east*   *found*

feeld in the lond of Sennaa, and dwelliden ther ynne. And oon
field   *land*   *therein.*   *one*

seide to his neiʒbore, Come ʒe, and make we tiel stonys, and
          neighbor   *ye*   *tile stones*

bake we tho with fier; and thei hadden tiel for stonus, and
         them   *fire*   *had*   *tile*

pitche for morter; and seiden, Come ʒe, and make we to vs a
                                                                          us

citee and tour, whos hiʒnesse stretche til to heuene; and
         tower   *height*   *heaven*

make we solempne oure name bifor that we be departid in to
         solemn   *before*   *are*

alle londis.

Four hundred years brought great changes to written English; this late Middle English passage can be read with only a little difficulty by speakers and writers of Modern English. There is only one unfamiliar letter, ʒ, which actually was a development from an older form of *g*, but which was used to represent several different sounds in Middle English. The Old English æ, ð, and þ have been replaced by modern *a* and *th*.

Although there are a number of spelling differences from Modern English, most of the vocabulary is familiar to us today. Several loanwords from French have appeared since the Old English text: Examples include *langage* (1.1), *morter* (1.6), *citee* (1.7), and *solempne* (1.8). The influence of Norse also appears in the words *same* (l.1) and *thei* (l.2). Spelling is not yet absolutely fixed, for the word *stones* is spelled *stonys* in l.4 and *stonus* in l.5

Inflections have almost, but not quite, diminished to their modern state. The definite article has only one form, *the*, regardless of the following noun. There are no endings on infinitives, nor are the different cases of nouns distinguished by suffixes. On the other hand, the singular and plural of the past tense are still differentiated by an -*n* on the plural (for example, *fonden*). The loss of inflections has been compensated for by an increased number of prepositional phrases.

There are still a number of differences in word order from Modern English. For example, in the imperative, the subject follows its verb (*Come ʒe, make we,* 1.4).

3. Early Modern English: King James Bible, 1611.

And the whole earth was of one language, and of one speach. And it came to passe as they iourneyed from the East, that they found a plaine in the land of Shinar, and they dwelt there. And they sayd one to another; Goe to, let vs make bricke, and burne them thorowly. And they had bricke for stone, and slime had they for morter. And they said; Goe to, let vs build a city and a tower, whose top may reach vnto heauen, and let vs make vs a name, lest we be scattered abroad vpon the face of the whole earth.

At first glance, this text looks like Modern English. There are no unfamiliar letters and spelling is standardized, usually according to modern patterns. However, the letters *u* and *v* are still being used to represent both vowel and consonant, with *v* appearing at the beginning of words (*vs,* l. 4, *vnto,* l. 7), and *u* elsewhere (*burne,* l. 4, *heauen,* l. 7). Also, the letter *i* is still being used as a consonant (*iourneyed,* l. 2) where we would have *j* today.

All of the vocabulary is familiar, although usage has changed somewhat. For example, we would probably say *over* instead of *vpon* in l. 8. Most of the French loans that appeared in the Middle English text appear here also.

The inflections are identical to those of Modern English, but we would not invert subject and verb as is done in *slime had they for morter* (ll. 5–6).

4. Modern English: Revised Standard Version, 1946–52.

Now the whole earth had one language and few words. And as men migrated from the east, they found a plain in the land of Shinar and settled there. And they said to one another, "Come let us make bricks, and burn them thoroughly." And they had brick for stone, and bitumen for mortar. Then they said, "Come let us build ourselves a city, and a tower with its top in the heavens, and let us make a name for ourselves, lest we be scattered abroad upon the face of the earth."

Little need be said about this Modern English translation because the language is almost completely familiar. It may appear a bit archaic or quaint because the language of Biblical translation always tends to be highly conservative and translators are influenced by the language of preceding translations. For example, few writers today would begin so many sentences with the word *And.*

The translators have substituted *bitumen* for the Old English *tar* and the Middle English *pitch*, a small illustration of the Modern English fondness for Latin technical terms. Indeed, probably *pitch* or *tar* would have been a better choice because everyone is familiar with those words, but few people know exactly what *bitumen* means.

These brief passages have illustrated a number of points about the English language. They have shown that English has changed greatly during the past thousand years and that it has borrowed many words from other languages, especially French, Norse, and Latin. The modern structure of English really appeared in Middle English, and the changes since Middle English have been more in the way of minor adjustments and refinements than of vast alterations. On the other hand, the core vocabulary of English today—our most basic verbs, adjectives, nouns, most pronouns, and even prepositions—is the same as that of Old English, and our favorite word order of subject-verb-object also existed in Old English. The word *history* implies both change and continuity, and both change and continuity are clearly visible in the history of English.

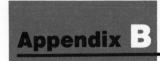

GLOSSARY OF USAGE

Even in writing, accepted usage is often arbitrary. For example, there is no logical reason why *any more* should be written as two words but *anyhow* as one word, or why *different to* should be frowned upon while *dissimilar to* is not. Further, usage is constantly changing; in the eighteenth century, many adjectives were acceptably used as adverbs (without an *-ly* ending), but today such usage is considered nonstandard. Finally, notions of usage are frequently vague and inconsistent—readers may object to slang as used by one writer and find it completely appropriate as used by another writer. The approach taken in this glossary is conservative, not as a protest against change and flexibility in language, but on the principle that if a word or construction is likely to offend even a few readers, it is best to avoid it.

This glossary lists only the most common problems of usage in student writing. For questions of usage not covered here, consult a good dictionary or other sections of this handbook. Space prevents discussion of many usage problems involving words that are frequently confused (e.g., *doubtful* and *dubious*). See Appendix C for an extensive list of such words.

The usage labels in the glossary entries below agree in general with those employed by most good dictionaries.

STANDARD	Acceptable at all levels of speech and writing
COLLOQUIAL AND SLANG	Acceptable in casual speech but not in writing
NONSTANDARD	Normally not approved of in either speech or writing
REGIONAL	Acceptable in speech in some geographical areas but best avoided in writing

A, AN.   *A* is used before words beginning with a consonant sound, *an* before words beginning with a vowel sound: *a metaphor, a euphemism, an instant, an hour.*

A LOT, ALOT.   The correct spelling is always as two separate words.

ABOUT, AROUND.   *Around* is used colloquially instead of *about* in expressions of time, but should be avoided in writing.

COLLOQUIAL	The drought lasted <u>around</u> a year.
PREFERABLE	The drought lasted <u>about</u> a year.

It is not necessary to add *at* to *about; about* is sufficient.

WORDY	He came in <u>at about</u> midnight.
PREFERABLE	He came in <u>about</u> midnight.

ABOVE, BELOW. *Above* is an accepted way of referring to preceding written material; *below* refers to following written material.

the <u>above</u> illustration   the discussion <u>below</u>

Some people feel that this usage is stilted and overly formal and try to avoid it by alternative expressions.

the illustration on page 23   the following discussion

ACCEPT, EXCEPT. *Accept* is a verb meaning "to receive, to take." *Except* is either a verb meaning "to exclude" or a preposition meaning "with the exclusion of, other than."

ACTUALLY. Do not use *actually* as a simple intensifier (*He actually had the nerve to strike me!*). Save it for expressing a contrast between fact and opinion (*George looks like an old man, but actually he is only 37*).

AD. Although the shortened form *ad* is frequently used in speech, the full form should always be used in writing. Similarly for other common shortened forms such as *auto, exam, gym, lab, math, phone, photo, prof,* and *Xmas.*

ADVICE, ADVISE. *Advice* is the noun, *advise* the verb. Similarly, *device* is the noun and *devise* the verb.

AFFECT, EFFECT. *Affect* is normally only a verb; *effect* is most often a noun, but is also used as a verb. The verb *affect* means either "influence" (*This quiz will not affect your final grade*) or "to pretend, assume" (*He affected a British accent*). The noun *effect* means "result" (*Painting the walls black had a depressing effect*). The verb *effect* means "to bring about, cause" (*The election effected a change of government*). The noun *affect* is a rarely encountered technical term in psychology meaning "an emotion."

AGGRAVATE. *Aggravate* is widely used in informal speech to mean "to irritate, annoy." In writing, *aggravate* should be reserved for the meaning "to intensify, make worse."

AIN'T. Nonstandard and universally frowned upon except when used humorously.

ALIBI. Strictly speaking, an *alibi* (Latin for "elsewhere") is a plea by a defendant that he was elsewhere when a crime was committed. Colloquially, *alibi* is frequently used as a synonym for "excuse," but this usage should be avoided in writing.

ALL, ALL OF. Either is usually correct, but *of* can often be omitted to avoid wordiness. Only *all of* is correct before personal pronouns (*all of us, all of them*). Only *all* is appropriate before abstract nouns (*All beauty is deceptive*).

ALL READY, ALREADY. *All ready* is a pronoun plus an adjective; *already* is an adverb meaning "by a particular time." Similarly, *all together* is a pronoun plus an adjective, and *altogether* is an adverb meaning "entirely."

They were <u>all ready</u> by noon. It was <u>already</u> noon.

The ten of us were <u>all together</u>. There were <u>altogether</u> too many.

ALL RIGHT, ALRIGHT. The only acceptable spelling is *all right.*

ALL THE FARTHER. A regional variant of *as far as*. *All the farther* should be avoided in writing.

REGIONAL   Is this <u>all the farther</u> you got today?

STANDARD   Is this <u>as far as</u> you got today?

ALL TOGETHER, ALTOGETHER. See **ALL READY, ALREADY.**

ALLUDE TO, REFER TO. *Allude to* means to mention indirectly, and *refer to* means to mention directly. You would allude to your neighbor's loud radio by asking him if he were hard of hearing. You would refer to the loud radio by telling him that it was too loud. *Refer* with a direct object means to direct to a source for help: *She referred me to the almanac for information on temperatures.*

ALMOST, MOST. *Almost* is an adverb; *most* is a pronoun or adjective. Colloquially, *most* is often used as an adverb before a pronoun, but this should be avoided in writing.

COLLOQUIAL   <u>Most</u> everybody likes chocolate.

STANDARD   <u>Almost</u> everybody likes chocolate.

ALOUD, OUT LOUD. *Out loud* is a colloquial variant of *aloud* and should be avoided in writing.

ALSO, LIKEWISE. *Also* and *likewise* are not coordinating conjunctions and should not be used as substitutes for *and*.

INCORRECT   He inherited a farm, <u>also</u> (<u>likewise</u>) a herd of cattle.

CORRECT   He inherited a farm <u>and</u> a herd of cattle.

ALTHOUGH, THOUGH. The words are interchangeable and both are correct. The abbreviated forms *altho* and *tho* should not be used.

AMONG, BETWEEN. In general, *among* refers to more than two persons and things, and *between* refers to only two persons or things. *Between* is, however, often used with reference to more than two things if the things are being considered individually. Only *between* is correct if relationships are being considered two by two: *There were several marriages between members of the class.*

AMOUNT, NUMBER. *Amount* properly refers to mass nouns, and *number* to countable nouns.

amount of water, rice, disagreement, furniture
number of cups, flowers, arguments, chairs

AND ETC. *And* is redundant because *etc.* is an abbreviation for Latin *et cetera*, which means "and the rest." Hence saying *and etc.* is like saying "and and so on."

ANGLE, SLANT. Slangy and unnecessary substitutes for *point of view* or *approach*.

ANY, SOME. The use of *any* and *some* as adverbs meaning "at all" and "a little" is colloquial and should be avoided in writing.

COLLOQUIAL   That didn't bother me <u>any</u>.

PREFERABLE   That didn't bother me <u>at all</u>.

COLLOQUIAL   He complained <u>some</u>, but did it anyway.

PREFERABLE   He complained <u>a little</u>, but did it anyway.

ANY MORE, ANYMORE.   The correct spelling is as two separate words. The use of *any more* in a sentence without a negative is a regionalism and should be avoided in writing.

REGIONAL   I see him almost every day <u>any more</u>.

STANDARD   I see him almost every day <u>now</u>.

ANY ONE, ANYONE.   *Anyone* means "anybody" or "any person at all." *Any one* means "a single individual and only one."

Choose <u>anyone</u> you like.

Choose <u>any one</u> of the three.

Exactly the same distinction applies to *everyone* and *every one; everyone* means "all persons" and *every one* means "each single individual." Similarly for *someone* and *some one.*

ANY WAY, ANYWAY, ANYWAYS.   *Any way* is an adjective plus a noun meaning "whatever way." *Anyway* is an adverb meaning "in any case." *Anyways* is a colloquial substitute for *anyway.*

Do it <u>any way</u> you like, but do it <u>anyway</u>.

ANYPLACE. See **-PLACE.**

ANYWHERES, EVERYWHERES, SOMEWHERES, NOWHERES. Colloquial or regional substitutes for *anywhere, everywhere, somewhere, nowhere.*

APPROVE, APPROVE OF.   *Approve* means to give official consent; *approve of* means to regard favorably.

The dean <u>approved</u> his petition even though he did not <u>approve of</u> it.

APT, LIABLE, LIKELY, PRONE.   In careful usage, all four of these words are distinguished. *Apt* means "talented" (*apt at wood-working*) or "suitable for the occasion" (*an apt remark*). *Liable* means "susceptible to something unpleasant" (*liable to error*) or "legally responsible" (*liable for damages*). *Likely* means "probable" (*likely to snow*). *Prone* refers to a strong habit or predisposition (*prone to temper tantrums*).

AS.   To be absolutely safe, reserve *as* to its functions as (1) a preposition meaning "in the role of" (*As a driver, he resented pedestrians*), and (2) a subordinating conjunction meaning "simultaneously" (*As the light turned green, a child stepped in front of his car*).

As is incorrect as a substitute for *that, which, who,* and *whether.*

INCORRECT   I'm not sure <u>as</u> I know Jackson.

CORRECT   I'm not sure <u>that</u> I know Jackson.

Do not use *as* after the verbs *nominate, name, elect, brand, vote, appoint,* or *consider.* Use *as* after the verbs *regard, pick, choose,* and *select.*

The class <u>named</u> him secretary.

The class <u>chose</u> him <u>as</u> secretary.

The class <u>considered</u> him qualified.

The class <u>regarded</u> him <u>as</u> a qualified candidate.

AS . . . AS, SO . . . AS.   Positive comparisons take *as . . . as*. Negative comparisons may take either *as . . . as* or *so . . . as*, although some writers prefer *so . . . as*.

Today's news is <u>as</u> bad <u>as</u> yesterday's.

Today's news is not <u>as</u> bad <u>as</u> yesterday's.

Today's news is not <u>so</u> bad <u>as</u> yesterday's.

AS TO.   Do not use *as to* to mean "about."

INCORRECT   The clerk inquired <u>as to</u> her health.

CORRECT   The clerk inquired <u>about</u> her health.

As to is redundant before the subordinators *who, what, when, which, whether, where, why,* and *how.*

WORDY   The clerk inquired <u>as to whether</u> she was healthy.

IMPROVED   The clerk inquired <u>whether</u> she was healthy.

AUTHOR, CRITIQUE, RESEARCH.   Although used colloquially as verbs (*He agreed to research the problem*), these words should be used only as nouns in writing. Substitute *write* for *author, do a critique* or *criticize* for *critique,* and *do research* or *investigate* for *research.*

AWFUL, AWFULLY.   The adjective *awful* has lost its former meaning of "inspiring awe" and has come to have the colloquial meaning of "unpleasant, disagreeable." The adverb *awfully* has been so overused that today it means only "very." Both should be avoided in writing. The use of *awful* as an adverb (*I'm awful sick of his complaining*) is nonstandard.

AWHILE, A WHILE.   *A while* may be substituted wherever *awhile* may be used, but only *a while* is correct after the preposition *for* or with *ago.*

Wait <u>awhile</u>. Rest <u>awhile</u> before you start again.

Wait <u>a while</u>. We waited for <u>a while</u>. He left <u>a while</u> ago.

BACK OF, IN BACK OF.   Both mean simply "behind," but *in back of* is colloquial and best avoided in writing. When in doubt, use *behind.*

BAD, BADLY.   *Bad* is an adjective and *badly* an adverb. Hence *bad* is the correct form after verbs of sensation (see 20a), and *badly* should be used with other verbs.

INCORRECT   I feel <u>badly</u> about the delay.

CORRECT   I feel <u>bad</u> about the delay.

INCORRECT   It doesn't hurt so. <u>bad</u> now.

CORRECT   It doesn't hurt so <u>badly</u> now.

BARELY, HARDLY, SCARCELY.   These are negative words and no other negative should be used in the same clause.

INCORRECT   hardly no trouble, barely didn't make, without hardly a word

CORRECT   hardly any trouble, barely made, with hardly a word

The same principle applies for the negative time adverbs *rarely* and *seldom.* Phrases with *barely, hardly,* and *scarcely* are followed by *when* or *before* and not *than.*

| INCORRECT | She had scarcely left the garage <u>than</u> her brakes failed. |
| CORRECT | She had scarcely left the garage <u>when</u> her brakes failed. |

BE SURE AND, COME AND, GO AND, TRY AND.   The use of *and* in these expressions is colloquial. Substitute *to* in writing.

| COLLOQUIAL | Be <u>sure and</u> leave a wide margin. |
| STANDARD | Be <u>sure to</u> leave a wide margin. |

BECAUSE.   *Because* properly introduces noun clauses, not adverbial clauses. Thus, after such words as *reason, excuse,* and *explanation,* the correct word is *that.*

INCORRECT	The reason Judy is crying is <u>because</u> she has a toothache.
CORRECT	The reason Judy is crying is <u>that</u> she has a toothache.
INCORRECT	Her excuse for not coming is <u>because</u> the roads are bad.
CORRECT	Her excuse for not coming is <u>that</u> the roads are bad.

BEING AS (HOW), BEING THAT, SEEING AS (HOW).   Nonstandard for *because.*

BESIDE, BESIDES.   *Beside* is a preposition meaning "at the side of." *Besides* is either a preposition meaning "in addition to" or an adverb meaning "in addition, moreover."

<u>Beside</u> the fishtank was a pump.
<u>Besides</u> the fishtank, there was a birdcage.
<u>Besides</u>, she had forty-two houseplants.

BETTER THAN.   Colloquial for *more than.*

BETWEEN.   See **AMONG.**   The expression *between you and I,* though often heard in speech, is incorrect in writing because the object form of the pronoun should always be used after prepositions: the correct usage is *between you and me.*

BROKE.   Slang in the meaning of "having no money."

BUNCH.   Colloquial when used to refer to a group of people or things, except for plants or fruit growing together, such as bananas or grapes.

BURST, BUST, BUSTED.   The principal parts of the verb *burst* are *burst, burst, burst. Bust* is nonstandard; *busted* is slang for "arrested."

BUT THAT, BUT WHAT. Nonstandard for *that* or *whether.*

INCORRECT	I don't doubt <u>but that</u> he's guilty.
CORRECT	I don't doubt <u>that</u> he's guilty.
INCORRECT	Who knows <u>but what</u> he's guilty?
CORRECT	Who knows <u>whether</u> he's guilty?

app

CALCULATE, FIGURE, GUESS, RECKON. Colloquial in the meaning of "think, suppose, believe, expect."

CAN, MAY. In speech, *can* is widely used to indicate both "ability to do" and "permission to do." In writing, use *may* to express the notion of permission.

CAN BUT, CANNOT BUT, CANNOT HELP BUT. *Can but* is a somewhat stilted way of saying "have no alternative" (*We can but hope for the best*). *Cannot but* is a rather illogical way of saying the same thing; use *can but* or *can only* instead. *Cannot help but* is often considered unacceptable; use simply *cannot help*.

QUESTIONABLE I <u>cannot help but</u> feel that I have forgotten something.

PREFERABLE I <u>cannot help</u> feeling that I have forgotten something.

CAN'T HARDLY. A double negative. Use *can hardly*. See also **BARELY, HARDLY, SCARCELY.**

CASE, INSTANCE, LINE. All three of these words tend to be overused and vague and are heavy contributors to deadwood. See 47c.

DEADWOOD In the case of the manufacture of paper, air pollution is a serious problem.

IMPROVED Air pollution is a serious problem in the manufacture of paper.

CHARACTER. Do not use *character* as a synonym for *person*.

COLLOQUIAL He was a very methodical character.

PREFERABLE He was a very methodical person.

COMMON, MUTUAL. Strictly speaking, *common* refers to something shared with others (*a common driveway, common interests*). *Mutual* means "reciprocal, having the same relation to each other" (*mutual respect, mutual agreement*). The distinction is often blurred in speech, but should be preserved in writing.

COMPARE, CONTRAST. *Compare* focuses on similarities; *contrast* focuses on differences. In practice, *compare* is often used to include both similarities and differences.

COMPARE TO, COMPARE WITH. Although *to* and *with* are used interchangeably in speech, in more formal writing, *compare with* means "to examine in order to note similarities" and *compare to* means "to represent as similar, to liken." In other words, *compare with* is the act of comparing, and *compare to* is the statement of similarity.

COMPLECTED. A regional and colloquial substitute for *complexioned*.

CONSENSUS OF OPINION. Redundant because the word *consensus* means "agreement of opinion." *Consensus* alone is enough.

CONTACT.   In the meaning of "get in touch with," the word is here to stay, despite the objections of some, because there is no suitable alternative when the means of communication is uncertain. However, if the means of communication is known, use a more precise word such as *speak, telephone, meet, call,* or *inform.*

CONVINCE, PERSUADE.   You *convince* someone *that* something is right, but you *persuade* someone *to* do something. Hence, you might *convince* your instructor *that* your grade is too low, but still not *persuade* him *to* change it.

COULD OF.   *Could of* is a nonstandard spelling of the spoken contraction "could've." Always write *could have.* Similarly for *will of, would of, should of, may of, might of, ought of,* and *must of.*

CRITERIA.   *Criteria* is a plural noun and should be used with a plural verb. The singular is *criterion.*

CUTE.   *Cute* is so overused colloquially that it is best to avoid it entirely in writing. If you mean "attractive," use *attractive.*

DATA.   Strictly speaking, *data* is the plural of *datum,* and you will never be wrong if you use it with a plural verb. However, *data* is today widely treated as a (singular) collective noun and is often used with a singular verb.

DEAL.   Widely used colloquially to mean "business transaction, political bargain, arrangement, treatment, situation." It should be avoided in writing; choose a more precise word.

DIFFER FROM, DIFFER WITH.   *Differ from* means "to be different from, to be unlike something." *Differ with* means "to disagree with someone."

DIFFERENT FROM (THAN, TO).   *Different from* is always correct, but *different than* is widely used, even in writing, when followed by a clause. *Different to* is not acceptable American usage. See also 21g.

DISINTERESTED, UNINTERESTED.   Although both words are often used to mean "not interested," *disinterested* more properly is reserved for the meaning "impartial, unbiased, objective," and *uninterested* to mean "not interested, indifferent."

DIVED, DOVE.   *Dived* is the preferred past tense of *dive,* but *dove* is also acceptable.

DOUBT.   *Doubt* may be followed by *that, if,* or *whether.* It should not be followed by *but what* or *but that.*

DROWNDED.   Nonstandard for *drowned.*

DUE TO, DUE TO THE FACT THAT.   *Due to* is always acceptable in an adjectival phrase (*The error was due to a misunderstanding*). However, some still object to using *due to* to introduce an adverbial phrase (*He was fired due to his incompetence*).

   Due to the fact that is unnecessarily wordy and can always be replaced by *because.*

EACH AND EVERY. *Each and every* is unnecessarily wordy; either *each* or *every* is preferable. If you do feel you must have both for emphasis, the verb is still singular.

EACH OTHER, ONE ANOTHER. Some very careful writers use *each other* to refer to two persons or things and *one another* for more than two. For most people, the two phrases are interchangeable.

E.G., I.E. *E.g.* means "for example" and *i.e.* means "that is." Both are usually acceptable abbreviations in writing, but do not confuse the two.

ENTHUSE, ENTHUSED. Although these words are widely used colloquially, many people object to seeing them in writing. Use *be enthusiastic* and *enthusiastic* instead.

EQUALLY AS. *Equally* should not be used in a comparison with *as*. If both elements of the comparison are expressed in the clause, use *as . . . as* or *just as . . . as*. If only one element of the comparison appears in the clause, use *equally*.

INCORRECT	Lentils are <u>equally as</u> nutritious <u>as</u> black beans.
CORRECT	Lentils are (<u>just</u>) <u>as</u> nutritious <u>as</u> black beans.
CORRECT	Black beans are an excellent food, but lentils are <u>equally</u> nutritious.

ETC. The abbreviation *etc.* is acceptable, even in formal writing, to avoid a long and tedious list that the reader can infer for himself. However, *etc.* should not be used just because the writer cannot think of any other examples; rather than write *Vermin include rats, cockroaches, etc.*, try *Vermin include such pests as rats and cockroaches*.

Do not misspell *etc.* as *ect.* Do not write *and etc.*

EVER SO OFTEN, EVERY SO OFTEN. The two do not mean the same thing. *Ever so often* is a somewhat childish way of saying "very often, frequently." *Every so often* means "now and then, occasionally."

EXACT, EXACTLY. *Exact* is an adjective; do not use it to modify the adjective *same*. The correct form is *exactly the same*.

INCORRECT	He did the <u>exact</u> same thing.
CORRECT	He did <u>exactly</u> the same thing.

EXCEPT, UNLESS. *Except* is a preposition and should not be used to introduce a clause. To introduce a clause, use the conjunction *unless*.

INCORRECT	He never writes us <u>except</u> he wants money.
CORRECT	He never writes us <u>unless</u> he wants money.

EXPECT. Colloquial or regional in the meaning "suppose, suspect, think." *Expect* is standard in the meaning "anticipate."

COLLOQUIAL	I expect you already know him.
STANDARD	I expect you to respond immediately.

EXTRA. Colloquial as an adverb meaning "especially, particularly." As an adjective, *extra* is standard English in the meaning of "additional."

COLLOQUIAL	February 29 was an extra boring day.
STANDARD	February 29 is an extra day in the year.

FABULOUS. *Fabulous* has been so overused and misused to mean simply "pleasing" that it has almost no force left, and it should be avoided in writing. The same is true for *fantastic, grand, great, lovely, marvelous, sensational, terrific,* and *wonderful.*

FARTHER, FURTHER. In practice, the two words are almost interchangeable. However, some prefer to reserve *farther* to refer to physical distance (*ten miles farther*) and *further* for other kinds of distance or degree (*a further observation*). Only *further* is correct in the meaning "in addition, moreover, furthermore."

FEATURE. *Feature* as a verb means "to make outstanding, to specialize in," and should not be used as a synonym for "offer, contain." In the meaning of "imagine," *feature* is regional slang (*Can you feature me as Snow White!*).

FEWER, LESS. In speech, *less* is often used before both plural and mass nouns. In writing, *less* should be reserved for mass nouns (*less control*) and *fewer* should be used with plural nouns (*fewer controls*).

FIELD. The phrase *in the field of* is often nothing but deadwood and should be eliminated entirely.

| DEADWOOD | He has been studying in the field of economics. |
| IMPROVED | He has been studying economics. |

When a noun meaning "realm of knowledge or work" is necessary, try giving the overworked *field* a rest by substituting a synonym such as *subject, domain, region, theme,* or *sphere.*

FINALIZE. Although *finalize* is formed according to the same principles as the acceptable *popularize, legalize,* and *modernize,* many people still object to it. Try *complete, conclude,* or *put into final form* instead.

FIX. *Fix* is colloquial as a verb meaning "arrange, prepare" or "punish." It is also colloquial as a noun meaning "awkward situation." It is slightly colloquial in the meaning "repair." *Fix* is universally acceptable in the meaning "make secure or firm."

FOLKS. Colloquial in the meaning of "relatives, parents" or even "people." The formal plural of *folk* in the meaning of "tribe, nation, ethnic group" is *folk,* but the word is rarely used as a noun in this meaning today.

FORMALLY, FORMERLY. *Formally* means "in a formal way." *Formerly* means "earlier, in the past."

FORMER, LATTER. *Former* and *latter* should be used only when two—and only two—items have been mentioned. Otherwise, use *first* and *last.* Even if you, as the writer, have only two things in mind, the reader may be confused if more than two things are mentioned in the same clause. Rewrite for clarity, avoiding *former* or *latter.*

| CONFUSING | He often talked to my aunt about my cousin because the <u>latter</u> was his best friend. (Does *latter* refer to *aunt* or *cousin?*) |
| CLEAR | He often talked to my aunt about my cousin because my cousin was his best friend. |

app

FUNNY.   Colloquial in the meaning of "curious, odd, strange, queer." Standard English in the meaning of "amusing."

GENTLEMAN, LADY.   *Gentleman* and *lady* should be reserved for reference to breeding and behavior and not used as synonyms for *man* and *woman*. Few men are gentlemen and few women are ladies.

GOOD AND.   As an intensifier meaning "very," *good and* is colloquial; it should be avoided in writing.

COLLOQUIAL   Cleaning the cellar made him good and tired.

PREFERABLE   Cleaning the cellar made him very tired.

GOOD, WELL.   *Good* is an adjective; its use as an adverb is colloquial or nonstandard. *Well* is either an adverb or an adjective meaning "in good health." Hence, *He plays good* is nonstandard, but both *I feel well* and *I feel good* are correct.

GRADUATE.   Either *He graduated from Cornell* or the more formal *He was graduated from Cornell* is correct. *He graduated Cornell* is nonstandard.

GUY.   Colloquial for *man, boy.* Similarly, the plural *guys* is colloquial for *people* (both male and female).

HAD BETTER.   An acceptable idiom meaning "should, ought." However, don't omit the *had.*

UNACCEPTABLE   We better call the fire department.

ACCEPTABLE   We had better call the fire department.

HAD OF.   Nonstandard for *had.*

NONSTANDARD   If you had of come earlier, you would have found me.

STANDARD   If you had come earlier, you would have found me.

HAD OUGHT, HADN'T OUGHT.   Nonstandard for *ought, ought not (oughtn't).*

NONSTANDARD   She hadn't ought to talk about sewers during dinner.

STANDARD   She ought not (to) talk about sewers during dinner.

In negative or interrogative sentences, *ought* may be used either with or without a following *to* before the infinitive.

HALF A, A HALF, A HALF A.   Use either *half a (half a day)* or *a half (a half day),* but not *a half a.*

HANGED, HUNG.   *Hanged* is the past tense and past participle of *hang* used with reference to executions or suicides. Otherwise, the past tense and past participle is *hung.*

HAVE, HAVE GOT.   Either *have* or *have got* is acceptable in many idioms, but why not save the extra word and simply say *have?*

ACCEPTABLE   She has got a bad cold.

PREFERABLE   She has a bad cold.

HEIGHT, HEIGHTH. *Height* is the correct form and *heighth* is nonstandard.

HISSELF. Nonstandard for *himself.*

HOME, HOUSE. A *house* is a physical structure; *home* is an abstract noun meaning the place where one lives. Hence one buys a *house;* whether it is a *home* or not depends upon whether one lives there.

HOPEFULLY. *Hopefully* is always acceptable in the meaning of "in a hopeful manner" (*Minnie asked hopefully if there were any brownies left*). As a sentence modifier meaning "it is to be hoped," *hopefully* is attacked by many, who apparently have not noticed that *hopefully* is completely parallel to such acceptable sentence modifiers as *undoubtedly* and *preferably*. To be absolutely safe, you can reserve *hopefully* for the first meaning.

-IC, -ICAL. Many adjectives have alternative endings in either *-ic* or *-ical* with no difference in meaning (e.g., *problematic, problematical*). However, the meanings of a few adjectives differ, depending on whether they end in *-ic* or *-ical*.

classic "typical, outstanding" (a classic case of embezzlement, a classic performance)

classical "traditional, established" (classical music, a classical education)

comic "pertaining to comedy" (the comic tradition, comic opera)

comical "funny" (a comical face)

economic "pertaining to the economy" (economic indicators)

economical "thrifty, money-saving" (economical car)

electric "powered by electricity" (electric motor)

electrical "pertaining to electricity" (electrical engineering)

historic "having a history" (historic buildings)

historical "pertaining to history" (historical research)

politic "tactful" (politic response)

political "pertaining to politics" (political divisions)

-ICS. Nouns ending in *-ics* take a singular verb when reference is to a discipline or field of study, but a plural verb when reference is to actual practice of the discipline.

Ethics is a branch of philosophy.

His ethics are questionable.

Similarly for other words such as *acoustics, athletics, economics, politics.*

IF, WHETHER. *If* and *whether* are almost interchangeable after a verb and before a clause. *Whether* is preferred when an alternative is expressed (*Tell me whether you want to play Probe or Scrabble*).

IGNORANT, STUPID. *Ignorant* means "not having learned"; *stupid* means "not able to learn" or "characteristic of someone not able to learn." *Ignorant* people are not necessarily *stupid*.

IMPLY, INFER. *Imply* means "to hint or suggest indirectly, without stating directly." *Infer* means "to make a conclusion, based on evidence." You might *infer* that your roommate is angry because he *implied* it by throwing his track shoes at you.

IN, INTO. Strictly speaking, *in* refers to something inside an enclosure, and *into* refers to going from outside to inside. In practice, *in* is frequently used instead of *into*. However, *into* should not be substituted for *in*. That is, do not write *John is into trouble over his income tax.*

IN BACK OF, IN BEHIND, IN FRONT OF, BEFORE. The *in* is unnecessary in *in back of* and *in behind*. *Back of* is acceptable, though somewhat more colloquial than *behind*. *In front of* is always correct and often clearer and less awkward than the formal *before*.

IN LIEU OF. *In lieu of* means "instead of" or "in the place of." It does not mean "in view of." Even used correctly, the expression is somewhat of an affectation and usually should be avoided.

IN REGARDS TO. Nonstandard for *in regard to* or *with regard to*. *As regards* is correct, but sounds affected in American English. All expressions with *regard* are wordy and often are better replaced with *about* or *concerning*.

INCLUDING, INCLUDE. The word *include* implies that only a partial listing is to be given. Hence the listing should not be followed by such expressions as *etc.* or *and others*.

INCORRECT	Hardwoods include oak, maple, and ash, among others.
CORRECT	Hardwoods include oak, maple, and ash.

INDIVIDUAL, PARTY. The noun *individual* means a single thing or person as opposed to an entire group; it should not be used simply as a synonym for *person*.

INCORRECT	This job requires an individual with strong self-control.
CORRECT	This job requires a person with strong self-control.

Except for lawyers and the telephone company, a *party* is a group of people, not a single person.

INSIDE OF, OUTSIDE OF. As prepositions referring to space, the *of* is redundant (*Don't wash the dog inside of the house*). In time expressions, *inside of* is colloquial for *within* (*You'll hear inside of a week*). As nouns, *inside* and *outside* require the preposition *of* (*We couldn't see the outside of the house because it was too dark*).

INSTEAD OF, RATHER THAN. Be sure to maintain parallelism when using these compound prepositions.

INCORRECT	We decided to buy two chairs instead of getting a sofa.
CORRECT	We decided to buy two chairs instead of a sofa.

INCORRECT	Rather than skiing, Bill prefered to snowshoe.
CORRECT	Rather than ski, Bill preferred to snowshoe.

INVITE. As a noun, *invite* is nonstandard. Use *invitation* instead.

IRREGARDLESS, DISREGARDLESS. Both are nonstandard for *regardless.*

ITS, IT'S, ITS'. *Its* is a possessive adjective; *it's* is the contraction for *it is* or *it has* (*It's lost its flavor*). *Its'* is always incorrect.

JUST. *Just* is colloquial in the meaning of "completely, very, really" (*She's just delighted with her new can-opener*).

KID. *Kid* is universally used in speech to mean "child, young person." In writing, use *child* instead.

KIND, SORT, TYPE. These words are singular and should be modified by *this* or *that*, not by *these* or *those*. In the phrase *this kind (sort, type) of a*, the *a* is redundant and should be omitted.

KIND OF, SORT OF. Colloquial for "somewhat, rather."

LAY, LIE. See 17a.

LEAD, LED. The correct past tense and past participle of the verb *lead* is *led*, not *lead*.

LEARN, TEACH. *Learn* means "to acquire knowledge." Teach means "to impart knowledge." Your teacher *taught* you arithmetic and you *learned* it.

LEAVE, LET. Before the word *alone, leave* and *let* are almost interchangeable (*leave him alone, let him alone*). Otherwise, *let* suggests a course of action and *leave* means "to allow to remain." *Leave* should not be used before an infinitive.

Let him speak for himself. Let the rope out slowly.

Leave him where he is. Leave the rope on the post.

LEND, LOAN. Traditionally, *lend* is the verb and *loan* is the noun. Today many people find *loan* acceptable as a verb, perhaps because they are uncertain about the past tense of *lend*. The principal parts of *lend* are *lend, lent, lent*.

LET'S US. Nonstandard for *let's*. Because *let's* is a contraction of *let us*, saying *let's us* is equivalent to saying *let us us*.

LIKE. Careful writers still use *like* as a preposition and *as* or *as if* as a conjunction to connect two complete clauses. However, if a verb has been omitted by ellipsis from the second clause, *like* is an acceptable connector.

COLLOQUIAL	He looked like he had just had a shock.
PREFERABLE	He looked as if he had just had a shock.
ACCEPTABLE	He looked like a man in shock.

app

LINE, ALONG THE LINES OF. In the meaning of "glib way of speaking," *line* is slang (*He's handing you a line*). As a catch-all term for "work, kind of activity," *line* is usually only deadwood. *Along the lines of* is a wordy way of saying *like* or *similar to*.

> WORDY   Would your wife prefer something along the lines of a digital watch?
>
> IMPROVED   Would your wife prefer something like a digital watch?

LITERALLY. *Literally* means "in a strict sense, exactly as spoken or written" and should not be used as an intensifier meaning "almost." *He literally crucified her* means that he actually nailed her to a cross.

Similarly, *veritable* means "true, actual," and should not be used as a simple intensifier. *My nephew is a veritable monkey* makes you a monkey's uncle.

LOOSE, LOOSEN, LOSE. *Loose* is either an adjective meaning "free, unattached" or a verb meaning "set free, unfasten." The verb *loosen* means the same as the verb *loose*. *Lose* is a verb meaning "mislay, suffer loss."

You will <u>lose</u> an arm if that dog gets <u>loose</u>.

LOTS OF, A LOT OF. Colloquial for "a great deal, many" and best avoided in writing.

MAD (ABOUT). Colloquial in the meanings of "angry, annoyed" or "enthusiastic, fond of."

MAJORITY, PLURALITY. Save *majority* for use with exact counts, where a contrast between the majority and the minority is made or implied. *Majority* should never be used with mass nouns (*The baby ate the majority of his oatmeal*). *Plurality* is a technical term; it means "the difference between the number of votes received by the winning candidate and the votes received by the next highest candidate."

MATERIALIZE, TRANSPIRE. Unnecessarily complicated ways of saying *occur, happen, appear,* or *take place*.

MAY BE, MAYBE. *May be* is a verb phrase indicating possibility. *Maybe* is an adverb meaning "perhaps." *Maybe* is somewhat colloquial; in formal writing, use *perhaps* instead.

MEDIA. *Media* is a plural noun and should be used with a plural verb. The singular is *medium*.

MEMORANDA. *Memoranda* is a plural noun and should be used with a plural verb. The singular is *memorandum*.

MIGHTY. Colloquial and regional as an adverb meaning "very, exceedingly." As an adjective meaning "strong, powerful," *mighty* is standard English.

MUCHLY. Nonstandard for *much* or *very much*.

MUST. Colloquial as a noun or adjective. Use *necessity* and *necessary* instead.

NICE. *Nice* has been so overworked as a general term to express mild approval that it is best avoided in writing. Choose a more precise word such as *amusing, polite, attractive,* or *entertaining.*

NO ONE. *No one* should always be written as two words.

NOHOW. Nonstandard for *in no way, not at all.*

NOR. *Nor* is correctly used as (1) the second member of the correlative conjunction *neither . . . nor,* or (2) to introduce a main clause after a preceding negative main clause. After a preceding *not, no, never,* etc., in the same clause, only *or* is correct.

INCORRECT	The refugees have no warm clothing nor shelter.
CORRECT	The refugees have no warm clothing or shelter.
CORRECT	The refugees have no warm clothing, nor do they have shelter.
CORRECT	He was neither a gentleman nor a farmer.

OFF OF. The *of* is unnecessary. The use of *off* or *off of* to designate source or origin is nonstandard (*I bought it off of a friend of mine*). Use *from* instead.

OFTENTIMES. An unnecessarily long way of saying *often.*

OK, O.K., OKAY. All are accepted spellings for the colloquialism. Except in the most informal writing, substitute more formal words such as *yes, all right, acceptable,* or *correct.*

OLD-FASHIONED. Spelled *old-fashioned,* not *old-fashion.*

ON ACCOUNT OF. Colloquial for *because of.* The use of *on account of* instead of *because* to introduce a noun clause is nonstandard.

| NONSTANDARD | I stopped reading on account of the light was so bad. |
| STANDARD | I stopped reading because the light was so bad. |

ONE. Highly formal usage still demands that the pronoun *one* be followed by *one (one's, oneself).* However, in all but the most formal contexts, it is acceptable to follow *one* with *he (his, him, himself).*

| FORMAL | One cannot always solve one's problems by oneself. |
| ACCEPTABLE | One cannot always solve his problems by himself. |

ONE OF THE, THE ONLY ONE OF THE. *One of the* is followed by a plural verb; *the only one of the* is followed by a singular verb.

Norman is one of the men who own their own boats.

Norman is the only one of the men who owns his own boat.

ONLY. In speech, *only* tends to appear toward the beginning of a clause, regardless of what part of the clause it modifies. In writing, it is best to place *only* just before the word or phrase it modifies. This is especially important if different placements could lead to different interpretations.

I only cooked the dinner. (I didn't wash the dishes.)

I cooked only the dinner. (Someone else cooked the lunch.)

OVER WITH. Colloquial for *ended* or simply *over.*

PASSED, PAST. *Passed* is the past tense and past participle of the verb *to pass. Past* is a noun, adjective, or preposition.

The time has passed rapidly.

in the past; past events; past our window

PER. Except in Latin phrases like *per capita*, *per* is best avoided in formal writing. In the meaning of "according to" (*per your instructions*), *per* is outdated business jargon. In the meaning of "for each," *a (an)* is preferable to *per* (*twice a day*, *$2 a dozen*).

PERSONAL. *Personal* is usually redundant and best omitted after possessive adjectives or nouns. For example, in the phrase *my personal feelings*, what else could your feelings be except *personal*? Reserve *personal* to contrast with *impersonal* (*highly personal remarks*).

PHENOMENA. *Phenomena* is a plural noun and should be used only with a plural verb. The singular is *phenomenon*.

-PLACE. Adverbs ending in *-place* (*anyplace, everyplace, noplace, someplace*) are colloquial. In writing, use the forms in *-where* instead (*anywhere, everywhere, nowhere, somewhere*).

PLAN ON, PLAN TO. *Plan on* is a colloquial substitute for *plan to*, perhaps by confusion with *count on*. In writing, use *plan to*.

PLENTY. As an adverb meaning "very," *plenty* is colloquial and regional (*plenty good enough*).

PLUS. *Plus* should be used only where addition and a specific sum are implied. *Plus* is not an acceptable substitute for *and* or *along with*.

UNACCEPTABLE	My brothers were there, plus my two cousins.
ACCEPTABLE	My brothers were there, along with my two cousins.
ACCEPTABLE	The total cost equals principal plus interest.

PRETTY. Colloquial as an adverb meaning "somewhat, rather" or "almost." Avoid it in writing.

PRINCIPAL, PRINCIPLE. *Principal* is an adjective meaning "chief, main" or a noun meaning (1) "the head of a school," or (2) "money used as capital, as opposed to interest." *Principle* is a noun meaning "rule, law, doctrine." It may help to remember that the adjective is always *principal*.

PROPOSITION. Always slang as a verb. Colloquial as a noun meaning "a situation or problem requiring special treatment." Reserve *proposition* for its more precise meanings of "a formal plan" or "a statement in logic."

PROVIDED, PROVIDED THAT, PROVIDING. All are acceptable in the meaning "on the condition that," but *provided* is preferred in more formal writing. The *that* can be omitted unless confusion would result. None of these need be used where *if* will express the same meaning.

QUOTE. In writing, use *quote* only as a verb. The corresponding noun is *quotation*. Similarly, use *in quotation marks*, not *in quotes*.

RARELY EVER, SELDOM EVER, SELDOM OR EVER. Instead of *rarely ever*, use *rarely* or *rarely if ever*. Instead of *seldom ever* or *seldom or ever*, use *seldom, hardly ever, seldom if ever*, or *seldom or never*.

REAL, REALLY. *Real* is colloquial as an adverb (*She was real pleased*). Use *really* or *very* instead. Or consider omitting the adverb entirely; *really* often sounds as if the writer is trying too hard to convince the reader (*You really must try this new shampoo*).

RIGHT ALONG (AWAY, OFF, NOW, OUT, etc.). As an intensifying adverb, *right* is colloquial. In writing, use more formal equivalents such as *directly, immediately,* or *at once*.

RUN. Colloquial as a transitive verb meaning "to operate, manage, maintain."

| COLLOQUIAL | Leroy runs a supermarket. |
| STANDARD | Leroy manages a supermarket. |

SAME, SAID. Except in legal or business writing, *same* or *said* should not be used as substitutes for *this, that, the foregoing*.

-SELF. The only correct forms of the pronouns are *myself, yourself, himself, herself, itself, oneself, ourselves, yourselves,* and *themselves*.

Although *-self* forms are often used in speech when the subject of the sentence is not the same as the receiver of the action, this usage should be avoided in writing, and *-self* forms should be used only as intensive or reflexive pronouns.

| COLLOQUIAL | He told a funny story to Paul and myself. |
| PREFERABLE | He told a funny story to Paul and me. |

SHALL, WILL. In American English, *will* is by far the more common, except in legal documents and in asking for direction or suggestions in the first person (*Shall we bring in the deck chairs?*). If *will* seems natural to you, use it; *shall* would probably sound affected to your readers too.

SHOW UP. *Show up* in the meaning of "appear" is colloquial.

SICK, ILL. In Britain, *sick* means "nauseated" or "vomiting," and *ill* is the general term for being unwell. In American English, however, *sick* is completely acceptable for "unwell," and *ill* tends to sound affected.

SIMILAR TO. *Similar to* should introduce only adjectival phrases, not adverbial phrases. For adverbial phrases, use *like*.

INCORRECT	She talks similar to her mother.
CORRECT	She talks like her mother.
CORRECT	This knife is similar to that one.

SITUATION. Most sentences in which *situation* is used will be improved by its removal. It is often vague and should be replaced by more precise wording.

| VAGUE | What about the shovel situation? |
| IMPROVED | Are there enough shovels for everyone? |

Often, the word *situation* is completely unnecessary and simply makes the sentence wordy.

| WORDY | The Midwest was suffering from a drought situation. |
| IMPROVED | The Midwest was suffering from a drought. |

app

SIZE.   *Size* in the meaning of "state of affairs" is colloquial (*That's about the size of it*). Also colloquial is the verb *size up* in the meaning "evaluate."

SLOW.   *Slow* is acceptable both as an adjective and as an adverb. The adverb *slowly* is more formal and more common in writing. However, *slow* is more common before participial adjectives (*slow-moving, slow-speaking*).

SMART.   Colloquial in the meanings of "intelligent" or "impertinent."

SO.   (1) As an intensifier not followed by a qualifying phrase, *so* is colloquial and should be avoided in writing.

COLLOQUIAL   I was so excited!

STANDARD   I was so excited that I forgot to say goodbye.

(2) Before a result clause, *so* should be followed by *that*. No comma precedes the *so that* before result clauses.

He wore elevator shoes so that he would look taller.

(3) *So* or *and so* in the meaning of "therefore, consequently" is somewhat colloquial and should generally be avoided in writing.

COLLOQUIAL   He wears elevator shoes and so looks taller than he really is.

FORMAL   He wears elevator shoes and consequently looks taller than he really is.

SO, TOO, VERY.   *So* and *too* are colloquial substitutes for *very* in negative clauses and should be avoided in writing. Either use *very* or omit the intensifier entirely.

COLLOQUIAL   The eggplant quiche doesn't taste so good.

COLLOQUIAL   The eggplant quiche doesn't taste too good.

STANDARD   The eggplant quiche doesn't taste very good.

SOME.   Colloquial as an adjective meaning "remarkable, extraordinary."

COLLOQUIAL   That was some speech that he gave.

PREFERABLE   He gave a remarkable speech.

See also **ANY, SOME.**

SOMETHING.   Colloquial as an adverb.

COLLOQUIAL   The trapped badger fought something fierce.

PREFERABLE   The trapped badger fought fiercely.

SOME TIME, SOMETIME, SOMETIMES.   *Some time* refers to a period or span of time (*I saw her some time ago*). *Sometime* refers to a particular but indefinite time in the future (*Come to see me sometime*). *Sometimes* means "now and then, at times" (*I see her sometimes, but not regularly*).

Sometime is also a slightly archaic adjective meaning "former" (*A sometime teacher, he now is a broker.*).

SUCH (A).   (1) As an intensifier not followed by a qualifying phrase, *such* is colloquial and should be avoided in writing.

COLLOQUIAL   We had such a good time in Utah!

STANDARD   We had such a good time in Utah that we plan to return.

(2) Before a result clause, *such* should be followed by *that*. Before an adjective clause, *such* should be followed by *as*.

His pain was <u>such that</u> he could not sleep.

I gave him <u>such</u> information <u>as</u> I was able to remember.

(3) *No such a* is nonstandard for *no such*.

NONSTANDARD	There is no such a word as "diversement."
STANDARD	There is no such word as "diversement."

SUPER, SWELL.   Both are colloquialisms for "excellent, splendid, enjoyable."

SUPPOSED TO, USED TO.   Even though it is usually not heard in speech, the *-d* must be written. Both *suppose to* and *use to* are nonstandard in writing.

SURE (AND).   *Sure* as an adverb is colloquial; use *certainly* instead.

COLLOQUIAL	Francis sure swims better than Gregson.
STANDARD	Francis certainly swims better than Gregson.

See also **BE SURE AND, COME AND, GO AND, TRY AND.**

THAN, THEN.   *Than* is a subordinating conjunction used in making comparisons. *Then* is an adverb of time or a conjunctive adverb meaning "consequently, therefore."

THAT (THERE).   (1) *That* and *this* as adverbs are colloquial (*I can't believe it's all that bad*). (2) *That there, this here, those there,* and *these here* are nonstandard.

THAT, WHICH.   *That* introduces only restrictive clauses. *Which* may introduce either restrictive or nonrestrictive clauses, although some writers prefer to use *which* only with nonrestrictive clauses.

THEIRSELF, THEIRSELVES.   Nonstandard for *themselves.*

THEM.   Nonstandard as a demonstrative adjective; use *those* instead.

NONSTANDARD	Try one of them epoxy glues advertised on television.
STANDARD	Try one of those epoxy glues advertised on television.

THERE, THEIR, THEY'RE.   *There* is an adverb or an expletive pronoun; *their* is a possessive adjective; *they're* is the contraction of *they are.*

<u>They're</u> pitching <u>their</u> tent over <u>there</u>.

THESE KIND, THOSE KIND.   See **KIND, SORT, TYPE.**

THING.   Slang in the meaning of "enthusiasm for" or "dislike of" (*Maryann has a thing about macramé*). In other uses, *thing* is so vague that a more precise word should be substituted whenever possible.

THIS.   Colloquial in the meaning "a, a certain" as in *I was standing at the bus-stop, when this man came up and asked for a light.*

THROUGH.   Colloquial in the meaning of "finished."

THUSLY.   Nonstandard for *thus. Thus* is already an adverb and needs no additional *-ly.*

TILL, UNTIL.   Either form is correct and the two words are interchangeable. The spelling *'til*, however, is incorrect.

TO, TOO, TWO.   *To* is a preposition; *too* is an adverb; *two* is a cardinal number.

The <u>two</u> girls were <u>too</u> small <u>to</u> see over the fence.

TOWARD, TOWARDS.   Either form is correct, although *toward* is preferred in American usage.

TYPE, -TYPE.   *Type* instead of *type of* is colloquial.

COLLOQUIAL   I wouldn't buy that type bicycle for a child.
STANDARD   I wouldn't buy that type of bicycle for a child.

The addition of *-type* to a noun to make a modifier is awkward. Usually the *-type* can be omitted entirely.

AWKWARD   A tepee has a cone-type shape.
IMPROVED   A tepee is cone-shaped.
IMPROVED   A tepee has a conic shape.

UNDOUBTABLY.   Nonstandard for *undoubtedly*.

UNIQUE.   In careful usage, *unique* means "the only one, the sole example, having no equal." Hence you should not write *he was a very unique child* (or *rather unique* or *somewhat unique*) any more than you would write *he was a very only child*. If you mean simply "unusual," then write *unusual, rare, remarkable,* or *extraordinary*.

USED TO COULD.   Nonstandard for *used to be able to*.

UTILIZE, UTILIZATION.   Unnecessarily long ways of saying *use*.

VERY, VERY MUCH.   Strictly speaking, *very much* (or *greatly*) should be used to modify past participles and *very* to modify adjectives. The problem lies in deciding whether a past participle is also an adjective. If the participle has a different meaning from the verb, it is probably a true adjective (*determined, very determined*), but in many other instances, the line is not easy to draw. One way of resolving the difficulty is to omit *very* completely; *very* is overused as an intensifier and many a sentence is improved by its removal.

WAIT ON, WAIT FOR.   In the meaning of "wait for, await," *wait on* is a regionalism.

WANT IN (OUT/DOWN/UP/OFF, etc.).   Regional and colloquial without an intervening infinitive such as *to go, to come,* or *to get*.

WANT THAT.   The verb *want* should not be followed by a clause beginning with *that*. *Want* should be followed by an infinitive.

NONSTANDARD   Do you want that we should wait for you?
STANDARD   Do you want us to wait for you?

WAY, WAYS.   (1) *Ways* for "distance, way" is colloquial.

COLLOQUIAL   That's a long ways to go by canoe.
STANDARD   That's a long way to go by canoe.

(2) *Way* for *away* is colloquial.

| COLLOQUIAL | Don't go way—I need you. |
| STANDARD | Don't go away—I need you. |

(3) The phrases *in a bad way* meaning "in poor condition" and *in the worst way* meaning "very much, greatly" are both colloquial.

WHERE (AT, TO). (1) *Where at* and *where to* are redundant colloquialisms. Omit the *at* or *to*.

| COLLOQUIAL | Do you know where the fly swatter is at? |
| STANDARD | Do you know where the fly swatter is? |

| COLLOQUIAL | Do you know where the dog went to? |
| STANDARD | Do you know where the dog went? |

(2) *Where* for *that* when no location is involved is colloquial.

| COLLOQUIAL | I see where the mayor is on vacation again. |
| STANDARD | I see that the mayor is on vacation again. |

WHICH, WHO, THAT. *Which* refers to nonhumans, *who* to persons, and *that* to either. See also, **THAT, WHICH.**

WHILE. *While* is somewhat colloquial and often vague in the meanings of "but" or "and." Save *while* for expressions of time.

WHOSE, WHO'S. *Whose* is the possessive adjective or pronoun from *who* or *which*. *Who's* is the contraction of *who is* or *who has*. Note that *whose* is perfectly acceptable as a possessive for a nonhuman referent and often is far less awkward than *of which*.

| AWKWARD | List all the planets the names of which you can remember. |
| IMPROVED | List all the planets whose names you can remember. |

-WISE. The suffix *-wise* is completely acceptable in established words such as *clockwise, otherwise,* and *lengthwise*. However, its use to form new adverbs indiscriminately is abhorred by many. Even if *-wise* saves space, it is best to avoid it.

| QUESTIONABLE | The house was satisfactory location-wise. |
| PREFERABLE | The location of the house was satisfactory. |

WOULD LIKE FOR. Colloquial for *want*. Use *want* instead.

| COLLOQUIAL | I would like for you to wash your ears. |
| STANDARD | I want you to wash your ears. |

YOU. In writing, *you* should be reserved for addressing the reader directly and should be avoided as an indefinite pronoun. Hence, *you* is correct in imperatives and in giving instructions or advice addressed specifically to the reader. As an indefinitie pronoun, use *one, anyone, everyone, a person,* or the plural *people* or *those (who)*.

| COLLOQUIAL | When you are deaf, you are cut off from the world. |
| PREFERABLE | A deaf person is cut off from the world. |

Appendix C

FREQUENTLY CONFUSED WORDS

The words listed below are frequently confused because of similarities in spelling, pronunciation, or meaning. If you do not know the difference between the items in any of the sets, check them in your dictionary.

absolve—acquit
accent—accentuate
accept—except
access—excess
accidentally—incidentally
adapt—adopt
adverse—averse
advice—advise
affect—effect
air—heir
aisle—isle
all ready—already
all together—altogether
allusion—illusion—
     delusion—elusive
alley—ally
aloud—allowed
altar—alter
alternate—alternative
ambivalent—ambiguous
amoral—immoral
anecdote—antidote
angel—angle
ante- —anti-
any way—anyway
appraise—apprise
apprehend—comprehend
arbitrator—arbiter
arc—arch
ascent—assent
assistance—assistants
assume—presume
assure—ensure—insure
attribute—contribute
avenge—revenge—vengeance
avocation—vocation
awake—awaken—wake—waken
award—reward
awhile—a while

bail—bale
band—banned
barbaric—barbarous
bare—bear
base—bass
bereaved—bereft
berth—birth
beside—besides
biweekly—semiweekly
bloc—block
board—bored
bolder—boulder
born—borne
bough—bow
brake—break
breath—breathe
bridal—bridle
buy—by—bye
cannon—canon
canvas—canvass
capital—capitol
carat—caret
cast—caste
casual—causal
cede—seed
censor—censure—sensor
cent—scent—sent
cereal—serial
ceremonious—ceremonial
childish—childlike
chord—cord
cite—site—sight
classic—classical
climactic—climatic
close—clothes—cloths
coarse—course
collaborate—corroborate
collision—collusion
complement—compliment

compose—comprise—consist—
    constitute
concept—conception
conscience—conscious—
    conscientious
contemptible—contemptuous
contend—contest
continual—continuous—
    constant
continuance—continuation
contrary—converse
corporal—corporeal
corps—corpse—corpus
costume—custom
council—counsel—consul
credible—creditable—
    credulous
credit—debit
currant—current
cymbal—symbol
dairy—diary
dear—deer
decent—descent
deduce—deduct
defect—deficiency
definite—definitive
deprecate—depreciate
desert—dessert
desirable—desirous
desperation—despair
detract—distract
device—devise
dew—do—due
diagnosis—prognosis
disc—disk
discomfit—discomfort
discreet—discrete
disinterested—uninterested
distinct—distinctive—
    distinguished
doubtful—dubious
dual—duel
dyeing—dying
earn—urn
earthen—earthly—earthy
eatable—edible—palatable
economic—economical
efficacy—efficiency
egoism—egotism
elemental—elementary

elicit—illicit
emigrate—immigrate
eminent—imminent—
    immanent
endemic—epidemic
enervate—invigorate
enormity—enormous
envelop—envelope
epitaph—epithet
esoteric—exotic
euphemism—euphuism
evince—evoke
exceed—excel
exceedingly—excessively
exceptional—exceptionable
executer—executor—
    executioner
exodus—exit
explicit—implicit—tacit
extant—extent—extinct
exterior—external—
    extraneous—extrinsic
faint—feint
fair—fare
famous—notable—noted—
    notorious
farther—further
fatal—fateful
faze—phase
female—feminine
figment—fragment
finally—finely
flagrant—fragrant
flaunt—flout
flounder—founder
forceful—forcible
foreword—forward
formally—formerly
fort—forte
forth—fourth
fortunate—fortuitous
full—fulsome
gamble—gambol
gamut—gauntlet
gourmet—gourmand
grate—great
grisly—gristly—grizzly
groan—grown
hair—hare
hale—hail

heal—heel
healthful—healthy
heard—herd
historic—historical
hole—whole
holey—holy—wholly
homogeneous—homogenous—
    homogenized
human—humane
idle—idol
imaginary—imaginative
immunity—impunity
impinge—infringe
imply—infer
incidence—incidents—
    instance
inept—inapt—unapt
inevitable—unavoidable
infect—infest
inflammable—inflammatory
ingenious—ingenuous
instinct—intuition
intellectual—intelligent
intense—intensive
intent—intention
interior—internal—
    intrinsic
irrelevant—irreverent
its—it's
judicial—judicious
knew—new
knight—night
know—no
lain—lane
last—latest
later—latter
lead—led
legal—legitimate—licit
lessen—lesson
liable—libel—likely
linage—lineage
livid—lurid
loan—lone
loath—loathe
local—locale
lonely—lonesome
loose—lose
luxurious—luxuriant
male—masculine
manner—manor

marital—martial
material—materiel
maybe—may be
medal—metal—mettle
medium—media
militate—mitigate
momentary—momentous
moral—morale
motive—motivation
mysterious—mystical
nauseous—nauseating—
    nauseated
naval—navel
nay—neigh
noisome—noisy
observance—observation
official—officious
ordinance—ordnance
orient—orientate
pain—pane
pair—pare—pear
passed—past
patience—patients
peace—piece
peak—pique
pedal—peddle—petal
peer—pier
percent—percentage—
    portion—proportion
perpetrate—perpetuate
persecute—prosecute
personal—personnel
perspective—prospective
piteous—pitiable—
    pitiful
plain—plane
poor—pore—pour
populous—populace
practical—practicable
pray—prey
precede—proceed
precedence—precedents—
    presidents
precipitate—precipitous
predominate—predominant
prescribe—proscribe
presence—presents
presumptive—presumptuous
principal—principle
progress—progression

prophecy—prophesy
prostate—prostrate
quiet—quit—quite
rabid—rampant
rack—wrack
rain—reign—rein
raise—rays—raze
rap—wrap
ravage—ravish
rebut—refute
recourse—resource—resort
regretful—regrettable
relation—relationship—
    relative
repellent—repulsive
respectful—respectable—
    respective
restive—restful—restless
reverend—reverent
revolution—revolt—
    rebellion
revolve—rotate
right—rite—wright—
    write
road—rode
role—roll
root—rout—route
rote—wrote
rung—wrung
seasonal—seasonable
sense—since
sensible—sensitive
sensual—sensuous
serf—surf
serge—surge
sew—so—sow
sewage—sewerage
shear—sheer
shone—shown
sleight—slight
sociable—social
sole—soul
staid—stayed
stair—stare

stationary—stationery
statue—statute—stature
steal—steel
stimulus—stimulant—
    stimulation
straight—strait
strategy—tactics
suit—suite—sweet
team—teem
tear—tier
terrify—terrorize
than—then
their—there—they're
threw—through
to—too—two
toe—tow
tortuous—tortured
track—tract
trail—trial
troop—troupe
turbid—turgid
tycoon—typhoon
undue—unduly
usage—use—utilize
vain—vane—vein
vale—veil
valuable—valued—
    invaluable
venal—venial—venereal
vial—vile
vice—vise
waist—waste
waive—wave
ware—wear—where
weak—week
weather—whether
which—witch
while—wile
who's—whose
worthwhile—
    worth (one's) while
yoke—yolk
your—you're

Appendix D — GLOSSARY OF GRAMMATICAL TERMS

ABSOLUTE CONSTRUCTION. Also called *absolute phrase* or *nominative absolute*. A word group that modifies an entire clause or sentence but that is not linked to it by a conjunction, relative pronoun, or preposition. Absolute constructions most often consist of a noun or other nominal followed by a participle, but may contain some other kind of verb. Sometimes the participle is only understood. See 11c.

The alarm jangling, Elaine woke up with a start.

Henry II returned to France, his barons in rebellion. (*Being* is understood.)

Come the revolution, we'll all be riding bicycles.

ABSTRACT AND CONCRETE NOUNS. An *abstract noun* expresses an idea, characteristic, quality, or condition as opposed to a specific object or example: *lateness, fear, situation, insecurity, duty*. A concrete noun refers to something definite that can be perceived with the senses or to a specific example of a thing or action: *hair, earthworm, my house, that gorilla, his accident*. See 3b.

ACRONYM. A word formed from the first letter or first few letters of a group of words. *AID* (from *A*gency for *I*nternational *D*evelopment) and *sonar* (from *so*und *na*vigation *r*anging) are acronyms. See 43d.

ACTIVE VOICE. See **VOICE.**

ADJECTIVAL. A word, phrase, or clause that is used as an adjective, that is, to modify a noun, pronoun, or other nominal. See 15b.

I have lost the top to my pen.

We met a man who had been married nine times.

Giggling uncontrollably, they left the fun-house.

ADJECTIVE. A word that modifies or limits a noun, pronoun, gerund, or other nominal. Types of adjectives include articles and descriptive, proper, demonstrative, indefinite, possessive, numerical, and interrogative adjectives. See 5.

   Int. Num.   *Proper*   *Art. Desc.*   *Poss.*
Which four Shakespearian plays will the slave-driving instructor ask his

Indef. Desc.   *Dem.*
many diligent students to read this week?

ADJECTIVE CLAUSE. A subordinate clause that modifies a noun or pronoun. Adjective clauses are usually introduced by relative pronouns or relative adverbs.

The man who ran into me had no insurance.

She returned to Ohio, where all her relations lived.

ADVERB. A word that modifies a verb, adverb, adjective, or entire clause or sentence. See 6.

ADVERB CLAUSE. A subordinate clause that functions as an adverb. Adverb clauses are usually introduced by subordinating conjunctions. In the sentence below, the subordinate clause modifies the verb *stop*. See 12b.

Stop <u>when the lights are flashing</u>.

ADVERBIAL. Any word, phrase, or clause that functions as an adverb. See 15c.

ADVERBIAL CONJUNCTION. Also called *conjunctive adverb*. An adverb that serves as a conjunction to relate two main clauses, either within one sentence or in two different sentences. Examples include *nevertheless, meanwhile, however, consequently, thus*. See 9b.

AGREEMENT. The correspondence in form of words to reflect their relationship to each other. Subjects and predicates agree in number and person; pronouns and their antecedents agree in number, person, and gender; demonstrative adjectives and their nouns agree in number. See 18, 19.

ANTECEDENT. The word or words to which a pronoun or pronominal adjective refers. In the sentence below, *John* is the antecedent of *he*.

John thinks that he is Genghis Khan.

APPOSITIVE. A word or group of words that follows another word or group of words and that defines or supplements the words it follows. Appositives refer to the same thing and serve the same grammatical function as the words with which they are associated. See 14.

The hyphen, <u>a mark of punctuation</u>, is used to divide words.

ARTICLE. The *definite article (the)* indicates that the following noun is a particular individual; the *indefinitie article (a/an)* indicates that the following noun is a member of a class.

<u>The</u> play that we saw was <u>a</u> melodrama.

AUXILIARY. Also called *helping verb*. Auxiliaries precede main verbs and indicate the tense, mood, and voice of the main verb. The English auxiliaries are *be, have, do,* and the modal auxiliaries *will, would, shall, should, can, could, may, might, dare, need (to), ought (to),* and *must*. See 4b.

CARDINAL AND ORDINAL NUMBERS. A *cardinal number* refers to quantity (*one, two, seven, four thousand*, etc.). An *ordinal number* refers to position in a series (*first, second, third, twenty-seventh*, etc.). See 45d.

CASE. The inflectional forms of nouns and pronouns that show their relationship to other words in the sentence. English has three cases: (1) the *nominative* (or *subject*), used for subjects and subject complements, (2) the *object*, used for objects of verbs and prepositions, and (3) the *possessive* (or *genitive*), used to indicate possession and various other modifying relationships. Pronouns have all three cases (*I, me, mine*), but nouns have only one form for both nominative and object cases (*girl*) and a form for possessive (*girl's*). The combined nominative-object case of nouns is also called the *common case*. See 3a, 7b.

CLAUSE. A group of words containing a subject and a predicate. An *independent* clause (also called a *main* clause) can stand alone as a complete sentence. A *dependent* clause (also called a *subordinate* clause) cannot form a sentence by itself, but is dependent on some other element. Dependent clauses function as nominals, adjectivals, or adverbials. See 12.

COLLECTIVE NOUN. A noun that is singular in form but that refers to a group of persons or things. *Committee* and *herd* are collective nouns. See 3b.

COLLOQUIAL ENGLISH. The natural spoken English of ordinary conversation. If a dictionary entry labels a word or phrase "Colloquial," that word is considered appropriate for conversation but not for formal written English. In the sentence below, the colloquialisms include the contractions *you're* and *don't*, the use of *going to* to express future tense, and the idioms *foul up* and *get down pat*. See 47a.

You're going to foul it up if you don't get the instructions down pat.

COMMA SPLICE. The joining of two independent clauses with only a comma and no conjunction between them. See 23c, 27a.

We knocked on the door, no one answered.

COMMON CASE. See **CASE.**

COMMON AND PROPER NOUNS. A *common noun* designates any member of a class of entities (*beer; a dog; the cities*). A *proper noun* names only one specific member of a class; proper nouns are usually capitalized and usually are not preceded by an article (*Schlitz; Rover; Minneapolis* and *St. Paul*). See 3b.

COMPARATIVE DEGREE. See **COMPARISON.**

COMPARISON. Changes in the form or syntax of adjectives and adverbs to indicate a greater or lesser degree of what is specified in the root word. The three degrees of comparison are *positive, comparative*, and *superlative*. See 21.

Positive	hard	bad	ambitious	impressively
Comparative	harder	worse	less ambitious	more impressively
Superlative	hardest	worst	least ambitious	most impressively

COMPLEMENT. A noun or adjective (or nominal or adjectival) following a linking verb and referring to the subject. Noun complements are also called *predicate nominatives* or *predicate nouns,* and adjective complements are called *predicate adjectives.* Both are called *subject complements.*

PREDICATE ADJECTIVE   Harry is <u>inefficient</u>.

PREDICATE NOMINATIVE   Harry became a <u>politician</u>.

An object complement is the complement of a direct object.

OBJECT COMPLEMENTS   Ellen wears her hair <u>long</u>.

They voted Joe <u>Man of the Year</u>.

NOTE: Some grammars also treat direct objects and indirect objects as complements.

COMPLEX SENTENCE. See **COMPOUND SENTENCE.**

COMPOUND SENTENCE. A *compound sentence* contains at least two independent clauses. A *complex sentence* contains one independent clause and at least one subordinate clause. A *compound-complex sentence* contains at least two independent clauses and one subordinate clause. A *simple sentence* contains only one independent clause and no subordinate clause.

COMPOUND	The windows rattled and the cellar leaked.
COMPLEX	Whenever it rained, the cellar leaked.
COMPOUND-COMPLEX	Whenever it rained, the windows rattled and the cellar leaked.
SIMPLE	The cellar leaked.

COMPOUND-COMPLEX SENTENCE. See **COMPOUND SENTENCE.**

COMPOUND WORD. A combination of two or more words used as a single word. Some compound words are written solid *(bloodhound)*, some are hyphenated *(bolt-action)*, and some are written as separate words *(boot camp)*.

CONCRETE NOUN. See **ABSTRACT AND CONCRETE NOUNS.**

CONJUGATION. The complete set of inflected forms or phrases in which a verb may appear to show number, person, tense, voice, and mood. See Appendix E for a complete verb conjugation.

CONJUNCTION. A word or group of words used to connect words, phrases, or clauses and to indicate the relationship between them. See **COORDINATING CONJUNCTION, SUBORDINATING CONJUNCTION, CORRELATIVE CONJUNCTION,** and **ADVERBIAL CONJUNCTION.**

CONJUNCTIVE ADVERB. See **ADVERBIAL CONJUNCTION.**

CONNOTATION. The emotional meaning of a word; its implications, suggestions, or associations, as opposed to its explicit literal meaning. For example, although the literal meaning of both *tranquil* and *stagnant* is "still, inactive," *tranquil waters* seem much more pleasant than *stagnant waters* because *tranquil* has connotations of peacefulness, gentleness, and calmness, while *stagnant* has connotations of sluggishness, lifelessness, and even decay. See **DENOTATION** and 47b.

CONSTRUCTION. A somewhat vague term referring to a group of words arranged grammatically.

CONTRACTION. The shortening of a word or group of words by omission of one or more sounds or letters; an apostrophe usually replaces the missing letters in writing: *I've, won't, there's, nor'easter, bos'n.* See 44.

COORDINATING CONJUNCTION. A conjunction that connects sentence elements that are grammatically parallel. The primary coordinating conjunctions are *and, but, or,* and *nor. Yet* is also used as a coordinating conjunction. See 9a.

app

COORDINATION.   The linking of parallel grammatical structures by means of specific words that express the relationship between the structures. See **CONJUNCTION, COORDINATING CONJUNCTION.**

CORRELATIVE CONJUNCTIONS.   Correlative conjunctions are coordinating conjunctions used in pairs to join sentence elements that are grammatically parallel. Examples include *either . . . or, both . . . and, not only . . . but.* See 9a.

COUNTABLE AND MASS NOUNS.   *Countable nouns* have both a singular and a plural form; the singular may be modified by the article *a* or the numeral *one: a bean/beans, one pen/pens, an idea/ideas. Mass nouns* have only a singular form and cannot be modified by *a* or *one: granola, ink, confidence.* See 3b.

DANGLING MODIFIER.   A modifier that either appears to modify the wrong word or that apparently has nothing to modify. See 20c.

Having fixed the flat tire, the car ran out of gas.

DECLENSION.   The change in form of nouns and pronouns to show number, gender, case, and person. English nouns decline for number and case; English personal pronouns for number, gender, case, and person.   See **INFLECTION,** 3a, 7b.

DEFINITE ARTICLE.   See **ARTICLE.**

DEMONSTRATIVE ADJECTIVES AND PRONOUNS.   The demonstratives are *this* (plural *these*) for "near" reference and *that* (plural *those*) for "distant" reference. The demonstratives are pronouns when they serve as subjects, complements, or objects, and are adjectives when they modify nouns or pronouns.

| DEMON. PRONOUNS | This is less expensive than any of those. |
| DEMON. ADJECTIVE | That drug is a prescription item. |

DENOTATION.   The basic, specific, literal meaning of a word, as contrasted with its emotional meaning or the associations one makes with the word. The denotation of the word *cockroach* is "an orthopterous insect of nocturnal habits that frequents human dwellings."   See also **CONNOTATION** and 47b.

DEPENDENT CLAUSE.   See **CLAUSE.**

DERIVATIONAL SUFFIX.   See **SUFFIX.**

DESCRIPTIVE ADJECTIVE.   An adjective that describes the quality, kind, or condition of the noun it modifies. Only descriptive adjectives can be compared and only descriptive adjectives take derivational suffixes. See 5b.

happy warrior, calmer weather, disreputable business

DIRECT ADDRESS.   A construction in which a name or other nominal is added parenthetically to a sentence to indicate the person or persons to whom the sentence is addressed:

I've told you, Dick, not to put teabags in the garbage disposal.

DIRECT DISCOURSE.   See **DIRECT AND INDIRECT QUOTATION.**

DIRECT OBJECT.   See **OBJECT.**

DIRECT AND INDIRECT QUOTATION.   Also called *direct* and *indirect discourse*. *Direct quotation* is the quotation of a speaker or writer using his or her exact words. *Indirect quotation* paraphrases a speaker's or writer's words without quoting them exactly. Indirect quotation usually takes the form of a subordinate clause.

DIRECT QUOTATION	Mme. Roland said, "The more I see of men, the better I like dogs."
INDIRECT QUOTATION	Mme. Roland said that the more she saw of men, the better she liked dogs.

DOUBLE NEGATIVE.   Two negative words in the same clause. When the intended meaning is negative, double negatives are not acceptable in expository writing. A negated adjective can sometimes be correctly used with another negative word to express an affirmative meaning.

UNACCEPTABLE	She <u>wasn't never</u> willing to help. (= She wouldn't help.)
ACCEPTABLE	She was <u>not unwilling</u> to help. (= She would help.)

DOUBLE POSSESSIVE.   A possessive form that uses both *of* before the noun and *-'s* on the noun. See 34a.

I went to England with a friend <u>of</u> my mother'<u>s</u>.

ELLIPTICAL EXPRESSION.   A phrase, clause, or sentence from which a word or words have been omitted but are understood and often can be supplied from a nearby phrase or clause. In the elliptical sentence below, the words *will last* are understood after *rayon*.

Nylon will last longer than rayon.

EXPLETIVE PRONOUNS.   The pronouns *it* and *there* used as subjects of a sentence (1) when no other subject is appropriate, (2) when the logical subject is a long clause, or (3) to emphasize a particular noun in the sentence.

(1)   <u>There</u> is no reason to fret.

(2)   <u>It is</u> unpleasant to admit that I have been foolish.

(3)   It was you who suggested taking this detour.

FINITE AND NONFINITE VERBS.   *Finite verbs* are inflected for person, tense, and number and can serve as complete predicates in main clauses. *Nonfinite verbs* (infinitives, participles, and gerunds) cannot serve as complete predicates.

FORMAL ENGLISH.   The variety of English used primarily for scholarly writing. It is characterized by relatively complex constructions, conservative usage, impersonality, objectivity, precision, seriousness, and conformity to accepted standards of correctness. See 47a.

FRAGMENT.   See **SENTENCE FRAGMENT.**

FUSED SENTENCE. Also called *run-on sentence*. The joining of two independent clauses without any punctuation or conjunction between them. See 27a.

GENDER. The grammatical division of nouns and pronouns into classes, the most familiar of which are masculine, feminine, and neuter. English overtly expresses gender only in the third-person singular pronouns (*he, she, it*) and in a few nouns (*actor/actress; widow/widower*). See 7b.

GENITIVE CASE. See **CASE.**

GERUND. A nominal made from a verb by adding the ending *-ing*. In the sentence "Judy enjoys hiking," *hiking* is a gerund. See 20a.

HELPING VERB. See **AUXILIARY.**

IDIOM. An expression whose meaning is not predictable from the meaning of its individual words and which may even not fit the usual grammatical patterns of the language, but which is accepted and understood by the users of the language. See 47a.

<u>In the long run</u>, we'll <u>make better time</u> if we <u>put off</u> eating so early.

IMPERATIVE. See **MOOD.**

INDEFINITE ADJECTIVES AND PRONOUNS. Adjectives and pronouns that refer to an unspecified person or thing. Examples include *another, each, much, any, some, such*, etc., and the compound indefinite pronouns like *anything, nobody*, and *someone*. See 5b, 7b.

INDEFINITE ARTICLE. See **ARTICLE.**

INDEFINITE PRONOUN. See **INDEFINITE ADJECTIVES AND PRONOUNS.**

INDEPENDENT CLAUSE. See **CLAUSE.**

INDICATIVE. See **MOOD.**

INDIRECT DISCOURSE. See **DIRECT AND INDIRECT QUOTATION.**

INDIRECT QUOTATION. See **DIRECT AND INDIRECT QUOTATION.**

INDIRECT OBJECT. See **OBJECT.**

INFINITIVE. The bare form of a verb with no ending (though it is often preceded by *to*). Infinitives are used in the formation of verb phrases and as nominals, adjectivals, or adverbials.

IN VERB PHRASE	Russ will <u>move</u> to Colorado if he can <u>find</u> a job there.
AS NOMINAL	Please try <u>to work</u> faster.
AS ADJECTIVAL	Sue wants a book <u>to read</u>.
AS ADVERBIAL	They went home <u>to eat</u> dinner.

INFLECTION.   The change in the form of a word to indicate a change in meaning or in grammatical relationships to other elements in the sentence. Inflection of nouns and pronouns is called *declension*; inflection of adjectives is called *comparison*; inflection of verbs is called *conjugation*. See **DECLENSION, COMPARISON, CONJUGATION.**

INFLECTIONAL SUFFIX.   See **SUFFIX.**

INFORMAL ENGLISH.   The variety of English used for lighter writing, such as magazine articles and newspaper columns. Compared to formal English, it tends to be characterized by shorter, less complex sentences, a more casual and personal tone, and occasional use of contractions and colloquialisms. See 47a.

INTENSIFIERS.   Modifiers like *much, too, really, very,* and *so* that add emphasis (but not additional meaning) to the words they modify.

INTENSIVE PRONOUN.   An intensive pronoun is used in apposition to a noun or pronoun to emphasize that noun or pronoun. The intensive pronouns are *myself, yourself, himself, herself, itself, oneself, ourselves, yourselves,* and *themselves.* See 7b.

INTERJECTION.   A word, grammatically independent of the rest of its sentence, used to attract attention or express emotion. Examples include *ha! ouch! oh!* See **ISOLATE.**

INTERROGATIVE ADVERBS AND PRONOUNS.   The so-called WH-words used in asking questions. The interrogative adverbs are *where, when, why, how,* and their compounds in *-ever (wherever,* etc.). The interrogative pronouns are *who, which, what,* and their compounds in *-ever (whoever,* etc.). See 6b, 7b.

INTRANSITIVE VERB.   A verb that is not accompanied by a direct object. In the sentence, "Puppies grow rapidly," *grow* is intransitive.

INVERSION.   A change in the usual word order of a sentence, such as placing the subject after the verb or the direct object before the subject.

Down the alley ran the big rat.

Insolence I will not tolerate.

IRREGULAR VERB.   Any verb that does not form both its past tense and past participle by the addition of *-d* or *-ed* to the infinitive form of the verb. See 4b.

ISOLATE.   A word or phrase that is independent of the grammar of the sentence in which it appears. Examples of isolates include *hello, yes, please, goodbye.* See 10.

LINKING VERB.   Also called *copula.* A verb that connects a subject with a subject complement (predicate adjective or predicate noun). The most common linking verbs are *be, become, seem, appear, remain,* and the verbs of sensation *see, smell, feel, sound,* and *taste.* Other verbs, such as *turn, grow,* and *prove,* are also sometimes used as linking verbs, as in the sentence "The suggestion proved worthwhile." See 4b.

app

MAIN CLAUSE. See **CLAUSE.**

MAIN VERB. Also called *lexical verb*. The verb that carries most of the meaning of the verb phrase in which it appears. See 4b.

William <u>hiccoughed</u>.

Why have you been <u>stirring</u> the rubber cement?

I am <u>appalled</u> by his audacity.

MASS NOUN. See **COUNTABLE NOUN.**

MISPLACED MODIFIER. A modifer which appears to modify the wrong word or words, causing confusion or ludicrousness. See 20c.

Jody replanted the ivy for the secretary <u>in the hanging pot</u>.

MODAL AUXILIARY. See **AUXILIARY.**

MODIFIER. Any word or group of words functioning as an adjectival or adverbial. See also **ADJECTIVE, ADVERB.**

MOOD. A verb inflection that indicates the speaker's or writer's attitude toward what he or she says. English has three moods: *indicative, imperative,* and *subjunctive,* of which the indicative is by far the most frequently used. The indicative is used for ordinary statements and questions (*He takes; Does he take?*). The imperative is used for commands and requests (*Look!*). The subjunctive is used to express uncertainty, possibility, wish, or conditions contrary to fact (*If he were*). See 4a.

NOMINAL. A word, phrase, or clause that functions as a noun.

NOMINAL CLAUSE. See **NOUN CLAUSE.**

NOMINATIVE ABSOLUTE. See **ABSOLUTE CONSTRUCTION.**

NOMINATIVE CASE. See **CASE.**

NONFINITE VERB. See **FINITE AND NONFINITE VERBS.**

NONRESTRICTIVE MODIFIER. See **RESTRICTIVE AND NON-RESTRICTIVE MODIFIERS.**

NONSTANDARD ENGLISH. English usage that differs from what is generally considered to be correct. See 48c.

I ain't a-fixing to take no sass from nobody.

NOUN. A word that names a person, place, thing, or concept (*taxi-driver, New Orleans, jackknife, disruption*). Nouns are inflected for number (*sandwich/sandwiches*) and case (*toddler/toddler's*) and are used as subjects, complements, and objects. See 3.

NOUN ADJUNCT. A noun used to modify another noun: *weather* prediction, *faculty policy* board, *discussion* section, *chain* reaction.

NOUN CLAUSE.   A subordinate clause that can serve all the functions of a single noun.

SUBJECT	<u>How you can read and knit at the same time</u> amazes me.
DIRECT OBJECT	I know exactly <u>what he will say</u>.
INDIRECT OBJECT	Eva told <u>whoever asked</u> the entire story.

NOUN PHRASE.   A phrase consisting of a noun or pronoun and all of its modifiers. See 11a.

She was carrying <u>an orange umbrella with two broken ribs</u>.

NUMBER.   As a grammatical term, *number* refers to the inflections of nouns, pronouns, and verbs that indicate one (singular) or more than one (plural).

SINGULAR NO.	<u>This is a monkey-wrench</u>.
PLURAL NO.	<u>These are monkey-wrenches</u>.

OBJECT.   A noun, pronoun, or other nominal that is governed by, and usually follows, a verb or preposition. A *direct object* specifies what or who is affected by the action of the verb. An *indirect object* specifies who or what is the receiver of the direct object; indirect objects normally appear only in sentences with direct objects. An *object of a preposition* completes a prepositional phrase; its relationship to another part of the sentence is specified by the particular preposition used.

DIRECT OBJECT	Georgia carved the <u>ham</u>.
INDIRECT OBJECT	Georgia handed <u>me</u> a fork.
OBJECT OF PREPOSITION	Georgia ate her salad with her <u>fingers</u>.

OBJECT CASE.   See **CASE.**

OBJECT COMPLEMENT.   See **COMPLEMENT.**

OBJECT OF PREPOSITION.   See **OBJECT.**

ORDINAL NUMBER.   See **CARDINAL AND ORDINAL NUMBERS.**

PARADIGM.   A technical term for all the inflected forms of a word. The paradigm for *mouse* is

mouse   mice   mouse's   mice's

PARAGRAPH.   A basic unit of written English, intermediate in size between the sentence and the total essay (or, for longer works, between the sentence and the chapter or section). Like a mark of punctuation, a paragraph sets off a portion of written material dealing with a particular idea, usually by means of indentation and a new line. Paragraphs may be as short as a sentence or two or as long as several hundred words. See 50.

PARALLELISM.   Using the same kind of grammatical construction for all items that have the same function. *Faulty parallelism* occurs when ideas serving the same grammatical function do not have the same grammatical form. *False parallelism* occurs when ideas that are not parallel in grammatical function are put into parallel form. See 23f.

PARALLELISM	He is young, handsome, and rich.
FAULTY PARALLELISM	He is young, handsome, and a banker.
FALSE PARALLELISM	He is young and handsome, and which makes him attractive to many people.

PARTICIPLE.   A nonfinite verb form used (1) in making verb phrases, (2) as an adjectival, or (3) in absolute constructions. The *present participle* ends in *-ing*. The *past participle* ends in *-ed, -d, -t, -en, -n,* or is formed by a vowel change (*stood, sung*).

IN VERB PHRASE	Smoke was slowly <u>filling</u> the room.
	Stanley had deliberately <u>left</u> his hearing-aid at home.
AS ADJECTIVAL	I was kept awake by that incessantly <u>barking</u> dog.
	Her teeth tightly <u>clenched</u>, Mrs. McNeill glared at Toby.
IN ABSOLUTE CONSTR.	The wind <u>rising</u>, they headed for shore.
	The stock market <u>having crashed</u>, many firms went out of business.

PARTS OF SPEECH.   The classification of all words into classes according to their inflections, meanings, and functions in the sentence. The exact classifications may vary according to different kinds of analysis, but nearly all analyses include nouns, verbs, adjectives, adverbs, pronouns, prepositions, and conjunctions. Most classifications also recognize interjections, which are treated here as a subcategory of isolates. See 2.

PASSIVE VOICE.   See **VOICE.**

PAST TENSE.   See **TENSE.**

PERFECT TENSE.   See **TENSE.**

PERSON.   The inflection of pronouns and verbs to distinguish the speaker or speakers (first person—*I, we*), those spoken to (second person—*you*), and those spoken about (third person—*he, she, it, they* and all other pronouns and nouns). Except for the verb *to be*, verbs distinguish person only in the third person singular present indicative. See 7b.

PERSONAL PRONOUNS.   Those pronouns that indicate grammatical person. English personal pronouns are inflected for three persons (*I, you, she*), two numbers (*I, we*), and three cases (*I, me, mine*). The third-person singular pronoun is also inflected for three genders (*he, she, it*). See 7b for a complete chart of all personal pronoun forms.

PHRASE.   A group of grammatically related words that do not contain both a subject and a predicate. Phrases function as a single part of speech within a clause or sentence. See 11.

<u>Inside the cave</u>, stalagmites had, <u>over the centuries</u>, created <u>an elfin city of calcium carbonate</u>.

PLAIN ADVERB.   An adverb that has the same form as its corresponding adjective. Examples include *hard, fast, straight, far.* See 6b.

POSITIVE DEGREE.   See **COMPARISON.**

POSSESSIVE CASE.   See **CASE.**

PREDICATE.   The part of a clause or sentence that expresses what is said about the subject. It consists of a verb or verb phrase and any objects, complements, or modifiers of the verb. See 1.

The quick brown fox <u>jumped slyly over the lazy, sleeping dog.</u>

PREDICATE ADJECTIVE.   See **COMPLEMENT.**

PREDICATE NOUN.   See **COMPLEMENT.**

PREFIX.   A bound form (one that is not an independent word) placed before another word or bound form to change its meaning.   See also **SUFFIX.**

<u>re</u>play, <u>uni</u>form, <u>un</u>pleasant, <u>de</u>clare, <u>trans</u>plant

PREPOSITION.   A part of speech used with a noun or other nominal (called the object of the preposition) and connecting the noun with another part of the sentence. The preposition together with its object forms a *prepositional phrase.* Prepositional phrases function as modifiers. See 8.

PREPOSITIONAL   Give the money <u>on the shelf</u> <u>to the paperboy.</u>
PHRASES

PREPOSITIONAL ADVERB.   An adverb that has the same form as a preposition. Examples include *up, across, outside, past.* See 6b.

PREPOSITIONAL PHRASE.   See **PREPOSITION.**

PRINCIPAL PARTS.   The forms of a verb from which all other forms can be derived. The principal parts of English verbs are the infinitive (*take*), the past tense (*took*), and the past participle (*taken*).

PROGRESSIVE.   See **TENSE.**

PRONOUN.   A member of a small class of words that serve the functions of nouns or replace nouns to avoid repetition of the nouns. See 7 and also **DEMONSTRATIVE** and **EXPLETIVE, INDEFINITE, INTENSIVE, INTERROGATIVE, PERSONAL, RECIPROCAL, REFLEXIVE,** and **RELATIVE PRONOUNS.**

PROPER ADJECTIVE.   An adjective made from a proper noun. Examples include *Parisian, African, Swedish, Platonic.* See 5b.

PROPER NOUN.   See **COMMON AND PROPER NOUNS.**

RECIPROCAL PRONOUN.   A pronoun that refers to interaction between two or more persons or things. The English reciprocal pronouns are *each other* and *one another* and are used only as objects. In highly formal usage, *each other* is restricted to interaction between two persons or things, and *one another* to interaction among more than two. See 7b.

The room was so dark that we could hardly see <u>each other.</u>

REFLEXIVE PRONOUN.   A pronoun that indicates that the object of the verb is the same as the subject of the verb. All reflexive pronouns end in *-self* or *-selves* and are used only as objects. See 7b.

I can't envision <u>myself</u> as Marc Anthony.

REFLEXIVE VERB.   A verb is said to be reflexive when its direct object refers to the same thing as its subject.

They <u>covered</u> themselves with suntan oil.

REGULAR VERB.   Any verb that forms both its past tense and past participle by the addition of *-d* or *-ed* to the infinitive form of the verb. See 4b.

RELATIVE ADJECTIVE.   An adjective that introduces a relative clause. The relative adjectives are *what(ever)*, *which(ever)*, and *whose(ever)*.

Albert soon lost <u>what</u> little confidence he had.

RELATIVE ADVERB.   An adverb used to introduce a relative clause. The relative adverbs are *where, when, why,* and *how.*

The grandfather clock was in the corner <u>where</u> it had stood for forty years.

RELATIVE CLAUSE.   A subordinate clause introduced by a relative pronoun or relative adverb. Relative clauses may be adjectival, nominal, or adverbial.

ADJECTIVAL   Use the scissors <u>that are in the drawer</u>.
NOMINAL   My dog will do <u>whatever you ask her to</u>.
ADVERBIAL   I'll sit <u>where I please</u>.

RELATIVE PRONOUN.   A pronoun that introduces a subordinate clause and serves as subject or object in that clause. The relative pronouns are *what, which, who, whom, whose,* and their compounds in *-ever* (*whoever,* etc.). *That* is usually also regarded as a relative pronoun.

RESTRICTIVE AND NONRESTRICTIVE MODIFIERS.   A *restrictive modifier* limits or uniquely identifies the word or words it modifies; if it is omitted, the meaning of the sentence will either be lost or be very different. Restrictive modifiers are not surrounded by commas. A *nonrestrictive modifier* describes the word it modifies or adds detail; if it is omitted, there is no essential change in the meaning of the sentence. Nonrestrictive modifiers are set off by commas. See 13 and 20d.

RUN-ON SENTENCE.   See **FUSED SENTENCE.**

SEMIAUXILIARY.   A verb, or a group of words including a verb, that precedes a main verb and functions like an auxiliary verb. Examples include *keep on, used to, be going to, have to.* See 4b.

SENTENCE.   An independent utterance, usually containing a subject and a predicate. A sentence begins with a capital letter and ends with a mark of terminal punctuation. Sentences are often classified as being one of four types: declarative, interrogative, imperative, or exclamatory.

DECLARATIVE   I want to see your master.
INTERROGATIVE   Where is your master?

IMPERATIVE	Take me to your master. (The subject *you* is understood.)
EXCLAMATORY	How fat your master is!

See also **COMPOUND SENTENCE** and 16.

SENTENCE FRAGMENT.   A part of a sentence punctuated as if it were a complete sentence. See 23a.

A part of a sentence. If it were a complete sentence.

SEPARABLE VERB.   A two-part verb consisting of a main verb and a preposition (or prepositional adverb) that function together as a single verb. Examples include *talk over, put on, mix up,* and *bring out.*

SEQUENCE OF TENSES.   The grammatical requirement that the tense of verbs in subordinate clauses be determined by the tense of the verb in the main clause. See 17b.

She <u>knows</u> that you <u>are</u> lying.
She <u>knew</u> that you <u>were</u> lying.
She <u>will know</u> that you <u>are</u> lying.

SIMPLE SENTENCE.   See **COMPOUND SENTENCE.**

SLANG.   Highly informal vocabulary typically consisting of newly coined words, extended meanings of old words, and exaggerated use of words. Slang is usually irreverent in tone, and most slang is short-lived. See 47a.

My <u>old man</u> <u>blew his stack</u> when he found out I had <u>gotten busted</u> by the <u>cops</u>.

SPLIT INFINITIVE.   The insertion of one or more modifiers between the word *to* and the infinitive form of a verb: *to absolutely disagree.* See 20c.

SQUINTING MODIFIER.   A modifier that is ambiguous because it could refer either to what precedes it or to what follows it. See 20c.

The man whom she addressed <u>eagerly</u> agreed with her.

SUBJECT.   The noun or nominal in a clause or sentence about which something is said or asked. See 1. Sometimes a distinction is made between a *simple subject* and a *complete subject*. The *simple subject* of a sentence is a single noun or pronoun; the *complete subject* is the noun or pronoun along with all of its modifiers. In the following sentence, the simple subject is *firm,* and the complete subject is *The toy firm that made these building blocks.*

The toy firm that made these building blocks has gone out of business.

SUBJECT CASE.   See **CASE.**

SUBJECT COMPLEMENT.   See **COMPLEMENT.**

SUBJUNCTIVE.   See **MOOD.**

SUBORDINATE CLAUSE.   See **CLAUSE.**

SUBORDINATING CONJUNCTION.   A conjunction that introduces a subordinate (dependent) clause and connects it to a main (independent) clause. Examples of subordinating conjunctions include *because, if, although, whenever, until.* See 9c.

app

SUBORDINATION. Making one (or more) clauses of a sentence grammatically dependent upon another element in the sentence.

<u>After he took his clothes out of the dryer</u>, he folded them neatly.

SUBSTANTIVE. A noun or any word functioning as a noun in a sentence.

<u>Charles</u> has always wanted to help the <u>poor</u>.

SUFFIX. A bound form (one that is not an independent word) added to the end of a word or another bound form. *Inflectional suffixes* indicate such meanings as "plural" or "past tense" (e.g., the *-s* on *bands* changes the meaning from singular to plural). *Derivational suffixes* usually change the part-of-speech category of the words to which they are attached (e.g., the *-ful* on *joyful* changes the word from a noun to an adjective). See 2a, 46d.

SUPERLATIVE DEGREE. See **COMPARISON.**

SYNTAX. The way in which words are arranged to form phrases, clauses, and sentences; the word order or structure of sentences.

TAG QUESTION. A question consisting of an auxiliary verb and a pronoun and attached to the end of a statement.

The bolts aren't rusty, <u>are they</u>?

You play tennis, <u>don't you</u>?

TENSE. The time or duration of the action or state named by a verb or verb phrase. English has five categories of tense: present, progressive, past, perfect, and future. The progressive and perfect tenses may combine with each other and with the present, past, or future tense to form compound tenses, such as the present perfect progressive (*I have been trying*). See 4a.

TRANSITIVE VERB. A verb that takes a direct object. Most transitive verbs can be put into passive constructions.

They <u>burned</u> their bridges.

The bridges were <u>burned.</u>

UNCOUNTABLE NOUN. See **MASS NOUN.**

VERB. A part of speech that serves as the main element in a predicate. Verbs typically express an action or state of being, are inflected for tense, voice, and mood, and show agreement with their subjects. See 4.

VERB PHRASE. The main verb of a predicate along with all its auxiliaries and semi-auxiliaries, if any. See 1.

VERBAL. A word derived from a verb but used as some other part of speech, especially as a noun or adjective. The nonfinite verb forms (gerunds, participles, and infinitives) are often called verbals.

The <u>irritated</u> and <u>bickering</u> campers refused <u>to go</u> <u>swimming.</u>

VOICE. A characteristic of verbs which indicates the relation of the action of the verb to its subject. English has two voices, *active* and *passive*. When the verb is in the active voice, the subject is the doer of the action. When the verb is in the passive voice, the subject receives the action of the verb. Only transitive verbs can be made passive. See 4a.

ACTIVE VOICE	People <u>eat</u> vegetables.
PASSIVE VOICE	Vegetables <u>are eaten</u> by people.

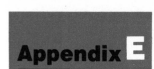

COMPLETE CONJUGATION OF AN ENGLISH VERB

Appendix E

Some of the following combinations occur only rarely, but all are grammatical and possible.

COMPLETE CONJUGATION OF THE VERB *TO TAKE*

INDICATIVE MOOD

ACTIVE VOICE		PRESENT	PAST	FUTURE
Simple	I	take	took	will take
	you/we/they	take	took	will take
	he/she/it	takes	took	will take
Progressive	I	am taking	was taking	will be taking
	you/we/they	are taking	were taking	will be taking
	he/she/it	is taking	was taking	will be taking
Perfect	I	have taken	had taken	will have taken
	you/we/they	have taken	had taken	will have taken
	he/she/it	has taken	had taken	will have taken
Progressive Perfect	I	have been taking	had been taking	will have been taking
	you/we/they	have been taking	had been taking	will have been taking
	he/she/it	has been taking	had been taking	will have been taking

INDICATIVE MOOD

PASSIVE VOICE		PRESENT	PAST	FUTURE
Simple	I	am taken	was taken	will be taken
	you/we/they	are taken	were taken	will be taken
	he/she/it	is taken	was taken	will be taken
Progressive	I	am being taken	was being taken	will be being taken
	you/we/they	are being taken	were being taken	will be being taken
	he/she/it	is being taken	was being taken	will be being taken
Perfect	I	have been taken	had been taken	will have been taken
	you/we/they	have been taken	had been taken	will have been taken
	he/she/it	has been taken	had been taken	will have been taken
Progressive Perfect	I	have been being taken	had been being taken	will have been being taken
	you/we/they	have been being taken	had been being taken	will have been being taken
	he/she/it	has been being taken	had been being taken	will have been being taken

SUBJUNCTIVE MOOD

		PRESENT	PAST
ACTIVE VOICE			
Simple	All persons	(that he) take	(if he) took
Progressive	All persons	(that he) be taking	(if he) were taking
Perfect	All persons	(that he) have taken	(if he) had taken
Progressive Perfect	All persons	(that he) have been taking	(if he) had been taking
PASSIVE VOICE			
Simple	All persons	(that he) be taken	(if he) were taken
Progressive	All persons	(that he) be being taken	(if he) were being taken
Perfect	All persons	(that he) have been taken	(if he) had been taken
Progressive Perfect	All persons	(that he) have been being taken	(if he) had been being taken

IMPERATIVE MOOD

Active Present	take
Passive Present	be taken
Infinitive	(to) take
Gerund	taking

FREQUENTLY MISSPELLED WORDS

Appendix F

Every word in the following list has been found in at least one list of words most frequently misspelled by students. For most words, only one form appears in the list. For example, only *preferred* is listed here, although *prefer, preferring, preference,* and *preferable* are also frequently misspelled. A few of the entries also appear in Appendix C, "Frequently Confused Words."

This list has been adapted from Falk S. Johnson, *Improving Your Spelling* (Holt, Rinehart and Winston, 1979). If you have serious problems with spelling, you may find this book useful; in addition to detailed analyses of spelling problems, it contains many exercises and diagnostic tests.

absence	appearance	category
absorption	appreciate	ceiling
acceptance	approach	cemetery
accidentally	appropriate	certain
accommodate	approximate	challenge
accompanies	arctic	changeable
accomplish	argument	characteristic
accustom	around	chief
achievement	arousing	choose/chose
acquaintance	arrangement	cloths/clothes
acquire	article	column
across	ascend	coming
actually	athletic	committee
adolescence	attack	comparative
advice/advise	attendance	completely
affect	attitude	conceive
against	author	condemn
aggressive	auxiliary	conscience
all right	basically	conscious
almost	before	considerably
already	beginning	consistent
although	believe	continuous
altogether	benefited	controlling
amateur	boundary	convenience
among	breath/breathe	controversial
amount	brilliant	council/counsel
analysis/analyze	Britannica	criticize
angel/angle	business	curious
annual	calendar	curriculum
answer	capital/capitol	cylinder
apparatus	careful	dealt
apparent	carried	decision

dependent
descendant
description
desirability
despair
destroy
development
difference
dining
disappearance
disappoint
disastrous
discipline
disease
dissatisfied
distinction
divide
divine
dominant
during
easily
effect
efficient
eligible
embarrass
enemy
entertain
environment
equipped
escape
especially
exaggerate
excellence
except
excitable
exercise
existence
expense
experience
experiment
explanation
extremely
fallacy
familiar
fantasies
fascinate
favorite
February
fictitious
field

finally
financially
foreigners
foresee
forty/fourth
forward
friendliness
fulfill
fundamentally
further
generally
government
grammar
grateful
guarantee
guard
guidance
happiness
hear/here
height
heroes
hindrance
hoping
huge
humorous
hungry
hypocrisy
ignorance
imaginary
immediately
incidentally
independent
indispensable
influential
intellect
intelligence
interest
interference
interpretation
interrupt
involve
irrelevant
island
its/it's
jealous
judgment
kindergarten
knowledge
laborer
laboratory

laid
larynx
later/latter
led/lead
leisurely
lengthening
library
license
likely
liveliest
loneliness
loose/lose
luxury
magazine
magnificence
maintenance
maneuver
marriage
mathematics
meant
mechanics
medicine
medieval
mere
miniature
mischief
morally
muscle
narrative
naturally
necessary
Negroes
neighbor
neither
nickel
niece
ninety
ninth
noble
noticing
obstacle
occasionally
occurrence
official
omitted
operate
opinion
opportunity
optimism
origin

app

paid
parallel
parliament
particular
passed/past
pastime
peaceable
peculiar
perceive
permanent
permitted
persistent
personal/personnel
perspiration
persuading
pertain
phase/faze
philosophy
physical
piece
planned
playwright
pleasant
poison
political
possible
practical
precede
preferred
prejudice
preparation
prevalent
primitive
principal/principle
privilege
probably
proceed
professor
prominent
propaganda
prophecy/prophesy
proving
psychology
pursuing
quantity
quiet
really
receiving
recognize
recommend

referring
regard
relative
relieving
religious
reminiscent
repetition
representative
resistance
response
restaurant
rhythm
ridiculous
roommate
sacrifice
safety
satire/satyr
satisfied
scenery
schedule
science
seize
sense/since
sentence
separation
sergeant
several
shepherd
shining
shoulder
significance
similar
simile
simply
sophomore
source
specimen
speak/speech
sponsor
stopped
stories
straight/strait
strength
strenuous
stretch
strict
studying
substantial
subtle
succeed

summary
suppose
suppress
surprise
suspense
syllable
symbol
symmetrical
synonymous
temperament
temperature
technique
tendency
than/then
their/there
themselves
theories
therefore
thorough
those
though
thought
through
to/too/two
together
tragedies
transferred
tremendous
tried
truly
undoubtedly
until
unusually
using
vacuum
varies
vegetable
vengeance
view
villain
weather/whether
weird
were/where
wholly/holy
who's/whose
writing
yield
your/you're

index

Numbers in **boldface** refer to sections of the handbook; other numbers refer to pages.

Index compiled by Robert Zolnerzak